THE YOUNG LORDS

JOHANNA FERNÁNDEZ

THE YOUNG LORDS

A RADICAL HISTORY

The University of North Carolina Press CHAPEL HILL

This book was published with the assistance of the Authors Fund of the University of North Carolina Press.

Designed and set in Arno and Trade Gothic types by Rebecca Evans
Manufactured in the United States of America

The University of North Carolina Press has been a member of the
Green Press Initiative since 2003.

Jacket photograph: *Young Lords Rally, Newark, NJ, June 20, 1970*; © David Fenton.

Library of Congress Cataloging-in-Publication Data
Names: Fernández, Johanna, 1970– author.
Title: The Young Lords : a radical history / Johanna Fernández.
Description: Chapel Hill : The University of North Carolina Press, [2020] |
   Includes bibliographical references and index.
Identifiers: LCCN 2019037862 | ISBN 9781469653440 (cloth) | ISBN 9781469669328 (pbk) |
   ISBN 9781469653457 (ebook)
Subjects: LCSH: Young Lords (Organization)—History. | Puerto Ricans—New York
   (State)—New York—Politics and government—20th century. | Community activists—
   New York (State)—New York—History—20th century. | Political activists—New York
   (State)—New York—History—20th century. | Puerto Ricans—Civil rights—New York
   (State)—New York—History—20th century. | Civil rights movements—New York (State)—
   New York—History—20th century. | Puerto Ricans—New York (State)—New York—Social
   conditions—20th century. | New York (N.Y.)—Ethnic relations—History—20th century. |
   New York (N.Y.)—Social conditions—20th century. | United States—Relations—Puerto
   Rico—Public opinion. | BISAC: HISTORY / United States / 20th Century
Classification: LCC F128.9.P85 F47 2020 | DDC 323.1168/729507470904—dc23 LC record
   available at https://lccn.loc.gov/2019037862

FOR MY BROTHERS, OSVALDO, GEOVANNY, AND TIRSO JR.,
BECAUSE WE FILLED THAT UNFORGIVING MINUTE
WITH SIXTY SECONDS' WORTH OF DISTANCE RUN.

AND FOR YOU, TIRSO APOLINAR FERNÁNDEZ, MY FATHER.
YOU MANIFESTED THE KINDEST, FIERCEST,
AND MOST PRINCIPLED HUMANITY.

CONTENTS

Introduction 1

1 **Beginnings:** José "Cha Cha" Jiménez and the
   Roots of Rebellion **13**

2 **Coming of Age in the 1960s:** The Emergence of the
   New York Young Lords **49**

3 **The Garbage Offensive 91**

4 **Building Blocks 115**

5 **Diseases of Poverty 135**

6 **The Church Offensive:** Prefiguring the New Society
   at the People's Church **155**

7   The Politics and Culture of the Young Lords Party 193

8   The Politics of Race and Gender 233

9   The Lincoln Offensive: Toward a Patient Bill of Rights 271

10 A Second Occupation 305

11 Organizational Decline 335

    Coda: Beware of Movements 379

    Acknowledgments 389
    Notes 393
    Bibliography 431
    Index 455

FIGURES

Young Lord briefs Cha Cha Jiménez at a public meeting, 1969 **14**

Fred Hampton calls a press conference with members of the Rainbow Coalition, October 10, 1969 **43**

Juan González shows a copy of *Palante* to a rider on the New York subway, February 1971 **50**

Central Committee members **87**

Statue of Liberty superimposed on a dirty street in East Harlem **92**

Young Lord Benjie Cruz and neighbor on 111th Street **97**

Youths overturn a car during the first Garbage Offensive **105**

Felipe Luciano on the cover of *Ramparts* magazine, October 1970 **116**

Young Lord Gloria Colón at a typewriter in the East Harlem office **118**

Pablo Guzmán **120**

Free breakfast program, second People's Church, October 1970 **124**

Aida Cuascut and comrades at the UN Plaza, post-march, October 1970 **129**

Clothing drive **136**

Door-to-door testing of tuberculosis, Lower East Side, December 1970 **150**

Young Lords in front of First Spanish United Methodist Church **156**

Phalanx of marchers in the Puerto Rican Day Parade, June 7, 1970 **184**

Police raid the occupied First Spanish United Methodist Church, January 7, 1970 **189**

Iris Morales leads political education class **194**

Coed communal living **197**

Building owned by the Young Lords on 117th Street and Third Avenue, East Harlem **198**

Image of machete and the words "Up with the Puerto Rican farmer, Down with the Yankee" **225**

Che Ja-Ja stands in front of the Bronx office, May 1970 **234**

Young Lords member sells copies of *Palante*, 1970 **251**

A women-led march **261**

Young Lords march **268**

Richie Perez at rally outside Lincoln Hospital **272**

Lincoln Hospital cartoon illustrated by Denise Oliver **283**

Young Lords build makeshift barricade at side entrance of occupied Nurses Residence, July 14, 1970 **289**

Denise Oliver speaks at press conference during Julio Roldán's wake, October 19, 1970 **306**

Pallbearers carry Julio Roldán's coffin **323**

Young Lords Party logo **336**

Julio Roldán march in Puerto Rico **347**

March with mournful expressions **355**

Triumphant rally in South Bronx, 1970 **380**

THE YOUNG LORDS

INTRODUCTION

In the final days of 1969, the Young Lords were on top of the world. As the decade entered its midnight hour, this group of poor and working-class Puerto Rican radicals brought an alternative vision of society to life in their own neighborhood. Their aim was to reclaim the dignity of the racially oppressed and elevate basic human needs—food, clothing, housing, health, work, and community—over the pursuit of profit. In the course of a fight with East Harlem's First Spanish United Methodist Church (FSUMC), they found an unlikely but irresistible setting for the public presentation of their revolutionary project.

The Young Lords had simply been looking for a space to feed breakfast to poor children before school. The church seemed an ideal place. It was conveniently situated in the center of East Harlem and housed in a beautiful, spacious building that was closed all week except for a couple of hours on Sunday. But its priest, an exile of Castro's revolutionary Cuba, denied the use of its building. In response, the Young Lords charged that the church's benign indifference to the social and economic suffering of the people of East Harlem—one of the poorest districts in the city—mirrored government indifference and enabled social violence. They argued further that the church's professed goals of service to mankind and promises of happiness and freedom from earthly worries in the hereafter cloaked a broader project of social control.

Two months after their initial request was denied, the militant activists nailed the doors of the FSUMC shut after Sunday service and barricaded themselves inside. In that moment, their neighborhood deployment of the building takeover—a strategy popularized by sixties radicals in universities—gave concrete expression to growing calls for community control of local institutions in poor urban neighborhoods.

In their determination to stoke revolution among Puerto Ricans and other poor communities of color, these radicals transformed the occupied building into a staging ground for their vision of a just society. Rechristened the People's Church by the Young Lords, the liberated space was offered up as a sanctuary for East Harlem's poor. Before long, community residents poured into the church in search of solutions to all manner of grievances, from housing evictions to the

1

absence of English translation at parent-teacher meetings. The Lords served hot meals to school-aged children, helping to institutionalize what is now a federal program that serves school breakfast to children, and ran a free medical clinic for members of the community. They sponsored a vigorous political education program for anyone who was interested, where they taught classes in Puerto Rican and black American history, the history of the national independence movement of Puerto Rico, and current events—an alternative to public school curricula that failed to make sense of the troubles of the poor and the brown in New York City. In the evenings, the Lords hosted "festivals of the oppressed" where they curated spurned elements of Puerto Rican culture and music, performed by underground poets, musicians, artists, and writers—an antidote to the erasure of Puerto Rican culture and history that accompanied the U.S. colonial project that began in Puerto Rico in 1898. New genres of cultural expression were cultivated at the liberated church, among them the spoken word poetry jam, which would in the coming years become a springboard for the development of hip-hop. In the process, the Young Lords created a counternarrative to postwar media representations of Puerto Ricans as junkies, knife-wielding thugs, and welfare dependents that replaced traditional stereotypes with powerful images of eloquent, strategic, and candid Puerto Rican resistance.

At a moment of growing state violence against activists, the decision of these radicals to turn the Lord's house into a site of protest was a brilliant tactical move that created a strategic sanctuary from the possibility of violent reprisals. Approximately one year earlier, in April 1968, after hundreds of Columbia University students occupied major campus buildings in protest of the Vietnam War and the university's gentrification of Harlem, students were dragged out of the occupied buildings by police with billy clubs.[1] At the church in East Harlem, such violence was politically untenable.

Immediately, local grandmothers began delivering pots of food to the Puerto Rican radicals through church windows, while a phalanx of National Lawyers Guild attorneys, on-site and in the church's periphery, filed court injunctions and reminded judges and police of the barricaded radicals' constitutionally protected right to protest. Teetering between sacrilege and righteousness, the Young Lords' unfolding drama was captured by TV cameras parked in and outside the house of worship.

As the Young Lords fortified their programs at the church, hundreds of supporters and engrossed spectators gathered to hear about new developments during their daily press conferences. Speaking through a bullhorn out of a church window to attentive journalists outside, Young Lord Iris Benitez explained, "The people of El Barrio have gotten to the point that they don't ask the why of things anymore, they just see things as they exist and try to survive. The Young Lords know the why and we're trying to relay that information to the people."[2] From their pulpit at the People's Church, the Young Lords observed that the poverty indices of Puerto Rico, a U.S. colony, and this Puerto Rican neighborhood were strikingly similar. Another Young Lord referenced the global scope of resistance a year earlier, when millions of people rose up in Rome, Madrid, Paris, Belgrade, Prague, Mexico City, Pakistan, Chicago, across U.S. cities, and beyond. Pablo Guzmán observed, "It ain't just y'all in this church, it ain't just East Harlem. . . . We relate to an international struggle. It may sound ridiculous but this all links up . . . from Vietnam to Puerto Rico to Watts."[3] Born in the wake of one of the deepest political radicalizations of the century, the Young Lords' creative militancy, critique of social problems spoken in the language of their peers, and socialist vision for America embodied the best of sixties radicalism.

■

Against the backdrop of America's escalating sixties urban rebellions, the Young Lords unleashed a chain of urban guerilla protests that amplified the primacy of class analysis and revolution in the fight against racism. From garbage-dumping demonstrations to a series of church and hospital occupations—termed "offensives" in deference to the Tet campaign of the Vietnamese—this small group exploded into the country's consciousness in July 1969, staging their social grievances with infectious irreverence and distinctive imagination. Although a new wave of repression befell the movement, the Young Lords actually benefited from protests in defense of the Panther 21, jailed that same year. The arrests had been part of a police frame-up.[4] With New York's police department exposed and discredited, the new radicals were able to launch their campaigns without the same level of disruption that the FBI and local law enforcement brought against the Black Panthers in the late 1960s.

Over the course of their brief yet productive life-span, the Young Lords won significant reforms and used local battles to expose the United States' quiet imperial project in Puerto Rico, which became a colony of the United States in 1898. In just a few short years, the group grew from a little-known organization to the stuff of legend. In the process, their media-conscious urban guerrilla offensives, combined with the group's multiethnic membership, redefined the character of protest, the color of politics, and the cadence of popular culture in the city.

And as the children of the vast post–World War II transfer of Puerto Ricans to the U.S. mainland, the Young Lords also helped their generation interpret the causes of that migration and the place of Puerto Ricans in U.S. society as "special citizens" and a diaspora of colonial people living in the metropole. Between 1947 and 1970, one-third of the people of Puerto Rico left the island. Most settled in New York, where Puerto Ricans migrated in larger numbers than black Americans during the same period. By 1970, the Puerto Rican population on the U.S. mainland had grown 500 times to approximately 1.5 million.[5]

Puerto Rican postwar migration formed part of a much larger migratory process that transformed the class structure and political standing of groups that have been historically racialized and concentrated in the most backward and exploitative sectors of the economy, namely black Americans, Mexicans, and Native Americans. The vast internal migration of people of color from countryside to city during and after World War II proletarianized these previously rural and small-town people, which increased their economic power. Urbanization gave them a sense of their strength in numbers, amplified their potential political power, and established the conditions for the rise of the civil rights movement.[6] The timing of Puerto Rican migration set the stage for the emergence of a group like the Young Lords in the 1960s, whose members were largely first- and second-generation, working-class Puerto Rican migrants between the ages of fourteen and thirty-four; most were in their late teens.[7]

The postwar migration of Puerto Ricans to the U.S. mainland was exponentially larger than in previous generations. The young were overrepresented in its ranks, and their consciousness would be shaped by an unlikely combination of politicizing experiences, from the rise of the civil rights, black power, women's, and gay liberation movements and the U.S. declaration of war in Vietnam to their own experience in an urban setting beset for the first time by industrial decline, permanent unemployment, and the growing spatial and economic isolation of its racialized residents. Like their black American counterparts in the sixties movements, the Young Lords became iconic among Puerto Ricans and within movement circles for several reasons. Their uncompromising militancy matched and channeled the anger unleashed by the era's urban rebellions. At a moment when the call for revolution began to replace the call for reform in the minds of many, the Young Lords linked the precarious conditions of postwar Puerto Rican migrants to their status as colonial subjects, identified common cause with black Americans, and called for socialism. And in their quest to take a stand in the city, the Young Lords discovered and asserted in the public square what it meant to be Puerto Rican in America.

Children of the Revolution

As the mainstream and underground sixties press captured the controlled chaos at the People's Church, an evocative portrait of the racial and ethnic composition of the protagonists struck a chord with people around the world. Unintentionally, the Young Lords had staged a visual coup. New York's major Spanish-language newspaper, *El Diario La Prensa*, took special notice: "These young men and women, Puerto Ricans—some white and others of the black race—and among them some Americans, love the ideal of independence for Puerto Rico. . . . They say that they form part of a coalition with the Black Panther Party and the Young Patriots."[8]

Although the Young Lords were self-professed Puerto Rican revolutionary nationalists, approximately 25 percent of its members were black Americans. The group's membership gave political expression to the common social, economic, and cultural urban experience of Puerto Rican and black American youth who grew up alongside each other in the 1950s and 1960s. Considered New York's Puerto Rican barrio, East Harlem was, in fact, home to Puerto Ricans, black Americans, and white Americans of Italian descent—one of the city's few multiracial and multiethnic neighborhoods. In 1960, 40.4 percent of its residents were Puerto Rican, 38.2 percent black American, and 21.4 percent white American.[9] With another 5 percent of its members composed of non–Puerto Rican Latinxs, the group's membership also reflected the changing demographic character and diverse ethnic composition of a city increasingly populated by people of color. The ethnic and racial diversity on display at the church seemed to express the possibilities for a society free from bigotry, of the kind that Dr. Martin Luther King Jr. imagined in his notion of the beloved community, the same kind that seemed ever more in doubt as riots crept across America's cities toward the end of the 1960s.[10]

But the Young Lords envisioned even more. Only a decade removed from the anticommunist witch hunts of the 1950s, the Young Lords, together with a significant minority of young organizers of their generation, began to embrace revolutionary politics. This vision of the political and economic organization of society was radically opposed to standard American political values. The Young Lords' calls for Puerto Rican independence, an end to hunger and want, and a socialist society embodied the politics of the era's revolutions for independence from European colonial rule that swept through Africa, Asia, and Latin America after World War II. In the United States, self-proclaimed revolutionaries of color linked racism to colonialism and class exploitation under capitalism and identified all as barriers to building a liberated society.

Organizationally, the Young Lords modeled themselves after the Black Panthers, who called for the building of vanguard revolutionary parties by black Americans and other people of color as vehicles through which those who believed that the system must be dismantled would come together to concentrate and coordinate their efforts.[11] The Lords outlined their bold vision for a just society in a thirteen-point program and platform in which they called for "self-determination for Puerto Ricans" and proclaimed, "We want a socialist society."[12] Through community-based campaigns and political propaganda, the Young Lords popularized the demand for Puerto Rican independence both in their own constituency and within broader movement circles. They also spread and demystified socialist ideas among poor and working-class people of color, arguing that society should be organized around human priorities and needs rather than capitalism's drive for profit.

Like the Black Panthers, the Young Lords believed that the fight against racism and colonial domination was central, rather than secondary, to the fight for a new socialist society. For this reason, they called themselves revolutionary nationalists, arguing that the fight for national independence was integral to the struggle for socialism. The Young Lords also believed that independence could not be attained through electoral means but only through revolution. They declared themselves the children of Puerto Rico's Nationalist Party of the 1930s and were the first mainland-raised Puerto Ricans to, as a group, call and organize for the island's independence.

The Young Lords' embrace of independence formed part of the 1960s revival of nationalism among Puerto Ricans with varying levels of political experiences and influences. Encouraged by the Cuban Revolution in 1959 and the gathering pace of the black freedom movement in the United States, elements of the Puerto Rican Left on the island, which had been forced underground by government repression, reconstituted themselves as the Movimiento Pro Independencia. In 1964, Movimiento Pro Independencia opened branches in New York and Chicago, attracting small numbers of older, first-generation Puerto Rican migrants. In the late 1960s, the politics and activism of the Young Lords, which had developed independently of the island and mainland independence movements, widened the terrain of independence politics among a new generation of mainland-born Puerto Ricans. They educated other 1960s activists about the language discrimination and racism endured not just by black Americans but also by Puerto Ricans on the U.S. mainland, and popularized the call for Puerto Rican independence among them.

The New York Young Lords formed part of a cohort of young working-class people—and people of color among them, in particular—whose unprecedented access to higher education sharpened their latent critique of society and afforded them an infrastructure for dissent. The postwar era's exponential increase in college enrollment delayed the responsibilities of work and family among the young for the first time in U.S. history and simultaneously opened up a space where they could question society.[13] The movements they built challenged racism; the U.S. war in Vietnam; and the oppression of women, gays, and lesbians and the transgender community. They also challenged what many believed were old, soul-slaying social norms and standards of behavior that constrained personal freedoms in the United States. Known collectively as the New Left, these diverse movements were built by a generation whose activism radically changed the cultural and political landscape of the United States. Its participants referred to the overlapping movements of the New Left as "the movement." These movements are historically significant because together they established contemporary standards of interactions among Americans and between American people and their government—they challenged white supremacy, made racism unpopular, changed "the relationship between white people and people of color," and influenced U.S. foreign policy and the ways the nation understood issues of gender and sexuality.[14]

Although the New Left is popularly understood as predominantly white and campus based, its origins are rooted in the intrepid and morally righteous sit-ins and radical campaigns of the youth wing of the civil rights movement that cohered in April 1960 with the emergence of the Student Nonviolent Coordinating Committee (SNCC). In the north, the Black Panthers and the Young Lords recast SNCC community organizing strategy. The temperament of their protests and worldview gave shape and meaning to the radical style and politics of the New Left. Built by young people of color in cities like Oakland, Chicago, New York, and Philadelphia, these movements were university-incubated and deployed to poor communities. And like the white student–led sector of the New Left, the seeds of these movements were also sown in the postwar years. They developed in response to the poverty produced by the flight of industries to the suburbs, which in turn created a class of permanently unemployed and discouraged young workers of color—an unprecedented development in modern urban history.

The politics of the Young Lords were driven by a search for root causes. They also were colored by a disdain for liberalism, an exploration of the broadest possible meaning of liberation, and the call for the transformation of both society and the individual. Like others of their ilk, the Young Lords broke new ground. They uncovered the psychological impact of racism on the oppressed; challenged sexism and homophobia in their ranks; exposed the character of racial oppression in the North, including and beyond that of black Americans; interpreted the standing of the racially oppressed with a colonial frame; fostered solidarity among all racially oppressed groups in the United States; popularized socialist ideas in communities in which they were active; and raised the standard of accountability in local government.

The Young Lords represent one of the most creative and productive expressions of the New Left; and while the group's rise was influenced by all the movements, the Young Lords are first and foremost heir to the black power movement. The term "black power" had been used in the past, but in 1966, when articulated by Student Nonviolent Coordinating Committee leader Stokely Carmichael, it signaled the growing dominance of a more militant political current long embraced by movement people, north and south. It was emboldened by continued white violence against black Americans and their continued exclusion from the political, social, and economic fabric of their society, despite the passage of civil rights legislation in 1964 and 1965.[15] Black power was, above all, a declaration of the right to self-determination—the right of black people to control and influence their lives and their world.[16] Before long, a broad cultural and political movement cohered around the concept, which variously came to mean the right to armed self-defense against white racist violence, black pride, and the development of independent black political leadership free from pressures to accommodate the interests of northern white liberals. The broad appeal of black power allowed for its use among a wide range of actors with differing political agendas who embraced a broad spectrum of solutions to racial oppression.[17]

Black power connected with the rebellious mood of an ethnically diverse set of racially oppressed people in the 1960s because it called on them to embrace the best of their history, lay down socially imposed notions of racial inferiority, exert control over the institutions that governed and oppressed their lives, and see themselves as the architects of a new world. As the black power movement reclaimed culture, language, and history for one of the most racially subjugated groups in American history, it inspired a cultural renaissance among Puerto Ricans as well as among Asians, Mexicans, and Native Americans. Black power enabled Americans of all shades to redefine their political relationship to the nation and to negotiate that often-fraught relationship from a position of strength. In the process, however, the color of the black power movement, and the civil rights movement more broadly, was changed as well.

Overview of the Book

These pages tell the story of the rise and fall of the New York chapter of the Young Lords Organization, later renamed the Young Lords Party, and of how the Young Lords, and so many others of their generation, came to believe in the concept of revolution. Chapters 1 and 2 explore the social and economic forces that shaped the lives of young people of color in the postwar city and laid the seeds of their radicalization in the era of civil rights and black power. Chapter 1 traces the origins of the Young Lords as a Chicago gang. Through the early life experiences of the group's famed leader, José "Cha Cha" Jiménez, the chapter examines how the mass dislocation of Puerto Ricans occasioned by federal housing policy forced them to settle in densely populated blocks on the edges of hostile, white ethnic neighborhoods, where young men of color, who were outnumbered by their white counterparts, joined gangs to survive and became embroiled in a life of petty crime. As the social movements of the 1960s opened up the possibility for self-transformation, Cha Cha Jiménez was politicized in prison and set out to transform his gang into the Puerto Rican counterpart of the Black Panthers. The bold move inspired and propelled a group of radical students looking for an activist agenda to do the same in New York. Chapter 2 examines the global forces that brought one-third of Puerto Ricans to the U.S. mainland and the social and economic crisis that befell the Puerto Rican community in postwar New York. The chapter explores the backgrounds of the talented cohort of first-generation college-educated students who, in July 1969, launched the New York chapter of the Young Lords Organization. Unlike their white baby boomer counterparts—whose activism was fueled by the alienation of postwar suburbanization, the repressive Victorian-era morality imposed on youth in the 1950s, and the expansion of the university—for youth of color, the seeds of rebellion sprouted in the crucible of migration, urban decline, and white backlash against their increase in the postwar city.[18] Caught in the middle of a political battle among adults over access to jobs and education, children of color experienced greater overt racism in the classroom and police repression in the streets. The early childhood experiences of the Young Lords in the schools and in the streets and as language and cultural translators for their parents radicalized them emotionally and compelled the evangelical commitment with which they launched their activism as young adults.

Historical accounts of the 1960s and of the civil rights and black power movements are today more textured than ever, with new historical research revealing the local actors, problems, and organizing that gave birth to ideas, strategies, and movements that are often imagined as national projects.[19] From the movement's inception, its local leaders—challenged with the task of increasing their ranks and cognizant that race oppression was not attributable to race alone—broadened their protest demands.[20] The objectives and character of protest challenged economic inequality and class divisions in society and among the oppressed. In New York, the Young Lords organized against the most visible manifestations of urban poverty and its distinctly new forms: chronic unemployment, escalating police surveillance and repression, the large-scale displacement of poor city dwellers from housing, intractable public health crises that came in the form of poor sanitation services, growing addiction to drugs, and an epidemic of childhood lead poisoning, among others. Chapters 3 through 6 examine the Young Lords' class-conscious, community-based campaigns and their impact on the city. Although civil rights and black power movement histories are popularly understood within the framework of black American citizenship rights, the work of organizations like the Black Panthers and the Young Lords paint a portrait of struggle that is more composite. Their organizing efforts show that the black movement set in motion an awakening of social consciousness wherein virtually no social issue escaped public scrutiny.

Chapter 3 examines the New York Young Lords' first community-based protests against poor sanitation services in East Harlem, the Garbage Offensive, which pressured the candidates of that year's mayoral election to address the citywide grievance. By pressuring local government to solve neighborhood problems such as poor sanitation, for example, these activists sought to establish standards of decency in city services that expanded the definition of the common good and stretched our nation's definition of democracy. Immediately following the Garbage Offensive, the Young Lords established a headquarters in East Harlem and developed an organizational infrastructure and political platform. Chapter 4 examines the nuts and bolts of that process. Chapter 5 reconstructs the medical activism of the Young Lords' 1969 door-to-door campaign to test children for lead poisoning in the tenements of East Harlem and the relationships the group fostered with medical personnel. The campaign ended with a sit-in at the Department of Health in protest of a childhood lead-poisoning epidemic in the city and eventually led to the creation of New York's Bureau of Lead Poisoning. Chapter 6 covers the Young Lords' occupation of the First Spanish United Methodist Church, their relationship with a younger cohort of church parishioners who supported their actions, and the response of the church to their protests. The children's breakfast program the Young Lords set up at this church and those of the Black Panthers established the precedent for what is now the federal School Breakfast Program.

Chapter 7 explores how the Young Lords applied to the U.S. context the political world view known as Third World socialism.[21] Formed at the height of the greatest radicalization since the labor struggles of the 1930s, the politics of the Young Lords and others of their time reflected the ideas and strategies for social change that became dominant with the advent of wars of decolonization in places such as Vietnam, Algeria, and Cuba. Radicals argued that subjugated groups in the United States—including black Americans, Native Americans, Chicanos, Asian Americans, and Puerto Ricans—were internal domestic colonies, politically and economically underdeveloped and dispossessed of their rights to self-determination. While Third World revolutions iconized peasant guerrillas, organizations like the Black Panthers and the Young Lords identified the lumpen-proletariat as the most revolutionary class in society. At a moment when economic restructuring and the flight of industries to the suburbs were producing permanent unemployment and greater economic and racial segregation in the city, the activism and politics of grassroots radicals like the Young Lords reflected the distinctive social features of the urban environment in which they emerged. The strong nationalist character of urban radical politics was also tied to the vast relocation of white Americans from city to suburb. In this environment, the ideal of people of color fighting together with white Americans for change grew more and more difficult to enact as the daily lives of these populations grew further and further apart. Instead, dramatic action was created by polyglot groups born of the increasingly multiethnic character of the American slum and its new racialized migrants.

Chapter 8 explores how the organization tackled racism and sexism within the organization. The Young Lords embraced the "revolution within the revolution," by which they meant the deliberate struggle to deconstruct and challenge the manifestations of power dynamics, racism, and sexism in everyday life among movement participants. The effort was also a trademark of the radical wing of the women's movement, articulated in the slogan "The personal is political."[22]

Chapter 9 analyzes the Young Lords' occupation of Lincoln Hospital in the South Bronx alongside a radical flank of white doctors to dramatize medical discrimination and the deplorable conditions of a hospital that, according to one of its doctors, "looked more like an abandoned factory than a center for the healing arts." Although historians sometimes interpret the revolutionary nationalism of the 1960s as a rejection of coalition building with white Americans, groups like the Young Lords collaborated with radicalized white allies. In their coalitions, however, the Young Lords, like the Black Panthers, set out to rework the power dynamics of cross-racial and cross-class alliances, rejecting what they perceived as the uninterrogated racial prejudices and liberal tendencies of middle-class white radicals and the potential for their disproportionate influence on interracial coalitions. At Lincoln Hospital, the Young Lords–led coalition drafted the first patient bill of rights and established the first and principal acupuncture drug treatment center in the United States.

Chapter 10 covers the circumstances surrounding the Young Lords' second occupation of FSUMC, this time against the backdrop of a prisoner uprising in the infamous New York City jail known as the Tombs.

Chapter 11 analyzes the New York organization's move to Puerto Rico and its decline. By the end of 1970, the Young Lords had grown to approximately 1,000 members and had expanded to Newark, Philadelphia, Hartford, Bridgeport, and Boston. Over the course of its life, the group drew approximately 3,000 members and influenced thousands more. Amid polarized deliberations about the organization's future and with a majority of its leadership advocating a stronger Puerto Rican nationalist orientation, the group decided to launch two branches in Puerto Rico: in El Caño and Aguadilla. The move to Puerto Rico, for which the group was ill prepared, combined with the decline in the coming years of the mass character of the civil rights and black power movements, weakened the ability of the Young Lords to remain connected to the grassroots. By 1973, Young Lord membership had declined considerably. Fueled by government repression, the youthfulness and political inexperience of its leadership, and a growing dogmatism, the Young Lords became entangled in violent internecine disputes that led to the organization's demise in 1976.

Telling the Story of the Young Lords

The word "radical" is used often in this text. In all cases, I employ the word's most common definition: concerned with root causes of social problems and system-wide change. This history of the Young Lords is reconstructed from the literature they left behind, including their newspaper, *Palante*, and internal documents; audio and visual recordings; municipal government documents that reference their work; extensive records on the Young Lords and studies conducted by the FSUMC following the group's occupation of its East Harlem subsidiary; the papers of a growing number of archival repositories across the country; the personal papers of a handful of Young Lords and their supporters; and the FBI's COINTELPRO documents on the Young Lords as well as surveillance documents kept by the New York Police Department (NYPD). Known as the Handschu files, these police documents were found as a result of my 2014 suit against the NYPD for its failure to honor my Freedom of Information Law (FOIL) request for the police records of the Young Lords. The suit and its astonishing resolution were widely covered in the media. They led to the 2016 recovery of the "lost" Handschu files, the largest repository of police surveillance documents in the country—namely, over 1 million surveillance files of New Yorkers compiled by the NYPD between 1954 and 1972, including those of Malcolm X.

Over the course of many years, I've conducted close to 100 critical oral histories with the Young Lords, doctors who worked alongside them, and people who were influenced by their activism. The people I interviewed were tremendously generous with their time. Over the years, their articulate and impassioned remembrances of that period kept this project alive.

CHAPTER ONE

BEGINNINGS

José "Cha Cha" Jiménez and the
Roots of Rebellion

On a cold night in late fall of 1968, José "Cha Cha" Jiménez, the president of the Young Lords, a street gang in Chicago, hit the after-hours bars and hangout spots in his neighborhood. He was looking for his guys, and members of other Puerto Rican and Mexican American gangs, who could surely be found drinking until the early hours. On any other night, Cha Cha would have been passing the time with his friends, mulling over the latest intrigues in turf battles between Chicago's growing Puerto Rican and Mexican gangs and their white rivals. Cha Cha was easygoing, with a wry and self-effacing sense of humor that charmed even members of competing gangs. His many stints in prison had granted him street cred and an arsenal of stories to tell. But this particular night was different.

The Young Lords' turf was facing its greatest threat. Just that week, local housing activists had convinced Cha Cha that a terrible fate awaited his neighborhood: the wrecking ball of urban renewal. Over drinks and loud noise, the gang leader called on his closest partners in crime, and even his opponents, to join him at an upcoming neighborhood meeting in Lincoln Park where the captains of urban renewal were scheduled to present their demolition plans.

To his dismay, his peers couldn't care less. A founding member of the Young Lords, Cha Cha had been the gang's president for most of the decade. Over the course of countless street brawls and dangerous stop-and-frisk encounters with police, he had won widespread respect, managing conflicts within his gang and even among other gangs in Lincoln Park. He wasn't used to derision and eye-rolling from his listeners. Cha Cha had promised local housing activists that he could fill the urban renewal meeting with his people. He had given his word.

But there was more at stake than just his reputation that night. Cha Cha was engaged in an internal struggle with himself, begun in his prison cell in the spring of 1968. Did he want to be involved with petty crime for the rest of his life, or was there something bigger he could commit to? He had begun to see the root

Young Lord briefs Cha Cha Jiménez on security at a public meeting, 1969.
(Photograph by Paul Sequeira; courtesy of Getty Images)

causes linking the fundamental problems beneath the seemingly disconnected burdens he faced daily. This was the first time he had tried to share that still-hazy understanding with his peers. And this was the first time that Cha Cha had asked his buddies to stand with him and fight—not in the gutter but at a community meeting. They laughed, but he persisted. And so the process began.[1] Though its members didn't know it, the Young Lords was being transformed from a street gang into one of the least likely and most intriguing socialist organizations of the 1960s.

Cha Cha Jiménez had been a Young Lord since the age of eleven. He was among a group of seven youths—six Puerto Ricans and one Mexican—who had organized the gang in 1959. The others included the group's unofficial leader, Orlando Dávila, as well as Benny Perez, David Rivera, Fermín Perez, Joe Vincente, and the Mexican-descended Sal del Rivero.[2] The group began as a "bunch of friends that got together to have fun, to have a good time, go to the beach, go to the park, and play ball."[3] But this circle linked by friendship soon transformed into a street-fighting organization. The Young Lords helped young men like Cha Cha map out the boundaries of their neighborhood and taught them which streets couldn't be crossed and which playgrounds and corners to avoid.

The Chicago office of the Puerto Rican Migration Division may have contributed to the problem. Charged with facilitating the settlement of Puerto Ricans in the city, it had warned them against living in their own ethnic neighborhoods or with Mexicans and encouraged their dispersal across the city's white neighborhoods.[4] But as Puerto Rican enclaves grew on the fringes of these neighborhoods, many were greeted with hostility. In one example in 1954, Italians firebombed a Puerto Rican bar and apartment. The incident led to a week of violence that drew 2,000 people into street battles at its height.[5] Spearheaded by white ethnic gangs, these scenes dramatized a long-standing ritual: the preservation of Chicago's racially and ethnically exclusive neighborhoods through networks of white youth accustomed to deploying terror and brawn in the streets.

In response to these conflicts, thousands of migrant Puerto Rican, Mexican, and black American youth formed their own gangs in self-defense.[6] Membership helped many migrants' children navigate the rules of racial etiquette in a city that was reproducing old social and economic structures of racism and creating new ones. In postwar Chicago and other major northern cities, three developments exacerbated racial antagonism: migration, urban renewal, and the social and economic anxiety that home ownership and, later, deindustrialization produced among white workers.

But the Young Lords provided more than protection from the street-level manifestations of larger social and political forces. As racialized young people came to discover where they stood within the urban power structure, they wrestled to understand who they were. The gang offered a sense of belonging. It served as a vehicle for cobbling together a defiant identity, defined by race pride and an assertion of strength in unwelcoming neighborhoods. The potential for politicization was present. But gangs were also incubators of turf rivalries, crime, and all manner of destructive behavior; their collective character mediated the risks that accompany such activities. By the age of fourteen, Cha Cha's life began to spiral into an abyss of petty criminal activity, imprisonment, and recidivism. When his time in prison intersected with the ideas and actions generated by the black power movement, Cha Cha began to see an alternative to the turf battles and petty crime that had up until then defined so much of his life. His own personal evolution drove the Young Lords' transformation into a political organization. Yet, his experience in the gang, where he rebelled daily against accepted norms, laid the groundwork for a much more socially consequential decision. Once politicized, he deliberately defied social taboos among Puerto Ricans against links that would associate them with black Americans.

Cha Cha's unequivocal pursuit of common cause with the most iconic and radical group in the black power movement—the Black Panther Party—paved the way for the later meteoric success of the New York Young Lords.

Imigrados Todos

Like many of his peers, Cha Cha grew up being called a "wetback" by his white peers. The epithet referred to "illegals," usually Mexicans, who entered the U.S. mainland by crossing the Mexican border with Texas through the Rio Grande. But his parents came from Puerto Rico, a colonial possession of the United States since 1898.[7] In 1917, the U.S. Congress consolidated U.S. rule over the island by extending citizenship, albeit limited, to the people of the island.[8] The term "wetback" stigmatized and racialized Cha Cha's parents, other Puerto Ricans, and Mexicans for the kind of back-breaking work they had been hired to perform in agricultural labor camps throughout the United States since the late nineteenth century.[9] Like other migrants before and since, they were contracted to work on the mainland by the U.S. government and simultaneously told to go back where they came from.[10]

In the mid-1940s, Cha Cha's father, Antonio Jiménez, left Puerto Rico and its intractable unemployment crisis to work in the tomato fields and greenhouses of the United States. Like other Puerto Ricans migrating under similar conditions, Don Antonio entered into a labor contract agreement through the local office of the Migration Division of the Department of Labor of Puerto Rico, which paid the cost of his travel, placing him at the privately owned Andy Boy Farms in Concord, Massachusetts.[11] The contracts often set no limits on work hours and provided a paltry monthly wage with deductions for room and board and the cost of the airline ticket.[12]

Antonio Jiménez was part of a class of transnational migrant workers from Puerto Rico and Mexico who were recruited to stem the labor shortages that threatened to undermine the war effort during World War II.[13] These migrants also formed part of a seismic internal migration to major American cities of a broad spectrum of previously rural people. Beckoned by the promise of well-paid industrial jobs, Puerto Ricans, black Americans from the South, Mexican Americans and Native Americans from largely rural states, and some poor whites from Appalachia migrated to industrial centers like Chicago, New York, and Philadelphia.[14] The concentrated urbanization and proletarianization of these mostly racialized populations gave some a sense of their potential numerical, economic, and political strength. These developments also set the stage for battles they would wage over their place in the postwar northern city.[15]

In 1947, after Don Antonio gained footing in Massachusetts and advanced to foreman in the tomato fields, he brought his wife and children to join him and settled outside Boston. Cha Cha's mother, Eugenia Jiménez, got to work doing laundry for the fieldworkers.[16] Seeking better pay and conditions, Antonio took a new job farming vegetables for Campbell Soup in Minert, Massachusetts, and then, in 1951, decided to move his family to Chicago. They settled in the growing Puerto Rican enclave on Clark Street in the Near North Side just north of downtown Chicago, near the households, hotels, factories, and department stores that employed the newcomers in the city's least desirable jobs as domestics, dishwashers, and piecemeal laborers.[17] Cha Cha's mother found work packing Christmas cards at Woolworth's and his father in a meat-packing plant.[18] They secured lodging in the dilapidated Water Hotel on "La Clark," which had been "bandaged and subdivided into apartments and single rooms," in the skid row neighborhood where Cha Cha spent his early childhood years.[19]

Lincoln Park

The Jiménez family toiled to make a home on La Clark during the early 1950s. During the same time, a coalition of urban planners, local government officials, and businessmen designated the entire downtown sector, of which La Clark was a part, for demolition and redevelopment. Its shabby hotels, local taverns, dive bars, and poor working-class residents were too close to the Gold Coast, Chicago's prime riverfront real estate. The Jiménezes' Water Hotel dwelling was soon "condemned and torn down." During their first six years in the city, the family moved nine times.[20]

The housing instability that defined the Jiménezes' early settlement was a product of federal slum-clearance policy intended to address urban disrepair and housing shortages for the poor.[21] But since the federal government contracted private developers to carry out its mandate, stated objectives were often sacrificed on the altar of private interests. As in the case of other cities, private developers disproportionately built middle-class and luxury condominiums in the working-class neighborhoods they razed. Many of the displaced were left to find housing on their own.[22] Lacking social resources or political networks to help navigate these structural changes, Cha Cha's parents were unable to escape the bulldozer's path. They were among the approximately 900 Puerto Rican families displaced from the heart of La Clark and its environs during the 1950s and early 1960s to make room for the Carl Sandburg Village—a for-profit, luxury residential skyscraper and commercial venture.[23]

By the late 1950s, the Jiménez family had been pushed to the southernmost boundary of Lincoln Park, a neighborhood that manifested all of postwar Chicago's simmering race and class conflicts. Most of its residents had lived there for generations. Descendants of old-stock, working-class Irish, Italian, German, Polish, and other Eastern European immigrants, they resented the neighborhood's changing racial composition. But the changes that befell this once well-defined white ethnic enclave came from other quarters too.[24]

After the war, Lincoln Park's eastern lakefront was settled by a small but growing influx of college-educated, white, middle-class Americans who chose urban homesteading over suburban living. These newcomers brought artistic sensibilities and a sense of entitlement to the old neighborhood. They purchased weathered, but beautiful, nineteenth-century buildings, which had been subdivided into multiple dwellings during the Depression, then renovated and turned them into large single-family Victorian homes.[25] Fiercely protective of their vision and investments, they committed to saving Lincoln Park from its "blighted area" designation and what would be almost certain demolition. They created and led the Lincoln Park Conservation Association and lobbied municipal government for urban renewal funds to elevate the neighborhood to a family-oriented, but eclectic and aesthetically reinvigorated, community of homeowners. What happened in Lincoln Park presaged gentrification. The neighborhood became attractive to white professionals and corporate investors; its property values soared, and rents increased more than 70 percent between 1950 and 1960.[26]

By the early 1960s, Lincoln Park was also becoming one of the most racially and ethnically diverse neighborhoods in the city. But except for a few integrated streets, its residents remained racially and ethnically segregated block by block. Cha Cha's family had settled in its fringes alongside other Puerto Ricans, white Appalachians, and smaller settlements of black Americans and Mexicans. All were poor, displaced families from La Clark and the Cabrini Greene area, respectively. They numbered approximately 5,000.[27]

In the schools, housing displacement led to a revolving door of enrollment. By third grade, Cha Cha had attended three schools. When anxieties about change manifested as "behavioral problems," his mother addressed them the best way she knew.[28] Raised in a Catholic poorhouse in Puerto Rico, Eugenia Jiménez endeavored to barter her years of church service for Cha Cha's matriculation in a Catholic school. Long after the migrants drifted northward out of the parish, she continued to organize the large and active Spanish-language mass in La Clark. But the Puerto Rican congregation met in St. Michael's gym rather than in its sanctuary. It was rumored that the German congregation would not have it otherwise. Puerto Rican congregants refused to address that uncomfortable fact of life. This embarrassed and angered the young Cha Cha.[29]

The reception of Puerto Ricans in postwar Chicago was far from uniform, and scholars disagree about the extent to which the group was racialized at the time of its population surge in the late 1940s. Sociologist Felix Padilla emphasizes that Puerto Ricans were perceived in accordance with the preexisting racial prejudices of the city's white ethnics, who lumped them together, deridingly, with black Americans.[30] Other studies state that initially, because of their traditional family structure, Puerto Ricans were perceived as good neighbors and distinguishable from black Americans; and that employers favored them because they worked for lower wages and were less demanding than their entitled white ethnic and black American counterparts.[31] More recent studies argue that Puerto Ricans were racialized over time in the contest for space and rights in a city undergoing dramatic demographic change in the postwar period.[32]

Yet the U.S. colonial project in Puerto Rico had already tarred islanders with the brush of racial inferiority. Its logic was captured by the popular cartoon depiction of "Porto Rico," the Philippines, Cuba, and Hawaii as uncivilized, wild-eyed black schoolchildren seated in a classroom, restrained by Uncle Sam's schoolmaster discipline as he lectured on the "lessons of self-government."[33] By the mid-1950s the racialization of Puerto Ricans in Chicago was under way, driven by the group's growing visibility in the city, overrepresentation in its lowest-paid jobs and the ranks of the poor, and its growing number of clashes with police and white ethnic groups.

Puerto Rican migrants had to find their place within a segregated urban landscape harboring long-held group antagonisms. Sources of hostility were diverse and ran deep, born from earlier migrants' desire for a sense of place. Many Italian, Irish, and eastern European immigrants had "sacrificed everything" to build a house in the city's remote outer rings. In search of stability and security, immigrants purchased as much land as they could afford. Mortgage payments required pooling contributions from multiple working family members over many years. For them, home ownership required the preservation of old-world values: tightly knit families and communities, loyalty, and keeping one's word—bonds that strengthened parochial attachments to place. Turf meant everything; and protecting it was now a badge of honor, fueling violent territorial conflict. Many adopted an austere work ethic just to survive, seeking to avoid the risks of labor mobility and reinforcing routines of economic survival with known outcomes.[34]

Chicago's gang culture began to be forged in the late nineteenth century by youths of German and Irish stock seeking to "protect" their communities from new waves of European immigrants. Machine politicians began to use these networks to enforce the city's racial and ethnic hierarchies and to maintain power.[35] In exchange for rounding up votes at election time, politicians had compensated white ethnic gangs with athletic clubs and "protections . . . [from] their depredations" on others.[36] After adolescence, these poor white youth often gained jobs from these political relationships, which helped integrate them into the city's formal political structure. As criminal justice specialist John M. Hagedorn notes, "Former Irish gang members would become cops, firemen, and yes, even the mayor of the city. The Irish gang, in effect, was reinvented as the Chicago Police Department."[37]

Although interethnic conflict persisted among European immigrants and their descendants, antiblack racism often brought otherwise warring groups together. In the late nineteenth century, as industrialists used black workers as strikebreakers, they became clear targets of white ethnic violence. By the early twentieth century, Chicago was one of the nation's most racially segregated northern cities. During World War I, white ethnics interpreted the mass re-cruitment of black labor in steel mills, foundries, and packinghouses as a black invasion and unleased six days of violence against black Americans in 1919.[38] As historian Arnold Hirsch explains, these communal acts of violence marked a turning point in the city's race politics wherein white ethnic gang identity cohered in opposition to black Americans. Puerto Ricans and Mexicans would have to make a place in a city with a long history of organized white racist terror. From 1946 to 1953, just as Puerto Rican migrants were beginning to settle in the city, localized white terror, hit-and-run attacks, and bombings of black American homes near white residences spilled into their lives when Italians firebombed a Puerto Rican home in 1954.[39]

The mass postwar settlement of black Americans, Puerto Ricans, and Mexi-cans in the city posed the single most observable threat to white ethnics. It visually disrupted their sense of community and place. Numbering only 32,000 people in 1960, Puerto Ricans in Chicago still represented a small percentage of the city's overall populace. But Puerto Ricans were visible because they were concentrated in enclaves that pressed against white neighborhoods.[40]

White racialized resentment and violence was also fueled by white flight to the suburbs, which reduced the city's white population from 68 percent to 51 percent between 1950 and 1960. The majority of Lincoln Park residents, over-whelmingly white renters, were among those who remained in the city. Many contended with feelings of being left behind. Those who owned homes feared the inevitable—that the influx of black Americans to the outskirts of white neighborhoods would drive down land values.[41] The pattern also made these communities vulnerable to "blockbusting." Created by real estate investors, the practice manipulated fear of a black invasion in northern cities and drove many white Americans to sell their properties at a financial loss to the very realtors who manufactured the panic. Many white ethnics' world view was informed not only by racism but also by a percolating resentment of predatory forces over which they had no control.

Antagonisms would also be shaped by the uncertainties of the postwar econ-omy. Although the country experienced economic expansion, and workers' wages rose in the postwar period, the picture of local prosperity was uneven. Cities like Chicago underwent industrial sprawl. According to government studies, economic growth followed white flight to the outer rings of the city, which meant that economic expansion was concentrated in Chicago's greater metropolitan area. By contrast, the city proper steadily lost manufacturing jobs. Between 1947, the city's year of peak employment, and 1958, Chicago lost approximately 150,000 manufacturing jobs.[42] As early as 1947, a section of the city's white workers began to experience real economic insecurity. The emerging service economy also fueled anxiety and urgency among many. This industry was creating poorly paying, un-unionized, low-skilled retail jobs on the one hand and jobs requiring workers with higher education on the other.[43]

White workers were unwilling to work in the low-paid sector jobs that employed the newcomers, yet they resented the city's super-exploited, Spanish-speaking labor force. To some, Puerto Ricans might have been distinguishable from black Americans, but to many they were nonwhite, Spanish-speaking outsiders.[44] Over time, white workers came to believe that the newcomers lacked family values and a strong work ethic and would taint the social fabric of their city.[45]

It was in this contest over access to urban space and resources that even some adults among the postwar migrants replicated preexisting white gang formations. They did so in self-defense. Soon after his arrival in Chicago, Cha Cha's father joined La Hacha Vieja, "the Old Hatchet," in response to the harassment he experienced at the hands of white residents and police while traveling to and from work.[46] La Hacha Vieja was the earliest-known street organization of adult Puerto Rican workers.[47] It offered Antonio Jiménez protection and strengthened his sense of belonging in Chicago during the period of hardship that followed his arrival.

At a moment when gangs were a way of life for many poor and working-class youth of all hues, second-generation Puerto Ricans like Cha Cha Jiménez mobilized their own. The development added fodder to the national panic around juvenile delinquency, which preoccupied the U.S. Senate in a series of hearings on the subject, begun in 1954, that lasted nearly a decade.[48] Missing from the Senate hearings was an analysis of racism, the effects of migration and urban redevelopment, and the psychological fallout that the first stirring of deindustrialization produced among the city's white workers. If racial tensions rose in Chicago as a result of the influx of black American, Puerto Rican, and Mexican migrants at a moment when the city's economic structure was beginning to change, racial turf wars were stoked even further by the mass-scale housing displacements produced by urban renewal. Under these circumstances, gang networks equipped those who later formed the Young Lords with protection in their neighborhood's hostile streets.

Becoming a Young Lord

While Cha Cha continued to get in trouble at school, Doña Eugenia continued to hold high aspirations for her son's future. Cha Cha had light complexion and green eyes, and she believed that by passing for white, he might become a lawyer or a priest. Phenotypically diverse, Puerto Ricans possessed the gamut of skin colors, facial features, and hair textures. Unlike most Mexicans, some Puerto Ricans had visible African ancestry. For white Chicagoans, however, Cha Cha's racial identity was hard to pin down, but it wasn't a pass. He spoke Spanish as well as English and had racially ambiguous facial features, curly hair that he straightened with a brush, and an unmistakably Spanish surname. When white youth mockingly referred to him as "the cha-cha-cha," a popular Cuban music genre and dance form, the name stuck. In spite of indignities like these, Cha Cha grew up believing that his light skin conferred on him social advantage. But the prejudice he witnessed against his family and friends gave way to internal conflict, confusion, and guilt about his own internalized sense of privilege. It didn't help that his Puerto Rican and Mexican-descended friends called him "Casper the Friendly Ghost," mocking his white skin.[49]

Bowing to his mother's vision of who he might become, Cha Cha explored the possibility of entering the priesthood. In preparation, he agreed to enroll at St. Theresa Junior High School, an all-white Catholic school in Lincoln Park. Influenced by the Marxist-inflected analysis of reality that he later embraced, he concluded that the alienation, confusion, and racism he experienced as a boy had fueled his search for refuge in the otherworldly. At school, Cha Cha's teachers, including many of the pastors, called him Joseph rather than José, a point that he remembers with shame because he didn't resist it. Racism in the school came in "different forms." Cha Cha was privy to conversations that would not have taken place in his presence were it not for his white skin and the complicity of his pastors. He remembers listening in on a conversation: "[The priests] are talking freely, using the N word, and I'm turning red [thinking to myself], 'Whoa, man, did this guy just say that?' And I'm wondering if he's gonna say something about Puerto Ricans, like 'spics.' I'm thinking, should I go off on this guy? This is a man of God talking like this; that really affected me."[50] Cha Cha's encounter with the church's contradictions gave way to deep feelings of anger, disappointment, and betrayal that, combined with his parents' inability to contain him, led him down the road of gang rebellion.

The vast contradiction between Cha Cha's visceral sense of hypocrisy and injustice in the world around him and his mother's spiritual aspirations for him also created a chasm between mother and son. From her own experience with racial discrimination in housing, low-wage employment, and the segregated arrangement of the Spanish-language Catholic mass she organized, Doña Eugenia was no stranger to the limitations of American democracy. Although the family's economic situation was better in the United States than it had been on the island, it came with the indignity of discrimination. But the challenges they faced, from difficulties with the English language to their experience as "alien citizens," Puerto Rican migrants' reality made many of them hesitant to fight adverse social conditions. Like a bitter pill, many swallowed their pride for the time being and dreamed of returning to the island.

About the dissonance of their perspectives and experiences, Cha Cha observes with sarcasm that as a child he was seeing how Puerto Ricans were being "pushed around" while his "mother [was] trying to get [him] to be an altar boy." Before long, Cha Cha developed a revulsion to his mother's conservatism, which he perceived as denial of reality when it came to the standing of migrants, not to mention her dream about him becoming a lawyer or priest. Cha Cha believed that Doña Eugenia was woefully unequipped to understand his world, let alone mediate its challenges. He wasn't entirely wrong. The conflict calls to mind the spirit if not the letter of comments made by the writer James Baldwin on the fallout of racism in the relationship between parent and child: "The most private, the most serious, thing this does to the subjugated is to destroy his sense of reality. . . . It destroys for example his father's authority over him . . . because . . . his father has no power in the world."[51]

Cha Cha experienced the extension of his pastors' conversations on the playground, where children "play out, relearn, and repeat society's assumptions" about race.[52] The terror of being chased by white youth began when his family found housing along the southernmost boundary of Lincoln Park when Cha Cha was around the age of ten. According to Cha Cha, "The whole block was white. In fact, there's a white gang on the corner that would terrorize us all the way to school. I'm getting chased by the gangs. Orlando's getting chased. All these other guys, like Benny are getting chased."[53] The experience was shared by Rory Guerra, who remembers waking up one day and refusing to go to school because he "simply did not want to fight anymore."[54] Guerra left school in ninth grade, joined the gang, and never looked back. The problem escalated more subtly for Sal del Rivero, later a founding member of the Young Lords, whose parents kept a tight rein on him and were among the modest number of Mexicans who lived in Pilsen at the time and built strong cultural and community institutions there. In Lincoln Park, however, Sal came face-to-face with a reality it seemed his parents preferred to suppress. When a member of the Dayton Boys, an Irish gang, snatched his bike from him while a line of white boys watched, an older Puerto Rican boy he barely knew intervened and quashed the escalating conflict. He understood then that boundaries were drawn along racial and ethnic lines and decided he had to hang out with those of his kind.[55] In Lincoln Park, Puerto Rican preteen boys were living in a particularly vulnerable situation. As historian Lilia Fernández observes about that neighborhood's demographic composition, white boys outnumbered Puerto Rican boys seventeen to one.[56] As Cha Cha explains, "We were Latinos in an area that was changing over from white to Latino and we became a gang . . . for protection . . . against other gangs."

The Young Lords emerged in 1959 on the borders of two neighborhoods, the Near North Side and West Lincoln Park. The first meeting of the group of seven was called by Orlando Dávila, the principal founder of the Young Lords. The group met at Arnold Junior High School, from where they would also walk together after school. One other person, Carlos Trinidad, the cousin of Joe Vincente, a founding member of the gang, was present outside the room where the meeting was held. According to Cha Cha, "He didn't want to come in, but he was an unofficial member." Trinidad was not the only one with trepidation. Cha Cha also joined reluctantly: "At first I didn't want to be part of the gang." Joining a gang was about drawing a line in the sand, a public declaration of conflict and combat. In the end, for Cha Cha, being part of a street organization was "a matter of controlling [his] life."[57]

Orlando Dávila was a young man of few words with a big heart and a strong commitment to protecting his own.[58] He was legendary for using his fists to express his rebellion against discrimination. As Cha Cha observes, "Besides being Puerto Rican, Orlando was discriminated against because he was a dark-skinned Puerto Rican."[59] The double burden of discrimination that trailed Dávila during his formative years points to some of the forces that led him to help form the gang and sealed his commitment to it. In street conflicts and interactions with white peers, darker-complexioned Puerto Ricans like him were read as black Americans, an assumption that clashed with the way Puerto Ricans viewed themselves. Ethnicity tended to trump race as a marker of identity for Puerto Ricans.[60] Yet, even when black Puerto Ricans sought to challenge public perceptions, American reality dictated that their ethnic identification was immaterial. Thus, despite the hostilities that existed between Puerto Ricans and black Americans, their common experiences with racism opened up the possibility of shared identification, especially in the context of the emerging social movements and among youth who frequented and were socialized in similar public spaces.

When this occurred, Puerto Rican parents often found their children's growing associations and cultural identification with black American peers hard to understand. Burdened by nativism in the mainland and prejudiced by the racism rooted in the legacy of Spanish colonial slavery in Puerto Rico and further developed under U.S. rule, parents often used their language and ethnic culture to avoid being mistaken for or associated with black Americans.[61] There were both real and imagined advantages to positioning themselves on some "middle ground" outside of the bipolar—black and white—racial paradigm in the United States.[62] But for the children of these migrants, sorting out their identities and allegiances in the context of two different worlds with competing systems of racial categorizations—that of their Puerto Rico–reared parents versus the different racial logic of the streets of the United States—was a complicated project of self-definition. Puerto Rican parents were often baffled by their children's seemingly inexplicable rebellion, and the children were angered and perplexed by their parents' antiblack racism and apparent "conformism."[63]

While joining the Young Lords provided collective support in fending off physical aggression, membership also meant defying the perceived inferiority of the newcomers. Like many black Americans migrating from the South during this same period, many young Puerto Ricans were seen as "country," or stupid, backward, and uncivilized.[64] According to Cha Cha, in this context, being a Young Lord offered him and others "a sense of pride" in the face of "being put down, of having low self-esteem, of being ashamed of my family, like many other Latinos . . . because [we] did not wear the same type of clothing . . . had accents . . . were not the American apple pie [type] taught in school."[65] One reason for the performative toughness of Puerto Rican, Mexican, and black American gang members was that it offered the potential to command respect and recognition among their peers. In a patriarchal society whose racism emasculated them by setting limits on their ability to meet its standards of manhood, the fierceness of the gang offered a psychological defense mechanism against social humiliation.[66] Not surprisingly, these adolescent boys with fledgling egos called themselves the Young Lords—a name whose bravado indicated both a rebuttal to their devaluation in society and a lavish affirmation of self.

In a society where consumption was a key feature of youth culture and the automobile a potent symbol of masculinity, social standing, and freedom of movement, gang activity also facilitated the acquisition of flashy cars.[67] Hotwiring and joyriding the tail-finned cars that were rolling off the production line in nearby Detroit formed part of the Young Lords' routine. These characteristics of the gang—despite the Young Lords' subsequent radicalization—were a reflection of, not a challenge to, the materialistic and competitive logic of American capitalism. The place where driving a car mattered most was at dances, where showing up with their girlfriends in nice cars was an essential emblem of their manhood: "We wanted to make sure we went to the dances with our women with nice cars—of the year. So we're driving to the dances and everybody has a stolen car and we're like, 'Hey what's going on? How you doin'? We've got our cars, you got yours?'"[68] Cha Cha explains that the Young Lords were often trying to keep up with another Latino gang, the Paragons, whose members were mechanics with "fancy cars [that] they would fix up like those in Los Angeles." According to Sal del Rivero, "Over the course of I don't know how many months, we had stolen over 350 vehicles." Selling parts from the cars they had stolen was also a source of income, and they often took orders from people in their neighborhood. Since Cha Cha had white skin and would be less likely to raise eyebrows among passersby, his job was to approach vehicles and break into the ignition.[69]

As boys grew into teenagers, their lives in the gang grew more complex. Whereas they had originally sought protection, identity, belonging, and community in the gang, it would soon be largely a question of experimentation with the boundaries of violence, petty crime, and drug use. Conflicts between young men over girlfriends raised the stakes. And when crossing boundaries involved dating a white girl, the repercussions were especially dangerous.[70] Disputes were resolved in public street fights that amplified pressures to prove one's masculinity through physical violence. As newcomers to the neighborhood with much to prove, members of the Young Lords started fighting early, practiced fighting with each other, and fashioned themselves as the gang that could "create the most damage" in a fight.[71] Dávila "fought everyone in the group . . . [as a] form of initiation."[72] According to Cha Cha, "The gang was our world, this was our new country. We were willing to fight to the death, no matter what, to defend each other. We did not care about going to jail, that was [like] a reward, a notch on our gun. . . . [It showed] what we stood for: these are the guys I am with and we are defending each other."[73] Before long, arrests for weapons possession increased among the gang's members.

The stakes of these social transactions were bound to be high, as access to more traditional markers of masculine identity, such as a steady job—or the confidence inherent in not having to disprove one's perceived racial inferiority—were increasingly out of reach.[74] By their midteens most Young Lords had dropped out of school and were facing the prospect of employment in the most menial jobs. In 1966, a national study placed the dropout rate among Puerto Rican youth ahead of that of all other racialized groups. A local study concluded that their dropout rate in Chicago was 71.2 percent.[75] Few Young Lords had permanent employment. An exception was the industrious David Rivera, also known as "Chicken Killer." He earned his nickname by holding a regular job at the North Avenue *vivero*, the neighborhood slaughterhouse.

The tipping point of Cha Cha's descent into socially marginal activity came at the end of his three years at St. Theresa, when he discovered during a conversation with his classmate Phil Monestero that he and his family were not invited to the school's yearly graduation party organized by the parents. Cha Cha explains, "Thinking about it is devastating even now. It was a rejection. They didn't want me, for whatever reason. There were no blacks in the class either. Anyway, after that . . . I don't want nothin' to do with the church or school. I don't want anything to do with nothing."

Cha Cha's humiliation would turn to rage. Like Malcolm X, Cha Cha soon refused to play by the rules of society and looked to crime as a means of escape, survival, and personal rebellion. Of the couple of summer months that transpired between his graduation from St. Theresa and his enrollment at Waller High School he explains: "It [felt] like ten years. That's when I really started getting into trouble, at the Burely playground; we were hanging out there every night, every day." The summer of 1963 launched Cha Cha's cycle of early teen-age imprisonment for petty theft, drug possession, and assault. On numerous occasions he was incarcerated at Audy Home, the famed Chicago detention center for adolescents that housed the world's first juvenile court.[76] He explains that he became "used to going to jail": "I just kept getting caught and once you go to jail, once they know you . . . [they] keep picking you up."[77] Amid a crime wave in Chicago that fed the hysteria around juvenile delinquency, he built up quite a rap sheet.[78]

Now older and hardened by imprisonment, the Young Lords went from being chased to doing the chasing. Because of his dark skin, Dávila understood inequality more viscerally than many in the group, and it was he who pushed the gang to cross forbidden boundaries. According to Cha Cha, "[The Young Lords] didn't wait for the Italians and Irish to come to us. . . . We walked up in their neighborhood and said, 'I want a pizza.' And they said, 'Whoa, who the hell do you think you are? You don't get no pizza here.' . . . [But] we got knives, so we're coming in for a clash."[79] The Young Lords were among a younger cohort of gangs with a strong sense of entitlement to public space and a bolder attitude of defiance to authority.

Puerto Ricans, Mexicans, and black Americans in Chicago were not allowed in public spaces reserved for whites. As historian Arnold R. Hirsch explains about the postwar period, for whites "the issue was no longer racial homogeneity of a given area but rather the prerogatives of community control" over the city's resources: its public spaces, parks, and beaches.[80] The beach at the end of North Avenue in Lincoln Park was one such space. As Cha Cha explains: "We could not go to the beach. That's for whites. That's by Lakeshore Drive. . . . The white gangs run that. . . . Our parents can't go there either. If you're Latino . . . adult or child, you walk in there, they're going to push you around. As little kids, we saw our [elders] being slapped around and kicked around." With his quintessential use of humorous dialogue in storytelling, Cha Cha explains how the Young Lords ran roughshod through de facto white spaces and, over the course of many rumbles, succeeded in opening up spaces that their parents had been afraid to enter: "We don't know anything about civil rights, all we know is we live here now, and this beach looks nice to us, and we're going to swim. I remember we're walking in there, it's a crowded beach. You can tell we don't belong there, and we know we're going to fight. People are going, 'What the fuck you doing, fucking spics, why are you here?' So we're throwing people into the water and cutting them up with bottles and knives. They fought for a while, we fought for a while, and they scattered."[81]

In another episode, Dávila convinced Cha Cha to join him on an after-hours walk through the playground of St. Michael's Catholic School, a whites-only space, where elements of the neighborhood's Drum and Bugle Corps operated as a gang at night. Although Cha Cha had reservations about crossing the line, Dávila, armed with a gun, was confident that they would sail through.

> So we walk in there, and they're going, like, "Whoa, look at these bad motherfuckers, they think they're bad, these fucking spics." That kind of shit. So we're smiling. To have a gun at that time, that's like having a cannon with you. So they stop us. They're in front of us, behind us, all around us. And then that's when Orlando takes out the gun. Pop pop, he just shot in the air, the whole playground evacuated, and we just walked through. And we're giving each other five and can't wait to get to the neighborhood to tell the guys, "We just walked through St. Michael's."[82]

These male adolescent contests of brawn and reckless daring helped open up segregated public spaces to people of color in the 1950s and 1960s. They suggest the rising self-confidence demonstrated in 1960 by the black southern teenagers who, having grown up after segregation had lost legal legitimacy, conducted sit-ins to desegregate lunch counters.[83] Cha Cha continues, "After that, everybody starts walking through St. Michael's. These guys are scared. When they see Puerto Ricans walking by, they leave because they think we're coming with guns."

Unlike Dávila, Cha Cha had an aversion to unnecessary physical confrontations. This put him in the position of handling delicate conflicts. In order to manage a gang "so that you're not fighting every second," he explains, it was crucial to "finesse [and] talk your way out of different situations or problems that came up."[84] Increasingly, Cha Cha came to play that role. The unsustainable pressure cooker of these experiences gave way to an ebb and flow of aggression among the gangs. Eventually they pursued less hostile activities, including the formation of sports teams and experimentation with style and culture as a form of resistance. These new activities fostered the development of a different skill set among the group's members, the discovery of hidden talents among others, the addition of dues to the gang structure, and the development of new leadership—all of which laid the groundwork for the Young Lords' later politicization.

In the early 1960s, when he was about fifteen, Jiménez established his leadership in the Young Lords when he identified a strategy through which the gang could acquire what would become their signature black with purple sweaters.

> We were anxious to get our sweaters, [but] we're not getting nowhere with the dues. The sweaters cost about thirty or forty dollars apiece. Our parents are not gonna buy them, so I said why don't we have . . . a business manager?

I didn't even know what that meant. I just heard it somewhere. "Let's make that person in charge of getting the sweaters," 'cause all we're doing is talking a whole lot of crap every meeting and we never get it done and we need [them] to identify ourselves and move us up [in status among other gangs]. So finally someone said, "Why don't we let Cha Cha do it? It's his idea, let him do it." So, I just got voted in like that.[85]

Shepherded by Cha Cha, the Young Lords acquired their sweaters with funds raised from a series of soul dance parties, which became popular in the neighborhood after Cha Cha arranged to have one of them announced on the radio. While tensions between rival gangs inevitably surfaced at these gatherings, the Young Lords measured their success by the diversity of gang colors they saw in the dance hall. In the streets, colors conveyed rumble or amity in an instant, but internally, within a group, colors conveyed allegiance, identity, and much more. In a classic example of the pursuit of life imitating art, the Young Lords chose purple and black as their gang colors. Purple was the color worn by the Sharks, the Puerto Rican gang in the 1961 blockbuster film *West Side Story*. The film trafficked in stereotypes; but it also offered the Young Lords a rare opportunity to identify with figures beyond their block. Cha Cha recalls what it meant for young men like them to suddenly see familiar faces on the big screen: "We were all walking proud with our sweaters, purple and black. Latinos were moving up in society. We were in the movies. *West Side Story* . . . that was big, and now all of a sudden it was more acceptable to be Latinos."[86]

The symbols and styles used by gang members, including colors, music, clothing, and language, signaled a provocative, public rebuke to their subordinate standing in society and attempts to contain them. Before this rebellion found mass expression in 1960s riots, street protests, and political organizations, it was visible in the distinctive styles and colors on display at dance parties in cities across the country, not to mention in the explosion of postwar gangs populated by people of color. The Young Lords wore baggy pants pleated below the waist and long-collared baggy shirts. Their style of dress was drawn consciously from black American Chicago youth who called themselves Gousters, who themselves were influenced by the flamboyant and extravagant zoot suit fashion created by black and Mexican American youth gangs in the 1930s and 1940s.[87]

As the civil rights movement awakened more people to issues of racial equality in the 1960s, a cross-section of social service organizations began to address gang violence and the travails of disconnected youth in Chicago. From 1960 to 1965, the YMCA's Chicago Area Project assigned counselors, called "detached workers," to shadow and document the activities of gangs like the Young Lords and to persuade their members to meet in the YMCA's facilities.[88] One of the counselors assigned to the Young Lords, Masao Yamasaki, was a Japanese

American man who had experienced internment during World War II.[89] This same project employed undergraduates from Wright Junior College to teach the Young Lords and other gangs to use parliamentary procedure in their meetings as a means of ordering their conflicts and discussions.[90]

According to Cha Cha, the streetwise Young Lords often played along with what they instinctively perceived to be a condescending "civilizing mission" on the part of social workers. Rolling his eyes and laughing, Cha Cha explains that the counselors were trying to "show us how to be respectable citizens, [but] if there was a gang fight, I was there and I said, 'I second the motion, let's kick their asses.' You know what I mean? That's the kind of parliamentary procedures we had."[91] Sal del Rivero adds that the gang prevention programs were counterproductive because in promoting competitive sports activities between gangs, counselors implicitly reinforced preexisting gang divisions.[92] Despite their limitations, social service interventions offered street-smart adolescents the opportunity to write articles about their gang in the YMCA's circular. Such activities took them out of the smallness of their block and its fabled corner store around which their lives revolved. The project also put the Young Lords in structured dialogue with each other, a rehearsal of things to come.

Becoming Puerto Rican

Even as the Young Lords embraced constructive activities, Cha Cha was arrested more than twenty times during the first half of the 1960s. One of the most serious arrests proved instrumental to his political evolution. At fifteen, he faced assault charges that could have imprisoned him until he was twenty-one. This was the outcome of a high-stakes contest with a white boy over a love triangle with a white girl. In a plea deal that would be unimaginable decades later for young men of his background, Cha Cha was sent to live in Puerto Rico for at least one year in lieu of a lengthy sentence at Sheridan Correctional Center. The deal was cut with the Cook County Juvenile Court and arranged by a local attorney whom Cha Cha's parents had hired with their meager savings. Cha Cha remembers that on the day of his departure, "They took me from the Audy Home, put me in a paddy wagon, took me to the airport, and they took the handcuffs off of me on the plane. I was crying. I don't know anything about Puerto Rico. I came [to the United States] when I was two years old and I was raised here. . . . I felt like I [was] being thrown out of the country for being in a gang."[93]

Cha Cha began to acclimate to life in the enclave of San Salvador in Caguas, Puerto Rico, where small-town social rules exposed him to that society's different approach to issues of criminal justice. When he fell in love with a girl in a different town, he stole a horse and hot-wired a car belonging to a priest to go see her. His offenses were handled through a series of embarrassing public lectures, first by the priest and later by an older woman in the neighborhood. Cha Cha recalls: "When I was in Puerto Rico, I didn't go to jail. Things were straightened within the family and the community, and I think it had to do with culture. I mean that lady [who gave him a public tongue-lashing] was worse than jail."[94] The difference in his experiences with the law in Chicago and in Puerto Rico led him to reflect on contrasting kinds of justice.

Living in Puerto Rico also compelled Cha Cha to consider how he had acquired his own tangled racial identity. What was unspoken back in Chicago was that Cha Cha, like other fair-skinned Puerto Ricans, could gain advantage in everyday life by passing as white, at least as long as he didn't reveal his unequivocally Spanish name. Yet, even though he was mocked by his peers for being able to pass and for the possibility that he might turn his back on *la raza* (race, lineage, or heritage), Puerto Ricans held contradictory feelings about their own identities: many both rejected and desired to attain the white standard against which they were judged inferior.

In Puerto Rico, Cha Cha "experienced culture shock." He had internalized the message that his light complexion and green eyes made him different, perhaps better. But then he discovered that his family was more racially diverse than he imagined, which suggested that he had black ancestry.[95] His uncles and aunts were dark- and light-skinned Puerto Ricans. Meeting his relatives for the first time also stirred up feelings of guilt for having rejected his parents' homeland. Cha Cha's strong resemblance to his grandfather was undeniable and instilled an intangible sense of rootedness in him. All of this led him to ponder, "Wait a minute, am I American or Puerto Rican?" Decades earlier, writer W. E. B. Du Bois used the term "double consciousness" to illuminate a similar internal struggle among black Americans, which he linked to their devaluation in a racist society where whiteness is the crucial marker of belonging. In this world, the black people must, at great existential pain, assemble a sense of themselves through the lens of a society that denies their humanity.[96]

Cha Cha continued, "It was when I went to Puerto Rico in handcuffs and came back that I became more Puerto Rican."[97] The circular migration of second-generation Puerto Ricans between their parents' country of origin and the continental United States facilitated a merging of this "twoness." Travel also put them in direct contact with two distinct societies where, as anthropologist Jorge Duany has shown, racism and racial identity were manifested differently.[98] For these and other migrants who shared a similar experience of transplantation and settlement, migration disrupted the notion that ways of seeing and understanding race were fixed. In some cases, the power of comparison alerted them to previously unexamined beliefs about race and racism.

Upon his return to Chicago in spring 1964, Cha Cha was more aware of "the contradictions in our parents [and within us]; that we were embarrassed of our parents who were jíbaros and we were more Americanized. . . . We had the pompadours. That was when I had hair [*laughs*]. We were trying to be Italian, trying to be something that we were not." Using political language and understanding acquired later, he clarified, "We had internalized racism." Despite his light skin, Cha Cha was beginning to throw his lot in with those at the bottom of the racial and social hierarchy.

While his perspective had deepened, his relationship with the criminal justice system was largely unchanged. Within a week of his return he was back in jail for stealing a toaster. Jiménez's immediate reimprisonment pointed to a serious problem with drug use and recidivism. According to Cha Cha's recollection, his relationship to crime during that period was "like an addiction": "[When] addicts go back to their environment they relapse eventually. . . . So you try to avoid going back to the people, places, and things, as they say in therapy. I'm back from Puerto Rico. . . . I'm back to the old neighborhood. Being back triggers a lot of stuff. You run into your friends. You want to get high and drunk or whatever. Then, you want to go out and get money."[99]

While Cha Cha resumed criminal activity alongside his cohort, the rising tide of an emergent urban black power movement would soon redirect the alienation, estrangement, and marginal activities of many people like him into more socially constructive action.

In response to the magnitude of black revolt and discontent of the period, Dr. Martin Luther King Jr. launched an economic justice campaign in 1966 that focused on the right to housing and employment in Chicago. His strategy sought to use southern-style marches to pressure federal, state, and city governments to address the crisis of northern slums. His emphasis on housing segregation took black marchers into all-white, suburban communities like Cicero, Illinois, where over 2,000 white residents jeered, cursed, and violently attacked them.[100]

Dr. King's organizing efforts in Chicago failed to deliver even moderate reforms. In the North, racism and poverty that stemmed from the systematic exclusion of people of color from access to decent housing, jobs, and education were not overtly codified in segregationist laws as in the South.[101] People of color were seldom explicitly denied jobs on the basis of race; they were simply not hired. As in Cha Cha's mother's experience, owners also engaged in the common practice of claiming that an apartment had just been rented when a person with dark skin appeared on the premises. In one instance, the light-skinned Cha Cha was told that an apartment was available; when his brown-skinned mother followed up on the inquiry she was turned away.[102] In addition, the experience of indignity and violence at the hands of police, often described by people of color as an occupying army, ignited and channeled the accumulated rage produced by a long-standing sense of powerlessness.[103]

Despite the controversy over Malcolm X's opposition to integration and his calls for black separatism, Malcolm's message of self-respect, self-reliance, and black pride, together with his unabashed condemnation of white liberal paternalism, resonated with many black northerners and with an increasing number of young Puerto Ricans raised in northern cities. As early as 1963, he predicted that, in the absence of a real redress of northern racism and poverty, American society might "erupt into an uncontrollable explosion."[104] The crisis was fully displayed in cities across the country, including in Chicago's Division Street riots of 1966—three days and three nights of spontaneous rebellion and organized protest in which Puerto Ricans were the major protagonists.

Although Puerto Ricans enjoyed new job opportunities upon their arrival in Chicago, the growing spatial isolation of their neighborhoods and the observable decline in industrial jobs that deepened after the recession of 1957 presented structural barriers to the advancement of their children. Out of this contradictory reality of raised hopes and dashed dreams emerged a distinct urban experience and identity in the new generation, whose frustrations, like those of black Americans, erupted during a conflict with police—a growing symbol, among Puerto Ricans, of racialized police brutality and Chicago's white power structure. In June 1966, a white police officer shot and wounded a young Puerto Rican man, Arcelis Cruz. In response, Puerto Rican youth threw rocks and bricks at police, targeted them with snipers, and looted and burned down white-owned businesses on Division Street, the central artery of the Puerto Rican community and, ironically, home to the Chicago branch of the Migration Division, the office in charge of facilitating Puerto Rican settlement on the U.S. mainland. In the end, "16 persons were injured, 49 were arrested, over 50 buildings were destroyed, and millions of dollars accrued in damages."[105] Of the riots, Cha Cha recalls: "To the best of my recollection, I was sitting on a second level bunk in Vandalia State Penitentiary at that time. But we were definitely proud of that moment. The community was fighting back. . . . And there was something that really lifted our hearts in that."[106]

While Cha Cha was in prison, Omar Lopez, one of the future political strategists of the Young Lords, was among a group of young radical community leaders and former students who, in the wake of the Division Street riots, called for grassroots organizing and deeper structural change. Lopez, who is Mexican, explains that it was "the street groups . . . that really kept [the riots] going for three days; and that was the beginning of the clash in the Puerto Rican community with its [established] leadership." In cities across the country the riots engendered a crisis of legitimacy in preexisting leadership structures in communities of color, which were often allied with city hall. In Chicago, there was an observable "decline in the relative social status of some of the earlier Puerto Rican elite" and an opening and yearning for new, younger leadership with different approaches to, and perspectives on, the problems facing the community.[107]

A cross-section of new voices, among them radical activists, convened public meetings and invited residents to voice their reactions and assess local problems. The Latin American Boys Club, located in the heart of the Division Street district, became the headquarters for community gatherings where marches and support groups for those arrested were organized.[108] The Spanish Action Committee of Chicago (SACC) was one of the largest and most influential Puerto Rican grassroots organizations to emerge from the riots and was influenced by the model of the War on Poverty's Community Action Programs (CAPs). Although the Young Lords Organization would emerge later, elements of its worldview were articulated by the Latin American Defense Organization (LADO), which emerged on Division Street immediately after the riots in September 1966. Organized by Omar Lopez's older brother, Obed Lopez, it stood to the left of the SACC. Radical groups like LADO spread across the country in response to the riots. The predecessor groups of the Black Panther Party, for example, deepened their activities immediately after the Watts riots of 1965.[109] These groups sought to channel the eruptions of social anger toward political ends by offering a structural critique of the urban crisis. Although LADO addressed many of the same local grievances as the SACC, it was critical of electoral politics. It opposed the SACC's ethnic nationalist allegiances, which according to Omar Lopez focused exclusively on building Puerto Rican leadership to the exclusion of leadership from other groups with common class interests. LADO argued for unity among people of Latin American descent together with historically oppressed people in the United States, especially black Americans. Responsive to the struggles for survival of Puerto Rican women who faced discriminatory exclusion and humiliation in Chicago's welfare offices, LADO organized a welfare union, led by Hilda Gamboa, whose activities often coalesced with those of the emerging welfare rights movement.[110] Its membership included working-class Puerto Ricans, Mexicans, Panamanians, and even some white Americans.[111]

LADO's perspective was driven by the political background of its founder, Obed Lopez, who was heavily surveilled by the FBI and Chicago police, which initially assumed he was Puerto Rican.[112] Upon arrival from Mexico in the late 1950s, Obed joined the Chicago branch of the Twenty-Sixth of July Movement. That was the revolutionary movement led by Fidel Castro and Che Guevara that in 1959 overthrew the Fulgencio Batista dictatorship in Cuba.[113] As a teachers college student in Mexico, Lopez had been involved in the campaign that elected radicals to student government in the Normales del Estado, Mexico's teacher-training colleges.[114] The "Normalistas,'" as they were called, laid the groundwork in the 1950s for the national student movement whose protests against autocracy, repression, and economic inequality culminated in the infamous Tlatelolco massacre of student protesters by Mexico City police in 1968.[115] This organic connection to radical organizing in Mexico and in support of Cuba nurtured a broad political perspective and was a precursor of things to come in the Young Lords.

Becoming an Activist

Within this setting of local and global unrest, Cha Cha continued his efforts to keep the Young Lords together. The gang experienced instability as members got married, joined the military, or went to prison.[116] As the Young Lords' recognized leader, Cha Cha's life, identity, and reputation were wrapped up in the gang's institutional survival. During continued stints in prison, he remained committed to what leaders and organizers recognize as the interminable work of keeping a group together: "If you are a head of a group you are always thinking about how you are going to put all the pieces of it together, like Humpty Dumpty. You know that the group is not all completely together. You are hanging on to it like a puppet on a string and it's hanging all over the place, it's all in pieces. So I'm in jail and the gang will not stay together unless [it] meets [regularly], so I'm dealing with that."[117]

In the spring of 1968, Cha Cha was imprisoned again on a drug charge, this time at North Cell House, a short-term detention center for adults and a subsection of the Chicago House of Corrections. It was here, in the wake of Martin Luther King Jr.'s assassination and in the context of a growing antiwar movement following the Vietnamese Tet Offensive at the end of January, that a complex web of unintended circumstances and conscious interventions paved the way for Cha Cha's explicit politicization.

In April 1968, the assassination of Martin Luther King increased the level of repression in the prison and raised political awareness among the prisoners.[118] Amid mass police roundups, Cha Cha was confined to "the hole" for sixty days. He was among a cohort of Spanish-speaking prisoners placed in solitary confinement for allegedly attempting to escape, although this may have been a measure to preempt dissent in the run-up to the Democratic Party Convention in August. Cha Cha channeled the stress of heightened repression by focusing on the abuse suffered by a group of non-English-speaking migrant workers who were also swept up in the roundups. He had earlier translated on their behalf and, in an attempt to protect them from the guards' harassment, joined others in demanding that, as especially vulnerable migrant workers, they be left alone. Cha Cha had grown up with stories of his father's and uncle's experiences as migrant farmworkers when they arrived on the mainland. The capricious abuse they suffered rankled his sense of justice and tapped into a desire to serve.

The incident also opened up the possibility of solidarity among black Americans, Puerto Ricans, and Mexicans. Amid the prison chaos, Cha Cha recalls being singled out for harassment by a black prison guard who berated him at full volume for "trying to act black." The guard unleashed a barrage of humiliating (and potentially dangerous) accusations that were meant to make Cha Cha a target for other prisoners. "You are not black," the guard continued, "you are just trying to pretend like you are black so they don't kick your ass, so they don't fuck you." The gravity of the psychological assault was compounded, Cha Cha remembers, by the silence that befell the unit while the guard laid into him. Stunned, enraged, and immobilized by the verbal pummeling, Cha Cha was finally shaken out of his stupor when he heard a black prisoner belt out, "Shut the fuck up, you pig!" Like a flood, the unit was filled with a cacophony of shouts from the prisoners indicting the guard. Cha Cha explains that although the humiliation was traumatic, the expression of solidarity he heard from the black prisoners left a bigger emotional imprint on him: "They defended me. . . . That really had a profound impact on me."[119]

Isolated in solitary confinement, Cha Cha was compelled to read. He would have to acquire books from the designated librarian, a job that all across the country was customarily sought and held by prisoners who were members of the Nation of Islam. The Nation was the organization whose mixture of jailhouse proselytizing with appeals to black pride and race-based separatism reformed the lives of a generation of black prisoners in the 1950s and 1960s, most notably Malcolm X.[120] Because of Cha Cha's light skin and green eyes, the librarian confused him for "a blue-eyed devil," but the conflict was mediated by Cha Cha's dark-skinned cousin who was also imprisoned at North Cell House. As when he was in Puerto Rico, Cha Cha was again confronted with an existential question: Who am I? He became more aware than ever of the need among Puerto Ricans to educate others "on just who we are . . . that we are in the same boat. . . . I felt . . . that we didn't fit in here and we didn't fit in there, and we needed to define our own identity."[121]

The first book he requested was *The Seven Storey Mountain* by Thomas Merton, the best-selling autobiography of a twenty-six-year-old man who withdrew from society to pursue spiritual transformation through contemplation. To Cha Cha, who had once considered becoming a priest, Merton's quest must have raised questions and guilt about his own life's path: before long he requested a visit by a Catholic priest to whom he confessed his drug use and expressed commitment to redirecting his life. Cha Cha's reading list included Martin Luther King Jr.'s *Where Do We Go from Here* and *The Autobiography of Malcolm X*. It was during this time that Cha Cha also learned about the newly formed Chicago chapter of the Black Panther Party (BPP) from the black-run radio station, WBON, which was on around the clock at the prison and mainly featured "old-school dusties," or love songs. The station's periodic news segments sometimes reported on the activities of the BPP, which according to Cha Cha often drew the attention of prisoners, especially the party's use of the word "pig." The unmasking of police abuse and authority implicit in the term offered a powerful psychological balm to many racialized people in the United States and especially to urban, male youth populations more likely to come into contact with police in increasingly patrolled public spaces. According to Cha Cha, "There was also talk about [the Panthers] having guns and fighting the police, and I'm against the police, naturally, because I've been beaten up so many times by them. . . . Everybody at that time was against [the police]."[122]

In the politicized atmosphere created by the era's social movements, several incidents awakened Cha Cha to the collective struggles of ordinary people against their subjugation. They included his stint in the hole, his clash with the black Muslim librarian, conversations with other prisoners about the books he was reading, the roaring voice of the black prisoner who defended him against a guard's assault on his dignity, and his witness and response to the abuse and repression of jailed migrants. These experiences fueled Cha Cha's resolve to redirect and refocus the gang's activities and stay the course. The changes he observed upon his release also played a role. Cha Cha explains, "When I came out . . . the neighborhood saw a complete change in sixty days, with people getting thrown out [of their homes, and] I'm saying [to myself], 'We need to do something like the Black Panthers.'"[123]

Cha Cha's first attempt at reforming his life and initiating a political project came when the Urban Training Center, a program of the Presbyterian Church, offered him work after his release from prison in the summer of 1968. Its radical Puerto Rican minister, Victor Nazario, invited Cha Cha to a training and networking conference for Latino activists in late October.[124] Nazario was influential among budding Puerto Rican and Mexican activists in Chicago because he provided an "analysis of things that was very powerful and inspiring," offered one-on-one political mentorship to young people, and held meetings that connected college students with the goings-on in the community. Moved by Nazario's example, Cha Cha lured a few members of the Young Lords to the conference, which put them in touch with a network of activists whose work offered concrete examples of the community organizing that was taking place in Chicago and across the country. It was at this event that Cha Cha reconnected with Omar Lopez of LADO, whom he knew from the neighborhood and who would be instrumental in deepening the gang's political analysis. At that time, Cha Cha attempted to form a group he called the Puerto Rican Progressive Movement, an effort that drew few members and gained little traction. In late 1968, he attended a few meetings of the local school board at Waller High School in Lincoln Park, and at one of those meetings was voted vice president of a coalition concerned with school reform and community control of the public schools.[125]

Cha Cha began to reconstitute the Young Lords as an organization in late fall 1968, when he learned about a new round of demolition plans in Lincoln Park. The gang was not new to changes in leadership and direction. In the mid-1960s it underwent a period of increased social activity, including parties and basketball games, and in 1966, it opened a coffeehouse called Uptight #2, under the leadership of Orlando Dávila.[126] The year 1968 brought change, however, as Cha Cha decided to incorporate "the Lordettes" into the group. The Lordettes had been formed as an independent entity in 1965, a women's auxiliary of the Young Lords with its own chairwoman and leadership structure.[127] The participation and integration of women would alter the group's character, helping to move it beyond its focus on narrow turf battles over adolescent, male-dominated spaces such as street corners and playgrounds. Opening the group up to women, many of whom had formed families with members of the Young Lords, immediately made critical the demand for childcare centers. It was becoming a major demand of radical women's groups across the country, especially among poor and working-class women and women of color. Together the male and female groups organized a series of fundraisers: a month of soul dances in collaboration with a black American gang, the Black Stone Rangers; a community picnic; a drug education program; and a food and toy drive for Christmas. Under the leadership of Cha Cha and others, the Young Lords also began to advance the idea of Third World unity, welcoming poor and working-class black Americans, while also accepting white Americans of the same class as members.[128]

Not long after the conference at the Presbyterian church, Cha Cha found himself in a heated debate with Patricia Devine, a housing organizer who had been hired by a predominantly white organization, Concerned Citizens of Lincoln Park (CCLP). Devine's CCLP emerged in the mid-1960s to "represent the common people of the neighborhood that were not represented by the Lincoln Park Conservation Association (LPCA)," a small but influential group of local homeowners, mostly middle-class, liberal professionals, that had developed the neighborhood's blueprint for urban renewal in its own image.[129] In her political pitch to the young men standing on one of the corners with Cha Cha, Devine explained that the very corner on which they were standing was under review for demolition. Devine painted a picture of imminent danger and argued that the ongoing displacement of Lincoln Park residents would only be stopped through a collective struggle by the older residents of the neighborhood, one that looked beyond racial divisions and the narrow world view of its gang formations.

Cha Cha responded to Devine with hostility and a mix of suspicion due to her race, class, and outsider status: "Who the fuck do you think you are? Are you trying to take our neighborhood from us?" As she attempted to explain her organization's mission to stop urban renewal, Cha Cha called her a "fucking communist, motherfucker." Devine's defiant rejoinder, "I'm proud to be a communist," startled Cha Cha, who was offended by the idea ("that was a sacrilegious word").[130] Cha Cha had already begun redirecting the energies of the Young Lords and rethinking racism and repression, both in the prisons and at the hands of the police. He had also observed the swift changes the neighborhood underwent during his short stint in prison. But he was not ready to have his world view challenged by a white, middle-class woman or to adopt the Marxist-inflected critique of urban renewal presented by Devine. Despite the increased visibility of what came to be known as Third World socialism in nations emerging from colonialism, Cha Cha's visceral response was a reflection of the extent to which anticommunism continued to permeate almost every sector of U.S. society.

Advised to calm down by his peers, Cha Cha agreed to continue the conversation with Devine and her friend at a nearby apartment. Eventually Cha Cha and a small group of his compeers softened up to the CCLP's mission of working against urban renewal. At the urging of Devine, Cha Cha worked hard to bring a group of his fellow Young Lords to the next scheduled meeting of the Lincoln Park Conservation Association (LPCA). Before long he was at the bars on Lincoln Park's North Avenue talking about the impending housing crisis.

But Cha Cha's challenges abounded. The learned behavior of survival adopted by gang members was perhaps his greatest stumbling block. In many ways, gang members were conditioned to think narrowly and parochially about turf control and protecting their own. Consequently, many Young Lords initially resisted explicit calls for coalitions and attempts at mobilizing the gang toward political ends. Cha Cha confronted the alienating experience of living in two opposed realities: being a respected gang leader among his peers one day and then awakening to being treated as an outcast, a suspected "communist," the next—at least by some in his community.

In January 1969, in close collaboration with Young Lord Ralph Rivera, Cha Cha convinced approximately twenty Young Lords to gather at the local urban renewal building. They were joined by a group of activists, including members of the North Side Cooperative Ministry, who since the mid-1960s had educated the neighborhood about housing issues. According to Pat Devine and Cha Cha, the LPCA was meeting to present its plans, with visual charts of the areas, and identify the blocks that would next be targeted for demolition. Although the entire neighborhood was being redeveloped and no single ethnicity was being targeted, per se, demolition plans targeted the Halstead-Armitage area where Puerto Ricans lived, including the Jiménez family.[131] At this meeting, a vote was cast in support of demolition.

Cha Cha, other members of the Young Lords, and the other activists went to the meeting with plans to unsettle and disrupt the proceedings. In light of the urgency of the situation—bulldozers being scheduled to raze entire city blocks—the Young Lords were perplexed by the meeting's decorum. However, the primary demands they presented during the meeting were quite moderate and focused on addressing the absence of Puerto Rican representation in the LPCA. As they left the meeting, they threw chairs across the room and "trashed" the place. According to Devine, even the activists in the room were startled by the aggressive, spontaneous actions of Cha Cha and his friends, who didn't hesitate to rumble to defend their homes on Chicago's Near North Side. Within a matter of days, however, a group of about twenty Young Lords commenced an intense period of formal politicization through study and discussion with radical activists. This engagement began to replace brawn with thoughtful organizing strategy. The Young Lords were courted by members of the Communist Party, as well as the Socialist Workers Party and its youth group, the Young Socialist Alliance.[132] Retrospectively, Devine reasoned that the clash had posed a basic question about the meaning of belonging and displacement among Puerto Ricans. Before long, Cha Cha began to argue that the Puerto Rican people "were 'pawns' in the hands of the 'white power structure'" and linked their housing displacement to the imperial role of the United States in Puerto Rico.[133]

Under Surveillance

Shortly after the clash at the urban renewal office, Cha Cha attended local meetings and marches involving a range of issues from welfare rights to calls for civilian review of complaints against the police. As he became increasingly active in the community, calling daily evening meetings among the Young Lords and appearing as an invited speaker at public events, he was subjected to increased hostility and surveillance by police.[134] The day after the incident at the urban renewal meeting, he was taken in for questioning and served with two outstanding arrest warrants, which he had previously successfully challenged. Later that same day, in a public display of intimidation, six squad cars surrounded Cha Cha when he arrived at a Waller High School meeting organized by the community education coalition of which he was now vice president. The police reportedly told a local minister, Bruce Johnson, that Police District Commander Clarence Braasch "intended to put Cha Cha in the penitentiary and that wherever the Young Lords go, the police would follow in force."[135] Eventually however, the police retreated when Bessie Lawrence, School District Seven's superintendent, called the nearby precinct to complain about their aggressive disruption of the meeting. Cha Cha was again arrested on January 30, 1969, when he attempted to defend two welfare mothers during a sit-in to demand welfare back payments. In January and February, Cha Cha was arrested, stopped and searched, or questioned by the police at least once, and often twice, weekly.[136]

In defense of Cha Cha, the Young Lords and their supporters attended a police-sponsored, community council meeting in the Eighteenth District Police

Station. The group claimed it brought more than 300 people to the meeting; the FBI reported 500.[137] Photos show a phalanx of young people in purple berets standing along the back wall of a room filled beyond capacity. The protesters were boisterous and irreverent, cheering and booing frequently. At the start of the meeting, a minister moved that the agenda be changed to address the grievances of those gathered, which included members from six organizations that had been active on issues of urban renewal, education, and police brutality alongside the Young Lords.[138] When the meeting chair, Ramon Valdes, used the meeting's "rules of order" to challenge the proposal, the group began yelling "read the rules." Adding to the meeting's raucous feel, the Young Lords affixed their placards and signs to the meeting room's walls. Their bold message—a biting critique of and dig at the police—reflected the newfound confidence and growing militancy of racialized people in cities across the nation. They read:

- City Law Does Not Allow Pigs on the Street
- Pigs Need Support Centers to Keep Them off the Street
- Keep Pigs on Hawthorne Mellody Farms
- Hands off Cha Cha
- Viva Young Lords
- Young Lords Serve and Protect[139]

In addition to adopting the Black Panthers' designation for the police, these provocative slogans effectively redirected at police the city's own patronizing declarations aimed at youth of color and their gangs.

Protesters exposed police attempts to silence Cha Cha. They demanded that police cease harassment of the organization. A barrage of questions about Cha Cha's many detentions forced Commander Braasch to acknowledge the existence of a gang intelligence unit, independent of the police district, that was likely observing the Young Lords' activities. In fact, as Chicago's gangs were becoming politicized, the mayor established a gang intelligence unit within the police department; Cha Cha was one of its main targets. That evening, the Young Lords mounted an important local defense of the First Amendment association clause. Braasch was also obliged to address the state of an investigation into the recent shooting of a fifteen-year-old black youth by a police officer.[140]

Building the Young Lords Organization

Cha Cha had become an organizer. The gang had taught him to size up a situation quickly and assess the skill sets, potential, commitment, and loyalty of individuals around him. As he was transforming the organization, he drew upon the resources, experience, and networks of others. One of the first people he approached about joining the Young Lords in late fall 1968 was Omar Lopez.

They had recently reconnected at the Urban Training Center. According to Lopez, immediately after their discussion, "I talked about it with my brother [Obed Lopez] and we thought it was a good strategic move [to join the Young Lords] because LADO wanted to involve different people in the struggle."[141]

The Young Lords made structural changes to adapt to their new political focus. On February 17, less than a week after their police precinct action, they cosponsored the two-day Third World Unity Conference at the Olivet Presbyterian Church in collaboration with Black, Active, and Determined, a youth organization in the Cabrini-Green housing projects.[142] One session featured the chairman of the Chicago Black Panthers, Fred Hampton, as the principal speaker.

Immediately after that event, on February 20, 1969, Chicago Panther leaders Hampton, Bobby Lee, and Henry "Poison" Gaddis met with Cha Cha and the Young Lords at Panther headquarters. It was a turning point: the Young Lords formally adopted the BPP model of organization and its Ten-Point Program and pledged to organize among Puerto Ricans as the BPP's Puerto Rican counterpart. On February 27, 1969, the Chicago BPP called for the formation of a "Rainbow Coalition," a class-based, poor people's alliance across ethnic and racial lines.[143] Its mission was to build solidarity among poor and working-class youth by promoting grassroots leadership among them in each of the city's racially segregated communities and tackling race antagonisms openly in the streets, at open forums, and through collaboration across racial lines. The groundbreaking project had not surfaced overnight. In 1968, BPP Field Secretary, Bob Lee, began to integrate his work as a gang counselor in Volunteers in Service to America with his BPP obligations. Lee introduced Black Panther–style political education to the predominantly white youth he was expected to advise in the city's North Side, where poor white migrants from the Appalachian Mountains of West Virginia, Kentucky, and North Carolina settled in the postwar period. Informal conversations turned into formal meetings that included black American gangs and to which Hampton, Gaddis, and other Panthers were invited.[144] Once formalized, the Rainbow Coalition included the Young Lords; the Black Panthers; the Young Patriots, a gang of white Appalachian youth; and Rising Up Angry, which emerged after the political split in Students for a Democratic Society.[145]

Of the series of gatherings that sealed the relationship, Young Lord Rory Guerra remembers: "They were kind of loose-knit meetings. They would say that they were gonna have a rally and they'd like us to attend and Cha Cha would be asked to speak. It wasn't a subservient relationship. They looked at us as peers. They didn't look at us as followers or leaders, but just peers. They empathized with us." Fred Hampton was instrumental in setting the terms of the relationship. Guerra continues, "Hampton was a very humble person and didn't walk around like he was God's gift to the movement, although he was an eloquent

Fred Hampton (*seated, far left*), chairman of the Chicago Black Panthers, calls a press conference with members of the Rainbow Coalition on October 10, 1969, challenging the armed struggle orientation of the Days of Rage actions organized by the Weatherman faction of Students for a Democratic Society. Also seated from left: Pablo Guzmán of the Young Lords of New York; José "Cha-Cha" Jiménez, founder of the Young Lords of Chicago; and Mike Klonsky of Students for a Democratic Society. Standing from left: one of the Matos brothers (Chicago Young Lords), Juan "Fi" Ortiz (New York Young Lords), and Benny (Chicago Young Lords). (Photograph by Dave Nystrom/Chicago Tribune; courtesy of the *Chicago Tribune*)

public speaker; he was also a great organizer. He was a person who came in an old car, got out, shook people's hands, wanted to really talk to people. I remember him saying, 'I'm glad to have met you. I'm glad to have met you.'"[146] Hampton's talents as organizer and public speaker and his radical coalition politics made him one of the most effective members of the Black Panther Party.

The emergence of the BPP in 1966 transformed the landscape of radical politics in the United States. The group's revolutionary rhetoric electrified millions of young people and transformed their outlook. Founded in Oakland, California, in 1966 by college students Huey P. Newton and Bobby Seale, the BPP sought to build a radical cadre organization of young black people united around a platform for radical reforms that they called the Ten-Point Program. Their program called for, among other things, "the power to determine the destiny of our Black Community"; "full employment for our people"; "an end to the robbery by the white man of our black community"; "decent housing, fit for shelter of human beings"; "education"; "an immediate end to police brutality"; and "clothing, justice, and peace."[147]

The BPP's embrace of armed self-defense, radical left politics, and coalition with white leftists made it a controversial organization among elements of the black freedom movement. But its bold activism channeled community rage against police brutality and abuse of authority and drew large numbers of black youth to the party. With law books in hand and the aid of short-wave radio signals that allowed them to pick up police communications, the Black Panthers organized armed civilian patrol units in East Oakland. Their objective was to stand at a legal distance with loaded and exposed rifles—allowed by California law—to monitor police arrests and inform community residents of their rights.

When the California legislature introduced a state law in 1967 barring citizens from carrying openly displayed weapons—dubbed the "Black Panther Bill"—the Panthers traveled to Sacramento to protest. National media captured the BPP's militancy, revolutionary rhetoric, denunciations of the police as "pigs," and provocative actions. These immediately raised the organization's profile, and by the end of 1968, the BPP had mushroomed from a single local organization in Oakland to a national organization with offices in twenty cities.

The BPP's provocative tactics were tempered by a series of "survival programs" aimed to address the worst aspects of urban poverty. These included a breakfast program for poor children, an ambulance service, and various health programs for detection of lead poisoning, tuberculosis, and sickle-cell anemia.[148] Because the BPP established a simple model of protest and organization that connected with the rebellious political pulse of much of black, urban America, others were eager to replicate its activities across the country.

There was another reason why others were inspired to model similar actions. According to Rory Guerra, Fred Hampton articulated the importance of survival programs in the context of a society intent on destroying poor communities of color "through drugs, poor nutrition and housing, all these things that people are talking about now: eating habits, healthcare, the Panthers were talking about all of that in those days." After the connection was made, the Chicago Lords began to combine "political education with talk about diet and who controlled the production of food. Eventually we built a free clinic, we provided health information to the community. We started a breakfast program. We had food giveaways. We had a dental program."[149]

By March 1969, three months after the Young Lords' first protest at the urban renewal office, they began to publish their own newspaper, as did the Panthers. It contained dozens of letters and reported on the range of community protests in which the Young Lords were involved. It offered an analysis of imperialism from Vietnam and Puerto Rico to Africa; covered the local and national actions of the BPP, including the campaign to free BPP chairman Huey P. Newton, who had been charged with first-degree murder, assault, and kidnapping in 1967; and reprinted the BPP's Ten-Point Program. The *YLO* was edited by the talented Young Lords spokesperson, Luis Cuza, but good writers like Omar Lopez and Hilda Vasquez-Ignatin had a hand in its editorial production too. Black American and white radicals, drawn to the Young Lords, also contributed, and the newspaper's political analysis reflected the fluency of some of its new members in Marxist-leaning politics. Reportage on the happenings in Lincoln Park's local movement pointed to heightened police repression. The first edition published five articles on community complaints against the police and, following the Panther newspaper's model, identified a former drug dealer turned police officer, Pete Rivera, as "Pig of the Month."[150] The paper also reported on local welfare rights and housing protests and a meeting in which community residents took commanders to task for the use of "intimidation and stop and frisk procedures" and illegal searches and seizures by police.

In the winter of 1969, the Young Lords began to cohere as a political organization. Because of Cha Cha's preexisting street networks, meetings and events either called or supported by the Young Lords drew large numbers. According to Omar Lopez: "In a sense the Lords came into an environment that already had a good base. . . . For example, some of the actions that the Young Lords were involved in were not necessarily Young Lords actions; LADO had initiated the work with the welfare unions and the citywide Welfare Rights Organization, and the Young Lords served as security. So the conditions were ripe for the Young Lords to flourish."[151] The work of LADO from 1966 to 1968 facilitated the politicization of the Young Lords. LADO helped build the gang's infrastructure quickly in the fall of 1969 by consenting to the full transfer of Lopez's work and political responsibilities to the Young Lords.

The transformation of the Young Lords into a political organization was uneven and challenging. Many members had one foot in gang life and another in political activity. Drug use, lack of discipline, and arrests were ongoing, especially in the first six months after their initial exposure to grassroots protest at the housing demolition hearing. A key moment, however, occurred in the early morning hours of May 4, 1969, when four Young Lords witnessed the fatal shooting of one of their own, Manuel Ramos, by an undercover police officer named James Lamb, as they celebrated the birthday party of the gang's founder, Orlando Dávila. Officer Lamb claimed he approached the area because he heard a gunshot. When Ramos emerged from the apartment where the party was being held, allegedly wielding a gun, the officer claimed he shot him in the head in self-defense. He also shot another Young Lord, Rafael Rivera, in the neck.[152] The Young Lords maintained that Ramos did not have a gun. The four witnesses from the Young Lords were arrested and charged with aggravated battery. From prison, they called Cha Cha, who was not at the party, and within a day he and other Young Lords raised bail.[153] But the police officer who fatally shot their friend was acquitted when a coroner's jury returned a verdict of justifiable homicide.[154] Led by Cha Cha, the Young Lords drafted a broad set of demands calling for the immediate dismissal and imprisonment of Officer Lamb; the hiring of public school bilingual teachers and instruction in Puerto Rican history and culture. They also demanded that "trials be conducted by residents of the community in which the offender lives"; the "disarming [of] all policemen"; and the implementation of community-based policing.[155]

The day after Ramos was killed, the Young Lords mobilized hundreds in a march against the police that included gang members from the Latin Kings and Latin Queens, the Cannibals, the Hell Stompers, the Harrison Gents, and Black Stone Rangers, and others. Thousands more joined them in subsequent street demonstrations; at a protest outside the Eighteenth District Police Department, where Illinois attorney general Edward Hanrahan was scheduled to speak; and at Ramos's funeral procession, where the police reported to the FBI that "the crowd was 'ugly' with considerable anti-police sentiment, and chanting 'Off the Pigs' at the police in the area."[156] Involvement of rival gangs in these demonstrations came with a good deal of tension that sometimes triggered violent street fights often instigated by agents provocateurs. The National Socialist White People's Party, previously known as the American Nazi Party, held a small counterprotest.[157] Fred Hampton, Cha Cha, Luis Cuza, and Ramos's family contained the violence with spirited speeches and calls for unity against the police.

Respect grew for the Young Lords among relatives and friends immediately after these events. The tragedy galvanized young and old; and support from an older generation of Puerto Rican and Mexican migrants legitimized participation of a growing cohort of young women. The gathering pace of protest on the Near North Side of Chicago led a special agent of the FBI to report that the "alliance between these apparently divergent groups into an anti-police, militant force would greatly increase the possibilities of disorders."[158] Within days of the Ramos tragedy, the Young Lords dedicated a special issue of the *YLO* to their slain brother. It began with a letter of gratitude by Ramos's family for the struggle waged in defense of their son by Cha Cha and the Young Lords. The Young Lords summarized the political meaning of their loss with the words of the revolutionary Ernesto "Che" Guevara: "Wherever death may surprise us, let it be welcome if our battle cry has reached even one receptive ear, and another hand reaches out to take up arms, and new men come forward to join in our funeral procession with the chattering of machine guns and new calls for battle and victory."[159]

The Young Lords would be politically transformed by the campaign to bring Officer Lamb to justice. Because of the group's established gang network, hundreds of young men and women who had watched the political activities joined what was now the Young Lords Organization. Emboldened by the support they received in the streets, the Young Lords were pivotal in turning the existing community sentiment against McCormick Theological Seminary, for its endorsement of urban renewal, into an occupation of its main building on May 14, 1969. The action was spontaneous; it followed one of the marches protesting the shooting death of Ramos.

According to Cha Cha, the impulse came suddenly and was envisioned as a way of bringing the tactic of building occupations on college campuses to the community—to "make community institutions, such as churches and seminaries, more accountable to the community."[160] In spite of confusion prompted by the unplanned occupation, diverse groups at the Ramos protest joined in. Most, including a group of seminary students, formed part of the Poor People's Coalition (PPC), which had been in negotiations with the McCormick Theological Seminary since May 12, two days earlier.[161] The long-standing battle centered on the use of $601,000 that McCormick had previously promised for community projects. The PPC demanded disbursal of those funds for a housing development led by a local architect, Howard Alan, selected by the activists. The activists envisioned a design that would preserve the fabric and dignity of the community with green space, parks, and aesthetically rich and affordable rental units. The coalition also called for a daycare center, a Puerto Rican cultural center, and a people's law office, which would offer free legal representation to activists and low-income earners.[162] The Young Lords played a leading role during the five-day occupation and in negotiations that led to the seminary conceding to most of the PPC's demands.

July 11, 1969, brought another important Young Lords action. The Board of the Armitage Avenue Methodist Church, where the Young Lords had been holding their regular meetings, declined the organization's proposal to rent church space for a daycare center and a Panther-style children's breakfast program and health clinic. The radicals occupied the church in protest. Acting independently of the board, the church's minister, Bruce Johnson, endorsed the Young Lords' activities. When he advised the police against taking action, the Young Lords turned the Armitage Street church into their headquarters.[163] Immediately, the Young Lords' minister of health, Alberto Chivera, a third-year medical student at Northwestern University, and his wife, began collaborations with other radical organizations and various social service groups. Together they established public health campaigns at the church with a social service focus akin to the BPP's survival programs, including clothing and food drives and the building blocks of a free community health clinic.

Cha Cha Jiménez's transformation from alienated youth to politicized gang leader exemplifies a process of radicalization in the sixties that gripped thousands of young people of color whose names we will never know. The conversion was incubated in the fallouts of migration, in clashes with white gangs and police, in prison and Puerto Rico, and as he grasped the broader meanings of urban renewal—the modern land question. These experiences also seeded his kinship with the Black Panther Party. When Cha Cha began to steer the Young Lords away from petty crime and turf wars, the BPP offered a popular political model to follow. It also afforded the most concrete organizational structure within which to discipline and reeducate gang members. In emulating the Black Panthers—the most politically persecuted and maligned organization of the 1960s—the Young Lords raised eyebrows among many Puerto Ricans and, for different reasons, among police. Puerto Ricans and other Spanish-speaking migrants had joined black power organizations as individuals. But no Puerto Rican organization had forged such a relationship.

Unencumbered by the need to keep up appearances or respectability politics, a Puerto Rican street organization met the challenge. The leap assured the Young Lords a place in a larger, iconic movement and in history. That bold move was precisely the example that Puerto Ricans in New York needed to propel them into motion.

CHAPTER TWO

COMING OF AGE IN THE 1960S

The Emergence of the New York Young Lords

While Cha Cha and his crew continued to seek justice for the police killing of Manuel Ramos, in New York a group of mostly Puerto Rican students was looking for an organizing agenda. The group had been brought together by Mickey Melendez, a student at the State University of New York College at Old Westbury (SUNY Old Westbury). It included fellow students Pablo Guzmán, back from studying abroad in Mexico; Denise Oliver, a black red diaper baby; and David Perez, a mature youth who had his nose in a book and his heart in Puerto Rico. Among others, they were joined by Juan González, recently expelled from Columbia University for his leadership during the student strike of 1968, and by two former students at the City University of New York, spoken word poet Felipe Luciano and his wife, Iris Morales, a community organizer recently returned from a trip to Cuba, who would come around later on.

Sometime in early June of 1969, a dozen or so of them trickled into the office of the Real Great Society (RGS) Urban Planning Studio, an antipoverty advocacy project in East Harlem.[1] For weeks they had alternated meetings between this community-based office space and a dorm at SUNY Old Westbury. The students were torn about whether to anchor their work on college campuses or in the socially marginalized communities where many grew up. This dilemma also preoccupied their white predecessors in Students for a Democratic Society (SDS) and the Black Panthers.[2] The spontaneous rebellions that had swept through East Harlem just two years earlier in 1967 in response to the killing of a Puerto Rican man by a police officer were sobering reminders that local community organizing was perhaps more urgent than university study.

Juan González shows a copy of *Palante* to a rider on the New York subway, February 1971. (Photograph by Michael Abramson; courtesy of Haymarket Books)

Up for discussion that day was a reading that would provide concrete answers to these burning questions. Sitting around a beat-up table, the dozen students read an interview with a Puerto Rican radical published in the June 7 edition of the weekly Black Panther Party (BPP) newspaper. His name was Cha Cha Jiménez.[3]

In the interview, Cha Cha described the swift politicization of his gang after the fatal police shooting of one of their own and how the Chicago Young Lords' growing commitment to militant, housing-rights action ushered in an onslaught of police provocation and harassment. Cha Cha reported that the newly renamed Young Lords Organization (YLO) focused on a radical political program seeking *structural change* rather than a liberal social-service response to community problems. In its organizational structure and politics, Cha Cha noted that the Young Lords followed the revolutionary leadership of the BPP.

Cha Cha's response to one question in particular—whether race or class was the key factor in social problems—indicated an embrace of Marxist analysis. It also revealed a deeper way of thinking about racial oppression both among Puerto Ricans and among other colonized people worldwide. In the deliberately indecorous language of the period, Cha Cha suggested that the experience of Puerto Ricans on the U.S. mainland offered clarity on the subject: "We have all kinds of people, a rainbow of people [among Puerto Ricans]. And this is why . . . this is a class struggle. . . . [We] see that the Pigs are the bodyguards of the capitalist pigs that are oppressing and exploiting our people. We . . . see that this octopus, the United States, has been sucking all the resources from Puerto Rico and we see who our enemy is . . . and we look out for allies, you know, we look to Cuba, we look at Mao, we look at all these other countries that have liberated themselves from the monsters."[4]

It had only been a year since Cha Cha read Thomas Merton, Malcolm X, and Martin Luther King Jr. and only months since he began to work with the Chicago Panthers. Yet Cha Cha had already integrated the class politics and language of the Rainbow Coalition in his analysis of the Puerto Rican experience. His perspective differed from that of many black Americans and helped broaden the scope of debate surrounding racial oppression. Like previous migrants to the United States from the Caribbean, his proximity to an island nation where racialized people sit at the top of a racially and economically divided society led him to emphasize the significance of class differences among racially oppressed people.[5] In line with the politics of the New Left, Cha Cha also called for solidarity with the era's most popular self-described socialist countries and those fighting colonial rule. He identified racial oppression and police violence as outgrowths of capitalism and colonial rule.[6]

That day, the students at the New York meeting felt an immediate political and personal affinity with Cha Cha. He seemed to apply ideas they had been debating for months. He was also one of their own. They would soon take a road trip to Chicago to explore a possible working relationship with the YLO, with far-reaching implications. After the trip they would bring together three preexisting groups of students, community activists, and artists to launch the Young Lords' New York chapter.[7]

These New York radicals represented a unique subgroup of working-class Puerto Ricans. Unlike Cha Cha Jiménez and his peers in the Chicago Young Lords, who came to political consciousness in prison and in the streets, these were mostly high school graduates and the first in their families to gain access to higher education. That was thanks to College Discovery, the first program designed to recruit underrepresented working-class students and students of color at the City University of New York.[8] Their approach was informed by their access and proximity to the radical analysis of social problems that developed alongside campus protest in the 1960s on issues ranging from the Eurocentric character of the university curriculum and open access to higher education for all to critiques of capitalism and colonialism.[9]

But the seeds of their political proclivities were also planted much earlier.

These English-speaking children of new migrants became accidental translators—of both language and culture—for the many postwar Puerto Rican newcomers to New York. The liminal role they played as cultural mediators formed the emotional scaffold of their radicalization in the late 1960s. The premature responsibilities foisted upon them helped ease their parents' adjustment to a foreign and inhospitable city but also exposed them to northern racism and their community's socioeconomic problems at an early age. With scant knowledge of their provenance, this role cast them as citizens and strangers. Not surprisingly, this generation grew curious about why New Yorkers belittled Puerto Ricans writ large and leapt at the opportunity to understand the relationship between their parents' homeland and the United States.

The reemergence of the civil rights movement in the mid 1950s, which ended the Red Scare's clampdown on social criticism and made the pursuit of equality the moral assignment of the 1960s generation, opened possibilities to address New York's so-called Puerto Rican problem. But even for black Americans living outside of the South, the dismantling of Jim Crow with the passage of the 1964 Civil Rights Act didn't go far enough. In New York, as in other northern cities, racial inequality came in the form of exclusion from industries with decent-paying jobs, poor wages, police violence, underfunded education, dilapidated housing, and inadequate and discriminatory healthcare.[10] Redress of these issues would require a radical reorganization of society.

Early exposure of future Young Lords to racism in the streets and in the school system also laid the groundwork for their break with mainstream politics. In New York, the civil rights movement had inspired struggles for equality in different areas of life, most visibly in the city's public schools and against police violence. Those who had gathered in East Harlem every Saturday had grown up in a city where battles to desegregate the public schools and reform the police failed, leaving the city more racially polarized.[11] Amid rising expectations for change produced by their successes in college, they returned home to dilapidated neighborhoods under the tight grip of economic decline. In the wake of the East Harlem riots these radicals were persuaded to address material impoverishment and psychological trauma produced by northern racism. They felt compelled to set aside the moderate solutions to the urban crisis adopted by an older generation of Puerto Rican reformers. Instead, they eagerly embraced Cha Cha's critique of the U.S. colonial project in Puerto Rico and his radical program and vision of a new society.

Of Operation Bootstrap and Puerto Rican Problems

As Cha Cha noted, the presence and condition of Puerto Ricans in cities like New York were bound up in the U.S. colonial project in Puerto Rico. The students who were taken with his interview were among a generation of Puerto Rican youth determined to understand how.

After World War II, U.S. policies in Puerto Rico led to an exodus from the island so great, in proportion to its population, that it exceeded the vast relocation of European immigrants to the United States in the late nineteenth century. Between 1947 and 1970, one-third of the people of Puerto Rico were dispersed to the continental United States, mostly New York.[12] Their settlements immediately transformed the racial and ethnic composition of neighborhoods in Manhattan, Brooklyn, and the Bronx. These changes, combined with growing signs of poverty among the newcomers, produced a racially coded nativist backlash by journalists and city residents that attacked the newcomers for allegedly abusing the welfare rolls, carrying infectious diseases, exhibiting criminal behavior, and "suffocating the culture of their adopted city."[13] Most Puerto Ricans, however, formed part of the working class. The experience of the family of Mickey Melendez, a principal founder of the Young Lords in New York, was not unusual. His father came from Puerto Rico in the 1940s as a merchant marine and married his mother, a Cuban homemaker. A member of National Maritime Union, he was among its growing and active Puerto Rican membership. The family first settled in East Harlem. In the 1950s, they moved to the South Bronx and kept a low profile among their new Italian and Jewish neighbors.[14]

Operation Bootstrap gave Puerto Rican migration its mass scale. That was the name given to the U.S.-led industrialization project of the island. Launched in 1947, the project transplanted to Puerto Rico New Deal strategies that had been employed to industrialize the U.S. South during the 1930s, among them rural electrification and paying farmers to cease agricultural production or hiring them to build roads and housing.[15] Expecting the displacement of more farmers than could be absorbed into the island's emerging industrial economy, its architects developed a contingency plan. Puerto Rican emigration to the U.S. mainland was to become lynchpin and safety valve of Operation Bootstrap.[16]

The economic project served the diverse interests of the players involved. Elements within the U.S. government welcomed it as antidote to social unrest on the island. Its proposed reforms were expected to placate a militant independence movement that during the 1930s drew strength from fierce labor strikes involving thousands of workers in the needles trades and the tobacco and sugar industries. The crisis peaked in 1936. When Puerto Rican nationalists killed the island's American police commissioner, Francis E. Riggs, members of Congress proposed a bill that would end or at least significantly curtail American political and military involvement in Puerto Rico. The bill did not prevail. But it set a threatening precedent to proponents of U.S. expansionism who valued Puerto Rico as a strategically important passageway to the Panama Canal—a cornerstone of global trade that linked the Pacific and Atlantic Oceans. Puerto Rico was also the site from which the United States had launched most of its military interventions in Latin America. To those for whom U.S. political control of Puerto Rico was paramount, Operation Bootstrap represented a path to political stability on the island.[17]

By the 1940s, the United States had found a keen indigenous leader willing to carry out Washington's mandate on the island: the president of the Puerto Rican senate, Luis Muñoz Marín. With his use of the carrot and the stick—violent political repression and land and social reforms to quell the island's social movements—Marín proved indispensable in wresting political control from Puerto Rico's divided nationalist movement. But Marín was not just a pawn. In 1938, he founded the center-left Popular Democratic Party, with its proposal to achieve independence gradually and through the electoral process. Marín and the Popular Democratic Party believed that Keynesian state intervention in the form of regulated land reform and state-sponsored capitalist industrialization were necessary precursors to Puerto Rico's future political independence.[18] In 1947, he became a major advocate and architect of Operation Bootstrap.

Over the course of the 1950s, the project transformed the island's sugar plantation economy to one organized around factory production in the cities, largely by drawing U.S. industry to the island with cheap labor guarantees, rent and real estate subsidies, and federal tax breaks.[19] Between 1950 and 1959, 9,000 corporate investors took advantage of what the U.S. financial press termed a "bounty for industry."[20] The island's industrialization had other uses as well. Heralded as the "showcase of democracy in the Caribbean," Puerto Rico's project of "economic development" offered the United States a critical laboratory and prototype for U.S.-led capitalist expansion across the globe, where market strategies could be developed, tested, and then deployed to new markets in Asia, Africa, and Latin America.[21] So-called Third World economies, such as Puerto Rico's, were seen as major sites of capital investment, guaranteeing new markets for industrial goods, lower production costs, and by extension, the economic revitalization of capitalism after the war.[22] Operation Bootstrap would thus serve as an early testing example and precursor to what would later be called global restructuring by world leaders—or neoliberalism by its critics.[23]

The consequences of this global economic agenda would eventually be felt in U.S. urban centers. Operation Bootstrap had fueled the vast displacement of Puerto Ricans to the U.S. mainland, and it would also negatively impact urban economies into which they migrated. In a terrible irony, Puerto Rico proved that cheap labor abounded in the Third World and encouraged U.S. industry to flee its urban manufacturing bases of operations in cities like New York for greener pastures with lower production costs—first to the suburbs and the South, and later abroad in stages. A long-term process of urban industrial decline began in the postwar period. During this period, industries became geographically dispersed in the outer rings of northern cities, and urban economies underwent a simultaneous structural shift from industry to service.[24] The first wave of Puerto Rican postwar settlements in the city coincided with the onset, in 1947, of the manufacturing industry's decline.[25] Because 70.6 percent of Puerto Ricans were employed in low-income occupations—in hospitals, in the restaurant and hotel trades, and most devastating, in New York's manufacturing industry—their community was especially vulnerable.[26] Job loss due to deindustrialization began in modest numbers in the postwar period and accelerated in the 1960s. Between 1947 and 1967, half of the jobs lost to manufacturing were in apparel, the city's main factory industry and main employer of Puerto Rican labor.[27] Puerto Rican women, in particular, were disproportionately affected by this decline. In total, New York lost half a million manufacturing jobs between 1950 and 1980, but the steepest job losses happened between 1965 and 1975—not coincidentally, the height of urban unrest.[28]

By the early 1960s, U.S. government labor agencies were documenting a new development in the history of the American city: the rise of permanent, structural unemployment among postwar migrants. Bureau of Labor Statistics studies published throughout the 1960s began to track the unprecedented changes in the labor participation of a segment of predominantly black American and Puerto Rican men in their prime working years concentrated in New York's poorest slums. According to the studies, these young men were neither employed nor counted as unemployed because they had long ceased their search for employment. The Puerto Rican example, in particular, was cited as extreme. Relative to the labor participation of black American and white men, job activity was lowest among Puerto Ricans.[29] In 1966, a different Bureau of Labor Statistics study referred to a new concept called "subemployment," concluding that in East Harlem the percentage of Puerto Ricans who were either unemployed, underemployed, or permanently out of the labor force for lack of success in finding employment was approximately 47 percent.[30] The majority of Puerto Ricans in the metropolitan area—over 50 percent—relied on jobs that were increasingly disappearing.[31] In sum, the combined impact of deindustrialization and automation—the infusion of technological advancements in industry that also eliminated unskilled jobs—produced concentrated pockets of permanent joblessness among the newcomers, an experience unknown to previous generations of urban dwellers.

New York had historically been a land of opportunity for new waves of unskilled workers. Despite the exploitation they suffered, many nineteenth-century European immigrants took jobs in the most advanced sectors of the industrial economy. Through hard labor over the course of their lives, many could expect to achieve greater economic stability. But when Puerto Ricans, black Americans, and other people of color were proletarianized, they were employed in the county's declining economies. The new and fixed structural barriers they encountered qualitatively undermined the possibility of upward mobility. Racism—in employment, housing, and education—and low wages compounded these conditions and produced deep poverty. By all estimates, the socioeconomic situation of Puerto Ricans in New York was dire. In 1960, 34 percent of Puerto Rican families were making less than $3,000 a year, the government-established income level demarcating poverty. By comparison, 27 percent of black American families and 12 percent of white families fell under that designation. With the lowest income of any racial or ethnic group in the United States and the lowest levels of education and quality of housing, almost half of Puerto Ricans in postwar New York lived in worse conditions than families living during the Great Depression.[32]

As we have seen, Puerto Rican poverty in New York was fueled by economic restructuring—a development that was intricately bound up in Puerto Rico's colonial relationship to the United States and U.S.-led economic policies on the island. Yet, in public discourse, Puerto Ricans themselves were collectively blamed for the precariousness of their condition in the city. Throughout the 1950s, mainstream journalists and social commentators referred to the precipitous influx of Puerto Ricans to New York and the putative burdens they imposed on the city—its public schools, the labor market, the welfare rolls, the city's crime rate and public health—as the "Puerto Rican problem." Some of these accounts concluded that the city "should throw them out."[33] Ironically, the term "Puerto Rican problem" had been coined a decade earlier for different reasons. Members of Congress, policy makers, and Washington journalists started using it during World War II as a catchphrase for an uncomfortable reality: that U.S. colonial rule in Puerto Rico contradicted the principles of freedom, democracy, and self-determination championed by the United States as part of the fight against fascism. Another term of the period, "the American dilemma," was a more fitting descriptor of the crisis of credibility that the colonization of Puerto Rico represented for the United States. That term was coined by Swedish economist Gunnar Myrdal, whose book of the same title exposed the incongruity between U.S. proclamations of freedom and the nation's long-standing oppression of black Americans.[34]

Amid the mounting firestorm of racist characterizations of Puerto Ricans in the 1950s, the Puerto Rican community leveraged a defense of itself in local newspapers, union halls, neighborhood centers, and local government. Its leaders formed part of two distinct political currents: those who sought the betterment of the community through the Democratic Party and those of the longer-standing Puerto Rican Left. The Young Lords would stand in the tradition of the latter, which included essayist Jesús Colón and members of the Hispanic American section of the International Workers' Order, who called for higher wages; denounced racial discrimination in employment, labor unions, housing, and education; and argued that Puerto Ricans had been rendered outsiders by their darker hue and colonial relationship to the nation.[35] This Puerto Rican antidefamation campaign formed part of New York's early civil rights movement; its largest meeting drew hundreds of people, representatives from thirty-three labor and civil rights groups, and prominent black activist politicians like Harlem congressman Rev. Adam Clayton Powell Jr. and black Communist Party leader Ben Davis, among other radical black American activists.[36]

The Puerto Rican Left's calls for independence and radical critique of the "Puerto Rican problem" stood in sharp contrast to the worldview of island-appointed representatives in New York, among them Joseph Monserrat, the director of the Bureau of Employment and Migration, renamed the Migration Division in 1949. In concert with New York's Democratic Party and its newly formed Mayor's Advisory Committee on Puerto Rican Affairs, their goal was to assimilate the new migrants with strategies used by early twentieth-century middle-class reformers to assimilate European immigrants. Their programs connected the Puerto Rican community with jobs and social services in education, housing, and health care. They also encouraged Americanization—learning English, adopting American standards of dress, following workplace rules, registering to vote, and resisting the relief rolls.[37] This response to the "Puerto Rican problem" made no mention of the pattern of economic and social exclusion of Puerto Ricans from public life on account of race, ethnicity, and their colonial "citizenship."

But with the resurgence of the civil rights movement in the mid-1950s, many of these themes would be raised and studied by an emergent cohort of social reformers indigenous to New York, among them the social worker and civil rights advocate Antonio Pantoja. Focused on building political leadership and social service groups in the city, these new leaders parted with the term "Hispanic" and launched organizations that embraced explicit ethnic identification—a sign that the social ferment around black American civil rights helped foster a regeneration among Puerto Ricans of the political significance of their collective identity and their relationship to the nation. In 1957, they launched their most influential organization, the Puerto Rican Leadership Forum, which modeled itself after the NAACP, and encouraged the formation of fully staffed, professionally run Puerto Rican nonprofit organizations. The new reformers trained and assembled a coterie of Puerto Rican leaders to lobby government on behalf of Puerto Ricans. They accepted the prevailing consensus that the marriage of social science expertise and public policy would resolve society's ills under capitalism. They prioritized legal and policy studies and advocacy on issues of discrimination and poverty and proposed improvements in social services, family cohesion, and elevation of Puerto Rican history and culture wherever possible.[38] By 1960, the reform spirit of these new leaders suited local government more than the orthodoxy of the Migration Division. A small number of Forum leaders were appointed to key governmental positions in exchange for political support, especially during the mayoral reelection campaign of Robert Wagner in 1961.[39]

By the 1960s, a pronounced gap existed between this small class of committed indigenous Puerto Rican leaders and the majority of Puerto Ricans. The former had growing access to the corridors of power, while the rest lived politically and socially isolated in New York's barrios. But with the upsurge of social movements during the 1960s, the radical, grassroots strategies for change of the 1930s and 1940s found new vehicles of expression.

Gilberto Gerena Valentin laid the groundwork in the 1950s. The militant labor organizer had been growing his Council of Hometown Clubs, a resource network of eighty community-based groups that used protest to address issues of housing, discrimination in public schools, employment, police brutality, and the emergency needs of newcomers.[40] Gerena Valentin had long supported Puerto Rican independence and had been a fellow traveler in the Communist Party, USA. In the early 1960s, he was drawn to the growing parent-led fight to desegregate the public schools in New York. There he joined Evelina Lopez Antonetty, a fierce organizer and Puerto Rican socialist, who was making appeals to poor people in the city, and Puerto Ricans in particular, to disrupt dominant perceptions of "the Puerto Rican problem." Like other radicals, their vision for Puerto Rican progress centered on grassroots organizing and agitation by the exploited and oppressed in the workplace and in the community; and solidarity with all oppressed groups. Like Puerto Rican radicals in the 1930, in the context of justice campaigns they raised the banner of Puerto Rican independence from U.S. colonial rule with their allies.

As a teenager in New York during the depression, Antonetty had joined protests against evictions, watched her mother organize a hotel workers' union, and embraced the anticolonial and anticapitalist consciousness of the era.[41] In a statement made decades later in the 1960s, she echoed Dr. King's denunciation of liberal ministers, in *Letter from a Birmingham Jail*, who denounced the upheaval produced by civil rights protests but were not equally bothered by the violence of white supremacy.[42] She noted: "Maladjusted is a word used perhaps more frequently than any other in modern psychology, and I am calling on the people of this city to be maladjusted. There are many things in this social system to which I am proud to be maladjusted. I can never adjust myself to the evils of discrimination and segregation. . . . I am sure history has a place for those who have the moral courage to be maladjusted . . . like Don Pedro Albizu Campos who believed that [if] even the birds are free, why not Puerto Ricans."[43] Antonetty's statement captured the sentiments of a younger generation of Puerto Rican migrants, whose 1960s rebellions, radical organizing, and social critiques would finally overturn the perception and political standing of Puerto Ricans in the city. The seeds of their political awakening were sown in the 1950s, when as children, they were beckoned to mediate the burdens and stigma of the "Puerto Rican problem."

The Migrant Crucible

As we have seen, Puerto Ricans who came of age in the 1960s were witnesses to one of the most complex socioeconomic crises in their community to date. The lives of the children of the vast postwar migration developed under conditions that were qualitatively different than those of previous generations of Puerto Rican migrants, even those who came of age in the 1950s. Because the postwar migration was disproportionately younger than in previous waves, the young forged a generational identity that was made stronger by unprecedented social changes. In this sense, they shared much in common with their white counterparts, the baby boomers.[44] But while the world view of white children had been shaped by Cold War repression and social sterility in suburbia, children of color were marked by their experience with the new poverty in the cities and the intensification of racial conflict with white America that emerged as a result of their exponentially greater numbers in the streets, schools, and government bureaucracies of New York. These experiences traumatized and alienated some but gave others an organic sense of the dynamics of power and inequality, fostering among them a sensitivity and radical responsiveness to issues of social justice.

During the beleaguered years of family settlement and adaptation to their new world, young Puerto Ricans with access to language skills and a closer proximity to the new culture occupied a special place as social mediators.[45] Often called upon to help parents and neighbors navigate the inhospitable, bureaucratic institutions of New York, Puerto Rican children were informal but indispensable interpreters of language and culture from hospitals to police stations, and from welfare offices and banks to their own schools. In *Palante*, the oral history compilation of the Young Lords published after the emergence of their New York movement, Iris Morales explains that the "older children in Puerto Rican families . . . become the link between . . . the Puerto Rican way of life and the American way of life." She sums up with poignancy this life on the threshold of two distinct worlds: "I became the one that translated. . . . I was the one that was the go-between."[46] Wilfredo Rojas, who joined the Young Lords in Philadelphia, describes his experience in the same terms: "Well, I was the go-between. Here I was a young seven-, eight-, nine-year-old, fourteen-year-old kid having to be the interpreter. There was no limited English proficiency access. I was the access. It placed a lot of responsibility because if you got the translation wrong, forget about it."[47] Others held even greater responsibilities, like another Young Lord, Carmen, who took charge of her home following her father's alcohol-fueled downward spiral.[48]

As Puerto Rican migrants witnessed the destruction of the world they knew, their children could not possibly have grasped the sheer emotional fallout of displacement. In her study of urban renewal in the postwar period, social psychiatrist Mindy Thompson Fullilove explains that displacement is perhaps the most traumatic experience that humans can undergo, with invisible consequences that can last for generations, from physical and mental problems to difficulty maintaining the social fabric of a community. Fullilove identifies the symptoms of displacement as "root shock," which, she explains, "undermines trust, increases anxiety about letting loved ones out of one's sight, destabilizes relationships, destroys social, emotional, and financial resources, and increases the risk of every kind of stress-related disease, from depression to heart attack. Root shock leaves people chronically cranky, barking a distinctive croaky complaint that their world was abruptly taken away."[49]

However, in the process of mediating between their parents and their new world, Puerto Rican children endured trauma, but they also gained insight into the workings of society. That insight illuminated the ways in which class, power, and prejudice defined their treatment and condition in American society. According to Morales, she and her peers "become, in a sense, the ones that come up against oppression the most." As intermediaries, she continued, "[we were] exposed to contradictions . . . in the sense of how society viewed us, and how we viewed ourselves, how the institutions viewed us and how we viewed ourselves, in the sense of what other people had and what we didn't."[50]

As foot soldiers in the settlement of this vast migration, these children were painfully aware of the stigma of their parents' "foreign status" and internalized a sense of inadequacy. Morales describes the shame of realizing that her parents "weren't as knowledgeable as the other people." In addition to bearing her own feelings of shame, she detected her mother's feelings of inadequacy in dealing with the institutions of their new society.[51] Morales continues, "My mother was ashamed to go to school and talk to the teachers, because she couldn't speak English and . . . didn't look as good as the other Americans, the other mothers."[52] The emotional fallout of this spatial and cultural relocation was no less formidable for black Americans. Mumia Abu-Jamal, in his memoir on the BPP, notes that many leading members of the party were children of southern migrants who were derided as "country"—"a connotation that has come to mean stupid, uncultured, and hickish in much of the northern mind."[53]

As in the case of Cha Cha Jiménez, the treatment of migrant parents as second-class citizens while their children mediated on their behalf undermined the parent-child relationship. Morales explains: "I started blaming my parents for not giving me anything better. I started hating them—feeling that it was their fault and that . . . if they'd really worked hard they could have gotten something better."[54] Similarly, Black Panther Assata Shakur recounts the ideological process by which, as a child, she internalized dominant conceptions of 1950s family life among middle-class white Americans that led her to judge her mother for not looking the part of the well-groomed, white, middle-class housewife depicted on TV. She writes, "Why didn't we live in a house with a backyard and a front yard instead of an ole apartment? I remember looking at my mother as she cleaned the house in her old raggedy housecoat with her hair in curlers. 'How disgusting,' i [sic] would think."[55] As the dignity of adults was undermined, children had to reckon with a subtle, contradictory, and often devastating mix of emotions.

Members of this generation would find in the Young Lords a cathartic forum in which to dissect and make sense of the thorny world of their childhood, which had engendered their second sight. Conversely, the painful insights these children gained as accidental intermediaries would later inform the righteous world view of the Young Lords. Despite the burden of their role as interlocutors, their bilingual and bicultural experiences helped cultivate in many of these young people a host of skills that would be essential in their organizing efforts. They gained at a very early age an analytical instinct, a greater capacity for communication, and a dexterity of thought that is fostered by constantly switching between two languages, two cultures, and two worlds. The children of other migrants and immigrants in America have shared in this experience—from Italians and eastern Europeans in the early twentieth century to Nigerians and Dominicans in the late twentieth century—but the experience of migrants in postwar America was simply amplified. From postwar global economic restructuring (of which Operation Bootstrap was a part) and the onset of deindustrialization to the rise of decolonization wars and the reemergence of the civil rights movement, the daily struggles of migrant life converged with global changes of revolutionary proportions. Fueled by the era's social movements, children of migration turned their second sight into an engine for political change.

The Struggle to Liberate Education

The role of migrant children as cultural translators awakened in some an instinct for social justice, but it would require a catalyst to develop fully. In New York City during the 1950s and 1960s, that catalyst was their schooling. Navigating these two realms, familial and educational, formed the emotional scaffold of their radicalization in the late 1960s. Historians have written about the fight launched by parents to desegregate public schools in New York, but we know little about its impact on the children who lived through that period of bitter contestation over the character and quality of public school education.[56]

In May 1954, the Supreme Court ruled in *Brown v. Board of Education* that racial segregation in the public schools was unconstitutional. Seven months after the *Brown* decision, on December 23, 1954, the New York Board of Education established the Commission on Integration and ordered an investigation of racial discrimination in New York schools.[57] That commission's report, which took four years to complete, concluded, "Whether school segregation is the effect of law and custom as in the South, or has its roots in residential segregation, as in New York City, its effects are inherent and incurable."[58] Its language reflected the firestorm that the federal mandate ignited—an acrimonious contest among white teachers, black American and Puerto Rican parents, and their white counterparts over the meaning and consequences of the *Brown* decision for their children. As these hostilities trickled down into the classroom, they intensified the experience of social rejection and stigmatization among black American and Puerto Rican kids. In the 1950 and 1960s, these children came face to face with white backlash to desegregation just outside their school buildings, the racism of their teachers, and political repression of students in the schools. Combined, these experiences laid the foundation of their full-blown estrangement from the dominant institutions of society.

The challenges confronting the Board of Education were also demographic and pedagogical. In 1943, the board had considered negligible the very small minority of Puerto Rican students in San Juan Hill, a Manhattan neighborhood, and "Spanish Harlem."[59] But only four years later, in 1947, it reported the matriculation of 13,914 Puerto Rican pupils.[60] In 1956, that figure jumped to over 113,000, exceeding the rate of matriculation in New York of black American migrant children from the South. Puerto Ricans presented new, head-scratching challenges for the schools. Independently of issues of race discrimination, the Puerto Rican migrants presented a pedagogical challenge to administrators, principals, and teachers because they had the dubious distinction of being U.S. citizens who did not speak English. In addition, like earlier migrants, both Puerto Ricans and black Americans came from small cities or rural settings where the educational systems were underdeveloped and literacy rates lower.[61] Before long, the board and its teachers were challenged with the task of providing instruction to a student population with vastly different needs.

At around the same time, during the 1950s and 1960s, the public schools lost to private and parochial schools approximately the same number of white students that they gained in Puerto Rican and black American student enroll-ment.[62] Often unacknowledged in public discourse, by 1966 Puerto Ricans made up approximately 20 percent of the student population in New York. Black American students made up 30 percent. For the first time in the city's history, over half of the student population in New York was black American and Puerto Rican.[63] This meant that, in the era of school reform ushered in by the *Brown* decision, the fortunes of New York's Puerto Rican and black American children depended heavily on each other.

Among black American and Puerto Rican parents across the city, the *Brown* decision signaled the possibility of change in education—the American institu-tion that, even in the face of prejudice and vilification, had historically promised progress and personal redemption. The decision ignited a brush fire of parent activity in support of school reform at local meetings of the Parent Teacher Association.[64] Constrained by the association's rules and its bureaucracy, by the early 1960s, these activists began to form independent organizations, in-cluding the Harlem Parents' Committee; the Parents' Workshop for Equality; the Citywide Committee for Public Schools; EQUAL, an organization of white parents who supported school integration; and United Bronx Parents, led by Evelina Antonetty. Collectively, their newsletters educated the public on the educational rights of children; their meetings and workshops trained parents, especially mothers, to become public speakers, organizers, and negotiators; and their grassroots actions sought to pressure the Board of Education to deliver substantive change.[65]

During the same period, a small group of well-organized, conservative white parents also launched a movement, one hostile to the project of integration. Along with many white Americans, they believed that their children's educa-tional standards would be depressed if the *Brown* decision forced their offspring to share the classroom with children they perceived to be incapable of learning.[66] By the late 1950s, once resolute in its condemnation of segregation, the board began to advocate measured consideration of all options in what it now insisted must be a slow and delicately implemented project in the distant future.[67] As early as 1959, the board began to "encourage integration" through a busing sys-tem that sought to transfer children, "whenever feasible," from overcrowded schools to underenrolled ones.[68] A negligible number of black American and Puerto Rican students in Brooklyn were actually bused to underpopulated white schools in Queens, hardly a desegregation mandate, but even that negligible effort sparked fierce protests by white parents.[69] Hundreds kept their children at home on the first day of school, and in one instance 2,000 white parents picketed city hall.[70]

Denise Oliver was one of several Young Lords who witnessed the fallout. In 1957, with the help of a white proxy, Oliver's middle-class, black American parents purchased a home in Hollis, one of the predominantly white Queens neighborhoods to which children of color were bused in 1959.[71] During her first day at Junior High School 59, Oliver remembers "getting off the bus, commotion going on, and a white kid with blood streaming down his face. There were fights going on in the yard. There were white students who had jumped on some black students, there were black students fighting back, there were [white] parents protesting the busing of kids into their neighborhood. The bus monitor rushed us into the building. You could feel the hostility immediately."[72]

Ramon Ramirez, a close friend of future Young Lord chairman Felipe Luciano, had a similar experience in seventh grade when he was bused to Astoria's Steinway Junior High School (JHS 141): "About 100 Irish-Italian people were demonstrating against us. Then you'd walk to class through a cordon of police. And if you didn't catch the bus at three o'clock there was always fear that you were gonna get caught and white paint [would be] hurled at [us by demonstrators]."[73]

The source of white opposition to integration was multilayered. Stanley Smigiel, the head of Parents and Taxpayers, the white Queens group that opposed busing, explained the group's goals to the New York Times: "To protect our children, preserve our neighborhood-school system, and keep our children from being bused into strange districts." He went on, "I don't have nothing against Negroes, but the only thing I care about is this. . . . I don't like [my child] going into classes with a lot of slow readers who will pull down his I.Q." Impelled by more blatant prejudice, others argued that the white community should not take on the burdens of black Americans, who "don't want to work hard enough to get out of [their] environment."[74]

The Brown decision signaled to many white parents that integration would disrupt their newly acquired middle-class status and their children's progress in school. Parents and Taxpayers' concerns echoed the world view of the generation of working-class white Americans who were massively relocated to racially exclusive suburbs in the outskirts of the city after World War II through a vast program of government-subsidized mortgages.[75] Home ownership and the taste of a good life deepened their racial fears and insular disposition toward "outsiders." The modest character of their new class standing also made them insecure, fearful of change, and risk averse.[76] Moreover, the changing structure of New York's economy produced anxieties displaced onto people of color, whom they viewed as the undeserving beneficiaries of new government policy. Sentiments against integration were not limited to the white residential sections of the outer boroughs. In a roundtable discussion that aired live on Channel 13's talk show The City, school reform activist and Jewish social worker Ellen Lurie recounted a discussion on the merits of integration in her son's fifth-grade class in a school in Washington Heights. According to her son, two-thirds of his classmates indicated that they were "saving their allowances to be able to go to private school if integration comes to their neighborhood."[77]

However, the experience of Puerto Rican children was not uniform. In search of better housing and schools, some black American and Puerto Rican families moved to newly built projects in Brooklyn and Queens. The González family, for example, moved into Brooklyn's Cypress Hill projects, where their son, future Young Lord Juan González, enrolled in Franklin K. Lane Public High School, one of the largest public high schools in the city. Black American and Puerto Rican students from Bronxville and East New York made up approximately 30 percent of its student body. Although Lane would become the site of racial strife in the late 1960s and early 1970s, the light-skinned González did not encounter racial hostilities there in the early 1960s. Rather, he captured the attention of one of "the toughest and most exacting" teachers, Pauline Buonoagura, and was nurtured by her. Buonoagura was advisor to the school newspaper, and according to González, although he didn't realize it at the time, "She decided in my freshman year that I was going to be her editor during my senior year, but she wanted me to go through a training process beforehand." With the guidance of Buonoagura, González enrolled in a junior-year summer program for high school students at Northwestern University's Medill School of Journalism. González remembers, "[Ms. Buonoagura] filled out all the applications, got me the scholarship, and then convinced my parents to let me go to Chicago for six weeks for this journalism boot camp."[78] González would soon become a key thinker and strategist and one of the most prolific and lucid writers of his cohort.

Future Young Lord Gilbert Colón, who enrolled in a predominantly Irish and Italian parochial school in the Bronx, encountered a different fate. In 1958, *The Puerto Rican Study*, a Board of Education–sponsored investigation of the educational needs of Puerto Rican children, observed a rise in incidences of racial violence immediately outside the school premises.[79] Colón's after-school rumbles add depth to the report's findings. He observes that school interactions between boys of color and white girls often precipitated physical hostility on the part of white boys. Colón's budding friendship with a coterie of white girls with whom he participated in a school play was the source of after-school fights with his white peers. As in the South, northern white opposition to the *Brown* decision was fueled by the fear that race mixing in the classroom would bleed into the "living room and bedroom as well."[80] Retrospectively, he observes what he was not able to fully grasp as a teenager: "The perception that I talked to these girls and hung out with them, even though nothing ever happened, was the trigger. . . . There's a fear that a white girl could actually like a male of color and actually end up going with them—I didn't realize that until a bit later."[81]

As early as 1963, black American and Puerto Rican parents were calling for immediate improvements in the quality of education of their children and turning their attention to teacher-driven racism in the classroom. These concerns were not new. Black psychologists Kenneth and Mamie Clark, who propelled part of the Board of Education's desegregation efforts, had spent a lifetime documenting the impact of racism on New York schoolchildren and advocating on their behalf.[82] Earlier, in the 1930s, Doxey Wilkerson, a professor of education at Howard University, denounced the Board of Education for ensnaring black children in "America's racial caste system" through their overconcentration in vocational schools and in classes for the mentally challenged; the poverty of the facilities that housed their classes; and the effects of the racial contempt they suffered at the hands of guidance counselors and teachers, among other findings.[83] The board's own 1950s investigations revealed that majority-nonwhite schools were staffed with inexperienced and ineffective teachers who deemed their students less capable of learning.[84] Despite the volumes of studies on the complexity and consequences of racism in the classroom, many teachers and social critics deployed the new sanitized language of northern racism, blaming poor academic performance on the alleged "cultural deficiency" of children of color.[85]

In the era of *Brown*, the Board of Education failed to implement a robust pedagogical infrastructure for assimilating children of color. It never considered, for example, a public antiracist campaign to reform the predominantly white and often prejudiced body of public school teachers. In the context of contested change ushered in by the *Brown* decision and the exponential growth of children of color in public schools, a fierce racist backlash in the classroom was to be expected. The Young Lords describe as formative their early school experiences in an environment that was intimidating and hostile to them. Of his experience, future Young Lord and Vietnam veteran Felix Velazquez explains: "[Growing up Puerto Rican] was just synonymous with dissatisfaction . . . and alienation. . . . I didn't know what to call it then, until I read Paulo Freire and Frantz Fanon [on] the psychology of oppression."[86] For his part, Carlito Rovira, one of the youngest members of the Young Lords, was in fourth grade when he heard a substitute teacher call one of his peers, beneath her breath, a "filthy Puerto Rican." Carlito describes shock: "I was emotionless. There was no emotion. I knew that she used the word 'Puerto Rican' and that my parents had some association with something that was Puerto Rican. I was traumatized because I was too young to fully understand why she said that, but it probably became one of the factors in my radicalization because it was cumulative with other things." When Carlito attempted in junior high school to stand up for his friend Jesse Quiñonez, who was being ostracized by a teacher, the teacher punched him. Carlito reacted with fury: "I told him that I was going to kick his ass and that I was going to kill him. The next day the NYPD [New York Police Department] was in the building, they wanted to know what gang I was in, and I was expelled."[87] Carlito found protection and mentorship in Mr. Calvin, a black teacher at the school to which he was transferred, who encouraged him to join a new group at the school, Students for Freedom. The young Mr. Calvin was a member of the BPP.

The ideology that precipitated the aggression against Carlito was echoed in a series of letters penned by white teachers that poured into the *New York World-Telegram* in November 1965. The letters vehemently challenged an editorial written by a black teacher on the racially prejudiced attitudes of her white peers toward their nonwhite students. Using language that today seems startlingly hostile, one letter blamed the culture and low aspirations of black and Puerto Rican children for the crisis in education. The writer asked whether these children "will . . . ever learn that living by the laws of the jungle is not behavior acceptable to our society?"[88]

This race ideology had been incubated in media representations of black Americans and Puerto Ricans, but it had also been institutionalized in educational studies and policies of the New York public schools. In 1935, a study of children in East Harlem conducted by eugenicist psychologists and sponsored by New York State concluded that the majority of Puerto Rican children were incapable of learning due to innate mental inferiority.[89] Not surprisingly, when the Board of Education established, after World War II, its so called 600 schools for the "emotionally disturbed," Puerto Ricans, like black Americans, were overrepresented in them.[90] By the 1950s, however, social scientists began to adopt new analytical frameworks to explain social problems and achievement differentials between white students and students of color. The new analyses identified poverty, social isolation, poor schooling, and racism, among other structural factors, rather than genetics, as the root causes. But in 1959, when the anthropologist Oscar Lewis coined the term "culture of poverty" in his study of Mexican families, social scientists began to elevate analyses of the culture produced by poverty over analyses of racism's and poverty's structural causes. The vagueness of the term also allowed for its adaptation by a cross-section of political currents on the right and among liberals, both of which now agreed, to varying degrees, that social problems among people of color were the product of dysfunctional cultural behavior within families and communities.[91]

Racial bigotry against Puerto Rican children in the classroom was compounded by language discrimination. For Puerto Ricans on the mainland, the stigma attached to the Spanish language was an extension of the politics of language in Puerto Rico where, from the time the United States took control in 1898 until the late 1940s, English became the official language of the island's political system and the compulsory language of instruction in public schools.[92] Young Lord David Perez spoke to the psychological consequences of this struggle over language on the mainland: "Language becomes a reward and a punishment system. . . . In the school system here, if you don't quickly begin to speak English and shed your Puerto Rican values, you're put back a grade. . . . You're treated as if you're retarded . . . and your own cultural values therefore are shown to be of less value than the cultural values of this country and the language of this country. . . . It creates a colonized mentality . . . a strong feeling of inferiority, . . . of not being as worthy as the [other] Americans."[93] Perez grew up in Puerto Rico until the age of ten, when he came to Chicago to live with his mother. Despite his academic interests, Perez was tracked in a vocational school.

These pedagogical concerns began to take center stage in New York when parents organized a citywide boycott of public schools on February 3, 1964, when over 464,000 students—almost half of the student body—stayed out of school.[94] Although the boycott was intended to challenge the Board of Education's stalling tactics on the question of integration, the complex and gargantuan effort before the protesters—of providing alternative instruction during the student boycott—gave birth to a new facet of the movement.[95] According to Gerena Valentin, organizing for one day what the New York school reform movement called "liberation schools" was an "arduous uphill organizing effort" that opened up a universe of political questioning, because they challenged organizers to think creatively about what a day of teaching would look like. Gerena Valentin continues, "We had now gone past an abstract intellectual question, now we were tackling the meat and potatoes, if you will, of a black community intent on learning about who was [W. E. B.] Du Bois and [Paul] Robeson; what was slavery all about and who were the responsible parties and what exactly happened during the Civil War. And Puerto Ricans were asking who was Pedro Albizu Campos and the struggle of the liberators for liberation, and what about the invasion of Puerto Rico by the United States?"[96] As we will see, the Young Lords would extend this approach and radical perspective to a much larger cohort of young activists of their generation by taking these efforts to radically rethink education to the streets.

By the mid-1960s, school integration had failed in New York. According to a 1965 pamphlet prepared by the Harlem Parents Committee, "Despite the optimism of the Commission on Integration—an optimism shared by many of us at the time—now, after seven years of studies and surveys, new programs and 'pilot projects,' . . . we find ourselves essentially no further along that road in the fall of 1965 than we did in the fall of 1958."[97] Frustrated with the Board of Education's stalling tactics, black American and Puerto Rican parent organizers reoriented their goals away from integration. The activists now argued that local communities should play a role in curricular development and the hiring and firing of administrators and teachers, challenging the exclusive power over education held by the Board of Education and the United Federation of Teachers.[98]

The new political current now called itself the movement to decentralize the public schools. It emerged alongside the actions of young people radicalized by the black power movement, who began to defend their rights in schools.[99] In the second half of the 1960s, junior high school and high school students in New York organized around issues of free speech, the imposition of dress codes, and the absence of structures within which to articulate their grievances and points of view in altercations with teachers. The articles they published in independent student newsletters and the lawsuits filed by some students against the Board of Education emphasized the violation of their constitutional rights. Many students, like Iris Morales, were also critical of the elitist and racist structure of school tracking.[100] Studies discovered that these students were critical of the schools' focus on tests over "the value of the educational process" and noted that "the high achiever . . . is often as disenchanted with his curriculum as the low achiever. Not wanting to be sealed off academically from the rest of his class, he is often resentful of being pressured into honors classes."[101]

It was in this cauldron of contestation over the rights of young people of color that those who later became Young Lords and Black Panthers were politicized. The backlash to student protest in the schools was swift. A secret memo by the Association of High School Principals outlined the problem from the perspective of administrators, observing that "contemporary student movements are . . . a battering ram to test and then destroy the 'establishment.'" Written by liberal administrators, the memo upheld what it called the "great libertarian tradition" of free speech and "responsible" dissent but recommended repression, calling on principals to "outline the limits of permissible dissent" and to exercise "courage" in limiting protests that create "social disorientation." Included among these were those protests that constituted "an attack on the viability of a school, using peripheral issues, nonnegotiable demands, and calculated disorder to wrest control from lawful authorities. The nature of the demands . . . manifestos, political platforms, position papers—and the manner of their presentation . . . allow only one response: denial, simple, clear, and unequivocal. Discussion perhaps. Negotiation no."[102]

Security guards were brought into public schools for the first time in March 1969, to bring to heel protests led by students of color, the new demographic majority in the public schools. Students who clashed with teachers or administrators were ejected by these security guards, often with police backup.[103] The implementation of law-and-order practices and the introduction of "parapolice methods" in the schools led to more suspensions and expulsions of black American and Puerto Rican students.

Shortly before she joined the Young Lords, Denise Oliver taught black American and Puerto Rican history at East Harlem Prep, an East Harlem school launched by the RGS that offered an educational space to this new class of young people permanently expelled from the public school system. After having been expelled for her activism at Howard University, Oliver was startled by her success with what the school system perceived as "incorrigible students . . . a lot of kids in the community who weren't in school at all. They were considered to be refuse, unteachable, unreachable; a lot of them were in gangs."[104] She, too, read Cha Cha's interview during the East Harlem gathering of students searching for a political agenda in June 1969.

In New York, the struggles in the schools had moved public discourse on solutions to the crisis in education beyond a narrowly conceived integration project. The discourse challenged pedagogy and elevated the project of education to the goal of personal emancipation and community uplift, a kind of antidote to racist instruction in the schools. The Board of Education's failure to implement integration had also paved the way for the argument among people of color that change would only be achieved through their control of community institutions. The young people who launched the Young Lords in New York would be influenced by their own experiences with racism in the classroom and by the politics bequeathed to them by the struggles for school reform in New York.

¡La Jara! ¡La Jara!

The struggle to liberate education was closely bound up with a long-standing struggle against police brutality, led by black civil rights leaders. In New York, that struggle peaked in the early 1950s, with a series of campaigns organized around a United Nations petition that argued that police violence against black Americans met the U.N.'s definition of genocide; calls for federal investigations of specific cases as well as the New York Police Department; and the creation of a local civilian board, independent of the police, charged with reviewing New York's many cases of police violence.[105] After a period of dormancy, the struggle resurfaced in public discourse in the early 1960s. Nationally televised images of police charging civil rights protesters with attack dogs gave credence to neighborhood protests against a spate of police shootings across the city. This time a disproportionate number of the victims were Puerto Rican youth. Old-guard Puerto Rican leaders had long resisted linking their grievances to those of black Americans, but these developments spoke for themselves. The widespread use of force by police against members of a given group combined with state-sanctioned protection of police, in spite of their abuse of authority, have been defining cornerstones of racial subjugation in the United States.[106]

By the 1960s, Puerto Ricans had been ensnared in the lowest rungs of the city's racial hierarchy. In an interview with the *New York Times*, the labor organizer Gilberto Gerena Valentin observed that police treat Puerto Ricans as they would if "they were running a plantation."[107] The experience was already codified in language among Puerto Ricans with the emergence of the term *la jara*, used to signal that the police were nearby. The Spanish idiom was an adaptation of "O'Hara," the "legendary cop who used his nightstick first and asked questions later."[108] By the early 1960s, the rising number of hostile, quotidian interactions between Puerto Ricans and the police, combined with the shift in consciousness occasioned by the civil rights movement, propelled some Puerto Ricans to find common cause with black Americans.

One of the touchstone cases of police brutality came on November 15, 1963, not long after the Harlem and Brooklyn chapters of the Congress on Racial Equality announced that they would add police brutality to their ongoing civil disobedience campaigns against discrimination in housing and employment in NYC's all-white building trades.[109] The new publicized case of police brutality involved the fatal shootings of two Puerto Ricans, Victor Rodriguez and Maximo Solero.

Rodriguez and Solero were bike-delivery men known for singing Puerto Rican folk songs en route to their destinations.[110] They were arrested for loitering when an Upper West Side resident called the police with a noise complaint. The men were shot and killed inside a police car beneath the underpass at 96th Street and Riverside Drive in Manhattan, while they were being driven to the precinct on 100th Street and Broadway. The details of the incident and the biographical sketches of Rodriguez and Solero humanized them—an element that has historically been central to the fight against police violence in the United States.

As the story spread through New York's Spanish-speaking community, Gerena Valentin and his Council of Hometown Clubs were among the groups that leapt into action. With the aid of the council's preexisting phone bank, the next day at 5:30 P.M. hundreds had gathered outside the precinct to "demand a hearing with the captain, who refused to talk to us."[111] The Puerto Rican protest evolved into a spontaneous occupation of the precinct. The scene must have recalled Malcolm X's legendary 1957 march alongside the Fruit of Islam to Harlem's 28th Precinct, where the marchers demanded proper medical care for Johnson X. Hinton. [112] According to Gerena Valentin, "The police was afraid of the large volume of people that got in. We were peaceful, but we exhibited a very firm stance."[113] The militancy exhibited by those present had been building over time. Many of them had participated in the movement to desegregate New York's public schools and in the organizing drive led by Gerena Valentin, which delivered a Puerto Rican contingent of 30,000 to the March on Washington only months earlier, in August 1963.[114] A subgroup of those present had also recently launched the National Puerto Rican Civil Rights Association, which was already consumed with complaints of police brutality in New York.[115]

The most dramatic case of the decade came in July 1964, with the fatal shooting of a fifteen-year-old black American boy, James Powell. Minutes before his death, Powell formed part of a group of black American and Puerto Rican students that had gathered across the street from Robert F. Wagner Jr. High School on the East Side of Manhattan. To the irritation of the neighborhood's predominantly white residents, Wagner was one of the sites of the city's newly created summer program for youth. When a building superintendent sprayed the students with a water hose and racial epithets, they struck back with soda cans and an ashcan lid. Powell, reportedly, went after the superintendent, who retreated into the building. At that moment, an off-duty police officer, Thomas Gilligan, happened upon the scene and shot Powell three times. Lieutenant Gilligan claimed that Powell had lunged at him with a knife. But eyewitnesses reported that the boy had no knife, that he was shot without warning while exiting the building, and that Lieutenant Gilligan allegedly kicked Powell's body to check for life. That act ignited an angry protest at the scene. Approximately 300 teenagers threw bottles at the police and yelled, "This is worse than Mississippi." Before long, thousands of young people in Harlem and Bedford-Stuyvesant were locked in six consecutive nights of rioting and fierce confrontations with police.[116]

New York was now the site of the first northern riots of the decade. That same month, riots exploded in Rochester, Philadelphia, St. Louis, and Newark, where Puerto Ricans were major protagonists. The years 1964–68 registered 329 violent upheavals of varying intensity in 257 cities.[117] These rebellions were markedly different in character than those that had come before. In previous periods, most urban riots targeted black people. They were orchestrated by racist members of the majority population of white residents against black Americans, who were often perceived as competitors in the labor market and undeserving beneficiaries of city services.[118] But in the postwar period, black Americans, and also Puerto Ricans, became the protagonists in riots that targeted property and the police—both symbols of an elusive power structure that excluded them.

The rising incidence and mass scale of these rebellions in cities across the country indicated that larger social forces were at work. The riots were an expression of the demographic increase of people of color in the cities, the unwillingness of new migrants to accept old patterns of racial subjugation, and the fact that collective anger over urban conditions and police brutality was no longer exclusive to black Americans. While there was no official accounting of police brutality anywhere in the United States, the experience was so pervasive that it was codified in urban culture and language, as the Puerto Rican example suggests. The devastating story of how James Powell was killed epitomized the terror and indignity of oppressive police practices, and as in the past, it sparked an upheaval fueled by urban poverty, chronic unemployment, and a disfigured housing landscape. Far removed from this world, in the comfort of home ownership in the suburban outer boroughs or in Manhattan's white, middle-class neighborhoods, most white New Yorkers were incapable of comprehending this reality. Many held an abiding belief in the law and a trust in the moral character of police. To them police misconduct was rare and police killings unfortunate, and those that were unjustified would be properly adjudicated through investigation. City officials' assessments of the crisis contributed further to the polarization.

On the last day of the riots in New York, Mayor Robert Wagner delivered a televised message that set the tone of the government response to these rebellions. The mayor proclaimed that "the mandate to maintain law and order is absolute."[119] His repeated deployment of the racially coded term "law and order" reinforced the racist views of police, white New Yorkers, and journalists, who condemned the uprisings as uncivilized.[120] But amid the uprising, a series of town hall gatherings organized by black radicals had drawn large militant crowds. The mayor thus crafted a paternalistic message on the benefits to black northerners of the social system, with its legal mandate for police to protect black Americans "with all the force that is necessary and justified." The mayor also credited law and order for the passage of civil rights legislation, declaring that "of all the groups in America, Negroes have the most to gain from law and order" and that "law and order are the Negroes' best friend."[121]

Law and order was the ideological weapon used by southern segregationists to suppress the civil rights movement, and now the mayor of New York reshaped the racially charged term for northern audiences. Its liberal logic identified poverty and "distrust" of the police—not police brutality—as the causes of black discontent. The underlying message of law and order held that if black northerners overstepped the boundaries of allowable, legal behavior, they were to blame for holding back progress. And finally, its tough-on-crime dictum criminalized communists and radical groups for inciting rebellion.

Undeterred, community outrage continued to simmer into the fall. In September 1964, the case against Lieutenant Gilligan for the shooting death of James Powell was dismissed. Days later, the media reported three more police shootings.[122] Among these was the near-fatal shooting by police of another Puerto Rican youth, Gregory Cruz, in a case of mistaken identity. The Cruz case, along with the discovery of other families who were in desperate need of legal defense, anchored and animated the work of the emerging National Puerto Rican Civil Rights Association, which reported in early 1965 that in the preceding fifteen months, the police had killed nine Puerto Rican children and maimed six others.[123] The National Puerto Rican Civil Rights Association now joined a broad coalition that included the Congress on Racial Equality, the NAACP, black American churches, and labor groups, as well as the more radical elements around the militant housing activist Jesse Gray.[124] The coalition broadened the fight against police brutality beyond police shootings. It called for an end to the use of violent interrogation methods against black American and Puerto Rican detainees and exposed disproportionate arrests of people of color due to police repression of local civil rights protesters and the rising incidence of unconstitutional stops and searches in their neighborhoods. The coalition also called for the creation of an *independent* civilian complaint review board (CCRB).

In 1966, Republican John V. Lindsay was elected mayor of New York. His platform had combined liberal and conservative themes, from critiques of old machine politics to strong support of business. His antipoverty program and proposal to reform the city's existing CCRB attracted black American and Puerto Rican voters, who gave him a critical margin in a close election.[125] Launched in May 1966, not long after he took office, Mayor Lindsay's new CCRB was the first to impanel civilians. Composed of four civilians and three police officers, the new board had no authority to prosecute. The board could make a recommendation to the police commissioner to bring charges against a police officer, but it was nonbinding. In the event that charges were brought forth, the police officer would be judged and prosecuted in a hearing impaneled by police, as had been the case in the past. In the parlance of people who were still close to the soil, Puerto Rican activists quipped that the new arrangement was "another case of assigning the goats to watch the lettuce."[126]

Despite its weak powers, the reorganization of the CCRB touched a nerve. Police commissioner Vincent Broderick called it a "cruel hoax." He charged that it would "depress the morale" of the police department, "impair its capacity to prevent crime," and undermine public safety.[127] For its part, the Patrolmen's Benevolent Association (PBA), New York's police union, pledged to "kill" the new CCRB at the polls. The PBA had already demonstrated its capacity to organize the grassroots. A year earlier, in 1965, its president complained that police were "sick and tired of giving in to minority groups with their whims and their gripes and shouting."[128] That logic helped galvanize police officers' wives and family members, who collected 400,000 petition signatures in 1965 against a civilian review proposal that was being heard in city hall. In its totality, the calculated messaging of the PBA would turn white fear into a full-blown ideology based on the association's perception that people of color were the undeserving beneficiaries of government policy. In its battle against the mayor, the PBA sponsored the Citizens Committee Against Civilian Review Boards, whose untiring grassroots was aided by a sophisticated media campaign that included "370 billboards, 20 storefronts and thousands of doorbell ringers."[129] To this end, the PBA enlisted the public relations firm Cole, Fischer, Rogow, which created memes for newspapers, radio, and TV in which the police were depicted as victims of a policy that pressured them into turning away from potentially dangerous situations, leaving citizens vulnerable in a riot-prone city where crime was on the rise.[130] The firm crafted thirty- and sixty-second TV ads. One ad featured a woman leaving a New York subway station at night and in the aftermath of a riot. Another presented the menacing gazes of black and

Puerto Rican youth with switchblades and guns on a street corner and ended with the following warning: "Not threatening any person, just a threat to the community."[131] Crafted with a keen understanding of race ideology, the ads set out to mobilize white voters in the city's outer boroughs by fusing new fears of crime with those that had been historically cultivated in the media, the courts, and the corridors of power, in both the North and the South, to undermine civil rights. The ads raised the specter of white women as victims of black and now Puerto Rican male violence and appealed to white men for their protection. At its core, the campaign combined two historically powerful ideological strains in American history: fear of political dissent and the alleged predatory proclivities of black men. In this racialized redeployment of McCarthyism, communists were replaced by black criminals, black rioters, and black radical protesters as the group to be feared by "law-abiding" white citizens. Because of their socio-economic and geographical proximity to black Americans and the civil rights movement, postwar Puerto Ricans migrants in New York were increasingly seen within this framework.

Six months later, on election day, the PBA succeeded in annulling the newly formed civilian body, through a popular referendum known as Proposition 4. The referendum campaign formed part of a nationwide movement led by con-servatives and liberals alike that created a social panic around the personal safety of white people. It set the tone for deeper estrangement between whites and nonwhites. Between the schools and the streets, the vilification and criminaliza-tion of young people accelerated. But with that acceleration and the defeat of the civilian review board came rebellion and more radical proposals among black American and Puerto Rican youth calling for the dissolution of the institution of police.

A New Generation Stands Up: The East Harlem Riots

On July 23, 1967, the year after the CCRB was defeated in New York, a rebellion exploded in Detroit that exceeded the scale of not only the 1965 Watts riots in Los Angeles but all those that followed.[132] On the same day, riots erupted in the Puerto Rican neighborhood of East Harlem. The rebellion shocked city officials, who purportedly never expected these relatively new migrants to riot, despite the forewarnings. A year earlier, Puerto Rican and black American riots had been triggered in east New York by racist white violence. And in Perth Amboy, New Jersey, Puerto Ricans had engaged in four nights of violent confrontation with police about a city ordinance that limited congregating in the streets.[133] However, as late as 1967, Puerto Ricans were still in the process of being socially and racially defined by government officials, social critics, and journalists— sometimes as criminal youths, other times as "passive" and "docile" migrants.

The four-day upheaval in East Harlem, where the dominant form of rebellion was the throwing of Molotov cocktails at the police, finally upended these facile characterizations of the Puerto Rican community.[134] On the final day of the crisis, the riots spread to the South Bronx's Mott Haven neighborhood, the Puerto Rican enclave connected to East Harlem by the Second Avenue Bridge. In total, thirty people were injured and four residents were killed, including a well-known black American neighborhood activist, Emma Haddock, all with the .38-caliber bullets used in police guns.[135] By all accounts, including the lead paragraph of a front-page New York Times article, the East Harlem riots were described as "anti-police."[136] As a younger and more militant segment of the population was thrust into public debates about the standing of Puerto Ricans on the U.S. mainland, the stage was set for the rise of the Young Lords in New York.

On July 23, 1967, two New York City policemen intervened in what they described as a Sunday brawl between two Puerto Rican men in East Harlem. The officers were off duty and wearing civilian clothes. According to their account, when one of the men, Reinaldo Rodriguez, lunged at officer Thomas Ryan with a knife, the other officer, Anthony Cinquemani, killed Rodriguez with repeated shots to the chest.[137] Eyewitnesses disputed the police's version of the incident, charging that the police deployed brutality against two friends who were engaged in rough banter while playing dice.[138] Within minutes, a crowd of approximately 400 Puerto Ricans and black Americans congregated at the intersection of 111th Street and Third Avenue, the line that divided the Italian and Puerto Rican sections of East Harlem, throwing rocks and bottles at the police. Rumors of the shooting spread. The upheaval gathered steam. The city deployed 160 helmeted police and three busloads of members of a universally detested crowd-control unit known as the Tactical Patrol Force (TPF).[139] They were met with rocks, bottles, and bricks hurled at them in the streets and from tenement windows.[140] Of these events the New York Times noted, "There is plenty of flammable material here, and not only among the Negroes."[141]

The next morning, Mayor John V. Lindsay walked the streets of East Harlem. In a street forum at the site of the shooting, Lindsay invited a subgroup of those present to a formal meeting at Gracie Mansion, the mayoral residence, to discuss grievances. Influenced by the logic of the War on Poverty, the major federal antipoverty legislation of the 1960s, the mayor's walking tour—a signature of his administration—intended to counteract feelings of "powerlessness" among the poor through "maximum feasible participation" in the political process.[142] Approximately fifteen youth affiliated with various antipoverty programs joined him later that morning, among them a young Hiram Maristany, the renowned photographer of Puerto Rican life in East Harlem.[143] Months earlier, Maristany had been arrested for refusing military induction. But when the staff of the Photography Workshop, the antipoverty program that trained him, produced a Columbia College acceptance letter at the eleventh hour, Maristany was absolved of military duty. The fledgling radical artist would join the Young Lords in 1969 and become its resident photographer.[144] For now, however, he and his cohort were standing before the mayor, arguing that a genuine conversation was impossible while the infamous TPF continued to menace the streets of East Harlem. A momentary agreement was reached. In exchange for the removal of the TPF from East Harlem, the young leaders pledged to help restore order in their neighborhood.[145] The truce ended, however, when a second wave of intense rioting began less than twenty-four hours after the first eruptions. But the fact that such a deal was struck with young people of color, however briefly, was remarkable—a testament to the rebellions' potential to reshape government practice.

On the second day of the rebellion, many who took to the streets were reportedly protesting the TPF's indiscriminate deployment of force on Third Avenue the night before. The infamous unit was targeted with sniper fire and Molotov cocktails from tenement windows. In the streets, thousands of youth engaged in approximately seven hours of uninterrupted battle with police. Equipped with bottles, bricks, debris, garbage cans, and all manner of refuse, they were able to repel the more than 1,000 police reinforcements dispatched to disperse them.[146] In at least one instance in which mediators were present, people in the street demanded that policemen stationed on roofs come down, and they did. While community leaders and antipoverty workers failed to convince throngs of residents to disperse, they were, in fact, able to persuade the police to avoid congregating, keep sirens quiet, not wear helmets, and call off police helicopters.[147] This open and taunting resistance to police reinforcements confirmed the views of an emergent group of radical social analysts, who argued that the decade's riots were rational and politically motivated and that, across the country, attempts at controlling the rebellions through increased police repression had intensified them.[148]

Reports of spontaneous attempts at mediation between residents and the police, of groups of people talking strategy on street corners, of improvised soapbox speeches, and of spontaneous marches in the streets point to the complex set of political grievances that motivated those who took over the streets. At one point, a young man reportedly confronted a Spanish-speaking police officer and said, "It's you who are abusing democracy, you with your gun and your shield."[149] Although largely led by a younger generation of Puerto Ricans, black Americans participated in these rebellions. A black American boy reportedly challenged a black American police officer to draw his revolver.[150] Reporters captured glimpses of a community engaged in a process of political self-definition. In one instance, a group of young people drew a line in chalk across Third Avenue, just above 110th Street, and over it wrote, "Puerto Rican border. Do not cross, flatfoot," an expression of a desire for meaningful control of their neighborhoods very similar to the animating concept of black power.[151] And those who rebelled had clear grievances. One soapbox speech suggested that people wanted reparations for the labor and military service that Puerto Ricans contributed to the country in spite of their standing as second-class citizens. In another scene, a group of youth carrying a large Puerto Rican flag tried to march into the 104th Street police precinct located between Lexington and Third Avenues.[152] As one journalist astutely noted, "The paraphernalia of nationalism now accentuated the void separating the crowd from the men in blue uniforms who represented the government of the city."[153]

The Puerto Rican flag held many meanings for Puerto Ricans. To many who migrated as adults, the flag was closely linked to nostalgia for the homeland and to the burdens of their working-class lives. To older Puerto Rican radicals on the mainland, the flag was a prized possession and endangered symbol of struggle. In 1948, ownership and display of the Puerto Rican flag had been declared a crime in Puerto Rico under the Gag Law, passed by the Puerto Rican legislature to suppress the independence movement.[154] But for the generation of younger Puerto Ricans who came of age in New York during the civil rights and black power movements, the Puerto Rican flag had taken on a more capacious and complicated meaning. To them, the flag was a symbol of pride and resistance to the psychic violence they had borne silently in the schools and in the streets at the hands of the police, an experience of racialization they shared with their black American peers. The act of holding aloft the Puerto Rican flag in the context of the riots challenged the distinct location of second-generation Puerto Ricans in the social structure of the city and set limits to how Puerto Ricans could be treated.

For now, aspects of these developments were repudiated by mainstream Puerto Rican observers and civic leaders seeking to protect the precarious reputation of the city's Spanish-speaking community from the stigma associated with black Americans and their well-reported troubles. Among others, the newly elected Bronx borough president, Democrat Herman Badillo, declared that the East Harlem rebellion was "different from the desperate, nihilistic wrath of the Negro riots" and argued that poverty and poor housing conditions, rather than race, motivated the upheaval.[155] Others such as the editorial board of *El Diario La Prensa*, the city's major Spanish-language daily, invalidated the Puerto Rican riot's implications about race by blaming the reds. One of its editorials excoriated residents of East Harlem for falling prey to "outside agitators sent to *El Barrio* to stir up trouble and to darken the name of the Puerto Ricans by making them a part of the racial riots that are now rampant in our nation." Translated into English and republished in the *New York Times* as an ad, the scolding editorial advocated individual discipline, proper comportment in public spaces and the airing of grievances through established mainstream channels—essentially the politics of middle-class respectability.[156] These editorial analyses echoed conservative social critics, who attributed the spate of bitter rebellions to the "permissiveness" of congressional antipoverty policies, which facilitated the lawlessness of rogue individuals who could only be restrained with law-and-order policies.[157]

Other sectors of the Puerto Rican community, however, linked the riots to "racial bigotry" within the NYPD. An "Open Letter to the Police Department" of unknown origin, but likely drafted by Puerto Rican activists, asserted that police "must show respect in order to receive it," denounced as criminal the language used by police in interactions with Puerto Ricans, and demanded that Puerto Ricans be treated as "human beings."[158] These sentiments expressed the much more common liberal analysis of the riots, increasingly dominant in government circles, which cited social alienation, years of racial discrimination, and political "powerlessness" as the underlying causes. This was the assessment of Mayor Lindsay, who was, nonetheless, confounded by the failure of his reform efforts. Months earlier, his administration had appointed the highest number of Puerto Ricans to key municipal government posts, including the young Puerto Rican reformer Marta Valle who, only months earlier in May 1967, organized a conference on Puerto Rican poverty—the largest-ever government-sponsored event on Puerto Ricans.[159]

Despite the various interventions of a visible coterie of Puerto Rican reformers with increased prominence in city politics, the East Harlem riots pointed to the growing disconnect between Puerto Rican leaders, who called for moderate reforms—such as integration of the police department, racial sensitivity training, and a greater share of antipoverty funds—and some members of the community cynical about these proposed solutions. Amid the rioting, one young antipoverty worker, Arnie Segarra, remarked, "Tell a kid you're putting $1 million [in the poverty funds] and he says 'that's got nothing to do with me.'"[160] Influenced by the era's upheavals and social movements, young people of color were approaching their world with a wider analytical lens. Their own lived experience reinforced the growing sense that racism and poverty were inbuilt features of society requiring change more fundamental than the funding of a government program.

From the War on Poverty to a Wider Mobilization

Conceived in the context of the postwar economic boom and the Cold War, which had narrowed the parameters of social critique in the United States, the federal initiative, to which Puerto Rican reformers were beholden, failed to posit solutions that reflected the magnitude of urban problems. The legislation linked urban poverty to a lack of access to political power among the poor rather than identifying it as a problem rooted in class relations, structural unemployment in New York as a consequence of urban deindustrialization, and the fallout of structural racism, which trapped most people of color in the city's worst schools, the most expensive and decaying housing stock, and the least-paying and least desirable jobs. Instead of access to well-paid employment, the legislation offered skills training and services to the unemployed. And rather than addressing police violence against people of color and white resistance to school integration, it put the onus of racism on poor people of color by encouraging behavioral changes, among them civic involvement and participation in a vaguely defined political process. These legislative initiatives differed from their counterparts in the 1930s, during which time the fierce strike actions of a socialist and communist-influenced labor movement pressured the federal government to redistribute wealth through unemployment insurance, higher wages, and the mass creation of jobs.[161]

At the local level, the War on Poverty's youth employment initiative sought to control urban social discontent. That was the purpose of the federal Community Action Programs (CAPs), introduced after 1965, which prescribed community involvement as an antidote to feelings of "powerlessness" among poor people of color. Developed by the Office of Economic Opportunity, the CAPs proposed to pull youth off the streets and into controlled protest activity in local government bureaucracies and preexisting community organizations.[162] In New York, Mayor Lindsay's "little city hall" project, which was funded partially with antipoverty funds, "tapped street-level activists, including gang members[,] and enmesh[ed] them in a series of relationships with the administration" as a means of ending urban "alienation."[163] The mayor's "summer task force" identified thirteen "trouble spots" where residents were likely to riot and funneled the young into a series of programs to "get kids off the street," especially in the aftermath of a police shooting.[164]

But as the political winds shifted in the era of black power, the War on Poverty's calls for "maximum feasible participation" in the CAPs and its calls to fund preexisting and new community projects produced unintended consequences and the further politicization of the young, out of which a new radical leadership arose. A future founding member of the New York Young Lords, Juan González, became an activist in federally funded programs. Growing up, González had been influenced by the conservative politics of the predominantly white ethnic milieu of his high school, but his political world view changed when he took a job as a tutor at a Harlem-based after-school program during his sophomore year at Columbia University. He took the job to connect with others like him and mitigate his feelings of alienation at the elite Columbia campus, where the distinct class position of his peers was palpable—"even the black American students were middle or upper middle class," he remembers. But he found a home and discovered radical politics tutoring working-class black American and Puerto Rican kids at a church whose young black minister was also leading a protest against Columbia's controversial project to construct a university gym in the Harlem community.[165] Before long González was at a community-led protest with other Columbia student tutors and Will Stein and Mark Naison, members of SDS, where they joined the young black minister in a sit-in in front of the bull-dozers. After a day in jail, talking to the other protesters about the many social and economic problems of the community, González began to turn his sight to problems beyond the college campus and became a strong student advocate on behalf of community residents during the Columbia student strike of 1968.[166]

As administrators of War on Poverty–funded programs engaged in activism that pushed the boundaries of civic participation, many young people gained organizational and leadership skills in the resulting projects. The founding members of the BPP, for example, wrote the main platform of that fledgling organization in the office of an antipoverty program in Oakland in 1966. As a consequence of the McCarthy witch hunts of the 1950s and of the failure of the Old Left to speak to what was then a new movement with a protest style different from what it was accustomed to, they were working in the context of a weakened organized-left tradition. Thus, fledgling activists were influenced by the institu-tionalized forms of struggle spearheaded by War on Poverty programs and by radicalized social service reformists even while they were beginning to develop a critique of the limitations of social service reform. Similarly, in East Harlem, the founders of the RGS brought together a team of talented, progressive young people to transform the architectural landscape of a dilapidated East Harlem. One of the founding members of the New York Young Lords, Mickey Melendez, shepherded youth into community centers such as RGS as part of his summer work in the mayor's Urban Action Task Force.[167] At RGS, Melendez also began to convene meetings of Puerto Rican student activists in the winter of 1969, and it was there that in June 1969 they discussed the Black Panther newspaper inter-view with Cha Cha Jiménez on the emergence of the YLO in Chicago.

A year earlier at the RGS-run school East Harlem Prep, Melendez had also met one of the school's teachers, Denise Oliver, the experienced activist who would play a central role in the history that was about to unfold. Oliver was born in Brooklyn in 1947 and grew up in Queens in a middle-class black American household. Her mother was one of the city's few black high school teachers, and her father, George Bodine Oliver, was a professor of drama, a Tuskegee Airman, and one of the first black actors to integrate Broadway in the 1940s. Oliver's father was either a member or "fellow traveler" of the Communist Party who became part of the city's growing and vibrant black Left. Oliver's future leadership role in the Young Lords would be informed by this political culture and the familiarity with Marxist theory that she gained as a child in the 1950s.[168]

In 1968, Oliver was expelled from Howard University for her participation in protests and occupations against the absence of black studies, the presence of the Reserve Officer Training Corps on campus, and restrictive parietals in the university's single-sex dorms.[169] Back in New York, she was hired by the RGS director, Harry Quintana, to teach at University of the Streets, a school initiated by activists to serve the growing number of youth of color who had been permanently expelled from the city's public schools.[170] Both the site and the topic of her new work would foreshadow much of what was to come.

Mobilization for Youth (MFY) in New York was also an important site that exposed young people to politics, among them some who would later join the Young Lords. In the 1950s, the organization had been a haven for radical psychologists and other professionals, some self-described communists and socialists, who had been driven away from activism by McCarthyism. But its success with "deviant" youth drew attention and funding from President Kennedy's Committee on Juvenile Delinquency and the Ford Foundation, and its model was eventually adopted by the War on Poverty's CAPs.[171] Located on the Lower East Side, MFY offered counseling and politics to large numbers of "deviant" youth who were expected to participate in a wide variety of grassroots actions led by civil rights organizations, parents' groups attempting to influence local school policies, and tenants' councils involved in the spate of rent strikes initiated by Jesse Gray.[172]

In late March 1969, MFY staff member Bob Collier helped organize a bus trip from New York to Denver, Colorado, for the first national Chicano Youth Liberation Conference. As a member of the Revolutionary Action Movement and the BPP, Collier had his finger on the pulse of developments in the movement. Although some black Americans traveled to the conference too, he knew that the conference would be an important site of political education for the mostly Puerto Rican youth who got on the bus from New York. The conference organizers, Crusade for Justice and its leader Corky González, advocated a mixture of socialism and nationalism that combined an affirmation of Chicano identity with calls for the economic and political autonomy of Aztlan, the Aztec name for what is the present-day Southwest.[173]

Days before the conference, its organizers called for a modest student walkout in response to a high school principal's racist remarks. To their surprise, it drew 1,500 students and ignited an uprising against the police in Denver's poor Chicano communities.[174] The high turnout at the conference reflected these developments. The New York youth who traveled to Denver gravitated to and were very interested to learn about a contingent from Chicago whose members carried a newspaper, donned purple berets, and displayed Puerto Rican flags.[175] Cha Cha Jiménez and the Young Lords were at the conference. But excitement quickly turned to disappointment when the conference organizers announced that black Americans would not be allowed to participate fully in the conference proceedings. Ironically, the organizers were drawing on a narrow interpretation of black nationalism's race-based unity principle, which was popularized by the black power movement, with its call for building power independent of white society. However, in the context of discussing the role of white Americans in the struggle to consolidate Chicano leadership and power, "black people were somehow lumped with the whites, because they didn't speak Spanish." Debates like these, about how racially oppressed groups might best establish leadership and leverage political power, had intensified three years earlier in 1966. That year, the Student Nonviolent Coordinating Committee expelled its white members and argued that its major decisions should be made by black Americans.[176]

The decision made by Chicanos at the Denver conference was especially distressing to the New York Puerto Ricans, who now faced a dilemma. They were being asked to part ways with black American activists with whom they had bonded during the long trip to Denver—and more generally with their neighbors in New York, whom they had grown to trust, despite differences—for a conversation with a subgroup of Americans they barely knew. The Chicago Young Lords were also uncomfortable with the position because earlier that same month they had made public their coalition with the Chicago Black Panthers.

The organizers' stance amplified the ambiguities of race as a social category. Iris Morales noted the reactions of some of the Puerto Ricans among them: "'How can they say no to blacks? Some of us are obviously black.' Right?"[177] Ralph Garcia, for example, who had traveled from New York, had a Cuban father but identified with the ethnic lineage of his black American mother. In addition, a disproportionate number of the Puerto Ricans on the trip were darker hued, including the poets Cenen and Papoleto, and felt a stronger affinity with black Americans than they did with Chicanos from the Midwest. They sensed that the inclusion of Puerto Ricans and other non-Mexican Latinos on the basis of shared language alone was "problematic." But as Carlito Rovira remembers, "We couldn't clearly articulate why politically."[178] But when the Puerto Rican contingents from New York and Chicago threatened to leave unless there was opportunity for further debate on the matter, an open discussion was convened. According to Morales, the position "wasn't presented in a racist way. It said, 'This is about Latinos getting together, and so therefore we want this to be just a Latino meeting.' Nonetheless, we felt we could not remain, and we got up and we left."[179] Embarrassed that the position had offended these East Coast Latinxs, Corky González sought a conversation with the activists. In the end, black Americans were allowed to participate and a formal apology was extended by the conference organizers.[180]

Within months of the Denver trip, Rovira, Morales, and a larger cohort of mostly Puerto Rican student radicals in New York added nuance to the nationalist position articulated at the Chicano youth conference. They argued that unity on the basis of language and culture alone was not the vehicle for political and economic justice among Latinxs.[181] In their quest to build an organization responsive to the concerns of poor and working-class Puerto Ricans in New York, they adopted the more expansive brand of nationalism known as revolutionary nationalism, which the Black Panthers popularized.[182] Influenced by Marxism, the Puerto Rican student radicals' brand of nationalism emphasized the vested class interests of upper- and middle-class Puerto Ricans in accommodating capitalism and U.S. imperialism. They also upheld the principle of solidarity among people of color and welcomed those who shared this world view into their ranks, especially black Americans.

The Young Lords Come Together

In July 1969, Iris Morales learned that a group of Puerto Rican students who were meeting in East Harlem had taken a road trip to Chicago to meet Cha Cha Jiménez, whom she had met in Denver four months earlier. She never joined the group. It was called the Sociedad Albizu Campos (SAC) and founded by Mickey Melendez. Its name paid homage to the recently deceased political prisoner and iconic leader of Puerto Rico's struggle for nationhood, Don Pedro Albizu Campos. Albizu Campos died in 1965 from torture and severe illnesses induced, almost irrefutably, by the U.S. government's Cold War radiation experiments during the leader's long years of imprisonment.[183] Members of the SAC planned the trip to Chicago when they read the interview with Cha Cha, which appeared in the Black Panther newspaper.

In Chicago, Cha Cha was excited to discuss the work of the Young Lords, but he first wanted to learn more about the SAC. The Chicago Young Lords met with many groups who solicited meetings with them, and the group's leadership was vigilant about not disclosing too much information to people who could be police agents. It helped that the SAC members had traveled all the way from New York, with someone the Young Lords knew from the neighborhood, David Perez, a student at SUNY Old Westbury on the East Coast. Over the course of their conversation, the Chicago Young Lords learned that their politicization and the emergence of the SAC happened concurrently in the winter of 1969 but on parallel tracks. The SAC was launched in January 1969 and cohered over time thanks to the tenacity of its founder, Mickey Melendez, who, like Cha Cha, was dedicated to recruiting new activists and had an unusual organizing background. In high school, Melendez had gained invaluable experience assembling a team of dynamic people with different skill sets, who successfully brought to fruition a series of dance hall events with Puerto Rican and Cuban musicians. Melendez had his finger on the pulse of the era's emerging youth culture and had an aptitude for managing projects and people and identifying ideas with potentially broad appeal. His persistence was key to the success of the SAC, which would soon become the major vehicle for launching the Young Lords in New York.[184]

Melendez had long worked to bring young Puerto Rican activists together. His vision was enriched and made possible as a result of his enrollment at the newly launched SUNY Old Westbury. In the summer of 1968, the college's admissions officers recruited Melendez and Denise Oliver during a scouting visit to East Harlem, where both were employed in antipoverty summer projects. The college had been launched in September 1968 under the leadership of Harris Wofford, former director of the Peace Corps in Ethiopia. Its faculty and staff sought to implement the era's calls for the democratic reorganization of education and society. To this end, the college employed unorthodox admissions standards that generated a dynamic, diverse, and civic-minded student body. The school's pedagogy was also new. It was anchored around practices that have since been mainstreamed in colleges across the country—an open, seminar-style classroom that stimulated critical thinking and a curriculum that encouraged independent study and student-led community-based projects.[185]

Melendez reminded Cha Cha that even before the members of the SAC decided to travel to Chicago to learn about the work of the Young Lords, SUNY Old Westbury had facilitated a connection with the gang leader. In the winter of 1968, Melendez's federal work-study job in the college's admissions office took him and a senior admissions officer to Chicago in search of prospective Latinx students. During that trip, Cha Cha was identified as the university's top potential recruit. But Cha Cha took a pass and recommended David Perez, a major protagonist in the organizing that was to unfold in East Harlem. Unlike Cha Cha, Perez had stayed away from gangs because his family's economic situation in Chicago demanded that he work at a young age: "I started shining shoes for about a year and then when I was thirteen, I started selling newspapers. By the time I was fifteen, I was working in a factory making brownies, and then I was working as a busboy during the summer and on the weekends." By the time of his impromptu admissions interview with SUNY Old Westbury, he had read and been profoundly moved by Malcolm X's autobiography and Ferdinand Lundberg's *The Rich and the Super-Rich*. In early 1969, Perez began his studies at SUNY Old Westbury and followed the political lead of fellow student Mickey Melendez on campus.[186]

During Melendez's first trip to Chicago, he had met a younger cohort of Puerto Ricans and Mexicans in the Latin American Defense Organization, who were in the throes of organizing grassroots movements independent of the old-guard Puerto Rican political leaders. Inspired by what he saw there, Melendez launched the SAC at SUNY Old Westbury and invited emerging leaders to speak on campus, including Juan González, a leading member of the Columbia

Student Strike Committee, and Felipe Luciano, a member of the Last Poets. Slowly Melendez drew into his orbit fellow SUNY Old Westbury students David Perez, Denise Oliver, and another important activist, Pablo "Yoruba" Guzmán. Later he recruited Diego Pabon, a radical activist at the City College of New York. Pabon eventually became the leader of the study group and is believed to have also been an affiliate of one of the Old Left groups.[187]

Among his peers, Pablo Guzmán had a unique upbringing. He graduated from one of New York's premier academic high schools, Bronx Science, where students were engaged with the political debates of the day, from the Vietnam War to the meaning of black power, thanks to the influence of a history teacher. Guzmán had also been politicized by his Puerto Rican father and maternal grandfather, who was Cuban. Both saw themselves as members of the black diaspora in the Americas. The job discrimination and racist indignities they endured in the Spanish-speaking Caribbean and in New York turned them into race men committed to the politics of black pride and racial uplift. When Guzmán was a teenager, his father took him to Harlem to hear Malcolm X speak.[188] He also remembers that his Afro-Cuban grandfather, Mario Paulino, regularly convened meetings at his home to discuss world politics with a circle of friends, many of whom were likely connected through their experience at the Tuskegee Institute, the historic black American school of industrial training, to which Paulino had applied from Cuba and at which he enrolled in the early 1920s.[189] Perhaps because of the strong black politics of his household, Guzmán identified strongly with the black American community, considered joining the BPP, and called himself "Paul." His "field studies" in Cuernavaca, Mexico, during his freshman year at SUNY Old Westbury, however, awakened him to the significance of his Latin American roots.[190]

The Chicago Young Lords recognized the seriousness of the New York group. They explained that the YLO was in the middle of two major local initiatives. In May, the organization had initiated a takeover of the Presbyterian McCormick Theological Seminary as a means of leveraging negotiations on behalf of the Poor People's Coalition. In June it had occupied Lincoln Park's Armitage Methodist Church, turned it into its headquarters, and begun a series of service projects akin to the BPP's survival programs, including clothing and food drives, free breakfast for children, and the building blocks of a free community health clinic. The New York students were impressed by Cha Cha and his epic personal transformation. He had led a life of rebellion against the middle-class aspirations and proprieties of his Puerto Rican migrant community and its prejudices against black Americans. That he modeled the Young Lords after the BPP was an extension of the solidarity with the black underclass that he had developed over the course of his life. This was a leap that the New York students would

CENTRAL COMMITTEE   YOUNG LORDS PARTY
FI   DAVID   JUAN   FELIPE   YORUBA

Central Committee members. From left: Juan "Fi" Ortiz, David Perez, Juan González, Felipe Luciano, and Pablo "Yoruba" Guzmán. (*Palante* 2, no. 4 [June 5, 1970]; courtesy of the Tamiment Library)

not have taken on their own. But the idea, once articulated and implemented, captured their imagination.

The activism of the reformed gang had gained traction quickly in Lincoln Park because it brought its preexisting social networks into its orbit of protest. The YLO's embrace of the Panthers' organizational structure, however, allowed it to channel its protest activity, identify its mission, and integrate its new recruits effectively without having to reinvent the wheel. The YLO's association with the BPP also brought attention to the organization from movement activists across the country. The experience demonstrated clearly that social movements have the potential to grow rapidly through the reproduction of existing organizational forms and the bringing together of existing social blocs.

Cha Cha informed his SAC visitors of others who were already working to build a chapter of the Young Lords on New York's Lower East Side. In June 1969, Jose Martinez, a seasoned Cuban activist and former SDS member from Florida, had begun to organize a chapter of the YLO on Manhattan's Lower East Side after meeting Cha Cha at the SDS convention that month.[191] Martinez scouted out and mentored young Puerto Rican junior high and high school students who were at risk for dropping out of school, primarily Carlito Rovira, Ralph Garcia, and Andres Cruz. The YLO leader suggested that Melendez and members of the SAC meet with Martinez's group about the possibility of a merger.

In the end, the New York chapter of the Young Lords grew out of the merger of three groups in New York. Led by Melendez, the SAC drove the project and convened meetings with Jose Martinez's fledgling Lower East Side Young Lords groups and with a third entity in East Harlem, the Photography Workshop. Funded by the Social Research Center at Columbia University's Teachers College, the Workshop had offered a space for politically minded youth to combine their artistic inclinations with activism. Its members included Juan "Fi" Ortiz, a fourteen-year-old member of the Workshop's formal leadership body who would soon become one of the youngest members of the Young Lords; Hiram Maristany, who would soon become the group's resident photographer; and other soon-to-be stalwart members of the Young Lords, especially Huey Cambrelen and Jose "Pai" Diaz.[192] Known to his peers as Debenya, Roy Peña also formed part of this East Harlem group. The Young Lords would later discover that Debenya was an undercover cop.

The newly merged organizations that formed the New York chapter of the Young Lords came out at an event to commemorate the Cuban Revolution, held on July 26, 1969, at Tompkins Square Park and sponsored by a broad coalition of left activists. On that day in 1953, a cohort of revolutionaries drawn from Cuba's urban middle class and led by Fidel Castro initiated the first guerrilla offensive of the Cuban revolutionary struggle, unsuccessfully attacking the Moncada Fort in Santiago de Oriente, Cuba. Three years later, the guerrillas reconstituted themselves as the July 26th Movement, overthrew the dictatorship of Fulgencio Batista, and began to lead a revolutionary project in Cuba. By 1969, Cuba was a self-declared socialist country and one of the main challengers of U.S. imperialism.[193]

On July 26, the New York group appeared clad in purple berets and black fatigues, resembling the BPP, holding aloft a banner with their insignia, an AK-47 rifle over the Puerto Rican flag, which they had adopted from the Chicago group. Their fatigues, beret, flag, and the rifle captured the stylized aesthetic of Che Guevara and were shorthand for the Young Lords' political worldview.[194]

According to someone present at that event, the Young Lords' spokesperson, Felipe Luciano, gave an arresting speech: "I was in a socialist organization at that time, and what caught my attention was that Felipe was giving a powerful and sophisticated revolutionary analysis of Puerto Rican oppression in the language of the streets."[195] With oratory skills and a worldview that were incubated in the streets, in prison, and in the university, Luciano was an evidently key figure in the emerging organization. He ended his remarks with a recitation of his spoken word poem, "Jibaro, My Pretty Little Nigger," an ode of love to Puerto Rican folkways but also a wake-up call and provocative challenge to Puerto Ricans, urging them to acknowledge their island roots, blackness, and shared condition of oppression with black Americans. Whatever its meaning, the poem captured the political imagination of second-generation Puerto Rican youth, most of whom were reared between two realities: the politically cautious households of their island-born parents and the rebellious world of New York's racially segregated and impoverished neighborhoods.

Before long, the Young Lords had transformed sprawling urban discontent in New York into a radical and well-organized social movement that became a magnet for thousands of disaffected urban youth. In the summer of 1969, this network of activists and artists would turn its camera lens and organizing efforts toward one of the most visible conditions of urban decay: the unsightly accumulation of garbage in East Harlem.

CHAPTER THREE

THE GARBAGE OFFENSIVE

The Young Lords may have seized the stage at Tompkins Square Park to demand a free Puerto Rico at the July 26, 1969, commemoration of Cuba's revolutionary experiment, but their show didn't stop there. Their vision and objectives remained a work in progress. Weeks earlier, in June, the Young Lords began to test their ideas before a more exacting audience—the people of East Harlem. For them, clean city streets were a more urgent matter than the independence of Puerto Rico.

The first grassroots campaign launched by the newly formed network of activists suggested that they were listening to neighborhood residents' grievances and simultaneously asking broader questions. What they called "the Garbage Offensive" demanded adequate neighborhood sanitation services but implied much more. It channeled the spirit of the Tet Offensive of a year earlier, a turning point in the Vietnam War. During Tet, guerrillas of the National Liberation Front quit the countryside and stunned the U.S. military with surprise attacks in urban areas, where television cameras captured the violent reality of war for the first time in history.[1] The Young Lords' imaginative title tendered a global analysis of the social problems they observed around them. The group's juxtaposition of an issue as unremarkable as sanitation with the era's most dramatic military operation underscored the relationship between the common problems of Puerto Ricans in East Harlem and the larger crisis of colonial rule the world over.

In a creative approach to organizing in East Harlem, the Young Lords mounted a nonviolent, urban guerrilla campaign in which, in their words, "we would hit and run, block to block, talking and spreading politics as we went, dodging the slow moving pigs sent to crush any beginning Boricua movement for freedom."[2] The Garbage Offensive was the laboratory within which the Young Lords developed an approach to local organizing that adopted the model of community service institutionalized by the War on Poverty. But the offensive also enlarged the model's social impact through the simultaneous deployment

Statue of Liberty superimposed on a dirty street in East Harlem. (*Palante* 2, no. 13 [October 16, 1970]; courtesy of the Tamiment Library)

of civil disobedience, political muckraking, and the symbolism and vocabulary of the era's defining decolonization struggles.

Theory and Praxis

In the weeks before their Tompkins Square Park declaration of existence, the New York Young Lords grappled with the challenges that have long preoccupied organized radicals: how to recruit others, how to link short-term campaigns for improved social conditions to the ultimate goal of revolution, and how to achieve broader community participation in their initiatives. Juan González, who had been one of the leaders of the Columbia University strike in 1968 and who had done thirty days in prison in June 1969 for his continued disruption of campus life at Columbia a year later, explained: "When we were meeting in the Sociedad de Albizu Campos, there was all this debate over how do we build a revolutionary organization. Do we do study groups? Do we get involved in electoral politics? The debate was over whether you build a political movement through debate, discussion, and education or do you build it through some concrete actions that affect people's lives."[3] The Young Lords chose a combination of political education and direct action.

The group's decision to build an organization beyond the college campuses where many of its leaders developed as organizers demanded that it put its finger on the pulse of East Harlem. Members began by talking with people on street corners, asking how they perceived the problems of the world around them and listening to their answers—a long-standing tradition carried out by different groups within the U.S. Left with varying degrees of success in the twentieth century.[4] In an interview with Pacifica Radio in spring 1970, Felipe Luciano, the chairman of the new organization, explained, "[Our objective was to find] an issue ... certain organizing tools that respond[ed] to the needs of the people in the streets that we knew: my mother, my uncle ... those kinds of people."[5] Of the issues that concerned the community, the most visible was the problem of uncollected garbage. Members of the East Harlem Photography Workshop—one of the three groups that came together to form the Young Lords—had zeroed in on this problem with their cameras in the months before the Garbage Offensive.[6]

However, if the Young Lords were to build a revolutionary organization among poor and working people, their challenge was to go beyond identifying grievances by fusing revolutionary theory and daily praxis.[7] The group of about fifteen to twenty young men and women who initiated the Garbage Offensive were reading texts on imperialism and decolonization that had restructured the political ideas of the Left around the world. With the advent of decolonization wars throughout Asia, Africa, and Latin America at the end of World War II, the center of gravity in revolutionary theory and politics now emphasized the role of Third World, peasant armies engaged in guerrilla war.[8] Guerrillas organized themselves into small, mobile forces that fought a war of ambush, booby trap, and quick field-gun barrage, a tactic of baiting the enemy with surprise attacks and stealth retreats. Guerrilla war was developed to avoid direct military combat with the modern military war machines of their colonizers; it became known as the only strategy that poor, colonized countries could employ successfully in the fight against colonial domination.[9] The shift away from the predominantly white industrial working classes of Europe and the United States—the major, early twentieth-century protagonists of revolutionary change upraised by the Bolshevik victory in 1917—was observed in the literature read by the Young Lords and their counterparts in the New Left. Their readings also addressed the new strategy as well as the impact and legacy of colonialism on people engaged in rebuilding their societies. They included Che Guevara's *Man and Socialism*; Mao Tse-tung's *Little Red Book*; Gen. Vo Nguyen Giap's *People's War, People's Army*; Juan Angel Silen's *We, the Puerto Rican People: A Story of Oppression and Resistance*; Kwame Nkrumah's *Neocolonialism: The Last Stage of Imperialism*; and Frantz Fanon's *The Wretched of the Earth*. According to Gilbert Colón, who was introduced to the group through his cousin, Pablo Guzmán, "[We read anything we could find] on the colonial situation in Puerto Rico. . . . We also read newspapers like the *Guardian*. It was like a quest. You read something that led you to something else. From Fanon, I remember *Wretched of the Earth*. I remember *Black Skin, White Masks*. A lot of stuff in that vein."[10]

It was a major challenge to apply, in the U.S. urban context, political theories that had developed in colonized societies with sizeable rural populations engaged in guerrilla war. The question was how to connect the revolutionary analysis of these readings to struggles for social reforms. Chairman Luciano suggests that the Young Lords were cognizant of the pitfalls of "talking about armed struggle but never really being able to legitimatize that idea among the masses of people."[11] From their meeting with Cha Cha Jiménez, the New York radicals got practical advice on how to get started. Influenced by Chicago Black Panther leader Fred Hampton, Cha Cha stressed that in order for larger numbers of people to become involved in the project of changing society, they needed to see examples of concrete actions toward that end, to have their consciousness raised through "observation and participation"—the notion that the masses can learn about and test out socialist ideas through engagement with activities modeled by revolutionaries in the community.[12] Variants of this concept had a long history among Marxists, but during the 1960s they were absorbed quickly when the Black Panther Party began to disseminate the pocket-sized *Little Red Book*, a collection of Mao's quotations on building a revolutionary party.[13] Pablo Guzmán, the group's minister of information, used the analogy of building a house to illustrate Cha Cha's point—that because small campaigns help awaken a sense of what might be possible, they function as conveyor belts for larger revolutionary ideas: "Something happens to their consciousness . . . once they get involved in doing. Somebody can theoretically explain how to build a house. But until you actually take a hammer and nails, you really don't know what they're talking about."[14] In the process of winning small victories, the idea of taking on larger structures becomes a real prospect.

The Young Lords' initial forays in the community demanded courage. Guzmán recalled the feeling: "To walk up to some strangers and just start rapping, and give 'em a leaflet—that's frightening shit."[15] But as Guzmán explains, the Young Lords acquired mettle when they convinced Felipe Luciano to join: "Felipe had certain characteristics of discipline and toughness, and a certain kind of leadership that we needed. . . . It was like, 'My name is Felipe Luciano, how are you doing. We're with the Young Lords. You should worry about Puerto Rico, Puerto Rico is in bad shape. The barrio is in bad shape. You know why the barrio is in bad shape?' I mean, we were like, this guy is out of his mind! He was like, 'Talk to this person over there, talk to that person over here!' And that's what we needed."[16]

As the nascent network cohered, Luciano emerged as the organization's most dynamic public persona. Luciano had a natural talent for articulating the grievances and aspirations of poor and working-class Puerto Ricans. He also had his finger on the pulse of the streets, which the Young Lords were intent on influencing. Luciano grew up in black American neighborhoods in Brownsville, Los Angeles, and East Harlem. His father, Joseph Luciano, "was not decidedly political, but had strong feeling on race and his people were nationalists from Puerto Rico." His mother, Aurora Olmo, was "Pentecostal. Bathed in the blood of Jesus, speaks tongues and raised me that way." On the issue of race, Luciano remembers that he "grew up hearing that black was beautiful but not from a black power standpoint." He goes on: " I grew up around blackness. I never saw it as foreign. I didn't have one parent who was light. . . . I've always seen blackness in my life, so I never saw it as anything else but gorgeous. My mother's gorgeous to me. My father is gorgeous to me and negritude was always described to me in the most glowing terms."

His oratory developed early in life. His parents "had a tremendous facility for language. Both read extensively." His mother fostered an inquisitive mind in him. And he developed a love of learning through a Junior High School teacher, Ethel Schapiro. She exposed him to Shakespeare and Hemingway and determined that he would learn Yiddish and Judaism. But Felipe lived a dichotomous life. Once outside, Felipe "beat people up, even got involved in stabbings," and though he "never killed anybody or saw anybody die until much later, this was part of the ritual, the rite of passage" of young black men like him. At around twelve, Luciano began to hang around the Canarsie Chaplains, a gang he describes as "an extensively black [American] with Puerto Rican overtones . . . because it was from Canarsie, an Italian stronghold where you could not play the black Puerto Rican game." On a night he hid away in Carnegie Hall at a Gregorian chants concert, a rival black American gang broke code and beat his brother unconscious. Luciano recalls, "When I saw my brother like that, I knew exactly what my destiny was. I made the call. I got prepared."

A fatal fight ensued. Luciano and six of his friends were arrested. Of the three who were found guilty, Luciano was convicted of attempted manslaughter in the second degree in 1964. With the help of mitigating testimonies from teachers and rabbis, Felipe got five years, a lenient sentence. Within two years he was released for good conduct and recruited by the Harlem antipoverty agency, HARYOU-ACT, which recognized his creative talent and urged him to apply to college through the SEEK program. He matriculated at Queens College, began to experiment with poetry, and was invited to join the Last Poets. The black power–era poetry troupe's spoken word recitations prefigured hip-hop. As part of his Harlem-based creative work, Luciano began to lead provocative political workshops that attracted intellectuals and activists, including leading figures of the black power movement like Stokely Carmichael and H. Rap Brown. Months earlier, Mickey Melendez had attended one of Felipe's performances, introduced himself, and pulled Pablo Guzmán into the conversation.[17]

Recognized as the poet with street cred, for whom talking to both grand-mothers and tough young men came easy, Felipe was elected chairman through consensus in the days before the group's coming out in Tompkins Square Park.

Organizing on Behalf of the People

As the group continued its street conversations with the people of East Harlem, its members found the answers they were searching for. In an interview conducted by Young Lord Iris Morales, the director of a 1995 PBS film on the Young Lords, Luciano explains humorously: "So we're on 110th Street and we actually asked the people, 'What do you think you need? What do you need? Is it housing? Is it police brutality?' And they said, 'Muchacho, déjate de todo eso—LA BASURA!" [Listen kid, fuggedaboutit! It's THE GARBAGE!] And I thought, my God, all this romance, all this ideology, to pick up the garbage? But that's what they wanted."[18]

A special series on blight in East Harlem published in the *New York Daily News* corroborated the residents' stories. It described as a "horror" the tons of rotting garbage and structural abandonment that characterized the forty-square-block zone of East Harlem where the Young Lords were most active. According to the journalists, the 160 streets covered by the survey were rarely swept, had only six garbage receptacles, and had uncollected garbage lingering

Young Lord Benjie Cruz and neighbor on 111th Street. (Photograph by Michael Abramson; courtesy of Haymarket Books)

for days and weeks at a time. A major factor in the web of social forces fueling this epic garbage accumulation was the neighborhood's population density and housing crisis. East Harlem was 50 percent more densely populated than other neighborhoods in Manhattan. The problem was even more acute block by block. Since East Harlem had a disproportionate share of the city's condemned housing units, over 90 percent of its residents were crammed into 60 percent of the neighborhood's residential areas, the majority of which housed dilapidated tenements that failed to meet legal standards set by the New York State Housing Act of 1901. In addition to yielding higher concentrations of household waste, East Harlem's built environment was itself littered with industrial-scale waste that included 107 abandoned buildings and fifty-five empty lots in a 160-street radius. These functioned as freelance dumping grounds and rat-infested repositories for all manner of refuse from rotting carcasses of animals to "bicycles, boilers, washing machines, furniture, metal drums, and other discarded bulk." In the East Harlem of the 1960s, it was not uncommon for pedestrian traffic to be obstructed by industrial-scale garbage pouring out of buildings and empty lots with "passersby assailed by fetid odors," especially potent in the summer months.[19] David Perez, a founding member of the Young Lords Organization (YLO) who relocated to New York from Chicago, observed years later, "Until I came to New York, I had never seen so much garbage and dirt in the streets. Not that Chicago was a clean place, but . . . the garbage was not . . . piled up on the front stoop, where people sat during the hot weather."[20]

New Yorkers had long identified the city's dirty streets and its inadequate sanitation system as a top problem. When the *Daily News* opened up its phone lines with the promise of forwarding callers' sanitation concerns to the proper city officers, thousands overwhelmed its lines with "the same refrain—'It's about time somebody tried to do something about this mess.'"[21] Before long, a new cast of characters heeded the call.

In July 1969, approximately thirty-five Young Lords, likely accompanied by a smattering of curious neighbors, walked into the local sanitation depot on 108th Street. They asked if they could register a complaint; they also asked for brooms and garbage bags.[22] Some of those present had probably already heard that the city was distributing a limited number of strong fire- and waterproof green plastic bags—an experiment begun by the mayor's office in partnership with the Ethyl Corporation as one of a series of solutions to the scarcity of garbage cans in the city.[23] The Young Lords claimed they were met with intransigence and racial slurs by the sanitation depot staff, who denied them brooms and bags.[24] The group left, likely hurling a few slurs of their own. Chances are the staff dismissed the group as a bunch of neighborhood rabble-rousers. They likely had no idea what the failure to give out a few garbage bags would spawn.

Over the course of three Sunday mornings, while many East Harlem residents were preparing for church, the Young Lords, armed with brooms pilfered from the sanitation depot and requested from neighborhood bodegas and supermarkets, swept sections of the neighborhood and piled the refuse on the sidewalk. In an interview with Pacifica Radio, Felipe Luciano described the first stage of the Garbage Offensive: "Believe it or not, we were like goody-goodies sweeping the streets all day on what we call Junkies' Row on 110th Street."[25] But sweeping streets alone was not going to sustain the campaign or its membership for long. In a neighborhood where more than 100,000 densely populated residents were producing garbage around the clock, the efforts of the Young Lords, like those of Sisyphus, seemed futile. And some within the group held quiet reservations— carting garbage was a far cry from the work they imagined their self-professed revolutionary organization would be doing. In response to the challenges before them, the Central Committee (the Young Lords' major leadership body) began to meet regularly—sometimes in closed meetings and sometimes with public input—to assess the work of the organization and identify short- and long-term goals.

Although not immediately evident to all their members, the Young Lords' street sweeping and garbage carting allowed the community to get to know them, even as it raised eyebrows. Residents were curious about the purpose of their actions, the meaning of their purple berets, and the message of their button, which featured a fist holding a rifle with the Puerto Rican flag as its background, with the words "I have Puerto Rico in my heart" in Spanish. Passersby asked, "What church are you all with?" or assumed they were with the mayor's Urban Action Task Force.[26] Other more politically discerning residents wondered whether their antiestablishment rhetoric and dress signaled a possible connection with the Black Panthers, whose presence in the city had been seriously thwarted in spring 1969 by a large police roundup that falsely accused twenty-one Panthers of plotting to blow up government buildings.[27] Getting their hands dirty in the community softened the Young Lords' image and offered an organic entry point that allowed them to engage in political discussions in the process of addressing concrete neighborhood problems. Guzmán recalled that the Garbage Offensive allowed the Young Lords to "rap with the people [of East Harlem] about the revolutionary changes going on in society at large and then to connect those changes with the need to make revolutionary change in the immediate society around them. Right now."[28]

In a way, it was fitting that these young, downwardly mobile Puerto Rican militants—the first in their families to go to college, with the expectation that they would become professionals—began with a community service campaign. But even as political rhetoric and dress disavowed the traditional markers of success, they presented their newfound political theories in the cultural language of Puerto Rican migrants. Unlike their white counterparts in the New Left, most members of the Young Lords were deferential to small-town, traditional Puerto Rican values with their respect for elders and a deep sense of obligation to family and community.[29] This particular feature of the Young Lords' élan charmed community residents and contributed to their success. The experience also proved cathartic for the Young Lords, as Guzmán explains: "It was like rediscovering where your parents had come from, rediscovering your childhood."[30] As residents got to know them, some participated in their street-sweeping activities, and the Young Lords gained members in the ones and twos.

Contrary to popular representations of 1960s radicals as one-dimensional, gun-wielding toughs, the Young Lords began to implement the practices and ideas that others in the New Left had made dominant over the course of the 1960s: that political work included *both* committing zealously to service in poor communities *and* supporting the idea of armed self-defense against racist violence, especially at the hands of the police. Best exemplified by the Black Panthers' breakfast program for poor children, urban radicals adopted the service model of activism made dominant by antipoverty programs, which fit with the conception of the revolutionary as a self-sacrificing "servant of the people" advanced by Mao Tse-tung and Che Guevara.[31] Because these activities were undertaken as part of a larger political project, their impact was qualitatively enlarged. As hundreds of young people of color—the most stigmatized population in U.S. society—began to join revolutionary organizations inside the world's major power, their humanistic programs simultaneously subverted their demonization in the mainstream and became a potent symbol of radical resistance the world over.

Back in East Harlem, the Young Lords argued that the absence of routine garbage collection in the city harmed poor people of color disproportionately and that the particular manifestation of the sanitation crisis in neighborhoods like East Harlem was fueled by racism against Puerto Ricans. Though perhaps abstract to some, their assessment was not off the mark. The changes that gripped northern cities during the postwar period produced greater structural inequality. Industrial decline and the mass exodus of working- and middle-class white Americans to the suburbs had eroded New York's tax base dramatically and produced a fiscal crisis. By the late 1960s, New York's disproportionately black and brown residents lived in an urban apartheid beleaguered by chronic unemployment, acute housing shortages, a disfigured physical landscape, impoverished schools, inadequate health and sanitation systems, and greater pollution.[32]

The New York City Department of Sanitation's own annual report for 1971 identified 1969—the year that the Young Lords launched their protest—as a particularly bad year for garbage collection, with the department meeting only 77 percent of its refuse collection schedule on any given day.[33] The refuse and industrial waste that was popping up across the city was that of a society whose capacity for garbage removal had not kept up with consumption patterns. Established in a different epoch, the city's sanitation equipment, administrative infrastructure, and protocols were overwhelmed by the scale of detritus of the new consumer society. For example, the city had not designated rules of disposal for abandoned cars, which often wound up in neighborhoods like East Harlem. These industrial carcasses, "stripped of wheels and engines, littered [city] blocks like giant dead bugs" and lured children and teenagers into dangerous play environments.[34] As the Young Lords' campaign picked up steam, its muckraking exposed how the city's extreme neglect produced environmental health hazards that disproportionately harmed poor Puerto Rican and black American neighborhoods with no resources to hire private garbage-carting services.

When sanitation workers finally showed up in East Harlem they dumped half the garbage into trucks and, according to the Young Lords, "left the other half … strewn in the streets," a practice that residents knew too well, and which the Young Lords attributed to the Sanitation Department's disdain for the people of East Harlem or El Barrio, as its Spanish-speaking residents called it.[35] There was likely a lot of truth in this observation. New York's 10,000 sanitation workers were part of an ethnically exclusive, largely Italian American union. A year earlier, they went on strike despite generous contract terms in comparison to those of other city unions. The sanitation men's walkout was motivated by the rebellious spirit of the late 1960s social movements, but they also seemed to have struck against the growing economic insecurity augured by inflation and the changing racial composition of the city's working class.[36] The sanitation workers were "angry at the city, angry at the changes in working conditions, angry at the apparent preference shown the minorities; they felt like second-class citizens, which the term 'garbagemen,' used to described them and their work[,] suggested, and wanted to strike almost for catharsis."[37] From their vantage point in the suburbs, East Harlem's structural woes were barely visible. Up close, the neighborhood was shamefully dirty, a place where residents didn't own their homes or care about their community.[38] As we have seen, suburbanization, struggles over school integration, and the creation of an independent civilian review board of the police intensified white reaction to the social and economic aspirations of black Americans and Puerto Ricans in the 1960s.

Practicing Civil Disobedience

When the Sunday sweeping activities of the Young Lords failed to elicit the participation of large numbers of people or command the attention of government officials, the YLO decided that more drastic action was necessary. Their leverage would be the rubbish itself, and there was plenty of it to go around.

With the garbage they swept up on a Sunday morning in July and the piles that had gone uncollected during the week, the Young Lords launched the second phase of their campaign. The day after their rally at Tompkins Square Park, on the afternoon of Sunday, July 27, 1969, the Young Lords dumped garbage in the middle of the street on Third Avenue at 110th Street. For good measure they threw in the old mattresses, armchairs, sofas, and sinks they found in the neighborhood's empty lots. While a group of Young Lords coordinated the unloading of abandoned furniture and garbage into the middle of the street, other members of the group explained the new direction of their protest to the familiar neighborhood faces that gathered to watch and participate in their audacious and visually captivating protest.

The group was transitioning from street sweeping to a form of civil disobedience. The new direction opened up conditions within which residents might take action independently, or alongside the Young Lords, or both. It differed markedly from the initial efforts at organizing "on behalf of" and "in service to" the people. The question of whether revolutionary change could be achieved through the self-activity of large numbers of people at the bottom of society or through the leadership of a politically edified and self-sacrificing minority had been a long-standing debate over the meaning and conception of socialism. It would remain an ongoing theme throughout the life of the organization.[39]

The Young Lords threw up garbage barricades to disable traffic on Third Avenue, a major neighborhood thoroughfare. Chairman Felipe Luciano explains that at different moments, the group's "lightning-like guerrilla raids blocked northbound and southbound traffic on Lexington and Madison Avenues, and many times on First Avenue, [and between] 111th Street and 109th Street."[40] Initially, they hoped that community residents who had previously seen them sweeping the streets would respond. Indeed, from the start, throngs spontaneously joined in. In an interview from the period, Guzmán gives a sense of the numbers of Young Lords and community residents involved in their first actions: "We would have fifteen Lords in the beginning, and about three hundred people coming in."[41] The crowds gathering around the dumped garbage soon captured the attention of hundreds of neighborhood residents who observed the mayhem from their windows. The group's objective was to create a crisis that would force the city to respond. When the police arrived at the scene, the Young Lords, who had meanwhile removed their berets, easily "melt[ed] into the community" like fish in the sea, avoiding detection. The Young Lords were applying, to an urban landscape, methods made famous in Vietnam and elsewhere, where guerrillas seeking decolonization attacked their military targets and sought cover from rural people in the mountains—whom they also hoped to recruit to their nationalist cause. Although the Young Lords used the metaphor of guerrilla warfare, their organizing efforts had more in common with nonviolent civil disobedience than with armed insurrection.

As August wore on, bored kids, angry young men, and even a few frustrated grandmas left their apartments to help the Young Lords haul the neighborhood's garbage to exactly those spots where it was not supposed to go. By stopping traffic and creating a gathering point for people, the Young Lords' initiative helped build a sense of community where neighbors could vent and engage in shared activity over a common cause. The Young Lords led the resulting informal street discussions with humor. Since the Department of Sanitation "didn't live up to its name," the Young Lords renamed it the Department of Garbage. They also linked the problem of sanitation to broader issues. Their sometimes crass political rhetoric was unequivocal about naming the enemy: "Our people will never be completely served until the politicians, businessmen and pig power is crushed . . . and all power is returned to the people."[42] To the Young Lords, the indignity of East Harlem's garbage crisis was a disgraceful symbol of the oppression of Puerto Ricans and black Americans on the mainland and on the island colony. In a press release distributed in one of their later garbage protests, they explained that the problem of sanitation was an extension of many other problems in East Harlem: "The average life expectancy of Blacks and Puerto Ricans is seven years less than for whites. The white drop-out earns more than the Puerto Rican high school graduate. Twenty-five percent of all housing in El Barrio is listed as deteriorated or dilapidated. Average income in East Harlem per family is less than four thousand dollars, half that of New York."[43] In these impromptu conversations, more young people asked if they could "get with" the group, and the Young Lords gained a few members at a time as well as dozens of friendly followers.

As the protests drew more people, they grew more spectacular. Through word of mouth, the Young Lords put out a call for a "mass action" on August 17. On that night, as Young Lords assembled the garbage at the intersection of 110th Street and Third Avenue, crowds gathered and grew quickly. Some of the onlookers pushed the protest in a new, more flagrant direction. Several men poured gasoline on the refuse heaps and set them aflame. In later recollections, several Young Lords said that they were not involved in lighting the garbage on fire, but they purposely did not try to stop their neighbors. And when someone planted the Puerto Rican flag atop one of the garbage heaps, the sense of solidarity, pride, and rebellion grew appreciably.

These demonstrations had become about much more than garbage. For many residents who participated, they were about sending a message that Puerto Ricans would not be pushed around. They were about taking a stand for Puerto Rican dignity in a mainland ghetto. And for the Young Lords, they were also about tying this experience of degradation to the experience of racism on the U.S. mainland and to the long-standing history of colonial domination of the island.

As seen in the 1967 East Harlem riots, the symbolism of the flag emboldened the protesters. That night, the Young Lords and their growing number of neighborhood supporters managed to block Madison, Lexington, and Third Avenues completely; uptown and downtown traffic was backed up for thirty blocks. The next day, the *New York Times* reported that "angry residents of a six-block area of East Harlem staged a two-hour garbage throwing melee. . . . Three abandoned automobiles were overturned and burned, blocking intersections, and mounds of burning garbage were heaped up at corners."[44] The protest quickly escalated into what must have appeared to law enforcement like a riot. Before long, two police helicopters hovered in the sky and heavy police reinforcements were called to the scene.[45]

Protests escalated when the police arrested Ildefenso Santiago, a Puerto Rican driver whose car was blocked by the garbage bonfire burning on 111th Street and Lexington Avenue. The *New York Times* reported that the driver was arrested because he was unlicensed; the movement press, however, later held that he was arrested on suspicion of burglary.[46] The throngs of people who looked on likely read the arrest as a form of police clampdown on the garbage protests through repressive retaliation against an innocent bystander and member of the community. The onlookers retaliated. The growing crowd "filled the streets with more trash, cars, old refrigerators, and anything else they could find."[47] In a scene often replayed during the decade's numerous riots, the sanitation workers and firemen who were called to the scene were pelted with bottles. If East Harlem residents hated the Department of Sanitation for making a bigger mess of the garbage, they knew that the fire department was among the most stridently discriminatory institutions nationwide, the epitome of a racially exclusive civil service fraternity. In 1963, out of close to 2,500 firefighters in New York City, only 38 were black American and only 1 was Puerto Rican.[48]

Amid the melee that was set off by Santiago's arrest, the Young Lords organized a march to the 126th Street police station that drew hundreds as rumors spread through the neighborhood about the arrest. Once there, a delegation of residents met with police officials to demand Santiago's release, while others gathered outside chanting "viva Puerto Rico," "power to the people," and "off the pig." Santiago was immediately released with a fine. As soon as the crowd set eyes on him walking out of the precinct, it carried him like a trophy all the way back to his car.[49] That same summer, in June alone, the *New York Times* reported on two different incidents in which throngs of Puerto Rican residents in the Bronx stormed police precincts. In both cases, spontaneous marches to the police station began after failed attempts by individual residents or groups of residents to stop a police arrest in progress. Refusing to succumb to what was surely perceived as abuse of authority or racially motivated harassment by the police for minor infractions, angry crowds followed "the patrolmen and their

Youths overturn a car during the first Garbage Offensive. (Photograph by Beverly Grant)

prisoner to the stationhouse," where demands for the prisoner's release were accompanied by hurled garbage, bricks, and bottles and the smashing of police car windows.[50] As the Young Lords quickly learned, their project would involve disciplining the volatility of a neighborhood recently consumed by riots.

Although the Young Lords tended to celebrate their actions as unique, aggressive interference with police arrests was a common feature of daily life in the late 1960s. These spontaneous expressions of quotidian resistance by people of color had set the stage for the success of the Young Lords' campaigns. The Young Lords' interventions, however, were different. They offered a political platform within which to organize the rebellious spirit of the ghetto beyond isolated outbursts of anger and toward a long-term project for social change fortified by their analyses of the structural roots of poverty, racism, and war. Like El Comité, a radical Puerto Rican group that emerged later, the Young Lords reinvigorated the example of militant community organizing established by the Black Panthers.[51]

The very next day, on August 18, the Young Lords returned to the neighborhood to continue to consolidate relationships with the people with whom they had bonded over the "liberation" of Ildefonso Santiago from the police station.

This time they held a rally and open mike where residents spoke and a number of Young Lords articulated their aims more explicitly. But passions escalated quickly and the *New York Times* again reported that "residents of the area around Park Avenue and 110th Street joined in the heaping and burning of garbage at several intersections. Several abandoned cars were overturned and burned, traffic was blocked and heavy police reinforcements were called to the area to protect sanitation men" who were again called to cart the garbage from the middle of the street. Once the lighting of the fires began, the Young Lords scrambled to figure out how to respond and how to avoid getting arrested. Their campaign had hit a nerve and they were connecting deeply with the community's rebellion against the indignity of living in filth. Guzmán told the *New York Times,* "We don't want violence for violence's sake and we don't want to dump garbage in the street. But if we have to go through a mountain of red tape, if there's never any action by the city, then we have no choice."[52]

The group conducted its hit-and-run, garbage-dumping routine from the end of July through the early days of September. Their new bold approach, coupled with the familiarity of a traffic-stopping routine in which they engaged almost daily in August 1969, set the stage for the inventive militancy that defined the Young Lords during their most productive years. Its chairman summed it up as the deployment of "basic techniques of urban guerrilla warfare: flexibility, mobility, surprise and escape."[53]

Demands against Environmental Racism

Tensions were already emerging within the organization about the direction these actions were taking. David Perez, for example, was uncomfortable with the garbage burning. He was concerned about the possible negative impact the arson might have on the community's perception of the Young Lords. But members had set off a process larger than themselves. The garbage offensive was an all-consuming affair, and most members had very little time and opportunity to figure out what they believed philosophically about the turn of events.

There were also more dangerous fires that needed to be extinguished. The YLO leadership suspected that they had been infiltrated by police provocateurs who were pressing the crowd to prematurely cross the Madison Avenue Bridge to the Bronx, where they would be isolated and could be vulnerable. While the Young Lords were committed to brash militancy, they were not out to incite rioting. A series of demands drafted and printed by the Young Lords, for distribution at their August 18 rally, give a sense of how the group gave definition to and concretized the ongoing garbage protests. Read out by Luciano at the rally, the Young Lords' first articulation of formal demands around local grievances was the following:

reporter, "How do we know what they stand for, what their aims are?" It appeared that the Young Lords were already raising eyebrows among some leaders who feared that these upstarts might be gaining ground in their territory. For its part, the police reported that the Young Lords were a new group about which little was known other than that "every once in a while they pop up."[59]

Although the Young Lords were unknown to some, hundreds of local residents had joined the six demonstrations they organized that summer, the most successful of which obstructed traffic for thirty city blocks.[60] During these days, several groups around the city held demonstrations around the same issue, including a group of parents in Brooklyn who protested the infestation of rats in their neighborhood.[61] The protests continued through the early weeks of September, and the incineration of garbage heaps by residents of East Harlem—often acting independently of the Young Lords in one of Manhattan's major connecting points for commuters—continued to create pressure on the city. At the height of the Young Lords' combined garbage demonstrations, the *New York Times* reported that "dirty streets may be the third issue in this [year's mayoral] campaign, behind the two racial issues, crime and welfare."[62]

Garbage Politics, from Above and Below

The success of the Garbage Offensive was due in part to its timing. As the Young Lords dumped garbage and attracted the press, the 1969 mayoral election race between incumbent Republican mayor John Lindsay and Democratic challenger Mario Procaccino grew more heated. While the Young Lords did not focus on electoral politics, this time they got lucky. The visibility of the Garbage Offensive had advanced the issue of sanitation in public discourse. By the end of the summer, as organized pressure mounted, the city's sanitation became a major issue in the run-up to the election in November. Accordingly, the mayoral candidates felt pressured to respond to the problem with concrete solutions to gain votes and support. When Procaccino wrote a position paper on what it would take to keep the city streets clean, recommending a 1,000-person increase in sanitation personnel, a defensive Lindsay launched a special countereffort. He called first for 1,100, and later 1,300, sanitation men to work overtime for the four Sundays of September to clear lots, remove "household bulk," and sweep and wash New York's streets. Just a month earlier, Mayor Lindsay's press releases had been lighthearted and even mocked the seriousness of the garbage protests; one explained that in addition to the garbage, the city had to contend with, among other things, the sudden invasion of caterpillars, that "have no desire to dine on space age man" because their "appetites are strictly vegetarian." The shift to his Sunday cleanup experiment was swift and had an air of desperation about it, evidence of how quickly the East Harlem protests had amplified a broader grievance in the city and made garbage a matter of legitimate mayoral concern.[63] And following the Young Lords' successive days of garbage protests in mid-August, the Department of Sanitation conceded to three meetings with the Puerto Rican community, where representatives of the Young Lords presented their demands. The assurance that community concerns would be addressed was delivered without any concrete plans. However, more garbage collection was ordered by the mayor's office.[64]

The YLO's tactics of creative disruption generated a fascination with its activism among East Harlem residents and movement activists. Ultimately, the YLO hoped that its actions would give Puerto Ricans confidence in the idea that problems in the community could be successfully addressed through collective, militant struggle. In assessing the Young Lords' work, chairman Felipe Luciano explained: "The people saw that once they took to the streets to demand the redress of their grievances, they would get an answer to their problems. And the answer was pickup. So it was effective and it was a victory for us. That was the beginning, the first formal campaign by the Young Lords Organization."[65] The day-to-day constancy of the Young Lords' two-month-long campaign demonstrated to East Harlem residents that they were serious, committed, and dependable. The group thus began to develop bonds of trust, a key ingredient in community organizing. Their defense of Ildefonso Santiago at the police precinct also began to establish the Young Lords' standing in East Harlem as tough leaders and defenders of the rights of the community.

The Young Lords were naturals in pulling together creative and deep-reaching protests in northern urban centers. They did so at the same time that the effectiveness of protest strategies was being debated—without the Young Lords' knowledge—in the broader movement. Even Martin Luther King Jr. grappled with the matter, as he explained in 1967:

> [Marches are] unsound for big cities because they are absorbed in the rapid pace of urban life. . . . To have effect we will have to develop mass disciplined forces that can remain excited and determined without dramatic conflagrations. To dislocate the functioning of a city without destroying it can be more effective than a riot, because it can be longer lasting, costly to the society but not wantonly destructive. . . . We reject both armed insurrection, either for shock value or conquest, along with weak pleas to insensitive government. Mass civil disobedience can use rage as a constructive and creative force. White decision makers may care little about saving Negroes but they must care about saving their cities.[66]

By blocking traffic with East Harlem's uncollected garbage, the Young Lords' direct action protests captured the imagination of neighborhood residents, interrupted the operation of one of the city's major transportation arteries, and shamed government officials into action.

Garbage-dumping demonstrations were not necessarily new in the city. There had been a variety of onetime garbage protests in New York in earlier years.[67] But their effectiveness had been minimal. They were memorable for nearby residents, but then, inevitably, the sanitation trucks came, the dumped garbage was cleaned up, and life continued. In contrast, the sustained nature of the Young Lords' efforts led to coverage of the garbage-dumping protests in a series of *New York Times* articles, which in turn led the newspaper to identify sanitation as a major issue in the election. The unrelenting dumping protests drew the attention of the mayor's office, which sent its Puerto Rican aide, Arnie Segarra, to meet with the Young Lords on multiple occasions. Unwilling to be moved out of their path of creative urban disruption, the Young Lords refused to sit down with Segarra, who they sensed was sent to co-opt their emerging movement.[68] According to one of Lindsay's key aides, Barry Gottehrer, "We were able to keep a connection to other community groups through War on Poverty money, but the Young Lords were very serious about their militancy and independence. We had to fight to get them to sit down with us."[69]

A combination of campaign promises and targeted pressure by muckrakers like the Young Lords eventually compelled local government to pose systemic solutions to a systemic problem. In consultation with urban policy specialists, the Department of Sanitation launched a more scientific approach to the crisis. It "introduced efficiency standards for mechanics, launched the new hoist compactor system of collection, decentralized repair operations, and improved dumping schedules"; garbage trucks were assigned specific dumping schedules twice a day rather than once a day, which reportedly increased the output of garbage dumping from between six and seven tons to nine tons per day per truck. During this period, the department introduced the systematic use of plastic garbage bags rather than metal cans for the disposal of trash, which helped mitigate the strewn garbage that the sanitation men were infamous for leaving behind. According to the department's report, the garbage bags also "saved time and wear and tear on their bodies" because of the "elimination of the double trip to the curb by the sanitation men."[70] In consultation with the public, the department also overhauled its sweeper routes and schedules by switching from an undependable three-times-a-week collection, which was stretching the department beyond its capacity, to a dependable and timely twice-a-week collection. The department made up for the fewer pickups by adding a thorough street cleaning and an improved bulk pickup service. In 1971, for example, the city came up with its current alternate-side-of-the-street parking system, which it then called an "effective city wide parking enforcement program"—meant to facilitate regular street cleaning.[71] If in 1969 the department was only meeting 77 percent of its refuse collection schedule on any appointed day, in 1972 this figure had gone up to 97.8 percent.[72]

A year later, in August 1970, Governor Nelson Rockefeller wrote a letter to Mayor Lindsay addressing the problem of solid waste collection and disposal. The letter announced an emergency urban cleanup program that would be financed by New York State. The governor explained that although sanitation is "a responsibility of local government, I think we have reached the point where collectively we can no longer tolerate the accumulated refuse and rubbish that blight some areas of our large cities all over the state. Such conditions are serious threats to the health and safety of the people and, therefore, have become a matter of state concern."[73] Following this initiative, however, in consultation with the Department of Health, the Department of Sanitation identified 186 blocks in the South Bronx and Harlem in need of emergency cleanup. These blocks were selected on the basis of field surveys that identified areas "exhibiting acute problems of garbage accumulation and rodent infestation."[74]

Galvanized by Garbage

On the surface, the Young Lords' strategic and irreverent campaigns resembled those espoused by Saul Alinsky, father of modern community organizing. But Alinsky had a narrow conception of community work. Labor journalist David Moberg captured its logic succinctly: "Don't talk ideology, just issues; build organizations, not movements. . . . Focus on . . . winnable goals."[75] By contrast, the Young Lords were hell bent on bridging *all* of these worlds.

The Garbage Offensive vested the newly minted New York chapter of the YLO with valuable experience. The group experimented with ways of linking local grievances to the fight for systemic change and in the process involved thousands of people in its urban guerrilla actions. Before long the daily practice of members of the Young Lords linked the refusal of local government to resolve basic problems of city life to the logic, interests, and priorities of the larger structures of capitalism and colonial rule the world over; the contradiction between the two, they argued, could only be resolved through revolution. According to Young Lord Juan González, "The Garbage Offensive was critical in making it clear to us that we had to be involved in concrete issues that affected people's daily lives; that you couldn't just proselytize [about] revolution without having some kind of impact on the day-to-day lives of people. [That lesson was] carried over to the lead poisoning, tuberculosis, and our work in the hospitals." In the words of radicals of the period, the Young Lords put their bodies on the line, evaded police arrests that could have hampered their continued presence and activism in East Harlem, and set an example for others to follow.

As the garbage actions of the YLO received increasing local coverage by mainstream media networks, and as the group involved greater numbers of people in their protests, the Young Lords grew in size. Their effectiveness was observed immediately. As González puts it, "We could see it right away, because people started saying, 'Hey, I want to join.' More and more people wanted to join, and they didn't necessarily all want to join for the right reasons. Some people had been in other gangs and thought, 'Hey, this is an even better gang.' . . . We began to realize that this was touching a nerve. . . . We easily tripled or quadrupled in size in a period of a few weeks."[76] However, in addition to gaining new members and dozens of supporters who joined them in protest, including the group's martial arts instructor and important cadre, Jose "Pai" Diaz, the Young Lords' urban disruptions also made them a target for surveillance by both the FBI and the New York Police Department. Both law enforcement agencies began to track Young Lord activities as early as June 1969.

Organizing with determination and creative flair amid the heightened political pressures of an election season, the Young Lords positioned themselves not only to gain the respect of their community but also to score a victory and raise their profile in the city. Within three months, the group had established organizing credibility through almost daily interactions with the people of East Harlem in the same blocks that years earlier had been one of the major sites of the East Harlem riots. The success of their first campaign gave the group a confident start that propelled its leadership to restructure the organization and take on greater challenges. In September the group moved to formalize its presence in East Harlem by establishing a storefront office between 111th and 112th Streets and Madison Avenue. The Young Lords established a division of work whereby different members specialized in distinct areas of concern such as community health and political education. These changes allowed the group to launch several campaigns simultaneously and involve larger numbers in the process. The organization's new division of labor also permitted its subgroups to devise campaigns on their own, which facilitated the development of leadership among its membership and let newcomers feel a part of an organization they could help shape.

The Lords' Garbage Offensive challenges the maligned image of urban radicals as angry people of color who engaged in crazed and senseless attacks against a society that had begun to grant reforms in the form of antidiscrimination legislation, for example.[77] Rather, the Garbage Offensive speaks to the kind of humility and dedication that was a hallmark of Young Lords organizing and, by extension, of late 1960s urban radical politics. In addition, in the public imagination, 1960s movements built by people of color, North and South, continue to be associated with grievances around racial discrimination and exclusion, narrowly defined. However, the Young Lords' garbage protest is but one example of the myriad of social and economic issues that animated activists of color in cities across the nation, especially those outside the South. But the campaigns of radicals such as the Young Lords combined protests of racism and its structural manifestations with links to broader social problems. In this case, their efforts raised standards of city services and government accountability and produced reforms that benefited people of all classes and races in New York. The Young Lords stood up against the idea that because the people of East Harlem were a predominantly colonized people from Puerto Rico they could be ignored, pushed around, and, treated like garbage by members of the Sanitation Department, the police, and local elected officials. Part of what the Young Lords built in East Harlem with their Garbage Offensive was an affirmation of the right of Puerto Ricans to be treated with dignity and respect.

—

CHAPTER FOUR

BUILDING BLOCKS

The success of the Garbage Offensive emboldened the Young Lords. No longer a fly-by-night organization, they were suddenly heroes, steadily taking root in the community. It was time for them to find a more permanent home.

In the waning days of summer, Central Committee member Juan "Fi" Ortiz began scouting neighborhood sites for their headquarters. They settled on a cheap storefront rental in the vicinity of their garbage-dumping protests at 1678 Madison Avenue between 111th and 112th Streets. The Young Lords' brick-and-mortar presence aroused curiosity about what the group might do next. It also generated a sense among local residents that the office might be a good place to register local grievances and find avenues for redress.

The Young Lords had committed themselves to a community wracked with social problems. Their undertaking would require consistency, deep commitment, and focus, not to mention a lot of work. To meet the challenge, the Central Committee set out to shore up the group's capacity by reproducing the preexisting model of organization established by the Black Panther Party (BPP) and the Chicago Young Lords. In the fall of 1969, members of the New York Central Committee also drafted the Young Lords' Thirteen-Point Program and Platform—a vision statement modeled after the Black Panthers' similarly named document that clarified the group's political orientation and world view. These close adaptations spared the New York Young Lords the lengthy process of developing an organizational structure and accelerated the integration of new members into the group. They also freed up its leadership to explore target issues, identify goals, and develop organizing strategies for the series of early campaigns that imbued the Young Lords with its distinctive essence.

The group launched its revolutionary start-up at the tail end of a decade-long process of radicalization. By 1969, the era's political assassinations, urban rebellions, and deadly antiwar campus protests had drawn new waves of young people into the movement. They shared a high degree of consensus that U.S. society was irrevocably broken. The Young Lords formed part of the small but committed cohort of young people across the country that responded to these developments with a structural critique of racism, capitalism, and war.

October 1970

PDC

How Harvard, Berkeley et al Set Up the Indonesian Massacre
Civil War in Ireland?; Middle Earth Art; $4 Woodstock. 75¢

Ramparts®

"The Young Lords,
once a street gang,
have become the most
potent revolutionary
organization of
Puerto Rican youth
in the U.S."

Felipe Luciano on the cover of *Ramparts* magazine, October 1970.
(Courtesy of William Cordova)

This radical cohort also presented a vision for a new society, which it argued could only be achieved through revolutionary leadership and organization. East Harlem, with its disproportionately youthful population, seemed ripe for the emergence of a new indigenous revolutionary movement.[1] Two years earlier its youth had demonstrated a fierce spirit of dissent as the protagonists of New York's second and final urban uprising of the decade. But the growing legitimacy of revolutionary ideas at home combined with the loss of U.S. authority abroad intensified local and federal campaigns of repression against political activists and their organizations.

In this context, the Young Lords developed a two-pronged approach to organizing. They implemented strict membership rules designed to shield the organization from the worst aspects of state disruption and infiltration. They also sought to maintain connections to the broadest audience possible through a series of issue-based campaigns that allowed for community participation with various levels of commitment to the organization. One of the Young Lords' most innovative initiatives involved a community-led, police-watch operation designed to deter gratuitous police abuse in the neighborhood and avoid arrest of community participants or the singling out of Young Lords.

Beyond their work on sanitation, the Young Lords turned their attention to other problems of public health. Early in the fall, the group launched its first children's breakfast program alongside the Black Panthers. It also joined welfare mothers in their battles against the decade's first round of state and federal budget cuts to social services.

The Office

While the Young Lords were signing a lease for a $200 monthly rental of a storefront office and a September 1969 move-in date, the FBI met secretly with their prospective landlord. This was likely part of an attempt to expand the state's network of informants, gain on-site access to the Young Lords' headquarters, and facilitate efforts to tarnish the Young Lords' budding reputation.[2] The FBI faced a stumbling block, however.

The Young Lords had already won the hearts and minds of some of their new neighbors. When they sought cover from police during the Garbage Offensive, East Harlem residents had opened their apartment doors to the young radicals. During the Young Lords' move into their new office, neighbors were helping them furnish it. As Young Lord Carlito Rovira recalls, a local superintendent donated "the old *mesa* [table]" around which people gathered as soon as they walked in. The group refurbished "old broken chairs, coffee tables . . . and stolen Volkswagen seats donated to us by some of the *tecatos* [drug users] in the neighborhood." Within a few weeks, as they established relationships with

local healthcare workers, the office also doubled as an informal clinic: "Doctors, nurses, medics, and ambulance drivers who sympathized with us would donate the medicine. *Ahí había medicina de cuanta madre había.* [There was medicine in there of all kinds.] We even had the thing to wet and wrap around you to make a cast. And no Young Lord walked around with broken shoes because people used to donate all the time."[3]

In his 2003 memoir, *We Took the Streets*, Young Lord Mickey Melendez describes the spirit of community that helped launch the office: "After organizing the office, the logical next step was to clean the sidewalk in front, and then clean the whole block. . . . We never lacked volunteers. They came with their brooms, or asked us to assign them one."[4] The relationship was reciprocal. East Harlem's Young Lords office became a place where neighborhood residents stopped by, some likely with hesitation, to learn more about the organization or ask for help with a range of problems, from welfare disputes and housing eviction notices to help with translation at a parent-teacher meeting.

The Young Lords were now paying rent, reproducing flyers and educational materials with mimeograph machines in their office, and traveling to participate in the city's wide array of political events. Sustaining this presence would require money. They appealed to individual donors and more established left organizations for resources. They also raised funds through a series of public events including concerts featuring well-known East Harlem salsa artists such as Ray Barretto. As word circulated within movement circles that the Puerto Rican radicals who had set uncollected garbage aflame in the middle of Third Avenue had opened an office in East Harlem, support poured in from beyond the local community.

Liberation News Service, the major news-gathering outlet of 1960s movements, announced the opening of the office and appealed for "office equipment, money and anything useful."[5] Before long leftists were delivering financial donations, political posters, and flyers to the Young Lords' office. According to Carlito Rovira, "Every square inch of wall in the office" was covered with posters of Che Guevara, Fidel, Don Pedro, Frantz Fanon, Marx, Lolita Lebron, and Malcolm X.[6] On their office walls, the Young Lords also curated prints of emerging Puerto Rican artists whose art collective and next-door printmaking workshop, Taller Boricua, inserted the Puerto Rican experience into the era's political art movement.[7]

To make their headquarters a vibrant neighborhood institution, the Young Lords engaged in an array of party-building and advocacy activities, the number and diversity of which was a product of many individuals' full-time organizing

Young Lord Gloria Colón at a typewriter in the East Harlem office.
(Courtesy of Henry Medina Archives)

efforts. Spurred by growing belief in the possibility of revolutionary change, the organization's core leadership and general membership had officially dropped out of college to concentrate on party building. Many lived collectively, while younger recruits like Juan "Fi" Ortiz and Carlito Rovira were already high school dropouts who still lived with and were supported by their parents.

The office was open most days from 9:00 A.M. to 10:00 P.M. Its telephone number (212-427-7754) was emblazoned on the storefront window and printed on flyers and literature. The phone rang off the hook. The office was staffed with morning, afternoon, and evening work shifts, each of approximately ten Young Lords, and managed by a rotating officer of the day (OD). The OD coordinated and distributed information and assigned tasks to the cadre, who traveled in pairs to answer calls from community residents or organizers requesting the presence of the Young Lords at citywide events.[8] At least two persons were routinely assigned to office security. Amid mounting party building and organizing activities, the OD position required a high level of organization to respond to the constant flow of information and demands. It also required someone who commanded respect. The OD ensured that members showed up for shifts on time. When members were late or failed to carry out the work of the organization, the OD dispensed discipline—laps around the block. The position would later grow into a site of power and influence outside of the Central Committee.

The office was the organization's center of gravity, the place from which members were deployed to engage with neighborhood residents or the broader movement in New York. In the fall of 1969, the chance arrest of a Young Lord at a welfare rights demonstration hastened the group's alliance with the growing ranks of the welfare rights movement. On September 9, 1969, Carlito Rovira was headed to the office from his parents' home on Manhattan's Lower East Side when he encountered approximately 200 welfare mothers, some of whom he recognized as his neighbors, blocking traffic on 6th Street and Avenue C.[9] They were demanding the restoration of a twenty-five-dollar school-clothing allowance for the children of welfare clients—the latest loss in benefits since the New York State legislature announced a $25 million reduction in welfare appropriations earlier that summer.[10] Without giving it a second thought, Carlito decided to delay his trip uptown to stand with these women.

Historically, welfare relief had been disproportionately afforded to white women who were widowed or abandoned by their husbands and whom caseworkers deemed morally fit and good mothers.[11] But with the 1965 passage of federal legislation that barred discrimination in employment and delivery of public services, poor women of color who had previously been deemed un-

Pablo Guzmán. (Photograph by Fred W. McDarrah; courtesy of Getty Images)

worthy gained access to welfare benefits in significant numbers. Only a couple of years later, a growing number of them were taking to the streets in a classic case of radicalization—the consequence of dashed hopes in the face of their greater confidence and raised expectations for economic independence.[12] Their grievances deepened in the late 1960s, when federal and state legislation cut spending on social programs to offset the crisis of stagflation—the unusual combination of economic stagnation accompanied by inflation—which economists linked to the government deficit produced by public spending on the Vietnam War.[13] The response in New York included protests by thousands of poor women of color who joined dozens of coordinated civil disobedience actions, including school boycotts, disruptions of welfare centers, clashes with police, and sit-ins on bridges, described as a "city-wide revolt."[14]

Meanwhile, at the national level, the welfare rights movement highlighted the crisis of poverty across the country, repudiated the notion of welfare as charity, exposed the risk of starvation under the program's paltry food allotments, and campaigned for a "guaranteed adequate income."[15] As poor women of color joined the movement's leadership and rank and file in large numbers after 1965, they brought forth other grievances in local speeches and congressional testimonies. The growing representation of women of color in the welfare rolls triggered a contentious and racially coded backlash almost immediately—in a public debate that depicted them as lazy, promiscuous, and prone to cheating the system.[16] In response, women of color elevated issues of dignity above others. Their stories of hardship challenged the shame and stigma attached to welfare relief and the conduct of caseworkers who criminalized them with racist contempt as they pried into their homes looking to take away their benefits on the pretext of suspected illicit relationships and welfare fraud.[17]

Like the Young Lords, women in the welfare rights movement were challenging the era's new racist representations, which blamed poor people of color for their economic conditions. These tropes doubled as the ideological bulwark of white backlash to civil rights gains. They overlooked the structural roots of the new urban poverty that disproportionately affected new migrants to the city and were beyond their control.

Immediately after Carlito joined the welfare mothers' Lower East Side action, police charged the demonstration "like a herd of buffalo," dispersed the crowd, pounded him to the ground, and arrested him. "I was one of the only males there; I was uniformed and since the Black Panthers were strong in the Lower East Side, they probably thought I was a Panther." That evening, Carlito's father registered a complaint at the Tombs, the jail where he was being detained, and the fourteen-year-old walked out to a boisterous crowd of welfare mothers waiting to receive him.[18] Back in East Harlem, the Young Lords had been worried about Carlito, who never skipped reporting to the office to get his day's assignment. That next morning, they were relieved to read about his arrest in the papers and finally see him arrive in the office, battered but alive.[19] Moved by what had happened to their comrade and by the continued efforts of welfare mothers to disrupt business as usual to draw attention to their issues, in September 1969 the Young Lords leadership assigned a group of members to assist those same organizers at PS 15 elementary school on the Lower East Side.

A month later, the Young Lords participated in a large civil disobedience action in East Harlem led by welfare rights workers who formed a human chain that blocked traffic on the 125th Street and Second Avenue entrance to the Triborough Bridge. The Young Lords supported them with what was by then their signature action—lining up garbage cans along the bridge entrance. After the hour-long bridge blockage, the Young Lords spontaneously redirected the protesters along 125th Street, Harlem's major thoroughfare, to the neighborhood's welfare grievance office on Seventh Avenue, half a mile west of the bridge entrance. According to Young Lord Pablo Guzmán, rerouting a predominantly Puerto Rican march through Harlem offered an opportunity to counteract the "divide and conquer game in the colony"—in which Puerto Ricans and black Americans were pitted against each other on the basis of ethnic differences—and build class unity among them. As he put it, "Everybody's on welfare and everybody's poor, and everybody should be fighting on the same side of the revolution."[20] Not long after the march, the Young Lords convened a public forum at PS 201 for parents and students on community control of the public schools, aided in part by their work with the Lower East Side welfare mothers, many of whom were also involved in New York's school reform movement.[21]

Largely unexplored in the historiography of urban 1960s activism, the upsurge of community-based activism led by black American and Puerto Rican mothers helped anchor routine activities of groups like the Black Panthers and the Young Lords. From Chicago and Oakland to New York, both organizations offered security at civil disobedience actions taken by these women at welfare centers.[22] In their mixture of redemption and vindication, the Young Lords and the Black Panthers collected clothing from "the avaricious businessmen in the community" and redistributed it to poor welfare mothers and others in need. They jointly held free clothing programs on Saturdays from 1:30 to 3:30 P.M. at the Theatre Arts Center on 110th Street between Lexington and Park Avenues.[23] The Young Lords also worked in tandem with the Black Panthers to establish a free daily children's breakfast program at Emmaus House on 116th Street between Second and Third Avenues in East Harlem. Established in the context of solidarity work with welfare mothers, these programs certainly possessed the patriarchal imprint of male provision and protection of women and children.[24] But with the growth of female membership in the Young Lords and the group's continued interactions with welfare rights and school reform organizers, a dis-

Free breakfast program, second People's Church, October 1970. (Photograph by Michael Abramson; courtesy of Haymarket Books)

proportionate number of whom were women, gender norms in the organization would soon be challenged. Above all, the solidarity extended to women of color by the Young Lords and the Black Panthers forged humanistic neighborhood relationships among them that allowed mothers to trust the disproportionately male members of these groups to feed and care for their children.

These activities created a humanism in the neighborhood that was amplified within the organization. The Young Lords initiated a range of activities that created meaningful work and unanticipated challenges. Both cemented bonds of trust and friendship among them. For example, neighbors often approached the Young Lords in the street asking for solutions to problems ranging from police brutality and domestic violence to legal representation in court and lack of hot water. Despite distrust from others in the community who questioned their larger political objectives, the Young Lords met the demands of work and relationships as a team, a team that grew stronger in the process.

Police Watch

In September 1969, the Young Lords began to experiment with a neighborhood police watch. The idea evolved out of the relationships the group fostered with many residents of El Barrio during the Garbage Offensive. The Young Lords' minister of information, Pablo Guzmán, described it as "a people's patrol, an underground movement of the people on the block in the Latin community, similar to the way the Panthers started out in Oakland."[25]

The Black Panthers' decision to legally bear arms to protect the descendants of slaves from police violence challenged the country's deeply rooted power relations. Though unstated, the tradition that became enshrined in the Second Amendment to the U.S. Constitution as the right to bear arms has always been understood to apply exclusively to Europeans and their descendants. The reasons are found in the eighteenth-century settler project that became the United States, which rested on the violent appropriation of land from the native people of North America and control of enslaved African labor. In self-defense, the indigenous population responded with an early form of guerrilla war, and Africans organized slave rebellions. In this contest, the emerging government weaponized Europeans of all classes, a measure necessary to secure, maintain, and extend the emerging borders of the state. As scholar of Native American history Roxanne Dunbar-Ortiz recounts, "In 1658, the colony ordered every settler home to have a functioning firearm; subsidized those who couldn't afford them; and fined homes without functioning weapons and individuals who traveled to public meetings without them. In time this became the basis of forced militia and slave patrol inscription among white men of all classes."[26] The Black Panthers' armed patrol units, therefore, touched a nerve. They opened a Pandora's box. In its challenge to one of the longest-standing building blocks of white supremacy, the BPP's bold action was too destabilizing for the state to allow to stand. A tsunami of violent acts of repression followed, led by the police and the FBI's counterintelligence program, generally referred to as COINTELPRO. The secret unit was established in 1956 to subvert the U.S. Left and other organizations and individuals engaged in protest.[27] Its self-professed aim was to destroy movements by frustrating movement goals and encouraging violent internecine struggles within its organizations. By one estimate, twenty-eight Black Panthers were killed in confrontations with police in 1968 and 1969.[28]

Still, the Young Lords proceeded to adapt a version of the BPP's police patrol. Unsurprisingly, neighbors looked on with hesitancy. According to Guzmán, the idea gained credibility after the stabbing death by "a brother on the block" of the beloved East Harlem resident Mingo El Loco when he tried to intervene in a neighborhood brawl on September 20, 1969. The Lords blamed the police for Mingo's death because they "let him bleed in the street," did not call an ambulance, and transported him to the hospital in a police car, where he died.[29] Mingo was a good neighbor and friend of the Lords—he loaned them his car, distributed their literature, and helped with neighborhood recruitment—and the community was "up in arms."[30] Amid the tragedy, approximately 200 neighborhood residents volunteered to help build a police patrol network in the five blocks surrounding the Young Lords' East Harlem office.

With the repressive backlash against the Black Panthers' police patrol in full view, the Young Lords concluded that the work of protecting the community from police violence be led by an autonomous, affiliate network of neighbors' circles. Those who signed up began their work in collective discussions, held in their own apartments, on strategies for sizing up a police crisis on the spot. The goal was to avert an escalation of police violence and resist unlawful arrests. The Young Lords believed that over time, these networks and interventions in neighborhood conflicts could replace the police. They argued that the work of self-determination begins by putting to use the untapped skills and creativity of community members toward larger collective goals. According to Guzmán, those who volunteered were mostly working men and women in their forties, whose family responsibilities did not allow them to commit to full-time organizing. Although they did not call themselves Young Lords, they supported the culture of resistance that the group sought to cultivate in the neighborhood. According to one former member, "We relate it to an iceberg, most of the iceberg is underwater but part of it is above water, that would be like the Young Lords office and the people that you see in berets."[31]

The Young Lords were already being monitored by the New York Police Department, so their support of community police patrols proved particularly provocative to law enforcement. The police department's strategic response appeared to be to undercut the organization's influence by targeting not the purple-bereted Young Lords but rather those who participated in their rallies and events. According to Guzmán, "[The police] dealt repression on the people. We have had several actions in the streets, mini-riots, mini-rebellions and the pigs didn't touch the Young Lords hardly, but the people were the ones getting busted."[32] Still, by grounding their anti-police-brutality initiatives in circles led by older people in the community, the Young Lords' organizing approach differed from that of the Black Panthers. Their more tempered approach to police misconduct curbed adventurist tendencies among younger rebellious recruits who might have been quick to engage in isolated and risky one-on-one confrontations with police. The activities and spirit of the community patrols networks flickered on and off until 1971, sometimes more brightly than others. They offered a rich laboratory within which the Young Lords advanced the reenvisioning of society and its reorganization in the "interest of the people." Beginning with their earliest campaigns, the Young Lords continued to forge a community organizing strategy. They combined Panther survival programs with their own fusion of traditional local grassroots campaigns that, through militant disruption, made demands on the city's sites of power.[33]

Building Structure

The opening of the office served to professionalize the work of the Young Lords. With their standards of operation and community connections raised, they focused on consolidating and adapting the organizational structure they inherited from the Chicago group and the Black Panthers. Leading members of the New York group did so in consultation with the Chicago Young Lords at a Chicago-based conference. Like the Panthers, the Lords envisioned themselves as both the revolutionary army and embryonic government of a future liberated nation. Their leadership body was called the Central Committee, a name associated with the standing administrative bodies of communist parties from the Soviet Union and China to Cuba. The Young Lords' Central Committee was composed of a chairman and four chief ministers. Each minister was in charge of a corresponding area of party life: defense, finance, information, or education. The original Central Committee included Felipe Luciano as chairman, Juan González as minister of education, Pablo Guzmán as minister of information, Juan "Fi" Ortiz as minister of finance, and David Perez as defense minister. As the Young Lords spread beyond New York City in 1970, "field" was added to the list of ministries, which was responsible for erecting new branches of the organization and expanding its geographical reach. Each mirrored the major branches of government and areas of development that a revolutionary government might erect.

Each ministry was responsible for organizing a series of programs and routine activities, such as the daily breakfast program, that sustained the organization and the involvement of its members. According to founding member Juan González,

> The information ministry handled all the flyers, put out the newspaper, did the press conferences or basically put out the perspective of the organization to the public. The education ministry handled the political education classes and all the internal education. Defense handled the security of the organization, the physical training, the defense of the different offices of the organization. Finance collected the money from the *Palantes*, raised money, and gave [stipends] for the food of the membership, basically handled all the finances. The field ministry was in charge of the community organizing programs, starting new chapters, starting new branches.[34]

While the ministries existed throughout the organization's history, rarely did they all exist at once. In this early period, while the organization was experiencing mass growth, the education and field ministries were prominent. The most constant were defense and finance. On the ground, each ministry consisted of ranking officers including deputy ministers, captains, lieutenants, and cadre. The term "cadre" referred to the at-large membership of the organization.[35] Young Lord Richie Perez explains further that "each ministry recruited people and had full Lords and Lords in training [LITs], so that you might be an LIT in the defense ministry . . . or in the information ministry, for example."[36]

At the Chicago conference, the Chicago Young Lords also briefed the New York group on the resolutions of a meeting held days earlier at the Black Panther headquarters in Oakland. Writing only days later, an FBI informant cited the conference's goals. The Black Panthers had called the meeting to "train members of the Young Patriots and the Young Lords in how to organize and operate on a nationwide scale."[37] Although no transcript exists of the meeting, Black Panther Mumia Abu-Jamal traveled from Philadelphia to participate in it. He remembers that matters discussed included security, the early identification of government provocateurs in new membership rosters, adherence to the party's internal chain of command and party discipline to minimize their impact, the importance of assigning formal leadership roles to talented recruits, and the integration of membership into the life and activities of the party through this process.[38] Through meetings like these, where organizational strategies and challenges were assessed in the context of a preexisting structural model, the Puerto Rican radicals in Chicago and New York got a head start on the otherwise lengthy process of organization building.

For the New York Young Lords, significant political decisions and organizational challenges lay ahead. COINTELPRO was engaging in a series of repressive, and frequently unlawful, actions to contain the BPP's impact within the New Left. FBI informants misleadingly reported that in the October meeting between the Chicago Young Lords, the Young Patriots, and the BPP, there was preliminary talk about the formation of a BPP-led North American liberation front, an underground, guerrilla-style combat unit based in "remote mountain areas" of the United States, whose purpose was to destabilize the U.S. government.[39] The proposal to engage in armed guerrilla actions was espoused by Panther leader Eldridge Cleaver and his supporters. It was one of the least supported political strategies within the BPP. For example, days after the West Coast conference, Fred Hampton organized a Rainbow Coalition press conference and countermarch in Chicago that challenged the armed struggle orientation of the Days of Rage actions organized by the Weatherman faction of Students for a Democratic Society. According to Cha Cha, the 2,000-strong march had originally been called by the Young Lords in honor of Pedro Albizu Campos, but

Aida Cuascut and comrades at the UN Plaza, post-march, October 1970.
(Photograph by Michael Abramson; courtesy of Iris Morales)

it acquired this broader purpose at the request of Hampton. Hampton thought it fortuitous that the march had planned to wind through working-class black American, Puerto Rican, and white neighborhoods because there had been "too much talk about armed struggle and not enough work [dedicated to] organizing the people."[40] The major political current within the BPP, espoused by Huey P. Newton, held that such a move was premature and not supported by the masses of black people; instead, the organization should focus on survival programs to address the socioeconomic needs of the black community. The process of meeting community needs, Newton argued, would build black self-determination and radical political organization independent of the state.[41] However, balancing Newton's position alongside the organization's politics of armed self-defense proved to be a challenge. Aided by covert COINTELPRO subversion tactics, the internal political split would soon produce a violent power struggle in the BPP.

As a new organization that embraced the vanguard leadership of the BPP, the New York Young Lords would have to navigate these politically treacherous waters. As seen in the Garbage Offensive, the group was committed to militant street action, but its leaders consciously avoided direct confrontations, armed or otherwise, with police. This perspective sought to avoid burdening its membership with legal defense campaigns that might distract from the group's focus on community organizing. During this nascent stage, the organization had a no-guns policy. However, the Young Lords, like the Black Panthers, as a matter of political principle, upheld the right of all racially oppressed people to armed self-defense against white supremacy and racist police violence. The police responded to this position with relentless repression, especially against the Panthers.

The potential political threat these organizations posed to the status quo was clear. Earlier in 1967, during a press conference at the first meeting of the Organization of Latin American Solidarity in Cuba, Student Nonviolent Coordinating Committee leader Stokely Carmichael noted that the urban riots in the United States were a form of nascent urban guerrilla war.[42] Of all the organizations of the New Left, the Young Lords and the Black Panthers were most determined to organize and discipline the violence and anger unleashed during urban insurrections, from Watts and Detroit to East Harlem. Yet even though the Young Lords rejected armed confrontations, they embraced the era's militant élan. As images of uniformed revolutionary leaders became iconic, the Young Lords, like the Black Panthers, adopted the uniformed garb of Third World guerrilla armies engaged in decolonization struggles around the globe. The black berets donned by Fidel Castro and Che Guevara during the Cuban Revolution inspired their purple and black berets, respectively. Both groups also wore black or green military fatigue jackets and combat boots bought at Army and Navy stores. Like the BPP and the Nation of Islam before them, the Young Lords marched in military formation at large public events. The group's subsequent annual participation in the Puerto Rican Day Parade, beginning in 1970, was especially dramatic in this regard. One member of the organization explains that the visual objective of the Young Lords, like the Black Panthers, was to "show the people and the enemy that we meant business and that we were at war."[43]

In its totality, the Young Lords' paramilitary image signaled a commitment to organization and discipline. It offered a counternarrative to mainstream depictions of people of color (and black American and Puerto Rican youth in particular) as incompetent, unruly, and delinquent. Sections of the Old Left—including its Puerto Rican constituents in the Movimiento Pro Independencia (MPI)—quietly derided the Young Lords' theatrical appearance, interpreting it as exhibitionism. Their dismissive posture reflected an experiential gap between two different political generations, and a racial one too.[44] The Young Lords were of an appreciably darker hue than their predominantly white counterparts on the Puerto Rican left. For young people of color who were daily criminalized and dehumanized in the media and in the streets and schools of a postwar city, the radical style of the Young Lords was a defiant act of self-definition.

By fusing symbols of revolutionary struggle with the style established by postwar gangs, the Young Lords and Black Panthers imbued urban culture with the politics of national liberation. Above all, their military appearance sent an unequivocal message to the state: the Young Lords would not bow down to the daily abuse, violence, and repression suffered by people of color at the hands of the police. The uniform reinforced their use of the term "pig"—following the example of the Black Panthers—as a way to deflate the indignity and fear that abuse of authority and police violence instilled in poor and working-class communities. The logic was that in associating the police with a farm animal, they could neutralize the psychological power held by police. According to Huey P. Newton, "We felt that the police needed a label, a label other than that fear image that they carried in the community. So we used the pig as the rather low-life animal in order to identify the police. And it worked."[45] Speaking about the psychological impact of a fierce exchange in East Harlem between Felipe Luciano and a police officer, Carlito Rovira explains that "when I heard him tell a police officer, 'Fuck you, you fuckin' pig, you can't do that to our people,' I felt like we became bulletproof."[46] Whatever their intentions in the realm of symbolism and politics, the Young Lords' bold paramilitary-styled gear made the organization highly visible. It undoubtedly elicited fear among conservative elements in the community. It was also attractive to the thousands of youth who were inspired by them from afar, came to their offices, marched with them, or formally joined the organization.[47]

The Thirteen-Point Program and Platform and Organizational Structure

In October 1969, Pablo Guzmán drafted the Thirteen-Point Program and Platform of the Young Lords in consultation with Juan González.[48] Modeled on the 1966 Ten-Point Program and Platform of the BPP, the document delineated what the Young Lords were for and against and clarified the group's political identity within movement circles. Widely printed in New Left publications, the one-page document assumed as a given the demands for radical reforms that defined the BPP's platform. It presented a broad vision of solidarity and change through revolutionary struggle, which the Black Panthers themselves had popularized and widely adopted by 1969. Written only three years apart, the difference between the two platforms reflected the swift radicalization of political consciousness that occurred in the last quarter of the 1960s.[49]

The first point of the platform added a new dimension to the New Left's widespread support of decolonization struggles: "We Want Self-Determination for Puerto Ricans, Liberation on the Island and Inside the United States." The Young Lords' explicit defense of "the rights of the diaspora" was new. Prompted by their experience as the children of the mass postwar exodus of Puerto Ricans from the island to the metropolis, the demand underscored a major twentieth-century development: the large-scale, geographic dispersion of colonial subjects generated by the fallout of colonial rule and resistance to it.

In the main, the document called for freedom built on a radical kind of solidarity, especially among subjugated people at home or abroad. In one of the first public uses of the term "Latino," point 2 called for "Self-Determination For All Latinos," which the group defined as the right, for example, of "the Chicano people [who] built the Southwest . . . to control their lives and their land." Although the assumed cohesion of people living in the United States with ancestral ties in Latin America remains a contested subject, the Young Lords identified unity among these people on the basis of a shared experience with Spanish and U.S. imperialism. Point 3 embraced unity among black Americans, Latinos, Asians, and Native Americans—people with a shared history of racialized exploitation in the United States, who "slaved to build the wealth of this country." It read, "Liberation for All Third World People." Its corollary, point 8, emphasizes a vision of solidarity attentive to differing class interests. It denounces "Capitalists and Alliances With Traitors" among the racially oppressed and lambasts the special role of politicians and middle-class people of color who are "paid by the system to lead our people down blind alleys." In point 4, the Young Lords declare, "We are Revolutionary Nationalists and Oppose Racism." Widely accepted within the New Left, the position held that the intractable history of racism in the United States made the building of race-based organizations central to the revolutionary process. In the same point, the Young Lords anticipate the misrepresentation of their world view by politicians who will "make our nationalism into racism" and counter with their class-based support "for the millions of poor white people [who] are rising up to demand freedom."

Other points take a position against imperialism outside of the Americas. Point 9 denounced the "amerikkkan military," calling for the "immediate withdrawal of u.s. [sic] military forces and bases from Puerto Rico, Vietnam, and all oppressed communities inside and outside the u.s." Point 11 declared, "We are Internationalist," and pledged to "defend our brothers and sisters around the world who fight for justice and are against the rulers of this country."

In the realm of radical reforms, the document concretized the abstract desire for freedom with the call for community control of local institutions and land to increase the possibility that people of color might determine the circumstances of their lives. They also demanded "true education of our Afro-Indio culture and Spanish language," with emphasis on the history of struggle against "cultural as well as economic genocide by the Spaniards and now the *yanquis*." The demand reflected the movement's important intervention in the production of knowledge in the United States and Europe with its erasure of the cultures, histories, and political and intellectual traditions of the rest of the world. Like the Panthers, the Young Lords demanded freedom for "political prisoners" and "prisoners of war." The former term referred to the growing ranks of people of color disproportionately imprisoned because of their race and class; the latter term described those imprisoned in the course of fighting for freedom. The same point denounced members of racially oppressed groups with jobs in prisons, which evidenced an early awareness among young radicals of color of the growth of the carceral system and the growing employment of people of color in state bureaucracies following passage of civil rights legislation mid-decade.

More than others of its kind, the statement consolidated in one short document the breadth of the New Left's social analyses and most radical aspirations. Beyond solidarity with colonized people it supported women's equality, advocated the seizure of political power, and imagined a new world. Point 10, which called for women's equality, would later be challenged for its simultaneous support of a purportedly revolutionary version of machismo. Point 12 employed Second Amendment language and rationale in support of "armed self-defense and armed struggle [as] the only means to liberation," stating, "When a government oppresses the people, we have the right to abolish it and create a new one." The last point of the program read, "We Want a Socialist Society."[50]

The Young Lords distributed mimeographed copies of their program and platform wherever they were active and printed it in *Palante*, a mimeographed newsletter they launched in November 1969. Later, beginning in February 1970, when the organization began to produce its newspaper of the same name, the platform appeared on the back pages of each issue. The document introduced its readers to a cohesive body of political ideas—a rare occurrence in the United States, where successive waves of Red Scares have delinked single-issue grassroots organizing from cohesive analyses of social problems such as those historically presented by the Left.

Drawing on Panther practice, all members of the organization were expected to memorize the document. In addition to imparting its members with a broad sense of purpose, the assimilation of the Young Lords' political world view educated new members and immediately reinforced the process of their integration into a cadre organization.

During the late 1960s, the question of whether to build a vanguard party or the movement was a major topic of debate in the New Left. Most understood these to be at odds with one another. The Young Lords attempted to do both; they devised and implemented broad reform campaigns and simultaneously attempted to build a cadre organization. In the latter, members shared a revolutionary perspective, which they sought to amplify—in theory and practice—among the poor and working class in their community.

CHAPTER FIVE

DISEASES OF POVERTY

As the golden age of American capital drew to a close in the late 1960s, the federal government began a protracted retreat from the idea that it would fund the common good.[1] Moved to action by the growing significance of healthcare in American politics, society, and the economy, 1960s radicals launched some of their most impassioned battles in the field of medicine, where the contest between for-profit interests and public good advocates reached high intensity in the 1960s. For the Young Lords, East Harlem resident Mingo's untimely demise became an entry point to this frontier of organizing. Reporting on his death to the *YLO*, the newspaper of the Chicago Young Lords, Juan González lamented that death should come early to those who depend on chronically delayed ambulances and long waiting hours in the city's emergency rooms. The tragedy brought into focus the potentially deadly fallout of a medical emergency involving police, city ambulances, and public hospitals in East Harlem and prompted the Young Lords to mobilize both "community and workers . . . to demand decent health care."[2]

In the fall of 1969, the Young Lords joined community groups, nurses' aides, technicians, and hospital medical and administrative staff in a battle over cuts to East Harlem's major municipal hospital. To concurrent debates that emerged on the changing structure of healthcare in the city, the Young Lords contributed a document called the Young Lords' Ten-Point Health Program and Platform, centered on preventive care, health education, and socialized medicine. And in what is perhaps their most enduring legacy, the group brought militancy to a preexisting campaign against childhood lead poisoning that pressured city hall to take action on a silent public health crisis.

At first glance, healthcare may seem a peculiar focal point of dissent for these actors. They were young and personally removed from the vicissitudes of aging and its attendant existential questions about illness and mortality. Their youthful embrace of revolution also instilled in them a fearless and invincible temperament. But larger forces steered the Young Lords' turn to health. They were, in part, following the example of the Cuban experiment, which made dignified healthcare for all a signature aspiration of revolutionaries around the world.

Clothing drive. (Photograph by Beverly Grant)

They were also propelled by postwar changes in the structure of medical care in the United States as well as by high rates of illness among the new migrants and the unintended consequences of their greater access to healthcare in the age of civil rights, which ironically also increased the incidence of medical discrimination.

Though much of the scholarly analysis of the Young Lords to date has focused on the group's better-known, drama-filled offensives, these more quiet and deliberate medical campaigns were a vital part of the young organization. Involving many hours of face-to-face organizing, they represent the kind of immersive work that truly characterized a typical day in the life of a Young Lord.

In 1970, residents surveyed in East Harlem ranked health and police among the top four social problems most in need of government attention.[3] In a classic example of poverty of riches, disease abounded despite the district's generous number of medical facilities in comparison to other low-income neighborhoods. The district had four large medical institutions: three teaching hospitals and one municipal hospital. Yet, even compared to other poor districts, East Harlem registered higher rates of morbidity and mortality, tuberculosis, venereal disease, asthma, hypertension, diabetes, arthritis, and infant mortality. Women were more likely to receive late natal care or none at all and give birth to lower-weight babies.[4] The district's high incidence of illness was unsurprising, given its disproportionate share of recent migrants both from Puerto Rico and from the South. A combination of historically specific developments increased vulnerability to disease among Puerto Ricans. Beyond the standard social stressors of migration, they would have to contend with mass-scale structural displacement in housing and employment, exposure to an environmentally toxic housing landscape, and white backlash to their claims to the city.

The people of East Harlem mostly availed themselves of care in the district's overburdened public institution, Metropolitan Hospital, whose emergency room registered a quarter of a million visits in 1968, mostly from neighborhood residents. The considerable number of hospital visits in relation to the district's size reflected a new development in the urban north. Beginning in the 1960s, people of color in New York began to make more yearly medical visits than white Americans—a departure from the national practice, where the opposite was the case.[5] Complex forces were at work, including expanded access to healthcare—one of the many gains of the civil rights movement. By the mid-1960s, as civil rights leaders secured federal legislation against racial and gender discrimination, the movement's left-leaning grassroots organizers were influencing public discourse and popularizing critiques of racism that emphasized its structural and economic roots. The ideological shift gave way to passage of the Social Security Act of 1965, which created Medicare and Medicaid, forms of public health insurance for the elderly and the poor, respectively, that expanded medical care for all, especially among people of color in the cities.[6] But for this population, greater access to medical care came with caveats, especially in the context of large-scale changes in the way care came to be administered in the country after World War II.

Before World War II, most Americans received medical care from private neighborhood doctors, the dominant providers of medical care in the country.[7] Low-income patients who walked into the office of a solo practitioner were often treated at reduced costs. Yet because of segregation in medical care, many people of color also relied on outpatient clinics at voluntary and municipal hospitals, staffed pro bono by these same local doctors, who received, in return, a series of hospital privileges, including access to expensive medical technology.[8] But by the 1960s, the administration of care had been taken out of the hands of individual medical practitioners, especially in urban centers. Large medical research institutions became dominant in the medical industry. In East Harlem alone, these changes, combined with white flight from the city, produced a 30 percent decline in solo practitioners during the postwar years.[9] This meant that poor and working-class residents in urban neighborhoods like East Harlem had fewer medical care options. They were compelled to seek medical treatment in large, public hospitals affiliated with research institutions where care was delivered impersonally on a mass scale.

The causes of change were manifold. Large political and economic forces were at work. Changes in the delivery of medical care paralleled developments in the postwar American economy, where interests of concentrated corporate power and consumerism dominated. In this period, large medical research institutions, pharmaceutical companies, private insurance interests, and manufacturers of medical equipment came to dominate the country's increasingly for-profit medical industry.[10] The Cold War imperative to outpace the USSR in science and technology funneled large subsidies and incentives to large private medical institutions and medical technology corporations. Research, development, and technology became the industry's chief priorities. The expansions of commercial health insurance in the postwar period and public health insurance in the 1960s, which favored full payment to large private hospitals, bolstered the profits and the dominance of large institutions.[11] Medical training followed suit, with an emphasis on research and organ-centered specialization, at the expense of patient-centered care and holistic medical wellness. Amid this transformation, wealthy and insured patients were turned into consumers of the latest advances in medicine. While this emerging system of medically fragmented care helped many, more often than not it failed to find solutions to basic systemic health problems.[12] Among the private practitioners who remained in New York, a disproportionate number began to practice "luxury medicine," serving populations on Park Avenue and in the city's outer boroughs.[13] In the context of these changes, most working-class and middle-class white Americans received care that was increasingly impersonal and patronizing and involved long wait times and occasional medical mishaps.

At the bottom of the chain, the urban poor were caught in a dilemma. A shortage of doctors in New York, among other factors, prompted the 1961 affiliation plan wherein private medical schools received public funds to administer municipal hospitals and staff their key clinical departments with medical interns, residents, and senior doctors.[14] The arrangement put public resources under control of private medical schools, which also meant that public dollars subsidized and expanded private infrastructure.[15] The growing influence and power of large medical institutions in the postwar period, coupled with the advent of Medicaid and the affiliation system, transformed public hospitals into the major providers of medical care to poor and working-class people of color in New York after 1961. Yet these people remained egregiously underserved. While their new, insured status gave them more access to medical care, it also made them more vulnerable to medical exploitation by the city's public hospitals and the research institutions that managed them. Lacking a sense of entitlement, poor people of color came to be treated not as consumers of medical services but as exploitable commodities and a captive demographic of for-profit medical practices (medical tests, prescriptions, and procedures).

The Young Lords' personal remembrances of traumatic visits to public hospitals as children afforded them a unique perspective on the impact of these large structural changes on individuals and their families. The changes increased contact between the predominantly white and unreconstructed medical staff of underfunded and overburdened public hospitals and the new migrants—a class of patients who increasingly became the objects of medical student training. The Young Lords had been witnesses to this social drama as children, when they served as their parents' indispensable cultural and language interpreters. Even before they got to see a doctor, waiting long hours in emergency rooms, the hospital's social hierarchy was starkly visible. In New York, hospitals' orderlies and housekeepers—the city's least-paid workers—were entirely black American and Puerto Rican.[16]

Although medical discrimination had a long history, under the new affiliation plan racial inequality had become (and remains today) an inbuilt feature of medical schooling. Per medical school protocol, interns and residents received training in the wards and clinics of public hospitals treating black American and Puerto Rican patients—disproportionately poor people with higher rates of illness whose inability to pay for services made them less likely to question or complain about their care.[17] At an early age, members of the Young Lords felt shame after sensing the racist contempt with which doctors treated their loved ones. The experience of patients of color, who often complained of "being treated like animals" in public hospitals on account of race, was uniquely dehumanizing, medically dangerous, and exploitative, adding social injury to illness. This experience was not new.[18] But the demographic increase of these populations in the city and the greater contact between people of color and public hospitals magnified the crisis of medical discrimination in the age of civil rights and established the groundwork for resistance.

As new engines of the local economies in the postwar period, hospitals also became employers of large numbers of women of color, a heavily exploited army of poorly paid nurses' assistants and orderlies, and of male janitors. In this era of civil rights, New York hospitals became major sites of labor organizing for racial and economic justice.[19] This backdrop, combined with the example set by the Cuban Revolution's advances in socialized medicine, transformed health into a site of organizing for 1960s radicals like the Young Lords and Black Panthers.

In the spring of 1969, a couple of months before the emergence of the Young Lords in New York, the East Harlem Health Council (EHHC) sponsored a town hall meeting to discuss a coordinated response to changes at Metropolitan Hospital, the single largest provider of medical care in East Harlem.[20] The hospital's executive administrators had announced a timeline for the implementation of cuts to Medicaid, which would reduce staff and health services. In pursuit of efficiency and lower costs, they also announced plans to combine the pediatric and adult emergency rooms, representing a step backward in medical practice that would sacrifice the special needs of children and expose them to the chaotic atmosphere of adult emergency rooms.[21] The more than 100 individuals who gathered at the meeting formed part of a diverse and growing network of activists from across the country that identified healthcare as a significant human and civil rights struggle. Activists included civil rights, black power, and community organizers; local residents; and radicalized medical students, physicians, nurses, and other hospital staff from across the country. The movement groups involved in health justice work included the Medical Committee for Human Rights; Student Nonviolent Coordinating Committee; Freedom House Ambulance Service in Pittsburgh, which established the precursor to contemporary EMT certification; Student Health Organization; Black Panthers and Young Lords; and later the Pediatric Collective, a group of thirty-one residents and interns at Lincoln Hospital in the Bronx.[22] In East Harlem and across the city, these loose groupings of health activists employed various forms of resistance to forestall budget cuts.

In the summer of 1969, while knee deep in the Garbage Offensive, Juan González and Carlito Rovira began to represent the Young Lords at the ongoing meetings and actions at Metropolitan Hospital. By that time, the EHHC was distributing fliers, gathering signatures against a newly announced emergency room construction project, and holding demonstrations in the hospital lobby. Hospital administration initially approved the mix of protest and advocacy in the lobby, hoping that the actions would raise awareness about its significantly reduced operating budget. But shortly thereafter it retracted support. The Young Lords joined the cacophony of lobby conversations on the workings of the medical system, its inbuilt inequalities, and the disproportionate incidence of disease among the residents of East Harlem, among other themes. One Young Lords flyer read, "Do you know that asthma, tuberculosis, mental retardation, diabetes, and drug addiction are higher in East Harlem than anywhere else in the city?"[23]

In hospitals and on street corners across the country, from Baltimore to Oakland and from Pittsburgh and Atlanta to Chicago, other 1960s health activists were engaging in similar dialogue. Collectively, they pried open withering movement critiques of the country's for-profit health industry, demystified the medical field, and challenged its exclusivity, esoteric jargon, and paternalism that excluded patients from involvement in their care. In New York, the movements adopted the political analysis of the Health Policy Advisory Center (HealthPAC) of the Institute for Policy Studies, a Washington-based think tank. Formed to study New York's affiliation system and led by Robb Burlage, the center concluded that the "health empires" it empowered were vested in a privately controlled healthcare system unconcerned with public health. In 1971 the center wrote, "Health is no more a priority of the American health industry than safe, cheap, efficient pollution-free transportation is a priority of the American automobile industry."[24] Its investigations revealed that the affiliation plan had failed to qualitatively improve municipal hospital conditions. Worse, they exposed widespread corruption of private medical institutions, which routinely siphoned off large sums of federal and city funds—granted to administer and provide medical staff to the municipal hospitals—to advance their own research and payroll needs.[25] A New York State investigation commissioned by Governor Nelson Rockefeller later confirmed these findings.[26]

Beyond protests and actions inside and outside of hospitals, New York's network of health justice workers established vehicles for long-term planning. They developed "lay health advisory boards," the purpose and function of which were contested among them. In many ways, these formations were animated by the era's various demands for direct democracy reflected in the New Left's emphasis on "participatory democracy," the War on Poverty's "maximum feasible participation" mandate, and the black power movement's calls for "community control."[27] Moderates envisioned the lay advisory boards as vehicles to voice the interests of the poor within existing hospital governing structures. The radical view, held by the Young Lords, among others, envisioned the boards as seedling, parallel governing bodies—a foreshadowing alternative intended to ultimately replace the city-appointed hospital administration. For their part, the Young Lords warned that moderate incarnations of the board were powerless, and their growing support by municipal hospital administrators across the city signaled a process of co-optation by city government.

At an EHHC meeting in mid-September, the Young Lords presented for discussion and adoption a proposal for the creation of a board that envisioned *direct* democratic governance of Metropolitan Hospital by medical staff, workers, and neighborhood residents. The proposal formed part of a broader manifesto, the Young Lords' Ten-Point Health Program, that framed local grievances with a broader, humanistic vision of healthcare. Drafted by Juan González in collaboration with doctors at the hospital, the program captured the imagination of those in attendance and sparked a robust conversation.[28]

The document went beyond slogans. It advanced concrete global and local demands, zeroed in on the problems of the existing system, and put forth viable alternatives. Point 1 established the demand for community control of the hospital, a subtext of the entire document. Points 2 and 10 outlined the necessary prerequisites for a democratic reconfiguration of the board and its exercise of real power, a differentiation from moderate proposals that sought merely a seat at the decision-making table. These points rejected entirely the existing government appointments and called for their replacement by those with a track record of advancing the interests of the "poor." Point 10 specified "total control" by the board of the hospital's budget, "medical policy . . . hiring, firing, and salaries of employees, construction, and health code enforcement."

Point 3 addressed a local issue, an end to construction of the new emergency room. At the meeting, the Young Lords proposed that the emergency room be redesigned by the Real Great Society, the organization led by young radical Puerto Rican architects in East Harlem who believed that urban design should reflect the social needs and political aspirations of city dwellers.[29]

Manifesto points 5 and 6 challenged the commodification of medicine by calling for a publicly funded healthcare system and an "end to all fees." Points 4, 7, 8, and 9 outlined a new vision of healthcare and its delivery. These urged "total decentralization" of medical care through the creation of small, neighborhood-based clinics and the appointment of health officers on every block accountable to the community-staff board. With illness prevention at its core, these points called for a comprehensive, "door-to-door" project of medical care and social services that prioritized care for drug users, prenatal care, childcare, and care for the elderly. These points also emphasized the role of education in the struggle for improved public health. They called for public classes detailing the health hazards of social inequality, or in their words, how "poor sanitation, rats, poor housing, malnutrition, police brutality, pollution, and other forms of oppression" lead to illness. A comprehensive program like this one would demand enormous human resources. Unlike the American Association of Medical Schools, which set strict yearly limits on the number of doctors trained, the platform required the mass expansion of healthcare training, employment, and promotion of East Harlem residents.

Those present at the EHHC meeting during the discussion of the Young Lords' health program adopted it unanimously—with one exception. According to Juan González, "Suddenly this woman in the back said, 'I disagree. . . . You're not dealing with the workers in these hospitals, many of them are black and Latino.' . . . And she insisted that we change [the language] to 'community-worker control of the hospitals,' and we did."[30] The woman was Gloria Fontanez. She was part of a network of young workers and unskilled staff, mostly black Americans and Puerto Ricans, who had been organizing at Gouverneur Hospital on the Lower East Side. Shortly thereafter, Fontanez joined the Young Lords. Within a few years she would scale the ranks of its leadership structure. Later that fall, at the urging of the Young Lords, she and Cleo Silvers, a worker at Lincoln Hospital in the Bronx, met with visiting representatives from the Dodge Revolutionary Union Movement (DRUM), the Marxist-influenced group that organized black workers at the point of production in Detroit's automobile industry.[31] Before long, the two women founded the Health Revolutionary Unity Movement (HRUM), which posited that black American and Puerto Rican health workers in New York were strategically positioned to link labor and community grievances. Like DRUM, HRUM sought to leverage labor power to fight racism in the labor movement and demand better conditions and wages; it argued that health workers of color were ideally positioned to expose race disparities in health and advocate for a fundamental transformation of the healthcare system.[32]

In its totality, the Ten-Point Health Program advocated restructuring healthcare in East Harlem and beyond around humane, patient-centered medical care focused on illness prevention through routine care and education. Its underlying premise held that through training and education, ordinary people had the capacity to administer and deliver the best healthcare for themselves.

The Young Lords' proposal drew inspiration from the Cuban Revolution's health experiment. In 1959, Cuba had abundant, overlapping medical systems in the cities; a weak state-run healthcare system for the poor whose services were unknown to many; a severe doctor shortage because many fled after the revolution; and virtually no rural medicine, vaccination program, or pediatric care. The Cuban Revolution's principal task was to create egalitarian access to comprehensive clinical, environmental, and community health.[33] To bring cohesion to a fractured system and reconceptualize medical care for all, the revolution created the Ministerio de Salud Pública (Ministry of Public Health). The ministry's focused interventions included hospital construction; a mass increase in doctor training—and later in medical research—through active recruitment of peasants and the poor; the mass expansion of medical care to rural areas; and an emphasis on health literacy through widespread public education campaigns. Finally, the system prioritized preventive care through the proliferation of its *policlínico integral* (integrated polyclinic), a local clinic that offered comprehensive curative and preventive medical services either on-site or through house calls, worked with whole families and documented their medical histories, and involved patients in the coordination of local public health campaigns. Each patient was assigned to a comprehensive team of providers that included a primary care doctor, nurse, OB-GYN specialist, dentist, and social worker. The clinics ensured medical care for all by deploying their medical teams to schools, communities, workplaces, and the island's most remote rural areas.[34]

The experience of Bella August, a psychology resident at Metropolitan Hospital who worked with the Young Lords, illustrates how 1960s organizers became familiar with Cuban health practices. In 1968, August traveled to Cuba to study in a clandestine month-long program organized by the Medical Committee for Human Rights.[35] Fifteen years earlier, during the Batista regime, she had lived in Caimanero, Cuba, with her husband, who was stationed there with the U.S.

Navy. Through volunteer work she witnessed firsthand the island's precarious healthcare system before the revolution. In her 1968 trip, she saw how vastly improved medical conditions were not only for the mass of patients but also for doctors, who now worked with the resources of a whole team, including a social worker. Upon her return, August began giving presentations about Cuba's healthcare system to radicalized medical students and communities across New York City. She became an active supporter of the Young Lords because they "took the lead on taking healthcare to the people."[36]

Similarly, Young Lord Iris Morales learned about Cuba's healthcare system firsthand. She traveled to the island for the tenth anniversary of the Cuban Revolution and reported on her trip at the Real Great Society.[37] The Young Lords also broadened their own knowledge as they interacted with sympathetic doctors, nurses, medical students, and workers. In their own words, "We learned that the fascist American Medical Association for years has been trying to keep the number of medical schools down, [that] the drug companies, like John, Park and Davis etc [sic] push harmful drugs for profit [and] have much influence in Washington and state legislatures . . . [and] that there are things called health empires: medical schools and private hospitals that through affiliations (contracts with the city) operate and run public hospitals."[38]

From the Cubans, the Young Lords adopted the term "diseases of poverty," a reference to the pervasive diseases caused by poor nutrition and the hardship of working and living conditions. Tuberculosis, lead poisoning, asthma, drug addiction, and domestic violence, to the Young Lords, were among the most common diseases of poverty of the North American ghetto. Their program sought to increase community awareness of the impact of power, poverty, and racial oppression on public health.

As a result of Metropolitan's lobbying, the advocacy and distribution of the Ten-Point Health Program continued well into December 1969. But even as new organizing networks emerged, including the Metropolitan Hospital Workers' Movement, the emergency room construction project continued, as did implementation of citywide hospital budget cuts. The Young Lords proposed increasing political pressure to halt the emergency room construction through direct action. On December 5, 1969, a group of approximately fifty Young Lords, medical staff, and hospital workers conducted a sit-in at the office of Anthony Constantine, the hospital's executive director.[39] According to Dr. Richard Stone, a medical resident at Metropolitan Hospital at the time, the activists held the director hostage in his office; one of the demands for his release was the appointment of hospital staff at a clinic in the Young Lords' headquarters.[40] Bella August, who participated in the sit-in, calls Stone's recollection "a slight exaggeration." She recalls: "[Dr. Constantine was] a huge guy. We weren't going to do a physical thing to the guy. We had no way of holding him hostage. We were unarmed."[41] Carlito Rovira remembers the protesters surrounding the office rather than sitting inside it.[42] Both recall that because residents and hospital workers were among the protesters, the hospital refused to call the police to avoid a public relations crisis. August adds, "We went in there and we exposed what was going on and they didn't like the publicity. The disastrous emergency room construction project alone made clear that health was not the main priority. There was no reason why this enormous medical facility couldn't do more for the community."[43] The *New York Times* reported that the activists occupied the hospital for seven hours, and "though some staff members were visibly annoyed, a number of them approved of the protest." They held a four-hour conversation with the executive director and even convinced him to telephone health commissioner Joseph Terrenzio to include him in the conversation.[44]

Health activists in the 1960s deepened their efforts for humane medical care at a moment of economic austerity and government retrenchment from the public good. Historians have suggested that 1960s health activists set their sights on issues that were too local to effect real change. But many recognize that all social justice movements begin with local grievances and build national alliances over time. In the case of Metropolitan Hospital, activists worked to halt a medically questionable construction project and simultaneously studied and exposed the larger structural forces that made equality in healthcare an impossibility. These included dilapidated housing, structural unemployment and poverty, and medical discrimination in a healthcare system organized around the commodification of medicine. Other specialists of the era point to the limitation of community control, which emphasized questions of local governance when the problem was one of "resources."[45]

But because the healthcare industry made billions in profits in 1969, health inequalities seem to have been produced by the profit-driven priorities of a disorganized behemoth, competing private interests each vying for control, unequal distribution of resources, price gouging, and the deliberate yearly restrictions on the number of doctors trained.[46] With a community-worker hospital board at its center, the Young Lords' Ten-Point Health Program offered a compelling example of what effective and humane medical care could look like. Although it was not merely a manifesto on governance, given the entrenched nature of racism in medicine and the public hospitals, the idea that these should reflect the ethnic and racial composition of the communities they serve was an elementary call for democratic reform. Although organizing in public hospitals coincided with an uptick in labor militancy, this work was anchored in poor communities with marginal political or economic power that lacked the social leverage needed to win structural changes in healthcare.

Back at the site of the Young Lords–led sit-in, Metropolitan's executive director refused to talk to the protesters about the construction blueprints for combining the pediatric and adult emergency rooms. Instead, the hospital granted a lesser demand. It assigned Stone and others to offer medical services through the Young Lords' programs at their office headquarters. Stone recalls: "So, there's Richie Stone, a nice Jewish kid from Queens, going up to Young Lords headquarters, 'cause I was volunteered to go up there and give immunizations. . . . Sometimes . . . it takes a radical movement to get people moving and thinking. That whole turmoil around the 1960s . . . woke people up. The Young Lords became . . . leaders in the community. If nothing else, it filled the political system with people who walked the walk."[47] In the words of the father of Puerto Rican nationalism, Don Pedro Albizu Campos, the Young Lords continued "to cook with the potatoes they had."[48] The Young Lords had been enlarging the cohort of doctors in their orbit, and with their support they launched an alternative site of screening and care, which combined with their savvy street organizing led to major municipal reform.

Saving the Children from Lead Poisoning

The Young Lords' protests and relationships at Metropolitan Hospital set the stage for one of their most consequential campaigns—tackling the long-standing crisis of childhood lead poisoning. Identified as a distinct condition in the first decade of the twentieth century, childhood lead poisoning, more serious and potentially fatal than its counterpart among adults, is usually acquired through contact with objects that contain lead. Lead is a neurotoxin whose damage to the brain is irreversible. The more acute cases of lead poisoning can cause mild or severe mental incapacity, persistent vomiting, epilepsy, kidney disorders, and in its most extreme case, a swelling of the brain that usually leads to death.[49] In the 1960s, scientists already believed that between 10 and 25 percent of children living in the slums of eastern and midwestern cities had absorbed dangerous quantities of lead. Even worse, research suggested that in that decade the standard allowable levels of lead in the blood were "three times higher than those that today prompt aggressive 'deleading.'"[50]

Although lead-based paint was discontinued in the 1940s, the failure of municipal governments to enforce housing codes—requiring landlords to remove old coats of lead-based paint from apartment walls—contributed to the crisis. In 1960s New York, 43,000 "old law" housing tenements, deemed "unfit for human habitation" in 1901, continued to house predominantly black American, Puerto Rican, and Chinese tenants.[51] The threat of lead contamination among children in these tenements was ubiquitous. In fact, public health advocates and government officials were aware of what came to be known as the "lead belt." According to a memorandum prepared for Mayor John V. Lindsay by his special assistant Wenner H. Kramansky, the Young Lords were not exaggerating when they denounced the housing crisis in East Harlem and the Bronx as deadly. The memorandum explained that New York's "lead belt begins in Jamaica East, skips Jamaica West, runs through Brownsville, Bushwick, Bedford Stuyvesant, Red-Hook, Gowanus, Fort Greene, Williamsburg-Greenpoint and becomes thicker and heavier in Lower East Side, skips Yorkville and is anchored in Riverside, East Harlem, Central Harlem, Mott Haven, Morrisania, and Tremont."[52]

In November 1968, New York City's health department announced that 600 cases of childhood lead poisoning had been recorded in a period of ten months, three of which had resulted in fatalities.[53] By September 1969, several other children had died of the same cause.[54] And while only 600 cases were recorded in New York in each of the years between 1966 and 1969, public health reports estimated that between 25,000 and 35,000 children were actually afflicted with the disease each year.[55]

The Young Lords' new focus was propelled by a nearly fatal case of lead poisoning treated at Metropolitan Hospital in September. After falling into a coma due to advanced levels of lead in his bloodstream, two-year-old Gregory Franklin emerged from the hospital with permanent and severe brain damage.[56] His case illustrated the social and economic dimensions of the epidemic. According to media interviews with the Franklin family, before Gregory's hospitalization, his parents had waged a fruitless eighteen-month battle with their landlord to repair the flaking and falling paint of their apartment walls. After Gregory's sister also tested positive for lead, it was suspected that a great number of children in their tenement were in danger, especially since the Harlem building had close to 100 outstanding violations.[57] The young boy's tragedy was the latest in a string of cases of plumbism, or lead poisoning, among children in the city.

Before the Young Lords launched their Lead Offensive, other groups attempted to bring attention to the issue. In the late 1960s, concerned activists, community groups, and politicians initiated a series of local efforts to pressure New York's government offices to implement preventive programs that had already been adopted in Chicago and Baltimore.[58] The Citizens Committee to End Lead Poisoning, for example, was founded in August 1968. It was launched at a community meeting in Brooklyn following the death of a child at King's Hospital. The committee's housing organizer and leading member, Paul Du Brul, led efforts to lobby local government and to educate communities most at risk.[59]

In the aftermath of Gregory Franklin's death, city councilman Carter Burden, along with Du Brul and others, held a press conference at the Franklin family's home at which he proposed "an apartment-by-apartment testing program to be conducted by the Neighborhood Youth Corps." In response to an incident of lead poisoning in the Bronx earlier that year, Representative Edward Koch also wrote a series of letters to Mayor Lindsay informing him that even Mayor Richard J. Daley of Chicago—notorious for his unscrupulous political practices—had a more advanced lead poisoning prevention program than existed in New York.[60]

The Franklin case outraged the Young Lords, who had trained their eyes on the lead issues since September. Because of their work at Metropolitan Hospital, the Young Lords Organization (YLO) was well poised to move quickly into lead organizing. With the November 1969 election fast approaching, they got to work. As in the Garbage Offensive, they approached the new Lead Offensive both strategically and practically, replacing their tools of brooms and garbage bags with scientific papers and diagnostic tests.

They knew that Bio-Rad Laboratories was donating prepackaged lead-screening kits to the city. For the Young Lords, "half the battle lay in obtaining [these] chemical kits" to test the children of East Harlem. In a series of letters and phone calls to the Department of Health, the Lords requested the kits. The department equivocated, but its administrators made promises about the possibility of their future use. The YLO held a series of meetings in September and October 1969 in East Harlem and at Metropolitan Hospital on the crisis of lead poisoning. They framed the problem in terms of racial, environmental, and housing justice. For several weeks they distributed leaflets and informed residents of their impending door-to-door testing campaign in collaboration with Metropolitan's residents in training from New York Medical College. One of their flyers read, "We are operating our own lead poisoning detection program with students from New York Medical College, beginning Tuesday November 25, on 112th Street. The Young Lords and medical personnel will knock on your door Tuesday and ask to test your children for lead poison. Do not turn them away. Help save your children."[61]

The Young Lords, of course, did not have the kits. But they had a dramatic plan to achieve their end. As early as the Garbage Offensive, the group's minister of information, Pablo Guzmán, had stressed the image the group should project to the media: "The camera should be used as an organizing tool, an avenue to the audience [they] wanted to reach."[62] With the expectation that creative disruption would garner media attention and with moral authority in their sails, the Young Lords and their medical allies decided to take their grievance to the Department of Health.[63]

A rumor that the Department of Health had refused to accept the 40,000 kits donated by Bio-Rad Laboratories fueled the Young Lords' thinking.[64] And community activists viewed the alleged decision of the department as proof of the callousness and opportunism of its officers. In October, at the height of the mayoral election, partly in response to the Gregory Franklin fatality, the department issued a press release announcing a crash lead-testing drive but had not established a concrete plan to obtain or use the tests.[65] According to the Young Lords, the kits were either being allowed to languish unused or were never claimed, despite the growing numbers of lead poison victims in the city. *Village Voice* journalist Jack Newfield corroborated their version of the story; the Department of Health admitted the error to him after the department's October press release came out.[66]

On November 24, approximately two weeks before their sit-in at Metropolitan Hospital and the day before their door-to-door testing was to begin, the Young Lords conducted another sit-in, this time at the office of Dr. David Harris, the deputy commissioner of the Department of Health. Led by Juan González and Rafael Viera, approximately thirty Young Lords participated, alongside a number of nurses, hospital workers, and medical students, including Gene Straus, Metropolitan Hospital's chief medical resident. The Young Lords pointedly asked the department if it would be as inactive about testing if the racial composition of the children of Harlem and East Harlem was not black American and Puerto Rican. In a more conciliatory tone, Straus proposed that the department had the opportunity to aid people like those gathered at that meeting, who were already investigating the problem at the neighborhood level. The group asked for 200 lead-testing kits and successfully persuaded the department to release them that same day.

By the next day, the Young Lords and their nonmedical volunteers had been trained and were conducting door-to-door screenings for signs of lead poisoning among children. These home visits represented a form of itinerant, grassroots organizing that brought the Young Lords campaign to a greater number of people than had visited their office or joined them at demonstrations. The painstaking door-to-door testing, which the Young Lords performed alongside health professionals, afforded the group a measure of moral authority and helped establish their reputation as dedicated young radicals. Bella August recalls that they went out in teams on Saturdays armed with tuberculosis and lead tests, a health questionnaire, and the Ten-Point Health Program: "That's how we began. Literally going door to door, we went into the projects and into the tenements. And we'd go together as a team and most people opened their doors."[67] The screening teams were composed of a Young Lord; a representative from HRUM; a doctor, resident, or intern; and staff members of the local hospital. The teams kept track of who needed treatment, and the doctors made referrals for hospital visits.[68] It was a re-creation of Cuba's medical teams. They found that health problems, among them diseases of poverty, abounded, and many residents had little idea about what services they were legally entitled to. Many had never accessed the services of Metropolitan Hospital and didn't even know they could.[69]

As the Young Lords and their team sat around in the homes of residents of East Harlem waiting for young children to urinate—a requirement of the lead

Door-to-door testing of tuberculosis, Lower East Side, December 1970.
(Photograph by Michael Abramson; courtesy of Haymarket Books)

poisoning test—the organization saw firsthand the health concerns of stay-at-home moms and grandmothers. Their visits underscored the centrality of sterilization, domestic violence, the stresses of childcare on mothers, and depression, among other issues. The group's growing knowledge about the gendered character of the public health crisis in poor communities laid the groundwork for what was to come.

In the spring and summer of 1970, the women of the Young Lords would begin to develop a position paper on the oppression of women of color that analyzed the social and political roots of these issues. These home visits and conversations with mothers about their own complex experiences would also help bring into the open the organization's internal crisis of male chauvinism. As we will see, that internal conflict would be led by the women of the Lords, among them Denise Oliver and Iris Morales.

As they had done earlier with their brooms, the Young Lords made their way through the neighborhood, tenement by tenement. And following Guzmán's call, the Young Lords used press conferences and press releases to publicize their findings. On one average day in December, the YLO tested nearly sixty children and discovered that 30 percent of them were positive.[70] Because doctors and medical technicians were present at the door-to-door visits in East Harlem, their findings were credible, exposed bureaucratic inaction, and magnified the Health Department's negligence. *Village Voice* columnist Jack Newfield noted that the Young Lords were "do[ing] the city's work in the Barrio," an indication that the group's activism was being noticed.[71] With news reports that one-third of children living in slums were potentially infected with lead, the department was forced to either disprove the Young Lords' findings or propose a program for treatment and prevention.

On December 21, a *New York Times* headline read, "City Held Callous on Lead Poisoning," and on December 26, "Criticism Rising over Lead Poison."[72] The president of the American Public Health Association, Dr. Paul B. Cornely, in New York from Washington, D.C., publicly criticized the New York City Department of Health for refusing the tests and charged that the race of the predominantly black and Puerto Rican victims played a role in the way the city handled its lead poisoning crisis.[73] Under pressure, the Department of Health later issued a statement explaining that the plans to use the 40,000 tests had been suspended because the Bio-Rad test did not accurately detect the amount of lead in the bloodstream and because it was difficult to collect urine samples from children between the ages of one and three, who have the highest incidence of lead poisoning. However, a letter written to the *Village Voice* by a Bio-Rad salesman cast doubt on the department's explanations. Acknowledging Jack Newfield's description of the Health Department as an office of bureaucratic indifference, the salesman wrote: "I think Newfield and the Young Lords are operating on false hopes. It is my personal opinion that the city does not want a large-scale screening of children for lead poisoning. Dr. McLaughlin does not want to know for sure how many children are lead-poisoned, because then the city will be obligated to do something about the situation. And there is only one solution to the lead poisoning problem—the walls and ceilings of the apartments must be removed and replaced."[74]

New York City's new commissioner of health, Dr. Mary McLaughlin, was a specialist in the area of lead poisoning and appreciated the enormity of the epidemic and the need for an aggressive response. But she failed to share with the public the political and funding hurdles she faced or to press for appropriate resources. Without prosecutorial authority, the department was incapable of addressing a major source of the problem: the housing violations that were feeding the crisis of plumbism.[75] The notoriously lenient prosecution of housing code violations in New York City failed to enforce laws prohibiting the presence of lead paint on the interior walls of dwellings. A 1965 study found that in that year's cases involving exposure to lead, landlords were fined a total of fourteen dollars and an average of fifty cents per violation.[76]

The YLO Lead Offensive, however, succeeded in forcing institutional change. In the memorandum Wenner Kramansky prepared in the early months of 1970 to Mayor Lindsay, he included a series of questions about lead poisoning, which were likely posed to him either by the mayor himself or by his press secretary, Thomas B. Morgan. The questions and the answers presented to the mayor suggest that the Young Lords had accomplished their aims: to create a conversation in the city about childhood lead poisoning and to capture the mayor's attention. The questions included: "Why are you evaluating the ALA (aminolevulinic acid) urine test? How many children in New York City are at risk of having lead poisoning? What is the city doing about the problem? And what happened to the Young Lords Project?"[77] That the Young Lords' Lead Offensive was referred to as a "Project," suggests that the mayor's office saw the efforts of the YLO as organized and intentional and not just the troublemaking of "radicals." In an interview many years later, one of Mayor Lindsay's close advisors, Barry Gottehrer, recalled that "the Young Lords were one of a kind. They were serious; they could not be persuaded to stop their muckraking for antipoverty money."[78]

Of all the political activities the Young Lords initiated in the fall and winter of 1969–70, the Lead Offensive had the most enduring impact. Although the YLO was not the only group that tried to bring attention to the issue of lead poisoning in the city, its bold and determined approach to the problem, just as in the case of the Garbage Offensive, attracted media attention and simultaneously exposed and shamed local government into action. The Young Lords' strategic collaboration with health workers, the seriousness and commitment that their home visits demonstrated, and their muckraking finally brought a crisis that had been simmering beneath the surface of city politics to its boiling point.

In January 1970, the Department of Health established a more exacting lead clause in the city's housing code and launched the Emergency Repair Program, a subsidiary of the Housing Development Administration, to remove lead paint from tenement walls. The new rule provided that if landlords failed to respond within five days to court orders to remove reported lead hazards from their buildings, the emergency team would make the repairs and bill the landlord for the job.[79] Moreover, the Health Department created an office, the Bureau of Lead Poisoning Control, whose sole responsibility was to launch programs in the city to combat lead poisoning. During the first half of 1970, the city tested more than five times the number of children it had tested in all of 1969.[80] There was also an attempt to promote more aggressively the model of community-based healthcare that the Young Lords advanced. A 1971 memo on "the Mayor's Walking Tour Possibilities" suggested that "15 teams of doctors from Bronx Lebanon, accompanied by Community Service Aides and Organized by the Health Department, will do door-to-door [lead poisoning] outreach. Also there will be a few stationary mobile units on the streets in those areas, manned by doctors and people from the Mayor's Urban Action Task Force. Sickle Cell, rubella and measles immunizations will also be given. Target expectation for each day is 500 people tested; politically it shows cooperation of voluntary and public sectors."[81]

■

In 1974, the *American Journal of Public Health* credited Young Lords activism for the anti-lead-poisoning reform achieved in New York during the early 1970s.[82] According to the journal, the politicization of lead poisoning was key to the passage of meaningful reform. Young Lord militancy forced a public conversation about the problem in broader circles, and their propaganda voiced the community's aspirations for humane healthcare.[83] When the Young Lords emerged in the summer of 1969, the New York organization was led by a committed body of five, and its activities were sustained by fifteen dedicated general members. Its first direct action campaign had unequivocally inserted the group and Puerto Ricans at large into the city's public debates. The opening of its East Harlem office a few months later in September, combined with growing involvement in the city's complex movement organism and multiple community initiatives, broadened its audience. By mid-October, its ranks had more than tripled, and the Young Lords were a known entity in the movement, in East Harlem, and in city hall.

The group's door-to-door activism offered resources to a marginalized community and generated a sense of entitlement to public healthcare by instilling in neighborhood residents an understanding that they had the right to claim public services and that these services must be provided with dignity. It also educated journalists, politicians, and New Yorkers at large about the public good and the ways in which race, poverty, and the dilapidated urban environment injured the health and life chances of people of color. In the 1960s the impact of racism and poverty on the built environment was a revelation and became a central facet of the analysis and efforts of the early environmental movement's politics. The Young Lords' activism around Metropolitan Hospital and the lead problem embodied that environmental awareness. Their challenges to medical discrimination, demands for dignity and equality in healthcare, and proposed socialized medicine in place of the country's for-profit medical system served as a potent example of how the reforms and aspirations of the Cuban Revolution seeped into American society. The Young Lords' efforts and those of the larger health rights movement challenged common conceptions of what organizers of color stood and fought for and won in the age of black power and civil rights.

CHAPTER SIX

THE CHURCH OFFENSIVE

Prefiguring the New Society
at the People's Church

On a late New York City night in October 1969, a few men in the Young Lords were smoking pot, talking politics, and listening to music after a long day of organizing. Juan González was eager to put Bob Dylan's 1969 hit single "Lay Lady Lay" on the turntable.[1] The men were drawn to its unembarrassed verbalization of male sexual desire and accompanying vulnerability. The song's working-class protagonist bares his fantasies to his lover, hoping to convince her to spend the night with him. Its candid title suggested that sex was at long last unbound from the remaining restraints of Victorian-era social conventions, which counseled repression of sexual urges, prohibited public discussion of sex, and restricted sex to the marital bed. It was a fitting soundtrack to the transgressions that lay ahead.

The ritual repetition of this classic, era-defining, bake-out scene by legions of people, young and old, signaled the triumph of personal liberation over puritan self-denial in the way many mainstream Americans chose to live their lives—a signature achievement of the counterculture and the sexual revolution.[2] Yet, the cultural shift was not without its challengers. As early as 1960, the emerging ranks of the New Right coalition joined evangelical Christians to condemn it, arguing that the erosion of "American morals" would lead to civilizational decline. Hell-bent on reasserting traditional values, its leaders appropriated a politically pliable term, "morality," as an ideological battle-ax against the cultural gains of the New Left.[3] But before these cultural warriors fine-tuned their narrative tools, the Young Lords snatched morality from the jaws of New Right elements and had their own battle with them on their turf.

In a wink, the Young Lords' conversation turned from "Lay Lady Lay" to the gingerbread church on 111th Street and Lexington Avenue. From afar, the

Young Lords in front of First Spanish United Methodist Church, December 1969.
(Photograph by David Fenton)

white trimmings on the redbrick building appeared illuminated. Its well-kept structure stood out among the dilapidated tenements and empty lots on Junkies' Row one block away. It would not be long before the Young Lords Organization (YLO) entered into a tense dispute with the East Harlem church over the use of its facility to feed neighborhood children. The Young Lords framed their request around the morality of the biblical Jesus, counterposed against the church's seeming indifference to poverty. The conflict drew the involvement of clergy from different denominations, government officials, mainstream media, East Harlem residents, movement organizations, and community group representatives. As two distinct definitions of morality cohered in New York's public discourse, most had no choice but to take sides. The drama-filled clash reflected a larger contest for social influence between the Left and social conservatives over the direction the country might take in the twilight of the 1960s.

There Is a Church in Spanish Harlem

Since their emergence a few months earlier, the Young Lords had already broadened the scope of New York's racial justice organizing. With their distinct mix of creative direct action and strategic messaging, they had shown how racism exacerbated the crises of sanitation and medical care in East Harlem; in calling attention to environmental racism and medical discrimination, they had linked civil rights to public health in New York. Their radical analysis and prefigurative examples of what a new humanistic society might achieve brought them both acclaim and increased government surveillance. However, alongside successes, the Young Lords faced organizational setbacks and failed campaigns. One such failure opened the path to their most iconic offensive.

The YLO initiated its first breakfast program in October 1969. Located at Emmaus House, an ecumenical social service organization in East Harlem, and run in partnership with the Black Panthers, the operation got off to a rough start. Among other details, it involved the securing and cooking of food, early morning pickup at children's homes, and timely transport to school. During its first week, only a handful of children participated. To discourage attendance, police distributed reports to staff at Emmaus House alleging illicit links between the Young Lords and New York's gangs. Troubled, the organization's director, Friar David Kirk, expressed apprehension about the group's use of the building. Likely bruised by the questioning of their good intentions, the Young Lords began searching for a new operating site. That errand was on their minds the night some members stumbled upon the gingerbread church while humming "Lay Lady Lay."

The following Sunday, representatives of the Young Lords approached the First Spanish United Methodist Church (FSUMC) with a sober request for space. The Young Lords greeted the head pastor with all the rituals of deference and respect that their parents previously had ingrained in them. To their surprise, the reverend gave them a chilly reception. He brusquely instructed them to submit a written request to the church's administrative board before dismissing them.

Whether by fate or happenstance, the Young Lords' weed-induced ruminations had delivered them to what was likely the least empathetic place of worship in East Harlem. The FSUMC believed that the most effective form of social service centered on "preaching the Good News to the poor," restoring "stability to their homes," and instilling a strong work ethic.[4] Its small congregation counted 138 "conservative, pietistic, [and] evangelical" worshipers—mostly working-class Puerto Ricans with upwardly mobile aspirations. Having moved out of El Barrio to Brooklyn and the Bronx during the 1960s, most returned to the church on Sundays.[5] Yet the distance they traveled was more spatial than economic. Still, the congregants' devoutness generated a thrifty self-denial and hard work on which their modest economic advancement depended. It also fostered a righteous superiority, which limited their capacity to gauge character beyond surface behavior. As later became evident, many of them sat in judgment of their former neighbors during Sunday service. They attributed their problems to individual shortcomings, worldly cravings, and deviation from the word of God.

Fatefully, in the conflict between the congregation and the Young Lords, the church itself fell under public scrutiny. The denomination's thorny history illustrated the power that social forces of magnitude bear on reality. By the nineteenth century, the FSUMC's predecessor sects (the Methodist Church and the Evangelical United Brethren Church) had become dominant Protestant denominations. They built urban headquarters and welcomed an influx of upper-class congregants, among them politicians, judges, and captains of industry. Their complex institutions adapted the new organizational structures and investment techniques of industrial capitalism.[6] Not surprisingly, they became junior stakeholders and managers of westward expansion, Indian removal, and territorial acquisition in Latin America.[7] And in 1899, a year after the United States took possession of Puerto Rico, the Church of the United Brethren in Christ exported its "civilizing mission": "to inaugurate a work that assures the Americanization of the island," which it linked to "the joys and privileges of being a Christian disciple."[8]

Two decades later, in 1922, the Methodist Church established the first Spanish-language congregation in New York, ministering to the third wave of Puerto Rican migrants to the city. Forced to move several times due to conflicts with the white congregations with which it shared space, its future became uncertain. With the influx of Puerto Rican migrants to New York during and after World War II, Puerto Rican Methodists finally achieved the demographic uptick they needed to secure a permanent home in East Harlem. Influenced by the labor and civil rights activism of the era, the church became a dynamic site of worship. In addition to spiritual refuge, it offered English-language classes and daycare services to the community, attracting Puerto Ricans of different denominations until 1964, when a fire partially destroyed its building. Through the fundraising efforts of its reverend Ezra Rodriguez, the building reopened in 1967.[9] Beloved by some, Reverend Rodriguez was reportedly "chased out of the church" by its high officials for his progressive and Puerto Rican nationalist leanings.[10]

His replacement, Rev. Humberto Carrazana, discontinued all community programs. A political exile, the new reverend had settled in the United States almost a decade earlier, after the Cuban revolution. He claimed to have supported the overthrow of Cuban dictator Fulgencio Batista but fled the island when "the Revolution turned Marxist," in fear of losing his ability to proselytize.[11] When the Young Lords knocked at his door, as if by apparition, the exiled pastor saw young people wearing berets who evoked Fidel Castro and the Cuban Revolution. On reflex, the reverend icily shot back, "Put it in writing."[12]

But the Young Lords lacked the experience to craft a diplomatic communiqué. Their October 22, 1969, letter explained their wish to use the church's facility to administer a free breakfast program. It also described a "liberation school" where children and adults could learn "black and Puerto Rican history" as well as more traditional academic subjects. The church's facility, they wrote, which sat empty during the week, should be put to the service of "one of the poorest neighborhoods in New York City." The Young Lords were themselves zealots. They lived among the people of East Harlem, stood on street corners, linked community grievances to the evils of colonialism and capitalism, and deployed militancy to recuperate Puerto Rican rights and dignity. They closed their letter by saying, "We ask that your church begin to relate concretely to Puerto Ricans and their problems. Without sounding offensive, it must be understood that while poverty and racism has afflicted our black and Puerto Rican communities, the churches have stood silent for the most part. Sins of omission must be stopped now."[13] The charge echoed the New Left's polemics against "well-meaning" civic, religious, and social service institutions for legitimizing the status quo through silence or token reforms. The tone epitomized the moralistic approach of the era's political youth.

The following Sunday, October 26, the Young Lords were back at the church, seated early for service. Clad in fatigues and Afros—not exactly Sunday best— they raised eyebrows among parishioners who knew nothing of the group's request. During the after-service coffee hour, they seized a moment with the pastor, asking to discuss their letter with the board and members of the congregation. The Young Lords, whose interventions were rarely improvised, were deploying a cardinal strategy among seasoned organizers—appeal to the broadest audience possible and avoid isolated negotiations with powerful individuals, skilled in evasion or pacification without concession.[14] But most parishioners had left promptly after the service ended. The reverend's stern demeanor signaled to them that he wanted to handle this situation privately. He denied their request to meet with other congregants and told the Young Lords that the board would reply to their letter.

In a November 3 letter, the board denied the request and outlined its rationale. Policy stipulated that all on-site programs be administered by church members.[15] The board continued with an itemized, polemical defense: "We want you to understand that our church is composed of 99 percent Puerto Ricans, who are very much aware of the problems of the community."[16] The barbed declaration—that an overwhelmingly Puerto Rican congregation should not be schooled on the problems of its community—aimed to put the Young Lords in their place, invalidate their accusations of indifference to the poor, and veil the board's commitment to an increasingly contested status quo.

The board's rebuttal typified a developing trend. It distorted and appropriated calls for increased racial representation in the service of regressive ends.[17] Answering the charge of shirking responsibility to the community, it derided new and boisterous approaches to injustices: "We feel that we are doing our share, without making too much noise, and through the proper channels, as well as taking care of the spiritual needs of the people, which is our main concern."[18] They seemed oblivious to Martin Luther King Jr.'s "Letter from a Birmingham Jail" of 1963, which excoriated white liberal clergymen for being more concerned with the propriety of antiracist protests than the violent bigotry that brought them into being.[19]

The next Sunday, the Young Lords were back at Sunday service. They stayed for the coffee hour and again asked to meet with the board. To avoid a public conflict before the congregation, this time the pastor conceded. The Young Lords prefaced their remarks with a clarification: theirs was a self-funded project that proposed to revive the teachings of the historic church of Jesus and its mandate to address the material suffering of the poor. Liberation theology was reclaiming that tradition in Latin America, yet in East Harlem it appeared that the FSUMC was "indifferent to the needs of working mothers for a place to leave their children during the day, the needs of children for a place to play other than the streets, the needs of families driven from their homes by fire, cold or eviction."[20] The pastor defended the right of his congregation to worship as it saw fit and charged the Young Lords with exploiting the sanctity of Sunday services to impose their political views. Board members took a different approach. They explained that the small congregation was already strained with a $640 monthly repayment of a loan it had borrowed to restore the church after a fire destroyed the original facility three years earlier. The National Methodist Investment Fund financed the loan, a detail omitted by members of the board.[21] Regrettably, they continued, the church was in no position to take on any projects or additional responsibilities associated with the use of the facility, which carried hidden costs, including securing supervisory staff.

Despite the board's explanations, the pastor's remarks intensified the growing antagonism between the church and the young radicals. Unencumbered by the strained civility of earlier communications, the Young Lords advanced their position by other means. Pablo Guzmán, the group's minister of information, understood the appeal of this evolving drama and its potential to amplify the Young Lords' political message to broader audiences. Among his peers, he stood out for his grasp of the power of words, images, and stories and had long advocated their strategic use in organizing. Over the course of the conflict, he, with other Central Committee members, crafted a sophisticated communications strategy. They combined their knowledge of scripture, which some had acquired in the religious milieu of their childhood, with the searing critique of organized religion they had adopted as teenagers and young adults in the 1960s. Though some still believed in God and others were atheists, most came to see Christianity as an ideological instrument of conquest, colonialism, and repressive state rule in Latin America, distinguishing it from the radical origins of the church of Jesus.

In a decade that made social engagement and personal sacrifice the benchmark of good character, the Young Lords homed in on the church's abstention from neighborhood problems to challenge its moral standing in the community. They began to disseminate their message on mimeographed flyers distributed outside the church and in subsequent Sunday service visits, during coffee-klatsch hour. An early flyer asserted that in blaming people for their suffering rather than blaming the "realities of life," the church found an excuse to abandon its mission as laid out in Matthew 25:31–40, which they quoted: "I was hungry and you fed me; I was thirsty and you gave me something to drink. When I was a stranger you took me in, and when I had no clothes you gave me something to wear."[22] The quotation mirrored the Young Lords' proposed projects at the church.

In an interview with *First Source*, a publication of the National Council of Churches, Guzmán used the ecumenical language of his reform-minded audience to win them over to the vision of change articulated by the New Left. Echoing the call for "participatory democracy," he explained that the Young Lords "were upholding an ancient Christian tradition since the time of Paul, that says that anybody that comes to a service has the right to speak up. In true Christianity the rights of the minority have always been respected." The conflict reflected dynamics of colonial rule, he continued. In depicting the Young Lords as imposters, the FSUMC leaders had inverted reality—it was they who "imposed themselves on the community by putting their church in the middle of the community" and closing "their doors to the people." To highlight the political role of organized religion, Guzmán observed that the American troops Cardinal Francis Spellman had consecrated went on to commit the My Lai massacre. The cleric's support for the Vietnam War, he concluded, "makes obvious that there is no separation between church and politics."[23]

The Young Lords continued to attend Sunday mass, and the congregation continued to clear out quickly after each service. Despite the pastor's tight rein on details about the evolving conflict, one of the few congregants who still lived in East Harlem had questions. Even though she bristled at their physical appearance, Petra Aponte de Pietri was struck by the obstinacy of these young Turks, observations she shared with her children. The widow and mother of five worked in the local Republican Party office. Under great hardship she raised her children in the FSUMC. But in the late 1960s, her children and other young adults became inactive members of the church. At a moment of growing identification with the grievances and aspirations of their generation, these young congregants were repelled by the congregation's conservative drift and discomfited by blanket depictions of East Harlem youth as ruffians. To Mrs. Pietri, the presence of a new cast of young people at Sunday services raised the possibility of luring her children back to the fold.

Carmen Pietri remembers her mother's colorful description of the Young Lords: "Estos muchachos vinieron otra vez a la iglesia, los hipe esos . . . los peluses que no se peinan, como el loquito de aqui, Pedro." (Those kids came to church again, you know who, the hippies . . . the hairy ones who don't comb their hair, like our own crazy Pedro.)[24] Mrs. Pietri was referring to her son Pedro Pietri, then twenty-five years old, a Vietnam veteran and up-and-coming poet. In referring to the Young Lords as *los peluses*, Mrs. Pietri was expressing anxiety about her son's and the Young Lords' explicit embrace of African traits, in this case the growing out of their Afros. *Los peluses* was code for blackness in a culture that had not come to terms with its own legacy of racism. Measures like men cutting their hair close to their scalp and women straightening the curls and waves out of their locks with chemical products were integral to upholding the tenets of respectability, which associated blackness with indecent and shiftless behavior. By growing their Afros and proclaiming that "black is beautiful," the Young Lords, like the Black Panthers and many others of African descent, were challenging the unexamined racist logic of both Puerto Rican and American cultural norms and their psychologically damaging dimensions among Afro-descended people of color.

Mrs. Pietri was anxious about these expressions of blackness and judged the Young Lords with the politics of respectability. Yet, she encouraged her children to return to the church to meet them. Other congregation members acknowledged that the Young Lords seemed peaceful but expressed fear of their presence and irreverence. A later report of the conflict commissioned by the United

Methodist Church's executive body recounts that on one occasion a Young Lord came with a poster of Jesus Christ carrying an AK-47 rifle over his shoulder.[25] The poster, which appears in photographs of the Young Lords' office, appropriates Jesus as a man of the people and imposes the politics of armed revolutionary nationalism on his image. Some also claimed that the Young Lords disrupted services by remaining seated when the congregation rose and standing when it was seated, an accusation the Young Lords denied.[26] Other sources, some partial to the young radicals and others critical of them, highlighted the group's cordial, respectful disposition and attempts "to play the game by the church's rules," especially during the initial stages of the conflict.[27]

Loyalty Sunday Clampdown

After approximately four weeks of failed attempts to appeal to a congregation that cleared out immediately after Sunday services, the Young Lords planned a different tactic on December 7 during Loyalty Sunday, known also as Testimonial Sunday. In this less-structured service, lay members bear witness to their faith from the pulpit and make a financial pledge for the year.[28]

The Young Lords' decision to press their demands came in the wake of devastating news to the movement three days earlier. On December 4, 1969, Mark Clark and Fred Hampton, two beloved and respected Black Panther leaders, were killed during a 4:00 A.M. police siege of the home where the Panthers lived collectively in Chicago. The deadly assault laid bare the potential consequences of political activity for radicals of color and raised the stakes for the New York Young Lords. Leaders of the group had met Hampton two months earlier during a trip to Chicago. The siege had been carried out with information provided to the police by an FBI informant who passed as a Panther member. And according to autopsy reports and the eyewitness account of Hampton's fiancée, who slept next to him as the police entered, Hampton had been killed execution style. Like Emmett Till's mother, who held an open-casket funeral to let the world see evidence of the fourteen-year-old's murder, the Black Panthers opened their blood-spattered, bullet-riddled house for journalists and the Chicago community to tour. On-scene evidence challenged the claim that police were under heavy gunfire from the Black Panthers and demonstrated that all but one bullet were shot by the police from outside.[29]

The Young Lords seized the rare opportunity at the forthcoming Loyalty Sunday service to sound the alarm about state-sponsored violence, while linking it to systemic childhood hunger in East Harlem and the massive U.S. bombing of Vietnam. The group also needed a sanctuary to protect its members. Its Loyalty Sunday insistence that the church host its breakfast program was a well-thought-out tactical move. A murderous police raid would be difficult to execute at a house of worship without public scandal.

In the struggle over space for a breakfast program, the church itself acquired symbolic significance as a political bunker, staging ground for dissent, and tribune of the oppressed. Pastor Carrazana, who had witnessed and opposed the radicalization of the Cuban Revolution, anticipated the development and took measures to prevent it. Thirty to forty Young Lords and their supporters arrived early at the FSUMC for Testimonial Sunday.

Amid a tense atmosphere, the Young Lords' talented orator Felipe Luciano— flanked by approximately six of his comrades assigned as protection—rose from a pew near the altar, seeking to articulate the Young Lords' request to the congregation.[30] As Luciano began speaking, Reverend Carrazana was already signaling to the organist, Benita Rodriguez, to lead the chorus in the singing of "Onward Christian Soldiers."[31] Instinctively, a Young Lord moved to unplug the organ, to keep Luciano's words from being drowned out, but was intercepted by an undercover officer of the Twenty-Fifth Precinct, Victor Badilla, who walked over to Luciano and told him that "we'll give you speaking time if you step down from the pulpit."[32] Despite Badilla's attempt at deescalation, the incensed pastor yelled that Luciano should not be allowed to speak. Reading this as a signal to disband the protesters, Officer Badilla ordered reinforcements on his walkie-talkie. At the same time, Arthur A. Baller, a police captain not in uniform, emerged from the pews and demanded that the group leave or risk arrest.[33] According to the Lords, Baller did not identify himself as a police officer. Whether or not he did, the situation spun out of control.

Accounts of the clash differ considerably. Police affidavits claim that the Young Lords were "engaging in tumultuous and violent conduct" at the front of the church, "flailing their arms and shouting," and that four police officers were injured in the course of the disturbance.[34] The undercover officer, Captain Baller, reported that while he was informing Felipe Luciano of his arrest for refusing to leave, another Young Lord attacked him with a chair.[35] Other officers described witnessing their own being hit by the Young Lords. Juan González allegedly jumped on the back of patrolman G. Alberti, who was hit on the shoulder and treated at the Joint and Disease Hospital. Joseph Hill allegedly hit patrolman Ronald Taylor, described as an informant, with a metal pipe. Patrolman Taylor had been assigned to protect Captain Baller and, it was stated, intentionally took a blow directed at Baller. Patrolman Taylor was reportedly knocked to the ground and suffered injuries to "the back and near his groin." Another officer was allegedly hit with a wooden club.[36] In another account, Patrolman Taylor reported that after he placed Young Lord Denise Oliver under arrest, she fled, and he had to "chase her for a block and half" before apprehending her.[37]

Depositions recorded within an hour of the incident by National Lawyers Guild attorneys, the Young Lords' legal counsel, offer a different perspective. According to their notes, the clash between police and the Young Lords ensued when Luciano was "dragged down from the [communion] railing" and hit over the head with a club while four or five police officers surrounded him as the congregation continued to sing "Onward Christian Solders."[38] Carmen Pietri's grandmother, a parishioner, tried to hit Luciano with a candelabra.[39]

Remembrances of one of the youngest members arrested on that day, Carlito Rovira, convey the Young Lords' point of view. He explained that there was an immediate attempt by nightstick-wielding police to remove the Young Lords from the church, which led the group to close ranks at the altar: "Three words describe what took place: *puño, patá, y candela* [flailing fists, kicks, and rumble]. There was complete and total chaos, and all you saw was hands and NYPD [New York Police Department] nightsticks flying all over the place and people making the sign of the cross as if Satan had intruded in this peaceful [M]ass. Meanwhile, the Young Lords were being beaten up by the police."[40] Charles Kroplinicki, a Catholic seminarian who attended the service with the Young Lords, gave a similar interpretation. He insisted that the police marched in with "sticks held ready" and immediately lunged at the group. When male members of the Young Lords tried to defend their female counterparts, he reported, the struggle intensified.[41] The women of the Young Lords, however, had the final say, asserting that they defended themselves and their male counterparts.[42] Meanwhile the agitated parishioner Petra Aponte de Pietri managed to phone her daughter Carmen from the church, imploring her to come over, "The cops were in there busting heads because the Young Lords interrupted the service again."[43]

After the altar clash, most of the group ran out of the church and past another line of police waiting outside, escaping their grip, probably because the snow on the ground made it difficult for police to apprehend them. COINTELPRO documents report that the Young Lords sent immediate word to the New York Black Panthers that approximately half their members had been arrested, asking that they "send over some Panthers to the 125th Street station and to find a lawyer."[44]

A total of thirteen Young Lords, eight men and five women, were arrested: David Velasquez, Elena González, Sonia Ivany, Joseph Hill, Mirta González, Felipe Luciano, Erika Seznov, Salvador Diaz, Benjamin Cruz, Denise Oliver, Carlito Rovira, Juan Romero, and Jose Diaz. They were variously charged with riot, obstruction of religious services, conspiracy, felonious assault in the second degree, possession of a dangerous weapon (a pipe), criminal trespass, and resisting arrest.[45] Five Young Lords were hospitalized. Luciano suffered a fractured arm, and Benjamin Martinez received a head gash. One police officer suffered a fractured hand, and three others reported pain.[46] When Carmen Pietri and her brother Frank arrived on the scene, they found an empty nave and "blood all over the church."[47]

Airing Dirty Laundry

The Young Lords' evolving struggle with the church was one of thousands of diverse campaigns spearheaded by countless local groups. Their direct actions over the course of the decade played a major role in shifting public opinion— on the causes of racial and economic inequality, the Vietnam War, women's rights, gay liberation, and beyond—and winning reforms. Although the New York Young Lords led the period's most prolonged protest against a church, they were not the only activists whose protests targeted religious institutions for "aiding and abetting" oppression. Seven months earlier, Student Nonviolent Coordinating Committee leader James Forman led the first and best-known of such actions on May 4, 1969. He unfurled the Black Manifesto at the progressive Riverside Church during services, demanding monetary reparations from white churches for their role in the enslavement and exploitation of black Americans. The action encouraged others, who over the next two years, staged similar protests.[48] Less than two weeks after the Forman declaration, the Chicago Young Lords used militant protest to compel the McCormick Seminary in Lincoln Park to disburse funds it had promised to a coalition of community groups for a low-income housing and neighborhood beautification development. As discussed in chapter 1, the Chicago actions led to concession on most of the coalition's demands.[49] The New York Young Lords followed in the footsteps of Chicago.

Against this backdrop, Reverend Carrazana's decision to call in the police on December 7 proved a critical error. Word of "the bust," as the Young Lords called it, spread quickly in the press and in religious communities. Religious officials from a diverse range of denominations condemned the church's leadership. The decision to invite the police to "physically remove the Young Lords from the church" was a terrible mistake, according to black American clergyman Robert Chapman, who said the police behaved not like men but "like what many militants are prone to call them."[50]

Those who voiced immediate support for the Young Lords included Rev. David Garcia of St. Mark's Episcopal Church on the Lower East Side and black radical Baptist minister Lucius Walker, an associate of Martin Luther King who supported James Forman's call for monetary reparations from white churches to black Americans. Other religious figures denounced the NYPD's violent intervention in a conflict over serving breakfast to hungry children and warned against the specter of collaboration between conservative houses of worship and government forces. The public record does not show whether or not Reverend

Carrazana was aware of the latest wave of state repression against the Black Panthers in New York and Chicago. However, his decision departed from the conciliatory disposition to protests adopted by churches in cities like New York.[51]

Others with more traditional views also took a stand against the violence. Late 1960s radicals were raising thorny questions about the complicity of long-standing American churches in slavery, their financial holdings, and unmet responsibilities to the poor. Congregants clamored for greater transparency, democracy, and racial diversification. Seminarians, young clergymen, women's groups, and many black members demanded that the church yoke spiritual ministering to problems of social and political import. In the context of growing scrutiny, the senior district leadership of the Methodist Church in New York refused to file criminal charges against the Young Lords and intervened to post bail and pay the medical bills of those injured.[52] They understood the political fallout of these developments better than Reverend Carrazana.

For its part, the YLO was emboldened in its resolve to use the church for its breakfast program. A Young Lord captured the fallout of the police bust at the church: "When blood is shed and you see broken bones, it makes you more determined. And that's precisely what happened to us."[53] The statement recalled the widespread radicalization occasioned by state repression against protesters captured retrospectively in images of police dogs, fire hoses, and the gassing of protesters, the press corps, and doctors from Chicago to Birmingham.[54] Determined to fill the church with supporters the Sunday after the December 7 bust, the Young Lords amplified their propaganda campaign and flyer distribution routine on the corner across from the church. Righteous anger emboldened them. They added impromptu speeches and sharpened their language, denouncing the December 7 incident as a "police riot."

In their bold recasting of the police as perpetrators of mob violence, the Young Lords inverted the term's underlying assumptions and seized its symbolic power to dramatize their story. As revolutionaries, they were honing sensibilities they acquired early in life—as their parents' cultural and language intermediaries—and putting them to political use. At their best, the Young Lords had a keen grasp of the power of language, symbols, and stories to enlarge their message. In an interview from the period, Pablo Guzmán credited the Reverend David Kirk of Emmaus House for illuminating the character of police actions at the church in a telegram to the group in which the reverend also remarked that "if Christ was alive today he would be a Young Lord."[55]

Within the FSUMC, the crisis loosened the pastor's grip on his congregants. A small cohort questioned his judgment and voiced long-held misgivings about the church's insularity. These and other congregants urged the pastor to reach out to young parishioners who had become inactive in their late teenage years, but whose generational insights might help defuse the conflict. Distressed by calls from the city's dissenting ministers and the specter of another encounter with the Young Lords, the pastor conceded. He invited young parishioners to the coming Sunday service where the Young Lords were once again expected, on December 14.

One young parishioner, Joe Pietri, who arrived early, remembers the scene humorously: "The media was everywhere. And everyone was playing to the media on both sides. Felipe Luciano was naturally Mr. Charismatic and Mr. Eloquence, a media darling. And there were others from the church who talked to the media too. It was a circus outside."[56] Approximately 500 people—the majority Young Lords sympathizers—lined up outside waiting to cram into the church. This was not what Reverend Carrazana had imagined, but warned by the New York Methodist Church leadership to avoid escalating the conflict, he did not block their entry.[57] Near the end of the service, after a tense whispered exchange with the Young Lords, the pastor agreed to meet with a small delegation. One Young Lord was allowed to address the congregation, stating, "We did not come to ask for money; we only ask for the use of space in this church." At the end of the service, sympathizers remained in their pews during the three-hour meeting that followed among the Young Lords' five Central Committee leaders, Young Lords cadre Denise Oliver, the church board, the pastor, and the previously inactive young parishioners.[58] The meeting began with tension and ended with acrimony. In their role as unofficial mediators, the church youth struggled with both sides. Carmen Pietri explains: "You got this Cuban minister, who was chased out of his homeland for political reasons. Pro-Batista probably. And in comes—Felipe, who was raised in a Pentecostal church and knew to go into a church properly dressed. My beef with the Young Lords is that if you want to be camouflaged in a Protestant church, your best camouflage is a shirt and tie . . . but they came in with Afros and berets looking like the children of Che Guevara. The clash was immediate. [All along, Carrazana] must have been freaking out, thinking he was back in Cuba. They were not gonna get to square one under no circumstance, because of what they were wearing. So from day one the Young Lords messed up."[59] Despite Carmen's disagreement with the Young Lords' "getup," she was struck that the board members kicked off the meeting with the denigrating descriptions of Puerto Ricans she heard growing up.

According to Carmen these comments were later reiterated by congregation members, Sister Jiménez, who pulled her aside and said in Spanish: "You know why they don't have money? Because I see them buying beer in the bodega with their welfare check instead of buying breakfast for their children. And then they want us to feed their children breakfast." Carmen emphasized, "And this was a Christian lady speaking."[60]

The Young Lords countered that the church had simply repackaged, for religious audiences, state propaganda, blaming the poor for conditions out of their control. They added that Puerto Ricans were driven out of their homeland by U.S. economic policies and that racism, dilapidated schools, and unemployment were the sources of their woes. Carmen hadn't heard anyone of her generation speak of poverty and migration as passionately and cogently as she did that day. "Here I am being exposed to [the arguments] of a group of educated Puerto Ricans who were pissed off about situations that I'm pissed off about." To her, it was "one big education! I didn't completely agree with their tactics . . . but everything they said made sense."[61] She and the other youth parishioners were treading on dangerous ground. The same youth group met again the next day with select board members, voicing the idea that perhaps they "could implement and carry out certain programs and work with the community in general." They were met with resentment, accused of sympathizing with the Young Lords' arguments, scolded for having aired the church's "dirty laundry in public," branded as "Judases," and excluded from subsequent negotiations.[62]

In an interview with *First Source* later that week, Pablo Guzmán summarized the political divisions between the Young Lords and the board: "The people of the Board of the First Spanish Church told us that we were Satan, and that if poor people wanted they could educate themselves. . . . Their idea is that Puerto Rican people dig being poor, and that they made it (through hard work) so why can't everybody else. . . . They think that Puerto Rican women on welfare spend their money on beer, they play the numbers and that they really dig the gutter. It took a whole lot to hold our tempers."[63] The board presumed that the poor brought poverty onto themselves through their lack of personal drive and work ethic. Purportedly driven by wayward values and irresponsible behavior, this subgroup of Puerto Ricans was cast as different. The reasoning implied that the poor did not deserve sympathy and that help would enable shiftlessness and deepen dependence—all of which justified the board's refusal to allow use of the church to feed poor children and offer classes to the community.

These were the oldest ideas about poverty in the United States. Promulgated by English colonists who believed the poor lacked the moral character, hard work, and discipline required for salvation, they also drove the logic of nineteenth-century poorhouse reformers who responded to the growth of poverty with proposals to institutionalize the poor.[64] In the 1960s, amid a new wave of displacement occasioned by postwar economic and demographic changes, these ideas gained widespread political currency when social scientists developed a theory of culture to explain poverty. They argued that low-income people were trapped in a self-perpetuating "culture of poverty," a web of interlocking pathological behaviors that hindered their economic advancement. Developed by anthropologist Oscar Lewis in his 1959 study of Mexicans and reiterated by political scientist Michael Harrington in his 1962 bestseller, *The Other America*, the theory emphasized the cultural effects of social and economic exclusion on the social fabric of poor communities.[65] It argued that the poor engaged in deviant behaviors that, when passed down to their children, reproduced inter-generational cycles of poverty. Harrington wrote, "There is . . . a language of the poor, a psychology of the poor, a worldview of the poor. To be impoverished is to be an internal alien, to grow up in a culture that is radically different from the one that dominates the society."[66] Despite Lewis's admiration for his subjects' resilience, he chastised Puerto Ricans for valuing "acting out more than thinking out, self-expression more than self-constraint, pleasure more than productivity, spending more than saving, personal loyalty more than impersonal justice."[67] Counterposed to the Protestant ethic—the founding system of values routinely deployed by the country's ruling elite to assert social control—these value-laden judgments of the poor distorted their humanity and classified them as a threat to the country's social and moral fabric.[68] In 1965, Daniel Patrick Moynihan penned a more analytical study of the black family. It underscored the crisis of unemployment among black men and centuries of discrimination, but also argued that other fundamental problems were at work: a "tangle of pathology," out-of-wedlock children, welfare dependency, and the authoritarian dominance of black matriarchs. These oversimplified representations of people living in poverty bore little resemblance to the distinctive protagonists in East Harlem's unfolding drama: the Young Lords with their vision of a new world and the hardworking Puerto Rican worshipers with whom they were embattled.

Writing on the heels of the communist-targeted Red Scare, these writers emphasized descriptions of poverty over analyses of its root causes, partly to avoid the association of their studies with Marxism.[69] Their goal was to rehabilitate a sense of public mission among white middle-class Americans, steeped in the culture of consumerism. In the end, these studies imparted academic legitimacy to old ideas linking poverty to pathological behavior and validated the erroneous public discourse that poverty was primarily a problem of people of color. Above all, the studies formalized a new and more resilient racism wherein culture replaced biological explanations for inferior social status.[70] The Young Lords' battle with the FSUMC is one of many examples, largely unknown, of how people of color used protest and direct action as a crowbar into public debate and to challenge the logic of these enduring arguments.

The Young Lords returned to the church on Sunday, December 21. COIN-TELPRO documents note that they were not allowed to speak and that at the end of the service they took their message outside into the icy December cold, where Felipe Luciano gave a moving speech next to the church.[71] "The parishioners have not stayed. . . . So, basically, we're talking to ourselves," he said. Luciano's speech expressed a range of emotions: an earnest commitment to the idea of a beloved community and a sense that the parishioners were betraying the young. "They turn their backs on babies . . . turn their backs on young people who are saying to them, yes, we agree, you are our mothers and fathers, yes, we want to work in cooperation with you."

Those witnessing the conflict might well have marveled at the role reversal orchestrated by the Young Lords. Luciano warned, "The problems of this world, much less East Harlem, will not be solved by people being adamant, being like stones. They will be resolved when you are open, when you are flexible, when you are receptive in some way. All we are asking for is for them to allow our babies—not mine, our babies—call it socialism if you want—to allow our babies to come inside and eat a hot breakfast."[72]

According to Luciano, the FSUMC congregation adopted "the whole American scene of vertical mobility, that you move out of the problem of the ghetto, you move out of the sensitivity that you once had." He linked their world view to that of the "Sadducees and the Pharisees . . . the elders of the tribe of Israel" whom Jesus condemned and, citing Matthew 21:12, reminded his audience that "[Jesus] actually went into the church and beat them! And you talk about us being violent . . . he told them, 'Get out of here you moneylenders, you are filth! All you are thinking of is filthy lucre, you are not thinking about the spirit of the law.'"[73]

To Luciano, the problem of want in East Harlem was inextricably tied to the spiritual crisis among Puerto Ricans produced by colonial subjugation on their island nation. Central to the project of Puerto Rican spiritual salvation, in his view, was ensuring that "our babies understand the nature of imperialism, understand the true nature of their country, Puerto Rico, understand the independence movement in Puerto Rico. We have Puerto Rican children who don't know who their revolutionary heroes are, who don't know their language, who do not know their culture, and we will die."[74] Felipe's speech on repression and political economy is an example of oratory elevated to art. His remarks inspired participants to stay the course and more. Impassioned, emotional, vulnerable, and honest, moments like these conveyed the humanism of socialist politics and presented a portrait of Puerto Ricans diametrically opposed to their one-dimensional portrayals in the media.

Violent police repression at their protests and potential fatalities weighed heavily on the Young Lords' collective conscience. They told the press that they "did not seek confrontations with the police, because that would be tantamount to suicide."[75] In an interview with El Diario La Prensa, Luciano explained that the Young Lords "never threatened anyone with physical violence. We don't carry weapons. The funds we use for our programs are obtained through private donations. The food we distribute during our children's breakfast programs we obtain through written requests to the chain stores that benefit from the Puerto Rican community that buys their products."[76]

In the context of the recent assassination of Fred Hampton, death was a real possibility for these radicals. Their only protection was broad public support.

Hundreds rallied in their support since December 7, and thousands were following the story closely, quietly rooting for the team with the purple berets. With his right arm in a cast and a patch on his head, Luciano appealed to Young Lords supporters to commit to what he believed would be a protracted struggle:

> The Young Lords will not be moved. We may lose your support, we don't know.... With the first fires of enthusiasm, everyone is in the church [but] as time begins to pass, support begins to peter out. But we're going to stay here. We want you here because ... you are going to keep us from getting killed. And don't take it lightly.... I don't know how I'll be able to live if one of our people is killed.... What do you tell a mother whose 15 year old boy, who is a member of the Young Lords, is killed by a .38 Smith-Wesson bullet. What do you tell her? He died for the revolution? ... All she sees is the loss of her son.... That's why we need you here.[77]

The COINTELPRO informant for that day reported that the Young Lords participated in the services and their demonstration ended "in a peaceful manner" with "no incidents or arrests."[78]

The Offensive

On Sunday, December 28, the Young Lords leadership placed children at the helm of a silent procession. It began just outside their office and marched into the chapel of the FSUMC.[79] The scene mirrored the controversial use of children protesters in Birmingham six years earlier, which galvanized support for the civil rights movement globally when the city's public safety commissioner fire-hosed, unleashed dogs on, and jailed many of the children.[80] In both sites the symbolic participation of youngsters reflected the movements' hopes for a better society.

At the East Harlem church, the Young Lords arrived early and sat quietly in the pews. It seemed a reprise of previous exchanges. At the end of the service, the Young Lords' minister of education, Juan González, rose to address the congregation. As if on cue, the group's defense committee also stood and with railroad spikes nailed shut the church doors from the inside.[81] As the Young Lords moved to consolidate their position, parishioners turned their heads in dread, and an ominous pall befell the room.[82] González announced that the Young Lords were occupying the building and that the pastor was to blame. Carmen Pietri recalls an exchange with Juan González. When she asked what was going on, he responded: "We're not talking any more. No more dialogue." She was devastated because in an earlier meeting at the Young Lords' office, when the group proposed a church occupation, the church youth argued against it, and the Young Lords assured them that they would not occupy the building.

Uncertain of "what was going to happen," Carmen later described the congregation's detention as a traumatic moment. Meanwhile, the eyes of judgment focused on the church youth: "Mira, te lo dije, mira lo que esos peluses le están haciendo a la iglesia." (Look at what's happening, we told you! Look at what those kids with the Afros are doing to the church.) Joe Pietri remembers that Juan "Fi" Ortiz yelled out from the altar that the FSUMC was now rechristened the People's Church.[83]

Others soon arrived with reinforcement "tools of the occupation," including martial arts nunchaku sticks for defense in case of a police attack.[84] That morning, Bella August, the trusted white supporter and psychology doctoral student at Metropolitan Hospital who participated in the Lead Offensive, was sent on a blind mission to the Young Lords' office, where Denise Oliver gave her materials to deliver to the church at a designated time. Like a *santera* priestess, Oliver placed chains over Bella's head and around her neck. But unlike the colorful beaded necklaces of Yoruba initiation ceremonies, these were steel industrial chains, concealed by her heavy coat. As Bella walked to the church she thought longingly about her own daughter and feared the violence that might befall the radicals if they chose to use these chains in battle. She was ushered through the one door that had not been nailed shut. As instructed, she handed the chains to Mickey Melendez. To her immense relief, he clarified how they would be used.[85] Like the autoworkers in Flint, Michigan who worked at the General Motors Fisher Body Plant, occupied the factory and welded steel frames around each of its doors in 1936 during the first sit-down strike in U.S. history, the Young Lords reinforced the nailed church doors with chains to block the police.[86]

So began the Young Lords' Church Offensive.

Nailing shut the FSUMC doors was both sacrilegious and liberatory. The nailing of the doors recalled the suffering of Jesus on the cross and the FSUMC's collective penance for straying from the path of God. To the Methodist leadership and to Carrazana, these developments signaled a violation of constitutionally protected religious freedom that evoked the moment in 1680 when Puritan authorities nailed shut the doors of a Baptist church in Boston. To others, the Young Lords' actions might well have evoked the moment when Martin Luther launched the reformation by nailing his Ninety-Five Theses to a church in Wittenberg, Germany.

The Young Lords invited the parishioners to stay and join their revolutionary ministering that evening. But the parishioners wanted out. Within an hour, those who wished to leave the building exited through the single, manned door that throughout the occupation remained accessible for those who wished to leave. The Young Lords also shepherded children out of the building. By then, they had negotiated an agreement: the pastor, who was in close contact with the NYPD, assured the Young Lords there would be no police raid. The activists' demands now included a space for a liberation school and a daycare center; they stated that they would leave only after officials granted them space to feed free breakfast to approximately fifty to seventy-five children. As parishioners filed out and walked down the church steps, about thirty-five remained outside singing hymns in Spanish.[87] They joined a growing crowd on Lexington Avenue, where police had shut down traffic, to witness an occupation of a place of worship by a group of Puerto Rican radicals.

The church occupation risked widespread condemnation by churchgoing residents of East Harlem. But the Young Lords' graceful execution thrust the organization into the national spotlight and highlighted its nerve and the political savvy of the group. The success of their occupation depended on a sophisticated deconstruction of church ideology. Aware of the potential backlash in a predominantly churchgoing community of recent migrants, the Young Lords prepared to make their case to the community. Led by Pablo Guzmán, later that afternoon—and every morning thereafter for the duration of the occupation—they held a press conference in the main chapel to keep the community abreast of their activities. At the press conference, Juan González called on his ten years' Catholic alter-boy service to elevate their message in the battle of ideas. Citing scripture, he argued that the East Harlem church had forgotten the teachings of the historic Jesus:

> It's just incredible to us how a simple thing like a request to grant a space has resulted in so much trouble in East Harlem. Our only understanding of it is that religion, organized religion has so enslaved our people, has so destroyed their minds in thinking of salvation in the hereafter, that they refuse to deal with the conditions they have now and the oppression they have now. . . . It's amazing to us how people can talk about Jesus who walked among the poor, the poorest, the most oppressed, the prostitutes, the drug addicts of his time; that these people who claim to be Christian have forgotten that it was Jesus who said that it is easier for a camel to pass through the eye of a needle than for a rich man to enter the Kingdom of Heaven.[88]

From the Young Lords' perspective, nailing the church doors inverted the public crucifixion of Jesus, the revolutionary and political prisoner who led a movement of the poor that challenged the power of the Roman Empire, its colonial rule of Palestine, and the corruption, wealth, and power of local elites. Under the Young Lords' leadership, the church would be open to grassroots communion, led by the oppressed, and driven by a commitment to the material and spiritual well-being of the surrounding community. This reimagining of the church's role was already a movement in Latin America. There, it embodied the teachings of the Brazilian teacher and philosopher Paulo Freire, who sought to find practical applications of the teachings of Frantz Fanon, the Martinican psychiatrist and fierce defender of the Algerian Revolution. Fanon's theoretical writings on colonialization's impact on the colonized transformed the canon of Western social and political thought.[89] At the press conference, the Young Lords called on New Yorkers to support and participate in their daily medley of activities at the church, including a medical clinic, a lead and anemia testing drive, the free children's breakfast program, a series of political education classes, and nightly cultural events. By merging militant action with projects that prefigured a new socialist society in the present, the Young Lords, like the Black Panthers, expanded the vision and work of the U.S. revolutionary Left.

Mayor John V. Lindsay immediately deployed an aide to the scene. According to Sid Davidoff, the mayor's field manager, the occupation presented Lindsay with a significant challenge. With media buzzing around the church, news of another bloody scene with protesters and police would surely travel around the world. It would damage the image of his liberal administration and his aspirations to higher office. There were also false rumors that the Young Lords were holding a priest hostage, even though Reverend Carrazana had left the church of his own accord. The mayor wanted to intervene personally, but Davidoff advised against it.

Over the course of the many conflicts of the late 1960s, the mayor's team had developed a policy of working with municipal representatives whom aggrieved parties "could recognize" and relate to. Davidoff suggested that Arnie Segarra, the mayor's Puerto Rican aide and ambassador in the Puerto Rican community, "go in there and begin a negotiation."[90] Segarra had been among a small group of young men who attempted to redirect and quell the violence of the East Harlem riots of 1967.[91] That Segarra was also "tall . . . and an extremely good-looking guy" whom "women loved" made his identity as a local sports hero turned political insider even more alluring.[92] Segarra was joined by Rev. Norman Eddy, the director of the Interfaith Council of Churches located near Columbia University.[93]

Given that Segarra had corresponded with the Young Lords earlier during the Garbage Offensive, he was able to talk his way into the church with a portable phone powered by a mammoth battery pack. Davidoff reported sending Segarra in with clear instructions: "When you go into that situation you get the lay of the land, ten minutes to fifteen minutes. You call out. Tell me what it is I need to start working on." However, in the course of discussion between the Young Lords and Segarra, the unexpected happened. Davidoff reported: "A half hour goes by, forty minutes go by and I finally get him on the two-way and I said, 'What the fuck are you doing there? What is going on?' He says, 'We're talking.' I say, 'What are you talking about?' He says, 'Well I think they're right and I'm staying here with them.' I couldn't believe this was happening to me. This was the worst day of my life. I didn't even know what they were right about. At which point I said, 'Arnie, you're fired. If I ever see you again, I'll probably arrest you if I can figure out how to do it.'"[94]

When media outlets asked how they would respond to a police siege or a court injunction, minister of information Pablo Guzmán replied, "We will do whatever is tactically sound."[95] According to COINTELPRO documents, a press conference the following day in the basement of the church was "covered by three TV networks, Associated Press, United Press, and local newspapers."[96]

At one of the press conferences, Guzmán proclaimed that the Young Lords "were one with the Cuban revolution" and supported independence for all Latin American countries and the building of a socialist society.[97] Guzmán continued, "Even though we're revolutionaries, what we do we do with love; to a lot of people there is a contradiction between love and revolution, but Che Guevara said true revolution is guided by feelings of love."[98]

Holding It Down

The Young Lords' high-profile actions at the East Harlem church drew a steady stream of media coverage spotlighting facets of Puerto Rican life previously unseen by most New Yorkers. Video clips and images on the evening news and in newspapers captured the Young Lords' impassioned project and political vision. They called their occupation the Church Offensive, which, like the Garbage Offensive, nodded to the National Liberation Front's 1968 Tet Offensive in Vietnam. The action evidenced the group's power to quickly shift public discourse through strategic messaging and deliberate leveraging of the era's new media. Interlaced with the teachings of the historic Jesus, their compelling narrative blamed capitalism, colonialism, and complicit church establishments for social problems and in the process dislodged culture-of-poverty theories from local discourse.

Inside the occupied church, the Young Lords' programs held wide appeal. They collaborated with professionals and community residents to feed, heal, and educate the people. From clergymen and elected officials to pop stars and civic leaders, the controversy drew diverse voices into the fray. It propelled multiple generations of Puerto Ricans out of the shadows and into the public square, at the church and beyond—a grassroots awakening that cohered self-definition for many and strengthened the place of Puerto Ricans in the polity.

Images projected in the mainstream media were radical. They unseated long-standing distortions of Puerto Ricans as junkies, knife-wielding thugs, welfare dependents, and violent rioters. Sustained for weeks after the occupation's end, these new representations helped civilize New Yorkers' perceptions of the city's second-largest racialized group. The church occupation was part of a diverse wave of actions by New Left activists of color across the country that changed the way overt manifestations of racism came to be viewed in U.S. society—one of the major sociocultural imprints of the 1960s movements on American history.

The waves of reporters, curious visitors, East Harlem residents, police informants, Young Lords supporters, and self-appointed interlocutors that visited the church first had to pass muster at the front door. Members of the YLO's security ministry were stationed there in shifts and at each of the nailed doors. They searched for weapons and drugs and outlined the occupation's protocols. Visitors were asked to respect the altar and spaces of worship, to exercise care with the furniture and in common spaces, and to refrain from behavior that could be construed as desecrating the church. Smoking was not allowed inside. Most who entered availed themselves of the Young Lords' services or delivered food, medical supplies, books, posters, flyers, or piles of clothing, which the group requested for distribution to the community. The group's military-style occupation involved a complex operation requiring high levels of strategy, organization, and discipline. From their daily briefings and their twenty-four-hour security detail to the consolidation of a support network and preparations for their daily health, education, and children's breakfast programs, the Young Lords' operation was meticulously well thought out.

By day, the church had the feel of a well-run school and hospital. Even critical accounts of the occupation lauded the discipline of the group's daily routine: "At the end of each afternoon regular activity stopped and all the hands (including visitors) were put to work mopping and cleaning the premises."[99] The *New York Post* reported that the Young Lords "held the church like a fort."[100] One of the dozens of letters the Young Lords wrote and delivered to local shop owners requesting food donation for the breakfast program gives a sense of their methodical approach and organizational capacity. In it, Young Lord Hiram Maristany writes, "Unfortunately we did not receive a responce [*sic*] to our letter. Since it has been over Two (2) weeks, we are again writing to you because we would appreciate an answer in order to meet with you to relate our program to you first hand."[101]

They kept passersby informed with a loudspeaker affixed to the building's exterior on which they played the speeches of Malcolm X, Pedro Albizu Campos, and Fred Hampton, among others, interspersed with political music. This included Eddie Palmieri's "Justicia," whose lyrics demanded justice for Puerto Ricans and black Americans; the pro-independence music of Pepe y Flora; and Daniel Santos's banned nationalist album, *Grito de Lares*.[102] The press referenced the Impressions' "Mighty, Mighty, Spade and Whitey."[103] Written by Curtis Mayfield, the song's bold lyrics warned against American global power and the consequences of racial polarization domestically. Although the Young Lords defended black power for its assertion of black human dignity in the face of supremacist calls for white power, the song's refrain must have spoken to the group's experience at the margins of the country's rigid race paradigm: "And mighty, mighty, spade and whitey / your black and white power / is gonna be a crumbling tower."

Midway through the occupation, an in-depth radio segment produced by KPFA in Berkeley, California, reported that the Young Lords had provided hundreds of free meals to children. It took its listeners behind the scenes of the operation. Young Lord Luis Nuñez, a former Vietnam medic, ran the kitchen in the occupied church; he explained that the Young Lords' health ministry consulted with nutritionists who set "standards" on the "right amount of starch, vitamins, and nutrients" of every meal, including for the signature children's breakfast program. Their objective was to offer poor children the dignity and satisfaction of eating like "a rich man" and the "chance to feel what it's like to eat bacon and eggs and juice and cocoa and bread and jelly and all sorts of things that they don't get at home."[104] In New York, both the Young Lords and Black Panthers were known for serving bacon, which many poor children and their families considered a treat.[105] The print media reported that the Young Lords had performed for children "a revised miracle of the loaves and fishes."[106] The program included an early morning political education class geared to children and their parents.[107]

After breakfast, the Young Lords prepared for an inflow of East Harlem visitors seeking medical care at the church's free health clinic or screening for tuberculosis, anemia, and childhood lead poisoning. The improvised clinic was staffed by approximately two dozen progressive doctors, nurses, medical technicians, and interns and residents from nearby Metropolitan Hospital—among them its chief medical resident, Gene Straus.[108] These included some of the same medical professionals with whom the Young Lords conducted the door-to-door medical visits discussed in the previous chapter, and others, such as Dr. Richard Stone, were assigned to the church by the hospital as a concession to the Young Lords.[109] The operation offered this medical cohort the rare opportunity to erect and manage community-based medical care that implemented protocols for personalized patient treatment. Counterposed to the impersonal, high-volume atmosphere of a large hospital, the change of venue alone facilitated a more humane exchange between patient and doctor.

Liberation School

In the evenings, the Young Lords ran a liberation school. The experience and skill sets of key members facilitated its development. Denise Oliver, for example, had been a full-time instructor at the University of the Streets, an antipoverty project for high school dropouts, and Iris Morales and Juan González had previously developed an internal, thirteen-week political education curriculum for the group's membership.[110] Set on the larger and more dynamic stage of the occupation, the school challenged the group to diversify the content and format of its political message. Puerto Rican and black American history anchored the curriculum. In their quest to debunk Eurocentrism, the Young Lords highlighted the significance of people of color the world over as agents of change, emphasizing the struggle against U.S. imperialism in Puerto Rico and the history of black resistance. They responded to the failure of public school curricula to make sense of the socioeconomic troubles of East Harlem by instructing on current events. They also examined negative media representations of Puerto Ricans and black Americans as criminals and welfare dependents. Screenings and discussions of such films as Gillo Pontecorvo's *The Battle of Algiers* also formed part of the evening education routine.[111]

Pastor Carrazana saw the school as a personal affront. New York's Methodist Church leaders deemed its communist-inflected instruction irreconcilable with Christianity and one of the clearest expressions of the occupation's violation of the constitutionally protected right to religious freedom.[112] Rev. Robert Chapman denounced this narrow legal interpretation of the conflict as "self-interested" and one that church officials did not believe themselves. Criticizing its underlying assumption—that "the church and politics exist on separate planets"—he underscored the conditions that brought the school into being: the systematic erasure in public education of the history and culture of "non-white American ethnic and racial groups." The reverend drew out the human consequences. He wrote: "Its practice is psychological genocide, in that its implications, to such groups, are: a) you really do not exist, or [if you exist] b) you have no worth at all and, c) the only value you can have as a person is attained when you absorb what we are, and become like us. . . . Even if it had an honest intention so to do, however, the offer would be profane, since a man's worth is in what he essentially is, in and of himself, not in and as someone else."[113]

Reverend Chapman observed further that while the conditions that fueled the Young Lords' actions might have been beyond the experiential comprehension of the Cuban pastor, the church had abdicated its higher responsibilities. Its posture, in fact, contributed to the "continuation of the crushing of humanity." By contrast, the liberation school offered an antidote to such dehumanization through explicit analyses of poverty and racism and recovery of the histories, cultures, and struggles of the dispossessed.[114] The reverend, thus, defended the Young Lords' right "to teach their reasons why Puerto Rico should remain free from United States statehood . . . and what America is functionally, rather than rhetorically, to Puerto Ricans, and to other non-white peoples at home and abroad."[115]

To those confronting oppression the world over, the transmission and production of knowledge had become as integral to the contest for power and dignity as strategies of resistance and war. The school proved to be one of the most controversial initiatives, arguably for rendering analyses of history at odds with canonical interpretations and dominant ideology and for flouting academic conventions regulating the instruction and production of knowledge. It also unleashed a public debate beyond the question of where children should go to school or who should control school curriculum and the staff hiring. The term "liberation" itself raised uncomfortable questions about the "American Creed." The real danger, Reverend Chapman warned, lay in the consequences of *not* finding systemic solutions to these problems: the failure to grant oppressed groups "self-respect, self-definition and dignity" would lead America to enact "more repressive measures against them . . . [and] to consider the final solution to her racial problem."[116] With the advent of hyper-incarceration of these communities, the reverend's predictions were not off the mark.

Staging a Nuyorican Identity

At 6:00 P.M. each evening, the Young Lords served dinner prepared by local Puerto Rican women, including some of their mothers, who brought pots of food or cooked meals. After 7:30, Young Lords discipline surrendered to creative revelry. Audible from a block away, the captivating sound of conga drums beckoned visitors to the church after work. Inside, the infectious rhythm of *bomba y plena*— the battle music of the occupation—aroused spontaneous eruptions of song and dance. Derived from the experiences of African slaves and their descendants, Puerto Rican elites stigmatized these popular music genres for their historic associations with black people, "lax" morals, and biting political commentary.[117]

Older Puerto Ricans recalled that this public embrace of their folk music by the younger generation triggered complex feelings: longing for the old country and vindication of their lives in New York.[118] And for the children of the Puerto Rican migration who grew up on the mainland, for whom institutionalized racism in the streets and schools distorted their self-perception, these sounds often tapped into the yearning for self-definition awakened by the black power movement. For the Young Lords, it was grounding music for their distinctive *bembé*, an all-out celebration of Puerto Rican folk traditions and emerging urban art forms at the church.

The Young Lords launched their cultural experiment amid protests against racist representations of people of color in museums and the exclusion of black American and Puerto Rican artists from New York's elite art world. That January, black American artists were swept into protesting the Metropolitan Museum's high-profile exhibition *Harlem on My Mind*, a voyeuristic rendering of black life that excluded works by black artists and whose catalogue featured an incendiary term paper written by a black high school student two years earlier.[119] By year's end, the Young Lords were curating vanguard elements of Puerto Rican cultural expression at the People's Church. The inadvertent evolution of the church into an unorthodox art space responded to the era's demand for civil rights in the arts. It did so with a dynamic model of resistance, art making, and cultural engagement that augured a new direction in the movement to democratize the arts in New York. Committed to demystifying and democratizing art, the Young Lords also welcomed impromptu performances and fostered a fluid environment that blurred the line between artist and audience. Chairman Felipe Luciano had long nurtured an interest in the arts. Respected for his broad and eclectic cultural knowledge, he was one of the original members of the Last Poets, the group of spoken word artists and musicians whose creative work prefigured the emergence of hip-hop.[120] The Lords approached these evenings with sensitivity, helping to foster the works of a new generation of Puerto Rican poets, musicians, artists, and writers.

The lineups often sparked impromptu collaboration across genres. Traditional Puerto Rican drummers seated in the audience often jumped into the fray with impromptu drumming cadences, adding unexpected dimensions to the heft of an emerging urban poetry. Spoken word poetry captured the essence of things with an economy of words, illuminated social relations, and aroused passions. Politicized by the world around them, artists had begun to rearrange reality with the symbols and music of Puerto Rico's resilient Afro-indigenous heritage. Their renderings of joy and tragedy in Puerto Rican life captured an aesthetic—decades in the making—wrought of the crucible of Puerto Rican migration to New York. These high-energy, open-mike jams captured the "structure of feeling" of the children of that migration who were swept into political activism by the civil rights, black power, women's, and gay liberation movements, the Vietnam War, and the social fallout of their parents' dislocation from Puerto Rico to U.S. slums. It was here that playwright and poet Pedro Pietri gave the first public reading of "Puerto Rican Obituary," the poem that according to the *New York Times* "ignited a movement."[121] The poem is an epic eulogy to Puerto Rican workers and a withering critique of class that tracks the illusory pursuit of the American Dream. Its snapshots of everyday working-class Puerto Rican life dramatize the soul-slaying consequences of obedience to authority:

They worked . . .
They were never late
They never spoke back . . .
They never went on strike
Without permission . . .

They Worked
Ten days a week
And were only paid for five . . .

————

Juan
Miguel
Milagros
Olga
Manuel
All died yesterday today
And will die tomorrow
Passing their bill collectors
On to the next of kin . . .
All died
Dreaming about america . . .
Hating the grocery stores
That sold them make-believe
steak
And bullet-proof rice and beans
All died waiting dreaming
and hating
Dead Puerto Ricans
Who never knew they were Puerto Ricans . . .

————

. . . And will die again tomorrow
Dreaming about Queens
Clean-cut lily white
Neighborhood . . .

————

They all died
Like a hero sandwich dies
In the garment district
At twelve o'clock in the
Afternoon . . .

In naming his subjects, Pietri dignified the city's most demeaned workers and reclaimed their humanity; the ritual repetition of names in the text compels recognition on different terms. His depiction of Puerto Rican migration as a kind of collective death, a universal theme, opened new ways of seeing Puerto Ricans among New Yorkers and others around the world, who accessed the poem through its several translations into Spanish, Italian, and German, among other languages. "Puerto Rican Obituary" also unmasked with levity the unconscious handiwork of dominant ideology and its influence on individual and group behavior and perceptions of reality.[122] Pietri's vision ends with an ode to the humanistic aspirations of Afro–Puerto Rican resistance:

Aquí que pasa Power is
what's happening
Aquí to be called Negrito y
Negrita
Means to be called LOVE.

The outpouring of performances of works like "Puerto Rican Obituary" on makeshift stages across the country produced yet deeper changes. They destabilized traditional conceptions of cultural production and one of its major assumptions: that people of color produce lower forms of art. And among poor people of color who might not have seen themselves as artists, performances like these emboldened their creative urges, especially in the context of the Young Lords' revolutionary politics. At its best, the People's Church prefigured the many possibilities for the arts in a new society: that a radical redistribution of time and resources could unleash the creative capacity of all. This expansive vision of art making, however short-lived, also broadened the narrow framework of civil rights in the arts and helped redefine the goals of a preexisting cohort of activist artists toward independent art spaces and institution building. The Young Lords catalyzed the work of artists who grasped the significance of art, both as expression of humanity and potential vehicle of resistance. Together they understood that the politics of cultural production—of who has access to it and who doesn't, of representations of subjugated people in art, and the absence of some artists and not others in the art world—is bound up with the struggle for human liberation.

The Young Lords' mixture of militancy, good works, political education, and cultural resistance had an observable impact on diverse sectors of the city. One mainstream report observed that the occupation "reached like a wave to the margins of society, even affecting some of the street gangs in Harlem, as in Chicago."[123] As the focal point of public debate on the Puerto Rican question, the occupation resuscitated the Puerto Rican pro-independence movement in New York. Its leaders now appreciated the possibility for growth among the children of Puerto Rican migrants. Many who did not agree with the full extent of the Young Lords' Third World, socialist, revolutionary orientation supported them nonetheless. At least sixty-three cross-denominational ecumenical leaders representing "national church agencies" endorsed their projects in a public letter. Addressed to Dr. Wesley Osborne, the district superintendent of the FSUMC, the letter also demanded a response to "the social crisis by means other than alli-

Phalanx of marchers in the Puerto Rican Day Parade, June 7, 1970. Front line from left: Young Lords Mickey Melendez and Carlos Aponte. (Photograph by Librado Romero/New York Times; courtesy of the *New York Times*)

ance with the State through court and police action."[124] Another twenty Puerto Rican leaders and antipoverty and community organizations backed the group's actions in a public statement.

The Young Lords enjoyed strong support among New Left activists. Members of the branches of the BPP were among the approximately 150 activists who permanently rotated in and out of the church. Student Nonviolent Coordinating Committee member H. Rap Brown visited and spoke at the church, as did national BPP leader Kathleen Cleaver.[125] Read by West Coast attorney Charles Garry, Huey P. Newton's solidarity greeting "thrilled the packed chapel with clenched fists raised in spread-armed salute."[126] Acting independently of the Young Lords, students from Columbia University and Union Theological Seminary staged a twenty-four-hour sit-in at Osborne's office demanding that the Puerto Rican radicals be granted space there. A long list of celebrities made appearances, among them film director Elia Kazan, screenwriter Budd Schulberg, boxer José Torres, actor Jane Fonda, writer Gloria Steinem, and rising salsa stars Joe Cuba, Joe Batan, and Ray Barretto.[127] And while the Puerto Rican theater actor Rita Moreno did not make an appearance, she sent funds.[128]

The occupation transformed the organizational character of the Young Lords. The group experienced significant membership growth, especially among women. At the same time, female members were drawn into the center of church operations. Their deeper engagement with politics as public speakers and development as leaders raised questions about the place of women in movements for social change. Many in the community, including leading members of the organization, believed that revolutionary behavior was tolerable in a young man but not in a young woman. Many parents of YLO members did not support their children's actions at the church. A disproportionate number of these parents had daughters in the organization, who were taken out of the church "by their ears."[129] As discussed in the following chapters, the growth of women's membership and leadership during the occupation accelerated a major political rift.

For others, like the handsome and charismatic Richie Perez, the church was the place where they found meaning and purpose beyond personal relationships. According to Richie, the night he came to the church he had been out dancing. His political work had been stymied up to that moment by a series of unfulfilling amorous relationships. That night he found his political home and with it, more stability in his personal life.[130] Gloria Rodriguez's tear-filled account captures what many Puerto Rican youth felt at the church: "I walked in and I felt like I was home. It was very gripping, it felt like that was where I really wanted to be [and] where I belonged. . . . [T]he concerns . . . that all these people had, about equal rights and . . . making a difference in the world and standing up for what they believe in and being really committed—that moved me. It moved everything I felt I was about at that time."[131] Some other participants fell in love. Discussing the broader significance of his story of love during the church occupation, Rovira explains: "When you go into the world of the unknown and there is a risk component, you grow attached to people, you build bonds. And that worked to our favor because it did not allow the police state to intimidate us at all. The bonds we built is what gave us strength. And for a group whose oldest member was twenty-five years old, for that chemistry to happen to people of that age group is a big positive, because there is nothing the enemy could have done to intimidate us."[132]

Bunkered in amid popular support and positive media reviews, the Young Lords would not be intimidated by the threat of a police break-in or legal action. Although Reverend Carrazana had allowed the police to lead negotiations at the start of the conflict, now they were held at bay. On various occasions, the NYPD "sent their officers to the door; telling us in detail what would happen to us legally if we continued the occupation . . . that you can do ten years in prison if you don't come out. They tried it all and it didn't work."[133]

In Legal Limbo

On Tuesday, December 30, the church obtained a court order requiring the Young Lords' attorney to appear before the New York Supreme Court the next day to "show cause why they should not be ousted from the church."[134] The order was served late in the afternoon, allowing their attorneys to postpone the hearing, arguing that it "was received too late to adequately prepare for the case."[135] With the New Year holiday upon them, the Young Lords could continue their political revelry at the church. Their attorneys argued that they were upholding one of the major tenets of the Methodist Church, service to the community, which the FSUMC had renounced in East Harlem. Reinforcing this position, a Young Lords flyer distributed that day stated, "The first responsibility of the church is to the people. The church is supposed to serve the people . . . and work with them. This is what it means to be Christian."[136]

On Friday, January 2, the hearing's presiding judge, Hyman Korn, concluded that the church occupation, "even for what [participants] consider laudable purposes, tends to a breach of the peace and impinges on the sanctity of this holy space."[137] He granted the church a preliminary injunction ordering the Young Lords to end the occupation. Served to the Young Lords at approximately 5:30 P.M., it was read aloud on the church steps by Sheriff Robert E. Lee. His Confederate namesake struck the Young Lords and their supporters as downright comical.

Taking advantage of their weekend reprieve, the Young Lords held another news conference on Saturday, January 3. The *New York Times* quoted Juan González: "We are all presently in contempt of court—all of us, including you press men." González then asked, "Why then have we not been arrested?" He answered, "Because the power of the Puerto Rican community outside of the church and the three hundred people that occupied the church last night are preventing the city from moving against us."[138] According to the *New York Post*, González also announced that the Young Lords had no intention of leaving the church until their demands were met and that "no injunction and no police clubs will stop us."[139] The Young Lords were in contempt of court, but the church would have to seek a "contempt citation against the Young Lords for non-compliance" before police could go in.[140]

On Sunday, January 4, the Young Lords opened the church for regular Sunday service. A small number of congregants attended, most of whom were among the church's youngest members. Board members argued that the Young Lords' claim that they allowed the congregation "to worship at the sufferance of a take-over group is sinister behavior."[141] But the church's youth group thought differently;

on that day, the two young women who led the youth group, Nancy Vasquez and Carmen Pietri, presided at the liturgy with the participation of Joe, Frank, and Pedro Pietri.[142] Carmen remembers that day well because she was ill, and before the services began Juan González led her to one of the church's health stations where on-call doctors treated her. In attendance were Puerto Rican community leaders and representatives of antipoverty organizations who had written a public letter in support of the Young Lords. Because removal of the Young Lords seemed imminent, these supporters sought to bring moral and political influence to bear for a peaceful resolution. Their statement was read by Lindsay's aide Arnie Segarra, whose firing had not yet been made public.[143]

The opening of the church for services that Sunday would prove advantageous in court. The church's attorney, Oscar González-Suarez, argued in the injunction request that the Young Lords' actions violated the constitutionally protected right to worship. This theme was developed in a statement released by Reverend Carrazana and the district leaders of the Methodist Church in New York, district superintendent Wesley Osborne and Bishop Lloyd Wicke. For these leaders, at issue was "whether this local congregation of Christians shall have the right to determine their own ministry and the programs to be operated in their own church."[144] The injunction request charged that "the defendants have threatened the peace and tranquility of the congregation and the community" and deprived the congregation of "its civil rights and the constitutional right to peacefully assemble and worship God according to their conscience."[145]

On Monday, January 5, the church's attorneys, in consultation with New York County sheriff De Lancey, obtained a court contempt order requiring representatives of the organization to appear in court the following morning.[146] In an affidavit challenging the church's application for a preliminary injunction, the Young Lords and their attorneys debunked charges that the group had for months "interrupted the religious services at the church." Had they been disruptive and unwelcome, the church would not have invited them and their supporters to a "'coffee klatch' with the pastor of the congregation and a few parishioners."[147] The deposition argued further that the Young Lords had been scapegoated by the church's lead minister and members of the board because "the Young Lords represent a serious threat to their conscience" and a challenge to the church to observe the Methodist Church's fundamental principle that "service to the people of the community is an important religious function, not to be ignored."[148] They quoted from the Methodist Social Creed found in *The Book of Discipline of the United Methodist Church*: "We believe the inner city to be a mission field crying out for bold new creative ways of witness. Here is emerging a pagan generation committed to values that run counter to those of Christ. Therefore we call our urban congregations to a deeper involvement in neighborhood life."[149] The Young Lords' attorneys also challenged charges of private property violation. Also citing the *Book of Discipline*, they suggested that for its failure to use private property in accordance with church doctrine, the church, not the Young Lords, should be held accountable for such a violation: "We believe God is the owner of all things and that the individual holding of property is lawful and a sacred trust under God. Private property is to be used for the manifestation of Christian love and liberality, and to support the Church's mission in the world. All forms of property, whether private, corporate or public, are to be held in solemn trust and used responsibly for human good under the sovereignty of God."[150]

On Tuesday, January 6, while legal procedures wound their way through the courts, the Young Lords tightened church security and celebrated Three Kings' Day, a major gift-giving event for children among Puerto Ricans. As Pablo Guzmán explained to the media, "This is a very important holiday in Puerto Rico and we are going to party. If the police come, we'll just continue partying. We're going to have folk dances and songs and experience our culture because that's what the Lords are all about."[151] The coincidence of Three Kings' Day with the end of their legal proceedings was a sign of things to come.

On that same day, a coalition of students from Union Theological Seminary and Columbia University met with Methodist bishop Lloyd Wicke to demand that the church drop the charges "against the 13 YLO members arrested on December 7, 1969," and that the church "furnish space to the Young Lords for their programs."[152] Knowing that their arrest was imminent, the Lords reported to the press that while "we may not open the doors" to the police, they would not resist arrest.[153] With public support from over twenty Puerto Rican leaders and antipoverty and community organizations, the Young Lords were about to leave the church on their own terms. Their attorneys and the sheriff's office arranged exactly what would happen.

At 5:30 A.M. on January 7, 1970, while a dusting of snow covered the ground, hundreds of riot-gear-clad police officers assumed positions on rooftops and in the area surrounding the church, which was closed to traffic. Inside, the Young Lords stood their ground. The presence of approximately twelve children and six attorneys who spent the night at the church was expected to safeguard against police violence.[154] Led by Undersheriff T. William Kehl, at around 7:00 A.M. eight unarmed deputies pried open the barricaded front doors. Two of the Young Lords' attorneys accompanied the deputies every step of the way. Once inside, Kehl informed the Young Lords that they were under arrest.

At approximately 7:15 A.M., 105 Young Lords and supporters walked out of the church, twenty at a time, and into police vans. Some of the militants exited the church singing the Puerto Rican nationalist song "Qué Bonita Bandera" (What a Beautiful Flag); others shouted "power to the people" on their way out; still others walked down the church steps in solemn silence with raised fists.

Police raid the First Spanish United Methodist Church on January 7, 1970, ending the occupation, which had begun on December 28, 1969. On the inside of the door, the Young Lords affixed a photo of the body of Ernesto "Che" Guevara, who in October 1967 was captured and killed by Bolivian military forces that had been trained and equipped by the U.S. Green Berets and CIA. (Courtesy of Associated Press)

They were transported to the courtroom of Justice Saul S. Streit in the New York Supreme Court building in downtown Manhattan.[155] In court the Young Lords performed an act that many of them would not have dared to enact as children. The *New York Times* reported that "as their names and addresses were called off, the Young Lords rose, many of them correcting the reader by giving the Spanish pronunciation of their names." Although the Young Lords had picked a fight with a conservative church over space for a breakfast program, the occupation was also about their determination to preserve their dignity, and that of their migrant parents, in the face of racism and language discrimination. The mangling of their names in school earlier in their lives, and the feeling that they were treated like garbage by the police, in hospitals, and by the administrative structure of the city was core to their organization's reason for being. And now as they stood before Justice Streit, they were intent on staging dissent and setting their names and identities straight for the court record.

The Young Lords' attorneys, Richard Asch and Daniel Meyers, explained that amid their round-the-clock negotiations with police, which ensured the peaceful arrest that morning, they had not had time to consult with the activists. The judge released all 105 defendants on their own recognizance and set their hearing for January 26, 1970.

■

For the Young Lords, the church became a staging ground for what a new society could look like and accomplish. They saw the services organized collaboratively for human need rather than competitively for profit, as a living example of the possibilities of a socialist society. Thousands took part, in some way, in the activities conducted at the church. Participants and reporters alike described the intoxicating atmosphere created by the Young Lords, with language echoing V. I. Lenin's description of revolutions as "festivals of the oppressed," during which ordinary people "come forward so actively as creators of a new social order."[156]

The United States in the late 1960s was in the midst of an all-sided upheaval of ideas: in the way the nation understood itself, in the place of racialized groups, women, and gays and lesbians within it, and in a halting but increasing recognition of the root causes of social problems. Throughout the decade, initiatives like the Young Lords' Church Offensive pressed a debate about the nation's social priorities and the contradictions of American democracy. At the heart of this public struggle were the children of Puerto Rican migrants, whose work helped to cement a place for Puerto Ricans in public discourse and New York City politics.

As the dramatic site where the most political elements of Puerto Rican culture were curated for eleven days, the People's Church marked the first public staging of a Nuyorican identity and the idea of a radical Puerto Rican art space. Such a project would later be institutionalized in places like the New Rican

Village, a "cultural arts center" on the Lower East Side that showcased the first Nuyorican theatrical productions and was "home to Afro-Caribbean music's avant-garde."[157] The Nuyorican Poets Cafe grew from a gathering in the East Village apartment of Puerto Rican writer Miguel Algarin to a vibrant, New York City institution for the performing arts. El Museo del Barrio would become a major museum on Fifth Avenue dedicated to Latinx cultures. The church occupation also presaged the emergence of Las Casitas Criollas del Bronx, the cultural project that transformed abandoned Bronx homes into vibrant sites that evoked Puerto Rico's countryside aesthetic, music, and culture.[158]

The week after the arrests, several hundred Young Lords again attended Sunday mass at FSUMC, requesting permission to run a breakfast program. Carranza did not concede an inch. Shortly thereafter, eighty-four Protestant denomination leaders pressured the FSUMC to seek resolution with the Young Lords outside of the courts. To that end, the parties were brought together by the newly formed Board of Mediation for Community Disputes, a Lindsay initiative that brought collective bargaining strategies in labor to disputes in the community. With Herman Badillo as mediator, a series of long, heated meetings ensued. In late February, the church dropped charges against the Young Lords and agreed to initiate a daycare center and a clinic for a drug rehabilitation program, to which the city agreed to contribute $200,000. The church never followed through.[159]

When the Young Lords ended their Church Offensive, their spirits were high. The occupation had electrified the neighborhood, inspired artists and progressives of all races across the city, and drawn the media into the orbit of the Young Lords, with journalists around the country and the world reporting on their activities. On the same night that the Young Lords abandoned the church, Republican governor Nelson Rockefeller proposed during his State of the State address to launch a breakfast program for 35,000 poor children in the city. In response, Harlem's Democratic state senator Basil Paterson told the media, "I think the Black Panthers and the Young Lords have influenced the governor," whom he also condemned for not having any original proposals of his own.[160] Even the judge who forced the church's evacuation, after declaring the Young Lords in contempt of a court order, seemed to equivocate in his condemnation of the Puerto Rican radicals. Reporting for Pacifica Radio, journalist Jeff Kamen explained, "The judge was impressed by what the Young Lords had done for the people, so he released them on their own recognizance, without bail."[161] The attention the Young Lords garnered from different sectors of society, especially from the media, strengthened the organization's sense of itself and convinced its leaders that they could challenge the structures of power and win.

CHAPTER SEVEN

THE POLITICS AND CULTURE OF THE YOUNG LORDS PARTY

The Young Lords' headline-grabbing campaigns, staged so theatrically at the church, elevated the organization's profile to new heights. Yet along with their newfound star power, the Young Lords were now confronted with the challenge of hundreds of young people descending on their East Harlem office clamoring to join the popular revolutionaries with the purple berets. In the aftermath of the Church Offensive, journalist Jose Yglesias reported that the "rush thereafter by young Puerto Ricans to join the Lords—who will also accept non–Puerto Rican blacks from the Barrio—was so great that the organization has had to close its rolls temporarily."[1] By May 1970, the group had absorbed approximately 600 new members and thousands of Friends of the Lords and Lords in training.[2]

It was less than a year since the Young Lords had set out to build a vanguard revolutionary party of people of color. Organized in a paramilitary-styled structure, the party's charge was to agitate for reforms in the here and now, raise revolutionary consciousness, and discipline the organization for the advent of larger social struggles. They were guided by older political theories and also by the writings that emerged out of what came to be known as Third World revolutions for independence in Algeria, Vietnam, Cuba, Congo, and beyond.

These movements and others in the former colonial world were influenced in various degrees by Marxist ideas. At the same time, such movements had to define themselves in relation to less radical "bourgeois" nationalist currents. The theme that all addressed was opposition to European imperialism and the racist ideology that justified it.[3]

The Young Lords identified political education as a central task. Beginning in February 1970, the organization's Central Committee implemented a systematic training program for its rank and file on the history of the Puerto Rican independence movement and its lessons as well as on the theories and practices of

Iris Morales leads political education class. (Photograph by Michael Abramson; courtesy of Iris Morales)

the Marxist tradition.[4] To disseminate their ideas within the community and beyond, the Young Lords circulated their Thirteen-Point Program and Platform and their newspaper, *Palante*. Distributed in mimeographed form in the fall of 1969, the paper was transformed after the Church Offensive.[5] The group also launched a radio show, *Palante*, on Pacifica Radio's WBAI.

New York City's postwar structural and demographic changes fueled the organization's decision to make community organizing, rather than workplace organizing, its focal point. The politics and community-based organizing of the Young Lords, together with those of other 1960s radicals of color, had reconfigured the racial composition of the U.S. socialist Left. The Young Lords' adaptation of Third World revolutionary politics and rhetoric to the U.S. urban context created a culture of resistance with iconic power. The style and charisma associated with the Young Lords made socialist organizations attractive to thousands of young people of color in America's slums. This was the first time in the

United States that *influential* socialist organizations were launched, led, and built from the bottom up by young, poor, and working-class people of color.

New Recruits

The weeks and months following the Church Offensive tested the Young Lords' mettle. Fame and notoriety brought new opportunities and challenges. The leadership worked to the brink of exhaustion to balance them. An exponential increase in inquiries and in-person requests swamped the Young Lords office. The police were interested in the goings-on too. Since the end of the Church Offensive, a police car had been permanently parked outside and visible from the ground-floor office window. Members were abuzz with tired excitement and nervous tension. Amid these changes, the Young Lords had to leave the comfort and intimacy of their small cohort—and the informality that their closeness fostered—to make room for an incoming wave of members on whom the future of the organization depended.

Becoming a Young Lord had never been an open process, but it had not been systematized either. The large influx of recruits compelled the organization to dust off its preexisting system for vetting and integrating new members. An interested individual would first become a "friend of the Lords" and then undergo a six-week trial period as a Lord in training (LIT), a method that the Panthers had borrowed from the Nation of Islam.[6] According to Richie Perez, the LIT process was about flagging potential government spies and testing a person's commitment: "You couldn't really be in this if you didn't believe in this. . . . It was a lot of hard work." The breakfast program was often the litmus test for determining a recruit's grit. An LIT had to "get up early in the morning, gather up the kids, take them to the place, feed them breakfast, take them to school and in between try to give them some political education and then those of us who had jobs, go to our own jobs, work our jobs, come back after that to sell newspapers in the afternoon and go to political education classes at night. Every day."

Graduation from LIT status was not always smooth—and not assumed. Leadership gave second chances to LITs with potential who, for personal reasons, did not complete the training. Just as important was the discipline and mentorship of the person in charge of the ministry to which a recruit was assigned. Over the life of the organization, much depended on "who was your supervisor and how diligent they were in moving people forward and how much [an individual] pushed. And sometimes there was inertia on both sides."[7] Recruits who passed LIT training became "cadre," an active, committed, and disciplined cohort of like-minded revolutionaries. Per the revolutionary party tradition, the cadre were trained to assess political conditions, implement a suitable practice of struggle, and build the organization. In the Young Lords, a distinction was made between "leadership" and "cadre." Promotion involved moving through the ranks of lieutenant, captain, deputy minister, and minister.

New Young Lords were funneled into a complex organizational terrain. They faced a daunting task: learning how to relate to the world in an entirely new way. Like many other 1960s radicals, the Young Lords lived communally, a signature element of the New Left's cultural imprint on its generation. The postwar expansion of the university had produced forms of collective living among proverbially poor college students enjoying life away from home. Among the politically active, it became a deliberate experiment that prefigured the new, communally organized society that radicals believed they would one day realize.[8] It also challenged the new forms of social organization produced by postwar suburbanization, private home ownership, and the nuclear family, which movement youth rejected as wasteful and oppressive.[9]

The arrangement was also expedient. It facilitated a lifestyle that helped sustain the exigencies of movement organizing. Most Young Lords were full-time members who dedicated all of their time to the organization, but that alone hardly conveyed the all-consuming nature of the commitment. The first item in the Young Lords' Rules of Discipline read, "You are a Young Lord 25 Hours a Day."[10] In other words, being a Young Lord was a way of life—filled as much with meaning and purpose as with nonstop activity and exhaustion. The work of the organization encompassed a vast array of mandatory, routine responsibilities: selling the group's newspaper and distributing other literature; writing for the paper and helping in its production; testing door to door for tuberculosis and lead poisoning; setting up breakfast programs and drug detoxification work; working double time during the organization's various offensives; and participating in internal political education meetings and ones organized for the community, including outdoor film screenings, which were often projected on the wall of a building.

Physical fitness was mandatory, given the group's paramilitary-styled structure. It was intended to prepare the Young Lords to defend themselves against police aggression as seen at the First Spanish United Methodist Church.[11] On a regular basis, members responded to community calls for translators and assistance at local police stations, schools, and welfare offices. They also responded to requests from schools for speakers and from organizers to send contingents to demonstrations and to lend security to the movement.

The Young Lords' dizzying productivity would not have been possible if the U.S. economy had not been strong. Even though a crisis was on the horizon in the late 1960s, American capitalism was riding the last waves of its golden age. Most Americans still enjoyed high purchasing power and relatively high minimum wages, which in 1969 peaked at what would be the equivalent of $10.39 in 2015 dollars. Combined, these conditions made full-time organizing affordable.

Coed communal living. (Courtesy of Henry Medina Archives)

Radicalized youth seized the opportunity to pour their energies into their goal of changing the world on fairly small stipends of sixty dollars a week.[12]

Most Young Lords lived frugally. They survived on the funds they collected from the sale of the organization's newspaper, half of which they kept for themselves.[13] Some Young Lords still lived with their parents and thus had minimal expenses. Few held full-time jobs. In accordance with the organization's rule, those who worked full-time contributed more than half of their salary to the organization and then went on to organize at night when they got home from work.[14] When necessary, the organization subsidized room and board. It set up a mess hall in a large apartment in a building it acquired sometime in 1970, at 75 East 110th Street. Members ate meals there, for free, at a long dinner table in shifts of twenty at a time.[15] One of the group's chief cooks, Vietnam veteran and Young Lord Julio Roldán, maximized his talents on behalf of the organiza-

tion. The new recruit "considerably improved the diet and reduced the cost of feeding full time workers in the organization."[16]

Guerrilla Style, Leninist Form

Other forces contributed to the organization's unusual output. The Young Lords demanded a high level of participation and commitment from its members. The Young Lords were building a revolutionary party, an assignment that 2 million students declared important during a national poll in 1969.[17] Success would require overcoming racism and ethnic divisions within the working class and the political influence of multiple anticommunist scares in the twentieth century. But by the mid-1960s, guerrillas had defeated or were defeating imperial powers from Cuba to Algeria and Vietnam.[18] These wars and revolutions against colonial rule were raising the possibility that Third World people might succeed at reorganizing society on a global scale. In the theater of war, the Tet Offensive's symbolic victory proved that the United States could be defeated by what President Johnson called "a raggedy ass little third-rate country."[19] The Tet Offensive also broadened the mutinous disposition of an ever-growing sector of U.S. soldiers.[20]

At home, the era's widespread political crises had eroded government authority and legitimacy. The body count among U.S. soldiers fueled opposition to the war and compelled young people to learn about U.S. foreign policy and the activities of the Central Intelligence Agency (CIA) that had overthrown governments and trained counterinsurgency forces to suppress popular movements abroad.[21] At home, the rebellions that swept through the cities like a hurricane exposed the entrenched character of racial and economic inequality, served as stark reminder of the limits of civil rights reform, and made clear to many that nothing short of a radical reorganization of society would bring about an equitable social order.[22] A new wave of protests after 1968, like the deadly protests at Kent and Jackson State Universities against the U.S. invasion of Cambodia, brought an expansion of state repression. Campaigns of criminalization, incarceration, and homicidal violence by local police and COINTELPRO, especially against known movement leaders of color, sowed deep indignation and incubated, among ever-growing numbers of people, more radical critiques of society. For the Young Lords, the frame-up of the New York Panther 21, the assassination of Fred Hampton, the persecution of Cha Cha Jiménez, and the surveillance and imprisonment of Puerto Rican radicals such as Martin Sostre, Carlos Feliciano, and Pancho Cruz were dramatic examples of state repression close to home.[23]

Building owned by the Young Lords on 117th Street and Third Avenue, East Harlem. (Photograph by Máximo Colón)

The U.S. government's increasing reliance on "armed bodies of men"—the open use of force—to maintain social control was a sign that dominant ideology had ceased to be effective as the preferred manager of social tensions in an unequal society.[24] According to Richie Perez, "The repression that was unleashed against the people . . . seemed to be so vicious that it was the domestic equivalent of the massacres of Vietnam."[25] And the era's multiple assassinations of national figures such as John F. Kennedy, Malcolm X, Martin Luther King Jr., and Robert Kennedy seemed symptomatic of an irreparably sick society.[26]

Among individual radicals and many others in the United States, the era's tragedies generated a moral dilemma. Amid a crisis of legitimacy and erosion of public trust in government, domestic organizers wrestled with questions of commitment and sacrifice for a greater good. Malcolm X had captured the sentiment with his distinctive clarity when he said, "If you are not willing to die for it, put the word freedom out of your vocabulary."[27] Young Lord Richie Perez put it differently: "Vietnam and the civil rights movement and black power had raised the issue of moral choices . . . the idea that you could be a good Nazi without being in the Nazi party, [that] you could be complicit with the war without actually dropping the bombs and that you could be complicit with institutionalized racism without calling someone a nigger. . . . Those were heavy things."[28]

Armed with the evangelical commitment and earnest passion of their youth, the founders of the organization built a full-time membership directed in its political perspective and organizing activities by a range of Marxist, Leninist, and Guevarist theories explaining the nature of society, the roots of exploitation and oppression under capitalism, and how to bring about revolutionary change. They distinguished their own liberatory position on the right to armed self-defense—especially among racialized people in the United States—from systemic violence. As Juan González explained to a Dutch reporter:

> We believe in armed self-defense. Not because we like violence, no one likes violence, but you have to make a differentiation between the open and direct violence that very often is [wrongfully] attributed to revolutionaries and the type of violence that [is perpetrated] on a regular basis [against] poor people. Whether it's the violence of having to go all winter in an apartment that has no heat or the violence of having to go to a hospital that doesn't give you services and you end up dying. You don't die with a bullet necessarily, but you die in different ways.[29]

The Young Lords adopted the appearance and style of the era's most iconic freedom fighters: the guerrillas of the Cuban Revolution. But they were *not* guerrilla combatants deploying armed raids against sites of government power. As Denise Oliver explained, they also did not "place or throw bombs in the name of Puerto Rican independence," a strategy the Young Lords denounced as "severely misguided."[30]

Like those of the Black Panthers, the day-to-day activities of the Young Lords consisted of political education, propaganda, and agitation. Within the social-ist tradition, these tools and tactics are also closely associated with the ideas of V. I. Lenin, the leader of the 1917 Russian Revolution, on the necessity of a revolutionary party in the protracted battle against capitalism. Based on decades of experience steering the Bolsheviks through the years preceding the Rus-sian Revolution, he theorized about the role and function of the revolutionary party. Lenin viewed the party as the "vanguard of the class"—a subsection of the working class, whose outlook reflects the class's highest economic *and* political interests. Its aim was to prepare its members to interpret social developments, identify peak moments of political crisis, amplify revolutionary propaganda, and transform the spontaneity of mass uprisings into revolution through the seizure of state power. The party's cadre trained for these moments through its engagement in interim struggles, developing disciplined routine activities and winning trust within the class as the tribune of the oppressed.[31] The Young Lords' minister of information, Pablo Guzmán, recounts having to adjust pro-spective members' misperceptions of the group's mission: "We found that a lot of people thought we were there just to throw garbage in the street. They couldn't understand that we were really there for a socialist revolution, we were really there to off the government of the United States. They just couldn't deal with that. So we tried setting up political education classes."[32]

In 1970, only a few Black Panthers and a handful of Young Lords read Lenin. In the main, the Young Lords' Maoist orientation concealed the Leninist roots of many of its organizational practices, such as the emphasis on the newspaper. However, like most of the New Left, the Young Lords' exposure to Lenin was refracted through figures like Mao Tse-tung, Joseph Stalin, Ho Chi Minh, Fidel Castro, and Che Guevara. Most of these figures identified the peasantry, small groups of students, radical intellectuals, and peasant guerrilla armies as the agents of revolution. This political current also emphasizes the power of will, commitment, and self-sacrifice in the revolutionary process.[33] By contrast, Lenin and classical Marxists emphasized the working class as the primary agent of revolutionary change and the party's social base. For them, socialist revolution depends on a combination of favorable objective conditions, including a crisis of legitimacy within the system, combined with revolutionary consciousness and political leadership within the working class.[34] The Young Lords leaned heavily toward the Maoist orientation, especially in its later years.

The leadership of the Young Lords brought a range of different views to the organization. Pablo Guzmán and Denise Oliver, for example, were attracted to

the left wing of the black freedom movement, in part for its attention to class differences within black America, and believed that the Young Lords should pursue
the strongest possible connections with the Black Panther Party (BPP), which
emphasized organizing the poorest sections of the black American community.
Oliver's brief studies at Howard University had put her in dialogue with a cohort
of West Indian students who became influential in the black power movement,
including Alfred Babington-Johnson and Hubert Brown, later H. Rap Brown.
The experience emboldened her revolutionary black nationalist views and she
came to the organization well versed in its debates.[35] Felipe Luciano, on the
other hand, who developed his oratorical skills in the world of the arts and
worked under the tutelage of the black cultural nationalist Amiri Baraka, cau-
tioned against the idea of turning the Young Lords into a replica of the Black
Panthers. He believed that because Puerto Rican culture and national identity
reflected a specific experience of migration from and colonization of Puerto
Rico, a radical reclamation of Puerto Rican culture would be among the most
powerful galvanizing forces in El Barrio. Luciano's cultural orientation found
support in David Perez's perspective, which according to Juan González "was
more grounded in common sense." Perez defined his political position based
on "what ordinary Puerto Ricans [might] think" about a given problem.[36] González, for his part, began reading Marxism in the summer of 1968 following
his expulsion from Columbia. He was also influenced by his partner, Gloria
Fontanez, health captain of the Young Lords, who had a strong sense of the
power and place of workers in social movements and also advocated a closer
relationship to the Puerto Rican nationalist movement.[37]

Although leadership made some decisions, as Leninists, the Lords practiced
democratic centralism, a process wherein policies and political direction are discussed and debated by cadre, decided by majority vote, and adhered to strictly.
In the first year, leadership fostered a tolerant and open political culture, bridged
differences, and worked together effectively. "Staying together" was both priority
and prize. Even so, according to Juan González, the group's "internal political
battles were intense. We had very long meetings [that were] draining."[38]

Educating a New Generation of Radicals

The Young Lords put education at the center of their broad vision of liberation.
Like the Black Panthers, they took education into their own hands and redefined
it. The group's internal edification regimen, which they called PE for political
education, required members to take seriously the study of history and radical
political theory. It included regularly scheduled reading hours and group discussion, a form of peer-to-peer learning that the Bronx education advocate Evelina
Antonetty observed among the Young Lords and began to promote in Bronx

public schools.[39] The political development of new recruits also depended on a strong rubric for learning social theory. Fast. Two of the group's most disciplined and talented leaders, Juan González and Iris Morales, developed a method and process for integrating and training new members and a new layer of leaders.[40] According to Guzmán, González "knew the most, he had the clearest mind."[41] Morales "was sharp, she was able to absorb ideas and break them down so that anyone could understand them."[42] Acting as minister and deputy minister of education, respectively, in early 1970, González and Morales launched a thirteen-week course, whose topics and readings connected to each point of the Lords' Thirteen-Point Program and Platform.[43]

For many Puerto Ricans, education had been fraught with the trauma and social rejection they endured as children in New York public schools. The sense that it was meaningless had led many members of the organization to drop out of school. But under the tutelage of the Young Lords, hundreds of young people, some of whom could barely read and write when they joined, were receiving a college-like education transforming them into impressive autodidacts.[44] The undertaking was not without its difficulties, however. Writing during the time, minister of information Pablo Guzmán quipped about the readings they assigned: "Ain't nobody could read the books, and then those who could read, let's say something like Che on *Man and Socialism*, threw the book away and said, 'this is boring.' Juan could not understand how Che Guevara could be boring. You know, it blew his mind." But the Young Lords persisted. Guzmán continues, "We tried everything, man, from jokes to getting high together, everything to try to bring the point across."[45] The organization became a formidable school in and of itself—and more. It became a fount of newfound freedom in the lives of new members during their late teens and twenties, a phase of life when transition brings on crises of confidence and identity.

Like other radicals before them, the Young Lords spent countless hours analyzing class subjugation and domination in society at large. But 1960s radicals added a new dimension to social criticism. As illustrated in the epochal women's movement slogan, "the personal is political," radicals also studied the imprint of larger social and political forces on their own lives and sense of themselves.[46] In so doing, the movements expanded the meaning of freedom and liberation for their generation to include the personal. To the Young Lords, deconstruction of custom and ideology was central to the process of liberation. It was a signature of their movement. Through collective analyses of shared experiences, they illuminated the dehumanizing nature of oppression within their community. This process is best captured in the 1971 oral history and photography book project, *Palante: The Young Lords Party*. In it, members tackle the fallout of being either demeaned for speaking Spanish or tokenized in school-tracking programs. They bear witness to antiblack racism among Puerto Ricans and other Latinxs, the patriarchal roots of discontent in modern family life, dehumanization suffered by parents in factories, psychic impotency and powerlessness on which structures of inequality depend (which they called "colonized mentality"), and internalized anger produced by powerlessness.

Their ultimate goal, however, was to help a generation gain understanding of the structural causes of alienation and suffering. To that end, they developed a method and process for training members politically. In their words, "The Young Lords were an initiation for a whole generation of people into their culture and their history. All of a sudden, I knew why my mother was angry, why my father was angry, and I no longer could blame them for anything. All of a sudden, I knew that they were victims in a big show. Because we were Puerto Rican and we were living here and we understood the beauty and the ugliness, but the Young Lords came to explain why."[47]

Even the group's most experienced members often transcended their socially imposed fears through radical education and engagement. As the leadership of the Young Lords came of age, many felt alienated in discussions of the social theories that were increasingly popular in movement circles. Iris Morales, deputy minister of education, explained the process by which she was drawn to revolutionary ideas: "As I started to get politically involved, [I was struck by] the absence of Latinos, and that the white activists used a language that I really didn't understand, but I listened because I said, I'll pick it up along the way. I remember feeling that there was something, some language, not a private code but it was some level of understanding that I knew I didn't have."[48] Minister of education Juan González also remembers his early relationship to the theories that he was now intent on disseminating among new recruits: "I felt I needed to read some Marxism because I really felt totally ill equipped even to engage in discussions with [white] SDS [Students for a Democratic Society] members . . . because I didn't have any kind of grounding."[49]

The deficit observed by these leaders was a consequence of several external developments. From the time of their first settlements in New York at the turn of the century, Puerto Ricans had formed part of an array of political fraternal orders and labor and socialist organizations. During the 1930s, they were active in New York's vibrant trade union movement, and thousands joined the Communist Party or its affiliates. But with the advent of the Cold War, the pall of silence and secrecy forced on the Old Left by the Red Scare at home also disemboweled the Puerto Rican Left. In 1948, at the start of the Red Scare, the U.S. government orchestrated the passage in Puerto Rico of the Gag Law, known in Spanish as Ley de la Mordaza. As its name suggests, the law had a chilling effect on the free exchange of political ideas that reached deep into the culture of Puerto Ricans on the island and in the continental United States. It banned the Puerto Rican flag, the Nationalist Party of Puerto Rico, writings about and gatherings to discuss independence, and references to independence in music. The decree unleashed fear and a clear message: that endorsing ideas associated with Puerto Rican freedom would come at a heavy personal cost. Enforced for a decade, until 1957, it ensured the incarceration of key nationalist leaders, pushed others underground, and weakened the organizations that might have passed on to the younger generation their analysis of social problems.[50] Strands of the Puerto Rican Left remained politically engaged, underground, on the island and the mainland. But disconnected from the grassroots, they were mostly reduced to small erudite circles with a disproportionately white, middle-class membership unfit to mentor a group like the Young Lords, which many viewed as the riffraff.[51]

Within the continental United States, the Red Scare marginalized and demonized the Left and shrouded Marxist theory in mystery and obscurity. It drastically limited exposure to Marxism and other radical theories of social change. When left politics became popular again in the 1960s with the political radicalization of the movement, knowledge of Marxism became the domain of young white activists on college campuses, an intellectual avant-garde that—disconnected from the working class—sometimes adopted airs of middle-class superiority and white paternalism.[52] The expression of white supremacy in a movement that became known for making racism unpopular was bad enough, but it reflected a larger presence in and dimension of the broader society that were not interrogated.

To the Young Lords and others who shared their world view, this reality confirmed the significance of "the national question," the call, used idiosyncratically among racially oppressed people, to build separate, race-based political organizations as a necessary challenge to racism and its fallout. For emerging working-class radicals of color—such as Morales, González, and others—the Young Lords did just that. González was one of the organization's strongest theoreticians, as was Denise Oliver, whose parents formed part of New York's vibrant black left culture during the 1940s and were friendly travelers of the Communist Party. Oliver had an "understanding of the unions . . . knew who Lenin was and read some of that . . . and had a fairly grounded set of politics, theoretically."[53]

By offering an alternative, unpretentious training ground where revolutionary ideas were accessible to working-class people in communities of color, the Young Lords' political education proved personally meaningful and politically transformative to new members. And for the children of migrants whose experience in the streets and the schools made them feel unfit and outside of mainstream U.S. society, the study of history and political theory in the Young Lords was a powerful antidote to class anxieties and feelings of intellectual inadequacy.

The Young Lords found other founts of Marxist politics. In hopes of influencing and perhaps winning the Young Lords over to their traditions, members of the Communist Party's black caucus, the Che-Lumumba Club, took up that assignment. Deacon Alexander and Charlene Mitchell of the Che-Lumumba Club held political education sessions with the Lords and their Central Committee.[54] Others passed on the revolutionary tradition, too, including Claudia Jones, Ella Baker, James Baldwin, Evelina Antonetty, Gilberto Gerena Valentin, Juan Antonio Corretjer, and James and Grace Lee Boggs.

Embodying Revolutionary Nationalist Ideas in the 1960s

Like the legion of radicals before them, the Young Lords drew parallels between the structure of racial inequality at home and imperialism abroad. Influenced by the vanguard revolutions of their time, they interpreted domestic racism as a kind of "internal colonialism." This understanding of racism had been discussed in movement circles since the early 1960s, when black radical activists and intellectuals, from Stokely Carmichael to Maxwell Stanford, began to interpret the spatial isolation and economic exploitation that defined black life in the United States as a form of racialized subjugation that mirrored the dynamic of imperialism in the Third World.[55] In the early part of the decade, the Revolutionary Action Movement produced the era's most sophisticated writing on the matter. Its networks popularized this interpretation through the deliberate distribution of its pamphlets and position papers in key movement cities among the vast wave of young civil rights workers who had been radicalized by the sit-ins. Like other left-leaning organizations, the Revolutionary Action Movement viewed black oppression as a major contradiction of American democracy—social tinder likely to create political crisis with far-reaching consequences for U.S. hegemony. Galvanized by the Cuban Revolution, its program advocated the application of Third World strategies for liberation to the black struggle domestically. It urged black revolutionaries to build armed urban guerrilla armies out of the bourgeoning discontent in the cities.[56]

The Young Lords rejected the concept of urban guerrilla war, as did the Black Panthers.[57] However, the groups' platforms reflected the broadest meaning of this analogy, which linked domestic racial inequality with colonialism and popularized the social theory in public discourse. The Young Lords declared that "the Latin, Black, Indian and Asian people inside the u.s. [sic] are colonies fighting for liberation."[58] As their deliberate use of the noun "offensive" suggests—when referring to the garbage, lead, and church campaigns—the Young Lords pledged solidarity with the Vietnamese in ingenious ways and adopted the logic, rhetoric, and style of Third World guerrilla warfare. The organization's direct actions and peaceful activities shocked and disrupted city life while avoiding direct engagement with forces larger than itself (the police).

In theory and practice, the organization never missed an opportunity to link local issues to the global imperial economy. In response to a question by a new recruit on how the Young Lords would counter the presence of two policemen who were permanently stationed in front of the First Spanish United Methodist Church following the Young Lords' occupation, Felipe Luciano said, "They're still there but they're going to have to go away someday. When the enemy advances you get out of the way. When he withdraws you move in. I didn't say that—Giap did!"[59] Luciano was referring to the Vietnamese general associated with the modern theory and practice of guerrilla warfare, Vo Nguyen Giap, who in 1954 orchestrated a dramatic defeat of the French at Dien Bien Phu.[60]

Depending on the context, 1960s radicals used the colonial experience as analogy, metaphor, or analytical reference point to illuminate the contours of racial oppression in the United States. When the Young Lords and the Black Panthers referred to the respective neighborhoods where they organized as "the colony," as they often did, they did so metaphorically and often with biting humor. On other occasions, they employed the term comparatively to interpret dynamics of inequality in the United States at a time when deindustrialization and white flight had produced deeper racial segregation and class stratification in the cities.[61] For example, Luciano used the reference as analogy when he wrote in *Palante* that racially oppressed groups at home are like colonized people in that they are stripped of the "right to self-determination." The term had an elaborate history, of which the New Left was likely unaware. However, he used it to mean that "the decisions affecting their lives are not made by them but for them by u.s. [sic] institutions." Absent any semblance of social, economic, or political agency, Luciano concluded, Puerto Ricans (and other racially oppressed groups) constitute a "nation within a nation." These formulations seemed applicable to Puerto Ricans—the only group on the U.S. mainland linked to a formal U.S. colony.[62]

The language and logic of colonization among radicals of color functioned as a vehicle for broadening the meaning of freedom beyond civil rights. Though imprecise, their call for "self-determination" envisaged a far-reaching equality. The concept became widely known in international discourse during World War I when V. I. Lenin called on socialists to fight for the unconditional independence of all colonies and exposed a series of secret treaties that belied the Allied powers' stated democratic aims. Discovered during the Russian Revolution, the treaties outlined how Britain, France, and Russia planned to divide up and rule over conquered territories after the war. The concept encapsulated the right of colonized countries to total social, political, and economic independence—free from European colonial domination.[63] A year earlier, the Easter Rising of 1916 put the issue on the map. Led by Irish nationalists, the armed rebellion challenged British rule in Ireland.[64]

In the domestic context, self-determination also came to imply a dialectical interplay between individual and collective liberation, best exemplified by Malcolm X's politics of self-respect, self-reliance, group autonomy, and black pride. As self-proclaimed heirs of Malcolm's political legacy, the Young Lords, like the Panthers, amplified these ideas at the grassroots. Writing in *Palante* on the anniversary of Malcolm's assassination in an article titled "Malcolm Spoke for Puerto Ricans," Pablo Guzmán emphasized the militant leader's insistence that liberation couldn't be legislated or handed down, that it had to be forged actively by the oppressed themselves. He wrote, "Malcolm ... told us if we want freedom we have to take it ('nobody can make you free')."[65] But the resolve to take charge of their destinies, Guzmán continued, came only after they "were awakened to a new truth: 'we are beautiful.'" He concluded that Puerto Ricans had to embark on a similar discovery. In a different article, Felipe Luciano wrote that the experience of "psychological imperialism" demanded collective regeneration through Puerto Rican–led organization and struggle.[66] These ideas had been articulated previously. Martin Luther King had denounced the internalization of white values among black southerners and "the corroding sense of inferiority, which often expresses itself in a lack of self-respect."[67] Similar ideas had been the subject of the New Negro movement of the 1920s led by Harlem Renaissance writers including Zora Neale Hurston, Claude McKay, Alain Locke, and others.[68] The emphasis on dignity cannot be underestimated. It was, as Martin Luther King also observed, a prerequisite for standing up.

The bold propaganda crafted by groups like the Young Lords expressed emergent Third World theories on self-formation. Their memorable catchphrases employed vivid imagery and emotional language that made their message infectious and likely to spread in public discourse. The political struggle waged by radicals of color on this issue contributed greatly to the era's cultural revolution. The notion of building a separate organization and separating from the oppressor had symbolic value and redemptive power. The unequivocal break with accommodation asserted the place of people of color in U.S. society and redeemed their humanity. The process also influenced the consciousness of many white Americans and made racism less acceptable in the public square.

These concepts were reinforced in the 1960s by the writings of Martinican psychiatrist and radical theorist Frantz Fanon, who developed an analysis of the effects of racism and colonization on the psyches of racially marked subjects and their oppressors. Fanon formulated a theory on identity and colonialism from his case studies of Algerian and French psychiatric patients during Algeria's war of independence against France and from studies of black psychology in French colonial society. His work demonstrated the alienation and propensity for self-deprecation among people who have suffered under the weight of imperialism.

His analysis was taken up to give expression to the day-to-day indignities of U.S. racism and was reflected in the literature of the Young Lords. According to David Perez, "Colonialism has messed [with] our minds so badly that psychologically we don't even know who we are. . . . We reject our cultural values. . . . We've been constantly told to hate ourselves while being reminded constantly by racist America that we ain't her kind of people either." Addressing the ways in which power dynamics are inscribed in language, which as Fanon observes holds within it "the weight of a civilization." Perez continues: "the cultural values of America are exalted [and] the cultural values of Puerto Rico are downgraded. People begin to feel ashamed of speaking Spanish; if you speak Spanish and stick to the old traditional ways, you're punished"[69]

For the recently arrived Puerto Ricans of the postwar period, ghettoized by virtue of their racialization, language, and economic status, national pride represented a way of laying claim to their humanity, a source of dignity and spiritual renewal. The Young Lords tapped into the latent nationalist sentiment in Puerto Rican communities, born of discrimination and exclusion from mainstream notions of who is an American, and this propelled the group's organizing efforts forward. When leading member Felipe Luciano emphasized the symbolism of a Puerto Rican flag at one of the initial garbage protests, the group received a warm response from community residents.[70]

Yet, in urging a radical overhaul of society, the Young Lords stretched the boundaries of nationalism. Recognizing that nationalist politics were open to interpretation from the right and from the left, they argued that liberation could not be achieved solely by addressing the problem of racial and national oppression and its psychological effects but that a larger reconfiguration of the social order was necessary. Richie Perez explains: "Many of our people see that our culture has been destroyed by this country and they react in an extreme way and become cultural nationalists—whose sole purpose is to revive the culture of the Puerto Rican nation and to keep it alive. . . . Our feeling is that nationalism is important . . . but pride alone is not gonna free us, the ability to play congas . . . [and] speak Spanish fluently is not gonna stop landlords . . . is not gonna stop the exploitation of our people on their jobs and every place else."[71] In this regard the Lords embraced the Marxist view that social inequality originates in the division of society into two principal classes, the one that owns the means of production and the one that sells its labor power for a wage. The former class, through its drive for profit, oppresses and exploits the latter.[72]

The Young Lords, like the Black Panthers, vehemently challenged cultural nationalists who proposed a liberation program based on the reclamation of cultural symbols and claiming a mythically constructed historical tradition among oppressed people. Both organizations referred to this wing of the nationalist movement with the derogatory term "pork chop nationalism." Their political world view and organizing strategy would be guided instead by "revolutionary nationalism."

Revolutionary Nationalism

For the Young Lords and the Black Panthers, revolutionary nationalism meant that the fight against racial oppression in the continental United States and against European colonial rule abroad requires two concurrent and interrelated struggles. The first centers on the fight for freedom against racism and imperialism in a society that rhetorically upholds as self-evident the equality of people and nations. This struggle for social equality and political self-determination, they argue, must be waged by the oppressed themselves, on their own terms and in separate, independent organizations. The second struggle is characterized by a broader, protracted fight against capitalism, which they identify as the root cause of subjugation and exploitation. It should be led, they argue, by revolutionaries and poor and working people of all races and nationalities, domestically and around the world.

The organization outlined the application of these ideas to Puerto Ricans in the widely read *Palante* article "On Revolutionary Nationalism." Written by chairman Felipe Luciano, it begins with a discussion of the political status of the island and its diaspora and the economic forces undergirding it. "Puerto Ricans," Luciano asserts, "wherever they are, whether in the united states [*sic*] or in Borinquen (Puerto Rico), constitute a colony." He impugns as the culprit the export-driven, U.S. monopoly capitalism that dominates the island, where Puerto Ricans earn "1/3 the wages of a northamerikkkan worker. Yet . . . they pay 25% more for consumer goods than northamerikkkans have to pay." He continues, "The colonial status of Puerto Ricans follows them from countryside to New York City," where they land in factories, are deprived of an education, and face unemployment, police repression, and incarceration. "In the city jails 44 out of every 100 prisoners are Puerto Ricans." He adds that "at the Bronx County jail, Puerto Ricans represent 85% of the prisoners." His discussion of root causes ends with a bleak conclusion, that colonialism has created a collective, existential crisis among the colonized. "Psychologically, we don't know who we are nor where we come from."

After establishing the systemic character of oppression, Luciano outlines the Young Lords' revolutionary nationalist program. He deploys the polemical style of argument that Malcolm X made famous. First, he lambasts the logic of the opposition and exposes what he sees as its self-serving individualism, namely the camp that purports to gain freedom within the system through demands for civil rights: "The assimilationists would have us believe that because they 'made it' as individuals (not realizing that capitalism always allows a select few to become college students, and professors, anti-poverty bosses and heads of city institutions in order to enforce genocide against their own) Puerto Ricans as a whole can make it."

By contrast, he continues, the Young Lords invoke nationalism because "Puerto Ricans have suffered as a group, racially and culturally, not as individuals. Therefore, the fight against amerikkkanism must be a group struggle, a nation struggle."

Nationalists observe that the very social conditions that have historically marginalized the racially oppressed from mainstream culture and life have inadvertently generated unique cultures, in some cases languages, and group-centered understandings of the self among these groups. Nationalists seek to organize, uplift, and harness this national identity to leverage power and group betterment. Revolutionary nationalism, however, represents the left wing of this analysis. Driven to tackle the systemic causes of social problems, it sees racism as an outgrowth of capitalism and calls for the radical transformation of society. Luciano, therefore, explains that group uplift alone will not "by itself resolve the question of liberation for our people on the island and self-determination for Puerto Ricans in amerikkka."[73] He goes on to denounce other pathways to freedom including "self-help [strategies] and Spic capitalism."

The group's nationalism had a strong class orientation; it disavowed collaboration with elite Puerto Ricans and reserved special animus for the *comprador* class, the would-be Puerto Rican middle-class managers and junior partners of the colonial system, or those who would re-create the system of capitalism once in power.[74] Puerto Ricans therefore could not gain true independence and freedom by electoral means but only through a revolutionary project that called for a fundamentally different society.[75] High on their list of detested collaborators with the U.S. colonial regime in Puerto Rico was Luis Muñoz Marín, who in 1948 became the first elected governor of Puerto Rico and the second Puerto Rican to hold the post (which had been held by an appointee of the U.S. Congress until then). Calling him "the biggest traitor in Puerto Rican history" and a "lackey," the Young Lords impugned Marín, "who shipped our people by the hundreds of thousands to New York because he could not provide jobs for them; who taught our people to be white middle-class Americanos, when they were poor, oppressed boricuas; who destroyed the *jíbaro* [peasant, small farmer, country people who farm the land in traditional ways] with Operation Bootstrap, moving thousands off the land into the slums of San Juan and Ponce, and let all our money go to u.s. [*sic*] capitalists. He was the apostle of non-violence for profit."[76]

Eliminating the economic roots of colonial oppression, the Young Lords argued, would come only by toppling capitalism. The struggle for national independence had to go hand in hand with the defeat of capitalism. The new

Puerto Rican society should not be organized on the basis of profit but rather around human priorities and needs. The Young Lords thus espoused at once a nationalist politics and international socialist principles. As the final point of their program and platform proclaimed, "We Want a Socialist Society." Luciano paints a picture of the kind of revolutionary process envisioned by this wing of the New Left. Freedom, he explained, will be won through a revolutionary process wherein the revolutionary vanguard of "the different colonies in the u.s. [*sic*]" joins with revolutionaries internationally and takes over "state power."[77]

The Young Lords and the Black Panthers were disseminating a social theory, revolutionary nationalism, whose origins were not known to many of their members. Developed during World War I and the years that followed by a cadre of black radicals in Harlem, somehow these ideas had survived two Red Scares. These radical thinkers had undergone a process of political awakening and analysis similar to that of 1960s radicals. Epochal movements abroad transformed their consciousness. The early twentieth-century stirrings of anti-imperialist organization in Africa and Asia and the political activity generated by an intercontinental African diaspora raised the prospects for black liberation in the United States. The Bolshevik revolution of 1917 also greatly influenced their analysis of the world.[78] Its unequivocal call for the independence of colonized people from European rule turned the socialist project into a path to liberation for colonized people. They were especially drawn to Lenin's call for "immediate liberation of the colonies" and his writings on "self-determination" and the "national question" on the right to independence of colonized nations and the right to separation of the weaker satellite nations in Russia's frontier.[79]

World War I and the two decades of imperial conquest that preceded it amplified the global dimensions of these questions. Responding to the long depression of the late nineteenth century, the British, French, German, and Dutch empires had sought to overcome the global crisis of overproduction by carving up the continents of Africa, Asia, and Latin America into spheres of influence and colonial possessions.[80] Although European Marxists were divided on how to assess the meaning of the colonies and their struggles for independence, Lenin's position on the matter eventually became dominant. As a matter of principle, he called on socialists to actively support the struggles of colonized people or those dominated by larger nations in Europe. Opposition to these projects, he argued, would go against the basic democratic principle of equality of all nations, peoples, and languages, without which solidarity among the working classes of different countries could not be achieved. He also observed that there was a distinct difference between the nationalist sentiments of colonized people who yearned to be free and the nationalism of larger countries whose chauvinism facilitated foreign subjugation and inequality among nations.[81]

In the context of these international debates, Harlem radicals began to think about the experience of black people in the United States within the framework of the national question. In 1919, they founded the African Blood Brotherhood (ABB). That year ushered in a fierce upsurge in labor struggles that paralyzed major cities. But it also witnessed a wave of white violence in the form of anti-black riots against the growing influx of black migrants in the country's major industrial cities, whom employers sometimes used as scab labor to cross exclusively white picket lines.[82]

In their effort to devise a revolutionary agenda suitable to these conditions, members of the ABB made a decisive contribution to twentieth-century understandings of racial oppression. With their fingers on the pulse of the era's intellectual and political debate among black radicals, they theorized racism as a social injury distinct from class exploitation but interconnected with it. They observed that the history of black people in the United States had produced a special oppression among them. As a superexploited subsection of the U.S. working class, black people were overrepresented in the most dangerous and lowest-paid jobs. Their exclusion from higher education, the professions, the unions, and public office set them apart from white people of the same class. Socially marginalized and spatially isolated in the poorest urban and rural districts, they lacked political power and suffered racism at the hands of white people of all classes, including both vigilante violence and police brutality.

On invitation by Sen Katayama, Lenin, Leon Trotsky, and the Bolsheviks, members of the ABB participated in the Communist International conferences of the 1920s held in Moscow. Their presentations on the "special conditions" of black people in the United States persuaded the congress organizers to adopt their perspective as the conference's official position on the matter. They concluded that their theoretical understanding—of the exceptional character of race as a social injury—required a corresponding practice among revolutionaries. Namely, it needed a strong antiracist platform and organizing strategy within the socialist movement, of which they were part. Most white American communists did not implement the position. Against the position adopted by Communist International, they continued to view racism as an extension of the class struggle and retained their previous position, that the U.S. Socialist Party "had nothing special to offer the Negro, and we cannot make separate appeals to all the races."[83] In 1928, however, the U.S. Communist Party (CP) reversed this position and proclaimed support for the right of black Americans to declare national independence in the southern Black Belt, where they formed a majority of the population and labored in a semislavery economy. Known as "the nation within a nation" thesis, the concept was advanced by Harry Haywood, one of the CP's prominent black leaders. The proposal implied that the CP would regard black Americans not as an oppressed section of the U.S. population but rather as a national minority, "a nation within a nation," with a distinct national culture and identity.[84]

The term was used in the 1960s by radicals of color. The formulation must have seemed especially tantalizing to the Young Lords. Puerto Ricans were the only group on the U.S. mainland linked to an actively colonized territory.[85] In his article on revolutionary nationalism, Luciano proclaimed that absent any semblance of social, economic, or political agency, Puerto Ricans in the continental United States constitute a "nation within a nation."

In their conceptualization of island independence, the Young Lords were influenced by the mythic militancy of the father of Puerto Rican nationalism, Don Pedro Albizu Campos, who in the early 1930s redirected the efforts of the Puerto Rican Nationalist Party from electoral politics to armed struggle for independence. Like their newly politicized counterparts in the black movement who studied the life and speeches of Malcolm X, the Young Lords were determined to reclaim their most radical leaders, including not only Albizu Campos but also the socialist and nationalist party leader Juan Antonio Corretjer, for the struggle against colonialism.[86]

To this end, the Young Lords studied and archived in *Palante* the lessons of the two major periods in Puerto Rico's war for independence. Of the first phase, led by Emeterio Betances, Juan González wrote: "In El Grito de Lares [1868], we were saying—we are not Spaniards. We are the mixture of African and Indian, born in Borinquen, speaking Spanish . . . an island nation, oppressed by the Spanish Empire." His assessment of these early revolutionary efforts concludes: "They had good leadership. They raised money, got arms, politicized the people. They understood that the enemy was well organized.... The revolution was defeated, though, because it was not organized enough. The patriots did not have military training. An arms supply from the Dominican Republic never reached them. They did not go into the countryside where the poorest and greatest number of Puerto Ricans, the jíbaros, the campesinos, were."[87]

In New York, the Young Lords were also influenced by the different political currents that emerged out of the defeat of the second struggle for Puerto Rican independence between 1932 and 1954. Led by Albizu Campos, the Puerto Rican Nationalist Party launched a combination of peaceful protests, assassination attempts, and armed raids against sites of U.S. military and political power, government officials, and the police. This form of armed propaganda intended to raise the cry of independence among the Puerto Rican people and create a crisis of authority within the colonial state. The party's first major action was the 1932 march inside the island's legislative building in San Juan, where nationalists protested the adoption of the Puerto Rican flag by the colonial government. A series of peaceful demonstrations followed over the course of the 1930s, during which fleeing, unarmed protesters were shot in the back and killed by police. The most well-known assault claimed the lives of nineteen people in Ponce, including a seven-year-old girl, and was declared a massacre by the American Civil Liberties Union. The party's armed actions included the 1950 raid of a fort in Jayuya, led by a woman, Blanca Canales, during which the nationalists held the town for three days, while others led uprisings in more than eight cities; and the attempted assassination of President Truman at Blair House in Washington in 1952. Two years later, in 1954, in a sympathy action, four New York–based Puerto Rican nationalists, among them the Puerto Rican icon Lolita Lebron, opened fire on the floor of the U.S. Congress and wounded five congressmen. Taken at the height of the Cold War, this action prompted the arrests of thousands of nationalists and the political demobilization of the Nationalist Party.[88]

By the 1950s, McCarthyism and the wholesale killing and incarceration of frontline fighters had transformed Puerto Rican independence into a seemingly impossible ideal. In New York, independence work was carried on in underground educational gatherings and fundraising activities organized by the Movimiento Libertador, a local group that formed after the Nationalist Party was banned in 1950.[89] But in the late 1950s and early 1960s, with the victory of the Cuban Revolution, the growing resistance of the Vietnamese against the U.S. military, and the gathering pace of the black freedom movement, the new Puerto Rican nationalist movement began to sink roots again on the island with the emergence of the Movimiento Pro Independencia (MPI) in 1959. With branches in Puerto Rico, and by 1964 in Chicago and New York, the MPI anchored the new Puerto Rican independence movement, attracting small numbers of older, first-generation Puerto Rican migrants.

Influenced by the civil rights and antiwar movements on the U.S. mainland, the MPI adopted protest models for independence that marked a tactical departure from what came before. During the 1960s, the MPI emphasized civil disobedience, antiwar protest, and resistance to U.S. corporate and military operations on the island.[90] Veterans of the independence movements living in New York, such as old-timer Tato Albizu and many others, passed on their stories of struggle and political literature to the Young Lords.[91] While many of these interactions were close and welcoming, others were more contentious because of the white racial composition and middle-class orientation of much of the Puerto Rican independence movement. To the erudite, middle-class activists in the independence movement, who had years of political and theoretical training under their belts, many Young Lords appeared poorly educated and politically unsophisticated.[92] Young Lord Iris Morales participated in a Friday night social gathering held at the 14th Street headquarters of the MPI. She recollects, "I remember going to some of those meetings and not understanding [because] there were class differences, language differences, I mean I couldn't understand the Spanish they were speaking, they were very middle-class."[93] But because the Young Lords had taken East Harlem by storm and raised the media profile of Puerto Rican poverty, their activism revitalized many preexisting organizations, such as the MPI in New York, and inspired the emergence of others like El Comité MINP and Resistencia Puertorriqueña. This period also witnessed the transformation of the MPI into the Puerto Rican Socialist Party in 1972 and the emergence of paramilitary clandestine organizations like the Fuerzas Armadas de Liberación Nacional and the Movimiento de Liberación Nacional, among others.[94]

In the late 1960s, the politics and activism of the Young Lords, which had developed separately from the independence movements on both the island and mainland, widened the terrain of independence politics among a new generation of mainland-born Puerto Ricans. They educated 1960s activists about the language discrimination and racism endured not just by black Americans but also by Puerto Ricans on the U.S. mainland and popularized the call for Puerto Rican independence.

For their part, the Young Lords offered an assessment of the Puerto Rican independence movement that was informed by the dominant politics and concerns of revolutionary movements of the period. According to González, "The Nationalist Party was destroyed by its own internal problems; by its emphasis on immediate shootouts with police instead of organizing a guerrilla army to lead the nation in the people's war in the countryside; by its failure to organize the Black Puerto Ricans as well as lighter skinned Boricuas; and by its failure to provide concrete programs to meet the immediate needs of the people."[95]

As a basis for organizing, this outlook presented a complex dilemma. By 1970, 41 percent of Puerto Ricans in East Harlem were second-generation migrants.[96] Although a significant number of Puerto Ricans returned to Puerto Rico in the 1970s, the majority who migrated in the postwar era remained on the mainland. Despite their alienation from mainstream American society, Puerto Ricans became part of the mainland U.S. labor force and many, especially those who were born in New York, identified it as their home. Puerto Ricans on the mainland represented a racialized ethnic group. But the Young Lords' perception of Puerto Ricans on the mainland as an integral part of the island had romantic revolutionary appeal. Whereas other racialized groups in the United States, like Native and Mexican Americans, largely lived on ancestral lands that had long been incorporated into the United States, Puerto Ricans such as the Young Lords were distinguished by the fact that they could lay claim to citizenship and ancestral ties to a colonized island nation that they would ostensibly one day liberate.

For now, however, using the same powerful biblical language they had used during the Church Offensive, the Young Lords explained, "We are in a period where revolutionary education is more important than revolutionary war. We are in a period of preparation. . . . Soon that revolutionary war will start and the oppressed people of the United States, led by the Young Lords Organization, the Black Panthers, the Comandos Armados para la Liberación, will slay Goliath, burn Babylon, throw the moneylenders out of the temple, and then we, the last, shall be the First."[97]

Postwar Conditions Give Rise to Nationalism

In the 1960s, nationalist sentiment grew among activists of color, many of whom came to view the building of separate race-based organizations as the most effective vehicle for social change. The persistence of racism in the culture and institutions of U.S. society, even in spite of the passage of civil rights legislation, fueled this perspective, as did the feeling that their white counterparts in the New Left couldn't overcome their paternalism toward people of color. Of his decision to leave SDS, Juan González explains that during his time in prison he engaged in concentrated study of "national, colonial, and racial issues," and while SDS was "increasingly talking much more about self-determination and national liberation . . . they were doing it in a very paternalistic and controlling way, so I realized that I couldn't stay in that organization; that I had to go to my own community."[98] Iris Morales had similar feelings about the paternalism of white activists.[99] The same sentiment had been articulated in the mid-1960s by black Student Nonviolent Coordinating Committee (SNCC) workers who grew weary of both interracial dating and white paternalism among white civil rights workers. SNCC's experiment in multiracial civil rights organizing in the early 1960s, while successful in many ways, set the stage for its repudiation of multiracial organizing later in the decade.[100]

Separatist sentiments also increased as a result of the postwar demographic transformation of northern cities. As workers of color migrated there in large numbers, working- and middle-class white residents moved to racially exclusive suburbs, propelled by a vast postwar project of home ownership engineered by real estate developers and secured with federally funded mortgages for whites only.[101] By the 1960s, the lived experience of white Americans and people of color who remained in isolated, poor, and overpoliced urban neighborhoods grew further and further apart. The tax-base erosion in the cities that accompanied white flight and the growing crisis of deindustrialization exacerbated this difference. The segregation of the country's housing landscape had its social consequences—"the gulf of incomprehension separating even liberal whites from the real lives of black people" and other racialized groups.[102] In this context, the material basis for interracial unity between people of color and white Americans appeared to be evaporating, and the 1930s communist slogan "black and white unite and fight" seemed harder and harder to enact. In addition, as we have seen, the experience in New York of white resistance to basic civil rights demands for racial equality in education and an independent civilian complaint review board of the police overwhelmed efforts by white liberal organizations such as Equal, which opposed school segregation in New York. Because most 1960s activism centered around community and not workplaces, where despite the persistence of racial labor segmentation there was greater integration, a struggle based on interracial collaboration with white Americans was very difficult to imagine.

However, as the postwar city became home to larger numbers of Mexican Americans, Native Americans, and people of Chinese, Filipino, Japanese, and Korean descent across the country, the call for black and white to unite and fight was replaced with calls for solidarity among people with long-standing histories of racial oppression and ethnic-based resistance to that condition. Efforts at coalition building after 1968 were regional in scope but resonated nationally among activists like the Young Lords, who reported about these various struggles and sent solidarity greetings. In New York's Chinatown, Asian Americans replicated the politics, organizational framework, and activities of the Young Lords and the Black Panthers in I Wor Kuen.[103] The radical wings of the movement in Los Angeles included Chicanos, the Brown Berets, and, later, the Center for Autonomous Workers, which organized Mexican workers. Among Japanese Americans and other Asian constituencies was the East Wind, which developed service programs similar to those of the Black Panthers. Meanwhile in the San Francisco Bay Area, black American, Native American, Chicano, and Asian students organized strikes calling for ethnic studies at Berkeley and at San Francisco State University and coalesced there in the Third World Liberation Front. Meanwhile, Chinese Americans in the Red Guard armed themselves and set up community organizing programs in San Francisco's Chinatown, developing ties with the Black Panthers and various radical Chicano groups. And while Native Americans had been engaged in disparate actions claiming rural lands, the occupation of Alcatraz Island in San Francisco by a group that called itself the Indians of All Tribes Coalition drew support from Third World activists nationally. It also set in motion dozens of occupations of federal properties by Native Americans, including the Bureau of Indian Affairs in Washington, D.C., and the national expansion of the American Indian Movement following the occupation of the Pine Ridge reservation as radical alternatives to the strategies of long-standing moderate Native American leaders and groups.[104]

Of necessity, Young Lords organizing was anchored in the fight against Puerto Rican oppression and poverty in the urban centers of the mainland. But because black Americans and Puerto Ricans lived side by side in East Harlem, the Young Lords' socioeconomic campaigns attracted their black American neighbors. The Young Lords welcomed them: over 25 percent of the Young Lords' members were black Americans.[105] It seems appropriate that the radicalized children of first-generation Puerto Rican migrants would identify with the BPP (even as their migrant parents were hesitant about that identification). Another 5 percent of the members were non–Puerto Rican Latinos.

The logic of revolutionary nationalism was premised on the notion of shared interests among oppressed people. As Panama Alba explained about his own experience at Lincoln Hospital with the Young Lords, in the 1960s his Panamanian origins did not pose a contradiction to his affiliation with a Puerto Rican organization: "This was the age of Che Guevara, an Argentine doctor who fought and led the Cuban revolution. It was a time of international solidarity among oppressed people."[106] The Young Lords' diverse membership captured a defining political sentiment among large numbers of urban radicals—solidarity among people of color. Along with others of their generation, the Young Lords advanced a new kind of revolutionary, multiracial politics in the United States—that of a Third World Left—which made common cause not only with other revolutionary nationalist groups but also with white radicals.[107]

Practicing a Particular Kind of Class Politics

The Young Lords' critique of capitalism, like that of the Black Panthers, developed in response to the conditions of urban poverty in which many of their members were reared. They articulated the grievances of Puerto Ricans on the mainland with eloquence and grace in part because they emerged organically from the Puerto Rican settlements of the 1950s and were attuned to their community's aspirations. Running as central themes throughout the Young Lords' Thirteen-Point Program and Platform are issues of social and economic want and the question of control over the major institutions that shape society. The group denounced "the violence of hungry children, illiterate adults, diseased old people, and the violence of poverty and profit."[108] Although early protests led by the NAACP and the Congress on Racial Equality in the North had focused on race and class—such as housing discrimination and exclusion from the labor unions in construction and other industries—with the emergence of the Black Panthers and later the Young Lords, a response to oppression sharply oriented around issues of class achieved organizational form and expression.

During the first two years of its existence, the Young Lords Organization (YLO) identified Karl Marx's lumpenproletariat, the group of permanently unemployed and discouraged workers eking out a living on the margins of society largely through criminal activity, as the social class with the greatest revolutionary potential. That position was formally adopted at the organization's first retreat in May 1970. Like the Panthers, the Lords expanded the classical Marxist definition of the lumpen by including the poor in general in its ranks—people on state relief and the partially unemployed. They argued that unlike the working class, which tended toward compliance with the rules of society, the lumpen had no investment in capitalism and possessed a fierceness, bravery, and disregard for authority that could be channeled toward revolutionary ends. Hence the group welcomed former gang members, drug users, and those repeatedly institutionalized by the state for petty crime. Pablo Guzmán discussed the place of the destitute classes in the book *Palante*: "The first segment of our people that will join, work with, and support the revolution is the lumpen, the street people: prostitutes, junkies, two-bit pushers, hustlers, welfare mothers. That's the group that got the Party through its first two years. . . . The street people come into the revolution because they've got nothing to lose. And it's a law of revolution that the most oppressed group takes the leadership position."[109]

Known as the Black Panther's lumpen thesis, and advanced especially by Eldridge Cleaver, the position romanticized the most oppressed sectors of society as those most likely to resist. The irony, however, was that the leaders of both organizations were not "the street people" but were among the most educated young, working-class Puerto Ricans and black Americans of their generation. The theory is contradicted by histories and assessments of social movements and revolutions across time and place, which suggest that grassroots leadership and mass social transformation are fueled by the higher expectations that come with improved conditions, organizational resources, and intellectual capital rather than the isolation and despair of extreme oppressive conditions.[110]

Former leaders estimate that despite the organization's lumpen orientation, only a very small number of its members, approximately 10 percent, were drawn from this class. Most Young Lords in New York were former college students, high school dropouts, and people who were employed part-time. Approximately 5 percent were Vietnam veterans, and a smaller percentage worked full-time.[111]

In line with their lumpen orientation, the Young Lords, like the Black Panthers, focused on the crisis of drug addiction in poor communities of color, which they accurately described as a growing epidemic. In the end, the group's political analysis of the problem was more compelling than its proposal for redress, which consumed a disproportionate part of its limited organizational resources. The Bronx, for example, where the Young Lords opened an office in spring 1970, had the highest rate of heroin addiction in the world.[112] The very first edition of *Palante* discussed the problem in an article titled "Gorilla on Your Back," a 1960s reference to heroin. The article posited that heroin was consciously used by those in power to "pacify" oppressed people and turn them on each other, when oppressed people might otherwise be turning their collective power against "politicians, greedy businessmen and racist murdering, pig cops."[113] While the Young Lords' reporting might have appeared conspiratorial, their analysis reflected ideas long adopted by the black power movement and the broader Left. According to Michael Rossman, a radical sociologist at the

University of California, Berkeley, "The effect of all this injection of heroin is that the ghetto people's energies become absorbed internally, turned against itself, undermining all revolutionary impulses against the external colonizing forces and the social conditions they have created."[114] In addition, by the mid-1970s, congressional investigations had exposed the complicity and involvement of individuals in the CIA and some high-ranking U.S. military officers in the heroin trade in Laos, where poppy flowers, from which heroin is derived, were plentiful. Eventually the Young Lords adopted the formulation coined by New York Black Panther Michael Tabor: "Capitalism + Dope = Genocide."[115] They saw the drug crisis in poor urban communities of color as part of a global web, one that linked the proliferation of drug use and black-market drug trafficking by officers in the Vietnam War to the funneling of drugs to urban centers in the United States.[116] The vehicle of community protest around which radicals focused their activities inevitably put them in frequent contact with criminal, unstable, and undisciplined elements within the lumpenproletariat. As Denise Oliver reported on the Young Lords' radio program on WBAI, "We are also dealing with drugs; it is obvious that our people of El Barrio did not bring in the reported 300 tons of illegal drugs that entered America that year. The man himself is directly responsible for keeping us high. Since junkies are victims and not the cause of the problem, we are starting a guerrilla drug clinic. This means getting an apartment, cleaning it up, screening junkies for commitment and then having them kick cold turkey. To date we have brought about half a dozen brothers and sisters back home. A new man and a new woman are emerging and their child is revolution."[117]

In line with its orientation of "serving the people," the Young Lords provided drug rehabilitation that included discussions on the impact of race and class inequality on personal psychology as a tool of personal regeneration. After establishing a person's frankness and determination to "kick the habit," their program paired the person with two Young Lords who kept watch over the drug user through the difficult process of withdrawal over the course of twenty-four-hour isolation. One Young Lord was then assigned as mentor and twenty-four-hour buddy for a six-month period.[118] The mentor was responsible for combining political education with moral support to help the user stay away from temptation. In the face of an epidemic, the project was, at best, a symbolic gesture of humanistic love and support for the downtrodden. Committed to reforming and politicizing those involved in petty crimes and gangs, the organization was attuned to the pulse of street life. As morally upright revolutionaries, the Young Lords prided themselves on cleaning up the blocks where they were active by expelling dope dealers, whom they denounced as social predators poisoning the community. Some male members of the Young Lords describe engaging in street battles with these elements and stripping them of money, which they argued had been taken from the most vulnerable people in the community. The group reported that its practice angered the Mafia, which according to the YLO and its street contacts, put out a contract of $20,000 for the murder of Felipe Luciano.[119]

On the ground, however, these efforts exhausted the group's limited organizational resources, confused social service with agitation and political strategy— the mainstay and primary function of a grassroots political organization—and, as experience has shown, weakened the group.

As a class, the lumpenproletariat is easily manipulated politically. Untethered to the responsibilities of work and family, which act as a force of discipline and collective consciousness among workers, it tends to rely on hustling, and often intimidation and violence, as a means of survival. For these reasons, lumpens were frequently used by the FBI as agents provocateurs to infiltrate, subvert, and undermine organizations such as the Young Lords and, especially, the Black Panthers. The Black Panthers' idealization of the lumpen has been identified by former members and scholars alike as a critical error that made the organization vulnerable to infiltration and undermined the building of a disciplined and united political organization.[120] During the period, the Young Lords, like the BPP, wagered that their organization's military-style structure would counter the inherent instability of these elements.

The lumpen thesis was an attempt (ultimately unsuccessful) to respond to a stubborn reality: the general Cold War retreat of the U.S. working class and its unions from any sustained challenge to capitalism; white working-class backlash to protest by people of color; and the persistence of racism in the unions. Late 1960s radicals were influenced by the pessimism that permeated New Left circles regarding the possibility of a worker-led challenge to capitalism. These were the result of the McCarthy-era purge of socialist and communist organizers from the unions. Variations of this idea were echoed by major New Left theorist and philosopher Herbert Marcuse, dissident sociologist C. Wright Mills, sociologist Daniel Bell, and Marxists Paul Baran and Paul Sweezy. The unprecedented increase in living standards among U.S. workers during the post–World War II economic boom, coupled with the rise of social-democratic governments in much of Europe during the same period, persuaded many radicals and conservatives alike that capitalism had found a way of circumventing deep economic crisis and sharp class conflict.[121]

However, working-class consciousness was in flux as evidenced by the upsurge of organizing and strike activity of the late 1960s and 1970s, especially in France. This development challenged the New Left's assessment of working-class consciousness and led many radicals to reevaluate their ideas. By 1969, the U.S. economy, overheated by the war, had stopped yielding the huge profits of the early 1960s and was dogged by inflation and stagnation. In attempts to recuperate profits, employers mandated production-line "speedups." In response to increased output demands, discrimination in the workplace, and an unresponsive union bureaucracy, young workers who had been radicalized by the black power movement and the Vietnam War organized unauthorized "wildcat" strikes in several regions of the country. As children of poor working-class Puerto Rican parents, it was not long before the Young Lords acknowledged that the affluence of some American workers was relative, temporary, and by no means uniform within that class.[122]

These ideas had been reinforced through the Young Lords' collaboration with a group of black American and Latinx workers involved in campaigns for improved working conditions and patient care in the city's municipal hospitals. As noted previously, in fall 1969, this network of young hospital workers had been frustrated by the limitations of their union's advocacy on behalf of its least-paid workers and sought to bridge community and workplace struggles. Because the Young Lords were involved in activism at three different hospital sites—Gouverneur Hospital on the Lower East Side, Metropolitan Hospital in East Harlem, and Lincoln Hospital in the Bronx—they facilitated a conversation among these black American and Latinx workers and encouraged them to formalize their common preoccupations through organization.

Disseminating Ideas

In early winter 1970, the YLO began to transform its mimeographed newsletter into a tabloid-style bilingual newspaper, *Palante*. The word *palante* is the informal Spanish contraction for the words *para adelante*; that contraction is most often used in the colloquialism *echar pa'lante*, which means "to push forward," a figure of speech for the concept of advancing in struggle, usually of a personal kind, against the odds. The New York Young Lords envisioned *Palante* as their tool for staying connected and in conversation with the community.

Because of the high level of political debate engendered by the events of the period, alternative newspapers were plentiful and considered an important means of reeducating the masses about the "issues." In 1969, more than 500 alternative papers were in circulation nationally, not including high school publications, which numbered another 500–1,000.[123] Many of these publications had consistent runs, but a significant number of them, like the Chicago group's *YLO*, were irregular and short-lived. Noting the chronically inconsistent distribution of the organization's national newspaper, the New York Young Lords decided to generate their own news organ. But doing it themselves soon revealed the labor-intensive requirements of newspaper production. From the editorial demands of a newspaper and the gathering of internally commissioned and submitted articles and artwork to design and layout, publishing a regular newspaper demands experience, a range of technical skills, organization, planning ahead, staying on top of the news, strict deadlines, and more. Pablo Guzmán served as editor of the paper. Denise Oliver, who studied in the competitive, specialized high school, Art and Design, remembers, "I was the only member trained in graphics and design, so I did the first layouts and produced a lot of its artwork." She would later train Richie Perez in these areas.[124]

It wasn't long before the New York group fell behind. In fact, *Palante* took six months to begin meeting its regular publication deadlines. Although the New York Young Lords prioritized its publication, *Palante* endured several periods of inconsistency after 1971 during times of political disorientation and after 1972 as a result of splits within the organization that are described in later chapters.

The newspaper was published twice a month, and all of its articles appeared simultaneously in Spanish and English. With little to no experience in newspaper production or training in journalism, the approximately ten young radicals who were on the *Palante* team at any given time worked doubly hard to produce one of the few bilingual newspapers of the period—no small accomplishment for an organization with few members who were fluent or formally trained in Spanish. In April 1970, the Young Lords' new branch office in the South Bronx became the "Information Center" that housed the newspaper's production.[125]

During its first two years, *Palante* was printed in color. Unrestrained by commercial standards, the paper brought together an array of eclectic graphics, photography, and rich renderings of art from the grassroots. Oliver produced some of its most memorable graphics, among them a depiction of Lincoln Hospital with two nefarious-looking pigs operating on a human. The young, politicized artists and printers at Taller Boricua also furnished the dramatic artwork that graced the covers of *Palante*. One cover reproduced Marcos Dimas's portrait of Ramón Emeterio Betances, the nineteenth-century revolutionary doctor and abolitionist who led the first armed revolt against Spanish rule in Puerto Rico.[126] At its best, *Palante* addressed social problems with humor. In one cartoon, a skeleton is slumped on a chair while a plump nurse holds on to a clipboard in the background. Its caption reads: "The long wait."

The distribution of *Palante* was at once a political requisite for membership and a means of subsistence for individual Young Lords. Members walked a regular newspaper route, and on a good day could sell between 100 and 200 copies of the newspaper, at twenty-five cents each. They were allowed to keep half the proceeds. The practice of selling the paper and engaging neighbors in the same city blocks, week after week, helped establish the reputation of the Young Lords as committed activists. With a print run of 24,000 at its peak, *Palante*'s circulation was impressive for an underground newspaper. Ramon Morales and Huey Jung organized its distribution and circulation, respectively.[127] Conceived as a vehicle through which to make the organization's ideas accessible to ordinary

Image of machete and the words "Up with the Puerto Rican farmer, Down with the Yankee." (*Palante* 2, no. 11 [September 11, 1970]; courtesy of the Tamiment Library)

people, *Palante* carried articles outlining the organization's position on the key issues of the day: the sources of women's oppression, the logic of revolutionary nationalism, the meaning and manifestations of class, the emergence of racism in the Americas in the context of slavery, and the uses of armed struggle, among other subjects. Reporting on demonstrations and campaigns that they initiated, the paper also kept the community informed of the Young Lords' activities.

Despite their strong support for armed rebellion, the Young Lords believed that education was "the first step in revolution."[128] *Palante* embodied this ideal, with numerous feature articles on Puerto Rico's history and radical tradition, from the Spanish conquest to the deleterious effects of Operation Bootstrap of the previous decade. The articles highlighted the early upheavals against colonial rule and the birth and evolution of the nationalist movement on the island.[129] *Palante* also dedicated several pages per issue to Third World revolutionary struggles, mostly in Southeast Asia and Latin America. In its totality, the newspaper offered a repository of unrelenting political analysis on local and global politics and a radical historical survey of Third World peoples and their struggles for freedom.

As a publication, *Palante* soared as quickly as did the Young Lords and became a crucial vehicle through which the organization achieved recognition within the Puerto Rican community and the broader movement. Filled with images of resistance and brash denunciations of politicians, the bourgeoisie of all races, "bought-off union bureaucrats," and the police (known as "the pigs"),

Palante was open and unapologetic in its partiality toward the dispossessed classes. At a moment when class struggle was at its highest level since immediately after World War II, and when structural inequality was acknowledged even by mainstream academics and politicians, underground newspapers like *Palante* reveled in taking sides and pulling no punches. Candid in its aims, the paper sought to advance the fighting spirit and revolutionary consciousness of working-class Puerto Ricans and other exploited and oppressed people.

Completely unrestrained by the conventions of journalism, a cross-section of Young Lords reported on their actions in different political campaigns—from community health to, for example, support for striking workers in the Bronx at the Art Steel factory—in prose that was fervent and youthful in its honesty.[130] The paper possessed an intrepid style of reporting that challenged the notion of politics as the domain of experts and professionals and opened up a forum where an unlikely segment of the population—young, poor, and brown—spoke up.

Yet the creativity and dissent were not without shortcomings. Periodicals such as *Palante* reflected the bravado of youthful radicals. Impatience in seeking to bring about change, combined with lack of political sophistication, often produced a righteous and preachy tone in *Palante*'s reporting. For example, the newspaper ran a number of editorials condemning common behavioral tendencies within the Puerto Rican community, such as the widespread tolerance of mistresses among married men or the routine practice among young working-class Puerto Ricans of seeking diversion and escape on the dance floor.[131] Although these articles attempted to locate the social origins of human behavior and understand the patterns of negative interaction between men and women, they sometimes lapsed into condescension and moralizing, not unlike the previous generation of middle-class Puerto Rican reformers that the Young Lords often criticized. *Palante*'s tone was common in the quasi-evangelical quality of much 1960s radicalism, with its tendency to substitute individual commitment, self-sacrifice, and upright behavior for objective political assessment and analysis of social phenomena such as, for example, Marx's theory of alienation under capitalism.

For the period's cadre organizations, the process of internal transformation was refracted through the ego-stripping Maoist exercise known as "criticism and self-criticism." As Oliver explains, if a member violated the codes of conduct, "you were given criticism and you had to stand up there and criticize yourself: 'I am guilty of putting my party at risk; I am guilty of betraying the trust of my comrades.'" Revolutionary commitment was measured by a member's willingness "to change their behavior and accept discipline." Members were also expected to call out bad behavior. Those who failed to do so were said to be liberal. Oliver continues, "That was the worst thing you could call somebody. It was straight from Chairman Mao and drummed into our heads: 'Liberalism is corrosive,' it enables bad behavior [and sets the socialist project back]. Some people stepped up to the plate and were not liberal, there was also anger and resentment."[132] The practice blurred the boundaries between principle and self-righteousness.

A shortcoming of *Palante*, as of many radical publications of the period, was a lack of analytical depth in its critique of American society. Publications were good at identifying the enemy but provided little in the way of understanding the specificity of American politics and assessing the movement on both the national and local levels. Yet the newspaper's bold and straightforward approach to reporting projected the organization's unshakable resolve and serious commitment.

The May 1970 "Retreat" and the Young Lords Party

The large influx of new members in early 1970 meant that it was time for the Young Lords to expand. The organization had spread in fits and starts with activists opening satellite offices, the first of which was established in Newark in fall 1969. But as the Young Lords grew qualitatively, the YLO field ministry, led by David Perez, emerged as a new, vital area of work. The field ministry identified new sites and neighborhoods for the organization's work and managed the process of setting up new branches. According to Iris Morales, Perez "would go out and just be with those areas for a while, get to know the local folks and assess if this should be a chapter or not; did it look like [there were] solid local folks there or was something else going on."[133] YLO members knew that they were being watched, even before white antiwar activists broke into the FBI office in Media, Pennsylvania, and confirmed that the government was pursuing a systematic campaign to "disrupt, misdirect, discredit, and otherwise neutralize" New Left activities in the black freedom, Puerto Rican independence, Native American, Chicano, antiwar, and student movements.[134] The monitoring of the Young Lords by the New York Police Department, for example, was transparent. Because the police department had a car permanently parked outside the Young Lords' office in East Harlem, the organization suspected that there had to be other, more subterranean attempts at disruption within the organization. Its leadership surmised that there would be attempts to undermine the organization at its weakest links—where new branches were being built. Part of the job of the field ministry was to protect the organization from this vulnerability.

In March 1970, the Young Lords opened an office in the South Bronx, and in May, more offices opened in Bridgeport, Connecticut, and in Boston, Massachusetts. Additional offices sprouted up in August 1970 on Manhattan's Lower East Side, and in Philadelphia. It was during this period that the organization began to conceive of itself as a national organization, even though its reach extended to only a handful of cities in the northeast. With three branches in New York—in East Harlem, the Bronx, and the Lower East Side—the Young Lords were strongest in that city. Throughout this period, the original East Harlem branch functioned as a national headquarters from which the Central Committee remained in communication with the different branches, coordinated the distribution of *Palante*, and established the framework for the education and integration of new members.

For a group that had organized full-time since its emergence in July 1969, and which had grown from approximately twenty individuals to an organization numbering in the hundreds in New York alone, the political gathering the Young Lords called "the retreat" of May 1970 was long overdue. The meeting was designed as a forum to assess the group's work and expansion since its formation less than a year earlier. With exponential growth came the challenge of assimilating its new members. Thus, the gathering was concerned with formulating "methods of work that would develop other leaders."[135] The retreat also provided an intensive course of political education as well as an opportunity to confer on some of the key political debates raised within the organization and in the movement at large. These discussions centered primarily on the position of women in society and the role of the lumpenproletariat in the struggle for social change. The convergence was the first of a series of meetings held over the course of the YLO's active life, especially during moments of political growth, disorientation, and organizational stagnation. These meetings became the venue through which the YLO would establish internal consensus on key political questions and where the leadership would initiate a guiding strategy for the group's work.

At the May 1970 retreat, the Young Lords confirmed that the lumpenproletariat would be the party's main social base. The position wedded the group to community-based organizing and to "serving the people" for the next year. However, a latent conflict of opinions over the organization's relationship to the working class became manifest at that meeting, when a minority of members supported the traditional Marxist position concerning the centrality of the working class, rather than the lumpenproletariat, as a primary force in the class struggle.

The debates on the lumpenproletariat and on the absence of gender equality were not new to the Young Lords. They had become central topics in the New Left at the time. However, in groups like the Young Lords, a rigorous consideration of the full breadth of such issues was difficult for those immersed in full-time organizing. Moreover, the political discussions that did occur were heavily dominated by the group's formal leadership. The ripples of debates surrounding the centrality of the lumpenproletariat at the retreat were evident immediately after the gathering. The Young Lords began to study more closely the meaning of socialism and the barriers to independence presented by an entrenched Puerto Rican ruling elite that endorsed the island's colonial status quo. For now, the group's critique of the island's indigenous ruling elite was a convenient way to bridge revolutionary nationalism with working-class politics. Missing still, however, was the Young Lords' assessment of their relationship to the U.S. mainland's mostly working-class Puerto Rican population. In the long term, the May debates laid the groundwork for a major political shift further down the line and an eventual embrace of a working-class orientation.

Another important dimension of the May retreat involved an assessment of the YLO's national leadership, the outcome of which had profound implications for the continued relationship between the New York and Chicago chapters. Beginning in summer 1969, when the Chicago Young Lords approved the New York charter of the organization, the New York YLO was allowed full autonomy to organize as it saw fit. The New York YLO had improved upon the models of protest established by the Chicago group and flourished in the first year of its founding, expanding the YLO's presence in northeastern cities. But the New York leadership came to believe that the Chicago-led national organization was not developing in proportion to its potential. While the Chicago Central Committee escaped criticism from the New York group during that group's first year of growth and activity, as the New York radicals began to address issues pertaining to organizational consolidation, expansion, and longevity on a national level, perceived shortcomings of the Chicago group came into sharp relief.

The New York radicals identified the absence of effective national leadership as a major obstacle to their project. According to the New York militants, the Chicago YLO had never assumed clear and resolute direction of the national organization; it also failed to cast off the vestiges of gang culture from its daily political routine.[136] Perhaps even more objectionable to the New York Lords was the national leadership's failure to meet its most important responsibility: the regular production of the organization's national newspaper, the *YLO*, which "progressive elements understood to be a key element in organizing the masses."[137]

At a moment when the YLO had more requests to organize chapters around the country than it could act upon, the question of effective leadership could not linger unresolved any longer. One of the resolutions of the New York–sponsored May retreat was to send a delegation to Chicago to persuade the Central Committee to relocate temporarily to New York for an intensive political and organizing training to bridge the gap in experience between the two groups and strengthen the national leadership. The original founders of the YLO refused the proposition. Cha Cha Jiménez observed that "the New York group had no clue about Chicago or what we were trying to do." Already skeptical of the possibility of rehabilitating a branch that they believed was disintegrating, the New York radicals resolved to sever their affiliation with the YLO. They renamed themselves the Young Lords Party. The "party" label, however, did not signify any qualitative expansion of their sphere of operations.

In their assessment of the national organization and justification for the split, which appeared in *Palante*, the New York Lords outlined their frustrations with Chicago:

> The Central Committee in Chicago was constantly changing; the only person who remained constant was Cha Cha Jiménez. Consistent leadership is necessary to set a revolutionary example for the members and the people. The members were not disciplined and many did not report regularly, so that important political work could not be done in the community all the time. This is one of the main reasons that the national monthly newspaper (*YLO*) came out only six times in eighteen months. Political education was not given to the members, so many of them still functioned the way they had when the Young Lords was a gang. . . . No political platform or program was developed. . . . When there is no political education and no program, the members flounder, become discouraged, and so do the people. Very few programs were developed in Chicago, and those that were started could not function because there was no consistent manpower.[138]

Contrary to the New York leaders' assessment, Chicago had quite a number of politically experienced members and supporters, and the organization's paper, *YLO*, was, ironically, more sophisticated than *Palante*, even though it was inconsistently published. *YLO* also regularly published letters from community residents and from other organizations, which suggested the group was connected to a community and the grassroots, despite its shortcomings. According to Cha Cha:

> We took over a church for five days, people might not have heard about it in New York, but it was all over the news in Chicago. When Manuel Ramos was killed, we went door-to-door organizing, that's why the march drew thousands. The medical clinic sent teams out door-to-door. Some of the guys were doing drugs and stupid things, we *were* the lumpen; but we were addressing that. We practically lived in the corners talking about politics. We were reading the little red book, studying and having classes. We read the collected works of Lenin, and we studied the national question. We were listening to records of speeches of Malcolm X, and we were meeting with all the socialists groups because they wanted to recruit us.[139]

Given its gang origins, the Chicago organization was bound to look and feel different from the mainly student-led New York group and face different challenges. Ironically, the New York group broke with the Chicago Young Lords because of their lumpen ways, precisely at the moment they identified that class as its social base.

Absent from the New York Young Lords' assessment was a consideration of the challenges, not to mention the trauma, that came with operating in a city such as Chicago, where the level of repression far surpassed anything they had encountered in New York. Six months before the proposed split, in December 1969, Panthers Mark Clark and Fred Hampton—with whom the Young Lords were in contact at least twice a week—were killed dictatorship-style by government agents. Months before that, the Chicago Young Lords were investigated and impugned for the bloody murders of Bruce Johnson, the pastor of the church where the Chicago Lords had established their headquarters, and his wife. The couple was stabbed nineteen and fourteen times, respectively, at the church, and their three small children were found crawling on the floor, bathed in their parents' blood.

The New York Young Lords were, in part, blinded by their meteoric success and the attention they garnered in the media, both of which imbued their leadership with a sense of invincibility that at times undermined its sense of reality, not to mention its organizational capacity. Retrospectively, leaders of the New York Young Lords wondered whether they should have reconsidered the split.

Reported in the *New York Times*, the split was amicable, sober, and without the usual acrimony associated with political faction fighting. Cha Cha reeled in his crew, which might have responded to the break with rumble. Cha Cha believes that the conflict could have been colored by a physical altercation that happened months earlier between Pablo Guzmán and a Chicago Young Lord known for "his problems with intoxication." Years later Cha Cha remarked, "The split was hard. I explained to the Chicago members that break-ups happen. I knew that from my time in the Young Lords, the gang." He continues, "In February of 1969, I got arrested with Fred Hampton twice at [two different] Welfare actions and now they [the prosecutors] were going after me over those charges. There were so many other things happening. The split came during a very hard time. But we accepted it. I remember telling them that they were our 'Revolutionary compañeros' [laughs]. I made that term up on the spot, it just came to me." Of the New York group's partial name change, he remembers, "most of us thought it was good that they kept our name, for unity."[140]

The disparate realities within which the Chicago and New York groups operated, and the apparent organizational cohesion of the New York group, meant that Chicago's opposition to the split was futile. The split also reflected the weakness of the Chicago group and its inability to take a more assertive role in the life of the national organization.

■

The Young Lords formed part of the wave of New Left students who took their politics and activism from college campuses to poor urban communities. As they set out to dramatize and address the conditions of the ghetto and barrio, they established a military-style organization whose form attempted to replicate domestically the ethos of Third World revolutionary movements. The organization's uniform and presentation were intended to inspire a sense of self-worth in its members and in the community. Young Lords adhered to strict disciplinary norms and were expected to dedicate most of their waking hours to the group's political work. In recollecting their time in the organization, veteran Young Lords describe their experience as one of "hard work" that was deeply satisfying, but also exhausting. The group's global perspective on local issues enabled it to educate its constituency with a comprehensive world view and to simultaneously attend to urgent day-to-day matters. Through their organizing and political propaganda, the Young Lords popularized the demand for Puerto Rican independence both in their own constituency and within broader movement circles. They also spread and demystified socialist ideas among poor and working-class people of color.

In their day-to-day political work, the Young Lords encountered sections of the Puerto Rican community that were not traditionally employed: housewives, welfare recipients, the elderly, young hustlers. Their lumpen orientation reflected the deep economic changes taking place in northern cities, where economic restructuring and the flight of industry to the suburbs created a class of permanently unemployed and discouraged young workers—an unprecedented development in modern urban history. In many ways, their attribution of revolutionary consciousness to the lumpen was a crude assessment of what they were seeing around them on the streets—that radical ideas may sound appealing to many people who live on the margins of society. But to paraphrase Marx, if things were as they seem, we wouldn't need science.[141] In their work, the Young Lords attempted to merge concrete community action with a broadly envisioned revolutionary theory. Internally they would also grapple with gender inequality and the divisive issue of color prejudice among Latinos. That would be a challenge they would have to confront in the months to come.

CHAPTER EIGHT

THE POLITICS
OF RACE
AND GENDER

Shortly after the Church Offensive, Young Lord Mirta González began to correspond with an Afro–Puerto Rican soldier, Carlos Rodriguez-Torres, who was imprisoned in one of the largest military prisons in the country, the stockade of the Fort Dix military base in New Jersey. She did so at the urging of Rodriguez-Torres's attorney, who knew the soldier would need moral and political support from folks like the Young Lords. Private Rodriguez-Torres was one of the Fort Dix Thirty-Eight, a group of thirty-eight imprisoned soldiers who were targeted for prosecution after they rebelled in the military prison.[1] Singled out as a "ringleader," Rodriguez-Torres was the last soldier to go to trial, charged with riot, incitement to riot, aggravated arson, conspiracy to incite riot, profanity against and assault on a noncommissioned officer, and refusing to obey a lawful order.[2] His attorneys believed that the heavy charges leveled against him were the product of racism and a form of punishment for Rodriguez-Torres's politicization in the aftermath of the rebellion.

Over the course of the 1960s, growing ambivalence toward the war's stated goals and contempt for the "body count," the dehumanizing military strategy that pressured soldiers to report the number of enemy combatants they killed in Vietnam, sparked an upsurge in insubordinate practices and resistance in the military.[3] Among other factors, disaffection was also fed by the growing knowledge that working-class boys were more likely to be conscripted and to die in Vietnam than those of the upper classes, as well as by the rebellious atmosphere created within the army by the black liberation and antiwar movements at home.[4] By late in the decade, 300 underground, antiwar GI newspapers circulated within the military. Dissent's organized and spontaneous expressions also included Vietnam Veterans Against the War and stockade rebellions, respectively. The most dramatic example of dissent was carried out by a small number of soldiers who threw hand

233

Che Ja-Ja stands in front of the Bronx office, May 1970.
(Photograph by Michael Abramson; courtesy of Haymarket Books)

grenades at their superiors to try to restrain the officer corps from driving soldiers too hard in the theater of war—a practice known as fragging.[5] But as in the case of Carlos Rodriguez-Torres, the most common form of insubordination came from soldiers who regularly engaged in drug use and went AWOL.[6]

Described as "dark-skinned, handsome and with a reputation for coolness," Rodriguez-Torres was born in New York but spent his childhood shuttling between the city and Puerto Rico, where his parents kept separate homes. At age sixteen, following the death of his mother, and desperate to kick his heroin addiction, Rodriguez-Torres volunteered for a three-year tour of duty in Vietnam with a friend. By 1969, his friend had been killed and he was back stateside at Fort Dix. That same year, the private experienced a downward spiral triggered by a verbal confrontation with his sergeant when he complained that he was being worked harder than others in his company due to racism. As punishment for insubordination, Rodriguez-Torres was commanded to dig a six-by-six-by-six-foot hole despite having blisters on his hands from similar punishing work the day before. Before long he entered a cycle of AWOL recidivism, drug use, and stockade imprisonment. According to Hendrik Hertzberg, the former U.S. naval officer, journalist, and veteran editor of the *New Yorker* who covered the trial of the Fort Dix Thirty-Eight, "Before Vietnam a soldier like Carlos Rodriguez would probably have been quietly discharged as unsuitable for military service."[7] But the high incidence of insubordination in the military produced harsh clampdowns by the officer corps in the form of soldier imprisonment.

The stockade at Fort Dix that housed Rodriguez-Torres was built during World War II for the temporary housing of 200–300 men. During the Vietnam War almost 1,000 soldiers were confined there, 90 percent of them imprisoned for going AWOL. Like many of these soldiers, Rodriguez-Torres was not predisposed to participate in collective action against the military. When asked about his political views before the stockade rebellion, he responded, "Man, I didn't have any, I really dug the Army."[8] But as numbers grew inside Fort Dix, similarities among the soldiers and shared conditions of repression established conditions for mass rebellion.

At Fort Dix, overcrowding was compounded by repression. Guards used heat and air conditioning as disciplinary tools; temperatures were "either kept so high they are sweating or so low they are freezing." Like Sisyphus, prisoners had to regularly push a "150-pound cement roller" from one end of the stockade to the other or rake the gravel in the yard. They were also forced to stand in the sun at parade rest for four or five hours at a time. A 700-calorie diet was imposed on some of the prisoners, which led to a loss of up to 50 percent of their body weight. The humiliation of black American and Puerto Rican soldiers was common. These men had worn tall Afros in the theater of war, but they were now targeted, dragged to the military barbershop, and forcibly given the long-unobserved "regulation" haircut. Black Americans, Puerto Ricans, and political prisoners were disproportionately placed in solitary confinement.[9] The army's effort at deterrence—incarceration and fierce penalization for the slightest infraction—fed the overcrowding, hardened the negative disposition of many enlisted men toward the army, and made some of them susceptible to the ideas of a small number of politicized organizers in their ranks.

On June 5, 1969, amid a day of particularly repressive and arbitrary activity by the guards, a solider threw a footlocker out of the window of one of the cellblocks. Soon after, other soldiers began burning mattresses and raising chants against the war and stockade conditions. Between 150 and 250 prisoners in three different cells participated in the spontaneous upheaval.[10] Armed with riot gear, 250 members of the military police were called to put down the uprising. According to subsequent reports, "No guards were injured. There was no violence perpetrated against any of the prisoners by other prisoners. No prisoners attacked or fought with guards. The riot had been a spontaneous reaction to conditions and was directed against property, not people."[11]

The rebellion only lasted for an hour, but it resonated far longer. Because it came a year after the sit-down strike of seventy-five prisoners at the Presidio stockade in San Francisco—one of the first domestic examples of collective GI antiwar protest against abuses in the stockade—the nation was watching.[12] At Fort Dix, two months after the rebellion, an investigation by Congressman Mario Biaggi of the Bronx confirmed the "charges of brutality, starvation diet, and general inhuman conditions" filed by the attorneys representing the Fort Dix stockade prisoners.[13]

On the day of the rebellion, Rodriguez-Torres was being processed for release from the stockade; he claimed he had not been anywhere near the melee. Yet he was identified as one of five ringleaders, reimprisoned, and eventually court-martialed alongside four other more politically conscious soldiers. Of that experience Rodriguez-Torres reported, "I've learned a lot from my partners Klug and Brakefield, and in a way I'm glad I was here, with the other prisoners. It's opened my eyes."[14]

The trajectory of Rodriguez-Torres's life, from alienated Puerto Rican youth and drug user to politicized GI, fortified the Young Lords' belief that social conditions in the United States were opening the door to political transformation through collective resistance and conscious political study. Their revolutionary organization would respond by channeling the growing discontent and disaffection of ordinary people and amplifying emotionally evocative stories of Puerto Rican resistance and survival like that of Rodriguez-Torres.

On March 9, 1970, a group of approximately twenty Young Lords traveled to the Fort Dix military base in New Jersey by bus. They were joined by members of the American Servicemen's Union, a group of former and enlisted soldiers begun in 1967 by Andy Stapp of the Workers World Party that sought to organize resistance inside the military. According to FBI records, Newark counterintelligence informed the New York police and Fort Dix officials in advance that the Young Lords planned "to pack the courtroom . . . [and] disrupt the . . . proceeding" of one of Rodriguez-Torres's final general court-martial hearings.[15]

In his arguments to the military board, the soldier's attorney Henry di Suvero would argue that his client's addiction was incubated in the hardships of his youth and that prison was no answer for someone whose problems were defined by social, rather than individual, failings.[16]

The Young Lords emerged from the courtroom in awed silence. Even though a guilty verdict was expected, they were shocked by the transparently autocratic proceeding, where those pressing charges appointed the prosecutor, defense, and jury and where court-martial boards were composed of officers and senior-grade enlisted men who would almost always vote to prosecute. Richie Perez remembers that when the proceedings ended, the Young Lords were immediately marched out of the courtroom building by military police (MP), with their batons held ready for combat. According to Carlito Rovira, "That little song and dance went on all the way to the bus."[17] Amid the shoving, an argument between a Young Lord and an officer spiraled into a physical confrontation. The tension then escalated when someone in the group clicked a camera. When an officer attempted to confiscate it, the Young Lord holding it shouted, "Man, fuck you! If you think you are going to confiscate this camera, you better call the army."[18] When the officer called for backup, another group of MP pushed the Young Lords more aggressively toward the bus with their batons.

The organization had rules about brawling. Perez explains that "only certain people among the Young Lords had the authority to start the battle, but once the battle was started everybody was expected to throw down. So as we're getting pushed to the bus one of the defense ministry people just knocked out one of the dudes . . . punched one of the GIs in the face." Rovira, who was in the back of the line, "heard someone cry out, 'Rumble.'"[19] According to Perez, the women and men in the Young Lords "started throwing down, punching bim, bam, bim bam. . . . Everyone was so aggravated by what we had seen and felt so helpless, that this was a way for us to express it."[20]

While the young radicals did battle outside the courthouse, another cluster of them held an unconscious member of the MP in the bus for a brief period. According to Rovira, amid the melee, the MP officer "got shoved into the bus, but we weren't exactly trying to take him away to East Harlem with us."[21] The scuffle continued unabated until additional police finally overwhelmed and arrested the radicals at gunpoint. Eventually, the Young Lords were fingerprinted and served with injunctions barring them from the military installation, which they refused to sign.[22] They were then driven long distances deep into the woods of the facility's outlying area and dispersed in pairs by the MP, so as to neutralize their ability to reconstitute themselves and return.

Historically, this magnitude of resistance within society's most regimented body—the military—signals a qualitative erosion of government authority and its legitimacy. These moments indicate a collapse of dominant ideology—the complex phenomenon of subject formation through which members of society learn their place in the polity, accept subordination within it, and rationalize its social contradictions, injustices, and inequities. Yet, as old ways of interpreting reality lose legitimacy, elements of dominant ideology endure. Some become major battlegrounds. In the sixties, the persistence of race and gender ideologies, both in society and within the ranks of the movements, became major sites of struggle.[23]

The Young Lords' rumble after the trial of Rodriguez-Torres was risky. The expectation within the group that everyone would "throw down" revealed a tendency within the male-dominated organization to rely on brawn rather than strategy. This episode exemplified the pitfalls of the Lords' faith in what they called "revolutionary machismo." The daring militancy at the Fort Dix military base affirmed their hubris and created, at times, a somewhat distorted lens through which the Young Lords assessed their political world. The incident bolstered their perspective—that the legitimacy of U.S. hegemony had eroded qualitatively around the world, that a shift in power relations was on its way domestically, and that the oppressed of the world would soon collectively reorganize society in their own interest. The battles with the outside world—with the racist pigs on the corner, with the inequalities of capitalism, and with the oppression and rapacity of colonialism—were clear-cut. Far murkier, however, were the battles within.

The organization's vision of a society free from bigotry was tested in the day-to-day interactions of its members, who didn't immediately shake off years of socialization into color and gender prejudices when they signed up to become Young Lords. The project of prefiguring the values of a socialist society in everyday struggles spoke especially to the women of the Young Lords. Since the founding of the New York Young Lords in July 1969, women had been vital to the group's lifeblood and its day-to-day work. Sonia Ivany, Denise Oliver, Iris Morales, Irma Martinez, Iris Benitez, Lulu Limardo, Marlene Cintron, and Elena González were among its early and founding members. Like the men of the group, they had left either school, home, or work to become full-time activists. But the masculinist culture of the Young Lords and chauvinist practices of some of its male members diminished the standing of their female counterparts, assaulted their dignity, and weakened the organization.

Within the broader movement, these issues had long been a source of quiet tension among organizers.[24] Despite the movements' egalitarian aspirations, men expected women to perform the movement's grunt work, from fetching coffee and preparing food to typing letters and reproducing flyers, a reflection of the conventional role of women in the larger society as mothers and caretakers. But by the late 1960s, the shift to direct action within the feminist movement's radical current had forced a debate in the public square on the sources of women's oppression that changed their standing in society.[25]

The emergence of the Young Lords in 1969, just as second-wave feminism deepened its political imprint in society, had compelled its mostly male founders to respond to the problem of women's oppression in the organization's formally written program and platform. But despite its articulated aim of building a new society of enriched human relations grounded in social equality and mutual respect—what the Argentine revolutionary Che Guevara called the "new man" and "new woman"—old patterns of male chauvinism persisted.[26] The upsurge of women following the Church Offensive emboldened a vocal cohort among them who launched a campaign proposing that leaders and cadre alike walk their talk. Vehemently resented by some, it called on members to embody the organization's politics and values in their personal lives and interactions with each other. The women of the organization called this "the revolution within the revolution." Having come to political consciousness in the hour of women's liberation, the women of the Young Lords were well positioned to have their leadership respected, voices heard, and demands met.

Race and color prejudice was the other major issue of contestation in the ranks of the Young Lords. Although the Young Lords Party had a multiethnic rank and file, its majority, first- and second-generation Puerto Ricans, grew up on the thresholds of two cultures with competing understandings of racial identity forged out of the different histories of slavery in the continental United States and Puerto Rico. On the whole, at home, Puerto Rican parents taught their children to identify with their national, linguistic, and ethnic origins and deny identification with race, if it was of the black variety. This calculus ran counter to norms in the continental United States. Here Puerto Ricans were often categorized racially, not ethnically, and compelled to identify as black or white. These diametrically opposed ways of seeing produced a torturous struggle of self-definition for many. For some, the experience, however painful, offered a measure of comparative perspective, a kind of "second sight" or "double consciousness" in the Du Boisian sense, that opened the door to the integration of competing ways of seeing, born of two diametrically opposed social orders.

A Hybrid Experience of Race

At the First Spanish United Methodist Church, the Young Lords had staged a striking vision of a new world that elicited both marvel and unease among many who witnessed it. The diverse racial and ethnic composition of that new world captured the interest of the city's major Spanish newspaper, *El Diario La Prensa*. The paper's carefully crafted description of the Young Lords presented their mingling of races as a new practice by a younger generation of Puerto Ricans in the city: "These young men and women, Puerto Ricans—some white and others of the black race—and among them some Americans, love the ideal of independence for Puerto Rico. . . . They ascertain that they form part of a coalition with the Black Panther Party and the Young Patriots."[27] While the article was sympathetic to the Young Lords' idealistic call for "liberation of the oppressed," its discomfort was evident in the labored description of the group's racial makeup. The Young Lords were a far cry from the older, island-born, disproportionately white or light-skinned political leadership that most Puerto Ricans were accustomed to seeing.[28] By contrast, as the onetime Young Lord attorney Geraldo Rivera observed, "The Lords were a different complexion: younger, darker, primarily English-speaking and mainland born."[29]

Within the Puerto Rican community of the 1960s, experiential differences between younger and older generations aroused competing perspectives on issues of race. The editors of *El Diario La Prensa* regularly expressed the most traditional and rigid view of the matter. Three months before it covered the Young Lords' occupation of the People's Church, the newspaper vehemently declared its opposition to efforts by black American and Puerto Rican student activists and faculty at various campuses of the City University of New York to combine black American and Puerto Rican studies programs into one ethnic studies department. An editorial read, in part: "Historically, culturally, and psychologically both are totally different in origin and development. Puerto Ricans, moreover, have not lived the Black American's experience and cannot identify with it."[30] Disconsonant with the era's shift in consciousness, this unabashed and absolute rejection of Puerto Ricans' common experience with black Americans did not make references to race but concealed a social distancing energized by racism. The maneuver was a projection of a distinctive Latin American expression of racism and race ideology, different from that which emerged in the United States. Cohered over centuries of Spanish colonial rule and reinforced by the nation-building projects that swept through the continent in the late nineteenth century, race ideology in Latin America had tolerated, codified, and promoted race mixing, or *mestizaje*, as a strategy of domination for erasing and depoliticizing black and indigenous resistance. Achieved variously through education, class mobility, or genetic mixing, the ideology of *mestizaje* promoted the "lightening" of the population, erased the presence of black people and their culture, and denied the existence of racism in these Latin American societies. In Puerto Rico, for example, where Afro-descendants made up conservatively 20 percent of the population, Puerto Rican society had historically denied or minimized the presence and influence of black people, black culture, and the black aesthetic.[31]

In the continental United States, the view expressed in the newspaper's editorial reflected the long-standing trend among newcomers to distance themselves from black Americans to protect their own tenuous standing and their chance at upward mobility.[32] The statement echoed long-standing prejudices, but it did not reflect the complexity of experience brought on by the changing pattern of Puerto Rican migration and settlement during the twentieth century. The sentiment was likely held by many who settled in New York during the first decades of the twentieth century. This wave of Puerto Rican migrants merged their political interests and identities with the city's Spanish-speaking enclave. That preexisting community self-identified as Hispanic—a term that denotes European ancestry—and Spaniards and their small businesses and civic organizations made up its majority, but Cuban and Latin American immigrants made a home there too. With a combined population of merely 0.7 percent of New

York's residents, this community's small size and the language barrier alone created an insular experience, even among its Spanish-dominant, darker-hued newcomers. Yet *El Diario's* proclamation did not reflect the lived experiences of black Puerto Ricans, who, despite their diverse perceptions of themselves, had been historically construed as black American in the public square and treated accordingly. In the late nineteenth century, for example, the Afro–Puerto Rican bibliophile Arturo Schomburg turned the conundrum into a lifelong identification and pursuit of common cause with black Americans. By contrast, the socialist writer Jesús Colón, who settled in New York during World War I, "saw himself as a Puerto Rican man who happened to be black."[33]

The editorial's assertion also lagged behind reality by at least thirty years. By the 1930s, Puerto Ricans made up 17.9 percent of the amalgam of Spanish-speaking people in the city.[34] In a country defined by the politics and economy of race, the increase of this population of Afro-descended people could not escape notice and would have consequences for all involved: the city, Puerto Ricans, black Americans, white New Yorkers, and other Latin America–descended people.

Puerto Rican postwar migration coincided with the comparably large movement of black southerners to the city and white flight to the suburbs. It also happened alongside the shift in the city's economy from manufacturing to service. Demographic and structural transformation propelled a process of racialization among Puerto Ricans that had been in flux until then. During the Depression years, for example, Puerto Ricans had been grouped racially with black Americans and perceived as biologically inferior, dependent, and diseased. In the postwar period, however, their hardships and troubles had been compared sympathetically to those of European "immigrants" before them. They had also been simultaneously disparaged as undeserving outsiders, incapable of self-rule, who were taking away jobs, burdening the city, and prone to criminal activity. But beginning in the late 1960s, the racialization of Puerto Ricans began to cohere. They began to be identified as dark racial foreigners, distinct from black Americans, predisposed to delinquency and violence.[35] Their close proximity to black Americans surely didn't help. As discussed earlier, in 1960 the census reported that Puerto Ricans and black Americans were more or less equally divided demographically in East Harlem, comprising 40.4 and 38.2 percent of the population, respectively.[36] Their growing demonization in public discourse mirrored the indignities they suffered in government bureaucracies and hospitals and at the hands of school staff and the police. That many Puerto Ricans suffered these indignities alongside black Americans *in the age of civil rights* provoked a reckoning with blackness that radically transformed their perception of their neighbors and themselves. The experience was finally captured in 1967 in the best-selling memoir *Down These Mean Streets*, Piri Thomas's searing portrait of poverty and racism growing up Puerto Rican and black in East Harlem.

Although not inevitable, the rise of the Young Lords and their dynamic demographic composition reflected the social reorganization of postwar Puerto Rican life. Compared to the disproportionately white leaders of other Puerto Rican organizations, the Young Lords' formal leadership body, the Central Committee, had a darker racial makeup. The majority, three out of five members, were Afro–Puerto Ricans. Two of the five, Juan González and David Perez, were fair-skinned Puerto Ricans who, absent their last names, might have passed for Italian American. The three others—Felipe Luciano, Pablo "Yoruba" Guzmán, and Juan "Fi" Ortiz—were unequivocally black. At first sight, their Afros, skin color, and facial features made them indistinguishable from black Americans. The same was true of the Young Lords' membership. The racial profile of the leadership drew a disproportionate number of Afro–Puerto Ricans into the group's ranks. Historically, many Afro–Puerto Ricans struggled to define themselves at the margins of two cultures with competing ideologies of race forged under very different social and historical conditions. They knew Puerto Rican antiblackness intimately. But they were also painfully familiar with their black American friends' summary dismissal of Puerto Rican claims to language and ethnicity as fundamental markers of self-definition.

For many members, the Young Lords provided a place to feel understood for the first time and to feel that they belonged. Pablo Guzmán articulated the experience of a segment of second- and third-generation Puerto Rican migrants powerfully when he wrote in *Palante*, "Before people called me a spic, they called me a nigger."[37] The experience had been documented by Puerto Ricans as early as the late nineteenth century during their first significant migration wave to New York. In the main, they forged middle-class mutual aid and cultural organizations alongside Cuban Afro-descendants living in New York that emphasized individual uplift, national solidarity, and diasporic unity among people of African descent.[38] New and emergent in the 1960s, however, was a conscious public campaign embraced by the Young Lords and others to transform the racial consciousness of Puerto Ricans by celebrating Afro–Puerto Rican identity and analyzing the sociohistoric roots of racial prejudice within Puerto Rican society. Their message also called for Puerto Rican and black American unity on the basis of a common experience of racism, colonial oppression, poverty, and working-class exploitation.

Black Americans also joined the Young Lords. Leading members of the organization estimate that black Americans made up between 25 and 30 percent of the group's membership. The organization's black leadership and fair share of Afro–Puerto Ricans appealed to black Americans as did its deliberate conceptualization of itself as sister organization to the Black Panther Party—the era's boldest expression of organized black resistance. The political disarray into which the Black Panthers fell, precisely at the moment when the Young Lords emerged, also propelled black Americans' membership in the Young Lords. But the basis of the group's cross-ethnic membership was rooted in the experience of everyday life. The hybridity of experience between black Americans and Puerto Ricans was anchored materially in their shared postwar migration patterns. Felipe Luciano hints at the common rural experience, which fueled identity convergences between many black Americans and Puerto Ricans:

> The blacks that we were dealing with came from three states: Georgia, North Carolina, and South Carolina. . . . The ones I knew were rural. They were from Charleston, Savannah, Buford. . . . When we came in, we were jibaros too. We dress[ed] in red shoes and green pants and we would come to New York without coats. They gave us coats. They gave us food. These were the people who fed us, who nurtured us, and so the relationship, while strained because of race, was tremendously intimate in terms of love. In spite of the racial differences . . . there came an attraction.[39]

Common lived experiences pushed black Americans and Puerto Ricans together. Both lived in an urban environment where poverty was qualitatively different than before, marked by economic restructuring and structural unemployment, combined with the shared experience of police brutality in the streets and the various forms that racism took in northern cities. Reflecting on their shared interests, Luciano continues: "We were living in bad housing, we were oppressed by police, institutionally we were discriminated against, we had objective, empirical issues that we had to fight together. . . . Even white Puerto Ricans were affected by that. Therefore, their natural partners had to be blacks."[40] As discussed in chapter 2, common traumatic schooling experiences laid the groundwork for cross-ethnic collaboration, particularly in the face of white backlash against integration in the late 1960s. Even before she joined the Young Lords, the fair-skinned Iris Morales regularly joined black radical organizations in high school and in college.[41]

The emphasis on race and class in the Young Lords' campaigns made the involvement of black Americans inevitable. But before finding widespread political expression in the 1960s, the common currents between the groups could be heard in music. Black American and Puerto Rican migrants forged a dynamic postwar urban culture during the decades they worked, studied, and created alongside each other despite their ethnic differences. As noted by the late sociologist and cultural theorist Juan Flores, "Black Americans and Puerto Ricans in New York had been partying together for many years . . . since the musical revolution of the late 1940s, when musical giants like Mario Bauza, Machito, and Dizzie Gillespie joined forces in the creation of 'Cubop' or Latin Jazz."[42] Gilbert Colón, a self-identified Afro-Latino Young Lord, was introduced early to the dance scene by his parents and aunt, who were regulars at the Palladium, New York's legendary Latin music ballroom. His parents were part of an earlier wave of immigrants and migrants from Cuba and Puerto Rico who settled in New York in the 1920s.[43] Colón recalls that the parties he frequented played rhythm and blues as well as salsa, and even WBLS, the flagship black music radio station in New York, "played salsa sometimes." He also notes that "white people—specifically a lot of Jewish people—were also into salsa and dancing. You would have black and Puerto Rican women dancing with white men—and vice versa. So on a sociological level, there was a level of interaction that was allowed in that setting that you didn't see elsewhere."[44] While Colón embraced the Latin rhythms of his parents' generation, others, such as the fair-skinned Young Lord Carlito Rovira, found refuge in black urban culture and rejected their Puerto Rican identity and ethnicity. "I was alienated because I knew I wasn't black or white, but I felt an affinity for black culture," Rovira says. "I was listening to Motown. We were taking our cues from African Americans. We were dressing like them, dancing like them, talking like them. Meanwhile my father was listening to Trio Mayarí and he wasn't too happy about what I was gravitating to culturally."[45]

Black American Denise Oliver was among those immersed in the rich cultural overlaps between black and Spanish Harlem. In his recollections of those years, Felipe Luciano remembers: "Denise loved Latin music. Danced her pants off . . . had an affinity for a culture that was African but had another patina to it. That is, she understood the African nature of Puerto Rican society when [Puerto Ricans] didn't." Of the organic manifestations of intercultural solidarity that came to define an emerging Nuyorican identity in the 1960s, Luciano says: "Puerto Ricans kept a nugget of their culture and their aesthetic deep within them, but the relationships that they developed with black people were so deep and so loving and so contradictory and so enmeshed that it developed a new culture, and you could hear it in the music. . . . Blacks and Puerto Ricans in New York—when you say the word, it already connotes a whole experience."[46]

It was in this context that the experiences of a generation reared in a moment of racial solidarity gave shape to boogaloo, which combined rhythm and blues and soul traditions with Afro-Cuban and Puerto Rican musical idioms. Boogaloo became hugely popular among both groups with Joe Cuba's "Bang Bang" and Pete Rodriguez's "I Like It Like That."[47] The same cultural moment would also give birth to a more explicit shift among a younger generation of Puerto Ricans. Gilbert Colón remembers "the slammin' house party where they played 'Say It Loud' when it first came out—'I'm black and I'm proud.' I remember it was summertime and everybody being like, 'Yeah, that's right.' And all of the Latinos I knew who could have an Afro started wearing them."[48] It was around that time that Colón began to challenge his mother when she advised against dating a girl darker than he was. He was one of many younger Puerto Ricans turning toward a black-identified racial consciousness.

Although Puerto Rican and black American interactions were certainly marked by conflict and prejudice, the Young Lords were in a special position to build an explicit politics against racism and colorism within their generational cohort. Whereas in the past Puerto Ricans and other Latinxs had sought answers to these questions as individuals or in small circles, the mass character of the black freedom movement opened the possibility for a collective response to and a public engagement of the issue among Latinxs. By examining their own views on race, studying the origins of racial ideology in Puerto Rico and in Latin America, making it integral to their practice, and welcoming black Americans into their ranks, the Young Lords embraced the assignment more systematically than any of their Puerto Rican contemporaries.[49]

Yet in spite of the growing sense of black pride among Puerto Ricans and common cause with black Americans, prejudice and conflict abounded even within the Young Lords. Sometime in the winter of 1970, a conflict between a fair-skinned female Puerto Rican recruit and a long-standing and trusted black American member who went by the name of Jaja sharpened internal debates around prejudice and racism in the organization. A veteran who had been a prisoner of war in Korea, Jaja had been politicized when the Korean army performed lifesaving surgery on his brain, sparing his life on account of his race. According to Carlito Rovira, after a series of interactions with the new recruit, Jaja detected that she was unconsciously afraid of him taking care of her daughter. He raised the issue publicly at a meeting and in so doing "opened up a can of worms about how Puerto Ricans had absorbed dominant racist fears about black Americans and black men, especially, and it gave us a deeper understanding of the different ways racism is manifested."[50] As this conversation spread through the organization, the Young Lords responded by "waging ideological struggle" against these tendencies in their internal and public meetings, in their literature, and by building an organizational culture of intolerance of racism.

The Young Lords' most observable intervention came in the form of analysis and political propaganda, which they disseminated through their newspaper *Palante* and radio program on WBAI. The newspaper was a key tool in challenging racism through political education. The many articles on the matter reflected a conscious and systematic attempt to challenge dominant ideas about race in Puerto Rico and antagonisms between black Americans and Puerto Ricans on the mainland. *Palante* published articles on the character of Native American society in Puerto Rico, Cuba, and the Dominican Republic before Spanish colonization; the nature and character of African slavery on these islands; African and Native American influences on Puerto Rico's language and culture; and African and Native American resistance to Spanish rule. The paper featured an article on the history of the Puerto Rican coastal town of Loiza, a town settled by runaway slaves from the British colonies, and the centrality of Loiza's Nigerian cultural and musical legacies to Puerto Rico's national culture and identity.[51] Readers of the newspaper also encountered an array of articles on black American history and the influence of Afro–Puerto Ricans on Puerto Rican politics and culture, including short biographies of black radicals across the Americas such as Sojourner Truth, H. Rap Brown, Malcolm X, Emeterio Betances, and the Afro-Cuban revolutionary Antonio Maceo.[52]

The Young Lords were determined to speak what was known but unspoken. Influenced by their own experiences as racialized "others" and inspired by the black power movement's humanistic assertion that "black is beautiful," the Young Lords launched an aggressive campaign of education on race ideology and racial inequality among Puerto Ricans—a fact of life that too often, they felt, was either avoided or denied within the Puerto Rican community. They made public a conversation about race that had been confined to hushed whispers among most Puerto Ricans, who were often ignorant of the racially charged character of their comments. Writing in *Palante* in an article titled "Puerto Rican Racism," Iris Morales took on the subject: "Puerto Ricans don't like to talk about racism or admit that it exists among Puerto Ricans. Boricuas talk of an island that is free from racism, or they say that the amerikkkan brought it in. Although the amerikkkan did make it worse, racism in Puerto Rico began with the spanish." Morales traces the origins of racism in Puerto Rico to the enslavement and exploitation in gold mines and plantations of Taino Indians and Africans. As justification for their own savagery, she argued, Spaniards depicted Tainos as "savage, unchristian, and of another race" and Africans as "inferior, uncivilized and of an alien race."[53] Unlike liberals who explained racism as a by-product of bad ideas and lack of interaction between people of different races, the Young Lords, like other radicals, argued that racism was an outgrowth of the economic organization of society.

Beyond theorizing racial formation in Latin America, the Young Lords emphasized the centrality of southern slavery, black American oppression, and antiblack race ideology to the lived experience of racism in the United States. Accordingly, they affirmed the primacy of the black American freedom struggle to the defeat of U.S. capitalism. The group also traced the impact of mainland structures of racism on all Puerto Ricans, where "light skinned Puerto Ricans start viewing themselves as white and their compatriots as Black, reflecting [the practices of] American society. . . . Many . . . say I'm american, I'm spanish, or I'm white in order to avoid identification as Puerto Rican."[54] The group countered by giving those who were drawn to the organization a sense of pride in their ethnicity and a sense of their humanity. They had implemented this work earlier, during the Church Offensive, where the Young Lords debunked Euro-centric constructions of knowledge and highlighted the significance of people of color the world over as agents of change in history. These classes were part of the broader movement's demand for ethnic and women's studies.[55]

In their straightforward and down-to-earth manner, the Young Lords thus posited an analysis of the various ways in which Puerto Ricans on the mainland not only denied the existence of racism but also denied their race and sometimes even their Puerto Rican ethnicity, language, and heritage. They exposed the tendency even among Afro–Puerto Ricans to deny their color and the known tendency among all newcomers to disassociate themselves from black Americans to escape further exclusion: "Many Black Puerto Ricans cling to being Puerto Rican in order to negate their blackness.... Both black and light-skinned Puerto Ricans adopt racist attitudes toward Afro-American brothers and sisters."[56]

In their zealous pursuit of solidarity between Puerto Rican and black Americans, the Young Lords didn't always convey the complexity of Puerto Rican mainland identity. Because of Puerto Rico's long-standing colonial relationship to the United States, the identity of many Puerto Ricans has been strongly organized around cultural and political independence, defined by the idea of the nation, not by race.[57] For Puerto Ricans living on the U.S. mainland, where the migrants experienced both exclusion and nostalgia for their homeland, their identification with the island was amplified by the revolution in ethnic pride heralded by the black power movement. While Puerto Rican mainland identity may have been influenced by prejudice against black Americans, Puerto Ricans' refusal to accept a racial signifier—black—was for some a repudiation of the singular U.S. tendency to treat race as a primary identity trait.

Puerto Ricans, like most people of Latin American descent, identify cultural heritage as the primary formative element in their social identity.[58] Reared in a setting with conceptions of race forged under Spanish rather than British colonialism, Puerto Ricans do not adhere to the U.S. mainland practice, reserved primarily for people of color, of subordinating cultural to racial identification. In fact, the United States' rigid racial discourse is the exception and not the rule in the Americas—a product of the greater exploitative character of American slavery and the legally sanctioned, post–Civil War racial apartheid that developed in the United States in the late nineteenth century.[59] In fact, the Young Lords' discourse on these issues, however limited, introduced new ways of seeing race through comparative analyses of race ideology as it developed under vastly different conditions in the United States and Latin America.

The Young Lords introduced their lay readership to a conversation on comparative racial formations in Latin America and the United States that was until then restricted to academia.[60] In the same article discussed above, Morales explained: "[In the United States] the formula for racism says 'one drop of Black blood makes you Black.' As a result, Puerto Ricans as a mixed people are considered Blacks, and all Puerto Ricans become victims of U.S. racism."[61] Although the racial experience of mainland Puerto Ricans was more complicated, often varying widely depending on a person's skin color and language, the Young Lords labored to understand historical conditions in Latin America, where imperial decline and the vast demographic advantage of Indians and slaves produced a different race ideology. Expounding further on the different conception of race forged under Spanish colonialism in Puerto Rico and the origins of racism in Latin America, Morales explained: "According to them, one drop of white blood meant you were white and better than your black compatriot. Acceptance was given according to the 'degree of whiteness.'"[62] She goes on to link the construction of race identity within the context of Spanish rule to the "axiom of life" in Puerto Rico and Latin America: "'Que hay que mejorar la raza . . .' Puerto Ricans believe that to better the race you must marry a light skinned Puerto Rican."[63]

Like many radicals before them, including the Puerto Rican socialist Jesús Colón, the Young Lords also argued that racism was the primary ideological tool used by capitalists to sow divisions among working people of all races to preclude a collective uprising by people at the bottom of society.[64] They explained that while black Americans and Puerto Ricans were "taught that the other is inferior and to be avoided or hated" both suffered under similar oppressive social conditions in terms of unemployment, a disproportionate vulnerability to the draft and drug abuse, and poor healthcare, housing, and education.[65] Of divisions among the poor and working class, they wrote: "We have been divided and conquered by the enemy in hundreds of ways—housewives against prostitutes, young against old, men against women, Puerto Ricans against Afro-Americans, unionized workers against non-union workers, workers against drug addicts, families against other families, one arabal against another. These contradictions should be . . . settled . . . so we can unite against the enemy."[66]

However, unlike that of the socialists and communists of the 1930s, the Young Lords' world view was influenced not just by Marxism but by the theoretical frameworks of anti-imperialist writers like Frantz Fanon and Albert Memmi, among others. They were part of a rising cadre of radicals of color who emphasized the fallout of the colonial project on colonial subjects—in the form of an alienated consciousness of inferiority and dependency. As a means of building an antiracist culture and consciousness, the Young Lords institutionalized their analysis of racism formally with the publication of their pamphlet *Ideology of the Young Lords Party*, which members were required to read and master. A section of the pamphlet defined "colonized mentality" as the kinds of uncritical, racially derogatory remarks expressed in day-to-day life among Puerto Ricans and the oppressed: "That Black is bad and ugly and dirty, that kinky hair is 'pelo malo,' [that] we call Black Puerto Ricans names like prieto, moulleto, and cocolo."[67] This antiblack racism among colonized subjects was a kind of false consciousness, in the Marxist sense, meant to disorient people who share common objective interests. "The colonizers divide us up, teach us to fight against each other, because as long as we fight against each other we won't deal with our real problems—slavery, hunger, and misery. We are so brainwashed by the newspapers we read, the books they write for us, the television, the radio, the schools, and the church, that we don't know what our real thoughts are anymore. We are afraid to be leaders because we are taught to be followers. . . . We are told that we cannot exist without amerikkkans in Puerto Rico, and we believe it, even though we know that our nation existed for hundreds of years without them. All of this brainwashing, this colonized mentality, holds us back from our liberation."[68]

The organization's analysis of how the dominant ideas of society are replicated in schools, the media, and the church suggests that its members may have been among the early readers of Louis Althusser, whose critique and writings on ideology—such as *Ideology and Ideological State Apparatuses*—were in the air and later anchored new fields of inquiry in the academy, such as postmodernism and critical race theory in the 1980s.[69]

Whether they were conscious of it or not, the Young Lords had a more pliable understanding of race and identity than black Americans. Despite their self-proclaimed Puerto Rican nationalism, one of their major publications identifies the Young Lords Party as "a Party of Afro-Americans and Puerto Ricans," a statement that a predominantly black American organization with Puerto Rican members would have been hard-pressed to proclaim. Because of the openness of the group and its genuine commitment to building coalitions among people of color, it attracted an ethnically and racially diverse membership. Beyond its black American membership of approximately 25 percent, another 5 to 8 percent were non–Puerto Rican Latinos, among them Cubans, Dominicans, Panamanians, and Colombians.[70] A significant number were also radicals with bicultural backgrounds whose parents were Cuban and Puerto Rican, black American and Puerto Rican, and in the case of Young Lord Rafael Viera, Kenyan and Puerto Rican.

In addition to shifting the relationship between whites and people of color in the United States, the New Left, of which the Young Lords were a part, also transformed the racial identities of people of color and the relationships among them. The change was incubated in a historical understanding of the origins and fallout of racism in the Americas. The Young Lords' literature, radio program on WBAI, and militant organizing popularized and contributed greatly to this theorization, from below, of race. In addition, the mingling of people of color from different backgrounds infused the organization with a sense of joy and freedom, as they built within their ranks a microcosm of the bold new society emblazoned in their Thirteen-Point Program.

Challenging the Patriarchy

From their origins as a 1960s street gang, the original Young Lords was fundamentally a male organization. Yet that masculine quality was never quite as pronounced in New York City. While many of the group's male members had not significantly studied the meaning of gender oppression or considered its consequences, the problem had been addressed in the Young Lords' Thirteen-Point Program. The emergence of the New York group had coincided with the feminist movement's radicalization, whose shift to militant disruption a year earlier put women's equality in the front of the bus and at the center of public dialogue. This shift in consciousness, combined with the work of the women of the Young Lords itself, made women's oppression inescapable for these radicals. Unlike other similar organizations of the period, the New York Young Lords' founding political document—its Thirteen-Point Program and Platform—took a position on women's equality. Point 10 read: "We Want Equality for Women. Machismo Must be Revolutionary . . . Not Oppressive."[71] The formulation was odd; but it evoked Che Guevara's new man and new woman and his entreaty to revolutionaries to eradicate "the vestiges of the past" by creating enriched human relations through common struggle, mutual respect, and a deliberate process of self-education.[72] Yet, in the thick of party life, women's equality disappeared in the gap between word and deed. In fact, patriarchal ideology was so firmly ingrained in the structure and fabric of society, and the psyches of those who opposed it, that it escaped detection even as the group was erecting a platform against it.[73]

Present at the Young Lords' creation, women formed a vital part of the cohort of radical students at the State University of New York College at Old Westbury (SUNY Old Westbury), out of which the Young Lords emerged in New York. Although some are only remembered by their first names, like Yvonne, Hope, and Chris, they participated in campus protests to diversify the faculty and student body and in on-site support at the Ocean Hill–Brownsville school experiment project.[74] Some, like Chris, formerly of the Student Nonviolent Coordinating Committee (SNCC), and Denise Oliver, contributed firsthand accounts of their participation in the southern civil rights movement and knowledge of the era's influential black thinkers and political debates. Others like Chiqui Reyes and Marlene Cintron were new to organizing but no strangers to issues of power and inequity. As part of the school's tightly knit cohort of students of color these

Young Lords member sells copies of *Palante*, 1970. (Photograph by Luis C. Garza)

How would you like to have me for a child?

"Mom wants YOU
to Hang Up your Clothes!"

KEEP AMERICA
BEAUTIFUL

CLEAN YOUR ROOM

Parents Protest $1.00
POSTERS each

A Store with Sensitivity

PALANTE 25
LATIN REVOLUTIONARY NEWS SERVICE
YOUNG LORDS PARTY

WELCOME BACK

HUEY

INSIDE

women helped build a dynamic political culture on campus and participated in early discussions on Puerto Rican nationalism. When Mickey Melendez created the Young Lords' predecessor, La Sociedad Albizu Campos, many attended its meetings on campus and in East Harlem. As Denise Oliver remembers, "We didn't have enough people of any one ethnicity to form a black or Puerto Rican anything. We were all part of the nonwhite caucus. That included women. And everybody said, 'Yeah, okay, cool. Right on.'"[75] Together with their male peers, women engaged in a process of discussion and decision-making that brought black American and Puerto Rican artists and organizers to campus, among them future Young Lords Felipe Luciano and Juan González. They also participated in the series of meetings in spring and summer of 1969 that launched the Young Lords' New York chapter.

As the fledgling group began to implement its mission during the summer of 1969, these SUNY Old Westbury women contributed their time and labor as part the college's independent study elective in the Urban Studies program, which involved immersion in a community-based project. Marlene Cintron, for example, participated in the Garbage Offensive and the strategy meetings that preceded it and helped staff the office under this arrangement. She returned to Old Westbury because she did not meet the standard of commitment that being a Young Lord entailed. In an example of unreasonable punishment, she was summarily dismissed from the group when she did not report to her assignment one day. The reason for her absence—that she had to accompany her mother on an unexpected trip to the South—didn't seem to matter.[76]

The Garbage Offensive drew other women as well, among them Sonia Ivany, a young Cuban mother, college student, and first formal female member of the Young Lords, as well as Iris Morales, the wife of deputy chairman Felipe Luciano at the time. Morales delayed joining until months later but was present all along and proved vital to the political development of the group. After a summer hiatus, another pivotal figure, Denise Oliver, returned to the group. By September 1969, the number of new female members tripled and continued to grow slowly during the fall months. Like their male counterparts, they, too, would soon leave school, home, or work to become full-time members, among them Myrna Martinez, Connie Morales, and Elizabeth González, Juan González's sister.[77]

Like their male counterparts, the idea of joining the Young Lords resonated among women because they too yearned for a political home "that took a stand on everything that was happening . . . but that [also] articulated our voice and the experience of our parents." Like other women, Morales traces the roots of her politicization to childhood: "As a child of migrants, I thought, 'We don't speak the language, we don't know how to navigate the court system, we don't know how to access our rights.'" Morales's larger vision of politics, however, grew out of the interface between world events and her immediate world. She recalls sharing the dread of two strangers in her neighborhood who during the Cuban Missile Crisis in 1962 stopped her to say, "We're gonna go to war." Like her male counterparts, she and other women who joined the Young Lords "had been involved [to some extent] in the black movement and the white movement." For Morales, "The horrific TV images of the civil rights movement" were brought home to her at Julia Richmond High School where some of her high school peers were members of SNCC and during her participation in a school play produced by the NAACP youth group. At around the same time, she participated in the citywide student strike of 1964 to desegregate New York's public schools. Through these networks she landed in the house of a Japanese American woman on the Lower East Side who spoke about her internment during World War II. In the process, she awakened to "the horrific . . . treatment of people in the history of the United States."

The intangible assets that women like Morales brought to the organization had ensured its sustained success a year earlier. Yet in many cases, their quiet skills and power were rendered invisible in the male-dominant culture of the Young Lords. In the case of Morales, she was soft spoken and preferred to engage in organization-building at the grassroots. Morales's marriage to the organization's charismatic chairman, Felipe Luciano, didn't help. Although the union raised her visibility, it overshadowed the indispensability of her contributions. Critics of the Young Lords' gender politics, and even some of its own members, referred to Morales as Luciano's wife. Yet Morales's organizing experience and political exposure *before* the Young Lords were formidable. As a teenager she became a tenants' rights organizer with the Westside Block Association, where she "work[ed] all day and night, knocking on doors, collecting signatures, and organizing rent strikes." It was there that she committed herself to bottom-up democracy and horizontal leadership. In housing organizing, she learned "that you never talk to authorities by yourself because they will manipulate you to [get you to abandon the interests of the people] or turn the people against you." Morales participated in counterpickets of the teachers union's strike of 1968, which challenged its opposition to the decentralization of schools; she marched with women striking for peace and against the Vietnam War; and attended Corky González's Crusade for Justice conference in Denver, Colorado, in the winter of 1969. Before that, she traveled to Cuba with New York's Cuban Mission for the tenth anniversary of the Cuban Revolution and was invited to speak on her experience at the Real Great Society in East Harlem, among other places. Morales had also identified common cause with black Americans early on. Even though she was very fair-skinned, Morales was active in black activist student groups in junior high school and high school. When she enrolled at City College, she joined ONYX, the black student organization, because there was no Puerto Rican political organization on campus. Later, she was among the founders of Puerto Ricans Involved in Student Action, which fought for the establishment of Puerto Rican studies at the school.[78]

Morales and the rest of the women who joined the Young Lords were among its most disciplined members. They answered phones, made flyers, served breakfast, distributed the group's circular, marched and on some occasions spoke at rallies, developed political curricula, and more. As discussed earlier, they were also instrumental to the success of the Young Lords' door-to-door medical home visits in East Harlem; their presence helped soften the image of the group and ensured that homemakers opened their apartment doors to these radicals. As in the case of SNCC and the Black Panthers, the organization's dizzying volume of activity developed its members' communication skills and sharpened their political acumen. Before long the arena for challenging preconceived notions and assumptions about women's inferiority presented itself.

The turning point came at the end of the Church Offensive, which brought a surge in female membership. By January 1970 approximately 35–40 percent of the group's members were women. With this growth, the discrepancy between the Young Lords' professed ideals and day-to-day practices became more manifest. The exponential rise in female membership made the absence of women in the group's formal leadership body more glaring. Other patterns now seemed intolerable. During the first altercation at the church, before the occupation, women fought the police. As Oliver remembers, they had "jumped on the[ir] backs and bit their ears."[79] Five out of the thirteen arrested were women—a number disproportionate to their percentage in the organization. The women of the Young Lords had literally proved themselves in battle. Yet, when the time came to assign posts in various ministries, especially the defense ministry, they were disproportionately assigned traditional women's work.[80] As Denise Oliver suggests, these patterns reflected the long-standing normalization of a profound power imbalance in the movement: "Fanny Lou Hamer is a key figure in the Mississippi Freedom Democratic Party and so is Ella Baker. They did a lot of the real work. Angela Davis [was known around the world, but] she didn't lead the Communist Party. By and large, all the movements were officially led by men."[81] In fact, on issues of gender oppression and homophobia, the movements' internal culture reflected the prevailing patriarchal ideas of society.

Women across the movement, especially black women and other women of color, continued to do "the work" but had been raising the problem of sexism for over a decade.[82] Iris Morales, who considered herself a feminist, had long felt conflicted politically about the "women's question" in the Young Lords and its prevailing, unstated belief: that a woman's place was "in the background." In fact, she had refused to join—formally—until about this time, but she did so after a visit to California where the women of the Brown Berets reminded her that she was already doing the work, and that she might as well struggle with these issues within the organization. As she remembers, frustration soon boiled over, and the female membership "decided to get together and talk."[83] In January 1970, the women of the Young Lords began to meet informally on Sundays, independently of men, to get to know each other better, discuss their frustration in the organization and society, and build sisterhood. They called these meetings the women's caucus. They were embracing a practice that had been popularized by the predominately white second-wave feminist movement—the women's consciousness-raising circle—in which women gathered to analyze and explore the ways in which structures of gender oppression played out in their personal lives.[84]

Oblivious to mounting tensions, the Central Committee "said go ahead, let the women go and have their hen talk."[85] Meanwhile, the caucus created a space for grievances, big and small. It addressed the ways in which machismo was manifested in the organization through its division of labor between men and women, interpersonal relationships, and the use of political power by men in the organization to sleep with women. Women began to articulate feeling humiliated and demeaned by some of their male counterparts, who routinely objectified and sexually propositioned potential female recruits, a behavior they came to denounce as "sexual fascism."[86] The women's caucus made explicit the men's nonconscious ideology and unexamined sexism and brainstormed how to hold them accountable. In this forum, women also challenged each other to unlearn dominant gender roles and the tendency to perceive feminism as a white woman's struggle and inspired each other to become leaders.

When she joined the Young Lords after the church occupation, Olguie Robles was shy and quiet, but the gender issues discussed in women's caucus helped her find her voice.

> We talked about the culture's impact on us as women in terms of female passivity and how it manifests itself in 1,001 ways; we talked about the forced sterilization of Puerto Rican women and women of color in hospitals and that you're not only a second-class citizen because you're Puerto Rican, a worker, and impoverished, but you're also a third-class citizen because you're a woman. Getting clarity helped me fight my own tendency to sit in the background and bite my tongue and be ashamed to speak because what do I know, you know, I'm just a woman.[87]

Although it didn't happen overnight, Olguie came to understand that "there was nothing wrong with sex and sexuality." For young Puerto Rican women who were socialized in Catholic households where women's oppression was enforced through the strict policing of their bodies and the association of women's sexuality with shame, discussions in the women's caucus deepened their analysis of power and proved liberating.[88]

The women's caucus met consistently through the spring of 1970, but its impact was uneven. Some women continued to do as they were told by the leadership, while others were emboldened to press their grievances. Some had come into the organization confident in their politics and ability to defend their rights as women, while others had acquired a greater sense of themselves as women organizers after joining. The most vocal female members were critical of the middle-class orientation of the feminist movement and its dominance by white women in the public sphere.[89] They also denounced the call among a small group of second-wave feminists to build separate, women-only organizations as a strategy toward women's liberation. The women of the Young Lords argued that for women of color, gender and ethnicity were inextricably linked. The problem of racism and national liberation, they posited, could not be resolved with half the Puerto Rican population but would have to be addressed by men and women together, as "Third World women make up over half the Revolutionary Army."[90]

These issues were discussed in an all-women panel of the Young Lords Organization (YLO) titled "Women of the Colonies" that aired in May 1970 on the organization's weekly radio program, also titled *Palante*. Although at different times the panelists emphasized some aspects of their identities over others, the consensus was that they were first and foremost revolutionaries committed to freedom for all people and were "opposed to establishing a separate movement for men and women."[91] They emphasized that from Puerto Rico to Vietnam, even when women have gone unacknowledged, they have been at the helm of revolutions. According to panelist Myrna Martinez, "We have revolutionary sisters who have played an important part in the liberation struggle in Vietnam . . . alongside their men."[92] While women of color in revolutionary nationalist organizations like the Young Lords adopted the women's movement interpretation that linked women's oppression to the institution of the family, their most politically sophisticated members also linked the emergence of the family with class society and with capitalism. Gender oppression, they believed, was rooted in the organization of society. With the birth of socialism, they contended, gender oppression would eventually wither away. While some were familiar with Friedrich Engels's *The Origin of the Family, Private Property and the State*, the text wasn't incorporated into their readings until at least a year later.[93]

Some middle-class women's groups disagreed with women in revolutionary nationalist organizations over the question of how to best achieve equality. The dominant liberal wing of the women's movement established that women's oppression was born of the age-old system of "patriarchy," that the major division in society was that between the sexes, and that the emergence of a new social order would not automatically bring about a society free of male domination.[94] Consequently, some argued for independent, women-only formations to combat "male privilege." Nationalist women retorted by rejecting the notion that all men exercised privilege, arguing that by virtue of their race most black and Latinx men were subjected to greater oppression than the ranks of the middle-class women's movement. They insisted that in the process of collective struggle, the question of women's oppression would be raised through day-to-day interaction between the sexes: "Because we are there with men, the women's liberation question will come up. . . . Since we are involved in the struggle in the day-to-day, if we have to type we type. . . . We don't say we're not going to do this or that. . . . We'll do whatever is necessary, and by being involved right in there you get rid of male chauvinism. You cannot deal with it on an abstract theoretical level; you have to deal with it concretely, and that's why we have sisters involved in every single ministry in the Lords. . . . While we're working, that's how we get recognition."[95]

Even though the women of the Young Lords were "proud to be women," some argued that "the Young Lords consider themselves first revolutionaries, second Puerto Ricans, and thirdly women."[96] This formulation echoed the ranking of oppressions that would later become dominant in debates surrounding identity politics during the retreat from social struggle of the 1980s and 1990s. Since revolutionary nationalists emphasized and privileged the ways in which racism undermined the manhood of men of color, if pressed to declare their political loyalties, many black and brown male nationalists would have privileged their identities as oppressed men of color.[97]

The radio broadcast revealed that the women of the Young Lords were in the process of revising and clarifying their ideas around women's oppression within the fight for the liberation of people of color. While at the beginning of their involvement in the organization some women embraced the notion that they were "first revolutionaries, second Puerto Ricans, and thirdly women," by summer of 1970—in the process of challenging male chauvinism within the Young Lords—their position had shifted toward a more nuanced analysis of the oppression they suffered. For now, the women sought to assess their experience of oppression, they articulated incongruous ideas. Iris Morales, for example, contradicted her comrades in the same radio program when she explained that in considering national and gender oppression, "it's not to say that one comes before the other, both work together."[98] Morales was articulating ideas that were being discussed among radical women of color in New York and across the country, which would be published formally a few months later, in the summer of 1970, by the Third World Women's Alliance and identified as the "triple jeopardy" of racism, capitalism, and sexism.[99]

They also asserted their contribution as comparable to men's—especially after they earned a measure of respect from men following what they called the "police riot" at the First Spanish United Methodist Church—but acknowledged that women still did not share "equal decision-making power" with men. And finally, as late as May 1970, they read aloud the tenth point of their platform, which invoked revolutionary machismo but did not yet acknowledge its contradiction publicly—that machismo could never be revolutionary because it constitutes a form of patriarchy organized around the subordination of women.

Although the panelists were confident in their exposition, their voices revealed anxiety, sometimes sounding as if they were on trial. The status of women in the Young Lords was as yet uncertain and filled with contradictions. Even as women sustained the organization's day-to-day work, men responded to the influx of female membership with a range of behaviors and dispositions, from newfound respect to heightened male bravado. And even though the women of the Young Lords drew inspiration from the public face of the women's movement, they also contended with that movement's failure to sufficiently address issues of racism and class exploitation. For example, YLO women participated in an International Women's Day rally where middle-class white women decried having been "niggerized" by society. Describing the event and the choice of words as a fiasco that "alienated" all the Third World women in attendance, the radio panelists assailed middle-class white women for "suggesting that they have experienced the same type of oppression and repression that black people and Third World people have suffered over hundreds and hundreds of years."[100] What the women's movement failed to recognize, they argued, "is that our men are in a very precarious position" and that because of racism "they've never been in a position to be oppressing anybody." The same women, they reported, talked first of "liberation for themselves and then mankind."[101]

Prodded by a combination of internal and external factors, the YLO women were about to bring the issue of gender oppression to its boiling point. Shortly after the Church Offensive, Denise Oliver was assigned the very prominent and strategic position of officer of the day (OD) after the incompetency of a male member of the group led to his dismissal from that position. The OD was charged with overseeing the day-to-day work of the organization; delegating assignments to each of its members; handling crises as they emerged; and keeping track of the sales of newspapers. Like a staff sergeant in the military, the OD was also charged with enforcing discipline both on the membership *and* on members of the Central Committee for failure to tend to assigned duties. Therefore, as a woman in a male-dominated, paramilitary-styled organization like the Young Lords, Oliver exercised rare power.

Oliver was assigned the post because of her assertive disposition. Her middle-class background growing up in a radical household, which affirmed individuality and encouraged her to defend her political beliefs, armed her with the confidence to refuse duties that were disproportionately assigned to women.

Unlike some women in the organization—who, in Oliver's generous phrasing, "had to work through issues of female passivity"—she was reared in a household where there was always an egalitarian distribution of chores, in which her father provoked political debates with her and where "nobody told [her] to wash the dishes... while [her] brother read a book." Oliver recalls, "I never learned how to type; I didn't want to learn how to type because I didn't want to be typecast."[102] Her middle-class background certainly allowed her the freedom to take that stance. Oliver was also known to be "very organized" and fiercely serious about the work of the organization, qualities that were indispensable for the role of OD. Oliver's work as OD gave her a bird's-eye view of the organization; the position also enabled her to expand her responsibilities exponentially. Because of the broad oversight that the position required, the OD worked closely with members of the Central Committee.

During her tenure as OD, Oliver became especially aware of the gendered assumptions made privately by the Central Committee about who could and could not perform particular tasks. She also came to understand that "part of the problem wasn't just that men automatically took the sort of macho role but [that] women were used to submissive behavior . . . and weren't opening their mouths."[103] It was this experience, in part, that led to the emergence of the women's caucus: "We used to talk about some of the young women in the organization; what we would need to do to get them to speak up, to take a more forward-moving role, not to drop to the back, not to defer to male privilege." The male-centric culture of the group encouraged the learned passivity of the least confident and self-aware female members, even as it provided openings for its more politically confident female members like Oliver.

Iris Morales would also play a key role in the organization's debates on women's oppression. Like Oliver, Morales was influenced by her father but for different reasons. Whereas Oliver's childhood home subverted the traditional gender roles of the 1950s, Morales's reified them. Her experience growing up in a very traditional, working-class Puerto Rican household predisposed her to setting straight the organization's internal double standard on women's equality. Like many of the young people who swelled the ranks of the organization, her parents came in the large wave of postwar Puerto Rican migration. In Puerto Rico, her father had been a cane cutter. In New York, he found work first as a dishwasher and later as an elevator operator in New York's hotel industry. This farmworker-turned-proletarian identified men as patriarchs and assumed exclusive power at home and in the world. His traditional worldview was rocked by the overnight reorganization of family life in an urban setting. Back on the island, Iris's mother, Almida, had cared for her and nine younger siblings (Iris's uncles). But to make ends meet in New York, Morales's mother worked as a seamstress.[104] Financial necessity functioned as an equalizing force. The new arrangement challenged her father's exclusive authority in the home. Eventually, Almida struck out alone and raised her four daughters as a single mother. Speaking of the power relations in her family, Iris observes:

> There's . . . a saying in Spanish to the effect that children should speak only when spoken to. The mother's just one step above the children. . . . And then . . . there's machismo . . . so that the man feels he has to go out with other women. . . . There were no sons [in my family]. My father . . . was the oldest son of the oldest son of the oldest son. I was supposed to be a son, but I wasn't, and then there were no sons to carry on the family name . . . so I guess that's one of the reasons he started running around, trying to develop a son somewhere else. . . . The Catholic Church is another thing too. . . . You have to go through all of the rituals . . . even if your family is not into a deeply religious bag. . . . Everything is a sin. . . . You get that on top of the strictness and the patriarchy . . . the kind of controls they have over you. . . . When I decided to leave home that was a scandal in the family. But it was worth it . . . because now I can see what is happening.[105]

Given the defining role that gender played in her childhood, it is no surprise that Morales refused to pander to the notion that national liberation should be privileged over women's liberation. As deputy minister of education, she exerted considerable political power, reeducating members on a range of issues, helping develop the organization's internal curriculum, developing classes for the community, and leading discussions. Ironically, the early political education sessions of the organization *didn't* address issues of gender, even though a woman was helping to create and lead them. But the Young Lords' philosophy of education—that the process of political education alongside struggle would engender enlightened individuals prepared for the task of building a new just society—opened up a world of critical analysis on women's oppression that eventually drowned out those who were against the organization's focus on women's issues. In fact, it inspired in its female members a desire to understand social relationships, the specific condition of women's oppression among women of color, and the influence of class, culture, and history in the gendered system of oppression.

Beginning in the spring of 1970, the Young Lords began to use in-depth articles written for *Palante* in the political education of new recruits. In the area of women's oppression and leadership, *Palante* articles discussed the state-led campaign in Puerto Rico that used women's sterilization as a form of contraception; deconstructed the institution of the concubine in Puerto Rico and its oppressive gendered logic; featured the biographies of political leaders such as Puerto Rican political prisoner Lolita Lebron and the black American freedom fighter Sojourner Truth; and in a sophisticated article on the politics of and

A women-led march. (Photograph by Máximo Colón)

motivation for the U.S. invasion of Cambodia in 1970, featured a photograph of armed female Cambodian guerrillas.[106] And in response to being called "Young Ladies" in Robin Morgan's classic essay "Goodbye to All That" in *RAT*, a New York–based underground newspaper whose editorial board was taken over by second-wave feminists,[107] the female members of the YLO mounted a fervent campaign in defense of themselves and their organization. The challenge deepened the already existing internal struggle within the organization over the place women would occupy in it.

Responding to the feminist critique by women in revolutionary nationalist organizations, the Young Lords emphasized that race and class created a complexity in their oppression which could not be understood or analyzed by white feminism. They argued that the mainstream of the women's liberation movement did not, for example, take into account the exploited condition of Third World women, who, by virtue of racism, were disproportionately demeaned as sex workers and used as a cheap source of labor with significantly lower wages than white women.

Despite their contentious rejection of the politics of what they called "right-wing" women's groups, the internal policies of the YLO were heavily influenced by the various factions of the women's movement, which had succeeded in making women's equality a central conversation in American society. The women of the Young Lords also became aware of their own blind spot in allowing the language of point 10 in the organization's platform to stand unchallenged. According to Oliver, amid debates and discussion in the women's caucus, "we looked in our own faces and we could kick ourselves; we had allowed this thing that said, 'Machismo should be revolutionary, not oppressive.' . . . It became patently clear to us that that was the stupidest . . . thing we had read in our lives, and we had let it slide by. They didn't mean anything by it; they were trying to be feminist in that statement. But we realized it was not."[108] They realized that machismo, like racism, couldn't be reformed. It had to be abolished altogether.

Point 10 also read, "Our men must support their women in their fight for economic and social equality, and must recognize that our women are equals in every way within the revolutionary ranks."[109] The Thirteen-Point Program's paternalistic language and attempt to sanitize "machismo" was a response among men of color to the politics of manhood. As one of the highest expressions of social power in American society, the concept of manhood invests men with power and with a great sense of responsibility as breadwinners, heads of households, and protectors of women and children. For young men of color, whose manhood is daily undermined by racism, hypermasculinity is a coping mechanism—a means of overcompensating for a social deficit. Similarly, in the context of a patriarchal society where women are relegated to supporting roles in the social order, the struggle against racism is often filtered primarily through the lens of men of color struggling to establish their manhood and humanity.[110] According to Iris Morales, these were the prevailing ideas within her cohort of movement activists: "The belief was that the fight for liberation required that men take the lead because they had been beaten so badly by the white man."

Amid this awakening and tug-of-war over the issue of women's inequality within the group, a backlash emerged from a fraction of the men of the organization, who grew angrier as women's grievances gained a greater hearing. The backlash took many forms: The most common happened interpersonally between men and women in the organization who were dating each other. In one rare instance, a male Young Lord slapped his partner for pushing the issue. On another occasion, at a martial arts class, the women of the Young Lords were punitively punched in the abs by some of the men who resented their efforts. Others ignored women when they spoke at meetings.[111] The main argument against those who advocated that the Lords had to address women's inequality internally posited that the "women's issue" was divisive and an expression of the middle-class, white feminist movement, which had little to offer the struggle for the liberation of people of color. This view was held primarily "by men and some women" of the Lords.[112] Some men, however, were supportive of the women's grievances and genuinely sought to reform their sexist behavior.[113]

In May 1970 the women of the organization presented a series of demands to the formal leadership of the Young Lords, the Central Committee, that included redrafting point 10 of the Thirteen-Point Program; the election of a woman to the Central Committee and the representation of women in all levels of leadership; the punishment of sexist behavior in the ranks of the Young Lords' members; the formation of a gay caucus as well as men's and women's caucuses for addressing the problem of sexism within the organization; and equal participation of women as writers and public speakers. One of the points also referred to the unequal participation of women in the defense ministry; in the words of Iris Morales, this area was "a male bastion," whose challenge by the women of the organization held great symbolic value.[114] The Central Committee agreed to discuss these demands at its May conference.[115]

On the issue of women's oppression, the Young Lords Party heeded the call in spirit, but the issue of gender equality remained a contested terrain throughout the organization's life. The leadership conceded that "the attitudes of superiority that brothers had toward sisters would have to change."[116] Consequently, the clause on "revolutionary machismo" was struck from the article on women's oppression in the group's Thirteen-Point Program and Platform and replaced with a direct and resolute position in support of women's equality that read "Down with Machismo and Male Chauvinism."[117] The revised point 10 was also moved up to become point 5 of the Thirteen-Point Program. The organization also agreed to mount an aggressive campaign to reeducate its members and challenge men and women to defy socially prescribed gender roles. As Oliver explains, one of these would be a men's caucus: "Men's caucus came after we recognized that it was all well and good that women were changing, coming to grips with their own passivity, coming to grips with learning how to say no to machismo, asserting themselves—but that doesn't do you any good if men aren't changing right along with it, and how do you change men? Men are going to have to take responsibility for changing themselves. That was later, when [the] men's caucus was established, and that was after the change on the Central Committee."[118] While the women's caucus endeavored to build female leadership, the men's caucus attempted to teach men "to cook, to care for children, to be open to cry and show emotions because these are all good things—needed to build a new society."[119] The caucuses also incorporated sex education. In them, the men learned what was to many of them an abstract concept: that their obliviousness to women's sexual pleasure was a manifestation and dimension of male domination of women.

The organization's lesser-known gay caucus began to meet spontaneously in the summer months of 1970. It did so without leadership's approval and was an initiative of a handful of the organization's openly gay members, including Miriam Dilot and Carmen "Flaca" Moreno. According to Carlito Rovira, "Many were in the defense committee, not because they were butch, but because they needed to prove themselves." A year earlier, during a routine police raid at the West Village's Stonewall Inn—a bar that catered to the marginalized segments of the gay and transgender communities, mostly people of color—patrons had fought back against acts of violent humiliation. The six days of protests and nighttime riots that followed tipped the balance in the long-standing homophile movement. The resistance emerged out of the shadows and away from the politics of assimilation, attaining visibility in the streets and affording a structural critique of gay and transgender oppression.[120] By late fall 1969, the efforts of the newly formed Gay Liberation Front (named after the Vietnamese National Liberation Front) had been acknowledged by the Young Lords and the Black Panthers. All were calling for unity among all oppressed people and the end of capitalism.

Much of this unity coalesced at the People's Church, whose revolutionary revelry drew the radical wing of the gay movement as well as gay and transgender people of color. Sylvia Rivera, a self-proclaimed transvestite and protector of homeless gay and transgender youth and sex workers on the Lower East Side, began developing a relationship with the Young Lords at the church. Immediately thereafter, Rivera faced death threats for a case she filed against a prison guard in the Tombs, whom she witnessed beating an inmate. When she sought protection from the Young Lords, the defense ministry assigned two of its members to her. Alternating shifts, Carlito Rovira and the Dominican member Marta Duarte served as Rivera's bodyguards for approximately a week. Rovira's account of his experience offers a window into the complexity of the gay, lesbian, and transgender struggle within the movement along with its possibilities. He remembers: "Other members declined the assignment. Marta accepted. I freaked out. But I was a soldier. At one point, we head to a party hosted by the queen she was living with, David, on East Tenth Street. Before we go in, she tells me, 'Don't go into a panic, they're not going to bite you.' Mind you, I'm fifteen. So we go in and I tense up at the first question I hear: 'Oooh, is he your date?' Sylvia responds, 'No, he's my security.' Then they all yell, 'Can we have him?' She says, 'No, he's off-limits, he's a Young Lord.' Y pa'que fue eso, they all go crazy. . . . That assignment was a gateway of understanding for me."[121] Sylvia Rivera formed part of the Young Lords as a friendly traveler.

Despite the Young Lords' genuine declarations of solidarity, LGBTQ issues remained shrouded in taboo within the organization. Battles waged around women's oppression, however, opened the path to the creation of the gay caucus and discussions of homophobia and heteronormativity. Opposed by some and feared by many, the gay caucus was actively defended by Pablo Guzmán and Denise Oliver. Both attended meetings of the Third World Gay Revolution, whose manifesto a year later called for a socialist society and "the abolition of the institution of the nuclear family." The caucuses, which aimed to refashion the culture of the group and the behavior of its members, never became institutionalized. The organization did, however, adopt a policy against gender discrimination and sexual misconduct. Sexist behavior in the organization was denounced formally, and those engaging in it were charged, tried, and disciplined by an internal disciplinary body.[122]

According to Iris Morales, the formalization of the Young Lords' official position on women's oppression reverberated outside the organization. Within the growing Puerto Rican movement, the Young Lords were accused of taking attention away from the colonial question and from mainland racism against Puerto Ricans. Similar critiques were leveled against the group for its focus on racism within the Puerto Rican community against Afro-Boricuas and black Americans. The Young Lords contributed to a political conversation that was unpopular at the time but that has since been adopted broadly within Puerto Rican circles. As Morales observes, "Thinking on it now, the Lords made a real contribution. We kept saying if we're gonna change society, we have to change ourselves. I challenge you to study any of the movement pictures of that time in terms of the other organizations and especially the organizations in Puerto Rico, and you will see a total absence of women and Afro–Puerto Ricans in leadership."[123]

With this newfound focus on women's unique struggles within both the Young Lords and society, in May 1970 Denise Oliver became the first woman elected to the Central Committee. First serving as minister of finance and later minister of economic development, she, and her ascendance, reflected both the struggle over the role of women in the organization and her own broad political experience, confidence, and wide-ranging knowledge and skills. Oliver's experience in the black American struggle mattered. It conferred on her a measure of respect that few other women in the organization enjoyed. In addition, in an organization that stressed the importance of revolutionary theory, Oliver had greater knowledge of classic theoretical texts than many of the men and had already been exerting political leadership. Because she had lived a life of struggle in the movement and had straddled many worlds, Oliver's election was also a strategic choice for the Young Lords' Central Committee. According to Felipe Luciano, "Denise knew how to live the double life: one of the revolutionary, one of the streets. . . . And then she knew just about everyone there was to know in the black movement. . . . Remember, when you're thinking of a Central Committee—let's make it equivalent to a board of directors—you need someone who has access, you need someone who has skills, and you need someone who is a worker. She fulfilled all of those things, plus she was close to us . . . so there really was no other choice."[124]

And in the atmosphere of fatal danger and suspicion produced by police infiltration of other radical organizations, trust was the paramount requisite for the appointed leadership of organizations like the Young Lords and Black Panthers. In the words of Felipe Luciano, "Denise hung with us when we were nothing. And the one thing about Puerto Ricans that you can put your money on is their understanding of loyalty. Denise had been with us from student days.... There were other women of comparable political experience, but no one as close to us as Denise. Denise was family."[125]

As we will see, not long after the Young Lords began to organize at Lincoln Hospital in the South Bronx, a young Puerto Rican woman, Carmen Rodriguez, died in July 1970 at the hospital following an abortion procedure performed by an inexperienced, and likely overworked, medical intern. The combined impact of Rodriguez's death, the challenge posed by white feminists to the YLO's female members, and the growing influence of women on the culture of the organization through the two key positions held by Oliver and Morales, as well as the increase in female membership, led to the production of one of the most lucid public documents in the Young Lords' history, the Position Paper on Women.

The position paper reflected a new-wave feminist analysis that linked the origins of women's oppression to the institution of marriage and the nuclear family under capitalism. The Young Lords, however, emphasized the distinct experience of poor women of color and their historically racialized roles as both "cheap labor and sexual objects." Class and race, they argued, were major concerns for women of color. The paper also critiqued the social expectation that Puerto Rican wives be pure and virginal at marriage, have children to enhance Puerto Rican men's self-concept of virility, and maintain the family name and honor. They also explored the negative consequences of these socially prescribed roles on the sexual freedom of these women. As the keepers of family honor, women had to sacrifice sexual pleasure while their husbands received sexual gratification from concubines, a common institution in Latin America known as *la corteja*, described by the Young Lords as a man's "sexual instrument."[126]

The position paper also sought to explain the socially prescribed roles of black American and Puerto Rican men. Men of color, they wrote, were perceived as "rough, athletic, and sexual, but not as intellectuals, and certainly not employable by capitalism." They explained how this racialized gendering affects the ways in which men of color oppress women of color: "All of the anger and violence of centuries of oppression which should be directed against the oppressor is directed at the Puerto Rican woman. The aggression is also directed at daughters."[127]

Finally, the document condemned the state-sponsored campaign of forced sterilization among Puerto Rican women.[128] Sterilization of women was one of the many consequences of Operation Bootstrap, as it made Puerto Rico a laboratory for testing economic strategies in Latin America, including often unethical research on birth control methods (such as the pill) and sterilization technology that later became widespread elsewhere in the world. The sterilization campaign of Puerto Rican women was supported ideologically by the American eugenics movement, which sought to control the ratio of "socially undesirable" people in society.[129] Using contemporary statistics, which reported that one out of three Puerto Rican women were sterilized, the Young Lords tried to highlight how the interconnection of race, colonization, and gender shaped Puerto Rican women's oppression.[130]

Because the Young Lords perceived their community to be threatened by a government-sponsored campaign of genocide, they had a split and perhaps nuanced view of abortion. The perceived threat of genocide fostered indirect arguments against abortion. The women of the Young Lords argued that because of poverty, the decision to have a child could not be made freely by women of color: the affordability of a child was always at stake. However, they argued that poverty made even legal abortions unsafe: "Abortions in hospitals that are butcher shops are little better than the illegal abortions our women used to get. The first abortion death in NYC under the new abortion law was Carmen Rodriguez, a Puerto Rican sister who died in Lincoln Hospital. Her abortion was legal, but the conditions in the hospital were deadly." The document continues, "We believe that abortions should be legal if they are community controlled, if they are safe, if our people are educated about the risks, and if doctors do not sterilize our sisters while performing abortions."[131]

On the basis of what they perceived as a genocidal threat, the Young Lords also disagreed with the position of the women's movement on abortion. Denise Oliver explained, "We feel we can't have a dogmatic approach on abortion. It would be incorrect for us to either be completely in favor of abortion or completely against it."[132] Their attention to their own community's struggles was, in this case, a disadvantage. The Young Lords failed to appreciate the broader political significance implicit in a legal decision around abortions—that legislation would either extend or curtail the power of the state in general and in particular over women's bodies. Despite this shortsightedness, the Young Lords articulated a comprehensive reproductive rights program calling for access to adequate healthcare, childcare, community control of abortion clinics, and contraception options alongside education geared at raising consciousness about state-sponsored sterilization campaigns that disproportionately targeted women of color and Puerto Rican women in particular. More clearly than that of any nationalist group of the period, their analysis offered potent connections not only to broader issues of race, gender, and class but between those issues and the democratic control of local institutions.

Months later, the organization established its women's union, whose pur-

Young Lords march. (Photograph by Michael Abramson; courtesy of Haymarket Books)

pose was to hold meetings on issues of women's inequality in the community, initiate a community-run childcare center, and publish *La Luchadora* (the Female Warrior), a short-lived newspaper. *La Luchadora* featured the work of the women's union in the community and addressed theoretical issues related to women's oppression and the organization's twelve-point program on women, which embraced a broad spectrum of demands that reflected the interests of poor women of color. Among other reforms, the twelve-point program called for "full employment and equal pay for women with day care facilities provided by the work institution"; welfare centers run by community workers "to insure the protection of women and their needs"; an end to the "oppression of prostitutes and drug addicted sisters"; "withdrawal of the American military from our communities and an end to their sexual abuse of women"; "freedom for all political prisoners and prisoners of war and an end to the sexual brutalization and torture enforced on sisters by prison officials"; "an end to "experimentation and genocide through sterilization, forced abortions, contraceptives, and unnecessary gynecological exams"; "true education of our story as women, the right to defend ourselves against rapes, beatings muggings and general abuse"; and "a socialist society."[133]

■

In the realm of consciousness raising on issues of race and gender, *Palante* played a pivotal role internally among its members and externally among broader audiences. The Young Lords deployed political education as a vehicle for personal transformation pending revolution and for overcoming divisions among oppressed people and within the working class. When the media spotlight was on their occupations, and they became "famous," they pushed the strategic power of the media and began to make the media work for them: what had begun as focused, local actions around social and economic issues quickly became a program and platform around a radical set of issues including race and gender equality, disseminated first through a newspaper, then through radio and film. Picked up by the mainstream and movement media, this was their "virtual platform." Their typewriters and flyers were thus precursors, in a way, to today's social media.

In their literature and activism, the Young Lords challenged expressions of racial prejudice among racially oppressed people as a precondition for unity among Third World people. In their adaptation of the notion that "the personal is political" to the experience of racism, they explored its personal and psychological consequences for people of color. The group also broadened the nation's understanding of race ideology. The very presence in the movement of radicals like the Young Lords, who were socialized under a system of racial formation that emerged in Latin America, challenged black Americans and white Americans to step outside of their United States–centered and narrow grasp of race and identity.

On the questions of gender inequality, the women of the Young Lords forced changes in the structure, rules, and global vision statement of their gender-integrated organization. Their methods and approach differed from those of their female counterparts within the New Left: white, second-wave feminists formed separate women's organizations, and the women of the Black Panthers critiqued the interlocking nature of race and gender oppression under capitalism, though they did not institutionalize gender-specific policies and rules within their organization.[134] The Young Lords stood apart, as their members struggled with misogyny within the organization, working to foreground the experience of class and racial oppression in public discourses on women's inequality in U.S. society.[135]

CHAPTER NINE

THE LINCOLN OFFENSIVE

Toward a Patient Bill of Rights

A human life is worth more than
all the wealth of the richest man.

—ERNESTO "CHE" GUEVARA

A year after their Garbage and Lead Offensives, the Young Lords launched a similar wave of tuberculosis activism in the context of grassroots service work in the community. The potentially serious lung disease—highly contagious and airborne—had long been linked to poverty and overcrowding. Small New York tenement apartments, with little circulating air or sunlight, were perfect breeding grounds. Puerto Rican migrants were further disadvantaged by coming from an island where the mortality rate from tuberculosis was the highest in the world. In May 1970, the group reported that it was conducting door-to-door medical home visits and that its members had administered 800 tuberculosis tests in East Harlem and the Bronx. According to the group, the administration of Prospect Hospital even permitted them use of a chest X-ray machine, a concession to their petition after word got out among locals that the Young Lords were conducting tests alongside doctors and technicians.[1]

The logic and objective of the Young Lords' public health efforts were explained in a June 1970 issue of *Palante*: "Services are extended out to the people, visiting them in their home and setting up Free Health Clinics in every block. This type of service which keeps people from getting sick in the first place is called preventative medicine." As they went door to door, they offered medical services alongside political education, explaining that "even though t.b. has been eliminated among the rich, the middle class, and white people in general, it is alive and spreading in the Puerto Rican and Black colonies of amerikkka, the richest country in the world."[2]

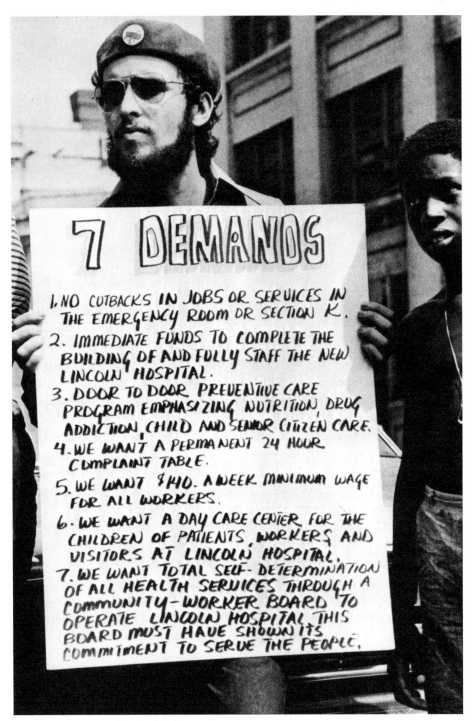

Richie Perez at rally outside Lincoln Hospital.
(Photograph by Michael Abramson; courtesy of Haymarket Books)

As they began to conduct tests at Prospect Hospital, they also tried to partner with the New York Tuberculosis Association, a public agency that operated a mobile chest X-ray unit. The Young Lords argued that the X-ray truck, operating from 12:00 P.M. to 6:00 P.M. on alternate days, did not accommodate the work schedules of laboring people; they proposed to staff the truck around the clock with the many local technicians and doctors who had already offered to volunteer. Citing the existence of city-managed programs with trained personnel and effective technology, the Tuberculosis Association denied the Lords' request.[3]

Determined to carry their intended project to fruition and prepared—perhaps even eager—to employ publicity to their benefit, the young radicals alerted both the press and the police of the time and place of an impending action.[4] On June 17, 1970, the Young Lords hijacked the association's mobile clinic and, with a Puerto Rican flag unfurled above the bus, drove off—another classic Young Lords moment, complete with cameramen capturing footage for the evening news.[5] Via the unit's loudspeaker, the Young Lords carried their message throughout Spanish Harlem, explaining the motives for their actions and inviting residents to get tested for tuberculosis at a new location. The next day they parked the truck across from their office on Madison and 111th Street and rechristened it the Ramón Emeterio Betances Health Truck—after the nineteenth-century Puerto Rican revolutionary physician. The mobile unit tested hundreds of people its first day in its new location. Within hours of the hijack, the Young Lords had negotiated an agreement with the director of health for the East Harlem district, Thomas Jones, authorizing the group to operate the unit, at the city's expense, for twelve hours a day, seven days a week.

Having established a record of community service through their previous door-to-door work and having demonstrated their ability to mobilize hundreds of inner-city youth at a moment's notice, the group could count on a measure of bargaining power in local politics, especially as the specter of urban rioting weighed on the minds of city officials. Referring to the Young Lords, Jones said, "Their methodology is in dispute, but we must relate to where the community feels they need the service. Occasionally confrontation does occur, but I think we can work it out."[6] Jones's rationalization was a kind of admission to the Young Lords' charge of government indifference to the needs of city residents. Moreover, that Jones's formulation—"relate to where the community feels they need the service"—echoed the Young Lords' manner of speech is an example of their impact on public discourse, values, and standards for municipal services.

Jones seems to have agreed to the arrangement primarily out of fear. The Young Lords' paramilitary style, confidence, and rhetoric were threatening to many, and yet they spent most of their time engaged in public service. Within the organization these two currents existed side by side, without any seeming tension or incongruity. The Young Lords would test the boundaries of their muckraking in the spring and summer of 1970. Surpassing prior challenges, they set their sights on a daunting task: addressing head on the injustices and substandard conditions plaguing neighboring Lincoln Hospital.

The Blight and Transformation of an Aging Institution

As the tuberculosis testing continued, the Young Lords were expanding their reach north to the borough with the largest conglomeration of Puerto Ricans in New York. Though East Harlem remained the cultural home of Puerto Ricans, by 1960 100,000 Boricuas had settled in the Bronx; most were concentrated in its southernmost section.[7] The Young Lords' turn to "the Puerto Rican borough" was a rational progression in the organization's growth and identification with Puerto Rican nationalism. In April 1970, the group opened its South Bronx office on Longwood Avenue (on the corner of Kelly Street). The expansion brought greater responsibilities. It challenged an emerging class of leaders and new members to take on broader obligations. That same month, the group began to host weekly outdoor, late-night film screenings as a form of political education. They featured *Los siete de la raza*, the story of seven Chicano youth accused of killing a police officer in San Francisco, and *Black Panther*, on the origins of the Black Panther Party (BPP), among others. Leading the efforts, Carlos Aponte reported in *Palante* that people from the block, on Intervale Avenue between Kelly and Beck Streets, stopped the police on a number of occasions from breaking up the screenings.[8] The Lords also extended to the neighborhood a practice they'd begun in East Harlem six months earlier, door-to-door medical home visits on Saturdays. Of their reception in the South Bronx they reported, "Our recruitment is growing rapidly and many brothers and sisters are offering us their services, making us a part of their everyday lives."[9]

By the late 1960s, the South Bronx was one of the most impoverished districts in the nation—a decaying strip of industrial land, where 80 percent of the housing existed in a state of moderate to severe deterioration. Against the onslaught of culture-of-poverty discourse, which interpreted urban poverty as a racial phenomenon, the Young Lords used a well-timed article, "The South Bronx Time Bomb," to highlight for *Palante* readers the larger social and structural forces at work in neighborhoods like this one. In it Richie Perez explained: "There are no jobs available. We are imprisoned in a vicious cycle. No education, no jobs, and no way to move out of the run-down, unhealthy and dangerous tenements of the South Bronx." As early witnesses to the borough's deepening crisis of deindustrialization and its social consequences, the Lords analyzed the root causes of what sociologists would later call "the urban crisis."[10]

The *Palante* article highlighted the public health crisis at the center of this dilapidated environment where "rats, roaches, uncollected garbage, no steam or hot water, and broken and unrepaired windows contribute to poor health." It also reported that the area's dirtiest and most overcrowded streets, "Simpson and Fox Streets, between 163rd and Westchester Ave. . . . have the highest death rates of any blocks in the entire city."[11] The Young Lords learned the morbid statistics and mastered the art of humanizing their fallout. The South Bronx had the highest rate of heroin addiction in the world; a mortality rate 50 percent higher than the rest of the country; and an incidence of syphilis and gonorrhea six and four times the national average, respectively. The leading causes of death among adolescents and young adults were heroin overdose and trauma.[12]

Apprised of the neighborhood's demography, its chronic social problems, and a preexisting grassroots effort for improved patient services at nearby Lincoln Hospital, the Young Lords settled on this aging hospital as a major organizing site. In a district with disproportionately higher medical needs than other parts of the city, access to medical care was as afflicted as the population it served. Lincoln's 350-bed facility was charged with caring for a catchment area of approximately half a million people. Not surprisingly, the facility was so overcrowded and the bed shortage so severe that patients were often treated in corridors. These conditions were not new, and Lincoln Hospital was not alone. Two decades earlier, a *Daily News* editorial noted that the city's public hospitals—"Harlem, Queens, Lincoln, Fordham, Kings County—are sick . . . with nurses and doctors scarce and overworked, patients crowded into every nook and cranny and service generally going to the devil."[13]

Lincoln's crisis, however, was extreme. The hospital had an outdated, turn-of-the-century open ward and a clinical interior that, according to one doctor, "looked more like an armory or abandoned factory than a center for the healing arts."[14] A study of municipal hospitals in New York offered a lengthy list of deplorable conditions. The periodic power outages in its main building were the consequence of generators installed in 1927 that were too weak to power the hospital's new technology in 1969. Air conditioners in the surgical recovery room did not work. The building's walls had paint with a lead base of 28 percent, a figure far exceeding the legal levels for retail paint. In a hospital that treated countless cases of child lead poisoning, and where the pediatric ward was meant to be a temporary refuge for lead-poisoned kids, at least two children treated for lead poisoning in the late 1960s reingested lead in the ward.[15] Meanwhile, the lack of a centralized administrative structure thwarted the hospital's ability to systematically address such problems. Under these and other conditions, disgruntled functionaries and medical staff customarily rendered services grudgingly. By all accounts, the Lincoln experience was abominable.

Starting with eastern European immigrants in the 1920s, successive generations of neighborhood residents referred to Lincoln as the "butcher shop of the South Bronx."[16]

The situation was no better for employees. Still in the process of transformation from charity foundations to professional institutions, hospitals were prone to underpaying the nonprofessional employees they hired.

Because of their long hours and labor-intensive, unsanitary, and repetitive duties, hospitals "had long been the urban employer of last resort" for superexploited newcomers, now demeaned by their occupation and their race.[17] Hospital salaries in New York were so low that a large percentage of their unskilled, predominantly black American and Puerto Rican labor force was eligible for public assistance.[18] Moreover, hospital administrators generally extended to their nonmedical staff the same paternalism accorded patients, a predicament reflecting the institution's origins in charity.[19]

This was the kind of largely ignored "social violence" the Young Lords were gearing up to expose. But in the decade before the Young Lords set their sights on the ailing hospital, Lincoln had become the site of at least three major reform efforts that helped prepare the groundwork for the Young Lords' intervention. The first took the form of semiprivatization. In 1959, Mayor Robert Wagner authorized the affiliation program, which turned over the management and staffing of New York's public hospitals to the city's major private medical schools. Under the new program, Lincoln became an affiliate of the Albert Einstein College of Medicine. As discussed in chapter 4, under the agreement, medical schools received operating budgets to staff and run the hospitals. In return, the schools reaped the benefits of unmonitored access to a poor population of patients prone to illness. They provided opportunities for medical research and a fertile training ground for interns and residents in the range of clinical departments housed in public hospitals. The new affiliation policy followed the trend in healthcare toward the expansion of large medical institutions. It also responded to the growing public debate on the crisis of healthcare and fragmented character of its delivery. In a market of spiraling costs produced by the fee-for-service dictum of the country's healthcare system, city hospitals continued to languish, albeit under slightly less deplorable conditions.[20]

The second attempt at reform lacked the global scope of the affiliation system, but its link to federal programs brought national attention to the hospital, and its experimental partnership with employees drawn from the community became the wellspring of struggles to come. In 1963, the Albert Einstein Medical College inaugurated the Lincoln Hospital Mental Health Services (LHMHS). It was a network of services with diverse points of contact between mental health providers and patients, designed to deliver related services and care at the neighborhood level—in schools, churches, and community centers. Its treatment protocol included traditional talk therapy, drug rehabilitation, mental health education, and community action. The program owed its unorthodox mission to the experimental stipulations of its two funding sources: the 1961 National Community

Mental Health Center Act and the Office of Economic Opportunity (OEO), the federal agency that implemented the so-called War on Poverty. The first legislation funded local mental health clinics, such as LHMHS, as part of its larger goal of consolidating a shift in psychiatry, already under way, from treatment of the mentally ill in asylums to treatment in private practices and privately run community centers.[21] The second source of funding sought to improve access to mental healthcare in urban and rural areas and mandated the "maximum feasible participation" of community residents in programs it funded.[22]

In 1967, LHMHS achieved national recognition when a documentary film, *Store Front*, chronicled the "struggles and success" of its teams' unorthodox community practice.[23] The clinics' progressive in-house psychiatrists, among them Dr. Mike Smith, believed that psychiatric treatment should emphasize talk therapy, rather than psychoactive drugs, to alleviate depression, addiction, and other psychological dysfunctions. The program's nonmedical, community staff contributed their own vision for improved mental health. They underscored the significance of patient involvement in the life of their community to foster meaning in and control over their lives. Influenced by the era's discourse on social inequality, these new approaches focused on the relationship between the individual and society. They emphasized the manifold social problems of urban life, which, according to a growing number of specialists and health professionals, contributed significantly to the psychological breakdown of the individual in society.[24]

Given the magnitude of problems at Lincoln, LHMHS's achievements, though groundbreaking, were at best piecemeal and symbolic. However, the program hired and trained an emerging segment of workers uniquely situated to launch and win more consequential reforms. Like other mental health centers in New York, LHMHS employed community members with funding from the New Careers program, a unique project of the OEO and offshoot of a 1962 federal policy designed to train, on the job, displaced blue-collar workers and the permanently unemployed as legal aides, social health technicians, vocational rehabilitation specialists, police community services aides, and community mental health workers.[25] To that end, LHMHS hired dozens of black American and Puerto Rican mental health workers. LHMHS applicants underwent a rigorous, three-month interview process that tested for communication skills, maturity, and a high threshold for withstanding high-stress scenarios with patients. Those hired, among them Richard Weeks, Ruth Dawkins, Aubrey "Doc" Dawkins, Danny Argote, and Cleo Silvers, were promised ongoing training to ensure the possibility of promotion and advancement in the health industry, now the fastest-growing sector of the American economy. Their social location, both as semiskilled workers in the city's poorest public hospitals and as residents in the hospitals' catchment districts, was strong motivation. They approached their work seriously, with the expectation that they would help build a clinic responsive to their community's complex health needs. "As Puerto Ricans and Black workers in the emergency rooms and clinics," one organizer reported, "we see what oppression in the hospital is like, the inferior medical attention our neighbors are subjected to or obligated to accept."[26]

As for others in their cohort, dramatic examples of resistance in New York shaped the consciousness of these young people. Seminal events were the Harlem riots; the battle to desegregate the city's schools; sit-ins in active construction sites; protest against racial discrimination in employment and labor unions; the fierce images of Malcolm X; and numerous rent strikes, among other struggles. Their counterparts in the south had raised the bar on what a young person might dedicate his or her life to. Here, too, this cohort was morally repulsed by poverty and war and eager to be part of something larger.

Unlike those who founded the New York chapter of the Young Lords, this cohort of young people of color, though very bright, did not go to college. Rather, they joined the labor force during or immediately after high school. Back at LHMHS, they proposed and organized social actions intended to improve patients' day-to-day lives, from challenging evictions to helping raise awareness about public health.

The BPP proved instrumental in the transmission of these methods and ideas at Lincoln. The group had already initiated a wide range of radical public health programs in black communities across the nation, including a sickle cell anemia project in New York, ambulance services in Pittsburgh and Oakland, and campaigns to test and raise awareness about tuberculosis, anemia, and lead poisoning.[27] In the Bronx, the organization had helped draft leaflets, conducted workshops on race and public health for the mental health workers, and even sat in at staff meetings in which core members discussed strategy.

The mental health workers brought a similar approach to a preexisting workplace struggle. Beginning in the late 1950s, the Service Employees International Union Local 1199 launched a campaign to unionize the nurse's aides, orderlies, porters, cooks, elevator operators, and laundresses in the city's privately owned, nonprofit "voluntary" hospitals. Disproportionately black American and Puerto Rican, these workers were vital to the basic operation of New York's hospitals but were among the city's least paid. The union's groundbreaking campaign combined the fight for civil rights with the demand for economic justice. It culminated in two major strikes in 1959 and 1962 that won unionization, increased wages, limited to eight the number of daily hours worked and mandated pay for overtime.[28] Public sector workers, however, remained on the margins of Local 1199's campaign. But with 80 percent of New York's nonprofessional hospital staff organized by the late 1960s, the unionization of their counterparts in the public hospitals was on the horizon. When Local 1199 sent its labor organizer, Bernie

Minter, to Lincoln Hospital in 1967, he found a cohort of workers who had already begun to organize themselves and whose broad vision of reform he could not easily accommodate. According to one of them, Cleo Silvers, "We wanted to join 1199 and we did eventually, but we wanted the union to take a position against the Vietnam War, against the increased prescription of psychotropic drugs in the neighborhood by Lincoln Mental Health Services, and to support our position: that social and economic conditions were determinants of a person's psychological health. We also wanted the union to back us up on what we had been promised but never got, which was training and upgrading. The union did not look positively on any of this. So from the start we were seen as renegades."[29]

For more than a year thereafter, the mental health workers attempted, but failed, to persuade the union leadership to press their employer to deliver on the promise of training and upgrading.

Tensions in the mental health program intensified in 1969 when OEO funding, which mandated community action, began to dry up. In response, the National Institute for Mental Health—a more traditionally oriented and research-driven psychiatric agency—took over funding the programs.[30] This development jeopardized the security of the nonprofessional staff and threatened the pioneering approach to mental health that the OEO had encouraged. With the change in funding source came a shift to a mental health approach that emphasized medicating patients. Activists and progressive doctors, among them Dr. Mike Smith, argued that the dispensation of psychotropic substances in poor black American and Puerto Rican urban neighborhoods was an attempt at social control.[31] When the mental health workers asked to meet with the clinic's top administrators to discuss these changes, they were reportedly dismissed with arrogance and contempt. Four were fired at various stages of the mounting struggle, which workers interpreted as retribution for speaking up.

The turning point in the struggle came on March 3, 1969. Over 100 nonprofessional mental health counselors, orderlies, and administrative and janitorial staff, mostly people of color, seized the Lincoln facility and evicted its director, Dr. Harris B. Peck, and high-ranking staff members. The stated purpose of the takeover was to democratize the program's governing structure and force it to meet its stated philosophy of making the community a partner in its own care. As justification for their actions, the workers deployed the words of Peck, who in an interview with *Reader's Digest* in early March 1969 had said, "When there's a foot planted in the seat of my trousers to knock me out of here, I'll know we've succeeded. It will mean that the people want to take over the running of their own community. And that's the way it should be."[32]

The mental health workers were now spearheading efforts for "community-worker control" that grew organically out of their relationship both to the workplace and the community they served. Like "black power," the meaning and application of "community control" varied depending on the political orientation of those defining it. Conservatives, liberals, and cultural nationalists measured it in terms of racial representation: that the ethnic composition of those who administer local institutions—schools, hospitals, police precincts, etc.—should reflect that of their constituency. To the Lincoln workers, however, community control involved a reconceptualization of the structure, leadership, and priorities of local institutions.

The team of community mental health workers who took over the clinic operated it for three days with the active support of some of the clinic's mostly white psychiatrists, psychologists, and professional staff. As liaisons between patients and psychiatrists, mental health workers had developed relationships with both. They commanded a measure of respect and power. They were, therefore, unimpeded in their efforts by other doctors and specialists who continued to treat clients during the takeover despite quiet reservations.[33] Workers' grievances included "discrimination in hiring and firing" policies, the closure of the neighborhood service centers, the inadequacy of the training and upgrading program for nonprofessional employees, and the firing of four mental health workers.[34] BPP support work was instrumental during the takeover. The Panthers organized security and brought food and throngs of community supporters.[35] The action was finally shut down at the end of the workday on March 6 when the Albert Einstein College of Medicine, with support of the city's public hospital administration, threatened to suspend specialists' licenses for "malfeasance and malpractice" and for continuing to render care under an illegitimate administration.[36]

In the weeks after the March 6 shutdown of the occupation, the mental health workers led a series of rallies and direct actions at the clinic. Twenty-three people were arrested. Forty-one nonprofessional workers and nineteen professionals, including three psychiatrists, were fired (although they were eventually reinstated).[37] The protests, however, were successful in leading to the reinstatement of the four black American mental health workers who had been fired in the year before the takeover, the clinic director's transfer out of Lincoln, and widespread questioning of the dispensation of psychotropic drugs in the South Bronx. On April 2, a month after workers took over the mental health clinic, twenty-one members of the New York chapter of the BPP were arrested and charged with terrorism. Almost all had been active at Lincoln Hospital during the takeover and subsequent rallies. They included Dr. Curtis Powell, Zade Shakur, Lumumba Shakur, Rashid, Afeni Shakur, Charlene Ife, Bob Collier, Dhoruba Bin Wahad, and Ali Bey Hassan, among others.[38]

But nonprofessional mental health refused to succumb to repression. In the fall of 1969, a network of workers of color formed the Health Revolutionary Unity Movement (HRUM). They were from New York's Metropolitan,

Gouverneur, and Lincoln Hospitals and the NENA Health Center. Influenced by the struggle at Lincoln and the black power movement, radicalized by the Vietnam War, and frustrated by the speedups and budget cuts brought on by economic stagnation in the late 1960s, they were among the patches of the American workforce that began to organize independently of union leaderships in this period. Hoping to carry the current political mood into the workplace, young black and Latino workers organized into insurgent groups. They challenged conservatism among elected union officials, organized opposition to the Vietnam War among their coworkers, and pressured the unions to address structural racism within the union, on the job, and in society at large.[39] HRUM argued that these had to be priorities of the unions in the health industry: "The unions 1199 and District Council 37, even though progressive in the question of salaries, do not fight against the conditions imposed on the workers nor the quality of the medical services our people are receiving."[40] Although Local 1199 was conceived as a "soul power" union (wedded to the political and economic concerns of working people of color) that was supportive of the controversial community control battle in the schools, Union officials opposed the bottom-up efforts of workers in the hospitals.[41]

HRUM borrowed its acronym from the Dodge Revolutionary Union Movement (DRUM), launched in 1968 by black autoworkers in Detroit.[42] Like DRUM, HRUM called for worker control of workplaces. Unlike DRUM, however, HRUM members joined the Young Lords and Black Panther Parties. HRUM's newspaper, *For the People's Health*, reported that members of the organization "live in the same communities where we work [the municipal hospitals] where we see our poor Black, Puerto Rican and Chinese Brothers and Sisters waiting too long and being told, 'sorry, no bed in this hospital, try another.'" HRUM believed strongly in patient advocacy. Its members observed that hospital workers had a "dual role" as patients and workers, "often in the same hospital," and argued that it was the "obligation of every health worker, Black, Puerto Rican, or Chinese . . . to make sure that our people are given decent health care—if you are a registrar refuse to collect high fees, if you are a nurse's aide demand that you have adequate help so that you may perform your duties well."[43]

HRUM protested healthcare's turn to profit and opposed the reduction of services in public hospitals. It also organized around traditional union issues, among them improved wages and working conditions. In its view, class exploitation of workers of color in the hospitals was inseparable from racial oppression shaping conditions in their neighborhoods. With continuity between workplace and community, they reasoned that the hospitals offered a unique venue to address both.

Efforts to transform the paradigm of healthcare delivery in the mental health clinic at Lincoln, combined with the rise of HRUM and the political vacuum created by the arrest of the Panther 21, set the stage for the Young Lords Party's activism at Lincoln a year later, in the spring and summer of 1970.

Think Lincoln, Think Community

In the weeks before the Young Lords went to work at Lincoln in the fall of 1970, a more traditional cast of political actors was already at work there. In early April, local Puerto Rican political clubs tied to the Democratic Party and community groups held a sit-in in the lobby of Lincoln Hospital after the commissioner of hospitals refused to support the candidacy for hospital administrator of a well-qualified Puerto Rican gynecologist and public health administrator, Dr. Antero Lacot, who was trained in Puerto Rico. Their efforts were inspired by Ramon Velez, a political boss and controversial player in local politics, who sought influence over Lincoln, one of the major employers in the South Bronx, especially since the future construction of a new hospital building would yield lucrative contracts. This earned Velez a spot as *Palante*'s "Pig of the Week":

> Number one Puerto Rican poverty pimp, head of the Hunts Point multi-service center, runs the South Bronx like a little political machine, giving jobs here and there to supporters and destroying anyone who gets in his way. He gets our people to fight Black people for a share of the rotten poverty program pie that shrinks every year. He . . . is head of a $12 million program. Meanwhile, Lincoln Hospital, the schools, the garbage, the buildings, and the police in Hunts Point are no better.[44]

The groups affiliated with Velez sought to reform care at Lincoln by demanding that the racial and ethnic composition of the hospital's administrative body reflect the racial and ethnic makeup of the community. Yet, given the medical establishment's conservative hiring patterns for top administrative posts, even the granting of moderate reforms at the height of a revolution in rights consciousness required substantial social pressure and militant action. In an attempt to quell the furor at Lincoln, the mayor intervened by overruling the commissioner's decision and approving Antero Lacot's appointment. Months later, the *New York Times* proclaimed, "If it were not for militants among the people of the South Bronx, Dr. Antero Lacot might not be administrator of Lincoln Hospital," referring to the militancy of activists the previous year.[45] Much more radical organizing was still to come.

Critical of Velez's group and its ties to the antipoverty industry and social-service-oriented community groups competing for funding, the Young Lords sought to influence Lincoln on their own terms. They explored a grassroots organizing approach at the hospital that focused on conditions rather than the

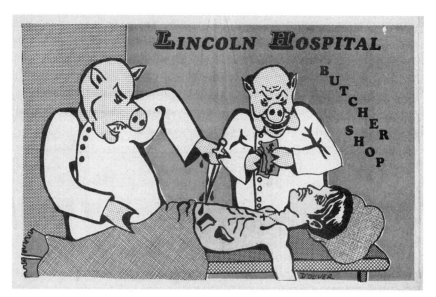

Lincoln Hospital cartoon illustrated by Denise Oliver. (*Palante* 2, no. 7 [July 17, 1970]; courtesy of the Tamiment Library)

appointment of people of color to administrative positions. Their objective was to address patient needs and grievances, expose malfeasance, impugn the profit-driven system of healthcare, and build their base in the process. In an article in *Palante* about how to solve the crisis of healthcare among people of color in New York, the Young Lords wrote: "The only way we can stop all this is not by electing someone into office, because we have tried that and it does not work. It is not done by going to college and getting doctor degrees, because that leads to an intellectual trip that takes us away from our people . . . and that we also tried. The only way to make this racist government serve us right is by knocking it down and building a new one of our own."[46]

In May 1970, in concert with neighborhood residents and hospital workers—among them the talented mental health worker and organizer Cleo Silvers, who became the head of HRUM at Lincoln and then its citywide cochair alongside Gloria Fontanez—the Young Lords and HRUM launched the Think Lincoln Committee (TLC). One of its goals was to challenge the newly formed citywide governing body for New York's public hospitals, the Health and Hospital Corporation (HHC), and its proposed budget cuts, scheduled for July of that year, which would further deteriorate an already miserable situation.

Run by a sixteen-member board appointed largely by the mayor, the HHC's stated purpose was to free the public hospital system of bureaucratic red tape in order to facilitate the provision of medical services in New York's underprivileged communities. But like its predecessor, the Department of Hospitals, the

HHC was hamstrung by rising healthcare costs and lack of funding.[47] According to HRUM, the HHC "is a group of business men, to which the city of New York has handed over the mismanagement of its public hospitals. It is a representative of the interests of the second most profitable industry in AMERIKKKA, the sickness industry that is, the drug companies, construction firms, medical schools and the reactionary American Medical Association. Nowhere in this conglomeration are the interests of the colonized people represented."[48] Galvanized by the hospital's abominable conditions and the immediate threat of budget reductions, the TLC proceeded to gather and spread information about the impact of the impending budget cuts on patients and hospital staff.

Of all the municipal hospitals facing austerity measures, the already impoverished Lincoln was slated for the steepest cuts. The TLC reported to patients and hospital workers that the cuts had precipitated a six-month job freeze in the Department of Medicine, which in turn blocked the replacement of five doctors whose services were vital to the functioning of the hospital. The budget redistribution was also expected to limit the operating hours of Section K, a screening clinic for patient diagnosis and referral, and increase the number of intakes in the ER—already ranked fourth busiest in the nation—where patients would be rerouted on evenings and weekends when Section K was expected to shut down.[49]

In the process of distributing leaflets, posting flyers, and talking to Lincoln workers and community residents about the cutbacks, the radicals were flooded with numerous concerns. For the Young Lords, many of whom had endured alienating visits to the hospital as children, these complaints were not foreign. These young people had witnessed the stigma and indignity of racial discrimination during hospital visits, long waiting hours in the ER, and the haphazard care of their parents and people like them. As we have seen, their generation functioned as indispensable language and cultural interpreters for their community, especially in New York's public hospitals, which, second only to the public schools, were the most frequented of the city's bureaucracies and institutions. It is no surprise that as politically conscious young adults, the Young Lords were drawn to the hospital that had become ground zero in the city's health crisis. The race and class critique of what became known on the left as the fight against healthcare inequity made sense organically and fueled righteous indignation among these young radicals.

Conversations with people in the hospital led the Young Lords to set up a patient/worker complaint table in the ER to document patients' many grievances. A rotating crew of Young Lords and community members sat at the table from 9:00 A.M. to 9:00 P.M. on weekdays and around the clock on weekends. Over the course of their first month they collected 2,000 complaints, the most common being unsanitary health conditions, the language barrier for non-English-speaking patients, the failure of doctors to explain medical information to their patients, the backlog created by the scarcity of doctors (one doctor per eighty patients, on average), and a five-to-six-hour waiting period in the ER.[50] TLC members championed the rights of patients and workers and often sought to resolve grievances immediately by accompanying patients to the office, floor, or clinic where they had been improperly served. TLC representatives would show up to any of the hospital's floors or departments to press patient grievances. The work of documentation and verification, day after day after day, was unexciting, but the Young Lords were filled with an impassioned commitment to serve. Although brash, their advocacy was not provocative, involved no confrontations with police, and had none of the glorious, self-righteous fury that accompanied radical 1960s activism. The hours logged at the complaint table embody the Young Lords' rapid evolution into a group committed to its community and to helping ease the banal injustices of everyday life.

In just a couple of months the hospital's ethics were transformed. By systematizing, for the first time, a way of documenting and bringing patient grievances into the open, the activists helped establish a code of behavior in the hospital. No other effort had zeroed in on the abominable conditions at Lincoln so methodically. The lay intervention of the activists in the relationship between patient and physician also challenged the rigid hierarchy of an institution founded on paternalism. Patients who were previously treated with condescension, disregard, or contempt by those occupying a higher social status in the hospital hierarchy began to be accorded better and more respectful treatment.

Redress of grievances was often procured successfully by discussing the issue with the appropriate staff person and in the presence of the patient.[51] A report on the crisis at Lincoln prepared in August 1970 for the HHC by its chief administrator, Antero Lacot, confirmed these findings. Describing those who set up the complaint table at Lincoln as "consumers of health care," Lacot wrote: "The watchdog activities of persons strongly committed to good, humanized and personalized health care, created immediate, visible, positive changes. Doctors kept a better working schedule. . . . The waiting period for patients diminished; the traditional long lines in our emergency rooms, outpatient clinics and the pharmacy became shorter."[52] In response to one of the many complaints it received, the TLC obtained screens for the ER's bathroom cubicles, which had been exposed.

When civil discussion failed to obtain desired results, the TLC adopted more confrontational strategies.[53] On another occasion, the TLC's request that garbage be removed from the corner of 142nd Street and Cortlandt Avenue, just outside the hospital, was finally granted—but only after the group, inspired by the Young Lords' sanitation protests, transferred a heap of garbage from the street into Lacot's office. According to the TLC, the garbage protest was an action of last resort: "We complained, we petitioned, we called the mayor's office. Nothing was done."[54] Although the TLC was primarily involved with issues concerning patient treatment, it also rallied around improved working conditions. Following the involvement of the TLC, cafeteria workers, who had long complained of the ninety-degree heat in the hospital's unventilated kitchen, were finally provided the fan they had requested a long time before.

In spring and early summer 1970, the coalition established a set of demands that reflected the concerns of a community-controlled movement and, to a lesser extent, the traditional demands that a union might present at a contract negotiation. The TLC declared:

1 Doctors must give humane treatment to patients.
2 Free food must be given to patients who spend hours in the hospital waiting to be seen.
3 Construction on the new Lincoln Hospital must start immediately.
4 There must be no cutbacks in services or in jobs in any part of Lincoln Hospital.
5 The immediate formation of a community-worker board which has control over the policies and practices of the hospital.[55]

These demands were in the spirit of those made by the mental health workers a year earlier but were more explicit about poor hospital conditions and in their demand that doctors live up to the highest ethics of their profession.

Initial successes soon stalled. The TLC's declaration was accepted graciously by the administration in June, but not much happened. These first three months of intense organizing yielded limited results beyond improved patient relations— a victory, for sure, but one that only made the activists aware of how much more they could accomplish. Starting in July, acting independently of the TLC, the Young Lords turned to more militant action, which they believed would jolt the hospital administration and city government into conceding greater reforms. The Young Lords acted on their own because their action would require clandestine planning and a chain of command that they believed could only be carried out by a disciplined cadre organization. Their plans for more dramatic protests coincided with the arrival, on July 1, 1970, of thirty-one medical interns and residents, who had applied collectively to complete their residencies at Lincoln.[56] This progressive group of young men and women chose Lincoln because they were looking to build a community-centered residency program and for a less traditional learning environment. According to one of the residents, Dr. Harold Osborne: "After medical school, a group of us got together and were talking about going together as a group to someplace to do our training. Because the training that you participated in, in medicine . . . internship and residency is very dehumanizing and sort of top-down, very traditional, very hierarchical . . . and we wanted to do it in a different way."[57]

The project was anchored by four progressive doctors in training at Jacobi Hospital in the Bronx who were entering their third year of residency: Charlotte Fein, David Stead, Fitzhugh Mullan, and Marty Stein. They chose Lincoln Hospital in part because of its history of activism but also because there was a power vacuum there. With a lack of resources and staff, it was a kind of medical Siberia. According to Mullan, Lincoln "didn't have a lot of senior staff. . . . If you were going to try to take over and build a community hospital with a different philosophy, with a different set of relationships, this was a good place to go, as compared to Jacobi or lots of other places that had a million invested and well-established interests." When the second-year interns at Jacobi introduced the idea of recruiting a community-minded cohort of residents to Lincoln's chief of pediatrics, Dr. Arnold Einhorn, he agreed with the proposal. Since Einhorn's department had long been staffed with foreign doctors, the introduction of an entirely U.S.-trained staff of interns and residents from reputable schools was expected to increase the prestige of his program.[58] According to Osborne, "The thing about Einhorn was that he was kind of an unusual character. He was clinically a very skillful pediatrician; someone who was pretty well known in academic circles, well published. But he ran the department like a little kingdom. He was the king. And he had these residents who were mostly foreign—particularly Filipino or Asian—who never questioned him and kind of hung on his every word and really thought that he was God."[59]

Troubles were on the horizon. The doctors of the Lincoln Collective, as they called themselves, were poorly dressed, long-haired, downwardly mobile doctors in training who were looking to "escape the medical training hierarchy [they] detested."[60] The doctors came to the South Bronx with a righteous sense of purpose and a belief that healthcare was a human right that was too often denied to the poor. According to Osborne, they understood that "medicine and politics were inseparable." Mullan explained that the goal was to "craft a community-oriented [medical] training program [for interns and residents] at a community-oriented hospital," where the presence of good doctors could save lives.[61] According to Osborne, they envisioned "a training program that was non-hierarchical, pro-patient and pro-public health." The doctors "saw prevention as important if not more important than medical treatment . . . [and] wanted to involve the workers in the hospital and the community in determining what services were made available and what kinds of doctors should work at the hospital." The collective came with no less of a goal than to "transform the healthcare of the South Bronx."[62] But from the outset, their dreams were tempered by the high stakes of medical care at Lincoln. According to Mullan,

"Whatever our plans were for ramping up our political activities, we were mostly consumed with ramping up our medical activities, getting comfortable being the staff of this very big, very active medical 24-7 institution." And then within two weeks of their arrival the doctors were thrust into a tumultuous battle for community control of the hospital.

The Occupation of Lincoln Hospital

On the afternoon of July 13, after a typically long day of carrying out the various daily functions of the organization—speaking engagements, leafleting, the selling of *Palante*, and assisting members of the community with translation or advocacy in schools or the welfare office—general body members of the Young Lords checked in as usual at their East Harlem headquarters. Upon arrival, members were given a sheet of paper with instructions that contained the coordinates of a gathering scheduled for that evening. Also included were the names of two or three Young Lords to bring along but to whom information should not be divulged. The leadership was concerned with police infiltration, but among the rank and file, rumor had it that a surprise party was in the works.

Over the next few hours, approximately 150 Young Lords gathered at an apartment on Manhattan Avenue. Chairman Felipe Luciano announced that those present would be occupying Lincoln Hospital the next morning. The leaders of the organization, including Luciano, Juan González, and David Perez, each gave an assessment of the crisis at Lincoln and why the takeover was necessary. Assignments were meted out and a division of labor was established among different subsets of Young Lords that coincided with the different ministries: health, information, field, and education. The rest of the meeting focused on the details of security and the need to comply with strict discipline during the takeover. All of them were expected to sleep in the apartment. Those not wracked with anxious anticipation managed to sleep a few hours before it was time for action.

At 3:30 A.M. on July 14, a large U-Haul truck and a number of cars were waiting outside the apartment. The Young Lords were instructed to maximize room by making use of the space between their legs for others to crouch in and to hang on tight during the bumpy ride to the South Bronx. At 5:00 A.M. the Puerto Rican militants proceeded to reenact a sensational routine, the same one that had first brought them national notoriety seven months earlier during their Church Offensive. With members of HRUM and TLC on call, approximately 200 people were gearing up for the action. Members of the Young Lords defense ministry were on-site, charged with "neutralizing" the hospital's security as soon as the Young Lords' caravan arrived at the prearranged location. The defense ministry was also ready to direct the action.

Driven by radical labor organizer William Santiago, father of Young Lord

Young Lords find Sterling rock-salt bags in Nurses Residence, the building they occupied earlier that morning, and build a make-shift barricade at side entrance, July 14, 1970. (Photograph by Jack Manning/New York Times; courtesy of the *New York Times*)

Gloria Rodriguez, the U-Haul truck backed into the hospital's loading dock, and when the back doors of the truck were opened, the Young Lords stormed the hospital "like marines storm a beachhead in war."[63] Equipped mainly with chuka sticks (a pair of eight-inch wooden batons held together with an elastic band and used in martial arts), the Young Lords deployed with confidence and even a measure of grace. Several entered the building wearing long white medical coats, a trademark display of the Young Lords' mischievous humor and deadly earnestness. Immediately after they secured the entrances and exits, they explained their purpose to those inside and allowed workers and patients access to the building.

Within the first hour, the Young Lords had secured all of the first-floor windows, doors, and entrances, blocking them with hospital furniture, boxes, and hundreds of industrial-size bags of "sterling rock salt" that were in the building.[64] The building's high-pressure water hose was unfurled, ready in the event that the police might charge the front entrance of the building.

The radicals announced a press conference for 10:00 A.M. and deployed messengers to the upper floors to inform doctors, nurses, and other hospital employees of the occupation and request their assistance in "running the hospital for the people."[65] As they did at the First Spanish United Methodist Church, they kept one door open to ensure that those coming to work were allowed in. Each employee was told that the Young Lords did not wish to interfere with the operation of the hospital. At 10:00 A.M., they explained their actions to the press, welcomed volunteers to help staff their programs, and invited the community to participate.

The timing of the occupation coincided, roughly, with the onset of the new budgetary cycle, when reductions in hospital services were scheduled to begin. Only days earlier, *Palante* had run a major article on Lincoln Hospital whose opening lines both reported on the imminent budgetary cuts and foreshadowed the Young Lords' July action. The portentous article began, "In July 1970, Lincoln Hospital will be the victim of the greedy businessmen who make money from the illnesses of the people of the South Bronx."[66]

Though the doctors of the Lincoln Collective were not part of the planning of the action, its logic resonated with their own understanding of the crisis. They all had read Barbara Ehrenreich's 1970 book, *The American Health Empire*, on the chaotic nature of the medical system, its organization around profit rather than patients, and its traditional hierarchical culture and systemic racist and sexist practices. The author paid special attention to the displacement of solo practitioners by "medical empires." Defined as a network of institutions spearheaded by an elite private medical school and anchored by a teaching hospital and, in New York, its public hospital affiliates, the medical empire accelerated the transformation of healthcare into an industry in the 1960s. Even though they were significantly subsidized by public taxes, the empires focused exclusively on research, the pursuit of prestige, the training of physicians, and the expansion of their real estate holdings through incursion in their surrounding urban ghettoes. Because they were powerful enough to set industry standards, they presented a formidable obstacle to patient-centered care and a drain on the public coffers.

With the help of HRUM and the TLC, the militants began instituting their community programs. In the auditorium, they began a provisional screening clinic for anemia, lead poisoning, iron deficiency, and tuberculosis, and in the basement they created a daycare center and classroom for political and health education. Over the course of the day hundreds of community residents who had heard of the takeover and of the free services made their way through the occupied building or stood watch outside amid a sea of armed police officers. Above them, hanging from the windows of the hospital's upper floors, fluttered the Puerto Rican flag and banners that read, "Seize the Hospital to Serve the People," "Welcome to the People's Hospital," and correspondingly in Spanish, "Bienvenidos al Hospital del Pueblo." According to a firsthand account by one of the doctors in the Lincoln Collective:

The Lords never requested formal backing in advance since to do so would have jeopardized the secrecy surrounding the planned action. In all likelihood, though, they counted on a fair amount of support from the hospital staff. And they got it. . . . The Collective members visited the occupied areas frequently, helped staff the day care and health care programs, and let it be known to the press and the police that physicians backed the Lords. I for one couldn't stay away. The Nurses' Residence suddenly had the fantastic, intoxicating air of a liberated zone. The press was listening; the city was listening; and the Lords had risen up and were telling the stories of the women and children waiting endlessly in the clinic, the old folks dying for lack of a Cardiac Care Unit, the humiliation of the Emergency Room, the flies, the pain, the degradation. It felt good, it felt right, it felt righteous. It was why we had come to Lincoln.[67]

For the duration of the day, radio and television news broadcasts reported on the group's dramatic disruption, capturing in the process the inhumane physical conditions under which service was customarily rendered at the hospital. At a press conference, the group's representatives described the hospital's deplorable conditions in detail. Even Lacot, the hospital's chief administrator, admitted that day that although he preferred that they leave, the Young Lords' actions were "helpful" to "dramatize a situation, which is critical."[68] For a city government that was planning to implement a long-term package of austerity measures in public services, the events at Lincoln Hospital would have consequences. In no uncertain terms, the Young Lords' action inserted the budget cutting and its consequences into the city's public discourse.

With confidence in their sails, the Young Lords outlined a new and more comprehensive set of demands at their press conference:

1 No cutbacks in services or jobs, specifically in the Section K screening clinic, the Emergency Room, of translators, doctors, or any other personnel.
2 We want immediate funds from the NYC Health Services Administration to complete the building of and fully staff the new Lincoln Hospital.
3 Door-to-door health services for preventative care emphasizing environment and sanitation control, nutrition, drug addiction, maternal and childcare, and senior citizen services.
4 We want a permanent 24 hour-a-day grievance table staffed by patients and workers with the power to redress grievances.
5 We want a $140.00 a week minimum wage for all workers.
6 We want a day care center for patients and workers at Lincoln Hospital.

7 We want self-determination of all health services through a community-worker board to operate Lincoln Hospital. This group of people must have shown their commitment to sincerely serve the people of this community.[69]

As the political and economic character of these demands suggests, the preoccupations of the TLC had evolved from an initial focus on humane treatment of patients to demands that also reflected a stronger set of traditional shop-floor concerns.[70]

The Young Lords' disruptive protests had proved effective once again. As before, fear that a prolonged and hostile conflict would spark similar actions by other discontented groups afforded the Lords a measure of bargaining power in city politics. Following their press conference, the militants entered into negotiations with Lacot; the mayor's chief assistant, Sid Davidoff; and representatives from the HHC, which had taken over the administration and allocation of expenditures for municipal hospitals a year earlier. After four hours of talks, the fragile balance at the bargaining table was suddenly upset just as an agreement was about to be reached. According to the Young Lords Party, the police were going to withdraw their forces from the hospital's surrounding area and would have allowed the group to run a series of programs in the hospital in return for the immediate evacuation of the premises. But when TLC delegates received word that an undercover police officer had tried to break through the central checkpoint door where a Young Lord was positioned, they called off the negotiations, concluding that "it was apparent that the administration had no control of what was going on and that Mayor Lindsay, through his mouthpieces, was trying to double-deal."[71]

At approximately 5:00 P.M., in an auditorium brimming with media and supporters, Young Lord Pablo Guzmán reported on what had transpired at the negotiation table. As he spoke, police reinforcements positioned themselves at every entrance of the building. Guzmán exhorted the audience to defend the hospital. But Guzmán's exhortations were merely a ploy to disorient the police. Believing that they had "won a political victory" and that they risked a bloody confrontation with the awaiting officers, the Lords decided against mass arrests. As the young radical excited the audience with his speech, the Young Lords in their white smocks began to slip out of the building, a few at a time, escorted by resident doctors. After just twelve hours, the occupation of Lincoln Hospital ended, just as stealthily as it began. Supporters stayed in the auditorium for several hours so that the Young Lords could exit without being detected. Only two were arrested.

The Aftermath

From July until December 1970, the crisis at Lincoln became central to the city's political debates. James Buckley, the Conservative Party candidate for U.S. senator, called the occupation a "vigilante action" and denounced Mayor Lindsay's decision to send his own chief assistant, Sid Davidoff, "to negotiate with the extremists."[72] And while Lacot, the hospital's chief administrator, and Einhorn, the head of pediatrics, acknowledged the validity of the activists' grievances, they took issue with the YLP's and TLC's "extremism" and questioned the authenticity of their ties to the community. In response, Cleo Silvers explained:

> Those people that recognize problems . . . [and] are willing to move on them in the interest of all the people and not a small segment of the community are those people who represent the community. . . . Our position is that we do not say that we represent the South Bronx. . . . We are an element of the community, which has . . . been able to articulate the problems. . . . [Our] job is to get out to the people in the community with this information, to organize the people in the community, and to involve them in making changes along with us, because . . . we won't be able to make any changes without . . . large numbers of people in the community. We feel that the only way that a person can be a bona fide representative of the community is by his practice, by what he has done to prove that he is representing the people of the community and not himself.[73]

In her statement, Silvers defined the role of the vanguard party as defender and advocate of the broadest and most progressive interests of poor and working people. To Silvers and the Young Lords, vanguard leadership had to combine analyzing the world's problems with charting political direction alongside the broadest possible number of oppressed people. Striking this balance would require an accurate assessment of both the political state of affairs and the level of consciousness of their community base at any given moment.

Just days after the July 14 occupation, a new crisis erupted. On July 17, Carmen Rodriguez went into Lincoln's gynecology service for an abortion. The Puerto Rican woman was a long-standing patient at Lincoln. She had been addicted to heroin and was an active member of Logos, a community-initiated heroin treatment center in the South Bronx at which progressive Lincoln doctors volunteered. According to one of the doctors who supervised Logos, resident psychiatrist and TLC member Mike Smith, Rodriguez was well known and had endeared herself to Logos's drug rehabilitation workers because of her caring spirit. She was fortified by Khalil Gibran's writings, carried his books with her daily, and regularly implored the people around her to treat each other with kindness.[74]

Though New York State had legalized abortion just two weeks earlier, Rodriguez had been approved for the procedure under the old abortion law because she had rheumatic heart disease and delivering a baby would endanger her life.[75] Smith explains that her procedure occurred just two weeks after a new cohort of residents and interns relieved the old class of doctors in training; because "the attendings were different, the doctors were different . . . they knew nothing of her medical background at all . . . and in those days at public hospitals you didn't always get records, so they assumed that she was there simply to get an abortion." Abortions were relatively simple procedures, but they had not been performed with any regularity before, and at Lincoln there was no established protocol and no formal training of doctors.[76]

The resident on call that day performed a saline-based abortion procedure, whose severely harmful effects on patients with heart disease were well known.[77] Rodriguez became short of breath, but without a chart the resident proceeded to treat her for what he assumed to be asthma and then repeated the same course again. According to Smith, the resident assumed that Rodriguez "was 'a Puerto Rican woman with asthma'—a common category but not a universal category. And so he gives her medicine for asthma, and that's medicine that makes the heart patient much worse. She was quite correctable. And again she was a person who knew the difference between asthma and heart disease." Although Rodriguez was likely conscious, and "could enunciate beautifully," she was being treated in a medical environment in which the patient was often infantilized; she was never consulted about what was happening to her body and how the medical care she was receiving might have been harming her.[78] She died on July 19, three days after the abortion.

On the day of her death, the TLC activists demanded a meeting with Lacot. According to the activists, they were told that Rodriguez's was "a complicated case," beyond their comprehension. The activists retorted, "We knew what they were talking about and also what they wanted to hide." They drafted a set of demands, calling for damages to be paid to her family; for the head of the abortion clinic, Dr. J. J. Smith, to be removed unless a community-worker committee was set up to oversee the program; and for the abortion clinic to be named after Carmen Rodriguez.[79] Within days, Rodriguez's record was leaked to the TLC by Mike Smith, who was well aware that her death was due to negligence.[80]

The tragedy of Rodriguez's death called into question the methods of care institutionalized in the public hospitals as a result of medical school affiliation contracts. In the affiliation system, patients were never assigned their own primary care physicians; a patient would likely see a different doctor—whoever was on call—from visit to visit. The resulting reliance on inexperienced students' treatment decisions increased the probability of disastrous outcomes. Moreover, the fact that no one doctor followed the progress of any patient over time meant that cases such as Rodriguez's could fall through the cracks. Although the affiliation contract was conceived with mutual benefits in mind for both the city's poor and the medical schools, in actuality the medical training of interns and residents and the schools' research needs became major forces in shaping hospital practices. One of the key reforms that came out of the activism at Lincoln was the emergence of "continuity clinics" in public hospitals, where patients are seen by the same primary care doctor. This program was conceived by the doctors in the Lincoln Collective.[81]

Another remarkable result, negotiated by the Young Lords, was that the hospital administration consented to a clinical pathological conference. In late July, the hospital hosted a public hearing, where administrators presented Rodriguez's diagnosis, treatment, and the medical complications that led to her death. The audience then asked questions, and doctors from other institutions presented counterarguments about the care she should have received. This type of public clinical conference, allowing a lay audience to cross-examine a team of medical doctors, has been cited as the first of its kind in the history of medicine. Though the meeting proved grossly contentious, with a lot of hissing and heckling, according to one of the doctors in the collective, "the fact of the meeting was an important event. It was a troubled, even tortured example of community control of medical services. At the least, it was a real and significant instance of physicians being called to account by community people. The agenda did not flow easily but the very meeting of the two sides to discuss a medical event stood as a victory for community participation in the hospital."[82]

After the clinical conference, the crisis surrounding Rodriguez's case escalated. The TLC charged the department with "genocide." In its estimation, the clinical conference was a victory, but Rodriguez's "murder," which was due to systemic negligence, required accountability, continued campaigning for fundamental change, and reprisals at the administrative level. On August 25, 1970, TLC activists met with the head of the division of obstetrics and gynecology, J. J. Smith, repeating their demands once again and adding that Smith should reinstate the only black doctor in gynecology, who the activists alleged was fired because "he stood up to" Smith.[83] The more-than-two-hour meeting was filled with acrimony, after which the activists took measures into their own hands and "fired" him. They escorted the doctor to his car, pushed him around, and told him never to come back.[84] According to Cleo Silvers, the conflict reached a fever pitch because of the arrogant and racist disposition of the doctors, even the progressive ones among them. She remembers, "If Dr. J. J. Smith had conceded to even some of our demands, and if [the administration] hadn't tried to cover up what we knew was all too common at Lincoln—the daily disregard for the lives of people of color—we wouldn't have had to take the actions we took."[85] Surprisingly, the activists were able to get away with such acts because they had relatively free rein in the hospital. Its chief administrator, Antero Lacot, had not asked them to disband the complaint table they had set up in the ER in late spring 1970 or the daycare center they established during the July 14 occupation.[86]

J. J. Smith resigned shortly after the altercation with the activists in his office. In response, twenty-seven residents and interns of his department, most of whom were foreign doctors, went on a ten-day strike in his support, from August 25 through September 3.[87] The interns continued to work at another affiliate of the Albert Einstein College of Medicine, Jacobi Hospital, but their actions shut down Lincoln's obstetrics and gynecology department. The interns and residents vowed to return only if the activists were barred from interfering in any aspect of work in their department. To this end, on August 27, 1970, the hospital sought a restraining order against the Young Lords, the TLC, HRUM, and all other activists.[88] Antero Lacot reported to the *New York Times* that the injunction was served to the Young Lords because they had "exceeded the ground rules." But Lacot was equivocal in his condemnation of the radicals. He had previously acknowledged that although their actions were extreme, they had helped move the Lincoln bureaucracy toward change. Perhaps because he sensed the value of their controversial presence and perhaps because he was unaware of the draconian character of the injunction, he reported to the *New York Times* that the activists would be allowed to continue to run their daycare and complaint table. But top city officials, the courts, and the mainstream media were collaborating with institutions in all spheres of public life, from the schools to the hospitals, to institutionalize heavy security measures against activists like the Young Lords and their supporters.

The injunction was served on the same day that the *New York Times* editorial board penned a scathing editorial against the Young Lords titled "Crisis at Lincoln." Because this editorial and another news article both referenced the terms and effective date of the restraining order, it is likely that efforts were coordinated between the newspaper, the city's attorneys, and the hospital administration. The editorial portrayed the striking Lincoln physicians as heroes and the Young Lords as villains, explaining that because of "doctor shortage, when many alternative jobs are available, it requires physicians with special dedication to the disadvantaged to be . . . willing to put up with Lincoln's many difficulties." But the profile of physicians at Lincoln, the majority of whom where foreign doctors seeking to gain licenses in the United States, was far more complicated. And there was no mention of the Pediatric Collective, which together with the Young Lords launched a door-to-door preventive medicine program in the South Bronx. The editorial derided the Young Lords as "a Puerto Rican imitation of the Black Panthers," who created "a climate of fear and conflict" in the hospital and took to "harassing doctors and nurses." Using the symbolic remnants and language of McCarthyism, it charged the group with "invading" the hospital and implicitly impugned its administrators for allowing the Lords "to become a fixture in it."[89]

In a letter responding to the *New York Times* editorial, Eli C. Messinger, national chairman of the Medical Committee for Human Rights, pointed out the contradiction between its "righteous condemnation of conditions at Lincoln" and its "even stronger condemnation" of the methods of those trying to effect change. Messinger itemized the "constructive" activities of the radicals and emphasized the failure of "the medical profession and the city" to redress "the abominable conditions of the hospital" until the Young Lords and others "began to directly institute changes." He also explored the merits of the Young Lords' most controversial demand, the community-worker board to set policy for the hospital, arguing that hospital workers and community residents were best positioned to "identify major health problems" and "shape corrective programs relevant to their communities." He went on to say that community control was less about "lay interference in the technical aspects of medical care" and more about compelling "physicians and administrators to abdicate their elitist roles of prescribing the structure of health services."[90]

The conservative politician James Buckley, eager for any publicity that might help his mayoral campaign, also weighed in. Like others, including the *New York Times* editorial board, he misapprehended the facts, failed to address the grievances that led to protest, and used the language of crime to describe the actions of the radicals at Lincoln. Buckley observed, "Not only was the superintendent of the hospital held hostage by extremists, but women in labor were actually turned away from the hospital doors because the rest of the medical staff could not function in this sort of chaotic environment."[91] What Buckley characterized as a hostage situation involving the superintendent of the hospital was, in fact, the activists' firing of the head of gynecology, J. J. Smith. Buckley also blamed the Young Lords' July 14 occupation for the disruption of services in the gynecology department. Speaking to the *New York Post*, Young Lord Pablo Guzmán retorted, "The only disruption of services came about when those doctors [who supported Smith] left . . . of their own volition, not because of any threat."[92]

Even though the hospital's chief administrator told the *New York Times* that the court injunction would allow the activists to continue to run the daycare and the complaint table, the injunction failed to bring the doctors back to work. Their work stoppage and temporary transfer to Jacobi Hospital may have offered some comparative perspective. Now, in addition to their harassment complaint against the Young Lords, they were demanding that their workloads be reduced at Lincoln. But when the city threatened to terminate its $28 million affiliation contract with the Einstein Medical College, Einstein forced the doctors to return to their posts.[93]

Other departments, including pediatrics and psychiatry, were also swept up in the conflict. Arnold Einhorn, the chief of the pediatrics department and its pioneer, was replaced by the acclaimed Dr. Helen Rodriguez Trias after protests by pediatric doctors within the Lincoln Collective. In their view, Einhorn was too rigid to allow the kind of training program the dissident doctors sought to establish, in which department policy was determined through collective discussion in weekly meetings that included the nurses. The doctors in training wanted to challenge the individualism, elitism, and sexism of the medical profession in consciousness-raising circles not unlike those that emerged in the women's movement. They also initiated a Pediatric Parents' Association to involve parents in the life of the department. Other innovations—like drawing straws to decide who was in charge of the daily rounds—were deeply flawed and didn't last. Ironically, Einhorn's ouster by a group of mostly young, Jewish doctors in training was decried by the American Jewish Congress and the Jewish Defense League as an instance of anti-Semitism. A civil rights investigation by the city ultimately led to Einhorn's reinstatement.[94]

Patient Bill of Rights

Before Carmen Rodriguez's death, the TLC had experimented with a variety of tactics in its fight for improved conditions and greater influence over the governance of the hospital. The activists held rallies, drafted a series of petitions and demands, convened meetings with hospital administration, and occupied buildings. All the while their presence in the hospital was anchored by their twenty-four-hour patient/worker complaint table in the emergency room. As we have seen, the activists' demands reflected grievances surrounding local conditions and an attempt to introduce the notion of preventive care through medical home visits at the neighborhood level. Another set of demands drafted in late summer 1970 by HRUM and the Young Lords proved uniquely influential in the field of medicine. Drafted in the cauldron of protest following Rodriguez's death, the demands aimed to establish a protocol of communication between patients and doctors, minimizing the incidence of such tragedies in the future and investing patients with knowledge and control over their care by recasting patients in the eyes of the medical profession as citizens with constitutional rights.

The Patient Bill of Rights demanded these rights:

1 To be treated with dignity and respect.
2 To have all treatment explained and to refuse any treatment you feel is not in your best interest.
3 To know what medicine is being prescribed and what it is for and what side effects it will cause.
4 To have access to your medical chart.
5 To have door to door preventative medicine programs.

6 To choose the doctor you want to have and to have the same doctor treat you all the time.

7 To call your doctor to your home.

8 To receive free meals while waiting for outpatient service.

9 To have free day care centers in all hospital facilities.

10 To receive free healthcare.

With its far-reaching implications for the relationship between patients and doctors, rearticulations of HRUM's Patient Bill of Rights have been adopted by hospitals across the nation under the same name. Part of what was remarkable about this list was its prescience. It significantly advanced the standards and ethics of patient care and patient rights in public discourse and helped enshrine concepts such as patient dignity, full disclosure and explanation of medical treatment and prescriptions and their side effects, and the right of the patient to refuse treatment. At the same time, it anticipated, in its call for free healthcare, what remains one of the most contentious debates about public health.

Coalition Politics:
Middle-Class Guilt and Revolutionary Bravado

The coalition of individuals and groups that came together to fight for better healthcare in the South Bronx was riddled with internal tensions. The relationships they built were full of promise but also strained by conflicts of race, class, and gender. The weakest link in the coalition revolved around the relationship between the TLC, itself an amalgam of radical organizations and individuals of color, and the predominantly white Lincoln Collective. For its part, the Lincoln Collective of doctors was independently organized and often deluged with the responsibilities of medical residency. The Lincoln Collective worked best within the coalition when it could offer concrete, skill-based support to the work, as in its contributions to the door-to-door preventive medicine program.

The Young Lords did not tell any of the staff at Lincoln about their takeover in advance. Osborne, among other Lincoln Collective doctors, was unsettled by the surprise occupation. He described the Young Lords as "top-down. . . . They might come and say, 'We're doing this today,' or, 'We're gonna do this tomorrow.'" He was resentful that they didn't involve the Lincoln Collective in discussions about strategy. Osborne also perceived the male leadership of the Young Lords to be "intimidating," "arrogant," and "secretive."

The Young Lords and their leadership were unapologetic in deploying both eloquent rhetoric and brawn in their day-to-day work. They inspired thousands of young people across the city with their dramatic antics and their perceptive insights, but they also threatened to beat up corner drug dealers for debasing their neighborhoods and the head of the Lincoln gynecology department for his attempts to cover up medical negligence. To a young, white, middle-class doctor unfamiliar with the parlance of the street, who was working in a disfigured urban landscape brimming with petty criminals and drug users, the masculine posturing and street savvy of male members of the Young Lords was likely discomfiting. The strident confidence and centralized power of the group's Central Committee surely unsettled white middle-class notions of legitimate leadership, and the brashness of some members of the Young Lords must have unnerved those who held on to any iota of middle-class propriety and respectability. The Young Lords challenged mainstream perceptions of race, which in turn destabilized the paradigm of power, world view, and identity of the middle class, of all roles, even the radicalized among them.

In his recollection of activism at Lincoln, Osborne returned to the male bravado and unilateral decision-making of the Young Lords' leadership as a source of tension. In fact, the Young Lords had enjoyed quite a number of victories since they had started organizing a year earlier. And the generally positive media attention they enjoyed must have enlarged their egos and made the group, and especially its leadership, feel invincible. But the organization's formal leadership had a mix of personalities. Its most visible leaders were Felipe Luciano, Juan González, Pablo Guzmán, and Denise Oliver. Juan "Fi" Ortiz and David Perez were self-effacing, background strategists. González was an articulate, but low-key, strategist and leader of the student strike and occupations at Columbia in 1968. Guzmán was a media maven who could pack a punch in a slogan. Luciano, the most charismatic among them, vacillated between poetic ruminations and a street-tough persona. And Oliver, a middle-class black American woman, was known for the haughtiness with which she brought down her opponents in an argument.

Despite Osborne's critique of the organization's leadership, he sang the praises of the organization's rank and file that was active at Lincoln—a disproportionately female representation of the organization who were also members of HRUM—whom he believed to be "much more earnest and hardworking and humble and sincere." While Osborne characterizes the activists at Lincoln as people who often adopted hard lines unnecessarily, overall he said they "were really trying their best to do the right thing. They were very consistent, I think, self-effacing, very altruistic."[95]

Osborne's perception of the Young Lords differed from that of Dr. Stephen Levin, "a Jewish kid from a working-class neighborhood in Philadelphia," who conducted home visits with the Lords and was the organization's resident doctor. The Young Lords "played a major role in my reassessing where I had come from, what was important, what I should do with my life.... Using one's life for a better purpose than getting rich, you know, made really resonating sense for me." He felt alienated by the middle-class professional aspirations of his medical school cohort. With the Young Lords, by contrast, he found home: "I don't know exactly . . . what there was about me and my personality that made me click so easily with a guy like Mickey Melendez or Yoruba Guzmán? I think I come from a neighborhood that was so much like the barrio—wild-ass kids runnin' in the street, playin' ball, doin' crazy things. . . . So there was something about the way they were that was so resonant with my own [experience growing up]. . . . I was white, unmistakably white, and a doctor, too . . . [but] my distinctiveness disappeared."[96]

Osborne described the behavior of the radicalized doctors in ways similar to his description of the leadership of the Young Lords, but he seemed less intimidated by his colleagues: "Despite our erratic behavior and arrogance, the workers came to like us because they felt, at least, we cared about the patient and were trying to do the right thing." He also observed that the manner with which the Lincoln Collective doctors dealt with Einhorn was "extreme" and unreasonable, and he attributed their inflexibility to youthful inexperience. However, in discussing the authoritarian disposition of the Young Lords, Osborne also recalls that "everybody was pretty sectarian in those days. That was the characteristic of most political groups that I knew of, which meant that . . . they were run in a very hierarchical fashion. Most of the leadership was male."

Middle-class guilt figured prominently in the relationship among the groups in the Lincoln coalition. According to Osborne, "They would give us political education and sort of make us feel guilty about being white and middle class."[97] Mullan explains the internal conflict he experienced over the notion that he should take a political lead from the Young Lords. "I struggle with it. On the one hand I thought it was good to think creatively, and I definitely had the sense that there were ways in which we needed to function differently as people in order to be responsive to people's movements, so I was at least open to the notion of considering . . . my own elitism." Although they never made their position overt, the doctors, according to Mullan, took issue with the analysis that "Third World people, and in particular Third World workers, were the leadership, which was a little bit unrealistic in the sense that while you might like that to be the case, that doesn't necessarily mean that it's true. Just declaring it doesn't mean it's right. But most of us felt we had to accede to whatever the leadership of these minority groups asked of us because we felt guilty."[98]

Mullan concludes that the notion that "you have to surrender your identity, or your leadership, or your pride, and take leadership from anyone who comes through the door because they're part of the party . . . is [not] a viable way to run anything."[99] For his part, Osborne often "felt a bit guilty and a bit intimidated and a bit used," but he believed that the good outweighed the bad: "On the whole we were doing the right thing. . . . We had to move forward by having parties and leadership and cadre and rank and file and organizing and all that.

And I don't think I knew enough quite yet, politically, about how groups worked to really have a consistent analysis or consistent critique."[100] Of the coalition's experience with the doctors, Young Lord Cleo Silvers emphasizes that "many of them, especially the men (and they were mostly men) were never able to accept the notion that we could be equal partners because we weren't doctors ourselves. They didn't truly get that you have to listen to the community in order to deliver quality healthcare. They couldn't overcome their middle-class entitlement and we struggled with them over this."[101]

The coalition work led by the Young Lords at Lincoln Hospital reflected the challenges presented by the demographic shifts of the postwar period. Lincoln employed and served members of a predominantly Puerto Rican and black American population, and tensions among hospital activists were exacerbated by the chasm between the life experiences of the cohort of working-class people of color with vanguard party politics who made up the core of the TLC and those of the group of politicized middle-class white doctors who made up the Lincoln Collective. In a nation where middle-class white professionals and poor people of color lived diametrically different lives, the workplace convergence of these two groups was bound to produce conflicts. On the one hand, white middle-class professionals were beholden to a world managed by experts and a world view that measured success through individual hard work, prudence, education, ambition, and self-improvement. By contrast, for many people of color, success was increasingly defined not by individual strivings alone but by their collective challenges to entrenched systems of oppression and grassroots campaigns for reform in education, health, and employment. In the context of growing claims to self-determination among people of color, there emerged critiques of less visible but no less damaging manifestations of racism and white paternalism among even progressive whites.

Through 1970 and 1971, the Young Lords continued their coalition work at Lincoln and in November 1970 became involved in another major action. In the lead-up to the action, the HRUM became an official subsidiary organization of the Young Lords, which meant that its members identified both as Young Lords and as HRUM members. This granted the Young Lords greater reach and political influence at Lincoln even amid administrative attempts to limit their access to the hospital after the Lincoln occupation. In August, the Young Lords and HRUM brought together a disparate group of seven neighborhood organizations in a collaboration they called the South Bronx Drug Coalition.[102] Its objective was to obtain institutional backing from Lincoln Hospital for a drug detoxification center. Following the dominant community control model of protest of that period, on November 6, 1970, the activists again occupied the sixth floor of the nurses' residence attached to Lincoln. There they proceeded to implement a program. With the aid of doctors, the group conducted physicals, assigned beds, and began to administer detoxification treatment, while representatives of the coalition negotiated with Lacot. At the end of the day, the police were called in, and fifteen people were arrested.[103] But others returned the next day and proceeded to lay the groundwork for a detox clinic.

The program became popular among the people of the South Bronx because it humanized the user and challenged the notion of addiction as a personal character flaw. The Young Lords and others involved sought to understand the relationship between individual behavior and the social context and structure of society. The identification of drug abuse as a social rather than a purely individual phenomenon was considered an integral component of the rehabilitation process. In a district that claimed the largest incidence of drug addiction in the nation, before long what came to be known as Lincoln Detox was treating 600 people a week.[104] Through political education, the program's treatment empowered users with an understanding of the complexity of addiction, including the sociopolitical context that led people to want to escape reality—poverty, permanent unemployment, racism, and a dilapidated living environment. The mandatory education classes also introduced their participants to a web of political ideas that highlighted the intersection between drug addiction and the expansion of drug trafficking as a consequence of U.S. foreign policy in places such as Vietnam.[105]

The detox program involved doctors, activists, and patients as partners in a multifaceted medical treatment and social rehabilitation project. Directed by Stephen Levin and Cleo Silvers, the program first adopted, of necessity, the mainstream methadone detox method, which was unpopular with activists because methadone could be just as addictive as heroin.[106] The activists sought an alternative that didn't replace one addictive substance with another. Before long they came to envision a program that would introduce Eastern medicine as the primary treatment method for addiction. Lincoln Detox was eventually funded by Lincoln Hospital in 1972 and became one of the principal acupuncture drug treatment centers in the Western world.[107]

■

The fast-paced course of activism initiated by the Young Lords at Lincoln used a range of tactics to involve workers and patients in the fight for better wages and improved care. The multiplicity of tasks—from rallies and petitions, the complaint table, and negotiations with hospital administrators to building occupations and door-to-door home visits—demanded a full-time activism that was as exhausting as it was exhilarating. Together, the TLC, HRUM, the Young Lords, and the Lincoln Collective sought to elevate the ethics of medical practice by establishing a compassionate, patient-centered, preventive model of care. They also sought to dramatize the problems of Lincoln and embarrass the city to compel it to build a facility that had been promised to the people of the South Bronx fifteen years earlier.

The crisis over governance at Lincoln Hospital was a continuation, albeit in a different sphere, of the movement for "community control" that had exploded during the Ocean Hill–Brownsville school decentralization crisis of 1967–68.[108] The growing call for community control was a radical interpretation of the War on Poverty's dictum of "maximum feasible participation." The concept demanded a reordering of decision-making, employment patterns, and delivery of local services in the major institutions governing community life such as schools, hospitals, and police precincts. The call for minority control over community institutions was not a radical demand, but it was an expression of the radicalization, and growing confidence, of movements built by people of color in urban centers across the United States. It was also one of the major practical applications of the concept of black power. It reflected a growing preoccupation among activists with extending the meaning of democracy and enhancing the fight for racial equality by rooting it in economic and political power at the local level. As the Lincoln example suggests, that demand was led by the growing sector of low-ranking workers in social service industries and municipal government, who were also often residents of that same community. The nonprofessional staff at Lincoln's mental health clinic called for a community- and worker-led board of the clinic, with authority to make and implement governing decisions and committed to fairly representing all staff. These activists raised issues of economic equality and wealth redistribution in their struggles, but in seeking greater influence and power over major local institutions they often became managers of a system that had not granted the major structural reforms needed to address racialized economic inequality.

At Lincoln, the Young Lords broadened the definition of community control. Their campaign took the call a step further, beyond a critique of the form of governance to a critique of its content and purpose. The struggle at Lincoln evolved politically from one that emphasized the ways in which racism colored healthcare services in the Bronx to one that articulated the social limitations of institutions governed by economic interests and how racism against people of color created deadly consequences. The dramatic work of the Young Lords and their supporters at Lincoln Hospital was driven by, and corresponded to, the deepening social and economic decay of the urban environment. Operating between two different epochs—the decline of the era of civil rights, black power, and the Great Society, and the emerging new era of social conservatism that began in the 1970s—the Young Lords were among the first activists to challenge draconian reductions in social spending and the associated privatization of public services. They were preparing for what they believed would be politically decisive battles.

CHAPTER TEN

A SECOND OCCUPATION

The Young Lords Party's long summer of protest in 1970—during which it intrepidly foreshadowed the possibilities and aspirations of "Socialism at Lincoln Hospital"—amplified its political reputation in New York and across the nation. Since its emergence a year earlier, the organization had undergone a meteoric rise in notoriety and popularity. It was slammed in the press by James L. Buckley of the Conservative Party and Sanford D. Garelik, the New York City Council president and former chief inspector of the New York Police Department (NYPD), among others.[1] At the grassroots, however, thousands of people had approvingly reached out to the Young Lords in the streets and in their offices. The group expanded its day-to-day work from East Harlem and the Bronx to the Lower East Side, opening a new office on September 16, 1970. The Young Lords were now fully known in wider circles of antiwar, women's, gay, lesbian, and transgender liberation, and in the black, brown, yellow, and red power movements. Their protests had also helped revitalize larger sectors of organizers and artists in the Puerto Rican community.

Emboldened by continued success, the Lords initiated a series of new projects between September and December 1970: They launched a student initiative, which was the springboard for one of the most sizable mainland, pro–Puerto Rican independence march in the history of New York. They reoccupied a floor of Lincoln Hospital's nurses' residence to initiate a drug treatment center that was lauded as the first of its kind in the Western world.[2] But as summer gave way to autumn, the organization also wrestled with inevitable challenges including assimilating new membership growth and discipline, internal conflicts, changes in leadership, and heightened repression. The demotion and loss of beloved chairman Felipe Luciano, unforeseen tragedy, and a second action at the First Spanish United Methodist Church (FSUMC) would set the Young Lords Party (YLP) on a new course toward decline, precisely at the moment it had reached the height of success.

The chairman's swift demotion, in early September 1970, was dramatic and commanded media attention. The group's highest leadership body took the action after Luciano and another member of the Central Committee, Pablo

305

Denise Oliver speaks at press conference during Julio Roldán's wake in the occupied First Spanish United Methodist Church, October 19, 1970. (Photograph by Tyrone Dukes/ New York Times; courtesy of the *New York Times*)

Guzmán, violated the organization's security protocol prohibiting unauthorized leave. One day in late August, the two men simply disappeared. Central Committee member Denise Oliver recalls that in the context of heightened repression and threats against the party, the situation sent many into a panic: "The organization was on red alert because there was a supposed mob contract out on Felipe. Security was heightened. Two members of the Central Committee went missing. And nobody knew where they were."[3] Approximately twenty-seven hours later, they reappeared with what some perceived as an elaborate excuse.

The men suggested that they had been lured into a trap, likely set by government agents. According to Guzmán, two white women approached them with a fund-raising proposal—a follow-up to a Randall's Island concert where the Young Lords had raised significant funds.[4] They all ended up at an Upper West Side apartment where, according to Luciano, one of the women offered him a joint that made him "hallucinogenic, sick, and suicidal." When he asked her to close the window because he wanted to jump out of it, "she opened it wider." Guzmán came to his aid and twice suggested that they leave: "I said no. Whatever took hold of me was so powerful that all I could do was stay in one spot for about twelve hours. I sat erect on a chair, my feet firmly planted on the floor, my fist balled up, and I told her, 'You brought me up here, you better take me down.' When I threw up, the strangest things happened. I felt totally infinite . . . and I made love to the same woman who tried to kill me."[5] The incident raised more questions than it answered. The chairman lamented, "Should I have known? Yes. In the back of my mind was I thinking that maybe we could get over? Yes. But we had no idea of the vulnerability of our position."[6] Whether this was a government disruption, bad story, or bad trip didn't seem to matter. These details surfaced amid distrust produced by the storm of internal dissent led by the women of the organization. That storm raged against sexism, philandering on the part of male members, and inequality between the sexes.

In concert with leading cadre, Oliver proposed that Luciano and Guzmán account for their breach of party discipline at a closed disciplinary hearing of the Central Committee and deputy ministers that included some of the organization's most vocal women. The women, unwilling to tolerate a disciplinary double standard fueled by sexism, questioned the men. In the past, the Central Committee had summarily terminated members who didn't report to assignments or violated party protocol.

Oliver recalls that the hearing revealed alarming details: "The other men on the Central Committee knew where Luciano and Guzmán were. So did their security detail."[7] Juan González asserts that he did not know their whereabouts. The hearing concluded with Felipe Luciano's demotion from chairman to cadre. Oliver remembers that the other men on the Central Committee would likewise be temporarily "suspended, charged, disciplined, and sent to study hall for two weeks." This left Oliver, the only woman on the Central Committee, to run the organization. The men do not remember having been demoted. Of the Central Committee members' response to their demotion, Oliver remembers, "Fi was a kid, you know. And Fi was, like, 'We fucked up.' And Pablo was, like, hanging his head in shame—remember, we were raised on criticism and self-criticism. You were given criticism and you had to stand up there and criticize yourself. We were very Maoist in that way."[8] The ritual of moralistic self-flagellation was a growing feature of life. Central Committee member Juan González was familiar with the practice. Months earlier, he had entered into an intimate relationship with a woman different from his known partner. González remembers, "When the women's caucus discovered that I was seeing someone else, I was brought up on charges and suspended from Central Committee for six weeks."[9] As we will see, the painful mingling of love and politics influenced the culture of the organization, added to the emotional intensity of movement life, had the potential to blur political decision-making, and was likely manipulated by COINTELPRO.[10] For Luciano, who was married to Iris Morales, a leading member of the women's caucus, the violation came at great cost, both personally and politically.

Luciano had failed the test of discipline and personal transformation to which he subjected others, and because he had become the face of the organization, the demotion would soon become public. The *New York Times* carried the story almost immediately, quoting Young Lord Carlos Aponte on reasons for the demotion: "male chauvinism, unclear politics, political individualism, and lack of development." It seemed that Aponte was speaking as an individual, not as official Young Lords spokesperson, a violation of the organization's Rules of Discipline: "No member may speak in public unless authorized by the Central Committee of Central Staff." Aponte was a veteran and experienced organizer previously active with California's left-wing Peace and Freedom Party, which ran radical candidates, including Panther leader Eldridge Cleaver, for president. As part of the secondary leadership of the YLP, he was a critical founding member of the Bronx branch. The development raised questions about him within the Central Committee that would not be addressed until later. Aponte asserts that he did not speak to the press.[11] A COINTELPRO agent likely did. The article also cited a supposed Young Lord statement on how informants might interpret the demotion. A few days later, the group corrected the record with a press conference of their own, in which Luciano stated that the demotion happened "in an atmosphere of love and education."[12]

The turn of events elicited different internal responses. Mickey Melendez accepted it as "a good soldier." He explains: "the women's question had just emerged. The men were still trying to figure out what that meant. But there was a sense that we had to set an example at the top."[13] There were some, like Young Lord leader Aida Cuascut, who opposed the public character that the demotion took on for the shame it generated for Luciano. The *New York Times* coverage must have felt permanent to him, even though many assumed it to be temporary.[14] The struggle's public dimension must have inadvertently silenced internal criticism by members of the organization because it signaled that stepping out of line carried a high cost. This moment of leadership transition was also open for COINTELPRO to exploit. But the decision had been made, and key members, including Gloria Fontanez, were vocal supporters of the demotion.

Luciano's recollections, years later, offer perspective on the emotional state he was in. "For about two to three days, I was under scrutiny.... After the criticism, self-criticism sessions, I was a nervous wreck. I ended up going to Soho." Influenced by the politics of black nationalism, which downplayed gender inequality, Luciano tended to see the issues raised by the women's caucus as a personal rather than political matter. In Luciano's words, "I felt that [the conflict] ... was a personal affair between me and Iris and that it should be dealt with in that manner, and they felt that this was a party issue and that my behavior indicated what was indicative of the sort of male chauvinism that existed in the party." Luciano acknowledged a problem of sexism in the organization: "Yes, the women were coming up with very legitimate issues . . . and [these] strong warriors were aided by the fact that . . . we were basically a male-oriented organization. We had to change." Both women and men in the organization believed that Luciano was undermining the political shift toward political equality among men and women. However, Luciano took the position—articulated most adamantly by cultural black nationalists—that the standing of men of color, whose manhood had been trampled by racial oppression, had to be elevated and prioritized in the struggle for liberation. He continues: "The change, I felt, had to come organically. It should not come abruptly. . . . That's why in our Thirteen-Point Program we had something about machismo, positive machismo. I came from the perspective that there was nothing wrong with machismo. Now, when I say 'machismo' I'm not talking about the . . . brutalization of women. I'm talking about the ability to stand as a man in your space and say, 'This institution, this community, is mine, it's part of my matrix, and I will not allow anyone to violate the sanctity of my home and family,' and so the way we organized a lot of Puerto Rican men in our communities was by telling them that your beating up your woman is not being a macho."[15]

However, even in retrospect, Luciano failed to grasp that his demotion happened a few months after the Young Lords women had led a successful internal struggle that altogether rejected machismo as a backward contradiction and had revised the notion of "revolutionary machismo" in the group's original Thirteen-Point Program and Platform.

A month later, Luciano was still unable to accept his demotion. After his public shaming, the charismatic leader had difficulty assuming the role of cadre. That role included selling newspapers, distributing flyers, carrying out assignments given by the officer of the day, and performing other quiet duties like waking early to cook for the children's breakfast program. His personal struggles with ego and humility factored into this. Making matters more difficult was the fact that, without a clear definition of his new role, others with long-brewing resentments and hostilities against him ran unchecked. The alienated chairman had to navigate these waters alone. In failing to give Luciano a new assignment, the Central Committee abdicated its role. The failure also undermined the organization's self-proclaimed commitment to love and compassion. It contributed to Luciano's withdrawal from party life.

The former chairman soon stopped showing up at the office and to meetings and demonstrations. A month later, he left the organization and Gloria Fontanez replaced him in the Central Committee.

Luciano had his shortcomings. This was not the first time he disappeared without notice. Yet, in spite of his individualistic streak, "he was forward thinking, clear on what the organization needed to do, and people in the street simply liked him."[16] Because he was revered and respected his departure was demoralizing to many in the group's rank and file and the community. With Luciano gone, the Young Lords lost a brave fighter and inspirational leader. Among his other virtues, he grasped the political value of solidarity between Puerto Ricans and black Americans. The organization didn't realize it at the time, but in losing Luciano it also lost the person best positioned to challenge the narrow notion of Puerto Rican nationalism that was under way in the organization, promoted as it was by an increasingly influential, and particularly authoritarian, emerging cadre.

Puerto Rican Student Conference at Columbia

Not long before Luciano's demotion in early September, two members of the Central Committee, Juan González and Juan "Fi" Ortiz, traveled to Puerto Rico. The reasons were manifold. They intended to learn about the different political formations on the island and to plant the seeds for a collaborative relationship between the YLP and the island's left-leaning, pro-independence parties. Influenced by his new wife and fellow comrade in the organization, Gloria Fontanez, González explored the terrain for branch building in Puerto Rico, an idea that was supported by one or two members of the Central Committee but would not be revealed to the party cadre until much later.[17] The more immediate task before González and Ortiz was to meet with island students who were leading mass antiwar protests against the Reserve Officer Training Corps (ROTC) at the University of Puerto Rico. González and Ortiz wanted to invite leaders of the pro-independence student group, Frente Universitario Pro-Independecia, to join them at the Puerto Rican Student Conference in New York, scheduled for a month later at Columbia University, on September 22 and 23.

Back on the mainland, the YLP was turning its attention not to another dramatic takeover but to a far less flashy goal: student organizing. In August, just before the start of the school year, the Lords had partnered with the Puerto Rican Student Union (PRSU) to begin a series of student initiatives at local high schools and colleges.[18] The PRSU emerged a year earlier in September 1969 to bring together Puerto Rican students who had been involved, over the past two years, in various protests across New York City: in the effort to ban the ROTC from recruiting on City University of New York (CUNY) campuses; to establish a Department of Black and Puerto Rican Studies at Hunter, Lehman, and Brooklyn Colleges; and to create an open admissions standard throughout the city's public colleges.[19] The Young Lords and the PRSU consolidated their relationship at the Puerto Rican Student Conference at Columbia University. The approximately 800 students in attendance heard speeches by members of the PRSU, the YLP, and Frente Universitario Pro-Independecia. The titles of the weekend's workshops typified both the big-picture thinking of student organizing in the 1960s and the broad variety of topics that the Young Lords deemed essential for radical social change: "Third World Unity," "The Draft and the Military," "The Role of Women in Revolutionary Struggle," "Political Prisoners," "Socialism," and "Media & Education."[20] Another workshop, "Latin American and Latin Unity," suggests that the Young Lords were forging a new identity based on common experiences of people migrating to cities such as New York from Latin America after having been displaced by Cold War–era, U.S. military and economic interventions in places such as Guatemala in 1954 and the Dominican Republic in 1965, among others.[21] In fact, through regular use of the term "Latin," the Young Lords were among the first to conceptualize the term "Latino/a." Their rendition of the term, however, underscored a shared political experience of regional underdevelopment produced by U.S. political and economic domination rather than contemporary appeals to *latinidad* on the basis of language and culture alone. The conference's closing remarks included speeches by radicals of Chicano, Cuban, and Dominican descent. A summary of the last panel observed that the Dominican presenter "eloquently linked the struggles for unity and freedom of the Dominican Republic, Cuba, and Puerto Rico, [which] can only be accomplished, said he, through militant opposition to outside oppression and eventual socialism (in the DR and PR)."[22]

The group embraced a pan-Latinx orientation despite the hard nationalist turn it was about to take. The conference took place on the 102nd anniversary of El Grito de Lares, the first recorded rebellion against foreign rule in Puerto Rico, and a number of conference sessions focused on the history of Puerto Rico's independence movement and the island's contemporary politics. At its closing session, Young Lord conveners encouraged participants to sign a pledge saying that they would organize Liberate Puerto Rico Now committees in high schools and on college campuses. This marked the first tangible initiative to make Puerto Rican independence an organizational focus and priority of the party. The myriad campus activities that followed took on an organizational life of their own, but the PRSU was influenced by the Young Lords' politics. Although the PRSU remained independent from the Young Lords, its members began to wear red berets. Over the next year, the Liberate Puerto Rico Now committees became the basis upon which the PRSU and Young Lords developed Marxist-Leninist chapters in New York's universities. These linked Puerto Rican independence to antiwar protests and the struggle of the Vietnamese and challenged the emerging political backlash: the surge in school regulations and the suppression of free speech and political association in high schools.[23] The chapters also supported the overhaul of Eurocentric academic curricula and the introduction of ethnic studies. The Columbia conference and the activities initiated in its immediate aftermath laid the groundwork for an impressive turnout at the Young Lords' Free Puerto Rico Now march to the United Nations on October 30, 1970. That march began a gradual shift in the Young Lords' political perspective.

Heightened Repression

Since their formation in the summer of 1969, the Young Lords had been the object of police surveillance, harassment, and arrest. Justifications for their surveillance came from New York City Council president Sanford D. Garelik. A highly visible politician, he attributed criminal and violent intent to the Young Lords' politics and militancy. Motivated by a regressive agenda, Garelik lumped the Black Panthers and the Young Lords together with the Weather Underground, a white splinter group of Students for a Democratic Society. He denounced them as "armed terrorist group[s]" and accused each of terrorism.[24]

Historically, authorities have invoked the term "terrorist" to criminalize organizers and dissidents.[25] By the classic, nineteenth-century definition, however, most U.S. radicals of the 1960s were not terrorists; they were not individual actors using violence to intimidate or instill fear among civilians as a strategy for advancing their cause.[26] Nevertheless, in the late 1960s, politicians began to use the term against radicals of all stripes, including the small sector of radicals who employed violence as a political strategy but who weren't terrorists either. Epitomized by the Weather Underground, these actors turned to armed propaganda against property and the symbols of government power. National independence movements deployed similar strategies against sites of colonial military and political power in places like Palestine, Algeria, and South Africa.[27] The term "guerrillas" more accurately describes these international actors.[28]

Garelik was building upon an existing blueprint. A decade earlier, conservatives across the country began to link civil rights demands to the communist boogeyman. But with the political ascendancy of Third World guerrilla communists in places like Vietnam and Cuba, terrorism came to replace communism as "the growing peril." Garelik also deployed the term "guerilla" against them. He told the *New York Times*, "These are urban guerrillas, the outgrowth of an era of disrespect for law and acceptance of Maoist Philosophy of guerrilla warfare." Again, given the growing legitimacy of decolonization movements, Garelik employed the language of race ideology—disrespect of law—to suppress and stigmatize activists of color. In addition to criminalizing radicals of color, the logic mandated respect for authority as precondition to claims on the right of redress. These regressive narratives did not emerge by happenstance. As we have seen, their logic was crafted earlier in the decade by a Madison Avenue public relations firm hired by the city's powerful police union to defeat the civilian complaint review board at the polls in 1966.

Though the Young Lords had not employed weapons during their campaigns, the organization's political platform supported "armed struggle." In an earlier conversation with the *New York Times* in March 1970, Pablo Guzmán said that "the only way to achieve liberation is by picking up guns—and we're moving our people in that direction." The statement spoke of events to come.[29] At around the same time, the Weather Underground began its underground bombing campaigns of state buildings and university sites where faculty were contributing research and technology to the military-industrial complex. Believing, like many others, that a world revolutionary crisis was on the horizon, Weathermen activities were launched in solidarity with Third World anti-imperialist revolutions abroad. At home, they were galvanized by the black power movement and welcomed the idea that their violent propaganda would redirect state repression away from the Black Panther Party (BPP).[30]

Historically, those committed to revolution have accepted what they perceive as inevitable in a revolutionary situation: that armed struggle is a necessity in the process of wresting power from the armed opposition forces of the state. For these actors, the use of violence and armed force is not the main issue of concern. More important is the question of timing. And even more central in debates within the revolutionary Left is the relationship between those "picking up the gun" and the mass mobilization of people at the bottom of society.[31] In this instance, the Young Lords, like others in the New Left, were either engaging in or considering the use of violence for several reasons. Some believed widespread rebellion was on the horizon. In reality, the movements were on the path of decline. Others saw mounting state repression as a reason to embrace the right to self-defense within their relatively small groups, which they confused with a defense of the masses in their communities. Amid the disorientation and siege mentality produced by state repression radicals became somewhat isolated from their communities. They began to see themselves increasingly as enlightened actors. Before long they began to substitute the painstaking task of grassroots mobilization with heroic acts of sacrifice taken on behalf of "the people."

Although the Young Lords did not experience the same homicidal state repression that befell the Black Panthers, the NYPD increased its repression and arrest of their members after the December 1969 occupation of the FSUMC in East Harlem. Six months later in June 1970, when the Young Lords led a spontaneous march in East Harlem protesting the beating by police of a teenager, riot-gear-clad police descended on their office. According to the Young Lords, when a bottle hit one of the police vans—likely hurled by the combative crowd of community residents gathered outside—the police "jumped out of their trucks like John Wayne on the range and went crazy, beating on every Puerto Rican they could catch, old and young alike." By the end of the clash, one Young Lord was unconscious on the pavement, and two others, David "Pelu" Jacobs and

Benjamin Cruz, were arrested and beaten in the police van and at the precinct, suffering serious head injuries and fractures.[32]

That same month, the group's youngest Central Committee member, sixteen-year-old Juan "Fi" Ortiz, was arrested and charged with the kidnapping, robbery, and assault of Jack McCall, who (according to the Lords and neighborhood reports compiled by the mayor's Urban Action Task Force) had taken to soliciting monetary contributions on behalf of the YLP without the group's authorization.[33] When police arrested Ortiz based on McCall's testimony, the Young Lords called a rally in East Harlem to protest what they believed to be a police setup. Ortiz was released soon after, but the demonstration against his arrest the next day attracted hundreds of black and Puerto Rican youth. At the start of the rally, David Perez, another member of the group's Central Committee, was arrested—plucked "out of a crowd of hundreds by plain clothes pigs," suggestive of a premeditated campaign by the police to arrest or frame the formal leaders of the group.[34]

Later that night after the demonstration wound down, throngs of teenagers—many of whom had likely joined the Young Lords' protest—began to riot. A dozen firemen and seven policemen were injured when called to the scene.[35] In the aftermath, the police made public statements linking the Young Lords with the disturbances. The group's public reputation was cleared when the *New York Times* and other media sources published testimonies of shopkeepers and eyewitnesses who maintained that the group was absent when the rioting began.[36] On several separate occasions, members were taken into custody for offenses so petty that they were dismissed immediately by judges who found the arrests ungrounded or the charges excessive.[37]

The Young Lords' public pronouncements about the right of people of color to armed self-defense increased in relation to the growing number of targeted campaigns of state violence and political disruption against them and other movement persons. Just a month before the police beat and arrested the Young Lords in front of their office, the country witnessed the tragedy at Kent State University. On May 4, the Ohio National Guard opened fire on unarmed students protesting the U.S. invasion of Cambodia, killing four protesters and wounding nine others. The Young Lords' perspective developed in the context of the highly publicized framing, a year earlier in April 1969, by NYPD and COINTELPRO of twenty-one BPP members. The Panther 21 were falsely accused, tried, and eventually acquitted of planning coordinated bombings and armed attacks on the Board of Education office in Queens and two police precincts—the Forty-Fourth and Twenty-Fourth in the Bronx and Manhattan, respectively.[38] The psychological impact on radicals of mounting arrests, beatings, and surveillance was profound. It distorted their sense of reality and ability to properly assess the political character of the period. Like others during the period, the YLP inaccurately assessed the moment. They interpreted mounting state repression as a sign that the United States was galloping into fascism. Significantly, they believed a revolutionary situation was under way among a broad sector of the population, which legitimized the party's call to "pick up the gun."

A Devastating Inquiry

On the evening of October 13, 1970, undercover narcotics police arrested two Young Lords, Julio Roldán and Robert "Bobby" Lemus, charging them with attempted arson. The circumstances appeared to fit the pattern of unsubstantiated charges against organization members. These arrests would galvanize New York activists, and in particular the people of East Harlem and the Bronx, in support of the Young Lords. They would also position the group toward another confrontation with the FSUMC and Mayor Lindsay's administration.

According to a major municipal investigation of the arrests, the two activists were apprehended for allegedly attempting to set fire to the vestibule of an East Harlem building in the aftermath of a garbage demonstration that, although initiated by the Young Lords, had taken on a life of its own.[39] Roldán and Lemus decried the charges as absurd because they and other members of the organization were building tenants. The men maintained that amid the protests, they entered the building to put out burning debris that had been swept into the vestibule. A few minutes later, three undercover narcotics officers jumped out of their vehicles, guns drawn, and apprehended them.[40] According to Lemus, the men were "insulted and picked on" during the car ride to the Twenty-Third Precinct and again during their 1:00 A.M. transfer to the Twenty-Fifth Precinct, the proper jurisdiction for the address of their arrest. Police zeroed in on Roldán's mild manner, hurled epithets at him, and mockingly called him "cookie" because he was the chief cook and organizer of the Young Lords' "mess hall," a sign that the NYPD kept close watch on the group's membership and its activities.[41]

Back at the precinct, police informed Roldán and Lemus that they could make a personal call through the arresting officer, Hubert Erwin, who dialed the office of the Young Lords. Two hours later, the Young Lords sent attorney Barbara Handschu and law clerk Carol Goodman to the precinct. Both were denied a private conversation with their clients.[42]

Because the Twenty-Fifth Precinct did not have a holding pen, the detainees were eventually returned at 4:30 A.M. to the Twenty-Third Precinct, where they spent the rest of the night in a cold, empty cell with no benches. Their requests to police to close the cell window fell on deaf ears. A few hours later they were transferred once again, this time to 100 Centre Street, for arraignment. On the ride, officers Erwin and James Murphy levied a barrage of questions and insults at Roldán. In the courtroom, two attorneys were trying to meet them before the proceedings began: Lemus was represented by Handschu, and Roldán by attorney Dan Pochoda, both National Lawyers Guild members. Neither lawyer was allowed access to their client. When Roldán's case was called in the afternoon, Pochoda asked Judge Hyman Solniker if he could speak to his client; the judge snapped back "I can't create the Utopia here" and denied the request because of the backlog. On that day, Judge Solniker had to hear 283 arraignments over the course of eight hours, with little time for lunch, which afforded only 1.7 minutes, or 102 seconds, for each case.[43] This exponential rise in arrests and the backlog created in arraignment proceedings in urban counties was unprecedented. It was one of the many consequences of the country's "law and order" campaigns, which manipulated crime statistics, identified drug use and trafficking a major crime, increased the number of police officers in urban centers, and criminalized residents involved in urban rebellions and organizers alike. Roldán interrupted the proceeding and yelled: "There is no justice in this court. There is no one here to represent us. Our lawyers have not had a chance to speak with us. This is only happening because I'm Puerto Rican."[44] Irritated and with no time to spare, Judge Solniker postponed the hearing until the end of the day.

While the detainees were being transferred to another section of the courtroom, the lawyers were finally able to talk to them. When they were recalled, Roldán's counsel tried to explain that the charges against the defendants were excessive because they were civic-minded members of their community whose friends and relatives lived in that building. Because Roldán had no prior record, Pochoda could have convincingly argued that his client be released on his own recognizance, pending trial; but no such argument was made because Pochoda intended to present this as follow-up argument, which the judge did not allow.[45] When Roldán again interrupted, saying that "he had set no fire," Judge Solniker asked that the prisoners be removed from the court. According to Lemus, Officer Erwin proceeded to bend Roldán's arm behind his back and "push and shove and knee him out of the courtroom." When someone in the courtroom yelled, "They're beating him," the judge demanded that the person making the complaint be taken out too. Officer Erwin later admitted to putting Roldán in a "hammerlock with one arm behind his back and put his [Erwin's] other arm on his collar, thereby forcing his head down . . . to move Roldán out of the courtroom."[46]

By his own admission, the district attorney requested a high bail of $2,500 because the deposition of the police officers suggested that this was "a heavy case" involving the Young Lords as defendants. This was a clear indication that the men's political associations were prejudicing the proceedings, in keeping with the trend of local police departments collaborating with the FBI to neutralize 1960s radicals. Ordered by FBI director J. Edgar Hoover, who identified the BPP as the nation's major "internal security threat," these directives sought to counteract militant domestic organizing, which in the context of the U.S. military crisis in Vietnam, threatened to further erode the nation's power and political legitimacy around the world.[47] Back in the courtroom, the prosecutor proposed a high bail because Roldán and Lemus allegedly gave "false" addresses, even though the defendants had given the address of the Young Lords' headquarters, well known to police. In the context of his arduous arraignment schedule, the judge was predisposed to side with prosecutors and police, with whom he worked closely day after day. In the end he set bail at $1,500, the standard for a serious felony case not likely to end in a lesser charge of misdemeanor.[48]

Julio Roldán's arrest and arraignment offers a window into the botched legal process that, beginning in the late 1960s and early 1970s, exponentially increased the arrest and jailing of people of color living in urban centers. This trend imposed on defendants disproportionately severe charges for victimless crimes and minor felonies, a new development in U.S. history.[49] In an attempt to convey the consequences of decisions made at arraignment hearings, a later investigation into the arrest and imprisonment of Julio Roldán ordered by New York's mayor, John V. Lindsay, recommended that "every judge assigned to arraigning prisoners who may be confined in the Tombs be invited to spend a 12 hour period in the MHD [Manhattan House of Detention for Men] before beginning his assignment."[50]

On their way to an upper-level holding pen in the court later that day, Roldán and Lemus were subjected to more rough treatment, then separated. Early in the evening of October 14, Roldán and twelve other men were finally transferred to the Manhattan House of Detention for Men next to the courthouse for prisoners awaiting trial. Known as the Tombs it was named for the resemblance of its original 1838 structure to an Egyptian tomb.[51] Described as a "melancholy picture of a fortress in bedlam" by the federal judge who ruled in favor of closing the detention center in 1974, the Tombs was an oppressive edifice of steel and concrete, "built like a series of safety deposit boxes."[52] As detainees were escorted to their cells they passed at least eight guarded steel doors. In the words of a Corrections Department spokesperson, "The Tombs was built in the Ma Parks, Bonnie and Clyde, Dillinger, and Al Capone era and its [architectural style] reflected America's attitude at the time that every criminal was a 'mad dog,' the feeling was lock them up and forget about them."[53] Those who wrote the Roldán report prefaced their remarks by saying, "If we kept our animals in the Central Park Zoo in the way we cage fellow human being in the Tombs, a Citizens Committee would be organized, and prominent community leaders would be protesting the inhumanity of our society."[54]

Upon arrival, Roldán underwent the routine admission procedure: he surrendered his wallet and personal belongings and was stripped and searched. Following the regulatory shower, the prisoners were allowed to wear their own clothes and proceeded to a meeting with the medical examiner to briefly document their medical history. Roldán registered athlete's foot as a problem and was given an ointment. The prisoners were transferred to the eighth floor, and Roldán was assigned a cell on the floor's lower level, Lower E-4, where he joined another prisoner who had been there since July.

The detention of Roldán and Lemus came just two months after a rebellion at the Tombs, during which prisoners held thirty corrections officers hostage in protest of deplorable conditions. At the time of the Young Lords' imprisonment, the Tombs was observing twenty-four-hour lockdowns, with no yard time, exercise, or "eating period outside of the cell."[55] This routine rendered detention an insufferable purgatory. Inmates spent most of their time in squalid cells the size of small walk-in closets, "enclosed in solid steel on three sides with bar gates forming the fourth side."[56] Although the cells were designed for one prisoner, they often housed two or even three men, one of whom often slept on the bare floor for lack of mattresses. A count done a few months before the rebellion revealed that the 932-inmate facility was housing close to 3,000 prisoners.[57] In addition to being overpopulated, these holding pens were infested with rats, roaches, and vermin. Perhaps the greatest crime of the Tombs was in how it was used: as a maximum-security prison that primarily held persons accused of minor felonies and misdemeanors who could not immediately post bail. This reality led prisoners to charge that "poverty and race are the crimes that are really being punished."[58]

From the time of arrest until release or transfer, Tombs detention was an assault on the senses. The jail had no access to fresh air or daylight. Sunlight rarely filtered through the facility's small frosted-glass windows; inmates often experienced disorientation since they couldn't determine whether it was morning or night. The noise level alone was enough to disturb the mental balance of a sane person. According to one account, "At 5:50 A.M., service crews drag metal garbage cans along concrete floors. Noise at the Tombs builds up as the day progresses: a blend of piped music, the high-pitched clicking of metal trays being stacked, the guards shouting, 'Stand by your cells,' for the morning count, and the clanging of steel doors against concrete, the blare of the television set and the inmates' voices reverberating off tile walls." This cacophony rose to a level of eighty decibels, a level comparable to that produced in the New York subways during rush hour.[59] These conditions regularly led to the psychological breakdown of detainees and the use of brutal corporal punishment by guards to restrain them. Detention at the Tombs was more trying than actual imprisonment.

On the day of his transfer to the Tombs, Roldán had been enraged by the trampling of his rights in the courtroom. By the time he was shuttled through the noisy, labyrinthine corridors and catwalks of the prison en route to his cell, the Young Lord had fallen silent. His cellmate later reported that when Roldán arrived he was upset and "alternatively frustrated, angry, crying, [and] laughing" and that periodically Roldán would give his cellmate "hostile looks." Other prisoners and cellmates also reported that Roldán began to rage, in Spanish and English, about "the oppression of minority groups, starving babies, killing of blacks, revolution, the establishment trying to kill minority groups and him, corruption and poison in the air." Later in the evening, he began to jump off his top bunk. He would land on the concrete floor, scramble back up the makeshift ladder, and jump off the bed again, over and over again.[60]

The next morning, on October 15, a prisoner sweeping the floors tried to speak to Roldán, who responded with gestures as if he were a mute. Later Roldán began asking the prisoner "stupid" questions including where he could get gas to make a bomb. The prisoner alerted the guards that Roldán should be transferred to the observation section of the prison. Later Roldán told his cellmate, "I will prove to you that I'm a man," and punched him. Nearby prisoners alerted guards from their cells and again suggested that Roldán be transferred to the observation block; instead, the guards transferred Roldán's cellmate to a separate cell.[61] Broken down both by the maddening noise at the Tombs and by the unnerving uncertainty of imprisonment, Roldán was experiencing the frustration, sense of impotence, and delirium that often led to violent explosions there.

Civilian access to the facility was severely limited. Detainees were often unable to communicate with their court-appointed lawyers or loved ones and didn't learn of the date and time of their trial until the day they were scheduled to appear in court. The Young Lords would not have been allowed a visit, but they sent a telegram to Roldán and Lemus, which the men had not yet received. That same evening, Roldán asked the sweeper-prisoner how he could get out of the jail. The prisoner responded that someone would have to post bail. Prisoners reported that Roldán "talked at length about revolution, the poor, the Young Lords. . . . One inmate described Roldán's behavior as that of one who had 'realized the truth about his people.' And his 'list of grievances' were received affirmatively by prisoners who yelled 'right on.'"[62]

The next morning, Friday, October 16, at 6:50 A.M., Roldán's name was called two or three times over the loudspeaker on the sixth floor of the prison. The Young Lords telegram had finally been processed; it read, "Sit tight, we are trying to get bail money." Although the guard noticed a discrepancy, he read the message over the sixth-floor loudspeaker, per standard operating procedure with telegrams. Roldán was on the *eighth* floor.

At 8:30 A.M., the guard conducting the morning prisoner count found Julio Roldán hanging by a belt from the rear bars of his cell.

That guard went in search of two other guards, a requirement before opening any cell. Then he had to get two keys, neither of which guards carried, to access a panel box that opened and closed the areas' mechanical gates and the cell doors. As word spread, prisoners began to shout, "Cut him down!" All the

Tombs guards, according to the later report, carried penknives "at all times for the express purpose of cutting down inmates who are attempting suicide."[63] One officer held Roldán's waist and the other cut the belt and lay him face-up on the lower bunk, at which point "two Captains arrived with resuscitators, one tried to find a pulse, while the other looked for a heartbeat and administered a cardiac massage." A doctor arrived shortly thereafter, performed a series of tests, and determined that Roldán's body "was beyond assistance." The doctor speculated that he could have been dead for at least one hour from the time he arrived at the scene.[64] Prisoners who were interviewed said that they had contact with him at approximately 7:00 A.M. when Roldán, who was in the E-4 cell, replied, "Yeah, brother," when he was asked to help pass pipe tobacco or a rolled cigarette between the E-5 cell and the E-3 cell. And at about 7:50 A.M., a prisoner-worker remembered greeting the Young Lord with "Hi, brother," as he served him breakfast and Roldán took the tray to the table. It is likely that Roldán died between 7:50 and 8:30 A.M.

A preliminary prison assessment conducted by the Tombs' house captain, who interviewed the prisoners of the Lower E block, determined that Roldán committed suicide. The assistant deputy warden then "made calls to official agencies." According to *El Diario La Prensa*, at least five police precincts (the Twenty-Third, Twenty-Fifth, and Ninth in Harlem and East Harlem and the Forty-First and Forty-Second in the Bronx) and two divisions of the NYPD were immediately placed on emergency alert, with the expectation that the news would lead to violent protests.[65] By midmorning, the Catholic chaplain was allowed into Roldán's cell to administer last rites, before a police sergeant, two police officers, the medical examiner, and an ambulance technician conducted another series of tests and then arranged to transport Roldán's body to the City of New York's office of the chief examiner. The prison captain reportedly called what he thought was the number of Roldán's nephew to deliver the news. According to the report, the person who answered the phone identified "the chapter or division title of the organization and his name followed by some phrase to the effect of 'officer of the day' . . . the same type of response he would expect when one calls a military institution of the MHD."[66] Roldán had given the number of the Young Lords' East Harlem office. Within hours, the Young Lords leadership sent out an emergency alert to its membership and supporters throughout the city.

At 4:00 P.M. a member of the chief coroner's office, Dr. John. F. Devlin, began to conduct an autopsy alongside the chief and deputy chief medical examiners, Dr. Milton Halpern and Dr. Michael Baden. The autopsy, completed shortly thereafter, was witnessed by two other doctors. They were Dr. David Spain of Brookdale Hospital in Brooklyn and Dr. Oliver Fein, a young progressive doctor who had recently begun to volunteer at the Tombs as an advocate for prisoners' medical rights and a member of Health Policy Advisory Center.[67] The Young Lords and Julio Roldán's family, respectively, requested the presence of these doctors. Neither of these doctors were pathologists, however. The chief medical examiner officially declared the death a suicide by hanging.

It was time for the Young Lords to tell the world.

A year after their emergence, the Young Lords had mastered the art of the press conference. Their eloquent, strategic, and smart communiqués injected an unlikely, young New Left perspective into New York's public discourse. On Saturday, October 17, 1970, the day after what appeared as Roldán's suspicious "hanging," Pablo Guzmán explained the Young Lords' version of the events at a press conference: "Yesterday we found out that our brother Julio Roldán ... was found murdered in his cell in the Tombs." Julio was thirty-three years old. News of the "murder" of yet another prisoner at the Tombs, this time of a Young Lord, spread like wildfire through East Harlem and through the larger movement.

Although Dr. Fein was present at the autopsy when the medical examiner declared the death a suicide, the Young Lords still doubted the process. They believed that Julio Roldán had been murdered by guards. Guzmán went on to discuss the "bogus" circumstances of Roldán's and Bobby Lemus's arrests and that the Young Lords had already heard from those inside the Tombs that "at 5:00 A.M. on the day the body was discovered inmates heard him screaming and there was a guard present." He added, "Now they're trying to say that he hung himself with his belt." According to Guzmán, because Roldán was taken to the eighth floor, the psychiatric section of the Tombs, prison officials should have automatically removed his laces and belt. But a later study reported that although prisoners at the Tombs had on two different occasions implored guards to transfer Roldán to the special observation section of the eighth floor, he never was. Roldán's murder, Guzmán suggested, was linked to that of Jose Perez, another prisoner who, on the same day, "was found dead of another supposed suicide." He continued, "Since 1967 or 1966 there have been countless stories of blacks and Puerto Ricans who were brought to their cells alive, and their families were then told that they had committed suicide. ... This has been happening to our people for so long. ... It's beginning to add up, and now it's got to be called genocide."[68]

In the wake of Roldán's death, two other prisoners unaffiliated with the YLP, Anibal Davila and Raymond Lavon, were also found hanging from the crossbars of their cells. By year's end, there would be eight reported suicides in the Tombs.[69] To a civilian population that was becoming more acquainted with the atrocities committed in the Tombs—especially after the prison riots that occurred only months earlier, in late August 1970—these cases seemed suspicious. In the case of Raymond Lavon, there was evidence that he had been violently subdued by prison guards in the days before his death, and the three-inch fracture in his skull revealed in his autopsy increased suspicions about the allegedly suicidal deaths at the Tombs.[70]

The Young Lords' tone at the press conference that day was as fiery as always, unafraid to indict vast swaths of society and adamant about making the connections between the lives of individuals and the circumstances of a people. But that press conference also presaged a permanent shift in the organization. Roldán's death emboldened the Young Lords with a darker spirit of rebellion. In a decade that witnessed numerous political murders—of civil rights leaders and organizers, of Black Panthers by the FBI, of Che Guevara at the hands of the CIA—Roldán's fate ushered in the ultimate repression to the organization's doorstep. The tragedy imbued members' preexisting political commitment with a sense of loyalty to the organization. And that loyalty, born of grief, grew more resolute.

Rebels with a Cause

The viewing of Roldán's body on Sunday morning October 18 at the González Funeral Home on 109th Street and Madison Avenue, a block away from the Young Lord' office, attracted throngs of people. They came from East Harlem and the Bronx. And the entire membership of the Young Lords, which now numbered approximately 1,000, came to pay their last respects. At about noon, when the flow of attendees was at its peak, the Young Lords closed the doors. They removed Roldán's casket from the González Funeral Home and led a stirring funeral march through the neighborhood, alongside members of Roldán's family, including his cousin Jesus Villanueva, also a Young Lord. Roldán's casket was carried by a roll call of members of New Left organizations of color: the Lords, the BPP, I Wor Kuen, Movimiento Pro Independencia, and Los Siete de la Raza. In keeping with the group's militaristic temperament, a larger group of Young Lords served as "revolutionary honor guards," the ceremonial guards that accompany funeral processions of fallen officers in the military. Solidarity with the Young Lords was palpable at the procession, which drew thousands of marchers, and thousands more witnessed it from their tenement windows.

Crowds of onlookers lined the sidewalks, picking up on and repeating the marchers' chants: "Julio Roldán, los Boricuas se vengarán" (Julio Roldán, Puerto Ricans will avenge your death), "Fuego, fuego, fuego, los yanquis quieren fuego" (Fire, fire, fire, the Yankees want some fire), and "Pick up the gun, go left, go right now, pick up the gun." Others hung out of their apartment windows, fists raised.

The Young Lords' final stop was the FSUMC. As its doors were forced open, hundreds poured inside the worship hall where the Young Lords intended to hold another viewing of the body, alongside a socially conscious ceremony.

Pallbearers carry Julio Roldán's coffin. (Photograph by David Fenton)

Once Roldán's casket was situated and opened on the altar, out came a small arsenal, including automatic weapons, carbines, and pistols, which had been tucked into the casket next to Roldán's body back at the funeral home before the procession. The next day, the *New York Times* captured photographs of two Young Lords flanking Roldán's casket and bearing arms. According to a report filed by an undercover agent on the day of the occupation, the Young Lords had in their possession "three carbines, five 12 gauge shotguns, two .30–30 rifles, one .22 caliber rifle, two .38 caliber pistols, one .22 caliber pistol and five or six alleged small home-made explosive devices. All are believed loaded and with a limited stock of additional ammunition. Attempts are being made to obtain more ammunition. A member of the American Service Union was heard to offer that he would get two M-16 rifles. His offer was accepted."[71]

Until now, the Young Lords had tactically avoided brandishing weapons publicly. They wanted to avoid unnecessary arrests and confrontations with police. But they also promoted the right to armed self-defense. If ever there was a moment for them to take up arms, this was it.

From Watts to East Harlem, urban rebellions had coursed through the country like a hurricane, drawing thousands of black Americans into pitched confrontations with law enforcement. Puerto Ricans and Mexican Americans took part in these uprisings as well. In 1968, the Vietnamese brought the war to the cities during Tet and led an armed occupation of the U.S. embassy in Saigon. That same year, a poll determined that 20 percent of the American student population supported the idea of a revolutionary party.[72] It had been approximately one hundred years since Europe colonized Africa and Asia, and so-called Third World people were taking up arms in the name of independence and self-determination—and most of the world rooted for them. And in the country's most regimented sector, the American armed forces, generals registered a significant increase in mutinous activity.

Taking up arms was a political statement rife with symbolism. It sent a message that the Young Lords were not going to accept the state's repressive violence, that they were not going to lay down to die, and that things had to change. The armed occupation of the People's Church was to the Young Lords what the armed march into California's state capitol in Sacramento was to the Black Panthers. It was the first and only time in modern American history that racially oppressed people in the United States asserted their right to bear arms in the public sphere. They deliberately adopted a tradition that has, for the most part, been understood to apply exclusively to Europeans and their U.S. descendants.

The act of displaying arms drew greater attention to the Young Lords within larger movement circles. It brought into their orbit hundreds more young people angry about police harassment, detention, arrests, and the conditions of poverty and discrimination in daily urban life. Some older East Harlem residents must have looked on these developments with mixed feelings of momentary pride and frightened disapproval. As exhilarating and cathartic as it was to prisoners and youth in New York, these armed occupations also horrified many in the Puerto Rican community.[73] A flyer that the Young Lords distributed at the church offered an explanation for their decision to bear arms: "We are armed because we must defend ourselves, and we advise all Puerto Ricans in New York to begin preparing for their defense. The U.S. government is killing us, and now we must defend ourselves or die as a nation."[74] Speaking at the church, Juan González asked rhetorically, "Why the arms? Why do we feel it necessary to come into this church with arms to make these demands to the city?" González then proceeded to review the history of the Young Lords' campaigns before the crowd of old and young seated in the church pews. The lesson learned, he explained, is that "every time we move to remedy the ills of our community, we are struck down." After he condemned the state for failing to meet human need, he went on to expose its repressive character: "Now they have killed one of our members and we've seen what's happened to our political parties in the past . . . to the Nationalist Party in Puerto Rico that was wiped out by the United States. We've seen what happened to the Black Panther Party. Year in and year out the police departments across this country have little by little killed them, such that there are now thirty Black Panthers left."[75]

The armed church occupation increased government surveillance. It also increased repression of the organization.

In describing the social crisis they saw around them, the Young Lords used language that foreshadowed the mass warehousing of poor, urban black American and Latinx communities in the 1980s and 1990s in U.S. prisons and the violent consequences of the militarization of police departments in urban communities across the nation. González ended his quietly rousing remarks with a defiant assertion: "Now is the time for us to say exactly how we're going to respond to the killing of our people. We are not going to sit by and allow more Julios and more Carmen Rodriguez abortion deaths. We have to stand up for the people, for the Puerto Rican people and say, 'That's enough!'" A few minutes later, the Young Lords informed those in attendance that they were taking possession of the church.

Taken two days after Roldán's death, the Young Lords' response was bolder and exponentially more spontaneous and therefore more dangerous than any of their previous actions. In this sense, bitterness more than strategy informed their declaration of war. The armed occupation could precipitate a violent confrontation with police, and the Young Lords were preparing for that scenario. David Perez was at the helm of defense. In the case of a siege, the Central Committee would evacuate the church, and Perez and his team of ten would remain behind to defend the Young Lords' position in an armed confrontation.[76] Because they were so ill prepared for the armed operation, the Young Lords' actions evinced political disorientation. It appeared that in avenging the tragedy of Roldán's death, the Young Lords were more committed to violence than they were to laying out a strategy for building a larger movement and winning a significant political victory.

The day before the occupation, a desperate and frightened David Perez went in search of Felipe Luciano to seek operational advice and assistance in acquiring more weapons through the former chairman's wide-ranging street connections. Luciano vehemently opposed an armed occupation of the church. He charged that the organization was headed toward a suicide mission that would risk the lives of its members, the majority of whom had absolutely no weapons training—including those on Perez's defense unit. He pleaded with Perez, pointing out that the Young Lords were barely adults and that some were still children. But the Central Committee had already made its decision, and so Luciano cooperated with apprehension and showed up at the church, but he chided Perez some more when he witnessed members of the security team stumble while handling and loading the guns.[77]

With members of the press in the audience, the group called on the Methodist Church to contribute a $150,000 grant to the Young Lords for a legal defense center, which the group planned to launch in the church basement. The mission of the center was to document abuses against prisoners by corrections officers and against civilians at the hands of the police. In addition, the center would provide psychological counseling to young men who had been drafted, one expression of the group's antiwar stance. The second demand called on the city to allow clergymen full visitation rights in prisons as well as the authority to investigate prison conditions, "especially the murders of Julio Roldán, Jose Perez, and three of the negotiators at the Queens House of Detention uprising on October 1."[78] The demand galvanized a group of clergymen from different denominations, who organized a meeting that week where they presented the proposal to the city commissioner of corrections, George McGrath. When the commissioner rejected the proposal, which the clerics perceived as just and reasonable, eighteen of them joined with the Young Lords in the church occupation.[79]

The Young Lords occupation took advantage of heightened public awareness concerning prison conditions following multiple rebellions by prisoners from August to October 1970 in the city's network of jails. For two days beginning on August 10, 1970, more than 800 prisoners took four floors of the Tombs, held eight guards hostage, and presented a list of ten grievances to the media and city officials. The ebb and flow of the uprising followed a familiar pattern. After hostages were taken and floors were secured, prisoners unleashed a torrent of anger against the jail that mainly targeted property; prisoner leaders, who restored calm and discipline, then became spokesmen and negotiators with city officials. The prisoners' grievances were known to the city. But Mayor Lindsay and Commissioner McGrath had failed to implement the recommendations made by two major reports released in 1969 and 1970 on overcrowding and poor, inhabitable conditions, respectively.[80] Chief among the prisoners' grievances was being held without having been convicted of any crime: half the prisoners in the city's jails were imprisoned for at least six months before trial, and many waited longer than a year. Other grievances included high bail set for defendants of color; inadequate legal aid services; overcrowding; inedible food; a wretched environment filled with rats, mice, lice, and roaches; poor medical care; guard brutality; and harassment and abuse of prisoners' visitors by guards. Prison officials regained control of the facility only when, after nine days of meetings with the prisoners, Mayor Lindsay, Commissioner McGrath, and others acknowledged that the prisoners' grievances accurately reflected claims of "cruel and unusual punishment."[81]

In the absence of meaningful change, another series of prison rebellions ensued less than two months later, on October 1, 1970, at the Queens House of Detention on Long Island, to which nine members of the Panther 21 had been transferred after the Tombs rebellion that summer. With the presence of Black Panthers and prisoners who had participated in the Tombs rebellion in August, the rebellion was better orchestrated and the demands more sophisticated. In exchange for the release of some hostages, the prisoners demanded and were granted the right to hold a press conference in the yard with TV, radio, and print media. They also asked for immediate bail review by a judge of forty-seven cases at the prison. At the press conference the prisoners outlined their grievances and presented a list of people they wished to serve as negotiators. The list included Mayor Lindsay, Georgia state senator and civil rights leader Julian Bond, attorney William Kunstler, Muhammad Ali, and others, but the final list included Representative Shirley Chisholm, Louis Farrakhan of the Nation of Islam, and former Bronx borough president Herman Badillo. The next day, the rebellion spread like wildfire to two other prisons: the Tombs and a new prison in Kew Gardens, Queens. And on October 3, 1,400 prisoners took three hostages at the Brooklyn House of Detention, while approximately 3,000 mostly Puerto Rican residents rallied outside the prison and threw bottles at police, who were called to back up the team of guards that was going to subdue the insurrection.[82]

To the surprise of government officials such as mayor's aide Barry Gottehrer—who was involved in all of the negotiations—unlike the prison guards, prisoners generally exercised restraint. At the Brooklyn House of Detention, where prison guards retook the prison, the guards seriously injured more than 200 prisoners and "ripped up their own building more vehemently than any gang of rampaging prisoners."[83] According to one of the hostages at the second uprising at the Tombs, Daniel Zemann, "You can't believe what it was like in there. There was complete bedlam—punching and screaming. It was a power struggle between Panthers and Muslims and the Young Lords and whatever else was in there." Many of the hostage corrections officers described the behavior of some who were deranged among the barricaded prisoners. Zemann recounts that when a prisoner attacked him with a pocketknife, another "inmate jumped in front and stopped him." Another hostage, Walter Starke, remembered that prisoners held three officers "with knives against their necks," and one threatened to "castrate . . . [a hostage] against the bars." But, amid the volatility, compassion and organization prevailed. Zemann told the New York Times that the prisoners "did for us better than we do for them. What they did, we should have done. They fed us first from what was available and let us call our wives. They set up a security system to protect us from the psychos." Later many of the hostages concluded that poor conditions and abuse led to the riots, and even the guards who had been held hostage lamented that although they were out of harm's way, nothing had been done for the prisoners.[84]

Prison conditions had been bad for quite some time. What was different was that the movements of the 1960s had, slowly, raised the expectations of a broad swath of U.S. society about how people should be treated, regardless of their social or economic status and regardless of their status as prisoners. The growing sense of entitlement to rights, what historians have called the "rights revolution," had penetrated even the prisons; and in New York the prisoners leading these rebellions self-identified as Black Panthers and Young Lords. This sense was articulated by Julio Senidez, a prisoner who was released shortly after the riots at the Queens House of Detention: "The other times I was in, prisoners were sort of conditioned to accept brutality. There was a feeling that if you said something or complained, you were a punk. It's different now, people are not giving in." According to the *New York Times* interview with Senidez, the shift in consciousness among the prisoners "came from an identification with the Black Panther Party and the Young Lords."[85] Some prisoners involved in the protests of the summer and fall of 1970 believed that they could only get justice if the United Nations intervened.[86]

The concerns of the rebelling prisoners assumed broader significance as they increasingly linked the roots of crime to social and economic inequality and emphasized the disproportionate imprisonment of people of color on account of racism in the courts. Radicals advanced these views as they carried on political work within the prisons. In some cases, imprisoned members of organizations such as the Young Lords and Black Panthers initiated organizing efforts; in other instances, unaffiliated groups of men were inspired by radical organizations to form their own chapters on the inside. As prisoners' rebellion opened the door to conversation about reform in the city's government, the Young Lords advanced a political program at the occupied church that called not just for improved conditions but also for prisoners' rights. The group's deliberate focus on prisoners' rights earned them respect and a "huge following in America's jails."[87] The Young Lords published several letters from circles of prisoners expressing solidarity with the organization and its political views and goals. In one instance a group signed their letter "Prisoner's Liberation Front a subsidiary of the Young Lords Party."[88] Prisoners identifying as members of the Young Lords, the Black Panthers, and the Black Muslims provided leadership during the uprisings, but there were contentious disagreements among these groups about how to move forward with negotiations.

At the Queens detention center, Victor Martinez, who identified with the Young Lords, played a crucial role in negotiations with prison authorities. He was one of six prisoners on the negotiation team, three of whom were subsequently murdered by guards. In early October, before the Roldán tragedy, the Young Lords responded to a letter Martinez had written them and paid for his bail. Upon his release, he became involved in an ongoing YLP project for prisoners' rights called the Inmates Liberation Front. He and Denise Oliver worked closely in the legal center at the church developing support services for those imprisoned and returning home. They also worked closely with lawyers from the Legal Aid Society, who argued before the Supreme Court that the Tombs was unfit for human habitation and should be shut down.[89] The YLP's Inmates Liberation Front devoted itself to the following five points:

1   To assure that no person be detained in jail because he or she is unable to make bail
2   To investigate and act on the brutal, unjust, and inhuman treatment being executed [sic] on the inmates
3   To assure that an inmates' committee be set up in the concentration camps, and that they be permitted to communicate with the outside world
4   To insure that inmates are given speedy trials, and have access to counsel of his or her choice, and that none of the people's constitutional rights and basic human rights be violated
5   To provide the inmates, upon release, with jobs, education, housing and readjustment to the community[90]

The lawyers preparing the case against the operation of the Tombs often met at the occupied FSUMC to gather depositions from former prisoners.[91]

The circumstances surrounding Roldán's death presaged how people of color would be treated by law enforcement and the penal system in the late twentieth-century epidemic of mass hyperincarceration. The new penal regime would be built through an exponential increase in policing and indiscriminate arrests in urban communities of color; intimate relationships among police, prosecutors, and judges at arraignment; overly punitive and fixed charges and sentencing, often with little correlation to the circumstances of arrest or crime; assembly-line adjudication in an overly burdened criminal justice system; high bail that targeted populations could not afford; warehousing arrestees pending trial under inhumane conditions; and the advent of desperate defendants coerced into signing their rights away in plea-bargain agreements.

The Young Lords' strategy of defying the law by seizing a symbolic institution added to the preexisting crisis of prisoners' rebellions, which the mayor and his aides identified as the most difficult and volatile crises of their tenure. In an attempt to restore a sense of authority in the city, the mayor belatedly denounced the armed occupation of the church by the Young Lords as "deplorable and a sacrilege" and rejected the Lords' demand for an independent inquiry into Roldán's death. He determined that an independent investigation was "unnecessary" because his office was in the middle of establishing a board of corrections (made up of civilians) to oversee grievances in the city's networks of prisons, and it would investigate Roldán's death "as its first order of business."[92] Though they had succeeded in forcing the mayor's hand, the radicals viewed the hasty activation of the board—which occurred on the same day the Young Lords took over the church—as a political maneuver to quell public sentiment rather than a genuine effort at an unbiased investigation. Moreover, they criticized the appointment of former Democratic gubernatorial candidate William J. vanden Heuvel as the chairman of the board on the basis that "a politician cannot be trusted to conduct an impartial inquiry."[93]

Above all, the Lindsay administration wanted to avoid clashes at the church that might spread to other prisons or that would reignite rebellions at the Tombs.[94] Despite their fierce rhetoric, the Young Lords did not want unnecessary violence either. Having made their point, the Puerto Rican radicals "entered into back-channel communications with the city."[95] They agreed to remove the guns. At around the same time that these negotiations were happening, the Young Lords' armed guards fought back police who sought to coax them into a confrontation by cocking their weapons as they attempted to push their way through the door. They finally removed the weapons with the support of elderly neighborhood women who managed to slip out of the church unsuspected with the disassembled parts of the weapons in their shopping bags.[96] The image in East Harlem was a microcosm and reverse example of the events leading up to the victory of the Vietnamese guerrillas against the French colonial army at Dien Bien Phu in 1954. There, a civilian network of a quarter of a million peasants carried artillery broken down into many pieces in their sacks along paths through the jungle, up the mountains, and through a complex system of tunnels, which they delivered to the Viet Minh up in the mountains.[97]

In another incident, Pablo Guzmán allowed police in the building but only after frisking them for unexposed weapons, which resulted in the next day's humiliating headline, "Police 'Frisked' by the Young Lords."[98] Eldridge Waithe, "the commanding officer of police in the north half of Manhattan," and his partner were not able to find any contraband inside the church, which would have been grounds for pressing formal charges against the group. Within a week of the occupation, the group had gotten rid of the guns. That seemed to be the Young Lords' nod to the mayor. As if on cue, the next day, on October 27, 1970, the mayor formalized his request to the board of corrections for an investigation into the death of Julio Roldán. The investigation was conducted by eleven attorneys who were voluntarily employed by the board to gather and analyze information from interviews with correction officers and prisoners.[99]

The Young Lords and their cleric supporters declined an offer to participate in the investigation. However, their attorney, Geraldo Rivera, participated in the inquiry, and the Lords' leadership remained in touch with him throughout. Attorney Oscar Garcia Rivera Jr., the son of the first elected Puerto Rican politician of the same name, also participated in the inquiry.[100] That rejection of a remarkable offer by the city was in line with the Young Lords' principle against collaboration with government institutions and its potential for co-optation. In refusing to participate, the Young Lords might have missed an opportunity to offer a powerful eyewitness account. Had the organization participated, it would have had entrée to the inner sanctum of an institution that operated outside civic society. The Tombs continued to dispense medieval punishment in the shadows precisely because residents and critics like the Young Lords had no access to its inner workings. This kind of on-the-ground reporting from behind the walls might have further broadened the Young Lords' political status in the city and offered an unprecedented platform for grassroots organizing on what had by the early 1970s become the new frontier in the fight against structural racism in the United States. While the Young Lords' left orientation and opposition to mainstream politicians influenced the party's decision against compromise, they were also likely influenced by the failure of long-standing petitions to the city for nothing less than an *independent* civilian complaint review board to monitor grievances against the police. The clergy's refusal to accept the city's deal also gives a sense of how discredited government institutions had become in the 1960s.

The inquiry yielded a gripping twenty-seven-page account on Roldán's life and his descent into insanity in a barbaric environment. The study, *A Report to the Mayor of New York on the Death of a Citizen, Julio Roldán*, was released three weeks later, on November 17, 1970. A sizable excerpt was printed in the *New York Times* the next day. The report concluded that Roldán "ended his life by his own hand and that no individual deliberately contributed to his death." Yet, while the report exonerated the officials who came in contact with the Young Lord during his court appearances and stay at the Tombs, it incriminated the institution of criminal justice for its degenerative effect on the individual. The report established that "the intricate system of criminal justice designed to protect the community and the individual succeeded only in deranging him and ultimately, instead of protecting him, it permitted his destruction."[101]

The organization had demanded an investigation into the detention center. But the Young lords were not interested in parsing out the fine details of Roldán's demise. They had articulated their position in countless statements. Released a month into the occupation, the report seemed to confirm their thinking. Gloria Fontanez articulated that position when, during their first press conference, she situated Roldán's fate in a larger context of systemic violence against poor people of color: "In the party, we make no distinction between the jails and our streets. Our people are killed in the streets all the time. A brother by the name of Johnny was killed in the Bronx by the police. A sister by the name of Carmen Rodriguez was killed in Lincoln Hospital by an abortion; we say that it's all the same thing, that it's genocide against Third World people, black and Puerto Rican people, and that's why we're charging the city with murder."[102]

The Young Lords were not alone in their insistence that Roldán was murdered. In summarizing lessons learned from the investigation, one mainstream editorial concluded that "suicide can be induced by a judicial and detention system of sufficient inhumanity, that such a suicide is very little different from murder, that justice is not so much blind any more as stoned out of her heard, and that we have in this country today immeasurable more order than law." [103]

The high-profile investigation of Roldán's death was a powerfully symbolic victory for New York City's organizers and for the prisoners' rights movement gathering steam across the country. The fate of Julio Roldán and protests that followed put pressure on the board of corrections and City Hall. It also led to the first official investigation of the death of a single prisoner, which corroborated the stories of horror that prisoners had recounted to journalists. Previous investigations focused on conditions but were imbued with the language of law and order. The board's investigation, however, humanized Roldán, and by extension all prisoners. It increased awareness among a broader segment of the population in New York City about basic rights violations and asserted the notion that prisoners have rights too. To the prisoners at the Attica Correctional Facility, in upstate New York, who would rebel a year later, the investigation must have offered some hope that their grievances would be heard and adjudicated by government officials.

The Young Lords' armed occupation was daring, frightening to its members, and risky. But the group also had a finger on the political pulse of the city, and its leaders likely knew, instinctively, how far they could go. The group's established record of grassroots muckraking also shielded them from the worst possible outcome. Loved by some and tolerated by others, the Young Lords were known to many Puerto Ricans and black Americans and to a cross-section of other New Yorkers from welfare rights activists, progressive doctors, and wider New Left circles to hospital administrators, citywide clergy, and the media corps—not to mention the Lindsay administration. This would be their last offensive. It lasted until early December 1970.

From the facility, they indicted the prison system at regularly held meetings and ecumenical services, developed a legal defense center, and ran their usual community service programs. Their advocacy continued to draw diverse supporters, including a radical Jesuit priest from Puerto Rico, Monseñor Antulio Parrilla, who led a series of services. Back in Puerto Rico, he reported having been "profoundly moved" by the work at the church. [104] The Young Lords continued their coalition work at Lincoln Hospital and found themselves involved in another major action. While some Young Lords were occupying the church, others occupied the sixth floor of the Lincoln nurses' residence in the first week of November.

■

The death of Julio Roldán, however tragic, presented the Young Lords with the opportunity to activate hundreds of Harlem residents who supported them through a broad campaign around an issue of growing concern. The moment also presented an opportunity to challenge the growing consolidation of an emergent racist ideology that criminalized, dehumanized, and scapegoated people of color as thousands of New Yorkers were questioning the war in Vietnam, the integrity of government officials, declining wages, and the economic and political structure of U.S. society. As discussed in chapter 2, in one of the most important political moves of the decade, New York mayor Robert Wagner recrafted for white northern audiences fearful of the riots the racially charged dictum of law and order, which southern segregationists used to suppress the civil rights movement. A year later in 1966, the NYPD ideologically defeated the civilian complaint review board referendum. The public relations firm it hired crafted a meme for white residents blending two historically powerful ideological strains in American history: fear of political dissent and the alleged criminal proclivities of people of color. But the fierce rebellions in New York's prisons had offered a counternarrative to the racist propaganda that New Yorkers had been fed. Among the groups of the New Left, the Young Lords had honed the most effective media presence in New York. They were positioned like no other group to launch what they might have termed a guerrilla offensive against law and order. It had the potential to push back the rebirth and consolidation of what has arguably been the most destructive and racially divisive ideology of the second half of twentieth-century U.S. history.

Yet, despite the organization's increased visibility and its growing ranks (approximately 1,000 members by the end of 1970), it was exhibiting signs of overstretch. The achievements at Lincoln and the continued growth in membership couldn't contain the gnawing sense among some members that things were changing. The death of Roldán, who was known in the YLP as a gentle and compassionate comrade, was demoralizing.

For the YLP, assertions by prison officials that Julio Roldán committed suicide were read as a government-inspired conspiracy intended to provoke fear among YLP members and break the political will of its membership. They understood that Roldán's murder was a manifestation of homicidal government repression. Since the mid-1960s, left activists had indeed been aware of how COINTELPRO worked to frustrate the movement's goals and to encourage internecine struggles within its organizations. Government infiltration of the BPP was the most visible example of this development. As repression intensified, radicals became increasingly pessimistic about their ability to effect change in the United States. Repression increased a sense of bitterness, cynicism, and disenchantment with the state of American democracy. Many turned their attention to the upheavals in the wider world, where revolutionary armed struggle had been in ascendance for decades.

For the Young Lords, what would come next was nearly as dramatic as the group's previous nine months of local actions: a shift from an ideology of community control to a nationalist battle against U.S. imperialism on the island of Puerto Rico.

CHAPTER ELEVEN

ORGANIZATIONAL DECLINE

From the moment of their emergence in New York, the Young Lords articulated a radical critique of U.S. imperial power in Puerto Rico and called for the island's independence. The matter, at the time, was one of political principle and propaganda, not an immediate working goal. While the Young Lords cultivated revolutionary positions on abuses of power that spanned the globe, the organization also focused on the world just outside its office doors. Its day-to-day work centered on improving living conditions for Puerto Ricans and other poor people of color in the slums of New York and raising their political consciousness; it sought to change the world by changing a few square miles within its periphery. Yet, within a year of the group's emergence, a few members of the Central Committee began to explore the possibility of expanding the organization's influence to reach onto the island of Puerto Rico itself.

The first public sign of the new orientation came in August 1970 when Central Committee members Juan "Fi" Ortiz and Juan González traveled to Puerto Rico to take the pulse of the island's political environment. Speaking to a student-packed auditorium in Rio Piedras, González drew on an analysis by the Students for a Democratic Society (SDS), whose 1962 Port Huron statement identified students as major agents of social change. He linked students' subordinate position in society to Puerto Rico's colonial relationship to the United States and to the global standing of Third World countries.[1] Eager to stake a place for the Young Lords among the small number of active nationalist groups on the island during the 1960s, González, in a rousing speech, affirmed the Young Lords Party's commitment to the struggle for Puerto Rican independence.[2] Triumphalist in its assessment of the era's revolutionary nationalist consciousness, his speech overstated the pulse favoring independence on the island. While calls for independence in the late 1960s enjoyed greater popularity than in decades past—due in part to the tenacity of the Vietnamese guerrillas, who appeared to push back the all-powerful U.S. military—island protests cohered primarily

Young Lords Party logo. (*Palante* 2, no. 4 [June 5, 1970]; courtesy of the Tamiment Library)

around the privatization of public utilities and strip mining in the interior of the island. And on college campuses on the island, students organized mainly against the draft and Reserve Officer Training Corps recruitment.[3] Anticolonial and nationalist sentiments were certainly integral to the political propaganda of these campaigns, but the independence movement in Puerto Rico remained in political disarray after having been all but destroyed by government repression during the 1940s and 1950s. Though the Movimiento Pro Independencia (MPI) had found some success in consolidating the disparate segments of the move- ment for independence and connecting with the 1960s social movements on the island, support for independence was nowhere near as strong, or widespread, as it might have appeared to the Young Lords Party (YLP). In fact, the group's new course would be the prelude to collapse.

The move to Puerto Rico was only an abstract idea when the trip began in August 1970. But just a few weeks later, the travelers' "Letter from Puerto Rico" depicted deplorable conditions in shantytowns near San Juan's upscale Condado neighborhood. They assured *Palante* readers that the area "will be easy to orga- nize."[4] The letter implied an intent to initiate political work in Puerto Rico and graft onto the island a political perspective born of mainland conditions. The very idea suggested an outsized sense of the Young Lords' political and organiza- tional capacity. An internal party document prepared for the cadre months later revealed that "initially, the committee had decided to take this step [of beginning to build in Puerto Rico] covertly, but upon further analysis we understood that we had to prepare and consolidate the party for this historic event."[5]

Gloria Fontanez had political island connections and was the project's main advocate. The dynamic agitator and cochair of the Health Revolutionary Unity Movement (HRUM), she had been elected health captain of the YLP a few months earlier, which made her responsible for important labor organizing in New York's public hospitals. Though not on the Central Committee, she had the ear of one of its most important members, Juan González. The two had met in fall 1969 at a meeting of the East Harlem Health Council and were married less than a year later, on July 25, 1970, in a "revolutionary wedding" ceremony presided over by Denise Oliver and Felipe Luciano.[6]

In the summer and fall of 1970, the Young Lords underwent a series of abrupt changes that included the demotion of their chairman, Felipe Luciano; the death of Young Lord Julio Roldán in the Tombs; and the armed occupation of the First Spanish United Methodist Church. The fallout raised questions and concerns among some members and confusion and demoralization in others. An open, collective discussion seemed a necessity. A December membership- wide retreat could have promised a forum where members might have articu- lated their thoughts and analyzed their leaders' decisions—an opportunity to build internal democracy and assess organizational capacity. In the face of these traumatic developments, the Central Committee held a closed retreat for itself instead. The decision indicated that serious political evaluations of the Young Lords' direction and decision-making would be centralized in the leadership's top echelons. Despite its rhetoric to the contrary, the Central Committee was moving away from the goal of building an organization of leaders—a process for which there is no shortcut. Within the Central Committee, the argument for centralization was likely strengthened in moments of crisis and by knowledge that government agents were operating in the organization.

In late December 1970, the Central Committee held its private retreat. It tackled three major areas: the internal political life of the organization; contemporary politics and history, namely, a contemporary assessment of consciousness and political crisis and a run-through of Puerto Rico's history of resistance; and finally, a discussion of the classic questions in revolutionary political theory and practice. The first order of business was a review of self-evaluations prepared by each of the branches on their activities, challenges, and progress. This area also assessed progress on the issue of male chauvinism in the organization's ranks and an evaluation of racism in the party. The next major area covered mainland and island politics: the state of the black freedom movement in the United States and a crash course on imperialism in Puerto Rico, as well as a history of the nationalist movement that also laid out the party's plans for building in Puerto Rico. The last section of the retreat reviewed Lenin's theory of the state and outlined Mao's and Lenin's positions on the role of the revolutionary party, the development of leadership and cadre, and the application of democratic centralism. It also reviewed the contours and development, by revolutionary groups, of mass "people's organizations"—party affiliates focused on single-sector organizing (e.g., women, students, or prisoners) that do not require of participants full political agreement with the party or round-the-clock membership commitment.[7]

By the retreat's end, the Central Committee had prepared a thirty-two-page internal document for members of the organization, summarizing its analysis of branch reports and self-evaluations. The document confirmed that the organization's formal and informal leaders were in high gear developing political sophistication through community engagement, struggling to build a disciplined party, engaging in self-criticism, and studying history and theory and their application to the world. The document also offered assessments of the broader political conjuncture and proposed direction for the next year. Sections written by Pablo Guzmán and Denise Oliver addressed changes in the civil rights and black power movements, an indication that the organization's leaders were wedded to mainland organizing. Finally, it outlined the goal of organizing in Puerto Rico.

The branch reports revealed global trends to the Central Committee. They were "well done," read the document, but "could have been better ... if National had provided more detailed guidelines." The branches were "a long way from rooting out chauvinism and passivity, at all levels from Central Committee to FOL's [Friends of the Lords]." The cadre remained confused about the meaning of "democratic centralism," and even the Central Committee violated it; but an educational tape produced by Pablo Guzmán promised to offer clarity. Ministries were disorganized. Cadre were not being given enough responsibility. "Higher levels [of leadership] were not giving enough guidance to lower levels." The organization lacked a rubric for evaluating political development of cadre and leaders. With a high point in membership of approximately 1,000 cadre in New York, Newark, Philadelphia, Boston, Hartford, and Bridgeport, the organization was struggling to integrate and cohere its component parts. The document quoted Mao on leadership to clarify the matter:

> [Leaders] work out ideas, and use cadre well. Such things as drawing up plans, making decisions, and giving out orders and directives, are all in the category of "working out ideas." To put ideas into practice, we must weld the cadres together and encourage them to go into action; this comes into the category of "using the cadre well." The challenge, Mao writes, lies in the tendency to "appoint people on their merit . . . [or] by favoritism." The best and "honest" policy is to make appointments on the basis of "whether or not a cadre is resolute in carrying out the Party line, keeps to Party discipline, has close ties with the people, has the ability to find his bearings independently, and is active, hard-working, and unselfish."[8]

The organization's major post-retreat goal was to hone political and theoretical training through focused readings on Marxist economics and the histories of Puerto Rico and the black liberation movement.[9] To this end, the general weekly branch meetings—identified as the "core of democracy in the Party"—would have to be upgraded from their "undisciplined and boring" states. The new perspective proposed to put the least and most experienced members in regular conversation at branch meetings. It required attendance by "all officers, Lords, and LITs [Lords in training]. . . . No speaking engagement, personal problem etc. (except an extreme emergency) . . . excuse(s)." This had to become the major site "for solving problems, and [forum for reading] . . . the 13 Point Program and Platform . . . [to] build the discipline and organization necessary for true democratic centralism." Better record keeping would be enforced, including daily and weekly reports "from branches, officers and individuals," to help the Central Committee assess the organization and identify trends and correctives.

The report gave a brief evaluation of the Second Church Offensive, noting that despite rave public reviews, "internally [the Young Lords] took the church at a time when we were weak, still in the midst of a setback (the demotion of Felipe). Communications between levels were terrible, Central Committee, and the Party were not unified. . . . Male chauvinism was one of the worst parts of the offensive."[10] In a situation that was, by its very nature, unwieldy, the Central Committee's brief critique of the occupation's shortcomings seemed a reflection of its struggle to assert leadership after Felipe Luciano's departure rather than a sober portrayal of what actually happened. That the membership rallied at the church in the absence of its demoted chairman and in the context of a risky, armed operation suggested that the organization had developed an internal culture and spirit that went on autopilot when fighting police, prisons, and the symbols of repressive state power in the city.

The Young Lords were no longer upstarts. By the fall of 1970, a vocal layer of experienced cadre had matured, and their leadership at the church helped avert calamity. Although male bravado was surely heightened by the uncertainty and anxiety that many male members of the Young Lords may have felt, women were more prominent than ever. At least three women formed part of the group of ten Young Lords assigned to defend the church in case of a police raid. And by the time of the occupation, the Central Committee included two women: Denise Oliver, appointed in June 1970, and Gloria Fontanez, who took Luciano's place, not his rank, in October 1970, immediately after Felipe's demotion.[11]

Having gone through such a defining event, the cadre felt entitled to a greater say in the organization's decision-making process. A growing number of members were already critical of the organization's strong emphasis on social service programs, but among the cadre and secondary leadership, the question of how the organization would refashion itself was up for debate.[12] However, the Central Committee had already decided to shift the organization's political priorities away from service-oriented campaigns, without convening a general discussion. Whether conscious or not, its shifting perspective was influenced by debates raging within the Black Panther Party (BPP) in late 1970—which had by February led to a violent, COINTELPRO-fueled internecine split. In line with the position of Black Panther minister of information Eldridge Cleaver, the New York Panther leadership contended that the time had come to respond to the state's violent campaign of repression against black radicals with its own campaign of armed revolutionary counterviolence—a move, Cleaver argued, that would attract a broader base to the party and lead to the overthrow of the country's economic and political system.[13] Supporters of the BPP's top leader, Huey P. Newton, opposed the position, arguing that the call for armed insurrection was premature and would lead to the loss of political allies and support from the black American community. Newton favored broadening the BPP's community social service programs pending the advent of revolutionary consciousness among a broad sector of the population in the United States.[14]

As the BPP's rupture worsened, the Young Lords' Central Committee analyzed the political disagreement and put forth its own perspective. To this end, David Perez reported that when the Young Lords emerged in 1969, the leadership didn't quite grasp the purpose of a revolutionary party: "[Now] we understand that the Party cannot get itself tied up in running service programs, because the biggest needs of the people are its political needs. At the same time, we recognize the importance of the material needs of our people (food, clothing, shelter) and must never forget them." The objective of a revolutionary party, he wrote, was to challenge capitalism, not merely "its effects"—such as hunger among poor children.[15]

As Perez's assessment suggests, the Central Committee had developed a critique of "voluntarism." The term refers to a tendency to substitute individual will, acts of heroism, and self-sacrifice for collective class struggle. The tendency ignores the collective organization, grounded in mass social blocks, necessary to significantly challenge the apparatus of power. In the 1960s context, this elevated instead moral commitments to "serving the people" through, for example, the various self-help programs that the Black Panthers popularized and the Young Lords adopted. Such programs do not necessarily constitute substitutes for class struggle, but in the absence of accompanying challenges to the power structure, they—alone—do not disturb the balance of power in society.[16] In the cases of both organizations, however, their serve-the-people programs achieved important symbolic functions. They exposed the state, offered a compelling example of the idea of organizing society on the basis of human need rather than profit, and helped give revolutionaries a human face in their communities.

Despite its break with these programs, the Central Committee's (CC) new direction proposed a close cousin of voluntarism as an alternative. In a section of the retreat's report penned in Spanish by Gloria Fontanez, the CC announced that on March 21, 1971, the Young Lords would work with the Nationalist Party of Puerto Rico to organize a demonstration to commemorate the Ponce Massacre of 1937. She added that the group would use the occasion to announce the expansion of its revolutionary program to the island, a project that it referred to as the "reunification of the Puerto Rican nation." During the retreat, members of the CC voted on this new direction. Pablo Guzmán, Denise Oliver, and Juan "Fi" Ortíz opposed it. Gloria Fontanez, Juan González, and David Perez supported it. As outlined in the CC's internal rules, it was up to the chair of the CC to break split decisions with a double vote. The chair at the time, Juan González, voted in favor.[17] Fontanez continued, "For the people of Puerto Rico this will be an important day. In order to achieve our goal we will need a disciplined party with a singular focus—our national liberation. This will be the Party's greatest contribution to oppressed people the world over, much like the People of Vietnam have contributed to our struggle."[18]

The cadre's reactions ran the gamut of opinion. Gilbert Colón thought "it was a pretty good idea at the time" but remembers "others saying it was a terrible idea." Gloria Rodriguez "was opposed to the move, instinctively." She continues, "I felt we didn't belong there. Most of us barely spoke Spanish and we didn't know the political terrain. I remembered, distinctly, that during my [childhood] trips to Puerto Rico, people used to call me 'la Americana.'" Her considerations were also personal: "I grew up in New York and identified with African Americans and the civil rights movements. My roots were here. I was in a relationship, and had a job; so that was a bridge beyond where I was willing to go for the party. I remember having conversations about what I would say if I was asked to go."[19]

Despite the organization's deficits—as membership had grown in leaps and bounds, its infrastructure needed reinforcement and cadre needed political training—the Young Lords also enjoyed a rich culture of debate and discussion. The atmosphere of learning and political exploration had intensified months earlier during the May 1970 retreat. Colón describes the culture: "This is how it used to go down. 'These are the things you should read to prepare yourself for this discussion, all kinds of discussions. And these are the two different points of view that have hit the table.' Now obviously they hit the table at the highest level, the Central Committee. But study it, research it, and come back and talk about it. And I have to admit, that was probably the most intellectually stimulating period of my life because it was like a really good college class but with much more significance."[20] He continues, "I think the move caught everybody by surprise, but the cadre trusted leadership and really looked up to people like Juan González and Denise Oliver."

Even though the decision to organize in Puerto Rico had already been made, members expected that an intense period of discussion would set the Young Lords' plans on the right track.

Reflecting on the Working Class and the Divided Nation

Independently of the new direction, however, the Young Lords were knee deep in building the party in East Harlem, the Bronx, Manhattan's Lower East Side, Newark, Philadelphia, and Bridgeport. In the context of a nationwide upsurge in labor strikes, some members wondered whether the Young Lords should continue to regard the lumpenproletariat as the major revolutionary force in society.[21] Party support work for 400 striking Bronx workers, the majority Puerto Rican, sparked discussion on the power of labor. An article by Richie Perez on the Art Steel Company strike reveals some dimensions of that debate:

> [S]treet and student groups have to begin to expand their concept of
> revolution ... [and] stereotyped thinking that says you can only be a
> revolutionary if you wear a beret and a field jacket and rap a lot of Mao.
> Revolutionaries are judged not only by their theory, but also by their

practice. Our striking brothers showed by their practice that they are revolutionaries committed to fighting our common enemy. . . . [T]hey showed they understand the need to unite all our people in order to win our struggle for national liberation.[22]

Even though Perez didn't quite hit the notes of the classic Marxist argument— that workers are central to the revolutionary process both because they're exploited and because of their objective social power as producers of goods and profit—he was attempting to challenge the student and lumpen base of the organization. He builds his argument on workers' support for national liberation, which he likely misassessed or overstated. On the U.S. mainland, Puerto Rican nationalism—like the Puerto Rican flag itself—was primarily symbolic. It was an emblem of the strivings of Puerto Ricans as a besieged group—adjusting to a new country under the strains of racism—and of their hankerings for homeland amid migration's hardships. That Perez felt compelled to showcase the political consciousness of these workers in relation to their "commitment" to national liberation indicated a trend in the organization. Increasingly, calls for the liberation of Puerto Rico were becoming the litmus test of a "true revolutionary." Whether consciously or not, the organization's leaders had long been seeking consensus on what was now its new political perspective.

Coming out of the retreat, the Young Lords' leadership drafted a document titled "Divided Nation Thesis"—a theoretical justification for the organization's partial transplantation to the island. Colón remembers the questions it immediately raised among the cadre: "It was pretty clear Puerto Rico was a nation. But what was the role of Puerto Ricans here? Can there be such a thing as a divided nation? If it was, then the YLP had the obligation to actually set up a branch in Puerto Rico. To be honest with you, on paper it had an appeal."[23] The "Divided Nation Thesis" posited that Puerto Ricans in New York represented one-third of a nation in exile severed from the homeland by U.S. political and economic imperialism. The remaining two-thirds of the nation was in Puerto Rico. The thesis advanced the idea that regardless of its distance from Puerto Rico, the Puerto Rican community in the continental U.S. had an immutable social, cultural, historical, and political bond to Puerto Rico, even if members of the mainland community did not speak Spanish or had never visited the island. According to the Central Committee, the political statuses of Puerto Ricans on the mainland and the island were inextricably linked. As long as Puerto Rico remained a colony of the United States, all Puerto Ricans would be treated as second-class citizens.[24] Reflecting years later, Juan González explained the logic and motivation behind the Young Lords' new position: "It may sound strange now, but our goal was to unite the divided nation, to unite the Puerto Ricans in the U.S. with the Puerto Ricans in Puerto Rico, and to spur the revolutionary process. We believed that the chance of developing a revolution for independence was more likely in Puerto Rico than in the U.S."[25]

The Young Lords' "Divided Nation Thesis," together with other documents written by members of the Central Committee in the weeks after the retreat—on Marxist concepts and theories—formed the basis of their pamphlet *The Ideology of the Young Lords Party*. As prelude to discussions of Puerto Rican history and class struggle, militarization and the economy, and other subjects, the document defined major terms, including capitalism, class, the state, vendepatria, contradiction, dialectics, and Afro-Boricua. One of its many fresh and engaging passages explains often obfuscated concepts like dialectical materialism:

> All Puerto Ricans concerned with their people must begin to see things in a scientific way. . . . [The scientist asks] 'what would be the best way of getting through this problem and to my goal?' and then the scientist lays out each step, one by one, until the goal is reached. This is the way we must lay out the revolution, using our passion, our feelings to keep us going, step by step, until we are free. This means that we will become dialectical materialists. What does this mean? First take the word dialectics. Dialectics is the study of contradictions.

The document's analyses of the unconscious character of sexism and racism and how each manifests among Puerto Ricans and people of color are also impressive and still resonate today. Its discussion of "colonized mentality"—internalized inferiority and inadequacy and senseless conflicts among the oppressed—is an organic distillation of Franz Fanon's theories on the psychological fallout of colonial domination on the colonized. That forty-three page primer, which borrowed its title from the Black Panther pamphlet *The Ideology of the Black Panther Party*, would come to epitomize both the Young Lords' great strivings and their great failings.

While the Young Lords' boots-on-the-ground project in Puerto Rico was fueled by many sources, their perspective reflected a broader trend in the domestic movement regarding struggles elsewhere around the globe. In the early 1970s, repression, exhaustion, and pessimism about the prospects of revolution at home set a significant number of black American activists' sights on revolutionary movements in Africa, and many moved there. Dozens of members of the Black Panther Party found political sanctuary abroad during this period in countries like Algeria, Ghana, and Tanzania. In Ghana, they joined a wave of black radicals who had settled there a decade earlier. Other currents in the black freedom movement focused exclusively on support work for African independence movements in Angola, Zimbabwe, and Guinea-Bissau and the Black Consciousness movement in South Africa.[26] The focus on international events was also fed by the persistence of racism and white reaction to the justice claims of black Americans and other racially oppressed groups.[27]

The nationalist fervor created by struggles abroad and difficulties at home reinforced ideas adopted by many radicals more than a decade earlier: that racially oppressed people in the United States represented distinct nations rather than racialized groups within the nation.[28] Taken to its logical conclusion, the theory assumed that these groups might, if they so desired, form independent nations apart from the United States. The status of Puerto Ricans occupied a special place in these debates. Puerto Ricans constitute the only racialized group with the possibility of identifying a landmass outside of the continental U.S. as their homeland. The group's "Divided Nation Thesis" telescoped this possibility.[29]

Building the YLP in Puerto Rico

The organization's attempt to bridge the Puerto Rican experience on the mainland and the island began to be implemented during the first months of 1971. By the end of March, the YLP had transferred approximately twenty members and a significant share of its resources to the island.[30] It hoped to establish two branches there. Central Committee members Juan González and Gloria Fontanez flew to the island in January 1971 to prepare. Fontanez led the work. She had a stronger connection to the island than others and established contact with longtime nationalist activist Minerva González, a relative of Young Lord Carlito Rovira. She also fostered relationships with Julio, Luis, and Andres Rosado—major figures in the independence movement known collectively as the Rosado brothers. These individuals had their finger on the political pulse of the different Puerto Rican nationalist groupings, domestically and on the island.[31] Thereafter, González traveled between Puerto Rico and New York frequently in 1971. During the same time, the YLP began to adjust party activities in New York. The move required labor and resources and the largest fundraising campaign in the organization's history. The aim: to raise enough money to defray the costs of room and board for members who would be transplanted to the island. Two different spaces would have to be identified and rented: a large apartment for the group's collective living quarters, and an office space. The Young Lords also had to purchase large-ticket items, including a car for transportation in Puerto Rico and the plane tickets of those who would be moving to the island. The group needed everything: office supplies, furniture, clothing, and above all money to sustain its organizing efforts for at least a year. By now, most Young Lords worked as full-time organizers and did not possess salaried jobs—evidence of the growing seriousness of many members. Therefore, the organization could not depend on its membership base to raise funds. The hard work of identifying and approaching external funding sources proved to be the group's main preoccupation between January and March 1971.

The YLP made a broad appeal for financial support through its broadcast program on New York's WBAI radio station and through various leftist newspapers.[32] *Liberation News Service*, a New Left clearinghouse for late 1960s radical politics and activism, carried the group's letter to the movement, which discussed its goal to build—in Ponce, Puerto Rico—the struggle for self-determination of Puerto Ricans and other Third World people. February was identified as the month of their "economic offensive." The group's list of acceptable contributions included "any amount of money however small; food and clothing; mimeographs, typewriters, stencils etc.; food and clothing drives by supporting organizations and students; and speaking engagements for representatives of the Young Lords."[33]

The Lords also tapped into the constellation of Old Left organizations, a number of which were eager to gain favor and a political ear within the New Left. From one of these organizations the Lords received a $10,000 donation that was later stolen.[34] The relationship the YLP fostered during its campaigns at Lincoln Hospital, during which it gained the respect and trust of medical residents and doctors, also proved indispensable. Driven by a combination of compassion for the underprivileged community they served and strong commitment to the ideals espoused by the Young Lords, as well as middle-class guilt, many interns, residents, and doctors at Lincoln made generous donations.[35]

The fundraising campaign diverted the energies of the YLP away from its established routine and local campaigns, but the organization achieved its fundraising and relocation goals. During this period the leadership also attempted to develop a hands-on perspective for building branches in Puerto Rico. However, at such a remove from the island, the task of understanding the relationship between the island's history and its contemporary political climate proved challenging. The Central Committee also identified the group of twenty Young Lords who were to move to Puerto Rico and arranged for them to receive intensive language training led by YLP members who were fluent in Spanish.[36]

By early March, members of the group began to land on the island. They joined forces with the remnants of the Nationalist Party—the significantly weakened party of the revered father of Puerto Rican nationalism (and namesake of their predecessor reading group at the State University of New York College at Old Westbury), Don Pedro Albizu Campos. Their first action was a demonstration on March 21, 1971, to commemorate the Ponce Massacre of 1937, one of the bloodiest chapters of the Puerto Rican independence movement, during which local police, under orders from U.S.-appointed government officials, opened fire on a pro-independence protest, killing 21 and wounding 200.[37] But by the 1960s, the Nationalist Party was more symbol than fighting organization. It had been wracked by repression at the hands of the FBI and the island government

Julio Roldán march in Aguadilla, Puerto Rico. (Courtesy of Henry Medina Archives)

following the wave of nationalist protests that began in October 1930 on the island and the armed attacks on the Blair House and Congress in Washington, D.C., that followed in 1950.[38]

At their first event on the island, the Young Lords donned khaki fatigues and purple berets and displayed their usual paramilitary style in the manner that had become the imprimatur of mainland, urban militant groups operating in American slums. Fittingly, the Young Lords used this occasion as the launching ceremony of their project. The march took the form of a procession toward the Ponce Cathedral, where the annual memorial Mass of the Ponce Massacre was held. The next day, at least five major newspapers in mainland cities where the Young Lords were active carried similar stories. All reported that the demonstration drew about eighty members of the Nationalist Party.[39] The Puerto Rican daily *El Nuevo Dia* identified the same number but accounted for the hundreds who lined the sidewalks, adding that the arrival of the Young Lords "increased the tense atmosphere in the wake of university rioting 10 days ago in which two police officers and a student were shot to death." A photo of the march published in *Palante* showed a much larger crowd, and the Young Lords stated that the procession had 700 participants.[40]

The Young Lords' paramilitary-styled display differed from what islanders were used to. Back in New York, the group's style inspired youth of color, who read it as a powerful symbol of political awakening and rebellion against their social marginality. On the island, such showmanship was out of place, but it underscored a haunting conflict among Puerto Ricans, borne of postwar colonial policy. Juan Maria García Passalacqua addressed the matter in an Op-Ed he penned on the Young Lords' island arrival. The well-known public intellectual was empathetic to the Young Lords but noted that they evoked "a mixture of hysteria and disdain" among islanders. Their presence, he explained, was "retribution" for, first, migrants' suffering in "putrid slums" while those on the island "looked the other way"; and second, for migration's unacknowledged economic benefits to the island. The piece was part mea culpa—and likely shared by a sector of Puerto Rico's managerial bourgeoisie self-conscious of its role in colonial migration policy. Of encounters between "Neoricans and Puerto Ricans," Passalacqua observed: "As the conversation progresses, the locals begin to fret [as they] sense the distinctions rather than the similarities coming to the fore." To him, the presence of Young Lords in Puerto Rico might help islanders grapple with these moments of "collective guilt" and tackle "the very important question [of] . . . what is Puerto Rican [or Puertorriqueñismo] and what [is] the future of our island." He asked islanders to "search deep into their souls" toward acceptance that "the Puerto Rico . . . of [the erudite] Julia de Burgos . . . is gone." He urged understanding for its replacement by "the tough, down-to-earth proletarian . . . slum dweller" represented by the Young Lords.[41]

Back on the mainland, the group announced its plans on the island in parallel demonstrations in New York, Philadelphia, and Bridgeport, organized jointly by the Frente Unido, a coalition of radical Puerto Rican groups that included El Comité, Puerto Rican Student Union, Justicia Boricua, HRUM in New York, and mainland branches of Movimiento Pro Independecia, the island's major nationalist group. The Young Lords' groundbreaking presence in New York spurred the emergence or resurgence of these groups, and now its move to Puerto Rico was strengthening collaboration among them. Attendance reports for the demonstration in New York vary widely from several thousand, as reported by *Liberation News Service*, to the 7,000 figure reported by the Young Lords.[42]

Ironically, the New York demonstration was larger than the one on the island where the MPI was conspicuously absent. Despite political differences, the MPI branch in New York was compelled to work with the Young Lords—a contending force on the Puerto Rican Left with broad appeal among youth, known in the Puerto Rican community and notorious in public discourse. However, in Puerto Rico, where the Young Lords were newcomers, the situation was much different. There, the MPI perceived the Young Lords as politically untutored and adopted a scathing position against them. It perceived the group's political declarations as brazen, presumptuous, and dismissive of the national independence tradition on the island.[43] The Young Lords' critique of the nationalist scene in Puerto Rico may also have discomfited the MPI. The largest independence groups on the island—the MPI and Partido Independentista Puertorriqueño—were led by the overwhelmingly white Puerto Rican bourgeoisie and petite bourgeoisie. Both had "failed to sink roots in the most exploited sectors of the island, the lumpen and the working classes, and among the most important social groups on the island, peasants and the Afro-Puerto Rican population."[44]

A week after the Ponce demonstration, the MPI's leader, Juan Mari Bras, welcomed the Young Lords with a biting opinion piece. Published in *Claridad*, it revealed competitive contempt for the Young Lords, and its mix of political analysis and paternalism portrayed the diaspora as helpless other. The letter denounced mainland Puerto Ricans' "dehumanized status" as "cruel and abusive" and likened their social segregation to South African Apartheid.

Mari Bras then pours paternalistic praise on the Young Lords for having made it out of the wilderness: "What is marvelous is that out of this almost complete rupture emerges among ghetto youth, a spirit of Puerto Rican nationalism." He chides the group for "believing itself a revolutionary party simply because its functionaries have taken on the bombastic titles of minister and field marshal." More lambasting is followed with a request to fall in line behind Puerto Rico's established nationalist leadership and movement:

> The Young Lords' error lies . . . in arriving as great liberators, giving the impression that they will carry out a messianic function . . . that will present Puerto Rico the magic touch it needs to emerge out of colonial stagnation. . . . [They] are undaunted by one century of uninterrupted liberation struggle nourished by so many heroes and martyrs and more than a decade of new independence struggle. They have launched their project to liberate us as those who initiate a building project on a blank slate. . . . The MPI welcomes our countrymen of the Young Lords and invites them to situate themselves within the proper political perspective and be mindful of their proper place. Only then will their presence be useful in Puerto Rico.[46]

That the lengthy editorial was written at all suggests a combination of pique and rivalry alongside valid concerns.

The Young Lords chose Ponce as its base of operations because it was Pedro Albizu Campos's hometown and the Nationalist Party's strongest organizational base. Ponce was also home to a number of chemical and copper plants, whose workers the Lords expected to influence. But although the city was once the fountainhead of the Nationalist Party, in more recent years it had become a stronghold of the most conservative wing of the island's government. The YLP opted against San Juan because U.S. political influence and capital predominated there, along with greater policing and government surveillance.[47] However, repression on the island was intense everywhere.

To the FBI, geographical considerations were immaterial. In 1961, the agency redoubled surveillance strategies of "groups seeking independence for Puerto Rico." Its new COINTELPRO program outlined specific instructions to informants in the Puerto Rican movement on "how to disrupt their activities and compromise their effectiveness." Informants were instructed to meticulously gather information on leaders and rank-and-file members concerning their weaknesses, morals, criminal records, spouses, children, family life, educational qualifications, and personal activities. Its objectives included "disruption and discord; creating doubts as to the wisdom of remaining in the independence movement; and causing defections." Instructions also outlined the methods to be used. The primary means advised "exploiting . . . a common fault within pro-independence groups: factionalism within an organization." Informants were also advised to "raise controversial issues at meetings, raise justifiable criticisms against leaders."

As in the experience of the CPUSA, the instructions continued, this method could lead the informant to "advance inside the Party primarily because of their forceful acts in criticizing poor leaders and other weaknesses in the Party organization." Additionally, the memo suggested that "the nationalist element could be pitted against the communist elements." Finally, the instructions explain the effectiveness of psychological methods in which "seeds of suspicion are planted concerning the real motivation" of groups, leaders, and individuals.[48]

The Young Lords were also infiltrated and surveilled by COINTELPRO and by police departments in New York, Newark, Philadelphia, and Bridgeport. Police in Puerto Rico also kept close watch on the group, and informants documented every detail of their movements, including air travel times, dates and flights.[49] Administrators of the program also recruited postmasters who allowed them to intercept the mail of the organization in New York, Philadelphia, and elsewhere and paid close attention to individuals that contacted the organization, "particularly those in prison with early release dates [who] would provide excellent targets for informant material."[50]

While government provocateurs watched them relentlessly, the Young Lords went through two months of hard, fruitless work in Ponce. In late May 1971, they began to build a branch in Aguadilla, a small city on the northeastern quadrant of the island, approximately ninety miles from the capital. Six months later they would open a second branch in El Caño, a very depressed neighborhood within San Juan.

Aguadilla was a small, poverty-stricken city with a high unemployment rate and an isolated population dependent on one hospital and one factory for work. Given these conditions, the Lords hoped that Aguadilla might better mirror New York's social environment.[51] Though the gulf between a small town in Puerto Rico and New York's inner city was vast, the Young Lords worked hard and found some receptivity. As a tightly knit town, still very much like a rural community, Aguadilla erected its social life on folk and kinship networks; neighbors had frequent, direct interaction with each other, and respected individuals could influence the town. The work of the Young Lords was made immeasurably easier as a result of a tragic, but advantageous, connection with these deep-seated networks: Aguadilla was Julio Roldán's hometown. Even before their arrival in this small town, these mainland radicals had achieved a measure of honor and standing as fighters against injustice. Aguadilla had hosted, six months earlier, an impassioned political funeral procession for Roldán of over 1,000 people. The funereal ceremonies concluded with speeches by Roldán's family and friends as well as by representatives of the Young Lords and the MPI, all of whom linked his death to police brutality in New York and U.S. rule over Puerto Rico.[52]

In the months after their arrival, the Young Lords' work in Aguadilla focused primarily on stopping the closure of the city's only hospital due to budgetary constraints. Given the group's health activism in New York, this was familiar political territory. The implications of the hospital closure were quite grave; those seeking medical care in Aguadilla and its greater area would have to travel an hour to the next-closest hospital, in the city of Mayagüez. The Young Lords held a rally in April, which, according to Juan González, "got 200 people . . . which for a small town is pretty good."[53] The hospital closed soon thereafter but reopened through pressure organized by the Young Lords, who built an alliance of community members and hospital workers. It closed permanently within a year, after protests subsided. The victory was significant, however brief, but the organization still did not grow.[54]

In El Caño, the fruit of the YLP's work was even less visible than in Aguadilla. Its major campaign in that city sought to halt an urban renewal initiative. Introduced by the Model Cities Program, the project introduced middle-class housing to diversify the class base of poor neighborhoods and spur economic development. This was known territory. When thousands of poor urban residents were displaced, the Lords identified the main bureaucrats behind the Model Cities Program and targeted them with demonstrations when they came to town. They also organized a number of protests that blocked construction work. The Lords in El Caño frequently likened their experience to that in East Harlem. The ramshackle neighborhood on the outskirts of the Puerto Rican capital actually had a higher incidence of poverty and was more akin to the poorest of towns in the U.S. South. Despite the familiarity they found in El Caño, their efforts were too isolated to arrest the national urban renewal initiative.

The hard work of the Young Lords in Puerto Rico wound up amounting to little growth. There was no significant success—symbolic or otherwise—that might have increased their membership base or reputation and influence among potential sympathizers on the island. Most important, the Young Lords working in Puerto Rico were very aware of the great discrepancy between the drudgery of their unproductive work and progress toward their identified goal—Puerto Rican independence—a reality that produced profound demoralization among them on the island. It was clear, especially to those in Puerto Rico, that the YLP had failed to create a plan that fit both its organizational perspective and Puerto Rico's social and political climate. Rather, along with the transplantation of a few of their members, the Young Lords had transplanted a method of organizing that had been effective in politicizing an isolated racialized group on the mainland but didn't work in the island context.

The group was handicapped by a number of obstacles. *Palante*—the sale of which was the mainstay of Young Lord organizing—rarely arrived on schedule because the New York Lords had difficulty getting the copies to JFK airport since they had to pick up the paper in Worcester, Massachusetts. According to Ramon Morales, "We had to go far away because the FBI and NYPD intimidated local companies not to print *Palante.*"[55] Even as they had grand dreams for Puerto Rico, the Young Lords were already overstretched on the mainland, their resources spread across six branches. Their bank accounts were low, they owed rent, and they were behind on payments to the printer for *Palante*.[56] Though it wasn't obvious then, sometime around February 1971 the organization's membership started to decline; as a result, at the very time the Young Lords were trying to spread their operations, they had fewer bodies to address the many disparate needs the group faced. On a number of occasions, monetary subsidies designated for the Puerto Rico branches did not arrive on time and the Young Lords on the island went without basic necessities, including food.[57] For its part, the state continued to ramp up its repressive mechanisms. In small-town Puerto Rico, just going into the Young Lords office to ask for literature might mean you would lose your job.[58]

Perhaps the greatest challenge was the group's lack of facility with Spanish, the island's dominant language. The group was also thwarted by its political inexperience; while the study of history was important to the project of building a branch in Puerto Rico, the application of political lessons derived from this history to contemporary conditions proved to be a more complicated matter. The latter required a keen understanding of contemporary politics through theoretical study, political debate, and most importantly, practice and learning through political engagement in diverse settings over time. Though the Puerto Rico members were sincere in their desire to sharpen their understanding, they had little time to learn and no established community from which to do so.

While the Young Lords had made grave mistakes, lessons were being learned. Of the organization's experience in Puerto Rico and shift away from lumpen organizing, González explained during the period: "If you're gonna build a revolution, it has to be based on, or at least given direction by, the main force, which is Puerto Rican working people. . . . It takes a long time to build [a revolution] unless you're talking about a coup . . . unless you're talking about a few people seizing power in a society. And if you do that, you don't have a revolutionary people, you just have a few revolutionaries."[59]

Back in the mainland United States, the work of the organization floundered as the YLP's sharp turn toward organizing in Puerto Rico seriously depleted its resources and the morale of its members. Some who weathered the shift during the first months of the move to Puerto Rico functioned primarily as auxiliaries for the new Puerto Rico–based branch of the organization. In the first few months of 1971, most of the group's focus was on preparing for the expansion to the island, and then in the few months thereafter it focused on continuing to raise money; throughout, a more intense course of study in the history and politics of the island was mandated by the Central Committee.

The departure of Denise Oliver was among the major losses of the period. In late March, she resolved her quiet reservations about the move to Puerto Rico by quitting the YLP and joining the Harlem chapter of the BPP, which was embroiled in its own internecine turmoil, one fueled by the FBI.[60] The month before, in February, the long-standing ideological divide in the organization came to a head—one faction was led by the then-exiled Panther leader Eldridge Cleaver and supported by Panthers in New York and elsewhere on the East Coast; the other faction was led by Bobby Seale and Huey P. Newton, supported by the Oakland headquarters and members on the West Coast. Cleaver opposed what he characterized as the reformist tendencies of Newton, whose ideas and program had become dominant in the organization. In response to widespread violent state repression against the BPP, Cleaver favored the development of a strong guerrilla underground organization. He critiqued Newton's focus on political education, legal defense, and "survival programs" that had constituted the core of the group's social service work, and which had been a model for the Young Lords—a free breakfast program for children, ambulance service, and lead testing. Newton, for his part, opposed tendencies toward what he saw as militarization because he believed the community would not support an emphasis on guns.[61] Ironically, within a month of joining the Panthers, Oliver also went in search of more revolutionary pastures abroad. She flew to Paris and then to Algeria, joined Eldridge Cleaver and his wife, Kathleen, and the international faction of the Panthers traveled throughout Africa to meet with new postcolonial governments.[62] Oliver had joined the extremist wing of the Panther split, a sign of widespread political disorientation in the movement.

As spring turned to summer, the organization lost several other crucial members who did not agree with the shift to Puerto Rico. Many of these members left feeling deeply disillusioned that their hard work on local campaigns and on building relationships in the neighborhood had seemingly been for naught. Other experienced members, like Carlos Aponte, were purged because they were believed to be agents of COINTELPRO, even absent any proof. The fact that Aponte was critical of the move to Puerto Rico did not help his case. As discussed previously, the Central Committee began to question his membership months earlier when the *New York Times* attributed to him an unauthorized quote about Felipe Luciano's demotion. These episodes eroded the sense of sisterhood and brotherhood in the group and amplified distrust and paranoia within the organization's ranks. Still others who felt a moral commitment to the Young Lords left because they found little to contribute to an organization whose established routine had collapsed.

New York Offices Close Their Doors

By June 1971, the East Harlem and Lower East Side offices had closed their doors. The party newspaper, *Palante*, continued its regular publication schedule, but the lack of a storefront presence in these Puerto Rican neighborhoods was a painfully obvious metaphor for the Young Lords' retreat from the community at large.

The disorientation that befell the Young Lords was certainly exacerbated by the Central Committee's own precipitous decisions. In an interview from the period, Juan González attributed the organization's inability to bounce back from its mistakes to the lack of discipline among "many young people in the party who had never worked and therefore did not have the capacity of consistency and patience, that we needed in our struggle."[63] While the Young Lords lost many of their more experienced members, they gained newer ones along the way who were politically green. A more experienced and mature membership would perhaps have been able to stay the course and redirect the organization's mission, but the paucity of democratic decision-making across the different levels of membership was a major impediment to their development. However, opening up the organization to democratic debate and discussion would have exposed the Central Committee's grave mistakes and authoritarian tendencies.

Moreover, although the Young Lords decided to embrace a working-class perspective, the social character of the organization never changed. Beginning in January of 1971, the YLP began to address more seriously the importance of

March with mournful expressions. (Photograph by David Fenton)

workers in the revolutionary project. If greater numbers of workers were to be integrated into the life of the organization, it would have to open up opportunities for involvement that did not mandate a "twenty-five hours a day" commitment. The twenty-five-hour model of commitment established by the YLP early in its development reflected the organization's strong student and lumpen base. However, unlike students who possess flexibility in their schedules and even the option of leaving school to dedicate themselves to full-time activism, workers who depend on their jobs for survival and to support their families could never conceive of themselves as full-time organizers. In order to attract more workers, the YLP's "mass organization" committees were designed such that they would not "demand that members spend too many hours in meetings."[64]

But absent an infusion of radical workers into the organization who might help change its internal culture and offer a different viewpoint on the challenges of workplace organizing, as the organization became more isolated, the group's "workerist" perspective became a whipping post for the infractions of its young students and the lumpen. Of the failure of its members to navigate the mistakes and organizational shifts of the Young Lords, González writes during the period, "The ideas of humility, collectivity, patience, consistency, hard work, principles that we the working people have developed were substituted with arrogance, individualism, impatience, inconsistency, and laziness, principles that the capitalist, the rich, the government put in our heads to weaken us."[65]

Following its big push to sink roots in Puerto Rico, the organization resurfaced in public life in the summer of 1971 to implement the mass organizations concept that the Central Committee had outlined at the December 1970 retreat.[66] Through these mass organizations, the Lords expected to encourage "the practice of revolutionary self-government" among different constituencies in the community. Among Maoists, mass organizations, sometimes known as "people's organizations," were believed to be "the organs of the State before the seizure of power," which would be influenced by a revolutionary organization, in this case the Young Lords.

Despite the quiet demoralization of many, Young Lords members limped along through another massive organizing push. There had been no mass recruitment of workers; in the absence of the significant uptick in revolutionary consciousness they had hoped for, the Young Lords leadership would build looser campaigns in the areas of labor, prisoners' rights, women's rights, housing, and organizing against the Vietnam War. People from the community would discuss issues of concern and plans for action. Within these structures the Young Lords would offer political education classes, but participation in their mass organizations would not require strict discipline or agreement with the full revolutionary program. The object of this new organizational perspective was to increase direct, community participation in YLP-sponsored projects among those who supported the organization but did not possess full revolutionary consciousness or were not ready to commit to full-time membership.

This new approach represented a shift from the YLP's founding orientation, which set prohibitively high moral and political standards and expectations for membership that expected members to abandon responsibilities and allegiances to work and family to become full-time organizers. As discussed earlier, the YLP's Rules of Discipline had previously demanded that Young Lords be on political duty "25 hours a day."[67] In order to accomplish its new mission, by summer 1971 the YLP began to assign to each of the three branches of the organization—in the Bronx, the Lower East Side, and East Harlem—a different area of work within the mass organization perspective. Meanwhile, the Central Committee created seven mass organizations:

- The Committee to Defend the Community, which would be dedicated to agitation against the police, with the help of Young Lords who were active in the Bronx branch
- The Lumpen Unidos Rompecadenas (United Lumpen Breaking the Chains), which would be developed in the East Harlem branch

- The Workers' Federation, which would operate out of the Lower East Side branch
- The Puerto Rican Student Union (college and high school students), which would be based at Hunter College
- The Third World Students' League, which would consist of junior high school students, though it never got off the ground
- The Women's Union, which would operate with the help of the Lower East Side branch
- The New Sixty-Fifth Infantry, which would work with Vietnam veterans and was named after a division of Puerto Rican soldiers in the U.S. Army that first emerged during World War I[68]

In the long run, the group expected to draw in the most politically developed individuals from these mass organizations as full-time members of the YLP.[69] At its best, the logic of these committees was to build activism from the vast majority of the community who were not full-time activists. That potentially large group of people would discuss those issues that resonated with them and would figure out tactics to create the change they desired; those organic ideas would then be infused with radical leadership, analyses, and critiques. But rather than focus on the one or two initiatives that would attract the largest number of participants, in launching seven mass organizations the YLP overstretched the capacity of its already disoriented membership.

The changing political perspective of the group, especially regarding its orientation toward workers, led it to encourage members in the Workers' Federation committees to take jobs in those industries deemed ripe for shop-floor activism. The strategy was influenced by the resurgence of working-class struggles in the late 1960s and early 1970s against demands for higher productivity on the shop floor. Activism by rank-and-file workers contradicted a commonly held assumption of the New Left, which suggested that American workers had become a conservative force, lulled by the higher standard of living achieved within a significant section of the working-class during American capital's golden years in the 1950s and early 1960s. However, sectors of the working class were growing more radical, as a result of the leftward shift in consciousness produced by the civil rights and black power movements, growing anger at the rising number of casualties in Vietnam, and finally frustration at the demands for higher worker productivity on the shop floor as employers attempted to offset economic stagnation. In 1968, black workers in Detroit's auto industry fought against racist hiring practices, automation, and speedups and against a union bureaucracy inattentive to workers' interests. In 1969, there was a resurgence of wildcat strikes; in 1970 workers at General Motors struck for sixty-seven days, tens of thousands of coal miners struck in three states demanding benefits for miners hurt on the job, and postal workers paralyzed post offices in 200 cities in an illegal strike.[70]

These developments were short-lived and emerged alongside a conservative backlash against the black freedom movement and the gains of the 1960s, which influenced white workers. Nonetheless, by 1971 the YLP formed part of a growing trend within the Left toward industrializing. The term "industrializing" is shorthand for a perspective adopted by left organizations that encourages or requires members to join the ranks of the working class in strategic industries for the purpose of carrying out political work among workers. Ironically, the strategy was implemented during another big wave of deindustrialization and working-class retrenchment.

The YLP's transformation away from its exclusive focus on the lumpen and toward the working class did not take place overnight. The group discussed and debated the issues in fits and starts, beginning in the summer of 1970. The YLP's community activism at Lincoln and Metropolitan Hospitals helped in this transition, especially since the organization had recruited a number of key shop-floor activists who belonged to HRUM.

Early in 1971, YLP members themselves began to take jobs in public hospitals, where Puerto Ricans and black Americans were heavily concentrated in non-professional health occupations. In addition, the move to Puerto Rico proved to be a turning point for the group. Work on the island clarified for the YLP the meaning of class conflict in the Puerto Rican community. Whereas on the mainland the YLP was able to organize Puerto Ricans with appeals to ethnic identity and, by extension, to their condition as an oppressed minority group, in Puerto Rico calls for Puerto Ricans to unite on the basis of national identity and shared oppression were not as effective. Whereas most Puerto Ricans in New York shared the same social class, in Puerto Rico class and race divisions among islanders were sharp, and they often determined perceived interests. As Pablo "Yoruba" Guzmán expressed in an interview with *Liberation News Service* on the work of the YLP on the island, "In Puerto Rico, it is not enough to say 'Puerto Ricans, let's get together,' because then Governor Ferre will come to the meeting."[71] Ironically, even though the Young Lords went to Puerto Rico on a nationalist mission, presuming the unity of the island, the experience deepened their understanding of class divisions and thus their working-class analysis.

The Attica Prison Uprising

Since fall 1970, the Young Lords had established a connection through mail correspondence with a network of prisoners in New York State known as the Inmates Liberation Front (ILF). In response to the ILF's request for a formal affiliation with the Young Lords, the Puerto Rican radicals adopted the ILF as a mass organization.[72] The ILF was a product of the changing face of U.S. prisoners. During the 1960s, New York State prisons registered prisoners with a different profile than in previous years. The new prisoner tended to be younger, was serving a shorter sentence, was disproportionately drawn from the state's major urban areas, and was overwhelmingly black American or Puerto Rican. Reared in the era of black power, many of these prisoners expected to be treated with respect and dignity, and many called themselves political prisoners, arguing that the actions that landed them in prison were less a product of individual character flaws and more the result of the nation's failure to provide decent employment, adequate housing, and equal education to so many of its citizens.[73] The coming together of these younger and more politicized prisoners with the small but growing number of radicals who had been imprisoned for their political activism created the conditions for widespread rebellions against the long-standing degradation experienced in some of the nation's most repressive prisons.

In summer and fall 1971, the Attica Correctional Facility in upstate New York became the site of the most dramatic prisoners' rebellion of the period. The siege took place in the context of growing tensions between guards and prisoners and growing awareness of small gains made by organized prisoner actions in New York State and across the country. A year earlier, 450 Attica prisoners working in the metal shop, the most despised work in the prison, to which black prisoners were disproportionately assigned, organized a work stoppage to protest inhumane conditions, low wages, and the transfer to a different facility of prisoners who had approached the supervisor about an increase in wages. Their wages increased from six to twenty-nine cents per day to twenty-five cents to one dollar a day. Three months later, when prisoners at Auburn State Prison in New York did not get permission to carry out educational activities during their proposed Black Solidarity Day, they marched the guards to the center of the yard after confiscating their keys and nightsticks and proceeded with their speak-out.[74] Frustration with the slow pace of change continued to grow in the context of prisoners' rising expectations following the appointment of a new commissioner, Russell G. Oswald, who had responded positively to prisoners' demands but had not delivered on reforms.

In July 1971, after corresponding with prisoners across the state by mail, a group of five prisoners calling themselves the Attica Liberation Faction wrote a letter to the commissioner in which they presented a set of demands. The demands included the right to counsel at parole hearings; improved conditions in medical care, food, clothing, recreational facilities, prisoner workshops, and the dining area; the right to shower more than once a week; the standardization of rules across the prison; and an end to the practice of segregating political prisoners from the general prison population.[75] According to the Special Commission on Attica, the disposition of prisoners toward organized protest was influenced by the emergence of groups of prisoners that identified as members of the Black Panthers and the Young Lords and as radical Muslims. Members of these groups conducted a prisoner-led class in "sociology," where discussions inevitably raised questions about their own status and conditions. In mid-August the guards at Attica reported that prisoners they recognized as Young Lords had mediated a dispute between Muslims and Black Panthers.[76] In the context of Julio Roldán's death and the growing politicization of prisoners in New York State, the Young Lords had prioritized prisoners' rights through the ILF. The frequent references in the Attica uprising investigations to prisoners who identified as Young Lords, coupled with the steady flow of letters penned by prisoners in *Palante*, were testament that the Young Lords had inspired many prisoners to come together to assert their rights through collective action and their humanity through political education and personal commitment to a cause higher than themselves. Not long before that, on August 22, 1971, while the sociology class was in recess for the summer, prisoners wore black armbands and held a daylong silent protest and hunger strike to commemorate George Jackson, a gifted writer and critic of the U.S. prison system, who had recently been murdered by a tower guard in the San Quentin State Prison in Marin County, California.[77]

A few weeks later, on September 9, the morning after two prisoners in two different units were dragged to solitary confinement, approximately 150 prisoners in those two units, mostly black American and Puerto Rican, took over parts of the prison. Within two hours, around 1,200 prisoners had joined in the uprising and taken hostage forty-two officers and civilians.[78] Before long they presented twenty-eight demands for prison reform that focused on conditions, but as the magnitude of the uprising became manifest, after much wrangling the prisoners settled on six "immediate" demands that called for "complete amnesty" for their actions and "freedom ... from all physical, mental and legal reprisals."[79] In negotiation with Commissioner Oswald, they demanded to be represented by well-known radical attorney William Kunstler, members of the Black Panthers and the Young Lords, the Nation of Islam, Bronx congressman Herman Badillo, journalist Tom Wicker, and others.

Young Lord Central Committee member Juan "Fi" Ortiz and Jose Paris, a former Attica prisoner and Young Lord, were deployed to Attica to join the negotiation. Back in New York City, the Young Lords immediately held local meetings and two large demonstrations in concert with the New York Black Panthers to pressure Governor Nelson Rockefeller to support the the prisoners.[80] But their efforts were for naught. The commissioner accepted the prisoners' original twenty-eight demands but refused to grant those deemed most important to the prisoners: full amnesty and the resignation of Attica's superintendent, Vincent R. Mancussi. Amid distrust on both sides, the prisoners refused to compromise on these two issues. According to Ortiz, they had drawn lessons from the multiple prisoner rebellions in New York City the year before, in which all the prisoners' demands were granted, but the repressive retaliation of wardens, together with unforgiving legal charges leveled against them by the state, would keep them behind bars for the rest of their lives.[81]

A desperate plea to the world written by Young Lord prisoners and delivered to Ortiz and Paris during the negotiations illustrates that the leaders of the rebellion understood the homicidal character of the state's reprisals against them: "We are automatically dead men if we remain here. As the representatives of the people, we will be the ones who will die first at the hands of the fascist pigs. . . . Please get us out of this concentration camp." They knew that the state would sacrifice the hostages in order to quash the uprising and felt that resolution could only come through some kind of humanitarian intervention by federal or international authorities: "The pig is already talking about sacrificing the hostages to get to us. . . . If possible we are willing to leave the country if we are granted safe passage out. We are not Amerikkkans, we are Puerto Ricans and Blacks, and as such we do not belong in fascist Amerikkka. Please you must get a federal judge to help us. . . . We need the full-unmitigated support of the world out there. . . . We have stopped begging for crumbs. We are human beings and will die to prove that fact."

Five days into the uprising, on September 13, the governor ordered an assault on Attica by state troopers. Within fifteen minutes, thirty-nine people were dead—twenty-nine prisoners and ten guards—making the death toll at Attica what a state commission would call "the bloodiest one-day encounter between Americans since the Civil War."[82] Four others had died in the run-up to the siege, bringing the death toll at Attica to forty-three.[83] Despite growing evidence of decline, the Young Lords had established an intrepid reputation as a tribune of the oppressed, and so they were called upon to participate in and bear witness to an epic struggle for human dignity in one of the nation's most notorious prisons. In the proceeding decades, prisons would become major pillars in the fight for racial freedom in the post–black power movement era.

From Young Lords to Revolutionary Workers

For all of their hard work and influential campaigns, in 1971 the Young Lords were facing challenges to their "mass work" perspective for many different reasons. They had sustained a dizzying pace of full-time activism and high stress, building occupations for more than two years. They had witnessed the murder of Black Panther Fred Hampton, the trial of the Panther 21, and the violent repression and internecine battles that were decimating the BPP. The fatal possibilities of activism came to their doorstep with the death of Julio Roldán and their armed occupation of the First Spanish United Methodist Church. The group then launched its most organizationally and politically complicated campaign—the move to Puerto Rico—at a moment when its longest-standing members and Central Committee were undergoing a combination of movement exhaustion, fear of growing government repression, and, in many cases, demoralization. While the organization struggled to reignite its work on the mainland, the momentum of times past had been lost. Although the group had restructured itself into mass organizations, its old fighting spirit was never revived.

The YLP was launching new, bold initiatives at a time when the organization's membership began a slow decline and the movement was losing its mass character. Had the group begun to create its mass organizations earlier during the window of opportunity between 1969 and 1970, when activism in urban neighborhoods was in ascendance, it might have emerged as a stronger force in the 1970s. But in 1969, while individual members of the YLP might have been familiar with the history of committee work among left organizations, the political inexperience of the organization as a whole precluded the application of such lessons and strategies. The adoption of this new approach toward organizing was partly a consequence of objective realities in the YLP—an attempt by the organization to compensate for its declining membership. Reflecting a year later on the decline in membership, Juan González wrote in *Palante*: "Many problems developed inside the Young Lords Party. . . . Offices closed. *Palante* . . . was almost never found in the street. . . . The Party would start a program, then drop it. . . . The Party was thrown off its course . . . and leaders and members became impatient when the problems mounted . . . and they wanted to quickly change things or escape."[84]

The disorientation that befell the Young Lords was certainly exacerbated by the Central Committee's own precipitous decisions, but the broader movement itself was experiencing decline. During a Young Lords interview conducted in November 1971 by the *Berkeley Tribe*, the interviewer identified lower alternative newspaper runs and protest activity as a trend "universal to the movement." In an interview, Juan González acknowledges that "there's a big struggle going on now in all the societies of the world. The question is, is the revolutionary movement going to become a real revolutionary movement or is it going to die away?"[85] Here, both interviewer and interviewee acknowledge that organizational capacities are not what they were a year before and that demonstrations are much smaller. Yet they attributed the downtick in activism not to broader, objective social forces but to the temporary retreat from public life of the movement's major organizations. These groups were in retreat, immersed in political debates about how society would be transformed in a revolutionary situation and "who's going to lead it, and what forms of struggle are going to be used. Whether it's going to be urban guerrilla warfare or mass mobilization or insurrections: what class bases are going to be the basis upon which to build."[86] But radicals were confusing the high-stakes frenzy produced by violent government repression against them with the advent of revolutionary consciousness among the masses.

The period must have been difficult to read politically. In the United States, in the late 1960s, mass urban rebellions had swept through dozens of cities; many young workers who had been politicized by the civil rights and black power movements were engaged in strike actions; rebellion was visible in the most regimented institutions of society, in the military and the prisons; the nation's standing as a world superpower appeared to have been irreparably damaged by a people's guerrilla army in Vietnam; and decolonization movements seemed to be raging in Palestine, Angola, Mozambique, and Guinea-Bissau, among others. But after almost two decades of sustained social conflict and social movements, the United States was entering a period of conservative backlash.

For its part, in preparation for what they saw as the coming revolution, the Young Lords had begun to focus some of their organizing efforts on the working class. In late 1971, the Young Lords ceased wearing field jackets and marching in formation at demonstrations. They now reasoned that their paramilitary style encouraged many people to "stand on the sidelines and watch us with all the fancy steps and stuff" rather than join them.

In October 1971, Central Committee member Pablo "Yoruba" Guzmán formed part of a delegation of over seventy American radicals who traveled to China. The delegates included Elaine Brown, Huey P. Newton, and Robert Bay of the Black Panthers and members of the Black Workers Congress, the American Friends Service Committee, and the Maoist group Revolutionary Union (RU). They met with a variety of Chinese communist leaders in government and leading activists in different areas of life. One of the government officials challenged Guzmán on the organization's emphasis on the powerless lumpenproletariat and on the organization's decision to deploy its efforts in Puerto Rico; they argued that a mainland organization could not easily launch or lead an independence struggle in a territory with which it shared a cultural heritage but not a direct, lived experience.

Following his return from China in November, Guzmán disseminated the critiques of the Chinese in a private meeting of select Young Lord cadre and a group known as the national staff—a layer of leaders secondary to the Central Committee who could be called upon to replace members of the committee in case of an emergency.[87] The timing of the meeting was intentional. It took place during one of Juan González's trips to Puerto Rico. Guzmán wanted to be able to influence those in attendance without the potential interference of González. After the meeting, Guzmán and his supporters identified their efforts as a rectification program, a vehicle for the organization to redefine and reconsider its political orientation and line of march. It gained adherents quickly and won the ear of two other members of the Central Committee, David Perez and

Juan "Fi" Ortiz. Guzmán was articulating a political explanation for what many already sensed: that the efforts in Puerto Rico were counterproductive. When González returned from Puerto Rico, he found an organization on the brink of redirecting its efforts back toward mainland activism. According to González, "Of course, when Gloria heard about it she got pissed off. And I was pissed off because nobody had talked to us about it."[88] Although González was one of the strongest political thinkers in the organization, after his marriage to Fontanez, who joined the Central Committee shortly after Felipe Luciano's demotion, González seemed increasingly to elevate party discipline and form.

Guzmán's call to return to the organization's roots made clear what many realized but were hesitant to say: since the move to Puerto Rico, most had succumbed to Gloria's will. Fontanez used political moralism to steer the organization. Ramon Morales remembers that "the clever manipulator" was "more Maoist than Mao." As a female worker in the healthcare industry, she turned her "proletarian" experience into the standard of revolutionary purity. She held alleged political weaknesses over the heads of her targets, including Juan González. With a carrot and stick (not to mention members' honest commitment), she coerced behavior and achieved her aims. Those who couldn't be controlled were demonized. From its inception, the organization had had its share of centralization. But the group had enjoyed an open political culture during its first two years. The cadre was encouraged to read a wide range of literature and raise disagreements. "The idea was that if you feel a certain way, don't keep it under the cap because it's not the main view," Colón remembers. "We were encouraged to study, come back, wage ideological struggle, that's what we called it, and battle for your idea. That was a real enlightening thing for so many of us. . . . [T]o develop yourself, even if that meant you could be in opposition with someone who you might have thought was a big shot."[89]

During that early period, the centralized leadership of the Young Lords was balanced out by the vibrancy and dynamism of the movement, which retained a mass character through the end of 1970. The possibilities for disagreement, and for input from all members of the group, reflected the sense of great possibility within the movement as a whole.

By contrast, after the New York branch offices were closed down in summer 1971, according to Colón and others, the Young Lords became gradually more dogmatic and rigid in their political outlook. Late 1960s radicals had failed to leverage the kind of power necessary to fundamentally change society, and as demoralization set in, the movements lost steam. This trend, combined with the growing pace of government repression, atomized and isolated groups like the Young Lords and encouraged paranoia in their ranks. As the mass base of the movement declined, the Young Lords' hypercentralized decision-making structure made dominant the political perspectives of a very small number of highly committed people who misread the period politically. For example, although someone such as González agreed that movement activity was on the decline, he, like other experienced leaders, believed that the downturn would be short-lived and that continued struggle was on the horizon. At a moment when the movements were most in need of critical assessment, debate and discussion were sacrificed for a greater insistence on party discipline and on not deviating from the party line.

Despite support for a shift back to the mainland, González's respected standing in the organization allowed him to stem the influence of Guzmán and his supporters: "I was able to win . . . David, and . . . we basically went back . . . to Fi and to the national staff, which played a bigger role at that time—Iris, Richie Perez, Juan Ramos, and Carmen Cruz. And we were able to win the majority of the national staff and the rest of the Central Committee to stop that."[90] Guzmán's clandestine meeting sought to win a critical mass over to his critique in advance of González's return. The failure of his plan, even though it had considerable support, exemplifies the eroded confidence of the group's base; for most Young Lords, party discipline and loyalty to and trust in the highest-ranking member of the Central Committee—the minister of defense—trumped a sober assessment of the organization's work.

For failing to raise his disagreement through the proper channels, Guzmán was suspended from the Central Committee for a couple of months. In the months to come, he and his partner, Iris Morales, would be transferred to Philadelphia to replace national staff member Juan Ramos, who, together with Central Committee member Juan "Fi" Ortiz, was sent to Puerto Rico to shore up the Young Lords' precarious efforts on the island. There they joined Gloria Fontanez, along with approximately thirty Young Lords, among them some new recruits, who were by now organizing on the island.

Although Guzmán lost his argument against organizing in Puerto Rico, the Young Lords absorbed other elements of his trip to China. During the six-week trip, Guzmán had met and developed a relationship with one of the leading members of the Maoist RU, Donald Herbert Wright. The RU had emerged out of heated ideological debates within SDS in 1968 and 1969 over the direction of the movement. The RU supported building a Marxist-Leninist organization rooted in local workplaces, with an eye toward building a national network of similar collectives.[91] According to Fontanez, Wright's friendship with Guzmán had multiple motivations: "During the China trip, Donald started to say I want to meet Gloria Fontanez; I want to meet her, I want to meet her. . . . So Yoruba arranged a meeting between me and Don at a party." That party took place in the early months of 1972.[92] The two started an affair soon thereafter, which, combined with the YLP's increasing attempt to implement a working-class perspective, accelerated the political influence of the RU on the organization.

Speaking in an interview with *Liberation News Service* in February 1972, Guzmán explained that the Young Lords came out of the working class, yet "up until this point . . . the people [who came around and] who were working had to quit their jobs to be in the Party."[93] But as the emphasis on mass organizations continued, now many of its members were gearing up to take jobs in factories within major industries. They expected that the shift would offer stability to the organization and counteract the youthful adventurism of the past. Once again they envisioned themselves as redeemers of the ideas their working-class families had bequeathed to them, but which they rejected when they adopted a lumpen orientation: "We all come from working-class families, and when we came into the Party we left them. [But] we realized that our families had helped build part of this country and . . . had instilled in us some ideas we had discarded. Patience, [and the notion] that this is a protracted struggle and that . . . life is protracted." Unwilling to abandon their lumpen work entirely, they initiated an oral history program, "going back three generations in some cases [to understand] how people arrived at the thing of being lumpen." In other words they sought to explore the process by which individual people of color living in urban centers became part of a poor marginal class detached from the formal economy.[94]

In the winter of 1972, the organization launched a forty-day course of Marxist study. The course was held in daily six-hour shifts that could be taken in either the daytime or evening. During the course, members of the Young Lords read and discussed Marxist classics, including Marx's theory of alienation in *Economic and Philosophic Manuscripts of 1844*, *Capital*, *Anti-Duhring*, and *The Poverty of Philosophy*, as well as Lenin's *State and Revolution* and *What Is to Be Done?*, among others.[95] The relationships between mass organizations and revolutionary communist parties, and between the revolutionary party and the working class in previous revolutionary moments, were among the major questions explored in the intensive study. In the context of a group that was increasingly disconnected from real-world events, this forty-day course of study further isolated the organization from reality. Spending so much time studying, sequestered from the world, under pressure to prove one's revolutionary commitment, encouraged cult-like behavior. This was also fertile ground for COINTELPRO.

In June 1972, a month before the First Party Congress, the Central Committee published a special issue of *Palante* titled *Faction Leaves Young Lords Party*, claiming that national staff member Juan Ramos and Central Committee member Juan "Fi" Ortiz, as well as several others, had "abandoned the Party's work in Puerto Rico." After a few months on the ground in Puerto Rico, Ramos and Ortiz and a few other members had attempted to make the point that the work on the island was futile with the Central Committee—to no avail. Not unlike Guzmán after his trip to China, they argued that U.S. imperialism was but a particular feature of a more general conflict in the United States, at the center of which was the class struggle between the U.S. ruling class and its multinational proletariat. From this understanding they concluded that Puerto Rican workers living in the United States should devote their time to struggles in the United States and not to the national liberation movement in Puerto Rico. Fontanez, who was back on the mainland when the critique was launched, perceived the petition for a shift in perspective as a declaration of war. In response, she took the first flight back to Puerto Rico and, flanked by YLP security, barged into the home where the Young Lords lived collectively on the island.[96] There she denounced Ramos's contingent for circumventing the authority of the Central Committee and for factional activity that advanced a political perspective different from that established by the Central Committee in its retreat a year earlier. Although there had been no membership-wide meeting to debate that shift in political perspective, Fontanez implied that the organization had consented to the move and therefore Ramos's contingent was in violation of democratic centralism. At the end of a long fight in the middle of the night, Ramos, Ortiz, and their supporters were thrown out on the street.

Back in the United States, the special edition of *Palante* was a scathing, personal attack on Ramos and his followers that denounced them as a "faction" bent on inciting conflict and dividing the party. The special edition also accused them of lazy dilettante behavior and caring more about their middle-class aspirations than the revolutionary struggle. This kind of public airing of hostilities in *Palante*, against leading members of the organization, was a clear sign that the leadership of the Young Lords was in crisis. COINTELPRO certainly had its hand in fueling bitter demonization campaigns like these. But as a matter of course, Fontanez had long been ruthless with those who challenged her authority. In between highly charged barbs filled with moralistic accusations, the Central Committee now adopted Guzmán's views and critique of the path the organization had taken. The Central Committee wrote that "as our Chinese comrades have pointed out the major conflict in the world today is [that] of oppressed nations against imperialists." Therefore, "the primary duty of workers in the U.S. is to support national liberation struggles against U.S. Imperialism."[97] For their differing political perspective, these members of the Young Lords were branded "enemies of the people." Never mind that this was a misapplication of the term Mao Tse-tung used to characterize counterrevolutionary forces in a revolutionary situation, "the social forces and groups which . . . are hostile to or sabotage socialist construction."[98]

The cadre on the mainland was not involved in the decision to publish these accounts and was shocked to see the special edition of *Palante*.[99] According to Gilbert Colón,

[The organization started] demonizing people who were in opposition. . . .
When that first happened I felt very pissed off, because how are all these
people who were comrades yesterday . . . enemies today? . . . That didn't sit
well with me. . . . I mean I knew these people, I partied with these people,
I love these people, and now you're telling me don't associate with them,
and that was the first inkling of what was to come later on. When [those
Young Lords] argued that the branch in Puerto Rico needed to be shut
down because we were wrong in our perspective—that way they were
dealt with . . . they were treated terribly.[100]

Not long after the Ramos contingent had been expelled on charges of breaking
rank and sowing dissent, the YLP once again adopted the perspective of the
demonized "faction." In July 1972, the Central Committee held the organization's first and last congress, which it called the Young Lords Party Congress.
There Gloria Fontanez became the singular leading person within the Central
Committee and announced that the Young Lords were closing their operations
in Puerto Rico, and in line with their shift toward organizing among workers at
the point of production, the Young Lords would also change their name to the
Puerto Rican Revolutionary Worker's Organization (PRRWO). Approximately
200 Young Lords were present at the conference—that was now the approxi-
mate number of its active membership—a steep decline from its approximately
1,000 members a year earlier. Led by Fontanez, the congress was a public event
intended to showcase the viability of the Young Lords within the Puerto Rican
Left on the U.S. mainland. Given both its successes in stimulating a resurgence
of radical Puerto Rican activism and its public disagreements, particularly during the denunciation of the Ramos faction, the Young Lords' congress attracted
many organizations within the broader left movement. Some were there to witness the Young Lords' political spectacle, while others fought to capitalize on
the audience that the Young Lords would surely attract to broker partnerships
with different groups that might lead to greater political influence. Missing was
the open and democratic debate, discussion, and assessment of earlier years.

Trapped in an Ivory Tower

The PRRWO hobbled along with smaller numbers and a greater emphasis on
study circles. The Young Lords Party Congress was, however, an important
precursor to a meeting called by the *Guardian* newspaper less than a year later,
on March 23, 1973, titled "What Road to Building a New Communist Party?" Its
"goals were greater clarity on . . . the building of a new party . . . [and] a higher
level of unity among the New Marxist-Leninist forces."[101] The most important groups present included representatives of the Black Workers Congress,

I Wor Kuen, and the RU, the ideological counterparts to some degree of the PRRWO, which gave solidarity greetings. At that conference, the PRRWO announced preparations for the formation of the National Liaison Committee (NLC), conceived as the organizational embryo of a future revolutionary party made up of representatives of these organizations. According to González, the formation of the NLC meant that "we agreed that we were all Maoist, and that our long-term goal was to unite into one organization to create a new communist party. . . . It was going to take time to get there because we were different organizations, with different leaderships, but that was the long-term goal. As PRRWO, we understood that Puerto Ricans in the United States were a national minority, but that the main focus of the group should be to organize industrial workers. So we not only went to work in factories, we went to work in factories in major industries."[102]

With the goal of building a revolutionary flank within the labor movement, the new PRRWO continued to work in New York's public hospitals and to address the onslaught of municipal budgetary cuts in social spending. Like some other Marxist organizations, PRRWO also sent members to Eagle Electric in Queens, which employed 25,000 workers, and to two factories in Brooklyn, Leviton and Chrome, specializing in light switches and chrome plating production, respectively; others were sent to Detroit and Chicago.[103]

By the time of the *Guardian*-sponsored forum in 1973, Juan González's relationship with Gloria Fontanez was over. Now accused of petit bourgeois tendencies by the Central Committee under Fontanez's leadership, González was demoted and transferred to Philadelphia. Shortly thereafter, Fontanez married Don Wright of the RU. Surveillance files note a feature of Fontanez's character consistent with her conduct in the Young Lords, and later PRRWO. The source reported, among other things, that Fontanez's "marriage to Wright was a power play to increase her influence with the movement and with RU."[104]

Developments occurred alongside the advent of a deep economic recession and a growing effort by conservatives in mainstream politics to roll back the gains of the 1960s. The times, to say the least, were politically confusing. Many movement activists sought to embrace a Marxist analysis of the world, and clandestine activity, especially among proponents of Puerto Rican independence, was growing, particularly within Armed Revolutionary Independence Movement and Armed Forces of National Liberation. In addition, the attention garnered by the Young Lords' own dramatic activism in the late 1960s encouraged other groups to enlarge their ranks, both on the mainland and in Puerto Rico. In a reversal of the YLP's trajectory, the MPI strengthened its efforts off the island and renamed itself the Puerto Rican Socialist Party at a conference in New York in 1973 that drew 3,000 people.[105] For its part, El Comité, the other mainland Puerto Rican radical group that emerged in New York after the Young Lords, was waging militant campaigns for better housing in what was known as Harlem-ville, the area between 72nd and 145th Streets between Central Park West and Broadway.[106] Nationally, a younger crop of workers emboldened by the black power and antiwar movements attempted but failed to maintain their wages and ward off an employers' offensive against benefits. Their actions, which took the form of wildcat strikes and shop-floor slowdowns, initiated by radical workers' caucuses operating independently of union leadership, soon declined.[107] Even as organizations were losing ground, COINTELPRO was determined to sow discord, distrust, and suspicion.

Despite the PRRWO's continued study of Marxism, its application of dia-lectical materialism for understanding the real world missed the mark. The PRRWO, alongside the New Communist Movement of the time, was not able to foresee the long-term rightward shift that was afoot in American politics. Moreover, PRRWO's attempts at influencing workers at the point of production were without a clear strategy and lacked the deployment of a critical mass of members in a specific industry that might collectively learn the basics of work-place organizing in order to influence a massive number of workers. Much like the Young Lords' experience in Puerto Rico, as novices in labor organizing the PRRWO spread itself thin at the same time that it lacked the experience nec-essary to attempt this latest challenge. In the absence of a clear and long-term political perspective and identification of obtainable goals, the PRRWO tended to romanticize workers rather than assess them as a class with potential, objec-tive power under certain optimal conditions. On the other hand, the PRRWO's increased study of Marxism, separate from real, direct collective engagement in society, led, in the words of Colón, to an "ivory tower" approach to its work. Ideological debate was fetishized among the group's leaders and its members; as these radicals became more conversant in Marxist literature that was still taboo in most of U.S. society, they came to believe that they held the enlightened posi-tion of "knowing what was best for everybody."[108]

At every turn, PRRWO blamed members who expressed critical opinions for the decline in membership of the group. The frustrations of the period were directed inward, even as the leadership was aware of FBI meddling in the life of the organization. The Young Lords' offices were raided by the FBI regularly, and provocateurs were in their midst.[109] Those who were suspected of being agents were purged in show trials that eroded what had been a culture of trust and fraternity. Those who stayed the course were asked to work harder.

Sometime in 1973, Don Wright, by then Gloria Fontanez's husband, became the RU representative in the NLC. The politics he upheld in these meetings turned out to be different from those of the RU. Composed largely of organiza-tions wedded to the fight against national oppression, the NLC had reached consensus on one issue—that black American workers and other workers of color must play a leading role in the coming revolutionary struggle. Because of the systematic use of racism to divide the working class and the persistence of racism in the ranks of white workers, radicals of color posited that a genuine socialist revolution in the United States demanded black working-class leadership. Their slogan was thus "Black Workers Take the Lead." However, Don Wright was misrepresenting the position of the RU. Increasingly, the RU saw revolutionary nationalists' assumption that black workers should lead revolutionary struggle as a barrier to working-class unity. The RU also opposed the busing program in Boston to end racial discrimination in education and what the RU perceived as busing's liberal and assimilationist designs. In so doing, the RU ceded ground to the racism of the anti-busing movement in Boston, which was led by reactionary white Bostonians and their allied politicians.[110] Critical of the RU's growing dismissal of revolutionary nationalism, in 1974 PRRWO broke ties with RU, and RU broke ties with Don Wright. That same year, Fontanez and Wright had a child, and Wright joined PRRWO.

Yet, the dysfunctionality of the PRRWO continued. According to Fontanez,

There was inside the organization a time of darkness that I wish I had not been a part of. Like in the cultural revolution of Mao Tse-tung, we adopted the inquisition methods, the methods of torture, and the methods of real cultural revolution, which was to go after the enemy of the people. If we believed that someone was the enemy of the people, we would go after that person. There were people that were in charge of the security of the organization who were involved, who later on washed their hands and threw it all on me.[111]

But Fontanez was at the center of the growing chaos; as the lead person in the Central Committee, she wielded an enormous amount of power. Throughout her tenure in the organization, she had exploited traditional gender roles to beguile men with status and power. Tragically, her use of fear and desire to control the people around her—as both siren and executioner—flew in the face of women's struggle for equality and respect in the organization. The year 1974 saw the resignations of Juan González, Iris Morales, Pablo Guzmán, David Perez, and others. Those left behind, including Gilbert Colón, Carlito Rovira, Richie Perez, and Hernan "Huracan" Flores, felt profoundly betrayed by those who left. Of the departure of his cousin Pablo Guzmán, Colón explains: "He tells me, 'I'm leaving,' but he doesn't say why. . . . I actually was naive enough to think that he owed an explanation. I got involved in this shit because of you, and now you telling me you leaving and you ain't gonna tell me why. And so I developed this animus against people like him who would just cut out and not say why. That set in my mind this whole attitude that if someone was critical, I would think, 'Oh you're down with them people that cut out.'"[112]

But many who left the PRRWO had done so because they understood that the culture of the organization was irreparably damaged, that open political disagreements were denounced either as individualistic and petit bourgeois or inspired by government provocateurs, and therefore it was impossible to set the organization on a healthier track. Meanwhile, Fontanez's relationship with Wright was a microcosm of the violence that gripped the organization. As she explains, "When I got together and married him . . . I started drinking with him . . . and became addicted." Wright had taken to abusing and torturing Fontanez; Fontanez then deployed the same treatment against dissenters. In 1974, Richie Perez was accused of being an agent and beaten up by PRRWO members on Fontanez's orders. Olguie Robles was held hostage, also on her orders. On another occasion, Fontanez showed up at Huracan's home in the middle of the night, bloodied, with her infant girl, after having been beaten by Wright. She then ordered Huracan and Carlito Rovira to raid Wright's apartment and strip it clean. Although she did not reveal it to the men, she left when she discovered that Wright was an FBI agent.

> I remember coming home, opening up my sofa, and finding a whole slew of rifles and guns that had been put there. . . . We were living on the Lower East Side and I find this notice that says "To All Agents—Re: Subjects," and then it went on, but I froze there. I said, oh my God. So I start looking through tapes that he had, and I put a tape on, and he's talking to me [over the phone] . . . while I was living at my cousin Carmen Cruz's house, and he called me there while he was in Chicago, and he's taping it.[113]

According to Carlito Rovira, David Perez had suspected that Wright was an agent earlier that same year, and prominent members of the RU had similar suspicions.[114] At the time of his death, Donald Herbert Wright, who was nursed by Fontanez's daughter, was employed as a sheriff in the South.

■

Organizations like the Young Lords and the Black Panthers captured the imagination of tens of thousands of people, young and old, in cities across the country and around the world. Although most did not join their ranks, they were inspired by the daring of these groups, their intrepid defiance of power, and their vision of a revolutionary society. These organizations grew because they disciplined and channeled widespread urban discontent wherever they were active. They also propagated revolutionary socialist ideas, theories, and practices—taboo only a decade earlier under McCarthyism—in a language and style that made them popular in communities of color across the country. These organizations came into being because of the tenacity and talents of their members, but also because of the widespread, leftward shift in consciousness that took place in the second half of the decade throughout the world, fueled in part by national independence wars or decolonization struggles in Vietnam, Algeria, Palestine, Kenya, and, later, Angola, Mozambique, and beyond. Both organizations mushroomed during and immediately after the uprisings of 1968. The Vietnamese set the tone during that year's Tet Offensive. Mass student protests followed, in some cases joined by workers, in Rome, Madrid, Paris, Belgrade, Prague, Mexico City, Pakistan, Chicago, and on U.S. college campuses. Another wave of urban rebellions swept through the country that year following Martin Luther King's assassination.

The Black Panthers and Young Lords, therefore, amplified their revolutionary dreams and practices during a period of global revolutionary awakening, but also at a moment when the United States faced its greatest political challenge internationally. In Asia, Vietnamese guerrillas dealt a blow to American hegemony during the Tet Offensive, both militarily and in terms of its political symbolism. Back home, black revolutionaries—the majority descendants of southern slaves—were exposing American capitalism from the inside. Shortly thereafter, the mainland-born children of America's last colony, Puerto Rico, followed suit. These threats were more symbolic than real, but they held power because they were spearheaded by the most demeaned and oppressed sectors of U.S. society. They were an affront that American power would not abide, and during those same years, J. Edgar Hoover set out to destroy these organizations. The volume of Young Lords' COINTELPRO documents (and agents assigned to disrupt the organization) is dizzying. The Young Lords' violent collapse, the unforgiving enmity and distrust sowed within its ranks, and the trauma inflicted on its members are largely products of the FBI's systematic campaign to destroy this particular section of the New Left.

Even when informants reported that the group was financially bankrupt, structurally decimated, and its members demoralized and embattled, surveillance and disruption continued unabated. It seemed that COINTELPRO wanted to ensure the organization's implosion and an erasure of its history fueled by the shame of comrades turning on each other.

But violent government repression alone did not destroy the Young Lords. From the moment of its inception, government agents were operating within the organization, documenting its campaigns, and attempting to wreak havoc within it. But the Young Lords' dynamism, the connection of its practice and politics to communities and to the streets during its two most productive years, and the still large-scale character of the movement in 1969 and 1970 likely intimidated agents even as it motivated the FBI to continue its disruptive work.

The Young Lords' disconnection from the grassroots beginning in 1971, but also the broader movement's decline, made the organization more vulnerable to COINTELPRO disruption than before. These same factors also made it vulnerable to the machinations of authoritarian individuals.

The YLP's political inexperience, the difficulties it faced when it came to reading the political moment in which it was operating, and its shift to a dogmatic embrace of the particular kind of "Marxism-Leninism" that was increasingly popular in the New Left were all used by COINTELPRO to bring about its demise.

Other factors contributed to the organization's decline. The YLP's early formulations around membership requirements—that members of the organization had to be Young Lords "twenty-five hours a day"—had by default excluded even highly motivated working people with jobs and family responsibilities. Although the organization established this rule, in part, as a means of disciplining the often highly undisciplined lumpen elements it attracted, the policy could potentially disconnect the group from the majority of Puerto Ricans living in New York. By ensuring that the group would likely only attract die-hard activists and lumpen elements, the policy fed a particular kind of activism that tended to detach it from social reality, especially when the group's outward-looking campaigns began to ebb. In many ways, the Young Lords reflected, but also attempted to overcome, a series of characteristics common among a wide variety of late 1960s radicals who were die-hard, often ruled by the impatience of youth and a belief in the possibility of delivering freedom to "the people." And like many of these groups, the Young Lords became more entrenched in these politics during periods of organizational stagnation, especially as the movement seemed to be dying down.

The Young Lords' move to Puerto Rico can be traced to interrelated, long-standing developments both internal and external to the organization. Among the immediate internal causes of the move was the devastating impact of Julio Roldán's death. As discussed in the previous chapter, the suspicions surrounding the death evoked the organization's instincts toward paranoia. Disillusioned by growing repression of the Left and the Black Panther Party split, the group's membership suffered unprocessed trauma and were ill equipped to challenge those who embraced a narrower conception of nationalism than the organization had previously espoused. And Felipe Luciano, who would have unequivocally challenged the position, was gone. Although the organization proposed a plan for community engagement in the mainland, the move drained and stretched its resources, making its mass work impossible to carry out by an exhausted and disoriented membership with unspoken reservations about the new perspective.

The Young Lords' pursuit of revolution in greener pastures in Puerto Rico was fueled, in part, by a political misassessment of the moment. Many movement activists believed that revolution was around the corner, but conservative restoration had been under way in the United States since the 1960s.

The move was precipitous and fueled by the assumption, held by a section of the Young Lords' leadership, that revolutionary potential was about will, with little real regard for social conditions or the level of political consciousness in society. Political disorientation, isolation from the masses, and its notion of the revolutionary process—that sheer will, dedication, and hard work among small groups rather than classes form the motor force of change—combined with youthful impatience, unseated the Young Lords from their earlier place of influence.[115]

For the Young Lords, whose heritage allowed them to identify and imagine a colonial nation to which they belonged, forsaking the opportunity of launching their own liberation project during this period of heightened political fervor would have taken hard, honest self-assessment and reflection. Amid widespread revolt in Third World nations, American radicals began to argue that struggles originating in the Third World were the vanguard of world revolution, and they were. The task of developing a revolutionary praxis among nonrevolutionary workers in the heart of empire was, however, a daunting challenge. After having given their lives, hearts, and souls to the movement, many individual American radicals were lured by the promise of revolution abroad, and some abandoned domestic struggles for those with greater perceived revolutionary potential in the Third World.[116] The Young Lords' decision to restructure the organization and take on the task of building an independence movement in Puerto Rico, a place whose local politics they knew very little about and whose language many members did not speak, was similarly influenced by the idealization of the Third World.

In reorienting the group to fight for Puerto Rican independence on the island itself, the Central Committee did not consider the absence at that time of a mass movement with that demand. The belief that the Young Lords could somehow leap over their organizational weaknesses and transform themselves into the revolutionary leaders that could free Puerto Rico contradicted the Central Committee's assessment of itself. In the retreat documents, YLP leadership was accurate about the organization's deficits. The organization's membership had grown by leaps and bounds in less than two years. Its infrastructure needed reinforcement and its cadre political training. The Central Committee, nevertheless, proposed a program that would further weaken and overstretch the organization. Felipe Luciano, the person who, along with others, might have successfully challenged the proposal, was gone. The organization did not possess a critical number of politically courageous and confident cadre capable of forcing an organization-wide debate about the move. One who attempted it, Carlos Aponte, paid a heavy price.

The consequences of hypercentralized political assessment and decision making were felt immediately in the organization. Among newer and less-experienced members, a culture of passivity and a tendency to be led uncritically took the place of any clear understanding of or commitment to political strategy. Cadre did not put up a fight, nor did it stand up for those with experience who challenged the leadership's perspective. Those who spoke up fell into disfavor or were charged with violating the tenets of democratic centralism. Disgruntled and demoralized by the organization's new direction, the first wave of Young Lords left the organization in January 1971. Others who believed they could influence the direction of the organization for which they had sacrificed encountered deeper hostility by a leadership that continued to clamp down on open debate and discussion. Vocal members, like Carlos Aponte among others, were wrongly accused of being government agents with no evidence and driven out of the organization.

Finally, the long-term, internal causes of the shift in the organization can be traced to the contradictions inherent in the political ideas that were hegemonic on the Left and that the YLP was increasingly adopting.[117] Commonly referred to as Maoism or "Mao Zedong thought," the political framework and revolutionary theories embraced by many in this period favored authoritarian structures that lacked democratic debate and decision making. Much of what became known as Maoist thought was also contradictory. For example, while Maoism promoted international working-class solidarity and a socialist movement rhetorically, Mao's government had a highly nationalist outlook and promoted alliances with many decidedly nonsocialist rulers, which in the early 1970s came to include even Richard Nixon. Thus, while Maoist-leaning radicals embraced the notion of revolution and were self-proclaimed socialists, they were equivocal about the kind of revolutionary process they espoused in practice.

Moreover, for Maoists, the revolutionary process depended more on the power of political will than on favorable material conditions, as Marxists had traditionally argued. Thus, U.S.-based Maoists embraced missionary-like political work among the people as a major catalyst of revolution, rather than mass popular insurrection. The slogan "serve the people," popularized by the BPP, was an extension of this logic, whose premise decreed that through dedicated service, the cadre of a revolutionary group could deliver a better world to "the people" in the here and now as well as in the socialist future. In the United States, this kind of prefigurative action inspired, disciplined, and activated many, but in the absence of other parallel initiatives involving broader sectors of the population as actors themselves, the survival programs were limited. The Young Lords' immense success during its early years was due to its combination of survival programs and militant campaigns that involved thousands of others and paralyzed sectors of the city. Unique for its time, the YLP's management and artful use of media also amplified its influence beyond its numbers.

However, under the narrow "serve the people" framework, "the people" did not have to be the subject of history but could be liberated by a dedicated group of enlightened revolutionaries. When the mass character of the movement declined, the logic of this politics also fueled revolutionary activities on the opposite end of the spectrum: that notion that small, isolated groups might create revolutionary change. In the United States, where radicals were learning what it meant to build a revolutionary organization under the pressures and in the heat of struggle, this paradoxical combination of options led to political confusion, organizational splits, and decline. COINTELPRO took advantage of all of this. Social isolation turned the organization moralistic and evangelical about their project. In the context of growing cult-like behavior in PRRWO, COINTELPRO threw the devil in the mix—the sense that members had to be purged and excommunicated for disobeying what by then had become scripture. The very language used by their brand of sectarian politics, the purging of members as "enemies of the people," fit in perfectly with COINTELPRO designs.

Influenced by COINTELPRO, narrow nationalist currents, and authoritarian figures like Gloria Fontanez and her influence on key members, the Young Lords made a wrong and costly political turn in 1971. Before then, however, the Young Lords created a profoundly effective, beloved, and exciting socialist organization that fueled the power of the New Left and made a lasting impression on U.S. consciousness and history.

CODA

Beware of Movements

Mass demographic transfers portend epic change.

In 2006, Mexicans and others from Latin America took to the streets of cities across the United States in the millions to protest racism, repression, exploitation, and workplace abuse. The vast settlement of these migrants happened over the course of at least two decades beginning in the 1980s. Like Puerto Ricans in 1947, they had been pushed out of their countries by the economic devastation wrought by structural adjustment, the North American Free Trade Agreement, and other U.S.-led economic policies. When they finally came out of the shadows to claim their humanity, the magnitude of their strikes and demonstrations shocked the country. No "American" saw them coming.[1]

The changes wrought by World War II and by U.S.-led postwar global restructuring produced similar tectonic shifts that reorganized the world. Domestically, the mass demographic transfer these shifts produced among people of color, from countryside to city, laid the seeds of unanticipated developments—like the rise of the civil rights, black power, and women's movements of the 1960s. The last thing the U.S. captains of postwar global restructuring imagined was that Operation Bootstrap's escape valve—migration—would lead to the rise, on the U.S. mainland, of a movement to free America's major colony and that it would be fiercely led not by the people of the island but by the Americanized children of the Puerto Rican migration and the Puerto Rican diaspora.

Puerto Ricans migrated into the civil rights movement and were radicalized by the antiwar, black power, women's, and gay liberation movements.

But the social location of the children of the Puerto Rican migration—as translators and cultural interlocutors between their parents and America's hostile bureaucracies—gave them a second sight. Combined with their experience of discrimination in the public schools and with police, these experiences established the emotional foundation for the radicalization of those who became Young Lords and the tens of thousands who identified with them.

Triumphant rally in South Bronx, 1970. (Photograph by Luis C. Garza)

Why the Fuss?

The story of the Young Lords is intoxicating to many because it resonates with the suffering and aspirations of millions of young people who are outsiders in America. Like the children of NAFTA, who migrated from Mexico and other parts of the Caribbean and Latin America in the 1980s and 1990s, the Young Lords also underwent the crucible of migration as children following Operation Bootstrap. They inspired their generation, and they inspire today because they gave their generation the language and analysis to make sense of the trauma produced by the large-scale economic and political forces that massively displaced their parents from their homeland. They also helped their peers understand their parents' place in American society as exploited, racialized, colonial people and the structural barriers they faced in an increasingly deindustrialized and dilapidated city. In their quest, they discovered and asserted in public discourse the distinctiveness of their identity in the United States. For these reasons, the Young Lords' legacy speaks to a cross-section of American youth.

Like migrants today, Puerto Ricans were blamed for the problems of American society.

Once upon a time, Puerto Ricans, like black Americans, formed part of this country's superexploited working class. Like Mexicans and other people from Latin America today, they were heavily concentrated in the lowest-paid, dirtiest, and most precarious and dangerous sectors of the economy. Seventy percent were employed in hospitals, restaurants, and the hotel trades. Their social station informed the dominant narratives about them in public discourse. As historian Barbara Fields aptly observes in her discussion of race ideology, "People are more readily perceived as inferior by nature when they are already seen as oppressed."[2] Not surprisingly, Puerto Ricans were perceived both as welfare dependents, knife-wielding criminals, and junkies on the one hand and as mild-mannered people who could be pushed around on the other.

Like the Black Panthers, the Young Lords changed this trope. Their intrepid organizing campaigns, literature, bold political analysis, and media savvy reclaimed the dignity of New York's hardest-working and most exploited workers and replaced stereotypes with powerful images of radical, strategic, and articulate militancy. As Barry Gottehrer, Mayor Lindsay's assistant, told me in an interview, the Young Lords couldn't be placated with antipoverty money, and you couldn't mess with them either. They took over a church *and* a hospital and made out like bandits on the evening news.

Growing fascination with the Young Lords Party is also rooted in its dramatic, smart, even humorous campaigns and strategic use of media. The party's inventive protests made even its haters take a second look; it made known its collective persona, built its ranks and reputation, and broadened support for its causes. The Young Lords did the work of black Twitter in the streets.

They inspire because they defied major social taboos. They denounced their parents' attempts to sever, in the public sphere, any associations between Puerto Ricans and black Americans. But the Young Lords did more. They embraced the politics of the most persecuted and maligned black power group of the 1960s and adopted its organizational model. Undeterred by fear, and determined in their hearts to right the wrongs of society, they barreled into a relationship with the "least of these"—the Black Panther Party. Although they didn't know it at the time, they were making common cause with the era's most iconic organization.

They were also determined to bring into the light of day conversations that had once been confined to hushed whispers among Puerto Ricans and other Latinos. They denounced antiblack racism in Puerto Rico and Latin America and theorized its root causes. They also challenged machismo, the oppressive character of the family, and the virginal discourse of the church. Like radicals before them, the women of the organization theorized "intersectionality" before it became a thing. At the same time, they were attentive to the primacy of class structures and grounded their analysis of gender inequality in a structural critique of the family, capitalism, and colonialism. Like most radicals active across the world since the second half of the nineteenth century, the Young Lords studied Marxism and identified socialism as an alternative to capitalism.

Puerto Ricans suffered violent political repression of their independence movement in the 1940s and 1950s. The message from authorities was clear: political talk could end with imprisonment or death. The Young Lords alongside others broke through the taboo of political activity; they reclaimed the Puerto Rican flag, restored its powerful cultural meaning, and linked it once again to the struggle for independence.

The Young Lords had their finger on the pulse not just of the moment but also of the future. They built a profoundly multiethnic movement: approximately 25 percent of their members were black American, and between 5 and 8 percent were non–Puerto Rican Latinxs, among them Cubans, Dominicans, Mexicans, Panamanians, and Colombians. The Young Lords' membership reflected the demographic character of a postmodern city, of which New York and Los Angeles are today the best expressions.

The Young Lords were among the first to use the term "Latino" based on common currents in the history and politics of the people of Latin America and their mass displacement from their homelands as a result of U.S. economic and imperial policies on that continent.

So What?

But what of their short-lived existence? As history shows, movements are not measured by duration. As the Russian revolutionary V. I. Lenin put it, "There are decades where nothing happens; and there are weeks where decades happen." Social movements and their organizations are not measured temporally but in terms of impact and the extent to which they shift consciousness, public debate, what's accepted, and how we live.

At its height of active membership, the Young Lords had 1,000 members. Over the course of its life, however, approximately 3,000 people joined the Party (or its other organizational iterations) across the northeast corridor.

The Young Lords' dizzying pace of organizing won reforms. Perhaps the group's most famous acts, their audacious garbage-dumping protests, pressured city hall to find solutions to the citywide crisis of sanitation and forced the Sanitation Department to conduct regular neighborhood garbage pickups in East Harlem and beyond. A quieter victory was the group's door-to-door campaign to test children for lead poisoning in the tenements of East Harlem, which Young Lords conducted alongside medical personnel. The *American Journal of*

Public Health took note. It credited Young Lord activism with pressuring city hall to finally pass New York's anti-lead-poisoning legislation in the early 1970s. The group was also the architect of the famed eleven-day occupation of an East Harlem church, which gave Puerto Ricans a big coming-out party in New York. It was there that they anchored a renaissance in Puerto Rican art and reclaimed the Afro-Taino roots of their culture. Even Stan Lee, creator of Marvel Comics' beloved characters, took note. In his *Amazing Adventures: The Inhumans and the Black Widow*, the characters "The Young Warriors" bear a striking resemblance to the Young Lords. In the series, the Young Warriors convince the Black Widow—previously a major KGB villain, now a hero in the fight against late sixties urban inequalities—that taking over an East Harlem building to provide free breakfasts for children is a noble cause.

Perhaps the most dramatic of Young Lords' campaigns was the twelve-hour occupation of the ailing Lincoln Hospital in the South Bronx. Occupied with the blessing of community groups and a radical flank of doctors and residents, the action led to the creation of one of the principal acupuncture drug treatment centers in the Western world and the construction of a new hospital building (which had been promised ten years earlier), among other victories. They believed that human rights are most important when we are most vulnerable and most human—when we are sick—and demanded free healthcare for all. In the context of the city's larger, decentralized health-rights movement, they also drafted the first-known patient bill of rights in collaboration with hospital workers and medical staff at Lincoln.

The Young Lords exposed police brutality and fought police repression in the streets. And in October 1970, following the death of one of their own in the infamous New York City jail known as the Tombs, the Young Lords reoccupied the East Harlem church, this time with firearms. They homed in on the deplorable conditions of the city's jails and put forward demands for prisoners' rights. Their action came one year before the Attica rebellion and immediately after a series of prisoners' rebellions across the city, which Mayor John V. Lindsay identified as the most difficult crisis of his tenure. The Young Lords' occupation compelled the mayor to initiate the city's first municipal investigation of the arrest of a citizen and of the prison conditions that led to his death. Ahead of their time, they formed part of the era's prisoner's rights movement and exposed imprisonment as a tool of repression against radicals, the poor, the black, and the brown.

Although much of the 1960s has been primarily understood within the framework of discrimination and citizenship rights, the issues around which the Young Lords built a movement reflect the full range of social and economic problems with which the civil rights and black power movements were concerned. This history of the Young Lords highlights the central role of class-based approaches to organizing in the era's most effective campaigns and coalitions.

It demonstrates the ways in which hospitals, schools, prisons, housing, and neighborhoods were focal points of movement activity. Increasingly, movement activists were concerned with finding solutions to problems as pedestrian as garbage collection and the removal of lead paint from tenement walls; fighting urban renewal; and addressing the crises of healthcare and its delivery, social welfare programs, childcare services for poor and working-class mothers, and unemployment.

In their writings on what has become known as the urban crisis, sociologists and historians depict a process that prostrated communities of color in northern cities. In their totality, these campaigns suggest that urban dwellers themselves were among the first to identify, analyze, and launch a fight back against these developments.

And while mainstream discourse does not associate the civil rights or black/ brown power movements with gains beyond those pertaining narrowly to issues of race, campaigns launched by organizations like the Young Lords helped stretch the country's definition of citizenship and democracy. By pressuring local government to solve local neighborhood problems, these radicals established standards of decency in city services for city dwellers that expanded the definition of the common good. Thus, however inchoately, late 1960s radicals articulated and struggled with issues pertaining to a socially and economically egalitarian polity.

What Works?

For today's organizers, the Young Lords offer a wealth of practical lessons.

First and foremost, if your intention is to build a movement that responds to the conditions of real people, there is no substitute for hands-on organizing on the ground and at the local level.

Bold direct action that stops the normal functioning of municipal life captures the attention of media and the public, shifts the terms of political debate, and broadens the public's understanding of social problems. The Young Lords conveyed the consequences, among other things, of the profit motive in healthcare, by putting a human face on the crises generated by government neglect and capitalism and by telling stories. And they used humor to make the sacrilegious sacrosanct.

Organization, political education, and discipline matter. Democratic debate matters, as does political training, which helps raise the caliber of political assessment and analysis in organizations. Prefigurative politics are crucial as well. Organizers who convey through their actions what they envision in their new society will prevail. Meanwhile, the presence of racism, sexism, homophobia, and heteronormativity weakens organizations. Fighting these toxins is difficult but makes organizations stronger. And the Young Lords' often self-critically humorous approach offers a sensible rejoinder to our contemporary cancel cultural. For example, at some point during the first conflict in the People's Church, one Young Lord asked all the men to give their seats to women and children. But when he heard muttering in some quarters and lack of movement in others, he piped up: "And if that's male chauvinism, forget about it." Success comes with its challenges. Managing quick organizational growth is unwieldy, particularly when a group is unprepared.

Trust is key to organizing. Love and politics are both glorious and blinding—establish rules and values around these inevitable human factors. One can't disappear the individual in the struggle for a more egalitarian society. The individual needs to breathe. Dissolving the individual into the group kills critical thinking and creativity and tends toward the cult.

Movements need to connect the local to the national. And if you look closely enough, the local is often connected to the international. But above all, movements must leverage power. While the Young Lords attempted to provide a critique of capitalism, their service-oriented strategy alone, however militant, lacked the muscle necessary to qualitatively affect the deep structural changes taking place in the cities, much less transform society. The kind of change that they espoused would have required linking neighborhood concerns to those articulated by a broader coalition organized around the interests and concerns of the exploited and oppressed of different races and ethnicities.

Although the Young Lords Party had brilliant tactics, the group's long-term political aims were hampered by the poverty of the left tradition in the United States, especially following the expulsion of communists, radicals, and progressives from American institutions during the Red Scare in the 1950s. Absent an influential tradition of left organizing in local communities seeking to connect neighborhood organizing with resistance in the trade unions, the practices and strategies of emerging 1960s radicals like the Young Lords increasingly fell into a vacuum. While the Young Lords launched an impressive course of grassroots campaigns in the late 1960s, the larger radical movement to which they belonged failed to coalesce around a broad campaign calling for wealth redistribution, the mass creation of jobs, and an extensive housing construction initiative. These were fundamental changes, which would have been necessary to alter the structural problems of urban decline and economic and racial inequality. The movement did not leverage the social power required to achieve these radical reforms.

The labor upsurge of the 1970s presented possibilities for a community and labor coalition that might have been capable of enacting significant socioeconomic and political changes. In fact, the Young Lords and many other groups began to organize in workplaces during this period, but their efforts were stymied by the inexperience of the New Left and by the advent of economic recession and conservative restoration, which undermined the mass character of the movement.

Knowing when to retreat from social protest is as important as knowing when to advance a bold political project.

Ironically, with the Young Lords' decision to move to Puerto Rico, the group narrowed its reach and appeal, choosing to organize along lines of ethnicity. In the process, the organization lost a significant number of black American and Latinx members who were not Puerto Rican. Coming at a time of widespread movement exhaustion, increased political repression, and pessimism about the prospect for revolution in the United States, this shift in perspective was also accompanied by an obsession with theoretical purity that was disconnected from a concrete assessment of the social and political conjuncture of the early 1970s. War, recession, and the rise of political conservatism were demoralizing the nation, and the times increasingly called for an organizational perspective suited to a period of retreat from social protests.

The Age of Great Dreams

Imprinted in the Young Lords' evolution from gang to political organization is a powerful story of agency and rebirth. This extraordinary and deliberate political transformation on the part of poor urban youth challenges the dominant historical narrative of radical movements of the 1960s, which features white students, urban rioters, and a narrowly conceived New Left as its major protagonists.

The Young Lords formed part of the New Left—the political, cultural, and intellectual 1960s movement that ended racial segregation, made racism and sexism unpopular, transformed the sociopolitical standing of people of color and women in the United States, challenged heteronormativity, and made the questioning of foreign policy acceptable in U.S. society. Within that movement, the Young Lords, like the Black Panthers, built revolutionary organizations led by people of color that popularized socialism in the United States.

Like other radicals of the time, the Young Lords adapted to the American context the vanguard organizational forms, political strategies, and cultural style of people fighting for self-rule in the Third World. As their various offensives suggest, they forced change by shocking and disabling normal city life. They adapted to urban protest the rhetoric and style of Third World guerrilla warfare. But their adaptations were also influenced by the conditions to which they necessarily had to respond in the U.S. context. While Third World revolutions iconized peasant guerrillas, the Black Panthers and the Young Lords identified the lumpenproletariat as the most revolutionary class in society. The lumpen orientation of late 1960s radicals reflects the deep economic changes taking place in northern cities, where economic restructuring and the flight of industries to the suburbs created a class of permanently unemployed and discouraged young workers—an unprecedented development in modern urban history. In this context, the organizing and politics of radicals like the Young Lords reflected the distinctive social features of the urban environment in which they grew up.

In addition, the vast relocation of white Americans from city to suburb, and the emergence of greater racial segregation in northern cities, influenced the strong nationalist character of urban radical politics. In this environment, the ideal of people of color fighting together with white Americans for change grew more and more difficult to enact, as the daily lives of these populations grew further and further apart. Instead, dramatic action was created by polyglot groups among people of color birthed of the increasingly multiethnic character of the American slum.

The history of the Young Lords is poignant and unique because of what it foreshadowed. The group built a local urban movement around social issues that would become central in public policy debates during the 1980s and 1990s. These include an increasingly intractable healthcare crisis, the neighborhood consequences of deindustrialization and municipal budget cuts, the growing disrepair of American cities, the swelling incarceration of people who could not be employed by urban economies, and an overtly self-interested American hegemony and foreign policy. In many ways, the Young Lords' politics and preoccupations, especially those concerning issues of employment and class stratification, foretold the story of the end of the American Dream, which had always been an elusive prospect for most racialized groups, but which also began to unravel for working- and middle-class white Americans with the long-term economic decline that began with the recession and oil crisis of 1973.

Now What?

Like many of us, the Young Lords had a complicated relationship to this country and lived as hopeful citizens but also strangers to America. Similarly, as children of migration, they are emblematic of the quintessential working-class experience that defines so much of American history and culture. Even today, their concerns mirror those of working people in the United States and around the world. And though their tactics and rhetoric may appear more extreme than most, their deepest desires are ones we can all relate to: decent healthcare, the possibility of dignity in employment, a living wage, responsible city services, and basic economic and social equality. The story of the Young Lords reveals a great deal about the profound victories, but also the pitfalls, of collective action for the common good.

The history of the 1960s continues to be revisited by people of all walks of life because it was the last time our country witnessed a surge of sustained radical movements for social change. I hope this history of the Young Lords will provoke a deeper conversation about that difficult time when the center would not hold—about its triumphs and setbacks as a group of unlikely organizers fought for what they considered the highest aspirations of humanity. Through this work, perhaps a new generation of Americans—and others as well—can find a more nuanced understanding of the significance of community-based class struggle and the complex ways those on the outside expanded our conception of the common good, American democracy, and human liberation.

Acknowledgments

This book has been long in coming.

The late Dr. Manning Marable, founding director of Columbia University's Institute for Research in African American Studies (IRAAS), was the biggest supporter of the book in its first incarnation. IRAAS funded my doctoral studies in the Department of History at Columbia, allowing me to write the first doctoral dissertation on the Young Lords. I thank this groundbreaking scholar and radical public intellectual for his mentorship. I am also grateful to the other members of my committee, whose early critiques of my research helped shape the final manuscript: Elisabeth S. Blackmar, Eric Foner, Robin D. G. Kelley and David Rosner. I am deeply indebted to Barbara Jeanne Fields, whose scholarship has greatly influenced my thinking and writing.

I am ever grateful to Joe William Trotter Jr. and his pioneering Center for African American Studies and the Economy (CAUSE) at Carnegie Mellon University in Pittsburgh. At a moment when I thought I might leave the academy, I was awarded the CAUSE postdoctoral fellowship. Working with Joe restored my faith in the profession. With CAUSE support, I was able to conduct research in Chicago and spend many hours with José "Cha Cha" Jiménez, Omar Lopez, Rory Guerra, Sal del Rivero and many others, learning about the origins of the Young Lords. I am especially thankful to Cha Cha Jiménez. Only a person with such tenacity, leadership, humility, and heart could have led the gang's political transformation. His humanity inspires me.

My chance encounter with the late professor emeritus David P. Demarest at Carnegie Mellon delayed the completion of this book but enriched it immeasurably. He, as well as attorney Martha Conely and concert pianist Bariki Hall, were critical to the work ahead. They encouraged me to visit Mumia Abu-Jamal at SCI Greene, the supermax prison in western Pennsylvania, where he sat on death row. Within two months, I was in a tiny enclosed room, talking intensely to Mumia behind a plexiglass window. Our conversations centered on uncovering the root of a problem. In hundreds of hours of discussion spanning many years, interrupted only by the unnerving clank of a prison gate signaling the end of each visit, we explored the broader history of the sixties and the fifty years of conservative reaction that followed. My mind and life have been profoundly enriched by having Mumia as a colleague, collaborator, and friend. I'd wanted him to read and comment on this manuscript, but the prison authorities thought otherwise. I sent it to him in the weeks before the prisoners' strikes of the summer of 2018, but prison authorities rejected it as a security risk. Since those strikes, the Pennsylvania Department of Corrections has turned correspondence with prisoners into a labrynthine operation and made the mailing of a manuscript nearly impossible.

I am grateful to the inspiring and dynamic people who built the Young Lords in New York, who've welcomed me into their lives and shared so much of their history. The list is long, but I'd like to especially thank Gilbert Colón, a Party soldier who shared his insightful analysis of the period with me over many interview hours. Juan González gave me multiple interviews at key junctures of this project, generously read parts of this manuscript, and commented extensively. Felipe Luciano offered support from the heart and made himself available, including at the last minute for an interview about Denise Oliver-Velez. Denise Oliver-Velez in turn allowed me to interview her over the course of many days in her upstate New York farm, offering spiritual counsel to boot. Mickey Meléndez was sober, straight-up, and kind. Iris Morales was generous and shared an important document with me at an important moment. Carlito Rovira was my biggest cheerleader, answered questions on call, and gave me numerous interviews. Walter Bosque del Rio, Olguie Robles, Gloria Rodriguez, and Minerva Solla have shared their stories and are some of the most powerful women I've met. Ramon Morales was also very generous with his time and insights.

Among the many doctors, attorneys, and supporters of the Lords who gave of their time generously during long interviews, I would like to thank especially the Young Lords lead attorney, Dan Meyers, of the National Lawyers Guild; the late Gilberto Gerena Valentín; Miriam Jiménez; Bella August, a current member of the indefatigable People's Organization for Progress in Newark, N.J.; members of Mayor John V. Lindsay's administration—the late Barry Gottehrer, Sid Davidoff, and Arnie Segarra; Dr. Stephen Levin; Dr. Fitz Mullan; the late Dr. Harold Osborne; the late Dr. Mike Smith; Dr. Bruce Soloway; Dr. Richard Stone; Dr. Ira Goldwasser and Harriet Broekman, who hosted me in Amsterdam; and Charlotte Phillips Fein and Dr. Oliver Fein. Also many thanks to parishioners of the First Spanish United Methodist Church Carmen, Joe, and Marina Pietri and Doña Benita Rodriguez.

Research for this book was supported by the Scholars-in-Residence program at the Schomburg Center for Research in Black Culture. I am grateful to the late Colin A. Palmer and my Schomburg cohort for their insights. I am especially grateful to the research assistant I was assigned, Peter Hobbs—now a filmmaker—who took this project very seriously and found some jewels for inclusion. I'd like also to acknowledge and thank women like Aisha-Adawiya and Diana Lachatanere for their long-standing service to the Schomburg and its highest mission.

At the City University of New York, I was supported by the PSC-CUNY 43 Award, the Eugene M. Lang Junior Faculty Fellowship, the Faculty Fellowship Publication Program, and the latter's exacting senior faculty group leader, the late scholar and activist Peter Kwong.

Funding for this project has been made possible by the Puffin Foundation.

I am ever grateful to my friend Heidi Boghosian, who read countless chapter drafts and remains my wordsmith on call. For reading many drafts and his warm friendship, I'm especially appreciative to Victor Wallis. For their many edits and comments, I am very thankful to Nora Eisenberg, Sándor John, Shannon King, Craig Wilder, and former political prisoner Laura Whitehorn.

For her insights on the book, moral support, and for talking me off the book-ledge on multiple occasions, I thank my dear colleague-friend Jessica Millward.

Jeanne Theoharis, Komozi Woodard, and Dayo F. Gore commented on earlier framings of my work published in their groundbreaking volumes.

Linda Gordon read an earlier draft of this book cover to cover and commented generously. She has been one of the book's greatest champions.

Clarence Taylor, Thomas Desch-Obi, Katherine Pence, and Thomas Heinrich, colleagues in the History Department at Baruch, have been steadfast supporters. For their comments on my work, I am also grateful to Ervand Abrahamian, Charlotte Brooks, Vincent DiGirolamo, Elizabeth Heath, Martina Nguyen, Mark Rice, Andrew Sloin, and Randolph Trumbach. A special thank you, also, to Ana Calero for her indispensable administrative support and elegant work in our department.

As historians, we depend on the meticulous work of a special class of people: research librarians. Their foresight, knowledge, and preservation instincts make our work sing.

This history might not have been written had Suzanne Oboler not introduced me to the story of the Young Lords during my senior year at Brown University. She and the late Francisco Chapman seeded the doctoral work that followed.

David Perry suggested, many moons ago, that this was a UNC Press book. It took me a minute to figure that out. Belatedly, I thank him.

I don't know what I would have done without these three people: UNC Press acquisitions editor Brandon Proia, Undergraduate Mellon Fellow Sandra Riano, and UNC Press editor Jay Mazzocchi. Brandon made publishing this book with UNC a fait accompli. He read, commented generously, and commented some more—multiple times. And then he held my hand throughout the elusive publication production process. At the eleventh hour, when I could not deal with one more errant detail, the quietly powerful Sandra Riano was sent to me by the faeries, or perhaps the orishas. She is everything. And Jay could not have been more meticulous and patient. Thanks also to copyeditor Iza Wojciechowska and especially David Lobenstine for his editorial work on an earlier draft of the manuscript. I am also grateful to Michael Koch for his work and to my student assistants over these years: Priscila Prado, Andrew Sylvester, Laura Szymanski, and Kalin Chow.

In the movement to free Mumia, I found my political family. The rich but grueling work of freeing a political prisoner has enriched my perspective and influenced this book. I am honored to be part of this pantheon of radical agitators: the fearless Pam and Ramona Africa, Mike Africa Jr., Wadiya Jamal, Keith Cook, Frances Goldin, Angela Davis, Vijay Prashad, Cornel West, and, among others, my crew in the Campaign to Bring Mumia Home, including Judith Ackerman, Lucien Baskin, Shirley Belton, Shesheena Bray, Gabriel Bryant, Jeff Camp, Gwen Debrow, Nyle Fort, Kyle Fraser, Basym Hasan, Kelina Jones, Sandy Joy, Malav Kanuga, Juliette Leak, Rebekah McAlister, Natalie Molinari, Gil Obler, Joe and Betsie Piette, Ajamu Sankofa, Sheena Sood, Robyn Spencer, Kevin Steele, Mark Taylor, Imani Vidal, Sophia Williams, and others, too many to name; and in the international movement, including Carolina Saldaña, Claude Guillaumaud, Jacky Hortaut, Michael and Annette Schiffman, and Mireille-Fanon Mendès France. And special thanks to Mumia's attorneys: the longest-standing counsel on the case, Judith L. Ritter, who also argued and won the issue that got him off death row; Samuel Spital; Cristina Swarns; and the winners of his precedent-setting and life-saving prisoner healthcare suit, Robert Boyle and Bret Grote.

I wish also to acknowledge the love of lifelong friends: Gregory Baggett, Rafael Arias Campusano, Erika Jeffers, Amanda Lewis, Seneca Mudd, Jaleh Sedehi, and David Thurston (who also did some research for me), among others. My gratitude to those who've cheered me on in the final stretch, including William Cordova, Sheri Heller, and Rev. Dorlimar Lebron Malave, the new pastor of the People's Church. Thank you, also, to Phyllis Rauch and Mohammad Niazi.

During a time of domestic despair, my siblings and I moved mountains. And then unforgiving hardship birthed hope and a year and a half of deeper love. Gratitude and love to my mother, Minerva, and my beloved brothers, Geovany, Osvaldo, and Tirso Jr. and their partners, the life-saving Dr. D'Andrea Joseph, Milagros, and Esther, respectively. My cousins and friends also supported us and showed up, big-time, when our father fell ill; among them are Alex, Iris, Isis, Isaura, Joel, Marcos, Martin, the Alcantara siblings, Eunice, Enrique, Alfredo, Cruz, Niña, Valdez, and Doña Olga.

My dear sister-friends Jeanette Reyes and Linda Smith sustained me and protected my heart.

In the middle of it all, the bright-eyed Valentina—my first niece—brought joy to the world. I hope the history in these pages will interest her one day.

On May 25, 2019, as I was wrapping up this project, Tirso Apolinar Fernández, my beloved father, joined the angels. He meant the world to me.

Mi Papacíto, este libro es para usted.

Notes

Introduction

1. Bradley, *Harlem vs. Columbia University*.

2. Joan de Jesus, "From 1969: The Young Lords Take Over Historic East Harlem Church," *PIX (11)*, July 30, 2015, http://pix11.com/2015/07/30/from -1969-the-young-lords-take-over-historic-east -harlem-church/.

3. Pablo Guzman in the film, *El Pueblo Se Levanta (The People Are Rising)*, Newsreel no. 63, 1971.

4. See Bloom and Martin, *Black against Empire*, 213–14.

5. Andrés Torres, *Melting Pot and Mosaic*, 65–66.

6. Jack Bloom, *Class, Race*; Payne, *Light of Freedom*.

7. This history of the Young Lords builds on arguments I put forth in my doctoral dissertation, "Radicals in the Late 1960s: A History of the Young Lords Party in New York." It also builds on the following pioneering works on the Young Lords: Browning, "From Rumble to Revolution," 231–45; Jennifer Lee, "The Young Lords, a New Generation of Puerto Ricans," 64–70; Lao, "Resources of Hope," 34–49; Oboler, "'Establishing an Identity' in the Sixties"; Whalen, "Bridging Homeland and Barrio Politics"; Jennifer Nelson, *Women of Color and the Reproductive Rights Movement*; Johanna Fernández, "Between Social Service Reform and Revolutionary Politics," 255–85; Enck-Wanzer, "Trashing the System," 174–201; Ogbar, "*Puerto Rico en mi corazón*," 148–69; Johanna Fernández, "Denise Oliver and the Young Lords Party," 271–93; Johanna Fernández, "The Young Lords and the Postwar City," 60–82; Enck-Wanzer, *The Young Lords: A Reader*; Lazú, "The Chicago Young Lords: (Re)constructing Knowledge and Revolution," 28–59; Lilia Fernandez, *Brown in the Windy City*; Wanzer-Serrano, *The New York Young Lords and the Struggle for Liberation*; Arguello, "Puerto Rico En Mi Corázon"; Negrón-Muntaner, "The Look of Sovereignty," 4–33; and Sonia Song-Ha Lee, *Building a Latino Civil Rights Movement*. Retrospective accounts by former Young Lord activists have also contributed greatly to my work. These include: Young Lords, *Palante: Young Lords Party*; Guzmán, "Puerto Rican Barrio Politics in the United States," 121–28; Guzmán, "Ain't No Party Like the One We Got," 293–304; Guzmán, "*La Vida Pura*"; Morales

"*Palante, Siempre Palante*! The Young Lords"; Mickey Miguel Melendez, *We Took The Streets*; and Morales, *Through the Eyes of Rebel Women*.

8. The Young Patriots, to be discussed later, were a radical group of poor white migrants to Chicago from Appalachia. Luisa A. Quintero, "Lucharemos por libertad de los oprimidos: 'Young Lords,'" *El Diario La Prensa*, December 21, 1969, 46.

9. Diane Ravitch, "East Harlem in Search of a Poverty Program," in East Harlem Poverty, box 7, Lurie Papers.

10. Martin Luther King, *Where Do We Go*.

11. Histories of the Black Panther Party include Spencer, *Revolution Has Come*; Joshua Bloom and Martin, *Black against Empire*; Charles E. Jones, *Black Panther Party Reconsidered*; Abu-Jamal, *We Want Freedom*; Alondra Nelson, *Body and Soul*; Murch, *Living for the City*; and Lazerow and Williams, *Black Panther Party*.

12. Young Lords Party, "13 Point Program."

13. Suri, *Power and Protest*, chap. 3.

14. Gosse, *Rethinking the New Left*, 2; see also Isserman and Kazin, "Success and Failure."

15. See Peniel E. Joseph, *Midnight Hour*; Carson, *In Struggle*, 215; Woodard, *Nation within a Nation*; and Tyson, *Radio Free Dixie*.

16. Black power was a modern manifestation of black nationalism, the notion that regardless of class, black people share a common culture, language, and common interests born of the history and experience of chattel slavery in the United States and that black people should concentrate and leverage their power to wrest concessions from the system in the fight for freedom.

17. For excellent summaries of black power and its origins, see Marable, *Race, Reform, and Rebellion*, 86–113; and Gosse, *Rethinking the New Left*, 111–29.

18. On the root causes of radicalization among the baby boomers, see Suri, *Power and Protest*, chap. 3; and Bailey, "Sexual Revolution(s)." See also James Miller, *Democracy Is in the Streets*.

19. Peniel E. Joseph, *Neighborhood Rebels*; Theoharis and Woodard, *Freedom North*.

20. Jack Bloom, *Class, Race*, 173–79.

21. Elbaum, *Revolution in the Air*, 41–58.

22. Echols, "Nothing Distant about It," 151. See also Evans, *Personal Politics*, chap. 5.

Chapter 1

1. This chapter's narrative account of the Young Lords' transformation is drawn, in part, from a series of interviews conducted by the author with the Chicago Young Lords in 2005 and 2014: José "Cha Cha" Jiménez (chairman), interviewed on October 22, 2005 (Chicago) and May 19 and 20, 2014 (New York); Sal del Rivero (founding member of the YLO), interviewed on October 22, 2005 (Chicago); Angie Naredo (founding member of the YLO), interviewed on October 24, 2005 (Chicago); Omar Lopez (founding member of the YLO and editor of the *Palante* newspaper), interviewed on October 25, 2005 (Chicago); and Rory Guerra (founding member of the YLO), interviewed on October 25, 2005 (Chicago). Recordings are in the author's possession. This chapter builds on the existing literature on the Chicago chapter of the Young Lords.

2. José "Cha Cha" Jiménez and Sal del Rivero, joint interview by author, October 22, 2005.

3. José "Cha Cha" Jiménez, interview by Mervin Mendez, December 6, 1993, in *Lincoln Park Project*.

4. Elena Padilla, "Puerto Rican Immigrants," 87.

5. "Disturbances at Jane Addams Housing Project," outline memorandum, Catholic Interracial Council Meeting, August 3, 1954, in Near West Side Community Committee Records. See also Staudenmaier, "Mostly of Spanish Extraction," 681–84; and Diamond, *Mean Streets*, 206.

6. See Diamond, *Mean Streets*; and Schneider, *Vampires*.

7. Puerto Rico, Cuba, Guam, and the Philippine Islands became U.S. territories as a result of the Spanish-American War of 1898. On the nineteenth-century expansion of U.S. economic power and its colonial project in Puerto Rico and other territories, see Herring, *From Colony to Superpower*, chap. 8; LeFeber, *New Empire*; Dietz, *Economic History*; Kramer, *Blood of Government*; Ayala and Bernabe, *Puerto Rico*; Gomez, *Manifest Destinies*; Monge, *Puerto Rico*; and Font, *La presencia militar*.

8. The legal status of Puerto Ricans has evolved since 1898 and was modified to "statutory citizenship" as late as 1989. Although Puerto Ricans are citizens, their status is contingent on residency. Those living on the U.S. mainland have claims to citizenship as outlined by the Fourteenth Amendment of the U.S. Constitution. But Puerto Ricans on the island have a restricted citizenship. Among other limitations, island dwellers cannot vote in national presidential elections, and their elected congressional representatives have no voting rights in Congress. See Venator-Santiago, "Mapping the Contours"; Grosfoguel, *Colonial Subjects*;

Burnett and Marshall, *Domestic Sense*; Venator-Santiago, *Puerto Rico*; and Lorrin Thomas, *Puerto Rican Citizen*.

9. On the history of migrant farm labor in the United States, see Colón, "'We Like Mexican Workers'"; Hahamovitch, *Fruits of Their Labor*; Lilia Fernández, "Of Immigrants and Migrants"; Duany, *Blurred Borders*, chap. 4 (on Puerto Rico's Farm Labor Program); Kirstein, *Anglo over Bracero*; Ngai, *Impossible Subjects*; Santiago, "Case Study"; and History Task Force–Centro de Estudios Puertorriqueños, *Labor Migration under Capitalism*.

10. The tendency of Puerto Ricans to move into Mexican neighborhoods and the language that many of them shared with newly arrived Mexican migrants often made these two groups indistinguishable to ethnic whites and black Americans. While there is no consensus among scholars of the Puerto Rican diaspora on the timeline and process of Puerto Rican racialization in Chicago, this association of Puerto Ricans with the term that has historically defined another group's racialization adds to the debate. For a thorough and concise discussion of the incorporation, political standing, and changing racialization of Puerto Ricans and Mexicans in the United States, see De Genova and Ramos-Zayas, "Latino Rehearsals," esp. 21–29.

11. José "Cha Cha" Jiménez, interview by author, May 19, 2014. The farm was one of many across the country owned by D'Arrigo Bros. Company, briefly mentioned in Anna Aurelia Lopez, "From the Farms," 266, 343–44.

12. See Maldonado, "Contract Labor," 103–21; and Korrol, *From Colonia to Community*, 13–47.

13. The best known of these was the bracero program, a diplomatic agreement between Mexico and the United States for the contract of temporary Mexican laborers. See Craig, *Bracero Program*; Joon, "Political Economy"; and Maldonado, "Contract Labor," 103–21.

14. For literature on the demographic transformation of American cities, see, for example, Kenneth T. Jackson, *Crabgrass Frontier*.

15. Local and national histories of movements outside the south include Sonia Song-Ha Lee, *Latino Civil Rights Movement*; Lilia Fernández, *Brown in the Windy City*; Purnell, *Fighting Jim Crow*; Clarence Taylor, *Civil Rights*; Countryman, *Up South*; Pulido, *Black, Brown, Yellow*; Theoharis and Woodard, *Freedom North*; Sugrue, *Sweet Land of Liberty*; and Biondi, *To Stand and Fight*.

16. Jiménez, interview by Mendez.

17. Felix Padilla, *Puerto Rican Chicago*, 78–83.

18. Jiménez, interview by author, October 22, 2005.

19. Cha-Cha Jiménez Defense Committee, *"Que Viva El Pueblo,"* 4; Hoch and Slayton, *New Homeless and Old*, 87–106; Suttles, *Social Order*, 148–49.

20. Cha-Cha Jiménez Defense Committee, *"Que Viva El Pueblo,"* 4.

21. Seligman, *Block by Block*, 76.

22. Mollenkopf, *Contested City*, 32–46.

23. Omar Lopez, interview by author, October 25, 2005; Condit, *Chicago*, 115; Lilia Fernández, *Brown in the Windy City*, 139–42.

24. Approximately 85 percent of these residents were renters. Statistics on percentage of renters and homeowners are discussed in Kitagawa and Taeuber, *Local Community Fact Book, Chicago's Metropolitan Area, 1960*, 27–31.

25. McEnaney, *Postwar: Waging Peace in Chicago*, 19–20.

26. Hertz, *The Battle of Lincoln Park*, 82.

27. Kitagawa and Taeuber, *Local Community Fact Book, Chicago's Metropolitan Area, 1960*, 246. Cha-Cha Jiménez Defense Committee, *"Que Viva El Pueblo,"* 5; Felix Padilla, *Puerto Rican Chicago*, 78–79, 82–83. After black Americans, residential segregation in Chicago appears to be highest among Puerto Ricans; see Tauber and Tauber, "Negro," 376, 380.

28. The impact of mass-scale, postwar housing displacement on school-age children is understudied by historians, but in New York, the issue was indirectly addressed, debated out of context, and muddied by racism and race ideology. In 1967, the rank and file of the city's major teachers' union successfully lobbied its board to demand the inclusion of a "disruptive child" clause during union contract negotiations with the Board of Education. The controversial clause would have given New York's white teacher corps authority to expel "seriously misbehaving" children (in New York's majority black and brown school districts) and send them to "special service" schools. Podair, *The Strike That Changed New York*, 161–64.

29. Jiménez, interview by author, May 19, 2014.

30. Felix Padilla, *Puerto Rican Chicago*, 56–66.

31. See, respectively, Gina Perez, *Near North*, 73; and Maldonado, "Contract Labor."

32. Lilia Fernández, *Brown in the Windy City*, 8, 176–77; De Genova and Ramos-Zayas, *Latino Crossings*.

33. Published in the satirical magazine *Puck*, the cartoon depicts the logic of social Darwinism and scientific racism, a pseudoscience, as the modern ideological gear of the nineteenth-century U.S. imperial project. See "School Begins."

34. For discussions of the predilection of home ownership among European immigrants and its consequences, see Lewinnek, *Chicago's Early Suburbs*, esp. chap. 4. See also Hirsch, *Making the Second Ghetto*, 186–95.

35. The early historiography on gangs emphasized the relationship between gang formation and the shifting boundaries of urban space. See Thrasher, *Gang*; and Asbury, *Gem of the Prairie*. The sociologically driven scholars of the postwar period identified poverty and lack of opportunity as engines of gang formation. These include Cohen, *Delinquent Boys*; and Cloward and Ohlin, *Delinquency and Opportunity*. Third-wave studies highlight the confluence of power, politics, culture, and geography in the making of the gang up to the drug wars. Andrew Diamond's *Mean Streets* is among the finest.

36. Quoted in Hagedorn, "Race Not Space," 196.

37. Ibid., 198.

38. The foremost study on the 1919 riot is Tuttle, *Riot*. See also Capeci, "Race Riot Redux."

39. For an account of the lesser known episodes of violence against African Americans seeking housing in transitional neighborhoods, see Hirsch, *Making the Second Ghetto*, 40–67; Drake and Cayton, *Black Metropolis*, 190; Diamond, *Mean Streets*, chap. 4; and Kornblum, *Blue Collar Community*.

40. They were concentrated in exactly seven enclaves. By 1970, the census counted 72,000 Puerto Ricans in Chicago. See Wagenheim and U.S. Commission on Civil Rights, "Puerto Ricans in the Continental United States," 23; and Lilia Fernández, *Brown in the Windy City*, 72.

41. The link between prejudice and land value is methodically documented in Hoyt, *One Hundred Years*.

42. See chart of manufacturing employment in Chicago and its suburbs in McDonald, *Employment Location*, 10, and see also 11–12; for slightly different statistics on industrial decline in Chicago, see Abu-Lughod, *New York, Los Angeles*, 219, 221.

43. The broader literature on postwar deindustrialization includes Thompson, *Whose Detroit*; Self, *American Babylon*; Sugrue, *Urban Crisis*; and Arnesen, "Symposium on Thomas J. Sugrue." On the cultural shifts produced by deindustrialization, see Rotella, *October Cities*; and Mollenkopf and Castells, *Dual City*.

44. Lilia Fernández, *Brown in the Windy City*, 8, 176–77; De Genova and Ramos-Zayas, *Latino Crossings*.

45. On race and the development of a shared white identity, see Roediger, *The Wages of Whiteness*; Lipsitz, *The Possessive Investment in Whiteness*; Jacobson, *Whiteness of a Different Color*; Ignatiev, *How the Irish Became White*; and Painter, *The History of White People*. Critiques of whiteness studies include Kolchin, "Whiteness Studies: The New History of Race in America," 154–73; Arnesen, "Whiteness and the Historians' Imagination"; and Foner, "Response to Eric Arnesen."

46. Jiménez, interview by author, May 19, 2014.

47. Mendez, "The Young Lords and Early Chicago Puerto Rican Gangs."

48. Diamond, *Mean Streets*, 195.

49. Jiménez, interview by author, May 19, 2014.
50. Ibid.; Jiménez, interview by author, October 22, 2005.
51. Baldwin, "James Baldwin Debates."
52. Omi and Winant, *Racial Formation*, 60.
53. Jiménez, interview by Mendez, 1.
54. Rory Guerra, interview by author, October 25, 2005.
55. Jiménez, interview by author, October 22, 2005; Del Rivero interview.
56. Lilia Fernández, *Brown in the Windy City*, 181.
57. Jiménez, interview by author, May 19, 2014.
58. Jiménez, interview by Mendez, 3.
59. Jiménez, interview by author, October 22, 2005.
60. For a discussion of the different and conflicting ways of seeing race that inform the identity of black Latinos in the United States, see Flores and Jiménez Roman, "Triple-Consciousness?," 319–28. For an overview of the politics behind the denial of blackness among Puerto Ricans on the island and its historical roots, see Arlene Torres, "La gran familia puertorriqueña," 285–306.
61. The Young Lords made the observation in *Palante*. See Morales, "Puerto Rican Racism," 6–7. For broader scholarly discussions on race and identity, see Di Genova and Ramos-Zayas, *Latino Crossings*. See also these special issues: "Race and Identity," *CENTRO: Journal of the Center for Puerto Rican Studies* 8, nos. 1–2 (Spring 1996).
62. Lilia Fernández, *Brown in the Windy City*, 10.
63. Lucas, *Puerto Rican Dropouts*, 38.
64. A similar analysis is made about the provenance of those who joined the Black Panther Party in Abu-Jamal, *We Want Freedom*, 6.
65. Jiménez, interview by Mendez, 1.
66. Pier, Mahalik, and Woodland, "Effects of Racism."
67. Diamond, *Mean Streets*, 175.
68. Jiménez, interview by author, May 19, 2014.
69. Jiménez, interview by author, October 22, 2005; Del Rivero interview.
70. A similar experience and assessment is recounted by New York Young Lord Gilbert Colón; see Gilbert Colón, interview by author, January 8, 2005.
71. Del Rivero interview.
72. Jiménez, interview by Mendez, 3.
73. Ibid., 1.
74. Diamond, *Mean Streets*, 174. Alternatively, one can argue that gang members rebelled against the monotony and discipline that the workplace imposed on their lives; see Schneider, *Vampires*, 116–77.
75. Coleman, *Equality of Educational Opportunity*, 449. See also Lucas, *Puerto Rican Dropouts*, 6; and Margolis, *Losers*, 58.
76. Knupfer, "Chicago Detention Home," 52–60.

77. Jiménez, interview by author, October 22, 2005.
78. Ibid.; del Rivero interview; Diamond, *Mean Streets*, 214.
79. Jiménez, interview by author, May 19, 2014.
80. Hirsch, *Making the Second Ghetto*, 41.
81. Jiménez, interview by author, October 22, 2005.
82. Ibid.
83. Carson, *In Struggle*, chap. 1.
84. Jiménez, interview by author, May 19, 2014.
85. Jiménez, interview by author, October 22, 2005.
86. Ibid.
87. Ibid. See also Cosgrove, "Zoot-Suit."
88. Committee for Detached Workers Report, 1966, in Board of Managers 1858–1975, subseries 3, committee minutes and reports, 1890–1975, box 73, folder 2, series 3, in YMCA of Metropolitan Chicago Records.
89. Jiménez, interview by author, October 22, 2005; del Rivero interview.
90. Central, Junior College Committee Report, 1960, in General Secretaries' Papers, 1881–1965, subseries 3, Frank A. Hathaway, Lloyd L. McClow, John O. Root ca. 1927–65, box 99, folder 2, 1853–1980, series 4, in YMCA of Metropolitan Chicago Records.
91. Jiménez, interview by author, October 22, 2005.
92. Ibid.; Del Rivero interview.
93. Jiménez, interview by author, October 22, 2005. Jiménez's reference to a police vehicle as a "paddy wagon" echoes the imprint of race and ethnicity in the life and power structure of the city. "Paddy" is a pejorative stand-in for "Irish." The origin of the term in "paddy wagon" is either rooted in the overrepresentation of Irishmen in the police force or a reference to those most likely to be hauled away in police vehicles because of the high incidence of poverty among Irish immigrants.
94. Jiménez, interview by author, October 22, 2005.
95. See broader discussion in Arlene Torres, "La gran familia puertorriqueña," 285–306.
96. Du Bois, *The Souls of Black Folks*, 1–4.
97. Jiménez, interview by author, October 22, 2005. First peoples around the globe have used shame effectively as an antidote to crime and an alternative to punitive justice. See Braithwaithe, *Crime, Shame, and Reintegration*.
98. Duany, *Puerto Rican Nation*, chap. 10. See literature review in Jennifer A. Jones, "Afro-Latinos: Speaking through Silences and Rethinking the Geographies of Blackness," 569–614.
99. Jiménez, interview by author, October 22, 2005.

100. Garrow, *Bearing the Cross*, chap. 9; Williams, *Bullet to the Ballot*, chap. 1.

101. On northern conditions, see Sugrue, *Origins of the Urban Crisis*, and Hirsch, *Making the Second Ghetto*.

102. "Jiménez, interview by Mendez.

103. See Horne, *The Fire This Time*; Marable, *Race, Reform, and Rebellion*.

104. Malcolm X Letter to Martin Luther King, July 31, 1963. Atlanta University Center. On Malcolm's life and politics, see Marable, *Malcolm X*; and Perry, *Malcolm X: The Life of a Man Who Changed Black America*.

105. Felix Padilla, *Puerto Rican Chicago*, 146; see also all of chapter 4.

106. Jiménez, interview by author, October 22, 2005; Del Rivero interview.

107. Omar Lopez interview. See also Felix Padilla, *Puerto Rican Chicago*, 156–58.

108. Felix Padilla, *Puerto Rican Chicago*, 155.

109. See Donna Murch, *Living for the City*.

110. "Protest by Welfare Recipient," May 18, 1967; and "Interview with Hilda Gamboa, Formerly Caseworker for Cook County Public Aid, Now Employed with LADO" [undated], both in Janet Nolan Ethnographic Research on Puerto Ricans. On the broader history of the welfare rights movement, see Nadasen, *Welfare Warriors*; Orleck, *Storming Caesar's Palace*; and Piven and Cloward, *Poor People's Movements*.

111. Omar Lopez interview; Caralee and Obed Lopez, interviews by Mervin Mendez, November 21, 1996, and October 17, 1995, *Lincoln Park Project*. See also the rich primary literature on LADO, including its newspaper, in the Janet Nolan Ethnographic Research on Puerto Ricans.

112. Felix Padilla, *Puerto Rican Chicago*, 172–73.

113. Omar Lopez interview. Although the support work of these natural allies in the United States of the Cuban Revolution goes unmentioned, the major study of the Cuban Revolution and the New Left is Gosse, *Where the Boys Are*, esp. chap. 5.

114. Omar Lopez interview.

115. On the student protests in Mexico City during the 1968 Olympics Games, see Trevizo, *Rural Protest and the Making of Democracy in Mexico*, chap. 2; Joseph and Buchenau, *Mexico's Once and Future Revolution*, chap. 8; and Pensado and Ochoa, *Mexico beyond 1968*.

116. Cha-Cha Jiménez Defense Committee, *"Que Viva El Pueblo,"* 11.

117. Jiménez, interview by author, October 22, 2005.

118. The nexus between urban rebellion and roundups, repression, and dissent in the prisons during the age of black power is an understudied area in a growing field. See Tibbs, *From Black Power to Prison Power*; Dan Berger, *Captive Na-*

tion*; Heather Ann Thompson, *Blood in the Water*; and Hinton, *From the War on Poverty to the War on Crime*.

119. Jiménez, interview by author, May 19, 2014.

120. Marable, *Malcom X*, chap. 1.

121. Jiménez, interview by author, October 22, 2005.

122. Ibid.

123. Ibid.

124. Omar Lopez interview; Jiménez, interview by author, October 22, 2005. See also Hilda Vasquez-Ignatin, "Young Lords Serve and Protect," *Movement*, May 1969, 4.

125. Omar Lopez interview; Jiménez, interview by author, October 22, 2005.

126. Vasquez-Ignatin, "Young Lords."

127. Angie Naredo, interview by author, October 24, 2005; Jiménez, interview by author, May 19, 2014.

128. Vasquez-Ignatin, "Young Lords."

129. Patricia Devine, interview by José "Cha Cha" Jiménez, transcript, in Lincoln Park Collection.

130. Jiménez, interview by author, October 22, 2005.

131. Devine interview.

132. Jiménez, interview by author, October 22, 2005; SAC, Chicago (157–3645) (P), to Director, May 9, 1969, "Young Lords Racial Matter," COINTELPRO Documents.

133. "Puerto Rican Disturbances, Chicago Illinois, Young Lords," February 12, 1969, file no. CG 157–1195, 157–3675, COINTELPRO Documents.

134. "Young Lords, Chicago Illinois, Racial Matters," April 28, 1969, file no. 157–3645, COINTELPRO Documents.

135. "Lincoln Park Residents Liberate Police Station," *Lincoln Park Press*, March 1969, 1, in Young Lords Newspaper Collection.

136. Jiménez, interview by author, October 22, 2005. See also "Hands off Cha Cha!," *Lincoln Park Press*, March 1969, 6.

137. "Puerto Rican Disturbances, Chicago Illinois, Young Lords," February 12, 1969 [sic], file no. CG 157–1195, 157–3645, COINTELPRO Documents.

138. "YLO Takes over Police Station," *YLO*, March 19, 1969, 1. This article was adapted and edited slightly from an article that appeared in the *Lincoln Park Press*.

139. Ibid., 12.

140. Ibid., 1, 12.

141. Omar Lopez interview.

142. Vasquez-Ignatin, "Young Lords."

143. Henry Gaddis, interview by author, January 27, 2007; José "Cha Cha" Jiménez, interview by author, January 27, 2007; "Young Lords, Chicago, Illinois, Racial Matters," April 28, 1969, file no. 157–3645, COINTELPRO Documents.

144. Bob Lee, interview by author, February 15, 2007.

145. Henry Gaddis and José "Cha Cha" Jiménez remarks, January 27, 2007, *Radicals in Black and Brown: Palante, People's Power and Common Cause in the Black Panthers and Young Lords Organization* exhibit symposium, dir. Johanna Fernández, Joseph Jordan, and Charles Payne, Sonja Haynes Center Collection, University of North Carolina at Chapel Hill. On the Rainbow Coalition, see also Williams, *Bullet to the Ballot*, chap. 4.

146. Guerra interview.

147. Phillip Foner, *Black Panthers Speak*, 2–4.

148. On the Black Panther's health programs, see Alondra Nelson, *Body and Soul*.

149. Guerra interview.

150. "Pigs Walk Beat," *YLO*, March 1969, 4.

151. Omar Lopez interview.

152. Chicago (157–3645) (P) (2P) to Director, May 5, 1969, "Young Lords, Racial Matters, OO Chicago," COINTELPRO Documents.

153. Fred [*sic*], "Wherever Death May Surprise U.S. [. . .]," *YLO*, May 1969, 3.

154. "Inquest Finds Policeman Lamb Justified in Killing of Ramos," *Chicago Tribune*, May 30, 1969, 5.

155. SAC, Chicago (157–3645) (P) to Director, May 8, 1969, "Young Lords, Racial Matters (OO. Chicago)," COINTELPRO Documents.

156. "Young Lords," May 14, 1969, file no. 157–3645; and Chicago (157–3645) (P) to Director, May 6, 1969, "Young Lords, RM, OO, Chicago," COINTELPRO Documents.

157. "Young Lords," May 14, 1969, file no. 157–3645, COINTELPRO Documents.

158. SAC, Chicago (157–3645) (P) to Director, May 7, 1969, "Young Lords, RM. OO Chicago," COINTELPRO Documents.

159. Fred [*sic*], "Wherever Death May Surprise."

160. Jiménez, interview by author, October 22, 2005; Omar Lopez interview.

161. Guerra interview; Jiménez, interview by author, October 25, 2005; Omar Lopez interview.

162. Lilia Fernández, *Brown in the Windy City*, 191–92.

163. Omar Lopez interview; SAC, Chicago (157–3645) (P) to Director, June 12, 1969, "Young Lords, RM, OO Chicago," COINTELPRO Documents.

Chapter 2

1. The Real Great Society in East Harlem was initiated by former gang members and a group of architecture students from Columbia University. Vaughan, "Real Great Society"; see also Aponte-Pares, "Lesson from El Barrio," 399–420.

2. On debates surrounding the chosen sites of protest of SDS, see Frost, *Interracial Movement*.

On the Young Lords, see Johanna Fernández, "Between Social Service Reform." On the Black Panthers, see Murch, *Living for the City*.

3. "Interview with Cha Cha Jiménez Chairman of the Young Lords Organization," *Black Panther*, June 7, 1969, 17. The article is referenced in Guzmán, "Ain't No Party," 296; Young Lords Party and Abramson, *Palante*, 9; and Luppens and Guzmán, *Young Lords Legacy*, 12. In *Young Lords Legacy*, Guzmán cites the *Guardian* as the newspaper that carried the interview with Jiménez. A more detailed account of the events that led those New York radicals to Chicago is found in Miguel Melendez, *We Took the Streets*, 83–87.

4. "Interview with Cha Cha Jiménez," 17.

5. Winston James's study of the political world of Caribbean immigrants in Harlem in the early twentieth century is among the finest discussions on this topic; James, *Holding Aloft the Banner*.

6. On the radicalized politics of the New Left at decade's end, see Elbaum, *Revolution in the Air*.

7. Juan González, interview by author, April 21, 1996; Carlito Rovira, interview by author, July 30, 2013; Young Lords Party and Abramson, *Palante*, 8–10.

8. In 1964, in response to the growing controversy over the absence of "minority" enrollment at the City University of New York, the state legislature authorized funding for the College Discovery program, a precursor to affirmative action that recruited low-income students with "intellectual promise" to community colleges. With public discussions on the failure of New York's public schools to meet the needs of children of color at a high pitch in all corners of the city, College Discovery reconfigured admissions policies to recruit applicants who would otherwise not have been admitted, with benefits to students of all races, including poor whites. Rather than focus on tests and grades, under the new guidelines, admission was based on credits completed, teacher recommendations, principal evaluations, and economic background. Dispenzieri, *Characteristics*, 2–17.

9. For a history of the political atmosphere at the City University of New York, where many of the leading members of the Young Lords studied, see Frabricant and Brier, *Austerity Blues*, chap. 3.

10. For examples of earlier civil rights organizing in the North, see Biondi, *To Stand and Fight*. See also Beth T. Bates, "'Double V for Victory' Mobilizes Black Detroit," in Theoharis and Woodard, *Freedom North*. Many of the racial justice movements that cohered during World War II and the years that followed were forced underground by an emergent Red Scare that began in 1947 with President Harry S. Truman's declaration of Cold War against the Soviet Union. For a discussion of how the Cold War both circumscribed the political

scope of the civil rights movement and increased international pressure on the U.S. government to address racism, see Dudziak, *Cold War Civil Rights*.

11. The literature of the racial justice movements of the 1960s in New York includes Podair, *Strike*; Johnson, *Street Justice*; Purnell, *Fighting Jim Crow*; Sonia Song-Ha Lee, *Latino Civil Rights Movement*; Freeman, *Working-Class New York*; Clarence Taylor, *Our Own Door*; Ravitch, *Great School Wars*; Clarence Taylor, *Civil Rights*; Biondi, *Black Revolution on Campus*, chap. 4; and Johanna Fernández, "Between Social Service Reform."

12. In the 1940s, the number of Puerto Ricans in the city quadrupled, and by 1960, the Puerto Rican population had grown tenfold to approximately 900,000; Fitzpatrick, *Puerto Rican Americans*, 141–42. On the relationship between black Americans and Puerto Ricans, see Andrés Torres, *Melting Pot and Mosaic*, 66; and U.S. Department of Labor, *Labor Force Experience*, 2. On the history of Puerto Ricans in New York, see Sonia Song-Ha Lee, *Latino Civil Rights Movement*; Thomas, *Puerto Rican Citizen*; and Korrol, *From Colonia to Community*.

13. *New York World-Telegram*, October 20, 1947, cited in Iglesias, *Memoirs of Bernardo Vega*, 229–30.

14. Miguel Melendez, *We Took the Streets*, 29–35.

15. Ayala and Bernabe, *Puerto Rico*, 100–103. For a discussion of the impact of New Deal policies in the U.S. south, see Jack Bloom, *Class, Race*, 61–66.

16. Plans for emigration also intended to address an assumed "problem" of overpopulation. On Operation Bootstrap, see Dietz, *Economic History*, chap. 4; and Briggs, *Reproducing Empire*, chap. 4.

17. Monge, *Puerto Rico*, 94–97; see also Bhana, *Puerto Rican Status Question*.

18. For a discussion of Marín, see Briggs, *Reproducing Empire*, 112–18. See also Caraballo, "Guerra, reforma y colonialismo."

19. Cuevas, *Economía política*, 22–23; Dietz, *Negotiating Development and Change*, 140; Dietz, *Economic History*, 208–9; Rodriguez, *Puerto Ricans*, 11–13; Ayala, "Decline," 62–90; Ayala and Bernabe, *Puerto Rico*, 179–200; Richard L. Bolin, "What Puerto Rico Faced in Being First to Create EPZs in 1947 . . . and Its Huge Success," Explorer's Foundation, September 9, 2004, http://explorers-foundation.org/archive/409t1-english.pdf.

20. Dietz, *Economic History*, 210–11.

21. This world systems theory interpretation of U.S. foreign policy is discussed in McCormick, *America's Half Century*, chap. 1. For example, the precursor of the maquiladora was established in Puerto Rico; see Fatemi, *Maquiladora Industry*; and Sklair, *Assembling for Development*.

22. The open-market industrialization of Puerto Rico also supported the United States' proposed alternative to the old imperial model of fixed trade blocs that had previously led to world war.

As suggested by the Atlantic Charter of 1941 and the Bretton Woods meeting of 1944 in New Hampshire, the United States sought to challenge and finally eliminate the legacy of international relations established by the colonial empires whereby each major power possessed a sphere of influence in world trade. In its stead, the United States favored open access to foreign investment and raw materials, unencumbered by protectionist policies. The United States argued that the abolition of spheres of influence that favored some investors over others would reduce future economic competition and military conflict between major powers that had snowballed into military clashes between competing empires. On the convergences between U.S. foreign and economic policy and the reorganization of the world economy after World War II, see McCormick, *America's Half Century*, chaps. 1, 3, 4.

23. Neoliberalism refers to the strategy employed by captains of American and British industry to overcome a long-term trend: the declining rate of profit that began in the early 1970s and continued into the late twentieth century. In response, American business partnered with the U.S. government to rescue its capital with a program of draconian wage cuts, the elimination of benefits like healthcare, and union busting. The strategy also included overseas expansion in Latin America and Asia (through policies such as the North American Free Trade Agreement), Wall Street speculation, and widespread deregulation of industry. On neoliberalism, see Harvey, *Brief History of Neoliberalism*; Duménil and Lévy, *Capital Resurgent*, chap. 3; and Brenner, *Boom and the Bubble*, chap. 1. See also Phillips-Fein, *Invisible Hands*.

24. Sugrue, *Urban Crisis*; Bluestone and Harrison, *Deindustrialization of America*; High, "'Wounds of Class'"; Gregory Wilson, "Deindustrialization."

25. For an account of how that process developed in New York, see Mollenkopf and Castells, *Dual City*.

26. Puerto Rican Forum, *Study of Poverty Conditions*, 25; U.S. Department of Labor, *Labor Force Experience*, 13.

27. U.S. Department of Labor, *Changing Patterns of Employment*, 1.

28. Fainstein and Fainstein, "Economic Restructuring," 193.

29. This kind of structural unemployment among Puerto Ricans resulted from a myriad of factors including the higher participation of Puerto Rican males in declining blue-collar industries and occupations; lack of educational opportunities and retraining; racial discrimination; and the group's exclusion from trade unions and government employment. As a group, Puerto Ricans encountered particular difficulty in the

labor market because, as a considerably younger population, they lacked the experience and job market skills of their counterparts in the population at large. U.S. Department of Labor, *Changing Patterns of Employment*.

30. U.S. Department of Labor, *Labor Force Experience*, 23–26.

31. The percentage of Puerto Rican women exceeded the proportion of men employed in this area, at 65.2 percent and 41.3 percent, respectively; U.S. Bureau of the Census, *U.S. Census of Population*, 2; also cited in U.S. Department of Labor, *Labor Force Experience*, 17. Many studies have suggested that the census reports are rife with numerical inaccuracies due to undercounting. Sociologist Clara Rodríguez estimates that 60 percent of Puerto Ricans were employed in manufacturing. See Rodriguez and Korrol, "Economic Survival," 44; and Fitzpatrick, *Puerto Rican Americans*, 60.

32. Puerto Rican Forum, *Study of Poverty Conditions*, 22–24.

33. *New York World-Telegram*, October 20, 1947, cited in Iglesias, *Memoirs of Bernardo Vega*, 229–30; Lapp, "Managing Migration," 52–53.

34. Myrdal, *American Dilemma*.

35. The International Workers' Union was founded by the Communist Party in 1930, encouraged progressive social, cultural, and political activities at the community level, and was modeled after Masonic lodges in the United States. See Keeran, "National Groups."

36. Biondi, *To Stand and Fight*, 191–207, 277–79. These postwar grassroots activities were the culmination of the labor and civil rights alliance of the 1930s. Supported by East Harlem's democratic socialist congressman Vito Marcantonio, this coalition had previously elected the first Puerto Rican official in the United States, Oscar Garcia Rivera, a candidate of the American Labor Party who won East Harlem's District Seventeen seat in the State Assembly in 1937. Wakefield, *Island in the City*, 266; see also Meyer, *Vito Marcantonio*.

37. Thomas, *Puerto Rican Citizen*, 152–61, 202. Sonia Song-Ha Lee, *Latino Civil Rights Movement*, 56.

38. Its predecessors include the Puerto Rican Association for Community Affairs in 1956. Other prominent leaders included Josephine Nieves and Marta Valle, who would later hold appointments in local government. Rodriguez-Fraticelli and Tirado Aviles, "Notes towards a History," 35–47; Sonia Song-Ha Lee, *Latino Civil Rights Movement*, 110; Rodriguez-Morrazani, "Puerto Rican Political Generations," 101–2. Lapp, "Managing Migration," 297–98. For a broader discussion of the politics of the social science–driven advocacy of the period, see Kelley, *Yo Mama's Disfunktional!*, chap. 1.

39. Gerena Valentin, *My Life*, chap. 20; Rodriguez-

Fraticelli and Tirado Aviles, "Notes towards a History," 38.

40. Rodriguez-Fraticelli and Tirado Aviles, "Notes towards a History," 40–41.

41. Adina Back, "'Parent Power,'" 186, 188.

42. Martin Luther King, "Letter."

43. Quoted in Sonia Song-Ha Lee, *Latino Civil Rights Movement*, 1.

44. On the coming-of-age conditions that shaped baby boomers' lives in the 1950s, see May, *Homeward Bound*.

45. Hurtado, Gurin, and Peng, "Social Identities," 129–51.

46. Young Lords Party and Abramson, *Palante*, 24.

47. Wilfredo Rojas, interview by author, October 2013.

48. As the eldest children of their respective households, Carmen [*sic*] and Morales explain that they often assumed many of their mothers' responsibilities because Puerto Rican mothers were often stymied by the dual impediment of being housewives and not speaking the dominant language. "Being the eldest, I had to handle all the situations . . . in the house—and I was ten going on eleven, so I couldn't really do as good a job as I thought" (Young Lords Party and Abramson, *Palante*, 36).

49. Fullilove, *Root Shock*, 14.

50. Ronald Fraser, ed., Iris Morales, interview, 1988, Columbia University Oral History Project, 2.

51. Ibid.

52. Young Lords Party and Abramson, *Palante*, 24.

53. Abu-Jamal, *We Want Freedom*, 6.

54. Young Lords Party and Abramson, *Palante*, 26.

55. Shakur, *Assata*, 37; see also discussion in Ramsey, "Revolutionary Relatability," 130.

56. Podair, *Strike*; Clarence Taylor, *Our Own Door*; Ravitch, *Great School Wars*. See also Clarence Taylor, *Civil Rights*.

57. New York City Board of Education, *Resolution* (New York: Board of Education, 1954), quoted in Harlem Parents Committee, *Education*.

58. *Toward the Integration of Our Schools: Final Report of the Commission on Integration* (New York: Board of Education, 1958), in Lurie Papers.

59. Morrison, *Puerto Rican Study*, 1.

60. Board of Education of the City of New York, *Extended School Services through the All Day Neighborhood School* (New York: Board of Education of the City of New York, 1947), quoted in Madeleine E. Lopez, "Investigating the Investigators," 65.

61. The school system had not had to address the educational needs of an influx of students with rural roots who did not speak the language since 1924, when the Johnson-Reed Act closed the door

of immigration to Jewish and Italian immigrants. See Ravitch, *History*, 174; and Madeleine E. Lopez, "Investigating the Investigators," 64.

62. Jacob Landers, "Improving Ethnic Distribution of New York City Pupils: An Analysis of Programs Approved by the Board of Education and the Superintendent of Schools," New York: City School District of the City of New York, May 1966, in 5, box 7, Lurie Papers.

63. For figures on Puerto Ricans, see U.S. Bureau of the Census, *U.S. Census of Population*, also quoted in Landers, "Improving Ethnic Distribution," 5. For figures on black Americans, see Ravitch, *History*, 292.

64. This is evidenced by the rich archival record, which includes the papers of United Bronx Parents and Ellen Lurie at Centro de Estudios Puertorriqueños and those of the Harlem Parents Committee, among others, at the Schomburg Library for Black Culture. See also Clarence Taylor, *Our Own Door*, chap. 4.

65. See Clarence Taylor, *Our Own Door*; Weiner, *Power, Protest*; and Podair, *Strike*.

66. Podair, *Strike*, 27; for a fuller discussion, see chap. 3.

67. This was a consequence of white opposition. See Podair, *Strike*, chap. 3.

68. Board of Education, "Toward Greater Opportunity: A Progress Report from the Superintendent of Schools of the Board of Education dealing with Implementation of Recommendations of the Commission on Integration," New York, June 1960. It is also for this reason that the Board of Education progress report of 1970 warned that "the neighborhood school concept continues to be the basis for pupil placement on the elementary level, and, to a lesser degree, on the junior high school level, so that within the near future neither complete integration nor a time-table for integration is a likely possibility."

69. Podair, *Strike*, 28–29.

70. "2,000 Rally in School Fight," *Long Island Daily Press*, June 24, 1959; "Transfer of Students Opposed," *Long Island Daily Press*, July 26, 1959; "State to Review School Transfers," *Long Island Daily Press*, August 27, 1959; "White Pupils End Queens Boycott," *Long Island Daily Press*, September 16, 1959.

71. "Let the Children Go Back to School," *Long Island Daily Press*, September 15, 1959; Denise Oliver, interview by author, August 18, 2007; Clarence Taylor, *Our Own Door*, 81.

72. Oliver interview, August 18, 2007.

73. Ramon Ramirez, interview by author, December 2011.

74. Peggy Streit, "Why They Fight for P.A.T.," *New York Times*, September 20, 1964; also cited in

Podair, *Strike*. This picture of white working-class reaction to a perceived threat to their advances is also discussed in Formisano, *Boston against Busing*.

75. See Kenneth T. Jackson, *Crabgrass Frontier*; Lipsitz, *Possessive Investment in Whiteness*; and Katznelson, *Affirmative Action*, 116.

76. Podair, *Strike*, 28, 50–52.

77. Notebook, Lurie Papers.

78. González interview.

79. Morrison, *Puerto Rican Study*, 155.

80. Tyson, *Radio Free Dixie*, 74–76, 35.

81. Gilbert Colón, interview by author, January 8, 2005.

82. Kenneth B. Clark, *Alternative Public School Systems: A Response to America's Educational Emergency, National Conference on Equal Educational Opportunity in American Cities* (Washington, D.C.: U.S. Commission on Civil Rights, November 16–18, 1967), in box 1, folder 19, Lurie Papers.

83. Clarence Taylor, *Reds at the Blackboard*, 78–79.

84. Reports also highlighted the misuse of a subjective intelligence test that disproportionately placed black American and Puerto Rican children in classes for the mentally disabled and in vocational rather than academic schools and the gerrymandering of school districts by school officials in ways that excluded nonwhite students from higher-performing and better-funded school districts. Board of Education Commission on Integration, "The Status of the Public School Education of Negro and Puerto Rican Children in New York City," October 1955, 3–13; and Kenneth Clark, "Segregated Schools in New York City, Urban League Conference, 'Students Apart'" speech, April 24, 1954, both in Lurie Papers.

85. Omi and Winant, *Racial Formation*, 32, 61–62. For a fuller discussion, see Stratton, *Education for Empire*, 192–200. By contrast, the earliest and most extensive study of Puerto Rican students in the New York City public schools, *The Puerto Rican Study*, acknowledges these objective challenges and the difference in quality and levels of schooling in relation to the age at which Puerto Rican children entered the New York schools. Morrison, *Puerto Rican Study*, 153.

86. Felix Velazquez, interview by author, August 2009.

87. Rovira interview, July 30, 2013. This account echoed the brutal corporal abuse, in 1936, of fourteen-year-old Robert Shelton by a white principal in a Harlem school, which ignited a public campaign by the Permanent Committee for Better Schools led by Lucille Spence, the black teacher and member of the communist-influenced Teachers Union. Clarence Taylor, *Reds at the Blackboard*, 288–89.

88. Barbara A. McKinnon, "Educating Kids in

the Ghetto: A Negro Teacher's Criticism," *New York World-Telegram*, November 17, 1965.

89. For a fuller discussion, see Stratton, *Education for Empire*, 192–200.

90. Lewis, *From Brownsville to Bloomberg*, 18–19.

91. Kelley, *Yo Mama's Disfunktional!*, chap. 1.

92. Barreto, *Politics of Language*. For discussions of the politics of language among Puerto Ricans, see also Korrol, *From Colonia to Community*, 155–56; Meyer, *Vito Marcantonio*, 163–64; and Back, "Up South."

93. Perez and Tobier, *Long Road from Lares*, 12.

94. The campaign, which surpassed even the March on Washington in terms of numerical participation, brought together unions, community groups, local parents' associations, and black churches, all of which offered their buildings around the city for use as classrooms. Clarence Taylor, *Our Own Door*, chap. 5; Theoharis and Woodard, *Freedom North*, introduction; see also Back, "Up South."

95. Previously, parents had addressed their pedagogical concerns by demanding increased hiring of black American and Puerto Rican teachers and the institutionalization of special curricula "designed to teach children with a history of racial and ethnic oppression in the United States." Gilberto Gerena Valentin, interview, August 23, 2013, Oral History Collection, Centro de Estudios Puertorriqueños.

96. Gilberto Gerena Valentin, interview by author, November 2013.

97. Harlem Parents Committee, *Education*.

98. Clarence Taylor, *Our Own Door*, chaps. 6, 7; Podair, *Strike*, chap. 4.

99. For a history of black power in the university, see Biondi, *Black Revolution on Campus*, chap. 4.

100. Morales interview, 5.

101. Citizens' Committee for Children of New York, Inc., "A Report on New York City High Schools," January 5, 1970, 4, box 2, folder 19, Lurie Papers.

102. "Confidential: For HSPA Use Only, '"Confrontation and Response,'" box 10, folder 4, Monserrat Papers.

103. Citizens' Committee, "Report on New York City High Schools," 2–3.

104. Denise Oliver, interview by author, August 11, 2006.

105. Biondi, *To Stand and Fight*, chap. 9. See also Clarence Taylor, *Fight the Power*, chaps. 3–5.

106. On the racialized origins of policing in the U.S., see Dunbar-Ortiz, *Loaded*, chapter 3.

107. Gertrude Samuels, "'I Don't Think the Cop Is My Friend': So Say Many of New York's Puerto Ricans, Accusing the Police of Prejudice and Brutality," *New York Times*, March 29, 1964.

108. "The Puerto Ricans: Behind the Flare-Up,"

Week in Review, *New York Times*, July 30, 1967, sec. 4; Arnie Segarra, interview by author, December 2011.

109. Johnson, *Street Justice*, chap. 6; Clarence Taylor, *Fight the Power*, chap. 4.

110. Gerena Valentin, interview by author.

111. Ibid.

112. Marable, *Malcolm X*, 127–29.

113. Gilberto Gerena Valentin, interview by Lillian Jiménez and Carlos Rodriguez-Fraticelli (n.d.), video, 1; Gerena Valentin, interview by author.

114. The effort to organize Puerto Ricans for the march was systematic and involved incentives from the national organizing committee, which had invited Gerena Valentin and Manuel Diaz of the Puerto Rican Forum to an organizing meeting with Dr. Martin Luther King in Atlanta earlier that year; Gerena Valentin, interview by author. See also Gerena Valentin, *My Life*, 135.

115. "Rights Drive Set by Puerto Ricans: Leaders Form Committee to Press for Equality," *New York Times*, August 23, 1963, 10; Gerena Valentin, interview by author.

116. Paterson, "Remembering the Harlem Riot." Numerous other incidents made headlines in the run-up to the riots. Three months after the Rodriguez and Solero shootings, in February 1964, Puerto Ricans took the streets again after the death of Francisco Rodriguez, an eighteen-year-old who had been named Boy of the Year by the Boys' Club, at the hands of an off-duty Bronx patrolman who was on probation. Robert Trumbull, "Rodriguez Boy Is Mourned by 300," *New York Times*, February 25, 1964, 21.

117. Button, *Black Violence*, 10.

118. Masotti, Seminatore, Haden, and Corsi, *Time to Burn?*, 122–27.

119. Text of Wagner's radio-TV appeal for restoration of law and order in city, *New York Times*, July 23, 1964, 12.

120. "A Civilized Community," *New York Times*, July 22, 1964, 32. The arson and looting that accompanied the uprisings were understood, at best, as actions taken opportunistically by criminal or radical elements and, at worst, as the product of uncontrolled emotionalism among black Americans and their propensity for violence.

121. Text of Wagner's radio-TV appeal.

122. The three reported cases included those of Gregory Cruz, a twenty-two-year-old Puerto Rican youth who was shot three times by police in a case of mistaken identity; Clarence Ritchie, a sidewalk vendor of dancing paper dolls, who was shot to death by a retired police officer before hundreds of people in Times Square; and Robert Owens, who was fatally shot by an off-duty officer in the Bronx. See David Herman, "Trigger-Happy Cops Gun Down More Victims," *Militant*, Sep-

tember 28, 1964, 1, 6; "Peddler is Slain, Ex Officer Held," *New York Times*, September 17, 1964; and Peter Kihss, "Detective's Trial Is Told He Was Badly Beaten," *New York Times*, February 10, 1965.

123. Johnson, *Street Justice*, 239; Gerena Valentin, interview by author.

124. Gerena Valentin, interview by author.

125. Cannato, *Ungovernable City*, 160. The city's first CCRB emerged in 1953 in the context of growing anti–police violence protests and the discovery of a deal cut between the NYPD and the Department of Justice, wherein the FBI would not investigate charges of police violence against black Americans; Biondi, *To Stand and Fight*, 191–207.

126. Gerena Valentin, interview by author.

127. Police commissioner Vincent Broderick "to Mayor John V. Lindsay, "February 8, 1966, 8–9, "Police Subject Files," box 85–86, folder 1613, location 6691, roll 43, master negative 45043, in Lindsay Papers.

128. Quoted in Johnson, *Street Justice*, 242.

129. Bernard Weinraub, "PBA Plans Door-to-Door Fight against Review," *New York Times*, September 26, 1966, 20.

130. Government policy of the 1960s generally left the complex causes of crime and riots unanswered. Cultural explanations for the rise of crime became dominant then and continue to influence sociological debates today. On the political economy of law and order and mass incarceration in the 1960s, see Hinton, *War on Poverty*. For sociological discussions of crime in the early 1960s, see the work of Gary LaFree, including LaFree and Drass, "African American Collective Action"; and Karstedt and LaFree, "Democracy, Crime, and Justice." For a critique of social sciences' cultural theories of problems in black urban life, see Kelley, *Yo Mama's Disfunktional!*, chap. 1.

131. Philip H. Dougherty, "Advertising: Civilian Review Board Fight," *New York Times*, October 18, 1966, 58.

132. Jack Bloom, *Class, Race*, 200; Marable, *Race, Reform, and Rebellion*, 92–93; Kerner Commission, *Commission on Civil Disorders*, 144.

133. Paul L. Montgomery, "1,000 Policemen Move in to Stem Brooklyn Unrest," *New York Times* July 23, 1966; "34 in Perth Amboy Held in Disorder," *New York Times*, August 1, 1966; Peter Kihss, "Puerto Rican Story: A Sensitive People Erupt," *New York Times*, July 26, 1967.

134. Homer Bigart, "2 Killed, 12 Hurt in Violence Here," *New York Times*, July 25, 1967; Sylvan Fox, "Chief Defends Method of Tactical Patrol Force," *New York Times*, July 25, 1967.

135. "Puerto Ricans: Behind the Flare-Up"; McCandlish Phillips, "Residents of East Harlem Found to Have Ingredients for Violence," *New York Times*, July 27, 1967.

136. Homer Bigart, "Renewed Violence Erupts in 2 Puerto Rican Areas," *New York Times*, July 26, 1967," 1.

137. Homer Bigart, "Disorders Erupt in East Harlem; Mobs Dispersed," *New York Times*, July 24, 1967.

138. "Policía mata puertorriqueño," *El Diario La Prensa*, July 24, 1967, 3.

139. Established in 1959, the TPF was disproportionately employed in the city's Puerto Rican and black American neighborhoods but also criticized by poor white residents in east New York. John Morganthaler, "Defended by Police Commissioner: N.Y. Riots Details Specialists," *Register-Guard*, July 22, 1964; Sylvan Fox, "Police the Target of Ghetto Wrath," *New York Times*, July 24, 1967, 17.

140. "Police in Harlem Pelted by Bricks," *New York Times*, July 24, 1967, 23.

141. "Trouble in East Harlem," *New York Times*, July 24, 1967, 25.

142. Gottehrer, *Mayor's Man*, 71.

143. Peter Kihss, "Causes Pondered by Puerto Ricans," *New York Times*, July 25, 1967.

144. Hiram Maristany, interview by author, August 11, 2000.

145. Bigart, "2 Killed, 12 Hurt"; Bennett Kremen, "Do Not Cross Flatfoot!," *Nation*, August 14, 1967.

146. Bigart, "2 Killed, 12 Hurt"; Bigart, "Renewed Violence Erupts."

147. Bigart, "2 Killed, 12 Hurt"; Bigart, "Renewed Violence Erupts."

148. Button, *Black Violence*, 7.

149. Bigart, "Renewed Violence Erupts," 20.

150. Bigart, "Disorders Erupt in East Harlem."

151. Bigart, "2 Killed, 12 Hurt," 18. Also cited in Kremen, "'Do Not Cross Flatfoot!,'" 126.

152. Bigart, "2 Killed, 12 Hurt."

153. Kremen, "Do Not Cross Flatfoot!"

154. Lespiere, *Mordaza*; Falcón, Rodríguez, and Reyes, *Puerto Rico*.

155. "Puerto Ricans: Behind the Flare-Up," 133.

156. "La policia esta de nuestra parte," *El Diario La Prensa*, July 26, 1967, published in English as "The Police Are on Our Side," *New York Times*, July 27, 1967.

157. Button, *Black Violence*, 5.

158. Bigart, "2 Killed, 12 Hurt."

159. Office of the Mayor, *Puerto Ricans Confront*.

160. Kihss, "Causes Pondered by Puerto Ricans," 18.

161. Katznelson, "Was the Great Society."

162. See Moynihan, *Maximum Feasible Misunderstanding*.

163. Katznelson, *City Trenches*, 137; Lindsay, *City*, 118.

164. Gottehrer, *Mayor's Man*, 34–44, 49.

165. Bradley, *Harlem vs. Columbia University*, chap. 1.

166. González interview.

167. Miguel Melendez, *We Took the Streets*, 73; on the RGS, see Aponte-Pares, "Lesson from El Barrio," 399–420.

168. On Oliver's biography and leadership in the Young Lords, see Johanna Fernández, "Denise Oliver."

169. On the protests at Howard University, see Degroot, *Student Protest*, 178–83.

170. Today that campus houses Lehman College. See Oliver interview, August 11, 2006.

171. Button, *Black Violence*, 24. See also Fainstein and Fainstein, "Economic Restructuring," 195.

172. Moynihan, *Maximum Feasible Misunderstanding*, 109–16.

173. Matt S. Meier and Rivera, *Mexican Americans, American Mexicans*, 215.

174. Vigil, *Crusade for Justice*, 95–97; Navarro, *La Raza Unida Party*, 87–88.

175. Carlito Rovira, interview by author, July 27, 2013.

176. Carson, *In Struggle*, 191–94, 214. For multiple interpretations of the Student Nonviolent Coordinating Committee split, see Iwan Morgan and Davies, *From Sit-In to SNCC*, chaps. 6–8.

177. Morales interview, 42–43.

178. Rovira interview, July 27, 2013.

179. Morales interview, 43.

180. Rovira interview, July 27, 2013. Note that this rendering of what happened at the meeting is corroborated by Papoleto but differs from Iris Morales's reminiscences in Morales interview, 43.

181. Rovira interview, July 27, 2013.

182. For discussions of cultural and revolutionary nationalism, see Woodard, *Nation within a Nation*; and Bush, *We Are Not*.

183. Denis, *War against Puerto Ricans*, 233–45; Monge, *Puerto Rico*, 93–94.

184. Miguel Melendez, *We Took the Streets*, 84; González interview.

185. Carlos Russell, interview by author, September 22, 2013. See also Carlos Russell, interview by Carol Quirke, 2012, 15–17, Old Westbury Oral History Project.

186. David Perez and Tobier, *Long Road from Lares*, 6–7, 10.

187. Miguel Melendez, *We Took the Streets*, chap. 3.

188. Pablo's cousin, Gilbert Colón, recounted this to me during an interview; Gilbert Colón, interview by author, June 15, 2010.

189. Guzmán, *Pablo Guzmán*, 10. Paulino's studies were made possible by a program initiated in the early twentieth century by professional Afro-Cubans in collaboration with the school's black American founder, Booker T. Washington; see Guridy, *Forging Diaspora*, chap. 1.

190. Guzmán, "*La Vida Pura*," 156.

191. "Young Lords Organization," November 1969, 2, file no. 157–4479, COINTELPRO Documents; Young Lords Party and Abramson, *Palante*, 9. According to Pablo Guzmán, the Lower East Side chapter of the Young Lords was formed without the consent of the founding Chicago group. See Guzmán, "Ain't No Party," 296; and González, *Roll Down Your Window*, xxii–xxiii.

192. Maristany interview.

193. De la Cova, *Moncada Attack*, 37–38. Developing further from its initial program, the Cuban Revolution of 1959 declared itself socialist in 1961; see Smith, *Talons of the Eagle*, 164–69.

194. Lao, "Resources of Hope," 37.

195. Joseph Harris, interview by author, November 20, 2015.

Chapter 3

1. Herring, *America's Longest War*, chap. 6; Pach, "And That's the Way."

2. Pablo "Yoruba" Guzmán, "One Year of Struggle," *Palante*, July 17, 1970, 12.

3. Juan González, interview by author, February 27, 2015.

4. Kelley, *Hammer and Hoe*; Naison, *Communists in Harlem*; Solomon, *Cry Was Unity*; Draper, *Roots of American Communism*; James, *Holding Aloft the Banner*; Kuykendall, "African Blood Brotherhood"; Makalani, *Cause of Freedom*; Iglesias, *Memoirs of Bernardo Vega*; Jesús Colón, *Puerto Rican in New York*.

5. "Young Lords: Ines Benites and Felipe Luciano."

6. Hiram Maristany, interview by author, August 11, 2000.

7. Mao Tse-tung, "On Practice"; Lukács, *History and Class Consciousness*.

8. Katsiaficas, *Imagination*, 29–36; Kelley and Esch, "Black Like Mao"; Elbaum, *Revolution in the Air*, chap. 2.

9. Mao Tse-tung, *On Guerrilla Warfare*; Vo Nguyen Giap, *People's Army*; Che Guevara, *Guerrilla Warfare*.

10. Gilbert Colón, interview by author, August 5, 2010. Although he did not officially join until later, Colón was trusted to do "cadre work" during the Garbage Offensive.

11. "Young Lords: Ines Benites and Felipe Luciano."

12. Fred Hampton, "Power Anywhere Where There's People," 1969, Black Panther Party, political pamphlets, P201234, Northwestern University Library Special Collections.

13. See specifically "Methods of Thinking and Methods of Work" in Mao Tse-tung, *Quotations*, 115–33. In an earlier epoch, Vladimir Lenin and Rosa Luxemburg debated the relative importance

of what they referred to as "spontaneity" versus "consciousness," by which they meant spontaneous eruptions of rebellion versus the planned actions of a revolutionary party. Citation on "spontaneity" versus "consciousness."

14. Guzmán, "Young Lords Legacy," 14.

15. Young Lords Party and Abramson, *Palante*, 75. The sources of their trepidation ranged from youthful inexperience to the chilling effect of left repression in the United States. The Young Lords were young; some were barely teenagers. And East Harlem was the most surveilled neighborhood in the United States, with an uninterrupted history of spying that began in 1904 when Italian radicals became the target of the police department's first red squad and continued with the surveillance of the district's democratic socialist congressman, Vito Marcantonio, in the 1930s and 1940s. In the 1950s, East Harlem experienced even deeper political repression when, in an act of armed propaganda, Lolita Lebron and four other Puerto Rican nationalists opened fire on the floor of the U.S. Congress, wounding five congressmen. For late 1960s radicals like the Young Lords, this meant that the repression of the left in the United States had a long reach that shaped their interactions with the community they called their own. Gerald Meyer, interview by author, September 12, 2015; Meyer is the author of *Vito Marcantonio: Radical Politician, 1902–1954*.

16. Luppens and Guzmán, *Young Lords Legacy*, 14.

17. Felipe Luciano, interview by author, June 27, 2004.

18. Felipe Luciano, interview by Iris Morales, in Morales, *¡Palante, Siempre Palante!* (film); Miguel Melendez, *We Took the Streets*, 97.

19. Fred Loetterle et al., "In El Barrio, It's Uphill All the Way," *New York Daily News*, June 9, 1940. See also Zipp, *Manhattan Projects*, 265; and chaps. 6–7 on the political economy of housing and urban renewal in East Harlem.

20. David Perez and Tobier, *Long Road from Lares*, 11.

21. Barry Gottehrer, interview by author, August 18, 2005; Henry Machirella, "Angry Thousands Call U.S. with Protests on Refuse," *New York Daily News*, March 20, 1969, in Sanitation Vertical File.

22. The Young Lords' insistence on obtaining brooms from the Sanitation Department was a reflection both of their political inexperience and the widespread sentiments generated by antipoverty programs, which often gave residents in the country's poorest districts a false sense of their leverage and power over local governance.

23. John V. Lindsay to Dr. Clarence C. N. Neher, vice president, Ethyl Corporation, May 7, 1969, departmental files, box 90, folder 1119, 1966–1973, Lindsay Papers. See also John V. Lindsay to Rob-

ert O. Lowery, fire commissioner, May 23, 1969, general correspondence, 1966–73, confidential, I–K, box 2, folder 18 ("Levy-Lu"), Lindsay Papers.

24. See Young Lords Party and Abramson, *Palante*, 76; Luppens and Guzmán, *Young Lords Legacy*, 15; and Pablo Guzmán, "*La Vida Pura*."

25. Felipe Luciano, interview by Denny Smithson, in "Young Lords Organization."

26. Pablo Guzmán, "Before People Called Me a Spic," 75; Carlito Rovira, interview by author, January 5, 2015.

27. On the trial of the Panther Twenty-One, see Kempton, *Briar Patch*; and Simroth, *Perversion of Justice*.

28. Guzmán, "Ain't No Party," 297.

29. See specifically "Serving the People," in Mao Tse-tung, *Quotations*, 95–97. For a discussion of the culture and structure of the Puerto Rican family, see Fitzpatrick, *Puerto Rican Americans*, 77–100. For a discussion of comparable sensibilities in the southern civil rights movement, see Payne, *Light of Freedom*.

30. Guzmán, "Before People Called Me a Spic," 74.

31. For an analysis of the discrepancy between the maligned image of the Black Panther Party in public discourse and its "serve the people" campaigns, see Charles E. Jones and Jeffries, "'Don't Believe the Hype.'"

32. For a thorough overview of the manifold social, structural, and economic problems in postwar urban cities of the North and Southwest, see Steigerwald, *Sixties*, 187–215.

33. Press release, New York City: Sanitation Department, February 2, 1972, box 16, folder 195, confidential subject files, 1966–1973.

34. Gottehrer, *Mayor's Man*, 4.

35. Guzmán, "Ain't No Party," 298–99. See also Luciano and Maristany, "Young Lords Party," 11; Jennifer Lee, "Young Lords," 66; and Jose Iglesias, "Right on with the Young Lords," *New York Times*, June 7, 1970.

36. Freeman, *Working-Class New York*, 212.

37. Charles Morris, quoted in Cannato, *Ungovernable City*, 197.

38. Peggy Streit, "Why They Fight for P.A.T," *New York Times*, September 20, 1964, SM20.

39. The challenges the group confronted in this early struggle raised larger theoretical questions, which were rooted in the long-standing debate over the meaning and conception of socialism. That debate was articulated by American socialist Hal Draper. Draper traced two major competing tendencies in the history of the socialist movement, which he defined as socialism "from below" and "from above." The former envisioned a system assembled and maintained through mass participation, while the latter depended on the

self-sacrificing struggles and dedication of a politically edified minority. Hal Draper, "The Two Souls of Socialism," pamphlet, 1966, boxed newspapers, Tamiment Library.

40. Luciano, interview by Smithson.

41. Guzmán, "Young Lords Move."

42. "Young Lords Press Release," November 12, 1969, 8–9, file no. NY 157–4479, COINTELPRO Documents.

43. Ibid.

44. "Garbage Burned in Harlem Melee," *New York Times*, August 18, 1969.

45. "Pigs Oink in Fear as YLO and the People March thru the Streets," *YLO*, ca. 1969, 17.

46. See "Garbage Burned in Harlem Melee"; Alan Howard, "The Barrio and the YLO Say No More Garbage in Our Community," *Liberation News Service*, August 21, 1969; and Abraham Peck, "Young Lords: Serve and Protect," *Rat Subterranean News*, August 28, 1969, 6.

47. Howard, "Barrio and the YLO."

48. As late as 1979, black Americans accounted for only 5 percent of the department and Puerto Ricans a scandalous 1 percent. New York City Commission on Human Rights, *Ethnic Survey*, tables 1.1–1.68; City of New York, Citywide Equal Employment Opportunity Committee, *Equal Employment*, 42; both also cited in Wilder, *Covenant with Color*, 226, 229.

49. Howard, "Barrio and the YLO"; "Garbage Burned in Harlem Melee."

50. David Bird, "Bronx Cleans Up after Rampage," *New York Times*, June 3, 1969; "Police Repulse 150 in Bronx Who Pelt Simpson St. Station," *New York Times*, June 17, 1969.

51. On El Comité, see Muzio, *Radical Imagination*.

52. Joseph P. Fried, "East Harlem Youths Explain Garbage-Dumping Demonstrations," *New York Times*, August 19, 1969. See also Guzmán, "La Vida Pura," 24.

53. Guzmán, "One Year of Struggle," 12.

54. "Young Lords Press Release," November 12, 1969, 7, file no. NY 157–4479, COINTELPRO Documents; major investigation summary sheet, August 19, 1969, City of New York, Police Department, Intelligence Division, Security, and Investigation, initiated in June 1969, R.Pe B34 F4, Richie Perez Papers, Centro Library and Archives, Hunter College.

55. Nancy Moran, "Garbage Piles Up, and Suburbs Seek Places to Put It," *New York Times*, August 22, 1969.

56. "Upward Wage Push," *New York Times*, December 2, 1969.

57. Guzmán, "One Year of Struggle," 12.

58. Guzmán, "Ain't No Party," 297.

59. Joseph P. Fried, "East Harlem Youths."

60. Carl Davidson, "Young Lords Organize New York," *Guardian*, October 18, 1969. For a reference to the series of demonstrations held by the Young Lords, see also "Plastic Bags Given East Harlem in War on Garbage Pile Up," *New York Times*, September 13, 1969.

61. "Residents in Flatlands Protest Spreading of Rats," *New York Times*, August 19, 1969.

62. Richard Reeves, "Lindsay: Learning about the Politics of Garbage," *New York Times*, August 24, 1969, E4.

63. See press releases, August–October 1969, August 1, September 4, 5, 13, 14, 21, 28, and October 1, 1969, subject index, Lindsay Papers. See also "Overtime Force to Clean Refuse," *New York Times*, September 6, 1969; "1,509.9 Tons of Trash Taken in First of 4 Sunday Tests," *New York Times*, September 9, 1969; "Mayor Enlarges Sanitation Drive," *New York Times*, September 14, 1969; and "City Concludes Experiment on Sunday Trash Pickup," *New York Times*, September 29, 1969.

64. Davidson, "Young Lords Organize New York."

65. Miguel Padilla, "How N.Y. Young Lords Developed," *Militant*, January 30, 1970.

66. Martin Luther King, "The Crisis in American Cities: An Analysis of Disorder and a Plan of Action against Poverty Discrimination and Racism in Urban America," speech, Southern Christian Leadership Conference, August 15, 1967, Atlanta.

67. The early civil rights movement in New York experimented with the issue of sanitation as a campaign. For example, the Congress on Racial Equality organized garbage-dumping campaigns, and in 1968 the papers reported garbage-dumping demonstrations at Lincoln Center, in Queens, and on the Lower East Side. See Leonard Buder, "Bridge Sitdown by CORE Blocks the Tri-borough," *New York Times*, March 7, 1964; "Garbage Protest Closes 5 Blocks: Lower East Side Residents Dump Trash in the Street," *New York Times*, February 7, 1968; and "Garbage Protest Wins Fast Pickup: Queens Residents Put Cans in Middle of Street," *New York Times*, July 3, 1970.

68. Arnie Segarra, interview by author, December 2011.

69. Gottehrer interview.

70. Department of Sanitation Annual Progress Report for 1971, February 2, 1972, box 16, folder 195, confidential subject files, 1966–73, Municipal Archives of the City of New York.

71. Jerome Kretchmer, administrator, EPA, to John V. Lindsay, October 7, 1970, "Re: Experimental Street Cleaning Project," subject files 1966–1973, box 37, folder 638, "Environmental Protection Administration (3)," Municipal Archives of the City of New York.

72. Press release, Sanitation Department, EPA, February 2, 1972, box 16, folder 195, confidential

subject files, 1966–73, Municipal Archives of the City of New York.

73. Rockefeller to Lindsay, October 12, 1970, subject files 1966–73, box 37, folder 638, "Environmental Protection Administration (3)," Municipal Archives of the City of New York. "As a reminder of the conflict that ensued between the two politicians during the handling of the nine-day strike in winter 1968 led by New York City's Uniformed Sanitationmen's Association (USA), the letter must have touched a raw nerve with Mayor Lindsay. During the breakdown in negotiations between the USA and the city, Lindsay called on the governor to deploy the National Guard to pick up the 100,00 tons of garbage that had accumulated in the city during the nine-day strike. The governor refused and proceeded to call a public health emergency and takeover of the Department of Sanitation by New York State. This forced the USA to agree to terms set by Rockefeller, which seemed to undermine the mayor's leadership and authority in the handling of the strike. For fuller discussions, see Freeman, *Working-Class New York*, 212–13; and Cannato, *Ungovernable City*, 196–204. See also Daniel Armet, director, Bureau of Pest Control, Department of Health, to Steve Isenberg, August 17, 1971 (memo, "Status Report on Phase 2 of Emergency Clean-Up Program," box 16, folder 195, confidential subject files, 1966–1973, Municipal Archives of the City of New York.

74. Armet to Isenberg, August 17, 1971, memo.

75. Quoted in Engler and Engler, *This Is an Uprising*, 33. See also Reitzes and Reitzes, "Alinsky Reconsidered," 266–79.

76. González interview.

77. David Farber and, to a lesser extent, Allen Matusow, are but two authors that blame the Weathermen and their supposed urban "revolutionary allies" (in this case the Black Panthers and others like them) for what they perceive as an unwieldy and violent finale to the decade. See Farber, *Age of Great Dreams*, 204–10; and Matusow, *Unraveling of America*, 342–43, 373–75.

Chapter 4

1. On the younger character of the migration, see Fitzpatrick, *Puerto Rican Americans*, 131.

2. "Young Lords Press Release," November 12, 1969, 4, file no. 157–4479, COINTELPRO Documents. On COINTELPRO, see Blackstone, *Cointelpro*.

3. Carlito Rovira, interview by author, July 30, 2013.

4. Miguel Melendez, *We Took the Streets*, 100–101.

5. "Radical Media Bulletin Board," *Liberation News Service*, September 6, 1969, 19. This citation is also referenced in "Young Lords Press Release," November 12, 1969, 4, file no. 157–4479, COINTELPRO Documents. Established in 1967, *Liberation News Service* emerged in response to distorted media coverage of the antiwar march at the Pentagon in 1967. Jack Newfield et al., "LNS," *New York Review of Books*, September 21, 1972. See also McMillan, *Smoking Typewriters*; Leamer, *Paper Revolutionaries*; and Dreyer and Smith, "Movement and the New Media."

6. Rovira interview, July 30, 2013.

7. Ramirez, "Nuyorican Vanguards."

8. Denise Oliver, interview by author, August 18, 2007; Juan González, interview by author, April 21, 1996.

9. Rovira interview, July 30, 2013; police record, Carlos Rovira, case #820-M 1969, Handschu Files. The police records of which this document is a part are known as the Handschu Files, which were lost and rediscovered in 2016 as a result of the author's 2014 suit against the New York Police Department for its failure to honor her research-driven, freedom of information law request on the Young Lords. The Handschu Files are the largest repository of police surveillance documents in the country, namely over 1 million surveillance files of New Yorkers compiled by the police department between 1954 and 1972, including those of Malcolm X. As of this writing, the files were not yet fully processed and organized. See Joseph Goldstein, "Old New York Police Surveillance Is Found, Forcing Big Brother Out of Hiding," *New York Times*, June 16, 2016; and Colin Moynihan, "Police Files on Radicals Are at the Center of a Suit," *New York Times*, August 11, 2014.

10. Randy Furst, "N.Y. Poor Revolt over Welfare Cuts," *The Guardian*, September 10, 1969.

11. Nadasen, *Welfare Warriors*, 4–5.

12. On rising expectations, see John Dittmer, "Rising Expectations, 1946–1954," in Dittmer, *Local People*; and Chandra and Foster, "'Revolution of Rising Expectations.'"

13. See Christopher Nigel Caton, "The Impact of the War in Vietnam on the U.S. Economy," Ph.D. diss., University of Pennsylvania, 1974.

14. "N.Y. Poor Revolt Over Welfare Cuts," *Guardian*, September 20, 1969.

15. Marilyn Salzman Webb, "Nationwide Welfare Protests," *Guardian*, July 12, 1969. Influenced by the ideas of Columbia professor Richard Cloward, the welfare movement sought to register every person in the country eligible for public assistance, and register every grievance of people already on public assistance, in order to pressure and ultimately overwhelm the welfare bureaucracy. For details of the larger movement, see Nadasen, *Welfare Warriors*; Orleck, *Storming Caesar's Palace*; and Piven and Cloward, *Poor People's Movements*.

16. Unlike previous generations of poor, white, stay-at-home welfare mothers, poor women of color were expected to transition to work.

17. Nadasen, *Welfare Warriors*, chap. 2.

18. Rovira interview, July 30, 2013.

19. Francis X. Clines, "Seven Arrested in School Boycott, *NYT*, September 10, 1969.

20. Guzmán, "Young Lords Move"; Pablo Guzmán, "Young Lords Are Taking Care of Business in New York," interview, *Liberation News Service*, September 27, 1969.

21. Juan González, "Free Clothing Program," *YLO*; see also "Young Lords Press Release," November 12, 1969, 14–16, file no. 57–4479, COINTELPRO Documents.

22. Sal del Rivero, interview by author, October 22, 2005; José "Cha Cha" Jiménez, interview by author, October 22, 2005.

23. González, "Free Clothing Program."

24. On Lords and Panther Women, see Nelson, *Women of Color and the Reproductive Rights Movement*; Morales, *Through the Eyes of Rebel Women*; "On Lord and Panther women, see Iris Morales & the Other book"; Spencer, *Revolution Has Come*; LeBlanc-Ernest, "'Most Qualified Person'"; Matthews, "'No One Ever Asks'"; Kathleen Neal Cleaver, "Women, Power, and Revolution"; Newton, "Women's and Gay Liberation"; and Lumsden, "Good Mothers with Guns."

25. Guzmán, "Young Lords Move."

26. Dunbar-Ortiz, *Loaded*, 35; see also Chapters 2 and 3.

27. Blackstone, *Cointelpro*; Churchill and Wall, *The COINTELPRO Papers*.

28. Joshua Bloom and Martin, *Black against Empire*, 479.

29. Guzmán, "Young Lords Are Taking Care of Business."

30. Juan González, "Revolutionary Health Program for the People: New York," *YLO*, January 1970, 12.

31. Guzmán, "Young Lords Are Taking Care of Business."

32. Ibid.

33. On the Panther survival programs, see Hilliard, *Black Panther Party*; and Witt, *Black Panthers*.

34. González interview. See *Palante: Latin Revolutionary News Service*, 1970–75.

35. González interview; Carlito Rovira, interview by author, July 27, 2013.

36. Richie Perez, interview by author, New York, July 17, 2000.

37. October 22, 1969, file no. 157–1204, COINTELPRO Documents.

38. Mumia Abu-Jamal, interview by author, January 24, 2015.

39. October 22, 1969, file no. 157–1204, COINTELPRO Documents.

40. Cha Cha Jiménez, phone interview by author, June 9, 2019. See also "Chicago Action," *Burning River News*, vol. 3, no. 2 (October 18, 1969).

41. On the positions of Cleaver and Newton, respectively, see Bloom and Martin, *Black against Empire*, 358–59, 386–89.

42. Julius Lester, "Black Revolution Is Real," *Movement*, September 1967, 4.

43. Rovira interview, July 30, 2013. For a cultural critique of style in the Young Lords, see Negrón-Muntaner, "Look of Sovereignty," 4–33.

44. Rovira interview, July 30, 2013; "¿Young Lords o 'landlords'? Ex miembros hablan de lo que hacen hoy," *El Diario La Prensa*, March 4, 1989, 46, referenced in Negrón-Muntaner, "Look of Sovereignty." In this 1989 article, the leadership of the MPI is cited for believing that the Young Lords were "a group of immature young people looking for publicity" and a "bunch of crazy exhibitionists." However, because of the popularity the Young Lords enjoyed in the 1960s, the mainland branch of the MPI in New York participated in Young Lords–initiated events.

45. Henry Hampton, Steve Fayer, with Sarah Flynn, *Voices of Freedom*, 358.

46. Carlito Rovira, interview by author, October 26, 2013.

47. Docents at the Bronx Museum, the leading venue of the Young Lords exhibits that were hosted in New York from July to December 2015, reported that dozens of neighborhood people who visited the exhibit recounted that they had been inspired by and wanted to join the Young Lords when they were teenagers. For a review of the exhibits, see Hansi Lo Wang, "Once Outlaws, Young Lords Find a Museum Home for Radical Roots," July 29, 2015, *NPR*, http://www.npr.org/sections/codeswitch/2015/07/29/427429960/once-outlaws-young-lords-find-a-museum-home-for-radical-roots.

48. González interview; see also Guzmán, "Ain't No Party," 294.

49. For a deeper discussion of this process, see Elbaum, *Revolution in the Air*, 20–22.

50. Young Lords and Abramson, *Palante*, 150.

Chapter 5

1. For a discussion of the shift and the racialized underpinning of its logic, see Edsall and Edsall, *Chain Reaction*, chaps. 4, 5.

2. Juan González, "Revolutionary Health Program for the People: New York," *YLO*, January 1970, 12.

3. Housing and education also ranked high as problem areas requiring greater government intervention; see Louise Johnson, *People of East Harlem*, 15–16.

4. Ibid., 79.

5. Three and a half, compared to 2.5 times, a year, respectively; ibid., 80.

6. See Engel, *Poor People's Medicine*.

7. See Ehrenreich, *American Health Empire*; and Risse, *Mending Bodies, Saving Souls*.

8. Other reasons included the privilege of admitting their private patients into the hospital and the possibility of practicing in a particular department or becoming its chief of service. Ginzburg, *Urban Health Services*, 3.

9. Kennedy, *In Critical Condition*, 121–22.

10. For an overview of the literature on the medical industry and its complexity, see Stevens, "History and Health Policy."

11. Rosner and Markowitz, "Hospitals, Insurance"; Reed, "Private Health Insurance."

12. Ehrenreich, *American Health Empire*, 12.

13. Kennedy, *In Critical Condition*, 121–22.

14. Ludmerer, "Teaching Hospitals in America."

15. Stevens, *American Medicine*.

16. Freeman, *Working-Class New York*, 213–14.

17. Ehrenreich, *American Health Empire*, 14.

18. Alondra Nelson, *Body and Soul*, chap. 1.

19. Leon Fink and Greenberg, *Quiet Zone*.

20. The EHHC was an affiliate of the Union Settlement Association, one of the nonprofit, Progressive Era organizations that settled students and middle-class social reformers in poor urban neighborhoods to help immigrants gain access to jobs, education, housing, and healthcare. See references to the meeting in "The Medicaid Blues," *Health/PAC Bulletin*, September 1969, 6; John Sibley, "50 Protest a Metropolitan Hospital," *New York Times*, December 6, 1969," 45; and Johnson, *People of East Harlem*, 80.

21. Bella August, "El Barrio: A People's Health Movement," *Health/PAC Bulletin*, February 1970, 9.

22. See Dittmer, *Good Doctors*. On Freedom House, see Trotter and Day, *Race and Renaissance*, 127–28. See also Naomi Rogers, "Caution"; Alondra Nelson, *Body and Soul*; Johanna Fernández, "Between Social Service Reform"; Johanna Fernández, "Postwar City"; Chowkwanyun, "New Left"; Mullan, *White Coat, Clenched Fist*; and Lefkowitz, *Community Health Centers*.

23. Young Lords flyer, box 4, folder 32, Union Settlement Records.

24. Ehrenreich, *American Health Empire*, v; also quoted in Stevens, "History and Health Policy."

25. Burlage, *Municipal Hospitals*.

26. State of New York Commission of Investigation, *Recommendations*, 1–32, 47–55.

27. On participatory democracy, maximum feasible participation, and community control, respectively, see Frost, *Interracial Movement*; Moynihan, *Maximum Feasible Misunderstanding*; and Podair, *Strike*.

28. Copy of original document in "Young Lords Press Release," November 12, 1969, 10, file no. NY 157-4479, COINTELPRO Documents. Reprinted in "East Harlem's Health," *Health/PAC Bulletin*, October 1969, 4; and "10 Point Health Program," *YLO*, January 1970, 13. See also Enck-Wanzer, *Young Lords*, 188.

29. Resolution document, box 4, folder 32, Union Settlement Records. On the Real Great Society, see Poston, *Gang and the Establishment*; and Aponte-Pares, "Lessons from El Barrio."

30. Juan González, interview by author, February 27, 2015.

31. Cleo Silvers, interview by author, February 29, 2016. On DRUM, see Georgakas and Surkin, *Detroit I Do Mind*.

32. HRUM, "Self Determination," in Smith Papers.

33. The term "clinical health" encompassed doctor-administered care; "environmental health" referred to hygiene and sanitation; and "community health" spearheaded public campaigns on health education. Brotherton, "Health and Healthcare"; Mir, "La evolución de los servicios," 53.

34. Danielson, "Medicine in the Community"; Fitz, "Cuban Polyclinic"; Whiteford and Branch, *Primary Health Care*, 20; Mir, "La evolución de los servicios," 53–56.

35. These clandestine trips and their impact have not been the subject of formal inquiry, but both Gosse, *Where the Boys Are*, and Dittmer, *Good Doctors*, treat the broader context of the subject.

36. Bella August, interview by author, August 1, 2013.

37. Ronald Fraser, ed., Iris Morales, interview, 1988, Columbia University Oral History Project, 20.

38. González, "Revolutionary Health Program"; see also Naomi Rogers, "Caution."

39. Sibley, "50 Protest a Metropolitan Hospital"; August, "El Barrio,'" 9.

40. Richard Stone, interview by author, February 2012.

41. August interview.

42. Carlito Rovira, interview by author, July 27, 2013.

43. August interview.

44. Sibley, "50 Protest a Metropolitan Hospital," 45.

45. For an assessment of resources and their misallocation, see Bowens, Wood, Olendzki, and Goodrich, "East Harlem and Its Health Resources," 45–50. For a critique of community control and assessment of its limitations, see Sugrue, *Sweet Land of Liberty*, 471–77; and Aronowitz, "The Dialectics of Community Control," 41–51.

46. Stevens, *In Sickness*; Odin Anderson, *Uneasy Equilibrium*.

47. Stone interview.

48. Pedro Albizu Campos quote referenced in Gilberto Gerena Valentin, interview by author, August 23, 2013.

49. Warren, *Brush with Death*, 14.

50. Ibid., 2, 33.

51. William E. Nelson, "Government Power," 372.

52. Kramansky to Lindsay, undated memo (ca. March 1970), General Correspondence, Outgoing Correspondence, G-L box 3F22, Lindsay Papers. See also a news article that reported that African Americans and Puerto Ricans were paying the highest rent per square foot of all tenants living in the metropolitan area; "Can Anybody Run New York City?," *U.S. News and World Report*, June 21, 1965, 58.

53. Edward O'Rorke, M.D. Commissioner of Health, News Release, Department of Health New York City: Poisonings Lead Vertical File, November 15, 1968.

54. For other cases, see "Infant Dies after Eating Paint from Tenement Wall," *New York Times*, May 28, 1969; "Brownsville Plagued by Paint Poisoning," *New York Times*, September 1, 1969; and Jack Newfield, "Lead Poisoning: Silent Epidemic in the Slums," *Village Voice*, September 18, 1969.

55. For more precise figures, see Eidsvold, Mustalish, and Novick, "Department of Health," 959. This document was replicated as a pamphlet by the New York City Department of Health; see pamphlet, n.d., New York City: Poisonings Lead Vertical File". See also Joseph P. Fried, "Paint-Poisoning Danger to Children Fought," *New York Times*, March 2, 1969; and "Lead Poisoning is Affecting 112,000 Children Annually, Special Report," *New York Times*, March 26, 1969.

56. Jack Newfield, "City Urged to Act in Lead Crisis," *Village Voice*, September 25, 1969; see also Jack Newfield, "My Back Pages," *Village Voice*, October 9, 1969.

57. Newfield, "City Urged to Act."

58. Christian Warren, *Brush with Death*, 163–67, 173–74, 180–89.

59. Ibid., 192–202; Newfield, "Fighting an Epidemic of the Environment," *Village Voice*, December 18, 1969, 12.

60. Jack Newfield, "Lead Poisoning Tests: Young Lords Do City's Work in the Barrio," *Village Voice*, December 4, 1969.

61. Young Lords flyer, author's personal files.

62. Guzmán, "Ain't No Party," 301, 303.

63. Newfield, "Lead Poisoning Tests."

64. Eidsvold, Mustalish, and Novick, "Department of Health," 957.

65. Ibid.; Newfield, "Lead Poisoning Tests."

66. Newfield, "Lead Poisoning Tests."

67. August interview.

68. Stephen Levin, interview by author, August 8, 2005.

69. Stone interview.

70. Rafael Viera, "Leaders of the New York Young Lords," interview, December 26, 1969"; see also "Lords Test for Lead," *Village Voice*, December 11, 1969.

71. Newfield, "Lead Poisoning Tests."

72. "City Held Callous on Lead Poisoning," *New York Times*, December 21, 1969; "Criticism Rising over Lead Poison," *New York Times*, December 26, 1969.

73. Cornely made his comments after delivering a speech at the National Conference on Black Students in Medicine and the Sciences; see Cornely quoted in "City Held Callous on Lead Poisoning."

74. Henry Intilli, "False Hopes," *Village Voice*, December 11, 1969.

75. Eidsvold, Mustalish, and Novick, "Department of Health," 957.

76. Jane S. Lin-Fu, *Lead Poisoning in Childhood*, pamphlet, U.S. Department of Health, Education, and Welfare, Health Services and Mental Health Administration, Maternal and Child Health Services, in New York City: Poisonings Lead Vertical File".

77. Kramansky to Lindsay, undated memo.

78. Barry Gottehrer, interview by author, December 14, 2005.

79. Project Status Report: Lead Poisoning Control, Health Services Administration, Housing and Development Administration, March 27, 1970, General Correspondence, Outgoing Correspondence, A–F, Eldridge, box B7F135, Lindsay Papers.

80. Press release and fact sheet on lead poisoning, Office of Public Information, Office of Administrator Gordon Chase, September 23, 1970, in New York City: Poisonings Lead Vertical File.

81. Mike Blumenfeld to Ronnie Eldridge, assistant to the mayor, July 14, 1971, Health Services Administration memo, subject files, box 6, folder 122 ("Hospital"), Lindsay Papers.

82. Eidsvold, Mustalish, and Novick, "New York City Department of Health," 956.

83. Ibid., 957.

Chapter 6

1. Carlito Rovira, interview by author, July 30, 2013.

2. On the sexual revolutions of the postwar era and the 1960s, see Bailey, "Sexual Revolution(s)." The song's title also underscored the gendered boundaries of the era's newfound sexual freedoms. In three short words, it objectified the female body and rendered women mere instruments of male sexual pleasure, a symptom of women's oppression. A month earlier, second-wave feminists had dramatized this grievance during a theatrical protest of the Miss America pageant, where they

dumped high heels, curlers, and fake eyelashes, among other symbols of women's oppression, in a "freedom trash can." On second-wave feminists, see Echols, "Nothing Distant about It."

3. McGirr, *Suburban Warriors*, 11, 219.

4. Dean M. Kelley, "The Young Lords and the Spanish Congregation: A Contest Between Revolution and Religious Liberty," *Christian Century*, January 23, 1970, 11, 13, in Bosley Papers. See also Henry C. Wyman, "First Spanish United Methodist Church and the Young Lords," January 9, 1970, *New York Crisis—Young Lords 1969–1970*, 1981–2002, in Division of General Welfare of the General Board of Church and Society Administrative Records.

5. Dean M. Kelley, "Young Lords and the Spanish Congregation," 9; Wyman, "First Spanish United Methodist Church."

6. Case, *Unpredictable Gospel*, 133–35.

7. "United Methodist Church Timeline," United Methodist Church General Commission on Archives and History, accessed July 30, 2019, http://www.gcah.org/history/united-methodist-church-timeline.

8. Samuel Cruz, *Masked Africanisms*, 23, cited in Jorge Juan Rodríguez, "The Colonial Gospel in Puerto Rico," January 3, 2017, *Christian Century*, https://www.christiancentury.org/blog-post/colonial-gospel-puerto-rico.

9. Commission on Archives and History, "Hispanic Ministries in Brooklyn and Manhattan," Spring 2014, *New York Annual Conference of the United Methodist Church Newsletter*, 3–4, in Christman Archives.

10. As told by two younger members of the parish at the time; see Carmen Pietri and Joe Pietri, interview by author, February 12, 2015.

11. Quoted in Dean M. Kelley, "Young Lords and the Spanish Congregation," 13.

12. Ibid.

13. Robert L. Wilson, *First Spanish United Methodist Church*, 10.

14. Iris Morales, interview by author, July 25, 2000.

15. The board seemed to have applied the policy indiscriminately. It had recently denied a similar request made by Massive Economic Neighborhood Development, one of the neighborhood's most established antipoverty organizations. Jonathan Black, "A Church in El Barrio—the Week of the Lords: 'This is a Family Thing,'" *Village Voice*, January 8, 1970, 29; also referenced in Guzmán and Smith, "Interview with Yoruba, Minister of Information, Young Lords Organization," 27.

16. Robert L. Wilson, *First Spanish United Methodist Church*, 11.

17. On how the New Right adjusted its rhetoric in the era of civil rights and pushed through with its regressive agenda, see Edsall and Edsall, *Chain Reaction*. The civil rights proposal called for the representation of members of historically oppressed groups in numbers comparable to their demographic percentages in society. The reform sought to correct a centuries-old practice across the country—the systematic barring, by law and custom, of members of these groups from access to decent employment, housing, education, government, sports, and the arts. Although most movement organizers supported the demand, many criticized its limitations, arguing that it didn't address endemic poverty and low wages among the oppressed. Many posited that racism was an outgrowth of capitalism and an intrinsic feature of a class-divided society and that its abolition would require changes of revolutionary proportion. These same critics observed that demands for racial representation alone reflected the aspirations of middle-class people of color—a small group in relation to its white counterpart—who stood to benefit from such reforms as junior partners in government and the professions. See Marable, *Race, Reform, and Rebellion*, chap. 8.

18. Robert L. Wilson, *First Spanish United Methodist Church*, 11.

19. Martin Luther King, "Letter."

20. Dean M. Kelley, "Young Lords and the Spanish Congregation," 10. The religious reform movement known as liberation theology emerged in the 1950s within the Catholic Church in Latin America; see Gerassi, *Revolutionary Priest*.

21. Leo D. Nieto, convenor, to United Methodist Board of Missions ad hoc committee, confidential memorandum, January 9, 1970, "Re: Notes on exploratory meeting," Young Lords Association 1970–71 (1987–029), Women's Division.

22. "The Church Must Serve the People," flyer, author's personal files; see also handwritten document for deposition, December 10, 1969, National Lawyers Guild Papers.

23. Guzmán "Interview with Yoruba, Minister of Information, Young Lords Organization, Regarding Confrontations at the First Spanish Methodist Church in El Barrio (Spanish Harlem)," 28.

24. Pietri and Pietri interview.

25. Unofficial statement of FSUMC in El Barrio, "Re: The Confrontation by the Young Lords," *First Source*, December 19, 1969, 41, *New York Crisis—Young Lords 1969–70*, 1981–2002, in Division of General Welfare of the General Board of Church and Society Administrative Records.

26. Robert L. Wilson, *First Spanish United Methodist Church*, 12.

27. Dean M. Kelley, "Young Lords and the Spanish Congregation," 10.

28. December 7 was also structured at the FSUMC as a day to share programmatic and finan-

cial plans for the new year. For a letter detailing the events leading up to the church occupation, see Bishop Lloyd Wicke to *First Source*, January 12, 1970, Young Lords 1970, in Bosley Papers.

29. Haas, *Assassination of Fred Hampton*, chaps. 12–14. On Emmett Till, see Tyson, *Blood of Emmett Till*.

30. Handwritten document for deposition, December 10, 1969, National Lawyers Guild Papers; Felipe Luciano, interview by author, August 28, 2005; Carlito Rovira, interview by author, September 14, 2013.

31. Luciano interview; Rovira interview, September 14, 2013.

32. Handwritten document for deposition.

33. Ibid.

34. Arthur Knobloch, affidavit no. 13260, Criminal Court of the City of New York, National Lawyers Guild, December 7, 1969.

35. William Colón, affidavit no. 27165, Criminal Court of the City of New York, National Lawyers Guild, December 7, 1969.

36. Fred Ledogar, affidavit no. 15049, Criminal Court of the City of New York, December 9, 1969; Knobloch affidavit.

37. Ronald Taylor, affidavit no. 29126, Criminal Court of the City of New York, December 7, 1969.

38. Handwritten document for deposition.

39. Pietri and Pietri interview.

40. Rovira interview, September 14, 2013.

41. Michael Kaufman, "8 Hurt, 14 Seized in a Church Clash," *New York Times*, December 8, 1969.

42. "Women of the Colonies."

43. Pietri and Pietri interview.

44. New York (157-4479) to Director (ATT-DID) Chicago, teletype (enciphered), December 7, 1969, 5:50 P.M., 1, 2, COINTELPRO Documents.

45. Handwritten document for deposition. See also "The Young Lords Organization Racial Matter," December 8, 1969, 3–5, Bufile no. 157-12295, file no. NY 157-4479, COINTELPRO Documents; and series of affidavits filed by patrolmen with charges leveled against the group, in National Lawyers Guild Papers.

46. The number of Young Lords hospitalized is identified in Robert Chapman, "Christian Churches and Confrontations by the Community," *First Source*, January 23, 1970, 21. On the hospitalization of Benjamin Martinez, see "Office of Probation, Report to Court, in the Case of Benjamin Martinez," December 7, 1969, National Lawyers Guild Papers. The names of the arrested are part of a list in a document titled "Young Lord Church Arrest 12/7/69," National Lawyers Guild. See also handwritten document for deposition; and "Young Lords Organization Racial Matter," 1–3.

47. Pietri and Pietri interview.

48. Carson, *In Struggle*, 294–95; see also Robert L. Wilson, *First Spanish United Methodist Church*, 1.

49. José "Cha Cha" Jiménez, interview by author, October 22, 2005; Omar Lopez, interview by author, October 25, 2005.

50. Chapman, "Christian Churches and Confrontations."

51. Reverend Carrazana and members of his congregation condemned the actions of the district executives because they were not aware of the district's conciliatory overtures toward the Young Lords, which unquestionably undermined the congregation's authority and strategy.

52. Dean M. Kelley, "Young Lords and the Spanish Congregation," 210; see also Bishop Lloyd Wick's letter to New York Annual Conference Congregations, *First Source*, January, 12 1970, 5.

53. Rovira interview, September 14, 2013.

54. Marable, *Race, Reform, and Rebellion*, 69–73; Farber, *The Age of Great Dreams*, 221–24.

55. Guzmán interview, 30.

56. Pietri and Pietri interview.

57. Robert L. Wilson, *First Spanish United Methodist Church*, 14.

58. New York (157-4479) to Director (157-12295) and Chicago (157-3645), att: Domestic Intelligence Division, teletype (enciphered), December 14, 1969, 1–2, COINTELPRO Documents. See also "Puerto Ricans Again Ask Church to Make Room for Food Program," *New York Times*, December 15, 1969.

59. Pietri and Pietri interview. Pastor Carrazana had already articulated precisely that sentiment to the *New York Times*: "The way they dress, with their insignia, it is obvious that they are not bona fide worshippers"; see Kaufman, "8 Hurt, 14 Seized."

60. Pietri and Pietri interview.

61. Ibid.

62. Nancy Vasques, Carmen, Frank, Susan, Jose, Pedro Pietri, and Magali Ayala, "Open Letter to the Congregation of the First Spanish Methodist Church," *First Source*, January 23, 1970, 2.

63. Guzmán interview, 31.

64. Katz, *Undeserving Poor*, chap. 1.

65. See Lewis, *Five Families*; Lewis, *La Vida*; and Harrington, *Other America*.

66. Harrington, *Other America*, 16–17.

67. Lewis, *La Vida*, xxvi.

68. On the Protestant ethic, see Palmer, "Theological and Moral."

69. According to Maurice Isserman, Michael Harrington's biographer, Harrington feared "sounding like a stereotypical Marxist agitator stuck in the '30s"; see Barbara Ehrenreich, "Michael Harrington and the Culture of Poverty," *Nation*, April 2, 2012. On liberal intellectual thought

of the 1950s and the political considerations that shaped these writings, see Matusow, *Unraveling of America*, 1–13.

70. Katz, *Undeserving Poor*, chap. 2; see also Robin D. G. Kelley, *Yo Mama's Disfunktional!*, chap. 1.

71. New York to Director, teletype, December 21, 1969, COINTELPRO Documents.

72. Luciano speech, transcript by Graciela M. Smith, *First Source*, December 24, 1969, 4.

73. Ibid.

74. Ibid.

75. Luisa A. Quintero, "Lucharemos por libertad de los oprimidos: 'Young Lords,'" *El Diario La Prensa*, December 21, 1969," 4, 46.

76. Ibid., 4.

77. Luciano speech.

78. BU 157-12295, New York to Director, Report: "Young Lords Organization," December 23, 1969, COINTELPRO Documents.

79. FBI documents cite the number of people involved as 100; see Telegraph from New York (157-4479) to Director, "Young Lords Organization (YLO): Racial Matters," December 28, 1969, 1–2, COINTELPRO Documents.

80. On the Children's March, see Levinson, *We've Got a Job*.

81. The committee included the group's chief minister, David Perez; Mickey Melendez; Herman "Hurricane" Flores; Disal Alkalili AKA Muntu; Gene Acosta; and Roy Peña Debenya.

82. Dean M. Kelley, "Young Lords and the Spanish Congregation," 208.

83. Pietri and Pietri interview.

84. The consideration seems unthinkable for activists in the post-1960s era, who would face an increasingly militarized and more deadly police force.

85. Bella August, interview by author, August 1, 2013.

86. On the sit-down strike, see Fine, *Sit-Down*.

87. Michael Kaufman, "Puerto Rican Group Seizes Church in East Harlem in Demand for Space," *New York Times*, December 29, 1969; Rovira interview, February 9, 2015.

88. Juan González, in *El pueblo se levanta*; also quoted in Luna, "Young Lords."

89. Freire, *Pedagogy of the Oppressed*; Fanon, *Black Skin, White Mask*; Fanon, *Wretched of the Earth*.

90. Sid Davidoff, interview by author, August 17, 2005; Kaufman, "Puerto Rican Group Seizes Church."

91. Arnie Segarra, interview by author, August 25, 2011.

92. Davidoff interview.

93. Kaufman, "Puerto Rican Group Seizes Church."

94. Ibid.

95. Ibid.

96. New York (157–4479) (2P) to Director (157–12295), att: Domestic Intelligence Division, teletype (enciphered), December 29, 1969, "Young Lords Organization: Racial Matters," 1–2, COINTELPRO Documents.

97. Arnold H. Lubasch, "Young Lords Give Food and Care at Seized Church," *New York Times*, December 30, 1969.

98. Ibid.

99. Dean M. Kelley, "The Young Lords and the Spanish Methodist Congregation," *Christian Century* 87, no. 7 (February 18, 1970): 208.

100. Max Lerner, "Whose Churches," *New York Post*, January 8, 1970, Young Lords 1970, in Bosley Papers.

101. Young Lords Hiram Maristany to A & P Food Stores, November 26, 1969, Perez Papers.

102. Rovira interview, September 14, 2013.

103. Michael Kaufman, "Church Occupiers Ordered to Court," *New York Times*, 35.

104. Jeff Kamen, in "Revolution for Breakfast."

105. Hiram Maristany, interview by author, August 21, 2013.

106. New York (157–4479) (2P) to Director (157–12295), att: Domestic Intelligence Division, teletype (enciphered), December 29, 1969, "Young Lords Organization: Racial Matters," 1–2, COINTELPRO Documents.

107. Political education classes were held every Tuesday evening in the Bronx and Manhattan. Each session brought an awareness of the historical, linguistic, and cultural heritage of Puerto Ricans. Carlos Aponte joined the Lords at this time and became a pivotal leader in this work. See Carlos Aponte, "Community Education," *Palante* (Bronx, N.Y.), June 5, 1970.

108. Black, "Church in El Barrio," 29.

109. Richard Stone, interview by author, February 2012.

110. Denise Oliver, interview by author, August 18, 2006; Morales interview.

111. Oliver interview.

112. Chapman, "Christian Churches and Confrontations."

113. Ibid., 18–19. On the freedom school movement, see Hale, *Freedom Schools*.

114. Chapman, "Christian Churches and Confrontations," 18.

115. Ibid., 20.

116. Ibid., 17–22.

117. Juan Flores, *Bomba to Hip-Hop*, 67–69.

118. Gilberto Gerena Valentin, interview by author, August 23, 2013.

119. These artists were also part of the newly formed Art Workers' Coalition, a racially diverse

network that asserted the right of artists to control the use and distribution of their work. M. S. Handler, "75 Artists Urge Closing of Museum's 'Insulting' Harlem Exhibit," *New York Times*, January 23, 1969, 14. See also Cahan, "Inventing the Multicultural Museum."

120. Luciano interview.

121. David González, "When Life Is Art, Bowing to Death Is Not an Option," *New York Times*, January 27, 2004, B1.

122. "Dominant ideology" refers to a commonsense understanding of reality that often perceives inequality as a by-product of "nature" or the natural order of things. By the 1960s, social critics and academics had critiqued, revised, and expanded the definition of ideology that Karl Marx and Friedrich Engels had originally conceptualized. Within the New Left, analyses of ideology—its unconscious expressions in movement work and its function in society—emerged as a signature practice of activism and prerequisite for personal and human liberation. Its members sought to overcome the ideological through political education and the study of history. Second-wave feminists deconstructed ideology in women's circles. Their slogan, "The personal is political," popularized the notion that power operates in all human transactions and relationships even in the seemingly personal spheres of sexuality, amorous relationships, and the family.

123. Max Lerner, "Whose Churches?"

124. Sixty-three signatories to Wesley D. Osborne, January 16, 1970, Young Lords 1970, in Bosley Papers.

125. Rovira interview, September 14, 2013. Visits by representatives of the Panther Twenty-One and the national office of the BPP are referenced in the FBI files of the organization. "Young Lords Organization: Racial Matters," January 9, 1970, 6, Bufile no. 157–12295, file no. NY 157–4479, COINTELPRO Documents.

126. Black, "Church in El Barrio," 30.

127. Ibid.; Juan González, interview by author, April 21, 1996; Michael Kaufman, "Church Occupiers Ordered to Court," New York Times, 35.

128. González interview.

129. Rovira interview, September 14, 2013.

130. Richie Perez, interview by author, New York, July 17, 2000.

131. Gloria Rodriguez, in *iPalante, Siempre Palante!*, documentary directed by Iris Morales.

132. Rovira interview, September 14, 2013.

133. Ibid.

134. New York 157–4479 2P to Director, att: Domestic Intelligence Division, teletype (enciphered), December 31, 1969, Young Lords Organization: Racial Matters, file b6 b7c, COINTELPRO

Documents. See also summons prepared by Oscar González-Suarez, attorney for plaintiffs, *Supreme Court of the State of New York: County of New York, First Spanish United Methodist Church, Inc., Rev. Dr. Wesley D. Osborne, District Superintendent Ramon Aponte, Lay Leader, Chairman Board of Trustees and Efrain González, Chairman Administrative Board v. Young Lords of America, Felipe Luciano, Juan González, Yoruba, David Perez, John Doe, Jan Roe, Jan Doe, John Roe, et al.*, December 24, 1969, National Lawyers Guild Papers.

135. New York 157–4479 2P to Director, att: Domestic Intelligence Division, teletype (enciphered), December 31, 1969, Young Lords Organization: Racial Matters, file b6 b7c, COINTELPRO Documents.

136. Anticipating that they might be charged with violating private property, the flyer affirmed that the church "does not pay taxes and just takes space in East Harlem."

137. "Young Lords Defy Take-Over Order," *New York Times*, January 3, 1970.

138. "Militants Vow to Continue Protest at Harlem Church," *New York Times*, January 4, 1970.

139. Quoted in newspaper photo enclosure captioned "The Young Lords" in letter of complaint by local business owner (name redacted) sent to J. Edgar Hoover. Sender's Address: Hosiery in Continental Styles, 5th Avenue, New York, N.Y. 10016. Dated December 29, 1969. File no. identified with letter: 157-12295-53.

140. "Young Lords Defy Take-Over Order," *New York Times*, January 3, 1970, 8.

141. Letter from Bishop Lloyd C. Wicke, January 12, 1970, Bosley Papers.

142. Pietri and Pietri interview; "Lindsay Aide Backs Youths Who Seized East Harlem Church," *New York Times*, January 5, 1970.

143. Arnie Segarra, interview by author, December 2011.

144. Rev. Humberto Carrazana, Wesley Osborne, and Bishop Lloyd Wicke, "The First Spanish United Methodist Church and the Young Lords: A Question of Religious Freedom," *First Source*, n.d., 3.

145. Summons prepared by Oscar González-Suarez, attorney for plaintiffs, *Supreme Court of the State of New York: County of New York, First Spanish United Methodist Church, Inc., Rev. Dr. Wesley D. Osborne, District Superintendent Ramon Aponte, Lay Leader, Chairman Board of Trustees and Efrain González, Chairman Administrative Board v. Young Lords of America, Felipe Luciano, Juan González, Yoruba, David Perez, John Doe, Jan Roe, Jan Doe, John Roe, et al.*, December 24, 1969, National Lawyers Guild Papers.

146. New York 157–4479 (P) 1P to Director 157–

12295, att: Domestic Intelligence Division, urgent teletype (enciphered), January 5, 1970, in Young Lords Organization: Racial Matters, file b6 b7c, COINTELPRO Documents.

147. *Supreme Court of the State of New York County of New York v. Young Lords of America*, index no. 19234/69, point 5, National Lawyers Guild Papers.

148. Ibid., points 24 and 7, respectively.

149. Ibid., point 28.

150. Ibid., point 6.

151. Kaufman, "Church Occupiers Ordered to Court."

152. "The Young Lords Organization: Racial Matters," 1970, 6, Bufile 157–12295, NY file 157–4479, COINTELPRO Documents.

153. Ibid., 5. See also "Church to Press Court for Young Lords," *New York Post*, January 3, 1970.

154. William Rivera-Torres, "Expulsan de iglesia a Young Lords," *El Diario La Prensa*, January 8, 1970, 3.

155. "The Young Lords Organization: Racial Matters," 1970, 6, Bufile 157–12295, NY file 157–4479, COINTELPRO Documents.

156. Lenin, *"Two Tactics of Social-Democracy."*

157. Ed Morales, "Places in the Puerto Rican Heart, Eddie Figuero and the Nuyorican Imaginary," *Centro Voice E Magazine*, Center for Puerto Rican Studies.

158. The collection of the art of Latino culture at El Museo del Barrio is the most impressive. It spans more than 800 years of Latin American, Caribbean, and Latino art, includes pre-Columbian Taino artifacts; traditional arts; twentieth-century drawings, paintings, sculptures, and installations; and prints, photography, documentary films, and video. For a history of the development of this renaissance moment in Nuyorican art and culture, see Ramirez, "Nuyorican Vanguards."

159. Peter Kihss, "2 Panels Are Set Up to Counter Threat of Community Disputes," *New York Times*, January 7, 1970, 21; "84 Church Aides Plead for Lords," *New York Times*, January 24, 1970, 40; Thomas F. Brady, "Badillo Confers with Young Lords," *New York Times*, February 1, 1970, 59; "First Spanish Methodist Church and the Young Lords Organization," Board of Mediation for Community Disputes, Detroit Industrial Mission Records, Series I, Box 6, Item 10, p. 109–12. Archive of Labor and Urban Affairs, Wayne State.

160. "Rocky's News for NYC Debated," *Adirondack Daily Enterprise*, January 8, 1970.

161. "Revolution for Breakfast."

Chapter 7

1. Jose Yglesias, "Right on with the Young Lords," *New York Times Magazine*, June 7, 1970.

2. Juan González, interview by author, February 27, 2015; Ramon Morales, interview by author, July 23, 2019.

3. Elbaum, *Revolution in the Air*, 41–42.

4. A useful collection of original texts is Tucker, *Marx-Engels Reader*.

5. Young Lords Party, "13 Point Program."

6. González interview.

7. Richie Perez, interview by author, July 17, 2000.

8. For a discussion of the New Left's yearnings for "liberated" zones and organizing toward that end, see Ashbolt, *Cultural History*, chap. 9.

9. On the social and cultural imprint of suburbia and the nuclear family in the 1950s, see May, *Homeward Bound*.

10. The "Rules of Discipline" were created in January 1970.

11. The Young Lords were trained in the martial arts by members Jose Angel Luis, Pie, Huey, and Chango, among others. Denise Oliver, interview by author, August 18, 2006; also described by Young Lord Iris Morales in Judy Clemserud, "Young Women Find a Place in High Command of Young Lords," *New York Times*, November 11, 1970.

12. Gosse, *Rethinking the New Left*, 188. The 1969 figure used here was calculated by the conversion table of the Bureau of Labor Statistics; see "CPI Inflation Calculator," Bureau of Labor Statistics, accessed March 17, 2019, http://www.bls.gov/data/inflation_calculator.htm.

13. Oliver, interview by author, August 18, 2006.

14. Perez interview.

15. Carlito Rovira, interview by author, July 27, 2013.

16. Vanden Heuvel, *Report to the Mayor*, 4.

17. Matusow, *The Unraveling of America*, 337. Same reference quoted as 19 percent in Kimmel, "The Sixties without Metaphor," 80.

18. Beyond their public support for black radicals, such as Robert Williams, and colonized people the world over, the Young Lords' support for Mao's policies seemed to challenge orthodoxy. Mao called out the Soviet Union for its "peaceful coexistence" with imperialism, and domestically his policies seemed to target the inertia and corruption of China's state bureaucracy. China appeared to be the beacon of a principled, evolving socialism responsive to the needs of the people.

19. Herring, *America's Longest War*.

20. On the American soldiers' rebellion in Vietnam, see Appy, *Working-Class War*; and Neale, *People's History*, chap. 6.

21. Examples include Iran, Guatemala, the Dominican Republic, and Chile. See Gaddis, *Cold War*.

22. For an overview of the urban rebellions and their root causes, see Steigerwald, *Sixties*, chap. 7.

23. See, for example, Felipe Luciano, "Huey," *Palante*, June 19, 1970, 14; Ministry of Education, "Libertad Para Los Siete," *Palante*, July 31, 1970, 15; Juan "Fi" Ortiz, "Carlos Feliciano Framed," *Palante*, August 15, 1970, 7.

24. Kavanagh, "Ideology."

25. Perez interview.

26. For a riveting account of how millions in the United States came to believe in the structural roots of militarism and inequality in the United States, see Elbaum, *Revolution in the Air*, chap. 1.

27. Special to the Defender, "Racial Militancy and Pride Urged at West Coast Rally," *Chicago Daily Defender*, Nov. 28, 1962.

28. Perez interview.

29. Juan González, West Side Story 1971.

30. Denise Oliver, interview by author, August 18, 2007.

31. The influence and survival of a revolutionary organization, he argued, depends on the ability of its members to accurately assess changing political conditions and adapt its practices, interventions, and programs quickly and accordingly, without compromising political principle. Lenin, *What Is to Be Done?*

32. Young Lords Party and Abramson, *Palante*, 77.

33. On the adoption of Third World Marxism by 1960s radicals, see Elbaum, *Revolution in the Air*, 41–58.

34. See, for example, this discussion: "The growing incompatibility between the productive development of society and its hitherto existing relations of production expressed itself in bitter contradiction, crises, spasms." In Marx, *Grundrisse*, 749–51.

35. Denise Oliver, interview by author, August 18, 2007. See also Johanna Fernández, "Denise Oliver."

36. González interview.

37. Gloria Fontanez, interview by author, October 20, 2010.

38. González interview.

39. Photo of small group of Young Lords in a circle, with Iris Morales speaking, captioned "New Ways of Learning," Evelina Antonetty Collection.

40. Iris Morales, interview by author, July 25, 2000.

41. Young Lords Party and Abramson, *Palante*, 77.

42. Rovira interview, July 27, 2013.

43. Morales, interview by author.

44. Felipe Luciano, interview by author, June 27, 2004; Oliver, interview by author, August 18, 2007; Carlito Rovira, interview by author, July 30, 2013.

45. Young Lords Party and Abramson, *Palante*, 77.

46. Echols, *Daring to Be Bad*.

47. Luis Acosta Garden, "The Young Lords," interview by Elizabeth Perez Luna, Pacifica Radio Archive (n.d.).

48. Ronald Fraser, ed., Iris Morales, interview, 1988, Columbia University Oral History Project.

49. González interview. SDS was the largest student organization of the New Left. For histories, see Sale, SDS; McMillian and Buhle, *New Left Revisited*; and Max and Isserman, *If I Had a Hammer*.

50. See Rodríguez-Morazzani, "Political Cultures"; and Lespiere, *Mordaza*.

51. Numerous Young Lords articulated this view in Chicago and New York, including Tony Baez of Chicago. Tony Baez, interview by author, August 10, 2010.

52. For an analysis of the process of radicalization in the 1960s and the revolutionary parties built during this period, see Elbaum, *Revolution in the Air*.

53. Oliver, interview by author, August 18, 2007.

54. Ibid.; Rovira interview, July 27, 2013; Gilbert Colón, interview by author, January 8, 2005.

55. Carmichael and Hamilton, *Black Power*; see also Allen, *Black Awakening*.

56. Kelley and Esch, "Black Like Mao," 17; Dean E. Robinson, *Black Nationalism*, chap. 3; Van Deburg, *Modern Black Nationalism*, chap. 26.

57. Panther leader Eldridge Cleaver advocated for urban guerrilla war, but his position did not prevail; Joshua Bloom and Martin, *Black against Empire*, 367–71.

58. Felipe Luciano, "On Revolutionary Nationalism," *Palante*, May 8, 1970, centerfold, reprinted in Young Lords Party and Abramson, *Palante*, 150. The group set "united states" in lowercase.

59. Yglesias, "Right on with the Young Lords," 84.

60. Herring, *America's Longest War*, 33–45.

61. Sugrue, *The Origins of the Urban Crisis*.

62. Luciano, "On Revolutionary Nationalism."

63. Lenin, "Right of Nations.'"

64. Bew, *Ideology*.

65. Pablo Guzmán, "Malcolm Spoke for Puerto Ricans," *Palante*, ca. January 1970, 2.

66. Luciano, "On Revolutionary Nationalism."

67. Martin Luther King, *Stride toward Freedom*, 22.

68. On the Harlem Renaissance's cultural analysis of racism, see Garcia, *Psychology Comes to Harlem*.

69. David Perez and Tobier, *Long Road from Lares*, 12.

70. Felipe Luciano, interview by Iris Morales, in Morales, ¡*Palante, Siempre Palante!* (film).

71. Richie Perez, "The Chains That Have Been Taken off Slaves' Bodies," in Young Lords Party and Abramson, *Palante*, 65.

72. Marx, *Capital*.

73. Luciano, "On Revolutionary Nationalism."

74. Franz Fanon, among others, well describes the class: "Because it is bereft of ideas, because it lives to itself and cuts itself off from the people, undermined by its hereditary incapacity to think in terms of all the problems of the nation as seen from the point of view of the whole of that nation, the national middle class will have nothing better to do than to take on the role of manager for Western enterprise, and it will in practice set up its country as the brothel of Europe." In Fanon, *Wretched of the Earth*, 154.

75. Juan González, "Price of Imperialism," in Young Lords Party and Abramson, *Palante*, 65. See also Luciano, "On Revolutionary Nationalism."

76. Juan González, "The Vote or the Gun," *Palante*, May 22, 1970, centerfold.

77. Luciano, "On Revolutionary Nationalism."

78. James, *Holding Aloft the Banner*, chap. 5; Zumoff, *Communist International*, chap. 14.

79. Lenin, "Theses on the National Question.'"

80. McCormick, *America's Half Century*, chaps. 1, 2.

81. Lenin, "Imperialism.'"

82. James, *Holding Aloft the Banner*, chap. 5; Zumoff, *Communist International*, chap. 14.

83. Debs, *Negro in the Class Struggle*; for a closer interpretation of this position, see William P. Jones, "Nothing Special."

84. Precursors to the concept include the emigrationist projects espoused by early black nationalists including Prince Hall, Lewis Woodson, and Martin Delaney. Disappointed by white racism toward black Americans and pessimistic about the prospects of equal interracial coexistence, these early black thinkers endorsed black American emigration from the United States to Africa. On this issue, see Maxwell, *New Negro, Old Left*; Naison, *Communists in Harlem*; and Kelley, *Hammer and Hoe*. On the origins of black emigration theories and black nationalism, see Floyd Miller, *Search for Black Nationality*; and Harding, *There Is a River*.

85. Luciano, "On Revolutionary Nationalism."

86. Andrés Torres and Velázquez, *Puerto Rican Movement*, 38–39.

87. González, "Vote or the Gun," 10–11.

88. Ayala and Bernabe, *Puerto Rico*, 116, 165–74.

89. Gilberto Gerena Valentin, interview by author, November 2013; Rovira interview, July 27, 2013.

90. Ramon Bosque Perez and Morera, *Colonial Rule*.

91. González interview; Gerena Valentin interview; Rovira interview, July 27, 2013.

92. Tony Baez, interview by author, July 29, 2014.

93. Morales, interview by author.

94. For studies of the emergence and dynamics of these movements and their leaders in New York, see Starr, "'Hit Them Harder,'" 135–54; and Andrés Torres and Velázquez, *Puerto Rican Movement*.

95. González, "Vote or the Gun," 11.

96. Powers and Macisco, *Los puertorriquenos en Nueva York*, 10.

97. González, "Vote or the Gun," 11.

98. González interview.

99. Morales, interview by author.

100. Carson, *In Struggle*, 191–94, 214.

101. Kenneth T. Jackson, *Crabgrass Frontier*.

102. Gosse, *Rethinking the New Left*, 47.

103. Huey Jung, "I Wor Kuen," *Palante*, n.d., 15; Maeda, "Black Panthers."

104. Pulido, *Black, Brown, Yellow*, chap. 4.

105. González interview.

106. Panama Alba, interview with author, August 16, 2005.

107. Geography was also important. In Chicago, where there was a more visible white working class, we see the emergence of the Rainbow Coalition.

108. See points 6, 12, and 13 of the Thirteen-Point Program and Platform, in Young Lords Party and Abramson, *Palante*, 150.

109. Young Lords Party and Abramson, *Palante*, 79.

110. On rising expectations theory, see Gurr, *Why Men Rebel*; for an overview of social movement theory, see Morris and Mueller, *Frontiers in Social Movement Theory*.

111. Perez interview; González interview.

112. Frank Browning and Banning Garrett, "The New Opium War," *Ramparts* 9, no. 10 (May 1971): 32–39.

113. Daoud, "Gorilla on Your Back," *Palante*, November 20, 1969, n.p. In Field Office File # 157-4479, "The Young Lords Organization," 3/31/70, 8. COINTELPRO files.

114. Quoted in Kuzmarov, *Addicted Army*, 94.

115. Miguel Melendez, *We Took the Streets*, 177.

116. Webb, *Dark Alliance*.

117. "Women of the Colonies." "Women of the Colonies" is a three-episode report by a group of young women members of the YLO living in Manhattan.

118. González interview.

119. "The Mafia Has Put out a $20,000 Contract for the Murder of Felipe," *Palante*, July 31, 1970, 2.

120. Booker, "Lumpenization"; Hilliard, *Black Panther Party*.

121. The emblematic radical expression of this perspective can be found in Marcuse, *One-Dimensional Man*.

122. On the background to this development, see Collins, "Growth Liberalism."

123. Peck, *Uncovering the Sixties*, xv; McMillian, *Smoking Typewriters*, 192.

124. Oliver, interview by author, August 18, 2007.

125. Young Lords Party and Abramson, *Palante*, 10–11.

126. Cover, *Palante*, vol. 3, no. 15.

127. Perez interview. Names of editorial staff appear in *Palante*, May 8, 1970.

128. Juan González, "Armense . . . ," *Palante*, October 30, 1970, 12.

129. Led by a black Puerto Rican, Emeterio Betances, El Grito de Lares is considered the first rebellion against colonization. "El Grito de Lares," *Palante*, September 25, 1970, 4–5.

130. For example, Luis De Graffe, "Urban Renewal = Spic Removal," *Palante*, July 31, 1970, 8; Carl Pastor, "Socialism at Lincoln—July 14, 1970," *Palante*, July 31, 1970, 5; Richie Perez, "High Schools," *Palante*, May 2, 1970, 16; Pablo "Yoruba" Guzmán, "Why the Young Lords Party," *Palante*, December 25, 1970, 13–14; Larry Louzau, "High School Students Unite," *Palante*, November 20, 1970, 8; and Richie Perez, "Los Trabajadores," *Palante*, December 11, 1970, 3.

131. "Boogaloo to the Gas Chamber," *Palante*, January 19, 1970, 6; and "Lisette and Lucesita," *Palante*, January , 1971, 7.

132. Oliver, interview by author, August 18, 2007.

133. Morales, interview by author.

134. The story is told in Medsger, *Burglary*.

135. Young Lords Party and Abramson, *Palante*, 11.

136. Young Lords Party, *Resolutions and Speeches*, 7; Young Lords Party and Abramson, *Palante*, 11.

137. Young Lords Party, *Resolution and Speeches*, 7. In place of the unreliable *YLO*, the New York Lords took on the challenge of publishing their own publication earlier in October 1969, a "mimeographed packet," which they called *Palante*, "the voice of the YLO-East," and on May 8, 1970, *Palante* began to be published as a full-length newspaper. See Young Lords Party and Abramson, *Palante*, 11.

138. Pablo "Yoruba" Guzmán, "One Year of Struggle," *Palante*, July 17, 1970, 12."

139. José "Cha Cha" Jiménez, interview by author, July 1, 2019.

140. José "Cha Cha" Jiménez, interview by author, July 1, 2019.

141. Marx, *Capital*.

Chapter 8

1. Hendrik Hertzberg, "What's Going Down at the Dix Stockade," *Win*, September 1969, 12, in Fort Dix 38 (GF) Vertical File.

2. The other four soldiers singled out as ring-leaders were Terry Klug, Bill Brakefield, Jeff Russell, and Thomas Catlow, who were members of the American Servicemen's Union (ASU). "Stockade Riot, Fort Dix, New Jersey" circular, Fort Dix 38 (GF) Vertical File.

3. The war of attrition, as it was called, was adopted after the failure of the Strategic Hamlet Program, which sought to relocate Vietnamese farmers and sever the possible influence of the National Liberation Front on them. See Herring, *America's Longest War*, 107–8.

4. On the black veteran experience and resistance, see Terry, *Bloods*.

5. Herring, *America's Longest War*, 301; Appy, *Working Class War*, 206–49; Neale, *People's History*, 149–84.

6. Untitled Workers' Defense League report based on inmates' interviews and documents of the Criminal Investigation Division of the Army, compiled by WDL lawyers and aides, Fort Dix 38 (GF) Vertical File.

7. Hertzberg, "Dix Stockade," 12.

8. Ibid.

9. Untitled Workers' Defense League report.

10. "Stockade Riot, Fort Dix, New Jersey" and "Fort Dix Fact Sheet" circulars, Fort Dix 38 (GF) Vertical File; Irwin Silber, "5000 March against War at Fort Dix," *Guardian*, October 18, 1969; "Free the Fort Dix 38," *Shakedown*, September 12, 1969, 1, 4; Hertzberg, " 'Dix Stockade," 12.

11. "Stockade Riot, Fort Dix, New Jersey" and "Fort Dix Fact Sheet" circulars.

12. On October 14, 1968, twenty-seven prisoners at the Presidio stockade in San Francisco abandoned their line on cue during morning formation and, singing "We Shall Overcome," began a sit-down demonstration in the yard in protest of the shooting death of a stockade inmate by a guard. Thus began a series of demonstrations by GIs against army conditions and against the U.S. intervention in Vietnam. The army was criticized for violating the rights of low-ranking enlisted men; denying its accused the right to a fair and impartial trial by a jury of peers; and assembling court proceedings where accusers appoint the prosecutor, defense, and jury and where court-martial boards are composed of officers and senior-grade enlisted men who would almost always vote to prosecute. In addition to seeking reforms in the military's justice system, antiwar groups and congressional investigation committees exposed the inhumane conditions and incidents of torture at the stockades. "Torture in Stockades," *New York Times*, October 10, 1970; also see "Stockade Life," Fort Dix 38 (GF) Vertical File (. For the full story of the Presidio stockade protests, see Gardner, *Unlawful Concert*.

13. "Stockade Riot, Fort Dix, New Jersey"; Untitled Workers' Defense League report.

14. Hertzberg, "Dix Stockade."

15. Newark (100-New) to Director, att: Domestic Intelligence Division New York, teletype, March 4, 1970, "Possible Demonstration, Ft. Dix, NJ by Young Lords Three Nine Next," COINTELPRO Documents. In the army a "general court-martial" is called to prosecute the most serious offenses and can end in dishonorable discharge with a penalty of several years of hard labor. Minor offenses are tried under "special."

16. "Racist Court Gives Rodriguez-Torres Four Years," *Shakedown*, March 6, 1970.

17. Carlito Rovira, interview by author, September 2013.

18. Richie Perez, interview by author, July 17, 2000.

19. Ibid.

20. Ibid.

21. Carlito Rovira, interview by author, July 27, 2013.

22. Maryann Weissman, "Fight MPs after Brass Railroad Puerto Rican Brother," *Bond*, March 18, 1970, 1, 8, in Fort Dix 38 (GF) Vertical File.

23. See classic discussion on "Dominant, residual, and emergent" culture in Williams, *Marxism and Literature*, 121–27. On ideology, see Kavanaugh, "Ideology."

24. For a survey of black radical women's interventions in a cross-section of movements, see Gore, Theoharis, and Woodard, *Want to Start a Revolution?* On the activism of Evelina Lopez Antonetty, an unsung Puerto Rican radical activist, see Back, "'Parent Power.'" For the experience of white women, see Evans, *Personal Politics*.

25. Echols, "Nothing Distant about It," chap. 5.

26. On the vision of the new individual in society, see Young Lords Party and Abramson, *Palante*, 53.

27. Luisa A. Quintero, "Lucharemos por libertad de los oprimidos: 'Young Lords,'" *El Diario La Prensa*, December 21, 1969, translation mine.

28. The best example was Herman Badillo, who was elected as borough president of the Bronx.

29. Rivera, *Exposing Myself*, 64; Pablo Guzmán, "Before People Called Me a Spic," 241.

30. "Puerto Rican Studies, Yes," editorial, *El Diario La Prensa*, August 29, 1969, 21.

31. Loveman and Muniz, "How Puerto Rico Became White."

32. Du Bois, *Dark Water*, 55–77; Frazier, *Negro Family*.

33. Hoffnung-Garskoff, "Migrations of Arturo Schomburg," 3–49; Delgado, "Jesús Colón," 80–81.

34. Sonia Song-Ha Lee, *Latino Civil Rights Movement*, 24.

35. Thomas, *Puerto Rican Citizen*, 57, 134, 142, 164.

36. Diane Ravitch, "East Harlem in Search of a Poverty Program," East Harlem Poverty, Box 7, Lurie Papers.

37. Guzmán, "Before People Called Me a Spic," 73.

38. See Hoffnung-Garskoff, "World of Arturo Schomburg"; and Mirabal, "Melba Alvarado."

39. Felipe Luciano, interview by author, September 21, 2008.

40. Ibid.

41. Iris Morales, interview by author, July 25, 2000; Denise Oliver, interview by author, August 18, 2007.

42. Flores, *Bomba to Hip-Hop*, 80.

43. On the history of Puerto Rican settlement in New York, see Thomas, *Puerto Rican Citizen*.

44. Gilbert Colón, interview by author, June 15, 2010. Flores, *Bomba to Hip-Hop*, chap. 5.

45. Carlito Rovira, interview by author, July 17, 2013.

46. Luciano interview; Tony Baez, a Young Lord from Chicago who built a branch in Milwaukee, articulates the same, almost word for word.

47. Flores, *Bomba to Hip-Hop*, 82.

48. Gilbert Colón, interview by author, February 8, 2005.

49. On race ideology in Puerto Rico, see Whitten and Torres, *Blackness in Latin America*, 13–15, 22–26, 104–6.

50. Rovira interview, July 17, 2013; also in Oliver, interview by author, August 18, 2007.

51. Carlos Aponte, "Loiza Aldea," *Palante*, August 15, 1970, 6, 20.

52. Denise Oliver, "Sojourner Truth: Revolutionary Black Woman," *Palante* (June 5, 1970, 7; Muntu, "Rap Brown: Warrior," *Palante*, July 17, 1970, 11; Umar Muntu Bakr, "Malcolm X," *Palante*, May 12, 1970, 7; Carlos Aponte, "Betances," *Palante*, July 3, 1970, 4.

53. Morales, "Puerto Rican Racism."

54. Ibid., 7.

55. Histories can be found in Acuña, *Occupied America*; special issue on ethnic studies, *Amerasia Journal* 15, no. 1 (1989), 7; Biondi, *Black Revolution on Campus*; and Ginsberg, "Triumphs, Controversies, and Change."

56. Morales, "Puerto Rican Racism," 7.

57. For a discussion of nationalist discourses in Puerto Rico's culture, see Maria Acosta Cruz, *Dream Nation*.

58. This does not imply, however, that racial identification does not impact the way Puerto Ricans perceive themselves. See Rodriguez, *Puerto Ricans*, 52–53.

59. During most of the colonial period, Puerto Rico functioned primarily as a military outpost and had a diverse nonsegregated population consisting of a small number of slaves and Native Americans, a substantial number of freemen of color and poor white tenant farmers, and government officials. In Puerto Rico, rigid racial demarcations did not form part of the New World colony's social fabric in part because the slave plantation system was not a central feature of the island's economy. When a plantation economy did develop in the nineteenth century, severe labor shortages led to compulsory labor laws, which forced white land squatters to work alongside slaves and freemen of color in the fields. This development encouraged racial mixing and blurred racial differences as black slaves and white and colored laborers were compelled to intermingle with one another in the fields, an arrangement that eventually led each to find common cause with the other. See Mintz, *Caribbean Transformations*, 82–94. For a discussion of racial ideology in the United States, see Fields, "Ideology and Race"; and Fields, "Slavery, Race and Ideology," 95–118.

60. Studies of race include Soler, *Historia de la Esclavitud negra en Puerto Rico Rio Piedras: Editorial Universitario*, 1965; Blanco, *El prejuicio racial en Puerto Rico*; and Chenault, *Puerto Rican Migrant*.

61. Morales, "Puerto Rican Racism," 6–7.

62. Ibid.

63. Ibid.

64. Delgado, "Jesús Colón," 80–81.

65. Morales, "Puerto Rican Racism," 6.

66. Young Lords Party, *Ideology*, 8–9.

67. Ibid., 28.

68. Ibid., 27–28.

69. Althusser, *Lenin and Philosophy*, 121–76.

70. Morales, "*¡Palante, Siempre, Palante!* The Young Lords," 214–15.

71. See the first printing of the platform in the organization's newspaper, "13-Point Program," *Palante* 2, no. 2, May 8, 1970.

72. Che Guevara, *Socialism and Man*. These ideas were articulated in *Ideology of the Young Lords*, ed. Young Lords Party (1971): 32.

73. This analysis builds on Jennifer Nelson's study of gender in the Young Lords (*Women of Color*), especially chapter 4.

74. Miguel Melendez, interview by author, October 24, 1999.

75. Denise Oliver, interview by author, August 11, 2006.

76. Marlene Cintron, interview by author, August 2, 2005.

77. Oliver, interview by author, August 11, 2006.

78. Morales interview.

79. Denise Oliver, August 11, 2006; see also NLG documents.

80. "Women of the Colonies."

81. Oliver, interview by author, August 18, 2007; Young Lords Party, *Ideology*, 32.

82. A range of biographies of black women in the black power and civil rights movements tell this story in Gore, Theoharis, and Woodard, *Want to Start a Revolution?* See also Jennifer Nelson, *Women of Color*; Valk, *Radical Sisters*; Springer, *Living for the Revolution*; Franklin and Collier-Thomas, *Sisters in the Struggle*; and De Veaux, *Warrior Poet*.

83. Morales interview.

84. Rosen, *World Split Wide Open*, chap. 5.

85. Iris Morales, interview by author, July 25, 2000.

86. Judy Clemserud, "Young Women Find a Place in High Command of Young Lords," *New York Times*, November 11, 1970, 52.

87. Olguie Robles, interview by author, July 1, 2001.

88. The generation of white children who grew up during the same period and joined organizations like Students for a Democratic Society were similarly oppressed by the Victorian values that were regenerated by the Cold War and that found fertile ground in the perfection-seeking character of suburban life and culture. Although white American families moved into the comforts of middle-class lifestyle rather than the urban poverty that defined life for postwar migrants of color, the large transfer of people from urban living to suburban isolation also constitutes a disruption of an old way of life, which likewise produced social and psychological upheaval, especially in white women's lives. See Friedan, *Feminine Mystique*.

89. Iris Morales, Denise Oliver, Olguie Robles, Gloria Rodriguez, and Minerva Solla, and special guests Marta Duarte Arguello, Wilma González, and Juliana "Cookie" Ramirez, "The Women of the Young Lords," July 23, 2015, feature panel in "*¡Presente! The Young Lords in New York*," Bronx Museum Exhibit, curators, Johanna Fernández and Yasmin Ramirez, Bronx Museum Archive. On YouTube under the same name.

90. Central Committee, "Women's Liberation," *Palante*, April 1971, 17.

91. Iris Morales, in "Women of the Colonies."

92. Myrna Martinez, in "Women of the Colonies."

93. Oliver, interview by author, August 11, 2006; Rovira interview, July 27, 2013. For some of these debates in the broader movement, see Weigand, *Red Feminism*.

94. For a broad sampling of the women's movement's analyses of women's oppression and its root causes, see Baxandall and Gordon, *Dear Sisters*.

95. Morales, in "Women of the Colonies."

96. Martinez, in "Women of the Colonies."

97. For a discussion of this perspective, see White, *Too Heavy a Load*, chap. 2. For a study of how issues of gender permeated the day-to-day life of the Black Panther Party, see Spencer, *Revolution Has Come*.

98. Morales, in "Women of the Colonies."

99. Springer, *Living for the Revolution*.

100. Martinez, in "Women of the Colonies."

101. Iris Benitez in "Women of the Colonies." This was also the position of the women of the Black Panther Party; see "Panther Sisters on Women's Liberation," in Heath, *Off the Pigs!*, 344, 346.

102. Oliver, interview by author, August 18, 2007.

103. Ibid.

104. Iris Morales, interview by author, July 25, 2000.

105. Abramson, *Palante*, 25; Morales interview by author, July 25, 2000.

106. Iris Morales, "Puerto Rican Genocide," *Palante*, May 6, 1970, 8; Connie Morales, "Women's Oppression: Cortejas," *Palante*, May 22, 1970, 16; Carlos Aponte, "Lolita Lebron: Puerto Rican Liberation Fighter," *Palante*, May 22, 1970, 5; Oliver, "Sojourner Truth"; Iris Benitez, "Cambodia '70," *Palante*, May 6, 1970, 14.

107. Robin Morgan, "Goobye to All That," *Rat*, February 6–23, 1970, 6–7.

108. Oliver, interview by author, August 18, 2007.

109. See Young Lords Party, "13 Point Program"; see also discussion in Clemserud, "Young Women Find a Place."

110. See Rudolph, "Masculinities"; Jenkins and Hine, *Question of Manhood*; and Tyson, *Radio Free Dixie*.

111. Rovira interview, July 27, 2013; Oliver, interview by author, August 18, 2007.

112. Morales interview.

113. Oliver, interview by author, August 18, 2007.

114. Morales interview.

115. Denise Oliver, interview by Iris Morales, in Morales, *¡Palante, Siempre Palante!* (film).

116. Young Lords Party and Abramson, *Palante*, 11.

117. Ibid., 51.

118. Oliver, interview by author, August 18, 2007.

119. "Colonized Mentality and Non-Conscious Ideology," in Young Lords Party, *Ideology*, 32.

120. D'Emilio, *Sexual Politics, Sexual Communities*; D'Emilio, *Intimate Matters*.

121. Carlito Rovira, interview by author, October 2, 2017.

122. This narrative is assembled from a series of conversations I had with Denise Oliver, Carlito Rovira, Marta Duarte, and others during the exhibit project *¡Presente! The Young Lords in New York*, which I cocurated with Yasmin Ramirez in summer 2015 at the Bronx Museum and facilitated

at two other museum sites in New York, El Museo Del Barrio and Loisaida Inc. The project was cited by the *New York Times* as one of the year's "Top 10, Best in Art." See Mark Armao, "The Art and Activism of the Young Lord: Three New York City Venues Look Back at the Puerto Rican Nationalist Group," *Wall Street Journal*, July 14, 2015.

123. Morales interview.

124. Luciano interview.

125. Ibid.

126. Connie Morales, "Women's Oppression: Cortejas," *Palante*, May 22, 1970, 16.

127. "Young Lords Party Position Paper on Women," *Rat Subterranean News*, October 6, 1970.

128. For an in-depth discussion of the Young Lords' position on reproductive rights, see Jennifer Nelson, *Women of Color*, 113–32.

129. Discussed in Iris Lopez, "Agency and Constraint," 320. For a comprehensive history of birth control in Puerto Rico, see Ramirez de Arellano and Scheipp, *Colonialism*.

130. "Puerto Rican Genocide," *Palante*, May 8, 1970, 8.

131. "Young Lords Party Position Paper on Women."

132. Young Lords Party and Abramson, *Palante*, 50.

133. *La Luchadora*, in boxed newspapers, Tamiment Library.

134. Kathleen Neal Cleaver, "Women, Power, and Revolution," 123–27; see also Abu-Jamal, *We Want Freedom*, chap. 7.

135. Other women of color were also involved in this work. See Keeanga-Yamahtta Taylor, *How We Get Free*.

Chapter 9

1. See Carlos Rovira, "Prospect Hospital," *Palante*, June 19, 1970, 8.

2. Carl Pastor, "Socialist Medicine," *Palante*, June 5, 1970, 8.

3. Alfonzo A. Narvaez, "The Young Lords Seize X-Ray Unit," *New York Times*, June 18, 1970, 17.

4. Luciano and Maristany, "Young Lords Party," 13.

5. Carl Pastor, "TB Truck Liberated," *Palante*, July 3, 1970, 11; Narvaez, "Young Lords Seize X-Ray Unit," 7; "Young Lords Free Health Truck," *Old Mole*, August 7, 1970, 5; "Control Seized," *Berkeley Tribe*, September 18, 1970, 13; "Young Lords Hijack TB Unit in New York," *Peace News Ltd.*, June 26, 1970; "Young Lords Truckin," *Good Times*, June 26, 1970, 3.

6. Narvaez, "Young Lords Seize X-Ray Unit," 17.

7. U.S. Department of Labor, *Labor Force Experience*, 7. One source estimates the neighborhood's racial and ethnic makeup in the early 1970s as 70

percent Puerto Rican, 20 percent African American, and 10 percent other. See Kaplan, *Organization*, 6.

8. Carlos Aponte, "Street Films in the Bronx," *Palante*, June 19, 1970, 9.

9. David Perez, "Y.L.O. Bronx Branch," *Palante*, May 22, 1970, 9.

10. See Wilson, *When Work Disappears*.

11. Richie Perez, "The South Bronx Time Bomb," *Palante*, July 17, 1970, 4.

12. Glazer, "South Bronx Story," 269–76; Mullan, *White Coat, Clenched Fist*, 114.

13. Quoted in New York State Department of Health, "A Preliminary Survey of the Municipal Hospitals of New York City," October 1966, 1, in New York City: Hospitals, Municipal, and General Vertical File.

14. Mullan, *White Coat, Clenched Fist*, 113.

15. Commission on the Delivery of Personal Health Services, *Community Health Service*, 266; "Lead Paint on Pediatric Wards," *Lincoln News*, mimeographed pamphlet, n.d., in Osborne Personal Files. According to the latter source, of the children treated for lead poisoning in ward 2-B in that period, two reingested lead in the ward.

16. Lincoln Home and Hospital was acquired by the city and transformed into a public facility in 1925.

17. "What Course for Health Workers," editorial, *Health/PAC Bulletin*, July–August 1970, 1, http://www.healthpacbulletin.org/healthpac-bulletin-julyaugust-1970.

18. Leon Fink and Greenberg, *Upheaval*, 6; Freeman, *Working-Class New York*, 213–14.

19. Rosner and Markowitz, "Hospital, Insurance," 74–95.

20. The affiliation contract failed to resolve the problems of poor municipal care in part because abolishing the double standard of care was not the priority. In a laissez-faire market, the priority of large research institutions centered around maintaining their viability in an expanding healthcare industry, not in abolishing the dual standard of care for the poor. Thus, affiliation did not bring a revolution in care for the poor; instead it meant that voluntary hospitals gained badly needed training territory, as well as funds, which helped them stay afloat in the midst of spiraling costs, a kind of Keynesian economics for the health industry. For discussions of the profit-driven structure of the health system and its consequences, see Rosner and Markowitz, "Hospital, Insurance," 74–95.

21. Levine, Murray, *History and Politics*, 51–52. For an assessment of the shift, see Grob, *From Asylum to Community*.

22. According to the policy of the antipoverty bill of 1964, sec. 2, "it is the policy of the United States to eliminate the paradox of poverty in the midst of plenty in this Nation by opening to everyone the opportunity for education and training, the opportunity to work, and the opportunity to live in decency and dignity" (quoted in Moynihan, *Maximum Feasible Misunderstanding*, 57–58).

23. The film featured one of the LHMHS's neighborhood service center storefronts in the southeast Bronx. See "The Storefronts," press release, October 24, 1967; and "Movie Premiered in Ghetto Area," press release, October 30 (no year), Director of Public Information, Arch 106.L63, Lincoln Hospital Papers.

24. R. R., "Heal Thyself," n.d., 1, Arch 106.L63, Lincoln Hospital Papers.

25. Janoski, *Political Economy of Unemployment*, 127–30. According to the policy of the antipoverty bill of 1964, sec. 2, "it is the policy of the United States to eliminate the paradox of poverty in the midst of plenty in this Nation by opening to everyone the opportunity for education and training, the opportunity to work, and the opportunity to live in decency and dignity," quoted in Moynihan, *Maximum Feasible Misunderstanding*, 57–58.

26. Gloria Cruz, "HRUM: Health Worker Organization," *Palante*, May 6, 1970, 3.

27. On the health activism of the Black Panthers, see Nelson, *Body and Soul*. On the convergence of black power activism and emergency medical care, see *Freedom House: Street Saviors*, directed by Gene Starzenski.

28. Ibid., 6.

29. Cleo Silvers, interview by author, October 13, 2018.

30. "Bronx Conflict Focused on Community Control," *Hospital Tribune*, May 5, 1969, 20, in Lincoln Hospital Papers.

31. Mike Smith, interview by author, August 19, 2005; Cleo Silvers, interview by author, October 19, 2005.

32. Gerald Fraser, "Community Control Here Found Spreading in the Field of Health," *New York Times*, March 9, 1969, quoted in Lincoln Hospital Mental Health and Non Professional Association and Supporting Professionals, "Einstein vs. the Community?," press release, March 10, 1969, Arch 106.L63, Lincoln Hospital Papers. See also Thomas S. Harper, "The Lincoln Hospital Protest: Community Mental Health Leadership as the Agent of Ghetto Imperialism," n.d., Arch 106.L63, Lincoln Hospital Papers.

33. An unidentified group of nonadministrative staff, the majority of whom would have been professional staff, wrote a statement opposing the methods but supporting the critique and grievances of the Puerto Rican and African American nonprofessional workers. See "Position Statement by Lincoln Hospital Mental Health Services Staff

in Opposition to the Current Work Stoppage and Takeover of Services," March 13, 1969, Arch 106. L63, Lincoln Hospital Papers.

34. Lincoln Hospital Mental Health and Non Professional Association and Supporting Professionals, "Einstein vs. the Community?"

35. The clinic remained closed for approximately two weeks, during which time its administration attempted negotiations with the staff. Cleo Silvers, "Learning through Struggle," *For the People's Health*, June 1970, 2; Cleo Silvers, interview by author, June 24, 2015.

36. Office of Public Information, "The Facts on Lincoln Hospital," Arch 106.L63, Lincoln Hospital Papers.

37. "Bronx Conflict Focused on Community Control," *Hospital Tribune*, May 5, 1969, 1, 20, in Lincoln Hospital Papers; see also Mullan, *White Coat, Clenched Fist*, 139.

38. Cleo Silvers, interview by author, April 24, 2018. On the Panther 21, see Kempton, *Briar Patch*.

39. For examples, see Levy, *The New Left and Labor in the 1960s*, chap. 8. For a case study, see Georgakas and Surkin, *Detroit*.

40. Cruz, "HRUM," 3.

41. Leon Fink and Greenberg, *Upheaval*, 199.

42. For a history of DRUM, see Georgakas and Surkin, *Detroit*. DRUM organized localized workplace actions and wildcat strikes in the auto industry against what the group termed "niggermation," the combined impact of shop-floor speedups and racial discrimination on the part of company management and the union, respectively. HRUM's replacement of "union" with "unity" in its name reflects the organization's preoccupation with building bridges with people of color and advancing the ever-evasive concept of unity among people of color presumably in "the community" rather than in the workplace.

43. "Workers-Patients United," editorial, *For the People's Health*, April 1970, 1, Microfilm Collection.

44. "Pig of the Week," *Palante*, June 19, 1970, 4.

45. "Besieged Hospital Head," *New York Times*, August 28, 1970.

46. Carlito Rovira, "Crime against Our Youth," *Palante*, May 8, 1970, 9.

47. Edmund Rothschild, interview by Bruce Solloway, in "Lincoln Hospital: The Decline of Health Care."

48. HRUM, "Total Self Determination," mimeograph, n.d., 1–2, in Smith Papers.

49. Mullan, *White Coat, Clenched Fist*, 45; Danny Argote and Cleo Silvers, "Think Lincoln," *Palante*, July 3, 1970, 2, 16.

50. Cleo Silvers, interview by Bruce Solloway, in "Lincoln Hospital: The Decline of Health Care"; Silvers, interview by author, June 24, 2015; Smith

interview; Carl Pastor, "Patient Worker Table," *Palante*, July 17, 1970, 20.

51. Ellen Frankfort, "The Community's Role in Healing a Hospital," *Village Voice*, November 26, 1970.

52. Antero Lacot, "Lincoln Hospital 1970—A Prelude of Things to Come," n.d., 1, Smith Papers.

53. Argote and Silvers, "Think Lincoln," 16.

54. "Lords Liberate Hospital," *Old Mole*, August 7, 1970.

55. Argote and Silvers, "Think Lincoln," 16.

56. *Pediatric Collective Bulletin*, n.d., Arch 106. L63, Lincoln Hospital Papers.

57. Harold Osborne, interview by author, July 30, 2000.

58. Fitzhugh Mullan, interview by author, December 13, 2005.

59. Osborne interview.

60. Harold Osborne, untitled manuscript, Osborne Papers. They belonged to a larger cohort of doctors who were politicized by the social movements of the 1960s and specifically by their participation during medical school in the public health projects in poor urban neighborhoods sponsored by the Student Health Organization. They were also connected through their networks to the older cohort of doctors who formed the Medical Committee for Human Rights, which participated in the southern civil rights movement and challenged segregation in southern hospitals.

61. Mullan interview.

62. Osborne, untitled manuscript.

63. Carlito Rovira, interview by author, July 27, 2013.

64. These bags are referred to as sandbags or bags of coal in a number of my interviews with the Young Lords. A photo of them was captured by the *New York Times* for an article on the takeover. See photo in Alfonzo A. Narvaez, "Young Lords Seize Lincoln Hospital Building," *New York Times*, July 15, 1970.

65. Mullan, *White Coat, Clenched Fist*, 142.

66. Argote and Silvers, "Think Lincoln," 2.

67. Mullan, *White Coat, Clenched Fist*, 144.

68. Narvaez, "Young Lords Seize Lincoln."

69. Carl Pastor, "Socialism at Lincoln—July 14, 1970," *Palante*, July 31, 1970, 5.

70. The involvement of the Young Lords with HRUM and with other hospital workers in HRUM accelerated the debate about the working class, which was initiated in May.

71. Pastor, "Socialism at Lincoln," 5.

72. "Buckley Denounces the Young Lords," *Massena Observer*, September 3, 1970.

73. Silvers, interview by Solloway.

74. Smith interview.

75. "Abortion Death at Lincoln Hospital," *Think . . . Lincoln*, July 27, 1970.

76. Smith interview.

77. Mullan, *White Coat, Clenched Fist*, 147.

78. Smith interview.

79. "Abortion Death at Lincoln Hospital."

80. "Bronx," *Health/PAC Bulletin*, October 1970.

81. Charlotte Phillips, interview by author, August 6, 2015; Mullan interview.

82. Mullan, *White Coat, Clenched Fist*, 148.

83. "A History of the Struggle at Lincoln Hospital," flyer, September 1970, Smith Papers; Silvers, interview by author, October 19, 2005.

84. "Crisis at Lincoln," editorial, *New York Times*, August 27, 1970.

86. Frances X. Clines, "City Gets Injunction in Lincoln Hospital Dispute," *New York Times*, August 27, 1970.

87. John Sibley, "Doctors Return to Lincoln Jobs: Normal Service is Restored in Obstetrics Department," *New York Times*, September 4, 1970.

88. Clines, "City Gets Injunction"; "History of the Struggle at Lincoln Hospital"; Silvers, interview by author, October 19, 2005.

89. "Crisis at Lincoln."

90. Eli C. Messinger, "Letter to the editor," *New York Times*, August 30, 1970, copy of original letter on letterhead in Smith Papers.

91. "Buckley Denounces the Young Lords."

92. Barbara Yuncker and Jay Levin, "11 Resign at Harlem Hospital," *New York Post*, August 28, 1970.

93. "Bronx."

94. Luis E. Yavner, chairman of the Committee on Urban Affairs, American Jewish Congress, to Samuel Belkin, president of Yeshiva University, February 4, 1971, and related correspondence, Vertical File, 1960–1975, Lincoln Hospital Papers.

95. Osborne interview.

96. Stephen Levin, interview by author, August 16, 2005.

97. Osborne interview.

98. Mullan interview.

99. Ibid.

100. Osborne interview.

101. Silvers, interview by author, October 19, 2005.

102. History of HRUM, undated document of the period, Mike Smith Papers.

103. Carl Pastor, "Seize the Hospitals," *Palante*, December 11, 1970, 6; "El Programa de las Drogas," *Lincoln News*, undated, 1971, Mike Smith Papers.

104. Levin interview.

105. In Vietnam, military officers and government officials with easy access to opium poppy fields established poppy-refining labs for the production of heroin that made its way into the nation's urban centers in CIA planes. Larry Collins, "The CIA Drug Connection Is as Old as the Agency," *New York Times*, December 3, 1993;

Michael Cetawayo Tabor, "Capitalism Plus Dope Equals Genocide," Black Panther Party, n.d., Pamphlet Series, Tamiment Library.

106. Smith interview.

107. Miguel Melendez, *We Took the Streets*, 177–78.

108. Podair, *Strike*, chap. 4.

Chapter 10

1. Garelik earlier managed the Red Squad, which was formally known as the Bureau of Special Services and Investigation and came into existence in 1946. At the height of the Cold War, it spied on a wide range of citizens with different political views, including communists, and during the 1960s it disproportionately targeted black power activists, the New Left, and others. Clarence Taylor, *Reds at the Blackboard*, 206.

2. The reported size of the independence march varies, with the Young Lords describing it as a 3,000-person march in "3,000 Join Protest Led by Young Lords," *New York Times*, October 31, 1970.

3. Denise Oliver, interview by author, August 18, 2007; Iris Morales, interview by author, July 25, 2000.

4. The concert organizers were white, and their program had displaced a long-standing yearly Puerto Rican festival held at Randall's Island on that same weekend. In protest, the Young Lords coerced its organizers into sharing the profits of the concert with the organization. Oliver interview; Carlito Rovira, interview by author, July 30, 2015. A photo of the event shows Denise Oliver speaking at the event.

5. Felipe Luciano, interview by author, August 28, 2005.

6. Ibid.

7. Morales interview; Oliver interview.

8. Oliver interview.

9. Juan González, email exchange with author, April 2019.

10. The most well-known example of this was a letter sent to Martin Luther King by the FBI suggesting that King kill himself rather than face the shame of his extramarital affairs, which the writers said they were about to disclose to the public.

11. Carlos Aponte, interview by author, July 30, 2019.

12. Rudy Johnson, "Ex-Head of Lords Backs His Ouster," *New York Times*, September 9, 1970.

13. Mickey Melendez, conversation with author, July 4, 2019.

14. Rovira interview.

15. Luciano interview.

16. Mickey Melendez, conversation with author, July 4, 2019.

17. Juan González, interview by author, February 27, 2015.

18. See "The History of the Puerto Rican Student Union," Young Lords Documents.

19. Initiated at City College, the open admissions strike protested racial discrimination in college admissions and demanded and won the enrollment of all CUNY applicants with a high school diploma, a victory which eventually transformed CUNY's predominantly white student body to one in which students of color formed the majority. Lavin and Alba, *Right versus Privilege*. See also Gunderson, "The Struggle for CUNY."

20. "Puerto Rican Student Conference," *Palante*, September 25, 1970, 3; National Staff, "2 Years of Struggle," *Palante*, July 31, 1971, 10.

21. In the 1970s, 1980s, and 1990s, CIA operations in Chile, Nicaragua, El Salvador, Honduras, Peru, and Panama and economic policies in Mexico and Colombia contributed to the exponential growth of Latinos in the United States. On U.S. foreign policy in Latin America during this period, see Herman, *Real Terror Network*; Smith, *Talons of the Eagle*; and Rabe, *Killing Zone*. On U.S. economic policy in the region, see William I. Robinson, *Latin America and Global Capitalism*; Petras and Morley, *Latin America in the Time of Cholera*; and Veltmeyer, Petras, and Vieux, *Neoliberalism and Class Conflict in Latin America*.

22. A. Torres and R. Rivera, "The Puerto Rican Youth Conference & El Grito de Lares," *Atrevido*, vol. 1, no 2 (October 1970), Lindsay Papers, Box: "Assistant . . . (Amalia Betanzos) 1970–1972," Folder: "Pamphlets."

23. See, for example, Larry Louzau, "High School Students Unite," *Palante*, November 20, 1970, 8.

24. Robert D. McFadden, "Garelik Says Terrorists Are Growing Peril Here," *New York Times*, March 13, 1970.

25. For a history of terrorism and the use of the term in the United States, see Brachman, "Terrorism."

26. For discussions of terrorism as a political tactic, see Mamdani, *Good Muslim, Bad Muslim*; and Herman, *Real Terror Network*.

27. For a discussion of the Weather Underground, see Berger, *Outlaws of America*.

28. For a clear discussion of guerrilla war, see Fred Halliday, *Revolution and World Politics*, chap. 9.

29. McFadden, "Garelik Says Terrorists."

30. See Rosenberg, *American Radical*.

31. See, for example, Guerara, *Guerrilla Warfare*, 2; and Trotsky, *My Life*, 473–75.

32. Esteban Ferrer, "Lords Attacked," *Palante*, July 3, 1970, 9, 16.

33. Alfonso A. Narvaez, "Victim Blames 'Kids,' Not Young Lords, for East Harlem Looting," *New York Times*, June 16, 1970, 42.

34. Ministry of Information, "Fi and David Ripped Off," *Palante*, July 3, 1970, 13, 16.

35. Robert D. McFadden, "Hundreds in East Harlem Rampage," *New York Times*, June 14, 1970. See also Richie Perez, "Insurrection," *Palante*, July 3, 1970, 12; and Miguel Padilla, "N.Y. Police in New Arrest of Young Lords Leader," *Militant*, June 26, 1970.

36. Alfonso A. Narvaez, "Victim Blames 'Kids,' Not Young Lords, for East Harlem Looting," *New York Times*, June 15, 1970.

37. Dan Meyers, interview by author, January 13, 2011.

38. Kempton, *Briar Patch*.

39. Denise Oliver, "Murder: Julio Roldán," *Palante*, October 30, 1970, 2; Vanden Heuvel, *Report to the Mayor*.

40. Vanden Heuvel, *Report to the Mayor*, 7.

41. Ibid., 4.

42. A year later, Barbara Handschu and other attorneys would file a precedent-setting case, challenging the constitutionality of NYPD surveillance of the Black Panther 21 and other organizations of the New Left. During the proceedings, the court subpoenaed police surveillance records of New Yorkers, and at the end of the case, the presiding judge ordered that they be preserved. In 2014, the author sued the NYPD for its failure to honor her research-driven, Freedom of Information Law (FOIL) request of these surveillance files. Her suit led to the recovery of the "lost" Handschu files in 2016. See Joseph Goldstein, "Decades Later, Big Brother Comes Out of Hiding," *New York Times*, June 17, 2016, A23; Colin Moynihan, "Police Files on Radicals Are at Center of a Suit," *New York Times*, August 12, 2014, A18.

43. Ibid., 10; Editorial, "Polarized City: The Tombs," *New York Times*, November 19, 1970, 46.

44. Ibid.

45. Ibid., 11.

46. Ibid., 9–13.

47. David Burnham, "F.B.I.'s Informants and 'Bugs' Collect Data on Black Panthers: F.B.I. Seeks Data on the Black Panthers," *New York Times*, December 14, 1969; Joshua Bloom and Martin, *Black against Empire*, 3, 210.

48. Vanden Heuvel, *Report to the Mayor*, 12.

49. Alexander, *The New Jim Crow*; Abu-Jamal and Fernández, *The Roots of Mass Incarceration*; Wacquant, *Punishing the Poor*.

50. Judges were assigned arraignment duty a month at a time. Ibid., 2, 10.

51. Ted Morgan, "Entombed," *New York Times*, February 17, 1974.

52. "Tombs Closing, Inmates Go to Rikers," *New York Times*, November 16, 1974.

53. Ibid.

54. Vanden Heuvel, *Report to the Mayor*, 1.

55. Ibid., 19.

56. Ibid., 2.

57. David Burnham, "The Tombs Called 'Dungeon of Fear,'" *New York Times*, August 8, 1970.

58. Vanden Heuvel, *Report to the Mayor*, 2.

59. Morgan, "Entombed," 5.

60. Vanden Heuvel, *Report to the Mayor*, 17.

61. Ibid., 18.

62. Ibid., 20.

63. Ibid., 22.

64. Ibid.

65. Esli Ramon González, "Hallan 'Young Lords' ahorcado en celda," *El Diario La Prensa*, October 18, 1970, 3.

66. Vanden Heuvel, *Report to the Mayor*, 24.

67. Oliver Fein, interview by author, August 2, 2015.

68. Pablo Guzmán, in *El pueblo se levanta*.

69. Lesley Oelsner, "8th 1970 Jail Suicide," *New York Times*, November 7, 1970, 17. See also William J. Vanden Heuvel, *Crisis in the Prisons: New York City Responds*, Annual Report of the New York City Board of Corrections to the Mayor, 1971.

70. Alfonzo A. Narvaez, "Mass Offered for Two 'Assassinated' Prisoners," *New York Times*, 39; Board of Corrections, *Shuttle to Oblivion: A Report on the Life and Death of a Citizen, Rommel Lavon Moore, in the Manhattan House of Detention for Men, also Known as the Tombs*, December 1970.

71. Commanding Officer, Special Service Division, to Chief Inspector, "Occupation of the First Spanish Methodist Church, 1791 Lexington Avenue, By the Young Lords Party," October 19, 1970, NYPD files, box 34, file 1, Perez Papers; confirmed by Juan González, interview by author, July 29, 2015.

72. Matusow, *The Unraveling of America*, 337. Same reference quoted as 19 percent in Kimmel, "The Sixties without Metaphor," 80.

73. Alfredo Lopez, *Puerto Rican Papers*, 336–39.

74. Young Lords, "Come to People's Church!," flyer, October 20, 1970, National Lawyers Guild Papers.

75. Juan González, in *El pueblo se levanta*.

76. Juan González, interview by author, October 2015.

77. Luciano interview.

78. Richie Perez, "Julio Roldán Center Opens," *Palante*, October 30, 1970, 4.

79. "Unidos Venceremos: The Lords' Victory," *City Free Press*, November 30, 1970.

80. The Dunne Report rang the alarm bell on the dangers of overcrowding in the city's prison in 1969; Peter Kihss, "Albany Report Calls Jails 'Crime Breeding Grounds,'" *New York Times*, November 10, 1969. In February 1970, Democratic U.S. representative Edward Koch gathered harrowing eyewitness accounts from approximately 1,000 prisoners for a report prepared for the House Judiciary Committee that was based on an analysis of approximately 1,000 questionnaire responses from detainees and recommended the passage of federal law establishing minimum standards for handling and housing prisoners. See Burnham, "Tombs Called 'Dungeon of Fear.'"

81. Craig R. Whitney, "Suit Seeks to Shut and Improve Tombs," *New York Times*, September 11, 1970.

82. For a fuller account of these events, see Cannato, *Ungovernable City*, 461–65; and Gottehrer, *Mayor's Man*, 262–87. See also "Message from the Tombs," editorial, *New York Times*, August 13, 1970; "New York: Tombs; An Ideal Breeding Ground for Riots," editorial, *New York Times*, August 16, 1970, 144; Frances X. Clines, "Inmate's Beating Called Riot Spark," *New York Times*, August 19, 1970; and Frances X. Clines, "Tombs Officials Agree with Inmates," *New York Times*, August 20, 1970.

83. Gottehrer, *Mayor's Man*, 272–73.

84. Paul Montgomery, "It Was Complete Bedlam—Punching and Screaming," *New York Times*, October 6, 1970.

85. Michael T. Kaufman, "Ex-Prisoner at Tombs Feels Close to Cellmates," *New York Times*, August 19, 1970.

86. Frances X. Clines, "Tombs Prisoners Boycott Hearings," *New York Times*, August 18, 1970.

87. Juan González, email exchange with author, March 18, 2019.

88. Gilbert Jiménez, "We Must Fight to Be Free," *Palante*, October 30, 1970, 15; "Letter from the Tombs," *Palante*, November 20, 1970, 5; Puerto Rican National Liberation Front in Attica, "A Letter from Prison," *Palante*, June 1971, 12.

89. Richie Perez, interview by author, July 17, 2000.

90. "To All Brothers and Sisters in the Concentration Camps of Amerikkka," *Palante*, October 30, 1970, 15.

91. Meyers interview.

92. Juan Vasquez, "Mayor Condemns Church Take-over," *New York Times*, October 23, 1970.

93. Ibid.

94. Barry Gottehrer, interview by author, Fall 2005.

95. Juan González, email exchange with author, March 18, 2019.

96. Miguel Melendez, *We Took the Streets*, 186–88.

97. Herring, *America's Longest War*, 29–32.

98. Juan M. Vasquez, "Police 'Frisked' by the Young Lords," *New York Times*, October 26, 1970;

"Armed Young Lords Seize the Church," *Liberated Guardian*, November 9, 1970.

99. Later, TV personality Geraldo Rivera, a young attorney and member of the board of corrections, received special mention for his participation.

100. Vanden Heuvel, *Report to the Mayor*, 1.

101. Vanden Heuvel, *Report to the Mayor*, 3.

102. Gloria Fontanez, in *El pueblo se levanta*.

103. Joseph Morgenstern, *Newsweek*, December 7, 1970.

104. A Parrilla Bonilla, "Huellas de un Peregrinaje," *Claridad*, December 13, 1970, 11.

Chapter 11

1. Juan González, "Mensaje a estudiantes puertorriquenos," *Palante*, September 11, 1970, 13. For a political history of the SDS and the convention discussions that gave rise to these ideas, see James Miller, *Democracy Is in the Streets*.

2. The organizations fighting for independence on the island were Movimiento Pro Independencia, the Independent Armed Revolutionary Movement for Puerto Rican Liberation, and Armed Liberation Commandos.

3. See Falcón et al., *Puerto Rico*; see also McCaffrey, *Military Power*, 68–70.

4. Juan "Fi" Ortiz and Juan González, "Letter from Puerto Rico," *Palante*, September 11, 1970, 4.

5. González et al., *Report*, 14.

6. Nydia Mercado, "Revolutionary Wedding," *Palante*, August 25, 1970, 9.

7. González et al., *Report*, 1.

8. Ibid., 3–4.

9. Ibid., 6–8, 19–20.

10. Ibid., 1–2.

11. See, respectively, "Central Committee," *Palante*, July 3, 1970, 17; and "Central Committee," *Palante*, October 16, 1970.

12. Richie Perez, interview by author, July 17, 2000; Denise Oliver, interview by author, August 18, 2006; Carlos Aponte, interview by author, July 6, 2019.

13. Joshua Bloom and Martin, *Black against Empire*, 358–62.

14. Ibid., 354–55.

15. González et al., *Report*, 17.

16. Gramsci, *Prison Notebooks*, 205. Gramsci criticizes those who "detach themselves from the mass by arbitrary individual initiative" as "'vanguards' without armies to back them up."

17. Denise Oliver, interview by author, August 18, 2006; Pablo Guzmán, interview by author, August 3, 2019.

18. González et al., *Report*, 15.

19. Gloria Rodriguez, interview by author, July 28, 2019.

20. Gilbert Colón, interview by author, August 5, 2010.

21. On the labor upsurge of the late 1960s and the New Left, see Levy, *New Left and Labor*, chap. 8.

22. Richie Perez, "Los Trabajadores," *Palante*, December 11, 1970, 3.

23. Gilbert Colón, interview by author, August 5, 2010.

24. Young Lords Party, *Ideology*, 17–18.

25. Juan González, interview by author, July 29, 2005.

26. Marable, *Race, Reform, and Rebellion*, 133–34. For fuller studies, see also Rickford, *We Are an African People*; Farmer, *Remaking Black Power*, chap. 4; and Tinson, *Radical Intellect*.

27. As discussed in previous chapters, the postwar migration of people of color into the cities, coupled with the trend toward suburban development, white flight from cities, and the strengthening of racially exclusionary practices in the real estate market of the 1950s and 1960s, created greater racial segregation in the cities. See chapter 6.

28. Budding radicals referred to this condition as the "nation within a nation" theory. The theory was first adopted by the Communist Party of the United States of America in the 1920s as it began to consider for the first time how the depressed condition of the Negro laborer would undermine attempts at organizing the working class in the United States.

29. Although there was a growing sense among urban radicals of color that multiracial working-class collaboration was critical to their objectives, the radicals who in the 1930s had built such struggles and made such arguments were cut off from the new movements of the 1960s. In particular, the Communist Party's blind political allegiance to the Soviet Union alienated young radicals who increasingly saw the USSR as an imperial superpower. Moreover, the Old Left's inability to relate to a movement with a different character and social base than that of the 1930s meant that the political experiences and lessons of previous attempts at a multiracial, working-class movement could not be imparted to the new radicals. In New York in particular, the racially divisive teachers' strike against community control of public schools further polarized the city and discouraged the efforts of radicals who were contemplating the possibility of racial solidarity in labor.

30. González, "2 Years of Struggle," 11.

31. Juan González, interview by author, July 29, 2015; Carlito Rovira, interview by author, July 30, 2015.

32. "Ponce March 21," *Palante*, March 5–19, 1971, 7.

33. "Young Lords Move to Ponce," *Workers World*, February 26, 1971, 10.

34. González interview, July 29, 2015.

35. Harold Osborne, interview by author, July 30, 2000.

36. Iris Morales, interview by author, July 25, 2000.

37. Young Lords Party and Abramson, *Palante*, 158.

38. Ayala and Bernabe, *Puerto Rico*, 167–71.

39. "City Young Lords, In Rally Marking Ponce Massacre," *Bridgeport Telegram*, March 22, 1971, 9; "Young Lords Join in March," *Daily News*, March 22, 1971, 172; "Meeting Marks 'Ponce' Massacre," *Bridgeport Post*, March 21, 1971, 44; "N.Y. Young Lords Join March in Puerto Rico," *Philadelphia Daily News*, March 21, 12; "Young Lords Take Part in March in Puerto Rico," *New York Times*, March 22, 1971, 8.

40. Richie Perez, "Que Viva Puerto Rico," *Palante* April 5–19, 1971, 3.

41. Juan M. García Passalacqua, "The Young Lords," *San Juan Star*, March 23, 1971, 21.

42. "Several Thousand Latinos and Supporters March for Puerto Rican Independence," *Liberation News Service*, March 24, 1971. Eddie Dias, "New York March 21," *Palante*, April 5–19, 1970, 8.

43. Tony Baez, interview by author, July 29, 2014.

44. González et al., *Report*, 13.

45. Juan Mari Bras, "Los Young Lords," *Claridad*, March 28, 1971.

46. Ibid.

47. In the 1972 gubernatorial elections, Puerto Rico's conservative statehood party, the New Progressive Party of Puerto Rico, received majority votes in Ponce; see Nolla-Acosta, *Puerto Rican Election Statistics*, 180.

48. SAC, New York (105-32872), Groups Seeking Independence For Puerto Rico (COUNTERINTELLIGENCE PROGRAM) Subversive Control Service (00: San Juan), COINTELPRO Documents, 11/15/60; SAC, San Juan (105-3353 Sub 1), Groups Seeking Independence for Puerto Rico (COUNTERINTELLIGENCE PROGRAM) Subversive Control Service, June 12, 1969; Director FBI to SAC San Juan, Letter to San Juan Re: Groups Seeking Independence for Puerto Rico, 105-6654, Document 5, COINTELPRO Papers, undated.

49. See for example, SA, San Juan (105-12884), Young Lords Party (YLP) IS—YLP (00: New York), Re: Re: San Juan Teletype to Bureau dated 8/21/70, COINTELPRO Documents, October 27, 1970.

50. SAC, New York (105-109042), Puerto Rican Revolutionary Workers Organization (PRRWO) IS—PRRWO (00: New York), COINTELPRO Documents, 4/16/73.

51. Gloria González, "Nueva rama en Aguadilla," *Palante* 3, no. 7 (n.d.), centerfold.

52. "Juran vengar muerte Julio Roldán" *Claridad*, November 1970, reprinted in *Palante*, November 20, 1970, 16.

53. Young Lords Party, interview, *Berkeley Tribe*, November 19, 1971, 10.

54. Ibid.

55. Juan González, interview by author, February 27, 2015; Ramon Morales, interview by author, July 23, 2019.

56. Report of James A. Walsh, 105-18046, Puerto Rican Revolutionary Workers Organization, Formerly Known as Young Lords Party, February 2, 1976. 23–27.

57. Minerva Solla, interview by author, April 2015.

58. Young Lords Party interview, 10.

59. Ibid.

60. "Statement on Denise," *Palante*, March 19–April 2, 1971, 19; Denise Oliver, interview by author, August 18, 2007.

61. Joshua Bloom and Martin, *Black against Empire*, 358–62; Kathleen Cleaver and Katsiaficas, *Liberation*, 8–11.

62. Oliver interview.

63. Juan González, "On Our Errors," *Palante*, February 16–March 2, 1972, 12–13.

64. González, "2 Years of Struggle," 11.

65. González, "On Our Errors," 12–13.

66. González et al., *Report*, 17.

67. See "Rules of Discipline of the Young Lords Party," in Luciano and Maristany, "Young Lords Party," 12.

68. González, "On Our Errors."

69. The Young Lords were implementing a model used by the Communist Party in the early 1930s to build protest campaigns of the unemployed and to agitate around the case of the Scottsboro Boys. Critics of the revolutionary left have deridingly called these committees "front groups," arguing that once in place, these committees become highly controlled by their parent organizations and that the absence of democratic debate and decision-making among them undermines the possibility for building local campaigns. Moreover, they argue that these committees function as membership recruitment venues for revolutionary left organizations rather than as real sites for organic activism.

70. In the early 1970s, rank-and-file committees succeeded in ousting corrupt union leaders in a number of major unions. General Motors workers in Lordstown, Ohio, struck against conditions that threatened to turn them into robots, and later in the 1970s the Teamsters paralyzed the freight-trucking industry. See Kim Moody, *Injury to All*, 86–87.

71. Pablo Guzmán, "The Young Lords Party: It's Been a Rough but Good Year," *Liberation News Service*, February 19, 1972, 15.

72. "To All Brothers and Sisters in the Concentration Camps of Amerikkka," *Palante*, October 30, 1970, 14.

73. New York State Special Commission on Attica, *Attica*, 116–18.

74. Ibid., 128–29.

75. Ibid., 134.

76. Ibid., 139.

77. Ibid., 107–8. On the significance of George Jackson, see Berger, *Captive Nation*, chap. 3.

78. New York State Special Commission on Attica, *Attica*, 184.

79. Ibid., 205.

80. The largest demonstration in support of the Attica prisoners was organized by the Black Workers Congress in Detroit, which reportedly drew 10,000 people. Young Lords Party interview, 10.

81. Juan "Fi" Ortiz, "Remember Attica," *Palante*, September 23–October 10, 2.

82. New York State Special Commission on Attica, *Attica*, ii. See also Attica Defense Committee, *Voices from the Inside* (New York: National Lawyers Guild Pamphlet, 1972), in Goldwasser Files.

83. A guard, who was struck in the head at the beginning of the uprising and released to the hospital by prisoners, died during the failed negotiations. Three white prisoners were killed during the takeover; two were perceived to be working with the state, and the third, who was known to be unstable and dangerous, had assaulted a prisoner with a pipe during the occupation. New York State Special Commission on Attica, *Attica*, 260, 284–86.

84. González, "On Our Errors," 12–13.

85. Young Lords Party interview, 10.

86. Ibid.

87. The national staff included Richie Perez, Juan Ramos, Iris Morales, and Willie Matos, among others.

88. González, "On Our Errors"; González interview.

89. Ramon Morales, interview by author, July 23, 2019; Gilbert Colón, interview by author, June 15, 2010.

90. González interview, July 29, 2015.

91. Elbaum, *Revolution in the Air*, 93–97.

92. Gloria Fontanez, interview by author, October 20, 2010.

93. Guzmán, "Young Lords Party," 14.

94. Ibid., 14, 15.

95. González interview, July 29, 2015; Carlito Rovira, interview by author, August 10, 2015.

96. Minerva Solla, interview by author, August 2015.

97. "Faction Leaves Young Lords Party," *Palante*, special edition, June 6, 1972, B.

98. Mao Tse-tung, *Quotations*, chap. 4.

99. Rovira interview, August 10, 2015.

100. Colón interview.

101. Irwin Silber, "What Road to Building a New Communist Party?," *Guardian*, April 4, 1974.

102. González interview, February 27, 2015.

103. Guzmán, "Young Lords Party," 16. Benjy Cruz, "Struggle at Leviton Plant," *Palante*, March 3- March 17, 1972, 6.

104. CG 105-27305, Revolutionary Union (RU) IS—RU, 00: Chicago, Puerto Rican Revolutionary Workers Organization, COINTELPRO Documents, November 20, 1973.

105. Velázquez, "Coming Full Circle," 48.

106. Velázquez, "Another West Side Story," 88, 90–94.

107. Brecher, *Strike!*, 249–71.

108. Colón interview.

109. Memorandum, Field Office File # 105-109042, Young Lords Party, 2/1/72, 76–78.

110. Elbaum, *Revolution in the Air*, 187–90.

111. Fontanez interview.

112. Colón interview.

113. Fontanez interview.

114. Leonard and Gallagher, *Heavy Radicals*, 145–54.

115. Lenin, *Left Wing Communism*.

116. Examples include movements in the Republic of Guinea-Bissau and Angola, the anti-apartheid movement in South Africa, and the evolving revolutions in Cuba and Algeria.

117. Maoism was attractive to radicals for many reasons; chief among these was that communist China under Mao appeared to be taking a resolute, anti-imperialist stance before the world at a moment when colonialism was widely denounced. Moreover, Mao purported to stand in the tradition of Marx and Lenin at a moment when revolution was an integral part of conversations for social change and when activists were clamoring to learn the ideas of the major modern critics of capitalism and theorists of socialism and the revolutionary process. Having recently led China's Cultural Revolution, Mao and his theories appeared to be a living example of the application of revolutionary ideas to real conditions. See Kelley and Esch, "Black Like Mao," 6–41.

Coda

1. They built these demonstrations underground, through informal networks and local Spanish-language radio. The great migration of Europeans to the United States in the late nineteenth century was also accompanied by mass upheaval. We also see this in the movement from periphery to center of formerly colonized people now settled in Europe.

2. Fields, "Slavery, Race, and Ideology."

Bibliography

Manuscript Collections and Archives

Board of Education. New York, N.Y.

Bosley, Harold Augustus. Personal papers. United Methodist Church Archives—General Commission on Archives and History, Madison, N.J.

Christman Archives. Commission on Archives and History. New York Annual Conference Center of the United Methodist Church. White Plains, N.Y.

COINTELPRO. Documents. Federal Bureau of Investigation, Washington, D.C.

Division of General Welfare of the General Board of Church and Society. Administrative Records. United Methodist Church Archives—General Commission on Archives and History, Madison, N.J.

Evelina Antonetty Collection. Centro de Estudios Puertorriqueños, Hunter College of the City University of New York.

Fort Dix 38 (GF) Vertical File. Tamiment Library and Robert F. Wagner Labor Archives, New York University, New York, N.Y.

Goldwasser, Ira Jack. Personal files. Private collection.

González, Juan. Papers. Centro de Estudios Puertorriqueños, Hunter College of the City University of New York.

Handschu Files. Municipal Archives of the City of New York.

James Weldon Johnson Community Center. Records. Schomburg Center for Research in Black Culture, New York Public Library, New York, N.Y.

Janet Nolan Ethnographic Research on Puerto Ricans. Chicago Collection. Depaul University Special Archives and Collections, Chicago, Ill.

Lincoln Hospital Papers. Albert Einstein College of Medicine Archives. D. Samuel Gotteson Library, Yeshiva University, New York, N.Y.

Lincoln Park Collection. Grand Valley State University Special Collections and Archives, Chicago, Ill.

Lincoln Park Project: An Oral History of the Young Lords Organization. Latino Institute Collection. Special Collections Library, DePaul University, Chicago, Ill.

Lindsay, John V. Papers. Municipal Archives of the City of New York.

Lurie, Ellen. Papers. Centro de Estudios Puertorriqueños, Hunter College of the City University of New York.

Melendez, Miguel. Personal files. Private collection. New York.

Microfilm Collection. New York University, New York, N.Y.

Monserrat, Joseph. Papers. Centro de Estudios Puertorriqueños, Hunter College of the City University of New York.

Morales, Iris. Papers. Private collection. New York.

National Lawyers Guild. Papers. Box 92. Folder 22. Tamiment Library and Robert F. Wagner Labor Archives, New York University, New York, N.Y.

Near West Side Community Committee. Records. Folder 675. Special Collections, University of Illinois, Chicago.

New York City: Hospitals, Municipal and General Vertical File. 1950–1970. Municipal Archives of the City of New York.

New York City: Poisonings Lead Vertical File. 1950–1970. Municipal Archives of the City of New York.

New York City: Sanitation Department. Subject Files. Municipal Archive of the City of New York.

New York City: Sanitation Vertical File. Municipal Archive of the City of New York.

Osborne, Harold. Personal files. Albert Einstein College of Medicine, New York, N.Y.

Pacifica Radio Archives. Los Angeles, Calif.

Perez, Richie. Papers. Centro de Estudios Puertorriqueños, Hunter College of the City University of New York.

Smith, Michael. Papers. Private collection.

Tamiment Library and Robert F. Wagner Labor Archives. New York University, New York, N.Y.

Union Settlement Records. Social Welfare History Archives, University of Minnesota Libraries, Minneapolis.

Women's Division Papers. United Methodist
Church Archives—General Commission on
Archives and History, Madison, N.J.
YMCA of Metropolitan Chicago. Records.
Chicago History Museum Research Center,
Chicago, Ill.

Young Lords. Documents. Centro de Estudios
Puertorriqueños, Hunter College of the City
University of New York.
Young Lords Newspaper Collection.
Community Archives, DePaul University,
Chicago, Ill.

Oral History Collections

COLUMBIA UNIVERSITY ORAL HISTORY PROJECT, NEW YORK

González, Juan. Ronald Fraser, ed. Student Movements of the 1960s. 1988.
Morales, Iris. Ronald Fraser, ed. Student Movements of the 1960s. 1988.

OLD WESTBURY ORAL HISTORY PROJECT, SUNY COLLEGE AT OLD WESTBURY

Russell, Carlos. Interview by Carol Quirke. 2012.

ORAL HISTORY COLLECTION, CENTRO DE ESTUDIOS PUERTORRIQUEÑOS,
HUNTER COLLEGE OF THE CITY UNIVERSITY OF NEW YORK

Aponte, Carlos.
Cruz, Benjamin.
Gerena Valentin, Gilberto.
Ivany, Sonia. Centro Labor Project.

Perez, Richie.
Ramos, Juan.
Rodriguez, Gloria.

Oral History Collections by the Author

INTERVIEWS WITH YOUNG LORDS, NEW YORK, N.Y.

Alba, Panama. August 16, 2005.
Aponte, Carlos. July 27, 2019.
Bosque del Rio, Walter. August 10, 2015.
Cintron, Marlene. August 2, 2005.
Colón, Gilbert. January 8 and February 8, 2005;
June 15 and August 5, 2010.
Copeland, Anthony. July 2014.
Fontanez, Gloria. October 20, 2010; June 2013.
González, Juan. April 3 and 21, 1996; July 29,
2005; February 27, July 29 and October 2015.
Guzmán, Pablo. January 27, 2002.
Jiménez, José "Cha Cha." May 19, 20, and 21, 2014.
Luciano, Felipe. March 3 and June 27, 2004;
August 28, 2005; September 21, 2008.
Maristany, Hiram. August 11, 2000; August 21, 2013.
Melendez, Miguel. October 24, 1999; January 5,
2002.
Morales, Iris. July 25, 2000.

Morales, Iris, Denise Oliver, Olguie Robles,
Minerva Solla, Marta Duarte Arguello,
Wilma González, and Juliana "Cookie"
Ramirez. August 5, 2015.
Morales, Ramon. July 23, 2019.
Oliver, Denise. March 26, 2004; August 11 and 18,
2006; August 18, 2007.
Perez, Richie. July 17, 2000.
Robles, Olguie. August 30, 2000; July 1, 2001.
Rodriguez, Gloria. July 28, 2019.
Rovira, Carlito. July 17, 27, and 30, September
14, and October 26, 2013; July 2014; January 5,
February 9, and July 30, 2015; October 2, 2017.
Silvers, Cleo. October 19, 2005; June 24, 2015;
February 29, 2016; October 13, 2018.
Solla, Minerva. April 2015.
Torres, Gabriel. August 17, 2005.
Velazquez, Felix. August 2009; August 2013.

INTERVIEWS WITH YOUNG LORDS, CHICAGO AND PHILADELPHIA

Baez, Tony. August 10, 2010; July 29, 2014. Chicago.
Del Rivero, Sal. October 22, 2005. Chicago.
Guerra, Rory. October 25, 2005. Chicago.
Jiménez, José "Cha Cha." October 22, 2005. Chicago.
Lopez, Omar. October 25, 2005. Chicago.
Naredo, Angie. October 24, 2005. Chicago.
Rojas, Wilfredo. October 2013. Philadelphia.

INTERVIEWS WITH BLACK PANTHERS

Abu-Jamal, Mumia. January 24, 2015.
Gaddis, Henry. January 27, 2007.
Harris, Joseph. November 20, 2015.

Huggins, Erica, and Dhorba Bin Wahad.
April 15, 2013.
Lee, Bob. February 15, 2007.

INTERVIEWS WITH DOCTORS, MEDICAL STAFF, FRIENDS, AND GOVERNMENT OFFICIALS

August, Bella. August 2013. New Jersey.
Davidoff, Sid. Fall 2005. New York.
Fein, Oliver. August 6, 2015. Brooklyn, N.Y.
Gerena Valentin, Gilberto. August 23 and November 2013. Puerto Rico.
Goldwasser, Ira, and Harriet Broekman. June 2010. Amsterdam.
Gottehrer, Barry. Fall 2005. New York and Washington, D.C.
James, Michael. October 25, 2005. Chicago.
Levin, Stephen. August 8, 16, and 21, 2005. New York, N.Y.
Meyer, Gerald. September 12, 2015. New York.
Meyers, Dan. January 13, 2011.

Mullan, Fitzhugh. Fall 2005. Washington, D.C.
Osborne, Harold. July 30, 2000. New York.
Pietri, Carmen, and Joe Pietri. February 15, 2015. New York.
Phillips, Charlotte. August 6, 2015. Brooklyn, N.Y.
Ramirez, Ramon. December 2011. New York.
Rodriguez, Miriam. April 2011. New York.
Segarra, Arnie. August 25 and December 2011. New York.
Smith, Mike. August 19, 2005. New York.
Soloway, Bruce. August 2013. New York.
Stone, Richard. February 2012. New York.

Newspapers and Periodicals

Adirondack Daily Enterprise
Amsterdam News
Berkeley Tribe
Black Panther
Bond
Chicago Tribune
Christian Century
City Free Press
Claridad
El Diario La Prensa
First Source
For the People's Health
Good Times
Guardian
Health/PAC Bulletin
Liberated Guardian
Liberation News Service
Lincoln News
Long Island Daily Press
Massena Observer
Militant

The Movement
Nation
New York Daily News
New York Post
New York Review of Books
New York Times
New York World-Telegram
Old Mole
Palante: Latin Revolutionary News Service
Peace News Ltd.
Pediatric Collective Bulletin
Rat Subterranean News
Register-Guard (Eugene, Ore.)
Shakedown
Think . . . Lincoln
U.S. News and World Report
Village Voice
Wall Street Journal
Workers World
YLO

Publications and Dissertations

Abu-Jamal, Mumia. *We Want Freedom: A Life in the Black Panther Party*. Cambridge, Mass.: South End, 2004.
Acuña, Rudolfo. *Occupied America: The Chicano Struggle for Liberation*. San Francisco, Calif.: Canfield Press, 1972.
Alinsky, Saul D. *Rules for Radicals: A Practical Primer for Realistic Radicals*. New York: Vintage Books, 1971.
Allen, Robert. *Black Awakening in Capitalist America: An Analytic History*. Garden City, N.Y.: Doubleday, 1969.
Althusser, Louis. *Lenin and Philosophy and Other Essays*. New York: Monthly Review Press, 1971.

American Social History Project. *Who Built America: Working People and the Nation's Economy, Politics, Culture, and Society*. Vol. 2. New York: Pantheon Books, 1992.
Anderson, Odin. *The Uneasy Equilibrium: Private and Public Financing of Health Services in the United States 1875–1965*. New Haven, Conn.: New Haven College and University Press, 1968.
Anderson, Terry. *The Movement and the Sixties*. New York: Oxford University Press, 1995.
Aponte-Pares, Luis. "Lesson from El Barrio—The East Harlem Real Great Society/Urban Planning Studio: A Puerto Rican Chapter in the Fight for Self-Determination." *New Political Science* 20, no. 4 (1998): 399–420.

Appy, Christian G. *Working-Class War: American Combat Soldiers and Vietnam*. Chapel Hill: University of North Carolina Press, 1993.

Arguello, Martha M. "Puerto Rico En Mi Corázon: Young Lords/ Puerto Rican Radical Nationalists During the Late Twentieth Century." Ph.D. diss., University of California, Irvine, 2015.

Arnesen, Eric. *Black Protest and the Great Migration: A Brief History with Documents*. Boston: Bedford/St. Martin's, 2003.

———. "Whiteness and the Historians' Imagination." *International Labor and Working Class History* 60 (Fall 2001): 2–60.

———, ed. "Symposium on Thomas J. Sugrue: Origins of the Urban Crisis." *Labor History* 39, no. 1 (1998), 43–69.

Aronowitz, Stanley. "The Dialectics of Community Control." *Social Policy* 1 (1970): 41–51.

———. *False Promises: The Shaping of American Working-Class Consciousness*. Durham, N.C.: Duke University Press, 1992.

Asbury, Herbert. *Gem of the Prairie*. New York: Knopf, 1940.

Ashbolt, Anthony. *A Cultural History of the Radical Sixties in the San Francisco Bay Area*. New York: Pickering and Chatto, 2013. Reprint, New York: Routledge, 2016.

Ayala, Cesar. "The Decline of the Plantation Economy and the Puerto Rican Migration of the 1950s." *Latino Studies Journal* 7, no. 1 (Winter 1996): 62–90.

Ayala, Cesar, and Rafael Bernabe. *Puerto Rico in the American Century: A History since 1898*. Chapel Hill: University of North Carolina Press, 2007.

Back, Adina. "'Parent Power': Evelina Lopez Antonetty, the United Bronx Parents, and the War on Poverty." In *The War on Poverty: A New Grassroots History, 1964–1980*, edited by Annelise Orleck and Lisa Gayle Hazirjian, 184–208. Athens: University of Georgia Press, 2011.

———. "Up South in New York." Ph.D. diss., Duke University, 1996.

Bailey, Beth. "Sexual Revolution(s)." In *The Sixties: From Memory to History*, edited by David Farber, 235–62. Chapel Hill: University of North Carolina Press, 1994.

Baldwin, James. *The Fire Next Time*. New York: Dial, 1963.

Baxandall, Rosalyn, and Linda Gordon, eds. *Dear Sisters: Dispatches from the Women's Liberation Movement*. New York: Basic Books, 2001.

Bell, Daniel. *The End of Ideology: On the Exhaustion of Political Ideas in the Fifties*. Glencoe, Ill.: Free Press, 1960.

Bellush, Jewel, and Dick Netzer. *Urban Politics, New York Style*. New York: M. E. Sharp, 1990.

Bew, Paul. *Ideology and the Irish Question, 1912–1916*. New York: Oxford University Press, 1996.

Berger, Dan. *Captive Nation: Black Prison Organizing in the Civil Rights Era*. Chapel Hill: University of North Carolina Press, 2014.

———. *Outlaws of America: The Weather Underground and the Politics of Solidarity*. Chico, Calif.: AKA Press, 2005.

Bhana, Surendra. *The United States and the Development of the Puerto Rican Status Question*. St. Lawrence: University Press of Kansas, 1975.

Biondi, Martha. *The Black Revolution on Campus*. Berkeley: University of California Press, 2014.

———. *To Stand and Fight: The Struggle for Civil Rights in Postwar New York*. Cambridge, Mass.: Harvard University Press, 2003.

Blackstone, Nelson. *Cointelpro: The FBI's War on Political Freedom*. New York: Pathfinder Press, 1975.

Blanco, Tomás. *El prejuicio racial en Puerto Rico*. Rio Piedras, PR: Ediciones Huracán, 1945.

Blauner, Robert. *Racial Oppression in America*. New York: Harper and Row, 1972.

Bloom, Jack. *Class, Race, and the Civil Rights Movement*. Bloomington: Indiana University Press, 1987.

Bloom, Joshua, and Waldo Martin. *Black against Empire: The History and Politics of the Black Panther Party*. Berkeley: University of California Press, 2013.

Board of Corrections. *Shuttle to Oblivion: A Report on the Life and Death of a Citizen, Rommel Lavon Moore, in the Manhattan House of Detention for Men, also Known as the Tombs*. December 1970.

Bonilla, Frank, and Hector Colón Jordan. "Mama, Borinquen Me Llama! Puerto Rican Return Migration into the Seventies." *Migration Today* 7, no. 2 (1979): 1–6.

Bonilla-Santiago, Gloria. "A Case Study of Puerto Rican Migrant Farmers Organization Effectiveness in New Jersey," Ph.D. diss., City University of New York, 1986.

Booker, Chris. "Lumpenization: A Critical Error of the Black Panther Party." In *The Black Panther Party Reconsidered*, edited by Charles E. Jones, 337–58. New York: Black Classic, 1998.

Bowens, M. G., C. B. Wood, M. C. Olendzki, and C. H. Goodrich. "East Harlem and Its Health Resources." *Annals of the New York Academy of Sciences* 196 (1972): 45–50.

Boyte, Harry. *The Backyard Revolution: Understanding the New Citizen Movement*. Philadelphia: Temple University Press, 1980.

Brachman, Jarret. "Terrorism and the American

Experience: Constructing, Contesting, and Countering Terrorism since 1793." Ph.D. diss., University of Delaware, 2006.

Braithwaithe, John. *Crime, Shame, and Reintegration*. Cambridge, UK: Cambridge University Press, 1989.

Bradley, Stefan. *Harlem vs. Columbia University: Black Student Power in the Late 1960s*. Urbana-Champaign: University of Illinois Press, 2009.

Branch, Taylor. *Parting the Waters: America in the King Years, 1954–63*. New York: Simon and Schuster, 1988.

———. *Pillar of Fire: America in the King Years, 1963–65*. New York: Simon and Schuster, 1998.

Braunstein, Peter, and William Doyle, eds. *Imagine Nation: The American Counterculture of the 1960s and 1970s*. New York: Routledge, 2001.

Brecher, Jeremy. *Strike!* Boston: South End, 1997.

Breines, Winifred. *Community and Organization in the New Left, 1962–1968: The Great Refusal*. New Brunswick, N.J.: Rutgers University Press, 1989.

———. "Whose New Left." *Journal of American History* 75, no. 2 (September 1988): 528–45.

Breitman, George. *Leon Trotsky on Black Nationalism and Self-Determination*. New York: Pathfinder, 1978.

———, ed. *Malcolm X Speaks: Selected Speeches and Statements*. New York: Grove Weidenfeld, 1990.

Brenner, Robert. *The Boom and the Bubble*. New York: Verso, 2002.

Brinkley, Alan. *Liberalism and Its Discontents*. Cambridge, Mass.: Harvard University Press, 1998.

Brisbane, Robert. *Black Vanguard: Origins of the Negro Social Revolution, 1900–1960*. Valley Forge, Pa.: Judson, 1969.

Brooks, Thomas R. *Walls Come Tumbling Down: A History of the Civil Rights Movement, 1940–1970*. Englewood Cliffs, N.J.: Prentice-Hall, 1974.

Brotherton, P. Sean. "Health and Healthcare: Revolutionary Period." In *Cuba: People, Culture, and History*, edited by Alan West-Dúran, 478–85. New York: Charles Scribner and Sons, 2011.

Brown, Elaine. *A Taste of Power: A Black Woman's Story*. New York: Anchor Books, 1992.

Browning, Frank. "From Rumble to Revolution: The Young Lords." In *The Puerto Rican Experience: A Sociological Source Book*, edited by Francesco Cordasco and Eugene Bucchioni, 231–45. Totowa, N.J.: Littlefield, Adams, 1973.

Burlage, Robb. *New York City's Municipal Hospitals: A Policy Review*. Washington, D.C.: Institute for Policy Studies, 1967.

Burnett, Christina Duffy, and Burke Marshall, eds. *Foreign in a Domestic Sense: Puerto Rico, American Expansion, and the Constitution*. Durham, N.C.: Duke University Press, 2001.

Bush, Roderick. *We Are Not What We Seem: Black Nationalism and Class Struggle in the American Century*. New York: New York University Press, 1999.

Button, James W. *Black Violence: Political Impact of the 1960s Riots*. Princeton, N.J.: Princeton University Press, 1978.

Cagin, Seth. *We Are Not Afraid: The Story of Goodman, Schwerner, and Chaney and the Civil Rights Campaign for Mississippi*. New York: Macmillan, 1988.

Cahan, Susan Elizabeth. "Inventing the Multicultural Museum: A Critical Study of 'Harlem on My Mind.'" Ph.D. diss., City University of New York, 2003.

Cannato, Vincent J. *The Ungovernable City: John Lindsay and His Struggle to Save New York*. New York: Basic Books, 2001.

Capeci, Domenic. "Race Riot Redux: William M. Tuttle, Jr., and the Study of Racial Violence." *Reviews in American History* 29, no. 1 (March 2001): 165–81.

Caraballo, Josepha Santiago. "Guerra, reforma y colonialismo: Luis Muñoz Marín, las reformas del PPD y su vinculación con la militarización de Puerto Rico en el contexto de la Segunda Guerra Mundial." Ph.D. diss., University of Puerto Rico, 2004.

Carmichael, Stokely, and Charles Hamilton. *Black Power: The Politics of Liberation in America*. New York: Random House, 1967.

Caro, Robert A. *The Power Broker: Robert Moses and the Fall of New York*. New York: Alfred A. Knopf, 1974.

Carrion, Arturo Morales. *Puerto Rico: A Political and Cultural History*. New York: W. W. Norton, 1983.

Carson, Clayborne. *In Struggle: SNCC and the Black Awakening of the 1960s*. Cambridge, Mass.: Harvard University Press, 1981.

Case, Jay Riley. *An Unpredictable Gospel: American Evangelicals and World Christianity, 1812–1920*. New York: Oxford University Press, 2012.

Caute, David. *The Year of the Barricade: A Journey through 1968*. New York: Harper and Row, 1988.

Cha-Cha Jiménez Defense Committee. *"Que Viva El Pueblo": A Biographical History of José Cha Cha Jiménez, General Secretary of the Young Lords Organization*. Chicago: Cha-Cha Jiménez Defense Committee, 1973.

Chalmers, David. *And the Crooked Places Made Straight*. Baltimore: Johns Hopkins University Press, 1991.

Chambliss, W. "Policing the Ghetto Underclass: The Politics of Law and Law Enforcement." *Social Problems* 41, no. 2 (May 1994): 177–94.

Chandra, Siddharth, and Angela Williams Foster. "The 'Revolution of Rising Expectations,' Relative Deprivation, and the Urban Social Disorders of the 1960s Evidence from State-Level Data." *Social Science History* 29, no. 2 (Summer 2005), 299–332.

Chenault, Lawrence R. *The Puerto Rican Migrant in New York City.* New York: Russell and Russell, 1970.

Chowkwanyun, Merlin. "The New Left *and* Public Health: The Health Policy Advisory Center, Community Organizing, and the Big Business of Health, 1967–1975." *American Journal of Public Health* 101, no. 2 (February 2011): 238–49.

Churchill, Ward, and Jim Vander Wall, eds. *The COINTELPRO Papers: Documents from the FBI's Secret Wars against Dissent in the United States.* Cambridge, Mass.: South End Press, 2002.

City of New York, Citywide Equal Employment Opportunity Committee. *Equal Employment in New York City Government, 1977–1988.* New York: Citywide Committee, 1988.

Cleaver, Eldridge. *Soul on Ice.* New York: McGraw-Hill, 1967.

Cleaver, Kathleen Neal. "Women, Power, and Revolution." In *Liberation, Imagination and the Black Panther Party: A New Look at the Black Panthers and Their Legacy,* edited by Kathleen Cleaver and George Katsiaficas, 122–27. London: Routledge, 2014.

Cleaver, Kathleen, and George Katsiaficas, eds. *Liberation, Imagination, and the Black Panther Party: A New Look at the Black Panthers and Their Legacy.* London: Routledge, 2014.

Cloward, Richard A., and Frances Fox Piven. *The Politics of Turmoil: Essays on Poverty, Race, and the Urban Crisis.* New York: Pantheon Books, 1974.

Cloward, Richard A., and Lloyd E. Ohlin. *Delinquency and Opportunity: A Theory of Delinquent Gangs.* Glencoe, Ill.: Free Press, 1960.

Cluster, Dick. *They Should Have Served That Cup of Coffee.* Boston: South End, 1979.

Cohen, Albert K. *Delinquent Boys: The Culture of the Gang.* Glencoe, Ill.: Free Press, 1955.

Coleman, James S. *Equality of Educational Opportunity.* With associates. Washington, D.C.: U.S. Printing Office, 1966.

Collins, Robert M. "Growth Liberalism in the Sixties." In *The Sixties: From Memory to History,* edited by David Farber, 11–44. Chapel Hill: University of North Carolina Press, 1994.

Colón, Ismael Garcia. "'We Like Mexican Workers Better': Citizenship and Immigration Policies in the Formation of Puerto Rican Farm Labor in the United States." *CENTRO Journal* 29, no. 2 (Summer 2017): 134–71.

Colón, Jesús. *A Puerto Rican in New York and other Sketches.* New York: International Publishers, 1982.

Commission on the Delivery of Personal Health Services (Report and Staff Studies). *Community Health Service for New York.* New York: Praeger, 1969.

Condit, Carl W. *Chicago, 1930–1970: Building, Planning and Urban Technology.* Chicago: University of Chicago Press, 1974.

Cone, James H. *Martin and Malcolm and America: A Dream or a Nightmare?* Maryknoll, N.Y.: Orbis Books, 1991.

———. "Martin Luther King and the Third World." *Journal of American History* 74, no. 2 (September 1987): 455–67.

Cordasco, Francesco. *The Puerto Ricans, 1493–1973: A Chronology and Fact Book.* Dobbs Ferry, N.Y.: Oceana, 1973.

Cosgrove, Stuart. "The Zoot-Suit and Style Warfare." *History Workshop,* no. 18 (Autumn 1984), 77–91.

Countryman, Matthew. *Up South: Civil Rights and Black Power in Philadelphia.* Princeton, N.J.: Princeton University Press, 2007.

Crawford, Vicki L., Jacqueline Anne Rouse, and Barbara Woods. *Women in the Civil Rights Movement: Trailblazers and Torchbearers, 1941–1965.* New York: Carlson, 1990.

Cruz, Maria Acosta. *Dream Nation: Puerto Rican Culture and the Fictions of Independence.* New Brunswick, N.J.: Rutgers University Press, 2014.

Cruz, Samuel. *Masked Africanisms: Puerto Rican Pentecostalism.* Dubuque: Kendall/Hunt, 2005.

Cuevas, Eliezer Curet. *Economía política de Puerto Rico: 1950 a 2000.* San Juan, Puerto Rico: Ediciones M.A.C., 2004.

Danielson, Ross. *Cuba: Twenty-Five Years of Revolution, 1959–1984.* New York, Eastbourne: Praeger, 1985.

Debs, Eugene. "The Negro in the Class Struggle." *International Socialist Review* 4, no. 5 (November 1903): 257–60.

De Genova, Nicholas, and Ana Y. Ramos-Zayas. *Latino Crossings: Mexicans, Puerto Ricans, and the Politics of Race and Citizenship.* New York: Routledge, 2003.

———. "Latino Rehearsals: Racialization and the Politics of Citizenship between Mexicans and Puerto Ricans in Chicago." *Journal of Latin American Anthropology* 8, no. 2 (June 2008): 18–57.

Degroot, Gerard. *Student Protest: The Sixties and After.* New York: Longman, 1998.

De la Cova, Antonio Rafael. *The Moncada Attack: Birth of the Cuban Revolution.* Columbia: University of South Carolina Press, 2007.

Delgado, Linda. "Jesús Colón and the Making of a New York City Community, 1917–1974." In *The Puerto Rican Diaspora: Historical Perspectives,* edited by Carmen Teresa Whalen and Victor Vásquez-Hernández, 68–87. Philadelphia: Temple University Press, 2005.

D'Emilio, John, and Estelle B. Freedman. *Intimate Matters: A History of Sexuality in America Liberation.* Chicago: University of Chicago Press, 1988.

———. *Sexual Politics, Sexual Communities: The Making of a Homosexual Minority in the United States, 1940–1970.* Chicago: University of Chicago Press, 1998.

Denis, Nelson A. *War against Puerto Ricans, Revolution and Terror in America's Colony.* New York: Nation Books, 2015.

Denning, Michael. *Culture in the Age of Three Worlds.* New York: Verso, 2004.

De Veaux, Alexis. *Warrior Poet: The Biography of Audre Lorde.* New York: Norton, 2004.

Diamond, Andrew J. *Mean Streets: Chicago Youths and the Everyday Struggle for Empowerment in the Multiracial City, 1908–1969.* Berkeley: University of California Press, 2009.

Díaz Soler, Luis. *Historia de la Esclavitud Negra En Puerto Rico.* Río Piedras: Palencia De Castilla, 1965.

Dietz, James. *Economic History of Puerto Rico: Institutional Change and Capitalist Development.* Princeton, N.J.: Princeton University Press, 1986.

———. *Negotiating Development and Change.* Boulder, Colo.: Lynn Rienner, 2003.

Dispenzieri, Angelo. *Characteristics of the College Discovery Program Students: 1964–1967.* New York: CUNY College Discovery Program, Research and Evaluation Unit, 1968.

Dittmer, John. *The Good Doctors: Medical Committee for Human Rights and the Struggle for Social Justice in Health Care.* New York: Bloomsbury, 2009.

———. *Local People: The Struggle for Civil Rights in Mississippi.* Urbana-Champaign: University of Illinois Press, 1994.

Dix, Aaron. *My People Are Rising: Memoir of a Black Panther Party Captain.* Chicago: Haymarket Books, 2012.

Draper, Theodore. *The Roots of American Communism.* New York: Viking, 1957.

Driscoll, Barbara A. *The Tracks North: The Railroad Bracero Program of World War II.* Austin: CMAS Books, Center for Mexican American Studies, University of Texas at Austin, 1999.

Duany, Jorge. *The Puerto Rican Nation on the Move: Identities on the Island and in the United States.* Chapel Hill: University of North Carolina Press, 2002.

Duberman, Martin. *Stonewall.* New York: Plume, 1994.

Du Bois, W. E. B. *Dark Water: Voices from within the Veil.* New York: Harcourt, Brace and Howe, 1920.

———. *The Souls of Black Folks.* Chicago: A. C. McClurg & Co., 1903.

Dudziak, Mary. *Cold War Civil Rights: Race and the Image of American Democracy.* Princeton, N.J.: Princeton University Press, 2000.

Duménil, Gérard, and Dominique Lévy. *Capital Resurgent: Roots of the Neoliberal Revolution.* Cambridge, Mass.: Harvard University Press, 2004.

Dunbar-Ortiz, Roxanne. *Loaded: A Disarming History of the Second Amendment.* San Francisco: City Lights Books, 2018.

Echols, Alice. *Daring to Be Bad: Radical Feminism in America, 1967–1975.* Minneapolis: University of Minnesota Press, 1989.

———. "Nothing Distant about It: Women's Liberation and Sixties Radicalism." In *The Sixties: From Memory to History,* edited by David Farber, 149–74. Chapel Hill: University of North Carolina Press, 1994.

Edsall, Thomas Byrne, and Mary D. Edsall. *Chain Reaction: The Impact of Race, Rights, and Taxes on American Politics.* New York: W. W. Norton, 1991.

Ehrenreich, Barbara. *The American Health Empire: Power, Profits, and Politics.* New York: Random House, 1971.

Eidsvold, Gary, Anthony Mustalish, and Lloyd F. Novick. "The New York City Department of Health: Lesson in Lead Poisoning Control Program." *American Journal of Public Health* 64, no. 10 (October 1974).

Elbaum, Max. *Revolution in the Air: Sixties Radicals Turn to Lenin, Mao and Che.* New York: Verso, 2001.

Enck-Wanzer, Darrel. "The Intersectional Rhetoric of the Young Lords: Social Movement, Ideographs, Demand, and the Radical Democratic Imaginary." Ph.D. diss., Indiana University, 2007.

———. "Trashing the System: Social Movement, Intersectional Rhetoric, and Collective Agency in the Young Lords Organization's Garbage Offensive." *Quarterly Journal of Speech* 92, no. 2 (2006): 174–201.

———. *The Young Lords: A Reader.* New York: New York University Press, 2010.

Engel, Jonathan. *Poor People's Medicine: Medicaid and American Charity Care since 1945*. Durham, N.C.: Duke University Press, 2006.

Engler, Mark, and Paul Engler. *This Is an Uprising: How Nonviolent Revolt Is Shaping the Twenty-First Century*. New York: Nation Books, 2016.

Estades, Rosa. *Patrones de participacion politica de los puertorriqueños en la ciudad de Nueva York*. San Juan: Universidad de Puerto Rico, 1978.

Evans, Sara. *Personal Politics: The Origins of Women's Liberation in the Civil Rights Movement and the New Left*. New York: Alfred A. Knopf, 1979.

Fainstein, Norman, and Susan S. Fainstein. "Economic Restructuring and the Rise of Social Movements." *Urban Affairs Quarterly* 21, no. 2 (December 1985): 187–206.

———. "The Future of Community Control." *American Political Science Review* 70, no. 3 (September 1976): 905–23.

Falcón, Luis Nieves, Pablo García Rodríguez, and Féliz Ojeda Reyez. *Puerto Rico, grito y mordaza*. Rio Piedras, Puerto Rico: Ediciones Librería Internacional, 1971.

Fanon, Frantz. *Wretched of the Earth*. New York: Grove, 1963.

Farber, David. *The Age of Great Dreams: America in the 1960s*. New York: Hill and Wang, 1994.

———. *Chicago '68*. Chicago: University of Chicago Press, 1988.

———, ed. *The Sixties: From Memory to History*. Chapel Hill: University of North Carolina Press, 1994.

Farmer, Ashley. *Remaking Black Power: How Black Women Transformed an Era*. Chapel Hill: University of North Carolina Press, 2019.

Farmer, James. *Lay Bare the Heart: An Autobiography of the Civil Rights Movement*. New York: Arbor House, 1985.

Fatemi, Khosrow, ed. *The Maquiladora Industry: Economic Solution or Problem?* New York: Praeger, 1990.

Fernández, Johanna. "Between Social Service Reform and Revolutionary Politics: The Young Lords, Late Sixties Radicalism, and Community Organizing in the New York City." In *Freedom North: Civil Rights Movements Outside of the South*, edited by Jeanne Theoharis and Komozi Woodard, 255–85. New York: Palgrave Macmillan, 2003.

———. "Denise Oliver and the Young Lords Party: Stretching the Political Boundaries of Black Radical Struggle." In *Want to Start a Revolution? Radical Women in the Black Freedom Struggle*, edited by Dayo F. Gore, Jeanne Theoharis, and Komozi Woodard, 271–93. New York: New York University Press, 2009.

———. "Radicals in the Late 1960s: A History of the Young Lords Party, 1969–1974." Ph.D. diss., Columbia University, 2004.

———. "The Young Lords and the Postwar City." In *African American Urban History since World War II*, edited by Kenneth Kusmer and Joe Trotter, 60–82. Chicago: University of Chicago Press, 2009.

Fernández, Lilia. *Brown in the Windy City: Mexicans and Puerto Ricans in Postwar Chicago*. Chicago: University of Chicago Press, 2014.

———. "Of Immigrants and Migrants: Mexican and Puerto Rican Labor Migration in Comparative Perspective, 1942–1964." *Journal of American Ethnic History* 29, no. 3, (Spring 2010): 6–39.

Fields, Barbara Jeanne. "Ideology and Race in American History." In *Region, Race and Reconstruction: Essays in Honor of C. Vann Woodward*, edited by J. Morgan Kousser and James M. McPherson, 143–77. New York: Oxford University Press, 1982.

———. "Slavery, Race and Ideology in the United States of America." *New Left Review* 181 (May/June 1990): 95–118.

Fine, Sidney. *Sit-Down: The General Motors Strike of 1936–1937*. Ann Arbor: University of Michigan Press, 1969.

Fink, Carole, Phillip Gassert, and Detlef Junker. *1968: The World Transformed*. Cambridge: Cambridge University Press, 1998.

Fink, Leon, and Brian Greenberg. *Upheaval in the Quiet Zone: A History of Hospital Workers' Union, Local 1199*. Urbana-Champaign: University of Illinois Press, 1989.

Fitz, Don. "The Birth of the Cuban Polyclinic." *Monthly Review* 70, no. 2 (June 2018): 21–32.

Fitzpatrick, Joseph. *Puerto Rican Americans: The Meaning of Migration to the Mainland*. Englewood Cliffs, N.J.: Prentice-Hall, 1971.

Flamm, Michael. *Law and Order: Street Crime, Civil Unrest, and the Crisis of Liberalism in the 1960s*. New York: Columbia University Press, 2007.

Flores, Juan. *From Bomba to Hip-Hop: Puerto Rican Culture and Latino Identity*. New York: Columbia University Press, 2000.

Flores, Juan, and Miriam Jiménez Román. "Triple-Consciousness? Approaches to Afro-Latino Culture in the United States." *Latin American and Caribbean Ethnic Studies* 4, no. 3 (2009): 319–28.

Foner, Eric. "Response to Eric Arnesen." *International Labor and Working Class History* 60 (Fall 2001): 57–58.

Foner, Nancy. *New Immigrants in New York*. New York: Columbia University Press, 2001.

Foner, Phillip. *The Black Panthers Speak: The*

Manifesto of the Party; The First Complete Documentary Record of the Panthers' Program. Philadelphia: J. B. Lippincott, 1970.

Font, Maria Eugenia Estades. *La presencia militar de Estados Unidos en Puerto Rico, 1898–1918: Intereses estategios y dominancion colonial*. San Juan, Puerto Rico: Ediciones Huracán, 1988.

Forman, James. *The Making of Black Revolutionaries: A Personal Account*. New York: Macmillan, 1972.

Formisano, Ronald P. *Boston against Busing: Race, Class, and Ethnicity in the 1960s and 1970s*. Chapel Hill: University of North Carolina Press, 1991.

Frabricant, Michael, and Steven Brier. *Austerity Blues: Fighting for the Soul of Public Education*. Baltimore: Johns Hopkins University Press, 2012.

Franklin, V. P., and Bettye Collier-Thomas, eds. *Sisters in the Struggle: African American Women in the Civil Rights-Black Power Movement*. New York: New York University Press, 2001.

Fraser, Steve, and Gary Gerstle, eds. *The Rise and Fall of the New Deal Order, 1930–1980*. Princeton, N.J.: Princeton University Press, 1989.

Frazier, Franklin. *The Negro Family in the United States*. Chicago: University of Chicago Press, 1966.

Freeman, Joshua. *The Politics of Women's Liberation: A Case Study of an Emerging Social Movement and Its Relation to Policy*. New York: McKay, 1975.

———. *Working-Class New York: Life and Labor since World War II*. New York: New Press, 2000.

Friedan, Betty. *The Feminine Mystique*. New York: Norton, 1963.

Freire, Paulo. *Pedagogy of the Oppressed*. New York: Blumsbury, 2000.

Frost, Jennifer. *An Interracial Movement of the Poor: Community Organizing and the New Left in the 1960s*. New York: New York University Press, 2001.

Fullilove, Mindy Thompson. *Root Shock: How Tearing Up City Neighborhoods Hurts America, and What We Can Do about It*. New York: Ballantine, 2005.

Gaddis, John Lewis. *The Cold War: A New History*. New York: Penguin Book, 2006.

Galbraith, John Kenneth. *The Affluent Society*. Boston: Houghton Mifflin, 1958.

Garcia, Jay. *Psychology Comes to Harlem: Rethinking the Race Question in 20th Century America*. Baltimore: Johns Hopkins University Press, 2012.

Garden, Luis, et al. "The History of the Puerto Rican National Minority in the United States." *Boricua* 1 (1974): 34–47.

Gardner, Fred. *The Unlawful Concert*. New York: Viking, 1970.

Garrow, David J. *Bearing the Cross: Martin Luther King, Jr., and the Southern Christian Leadership Conference*. New York: Morrow, 1986.

———. *The FBI and Martin Luther King, Jr.* New York: Penguin Books, 1981.

Georgakas, Dan, and Marvin Surkin. *Detroit I Do Mind Dying: A Study in Urban Revolution*. Boston: South End, 1998.

Gerassi, John, ed. *Revolutionary Priest: The Complete Writings and Messages of Camilo Torres*. New York: Random House, 1971.

Gerena Valentin, Gilberto. *My Life as a Community Activist, Labor Organizer, and Progressive Politician in New York City*. New York: Centro de Estudios Puertorriqueños, 2013.

Geschwender, James. *Class, Race and Worker Insurgency: The League of Revolutionary Black Workers*. Cambridge: Cambridge University Press, 1977.

Giap, Vo Nguyen. *People's War, People's Army: The Vietcong Insurrection Manual for Underdeveloped Countries*. New York: Praeger, 1962.

Ginsberg, Alice E. "Triumphs, Controversies, and Change: 1970s to the Twenty-First Century." In *The Evolution of American Women's Studies: Reflections on Triumphs, Controversies, and Change*, 9–39. New York: Palgrave Macmillan, 2008.

Ginzberg, Eli, and Conservation of Human Resources Project (Columbia University). *Urban Health Services: The Case of New York*. New York: Columbia University Press, 1971.

Gitlin, Todd. *The Sixties: Years of Hope, Days of Rage*. New York: Bantam Books, 1993.

———. *The Whole World Is Watching: Mass Media in the Making and Unmaking of the New Left*. Berkeley: University of California Press, 1980.

Glasser, Ruth. *Aquí Me Quedo: Puerto Ricans in Connecticut*. Middletown: Connecticut Humanities Council, 1997.

Glazer, Nathan. "The South Bronx Story: An Extreme Case of Neighborhood Decline." *Political Studies Journal* 16, no. 2 (Winter 1987): 269–76.

Glazer, Nathan, and Daniel P. Moynihan. *Beyond the Melting Pot: The Negroes, Puerto Ricans, Jews, Italians, and Irish of New York City*. Cambridge, Mass.: MIT Press, 1970.

Gomez, Laura. *Manifest Destinies: The Making of the Mexican American Race*. New York: New York University Press, 2007.

Gomez-Quiñones, Juan. *Mexican American Labor, 1790–1990*. Albuquerque: University of New Mexico Press, 1994.

González, Juan. *Harvest of Empire: A History of Latinos in America*. New York: Viking, 2000.

———. "The Price of Imperialism." In *Palante: Young Lords Party*, by Young Lords Party and Michael Abramson, 65. New York: McGraw-Hill, 1971.

———. *Roll Down Your Window: Stories of a Forgotten America*. London: Verso, 1995.

González, Juan, Juan "Fi" Ortiz, Denise Oliver, Gloria González, Pablo "Yoruba" Guzmán. *Report of Central Committee Evaluation and Retreat*. December 21–23, 27–31, 1970.

Gore, Dayo F., Jeanne Theoharis, and Komozi Woodard, eds. *Want to Start a Revolution? Radical Women in the Black Freedom Struggle*. New York: New York University Press, 2009.

Gosse, Van. *Rethinking the New Left: An Interpretative History*. London: Palgrave Macmillan, 2005.

———. *Where the Boys Are: Cuba, Cold War, and the Making of the New Left*. New York: Haymarket Books, 1992.

Gottehrer, Barry. *The Mayor's Man: One Man's Struggle to Save Our City*. Garden City, N.Y.: Doubleday, 1975.

Graham, Hugh Davis. *The Civil Rights Era: Origins and Development of a National Policy, 1960–1972*. New York: Oxford University Press, 1990.

Gramsci, Antonio. *Selections from the Prison Notebooks*. Edited by Quentin Hoare and Geoffrey Smith. New York: International Publishers, 1971.

Grant, Joanne. *Ella Baker: Freedom Bound*. New York: John Wiley and Sons, 1998.

Green, Charles, and Basil Wilson. *The Struggle for Black Empowerment in New York City: Beyond the Politics of Pigmentation*. New York: Praeger, 1989.

Griswold del Castillo, Richard, and Richard Garcia. *Cesar Chavez: A Triumph of Spirit*. Norman: University of Oklahoma Press, 1995.

Grob, Gerald N. *From Asylum to Community*. Princeton, N.J.: Princeton University Press, 1991.

Grosfoguel, Ramon. *Colonial Subjects: Puerto Ricans in Global Perspective*. Berkeley: University of California Press, 2003.

Guevara, Che. *Guerrilla Warfare*. New York: BN Publishing, 2012.

———. *Socialism and Man in Cuba*. New York: Pathfinder, 1982.

Gunderson, Christopher. "The Struggle for CUNY: A History of the CUNY Student Movement." Macaulay Honors College. Accessed March 11, 2019. http://macaulay.cuny.edu/eportfolios/hainline2014/files/2014/02/Gunderson_The-Struggle-for-CUNY.pdf.

Guridy, Frank Andre. *Forging Diaspora: Afro-Cubans and African Americans in a World of Empire and Jim Crow*. Chapel Hill: University of North Carolina Press, 2010.

Gurr, Ted Robert. *Why Men Rebel*. Boulder, Colo.: Paradigm Publishers, 2010.

Guzmán, Pablo "Yoruba." "Ain't No Party Like the One We Got: The Young Lords Party and *Palante*." In *Voices from the Underground: Insider Histories of the Vietnam Era*, vol. 1, edited by Ken Wachsberger, 293–30. Tempe, Ariz.: Mica Press, 1993.

———. "Before People Called Me a Spic, They Called Me a Nigger." In *Palante: Young Lords Party*, by Young Lords Party and Michael Abramson. New York: McGraw-Hill, 1971.

———. *Pablo Guzmán on the Young Lords Legacy: A Personal Account*. New York: Institute for Puerto Rican Policy, 1995.

———. "Puerto Rican Barrio Politics in the United States." In *The Puerto Rican Struggle: Essays on Survival in the U.S.*, edited by Clara Rodríguez, Virginia Sanchez Korrol, and Jose Oscar Alers, 121–28. Maplewood, N.J.: Waterfront, 1984.

———. "*La Vida Pura*: A Lord of the Barrio." *The Puerto Rican Movement: Voices from the Diaspora*, edited by Andrés Torres and Jose E. Velázquez, 155–72. Philadelphia: Temple University Press, 1998.

———. "The Young Lords Legacy: A Personal Account." *Critica: A Journal of Puerto Rican Policy & Politics* 11–12 (April–May 1995).

———. "Young Lords Move in New York." Interview. *Movement*, November 1969.

Guzmán, Pablo "Yoruba," and Graciela M. Smith. "Interview with Yoruba, Minister of Information, Young Lords Organization, Regarding Confrontations at the First Spanish Methodist Church in El Barrio (Spanish Harlem)." *First Source*, December 19, 1969, 27.

Haas, Jeffrey. *The Assassination of Fred Hampton: How the FBI and the Chicago Police Murdered a Black Panther*. Chicago: Chicago Review Press, 2011.

Hagedorn, John M. "Race Not Space: A Revisionist History of Gangs in Chicago." *Journal of African American History* 91, no. 2 (Spring 2006): 194–208.

Hahamovitch, Cindy. *Fruits of Their Labor: Atlantic Coast Farmworkers and the Making of Migrant Poverty, 1870–1945*. Chapel Hill: University of North Carolina Press, 2010.

Hale, Jon N. *The Freedom Schools: A History of Student Activists in the Mississippi Civil Rights Movement*. New York: Columbia University Press, 2016.

Halebsky, Sandor, and John M. Kirk, eds. *Cuba: Twenty-Five Years of Revolution, 1959–1984*. New York: Praeger, 1985.

Haley, Alex. *The Autobiography of Malcolm X.* New York: Ballantine Books, 1965.

Hampton, Henry, and Steve Fayer with Sarah Flynn. *Voices of Freedom: An Oral History of the Civil Rights Movement from the 1950s through the 1980s.* New York: Bantam Books, 1990.

Handlin, Oscar. *The Newcomers: Negroes and Puerto Ricans in a Changing Metropolis.* Cambridge, Mass.: Harvard University Press, 1959.

Harding, Vincent. *There Is a River: The Black Struggle for Freedom in America.* New York: Harcourt, Brace, Jovanovich, 1981.

Harlem Parents Committee. *The Education of Minority Group Children in the New York City Public Schools.* New York: Harlem Parents Committee, 1965.

Harman, Chris. *The Fire Last Time: 1968 and After.* London: Bookmarks, 1988.

Harrington, Michael. *The Other America: Poverty in the United States.* New York: Macmillan, 1970.

Harrison, Cynthia. *On Account of Sex: The Politics of Women's Issues, 1945–1968.* Berkeley: University of California Press, 1968.

Harvey, David. *A Brief History of Neoliberalism.* Oxford: Oxford University Press, 2007.

Heath, G. Louis, ed. *Off the Pigs! The History and Literature of the Black Panther Party.* Metuchen, N.J.: Scarecrow, 1976.

Herbstein, Judith. "The Politicization of Puerto Rican Ethnicity in New York, 1955–1975." *Ethnic Groups* 5, no. 3 (1983): 31–54.

Herman, Edward S. *The Real Terror Network.* Cambridge, Mass.: South End, 1982.

Herring, George C. *America's Longest War: The United States and Vietnam, 1950–1975.* Boston: McGraw-Hill, 2002.

———. *From Colony to Superpower: U.S. Foreign Relations Since 1776.* New York: Oxford University Press, 2006.

High, Steven. "'The Wounds of Class': A Historiographical Reflection on the Study of Deindustrialization." *History Compass* 11, no. 11 (2013): 1–14.

Hilliard, David, ed. *The Black Panther Party: Service to the People Programs.* Albuquerque: University of New Mexico Press, 2008.

Hilliard, David, and Lewis Cole. *This Side of Glory: The Autobiography of David Hilliard and the Story of the Black Panther Party.* Boston: Little, Brown, 1993.

Hinton, Elizabeth. *From the War on Poverty to the War on Crime: The Making of Mass Incarceration.* Cambridge, Mass.: Harvard University Press, 2016.

Hirsch, Arnold R. *Making the Second Ghetto: Race and Housing in Chicago 1940–1960.* Chicago: Chicago University Press, 1983.

History Task Force–Centro de Estudios

Puertorriqueños. *Labor Migration under Capitalism.* New York: Monthly Review Press, 1979.

Hobsbawm, Eric. *Age of Extremes: The Short Twentieth Century, 1914–1991.* London: Michael Joseph, 1994.

Hoch, Charles, and Robert A. Slayton. *New Homeless and Old: Community and the Skid Row Hotel.* Philadelphia: Temple University Press, 1989.

Hoffnung-Garskoff, Jesse. "Migrations of Arturo Schomburg: On Being Antillano, Negro, and Puerto Rican in New York, 1891–1938." *Journal of American Ethnic History*, no. 21 (Fall 2002): 3–49.

———. "The World of Arturo Schomburg." In *The Afro-Latin@ Reader: History and Culture in the United States*, edited by Miriam Jiménez Román and Juan Flores, 70–91. Durham, N.C.: Duke University Press, 2010.

Horne, Gerald. *Fire This Time: The Watts Uprising and the 1960s.* Charlottesville: University Press of Virginia, 1995.

Howard, Alan. "The Barrio and the YLO Say No More Garbage in Our Community." *Liberation News Service*, August 21, 1969.

Hurtado, Aída, Patricia Gurin, and Timothy Peng. "Social Identities—a Framework for Studying the Adaptations of Immigrants and Ethnics: The Adaptations of Mexicans in the United States." *Social Problems* 41, no. 1 (February 1994): 129–51.

Iglesias, C. A. *Memoirs of Bernardo Vega.* Translated by Juan Flores. New York: Monthly Review Press, 1984.

Ignatiev, Noel. *How the Irish Became White.* New York: Routledge, 1995.

Isserman, Maurice. *If I Had a Hammer: The Death of the Old Left and the Birth of the New Left.* New York: Basic Books, 1987.

Isserman, Maurice, and Michael Kazin. *America Divided: The Civil War of the 1960s.* New York: Oxford University Press, 2000.

———. "Success and Failure of the New Radicalism." In *The Rise and Fall of the New Deal Order, 1930–1980*, edited by Steve Fraser and Gary Gerstle, 212–42. Princeton, N.J.: Princeton University Press, 1989.

Jackson, Kenneth T. *Crabgrass Frontier: The Suburbanization of the United States.* New York: Oxford University Press, 1985.

Jackson, Larry R., and William Johnson. *Protest by the Poor: The Welfare Movement in New York City.* Lexington, Mass.: Lexington Books, 1974.

Jacobson, Matthew Fry. *Whiteness of a Different Color: European Immigrants and the Alchemy of Race.* Cambridge, Mass.: Harvard University Press, 1998.

James, Winston. *Holding Aloft the Banner of Ethiopia: Caribbean Radicalism in Early Twentieth Century America*. London: Verso Books, 1998.

Jamison, Andrew, and Ron Eyerman. *Seeds of the Sixties*. Berkeley: University of California Press, 1994.

Janoski, Thomas. *The Political Economy of Unemployment*. Berkeley: University of California Press, 2018.

Jenkins, Ernestine, and Darlene Clark Hine, eds. *A Question of Manhood: A Reader in U.S. Black Men's History and Masculinity*. Bloomington: Indiana University Press, 1999.

Jezer, Marty. *The Dark Ages: Life in the United States 1945–1960*. Boston: South End, 1982.

Jiménez de Wagenheim, Olga. *El grito de lares, sus causas y sus hombres*. San Juan, Puerto Rico: Ediciones Huracan, 1986.

Johnson, Marilynn S. *Street Justice: A History of Police Violence in New York City*. Boston: Beacon Press, 2003.

Johnson, Louise. *People of East Harlem*. New York: Mount Sinai School of Medicine, 1974.

Joon, Kim K. K. "The Political Economy of the Mexican Farm Worker Program, 1942–64." *Atzlan* 29, no. 2 (2004), 13–53.

Jones, Charles E., ed. *The Black Panther Party Reconsidered*. New York: Black Classic, 1998.

Jones, Charles E., and Judson L. Jeffries "'Don't Believe the Hype.'" In *The Black Panther Party Reconsidered*, edited by Charles E. Jones, 25–55. New York: Black Classic, 1998.

Jones, Jennifer A. "Afro-Latinos: Speaking through Silences and Rethinking the Geographies of Blackness." In *Afro-Latin Studies: An Introduction*, edited by Alejandro de La Fuente and George Reid Andrews, 569–614. Cambridge, UK: Cambridge University Press, 2018.

Jones, William P. "Nothing Special to Offer the Negro: Revisiting the Debsian View of the Negro Question." *International Labor and Working Class History* 74, no. 1 (September 2008): 212–24.

Joseph, Gilbert, Catherine C. LeGrand, and Ricardo D. Salvatore. *Close Encounters of Empire: Writing the Cultural History of U.S.–Latin America Relations*. Durham, N.C.: Duke University Press, 1998.

Joseph, Gilbert M., and Jürgen Buchenau. *Mexico's Once and Future Revolution: Social Upheaval and the Challenge of Rule since the Nineteenth Century*. Durham, N.C.: Duke University Press, 2013.

Joseph, Peniel E. *The Black Power Movement: Rethinking the Civil Rights–Black Power Era*. New York: Routledge, 2006.

———. *Neighborhood Rebels: Black Power at the Local Level*. New York: Palgrave Macmillan, 2010.

———. *Waiting 'til the Midnight Hour: A Narrative History of Black Power in America*. New York: Henry Holt, 2006.

Kaplan, Seymour. *The Organization of Delivery of Mental Health Services in the Ghetto: The Lincoln Hospital Experience*. New York: Praeger, 1976.

Karstedt, Susanne, and Gary LaFree. "Democracy, Crime, and Justice." *Annals of the American Academy of Political and Social Science* 605, no. 6 (May 2006): 6–23.

Katsiaficas, George. *The Imagination of the New Left: A Global Analysis of 1968*. Boston: South End, 1987.

Katz, Michael. *The Underclass Debate: Views from History*. Princeton, N.J.: Princeton University Press, 1993.

———. *The Undeserving Poor: America's Enduring Confrontation with Poverty*. New York: Oxford University Press, 2013.

Katznelson, Ira. *City Trenches: Urban Politics and the Patterning of Class in the United States*. New York: Pantheon Books, 1981.

———. "Was the Great Society a Lost Opportunity." In *The Rise and Fall of the New Deal Order, 1930–1980*, edited by Steve Fraser and Gary Gerstle, 185–211. Princeton, N.J.: Princeton University Press, 1989.

———. *When Affirmative Action Was White: An Untold History of Racial Inequality in Twentieth-Century America*. New York: W. W. Norton, 2005.

Kavanagh, James H. "Ideology." In *Critical Terms for Literary Study*, edited by Frank Lentricchia and Thomas McLaughlin, 306–20. Chicago: University of Chicago Press, 1995.

Keeran, Roger. "National Groups and the Popular Front: The Case of the International Workers Order." *Journal of American Ethnic History* 14, no. 3 (Spring 1995): 23–51.

Kelley, Robin D. G. *Hammer and Hoe: Alabama Communists during the Depression*. Chapel Hill: University of North Carolina Press, 1990.

———. *Yo Mama's Disfunktional! Fighting Cultural Wars in Urban America*. Boston: Beacon Press, 1998.

Kelley, Robin D. G., and Betsy Esch. "Black Like Mao: Red China and Black Revolution." *Souls* 1, no. 4 (Fall 1999): 6–41.

Kempton, Murray. *The Briar Patch: The People of the State of New York v. Lumumba Shakur et al.* New York: E. P. Dutton, 1973.

Kennedy, Edward M. *In Critical Condition: The Crisis in America's Health Care*. New York: Simon and Schuster, 1972.

Kerner Commission. *Report of the National*

Advisory Commission on Civil Disorders. Washington, D.C.: The Superintendent of Documents U.S. Government, 1968.

Kimmel, Michael S. "The Sixties without Metaphor." *Society* 26, no. 3 (1989): 78–84.

King, Martin Luther, Jr. "Letter from a Birmingham Jail." In *A Testament of Hope: The Essential Writings and Speeches of Martin Luther King, Jr.*, edited by James M. Washington, 289–302. New York: HarperCollins, 2003.

———. *Stride toward Freedom.* New York: Harper and Row, 1964.

———. *Where Do We Go from Here: Chaos or Community?* Boston: Beacon, 2010.

———. *Why We Can't Wait.* New York: Harper and Row, 1964.

King, Mary. *Freedom Song: A Personal Song of the 1960s Civil Rights Movement.* New York: Morrow, 1987.

Kissack, Terrance. "Freaking Fag Revolutionary: New York's Gay Liberation Front, 1969–1971." *Radical History Review* 62 (1995): 104–34.

Kitagawa, Evelyn, and Karl E. Taeuber. *Local Community Fact Book, Chicago's Metropolitan Area, 1960.* Chicago: Chicago Community Inventory, University of Chicago, 1963.

Knupfer, Anne Meis. "The Chicago Detention Home." In *A Noble Social Experiment? The First Hundred Years of the Cook County Juvenile Court, 1899–1999*, edited by Gwen Hoerr McNamee, 52–60. Chicago: Chicago Bar Association, 1999.

Kolchin, Peter. "Whiteness Studies: The New History of Race in America." *Journal of American History* 89, no. 1 (June 2002): 154–73.

Kornbluh, Felicia. "To Fill Their Rightly Needs: Consumerism and the National Welfare Rights Movement." *Radical History Review* 69 (1997): 76–113.

Korrol, Virginia E. Sanchez. *From Colonia to Community: The History of Puerto Ricans in New York.* Berkeley: University of California Press, 1994.

Korstad, Robert, and Nelson Lichtenstein. "Opportunities Found and Lost: Labor, Radicals, and the Early Civil Rights Movement." *Journal of American History* 75, no. 3 (December 1988): 789–93.

Kousser, J. Morgan, and James M. McPherson, eds. *Region, Race and Reconstruction: Essays in Honor of C. Vann Woodward.* New York: Oxford University Press, 1982.

Kushnick, Louis, and James Jennings, eds. *A New Introduction to Poverty, the Role of Race, Power and Politics.* New York: New York University Press, 1999.

Kuykendall, Ronald A. "The African Blood Brotherhood, Independent Marxist During the Harlem Renaissance." *Western Journal of Black Studies* 26, no. 1 (2002), 16–21.

Kuzmarov, Jeremy. *The Myth of the Addicted Army: Vietnam and the Modern War on Drugs.* Amherst: University of Massachusetts Press, 2006.

LaFree, Gary, and Kriss A. Drass. "African American Collective Action and Crime." *Social Forces* 75, no. 3 (March 1997): 835–54.

Lagemann, Ellen Condliffe. *Philanthropic Foundations: New Scholarship, New Possibilities.* Bloomington: Indiana University Press, 1999.

Lao, Agustin. "Resources of Hope: Imagining the Young Lords and the Politics of Memory." *CENTRO Bulletin* 7, no. 1 (1995): 34–49.

Lapp, Michael. "Managing Migration: The Migration Division of Puerto Rico and Puerto Ricans in New York City, 1948–1968." Ph.D. diss., Johns Hopkins University, 1991.

———. "The Rise and Fall of Puerto Rico as a Social Laboratory, 1945–1965." *Social Science History* 19, no. 2 (Summer 1995): 169–99.

Lavin, David, and Richard D. Alba. *Right versus Privilege: The Open Admissions Experiment at the City University of New York.* New York: Free Press, 1981.

Lazerow, Jama, and Yohuru Williams, eds. *In Search of the Black Panther Party: New Perspectives on a Revolutionary Movement.* Durham, N.C.: Duke University Press, 2006.

Jacqueline, Lazú. "The Chicago Young Lords: (Re)constructing Knowledge and Revolution." *CENTRO Journal* 25, no. 2 (Fall 2013): 28–59;

Leamer, Lawrence. *The Paper Revolutionaries: The Rise of the Underground Press.* New York: Simon and Schuster, 1972.

LeBlanc-Ernest, Angela D. " 'The Most Qualified Person to Handle the Job': Black Panther Party Women, 1966–1982." In *The Black Panther Party Reconsidered*, edited by Charles E. Jones, 305–27. New York: Black Classic, 1998.

Lee, Jennifer. "The Young Lords, a New Generation of Puerto Ricans: An Oral History." *Culturefront* 3, no. 3 (Fall 1994): 64–70.

Lee, Sonia Song-Ha. *Building a Latino Civil Rights Movement: Puerto Ricans, African Americans, and the Pursuit of Racial Justice in New York City.* Chapel Hill: University of North Carolina Press, 2014.

Lefkowitz, Bonnie. *Community Health Centers: A Movement and the People Who Made It Happen.* New Brunswick, N.J.: Rutgers University Press, 2007.

Lemann, Nicholas. *The Promised Land: The Great Black Migration and How It Changed America.* New York: Alfred A. Knopf, 1991.

Lenin, Vladimir Ilyich. "Critical Remarks on the National Question." In *V. I. Lenin Collected Works,* vol. 20, 19–51. Moscow: Progress, 1977.

———. "Imperialism: The Highest Stage of Capitalism." In *V. I. Lenin Selected Works,* vol. 1, 667–766. Moscow: Progress, 1963.

———. *Left Wing Communism: An Infantile Disorder.* New York: International Publishers, 1985.

———. "The Right of Nations to Self Determination." In *Lenin's Collected Works,* vol. 20, 393–454. Moscow: Progress, 1972.

———. "Theses on the National Question." In *Lenin's Collected Works,* vol. 19, 243–51. Moscow: Progress, 1977.

———. *Two Tactics of Social-Democracy in the Democratic Revolution.* Geneva, Switzerland: Central Committee of the RSDLP, 1905. https://www.marxists.org/archive/lenin/works/1905/tactics/index.htm.

———. *What Is to Be Done?* In *Collected Works of V. I. Lenin,* vol. 5, 347–530. Moscow: Foreign Languages Publishing House, 1961.

Lentricchia, Frank, and Thomas McLaughlin, eds. *Critical Terms for Literary Study.* 2nd ed. Chicago: University of Chicago Press, 1995.

Leonard, Aaron J., and Conor A. Gallagher. *Heavy Radicals: The FBI's Secret War on America's Maoists.* Alresford, UK: Zero Books, 2015.

Lespiere, Yvonne Acosta. *Mordaza.* San Juan, Puerto Rico: Editorial Edil, 2008.

Levine, Murray. *The History and Politics of Community Mental Health.* Oxford University Press, 1981.

Levinson, Cynthia. *We've Got a Job: The 1963 Birmingham Children's March.* Atlanta: Peachtree, 2012.

Levy, Peter. *The New Left and Labor in the 1960s.* Urbana-Champaign: University of Illinois Press, 1994.

Lewinnek, Elaine. *The Working Man's Reward: Chicago's Early Suburbs and the Roots of American Sprawl.* New York: Oxford University Press, 2014.

Lewis, Oscar. *Five Families: Mexican Case Studies in the Culture of Poverty.* New York: Basic Books, 1975.

———. *La Vida: A Puerto Rican Family in the Culture of Poverty—San Juan and New York.* New York: Random House, 1966.

Lhamon, W. T., Jr. *Deliberate Speed: The Origins of a Cultural Style in the American 1950s.* Washington, D.C., and London: Smithsonian Institution Press, 1990.

Lichten, Eric. *Class, Power and Austerity: The New York Fiscal Crisis.* South Hadley, Mass.: Bergin and Garvey, 1986.

Lindsay, John V. *The City.* New York: Bantam Books, 1970.

Lipsitz, George. *A Life in the Struggle: Ivory Perry and the Culture of Opposition.* Philadelphia: Temple University Press, 1988.

———. *The Possessive Investment in Whiteness: How White People Profit from Identity Politics.* Philadelphia: Temple University Press, 2006.

Lopez, Alfredo. *The Puerto Rican Papers: Notes on the Re-emergence of a Nation.* New York: Bobbs Merril, 1973.

Lopez, Anna Aurelia. "From the Farms of West Central Mexico to California: The Social Transformation of Two Binational Farming Regions." Ph.D. diss., University of California, Santa Cruz, 2002.

Lopez, Iris. "Agency and Constraint: Sterilization and Reproductive Freedom among Puerto Rican Women in New York City." *Urban Anthropology* 22, nos. 3–4 (1993): 299–343.

Lopez, Madeleine E. "Investigating the Investigators: An Analysis of the Puerto Rican Study." *CENTRO: Journal of the Center for Puerto Rican Studies* 19, no. 2 (2007): 61–85.

Louis, Debbie. *And We Are Not Saved: A History of the Movement as People.* Garden City, N.Y.: Anchor, 1970.

Loveman, Mara, and Jeronimo O. Muniz. "How Puerto Rico Became White: Boundary Dynamics and Intercensus Racial Reclassification." *American Sociological Review* 72, no. 6 (2007): 915–39.

Lucas, Isidro. *Puerto Rican Dropouts in Chicago: Numbers and Motivations.* Commissioned by U.S. Department of Health, Education & Welfare, National Institute of Education. Washington, D.C.: Educational Resources Information Center, 1971.

Luciano, Felipe, and Hiram Maristany. "The Young Lords Party: 1969–1975." *Caribe* 7, no. 4 (1983).

Ludmerer, Kenneth. "The Rise of the Teaching Hospitals in America." *Journal of the History of Medicine and Allied Sciences* 38, no. 4 (1983): 389–414.

Lukács, Georg. *History and Class Consciousness.* Cambridge, Mass.: MIT Press, 1971.

Lumsden, Linda. "Good Mothers with Guns: Framing Black Womanhood in the *Black Panther,* 1968–1980." *Journalism and Mass Communication Quarterly* 86, no. 4 (2009): 900–922.

Luppens, Joseph, and Pablo "Yoruba" Guzmán, eds. *Pablo "Yoruba" Guzmán on the Young Lords Legacy: A Personal Account.* Proceedings from the April 8, 1995, IPR Community Forum. New York: Institute for Puerto Rican Policy, 1995.

Maeda, Daryl J. "Black Panthers, Red Guards, and Chinamen: Constructing Asian American Identity through Performing Blackness, 1969–1972." *American Quarterly* 57, no. 4 (December 2005): 1079–103.

Makalani, Minkah. *In the Cause of Freedom: Radical Black Internationalism from Harlem to London, 1917–1939*. Chapel Hill: University of North Carolina Press, 2011.

Malcolm X. *Malcolm X on African American History*. New York: Pathfinder, 1970.

Maldonado, Edwin. "Contract Labor and the Origins of Puerto Rican Communities in the United States." *International Migration Review* 13, no. 1 (Spring 1979): 103–21.

Mamdani, Mahmood. *Good Muslim, Bad Muslim*. New York: Doubleday, 2004.

Mao Tse-tung. *On Guerrilla Warfare*. Eastford, Conn.: Martino Fine Books, 2017.

——. "On Practice: On the Relation Between Knowledge and Practice, Between Knowing and Doing." In *Selected Works*, vol. 1, 295–309. Beijing: Foreign Languages Press, 1967.

——. *Quotations from Mao Tse Tung*. New York: Bantam Books, 1967.

Marable, Manning. *Malcom X: A Life of Reinvention*. London: Viking, 2011.

——. *Race, Reform, and Rebellion: The Second Reconstruction in Black America, 1945–1990*. Jackson: University Press of Mississippi, 1991.

Marazzani, Roberto. "Puerto Rican Political Generations in New York: Pioneros, Young Turks, and Radicals," *CENTRO: Journal of the Center for Puerto Rican Studies* 4, no. 1 (1991/1992): 97–116.

Marcuse, Herbert. *One-Dimensional Man: The Ideology of Modern Industrial Society*. Boston: Beacon Press, 1964.

Margolis, Richard. *The Losers: A Report on Puerto Ricans and the Public Schools*. New York: Aspira, 1968.

Marx, Karl. *Capital: Critique of Political Economy*. vol. 1, *The Process of Production of Capital*. New York: Penguin Books, 1992.

——. *The Class Struggles in France, 1848–1850*. New York: International Publishers, 1964.

——. *Grundrisse*. New York: Vintage, 1973.

Masotti, Louis H., Jeffrey K. Hadden, Kenneth F. Seminatore, and Jerome R. Corsi. *A Time to Burn? An Evaluation of the Present Crisis in Race Relations*. Chicago: Rand McNally, 1969.

Matthews, Tracye. "'No One Ever Asks, What a Man's Role in the Revolution Is': Gender and the Politics of the Black Panther Party, 1966–1971." In *The Black Panther Party Reconsidered*, edited by Charles E. Jones, 276–304. New York: Black Classic, 1998.

Matusow, Allen. *The Unraveling of America: A History of Liberalism in the 1960s*. New York: Harper and Row, 1986.

Maxwell, William J. *New Negro, Old Left: African-American Writing and Communism between the Wars*. New York: Columbia University Press, 1999.

May, Elaine Tyler. *Homeward Bound: American Families in the Cold War Era*. New York: Basic Books, 1999.

McAdam, Doug. *Freedom Summer*. New York: Oxford University Press, 1988.

McCaffrey, Katherine T. *Military Power and Popular Protest: The U.S. Navy in Vieques, Puerto Rico*. New Brunswick, N.J.: Rutgers University Press, 2002.

McCartney, John. *Black Power Ideologies: An Essay in African-American Political Thought*. Philadelphia: Temple University Press, 1992.

McCormick, Thomas J. *America's Half Century: United States Foreign Policy in the Cold War and After*. Baltimore: Johns Hopkins University Press, 1995.

McDonald, John F. *Employment Location and Industrial Land Use in Metropolitan Chicago*. Champaign, Ill.: Stipes Publishing, 1984.

McEnaney, Laura. *Postwar: Waging Peace in Chicago*. Philadelphia: University of Pennsylvania Press, 2018.

McGirr, Lisa. *Suburban Warriors: The Origins of the New American Right*. Princeton, N.J.: Princton University Press, 2001.

McLaughlin, Mary. "Lead Poisoning in Children in New York City, 1950–1954." *New York State Journal of Medicine* 56 (1956): 3711–14.

McMillian, John. *Smoking Typewriters: The Sixties Underground Press and the Rise of Alternative Media in America*. Oxford: Oxford University Press, 2011.

McMillian, John, and Paul Buhle, eds. *The New Left Revisited*. Philadelphia: Temple University Press, 2003.

Medsger, Betty. *The Burglary: The Discovery of J. Edgar Hoover's Secret FBI Media Pennsylvania*. New York: Alfred A. Knopf, 2014.

Meier, August, and Elliott Rudwick. *CORE: A Study in the Civil Rights Movement*. Urbana-Champaign: University of Illinois Press, 1975.

Meier, Matt S., and Feliciano Rivera. *Mexican Americans, American Mexicans: From Conquistadors to Chicanos*. New York: Hill and Wang, 1993.

Mele, Christopher. *Selling the Lower East Side: Culture, Real Estate, and Resistance*. Minneapolis: University of Minnesota Press, 2000.

Melendez, Edwin, and Edgardo Melendez, eds. *Colonial Dilemma: Critical Perspectives on Contemporary Puerto Rico*. Boston: South End, 1993.

Melendez, Miguel. *We Took the Streets: Fighting for Latino Rights with the Young Lords*. New York: St. Martin's, 2003.

Mendez, Mervin. "Latin Kings History." Interview by [interviewer]. Chicago Gang History Project. https://www.uic.edu/orgs/kbc/latinkings/lkhistory.html.

Meyer, Gerald. *Vito Marcantonio: Radical Politician, 1902–1954*. Albany: State University of New York Press, 1989.

Mill, C. Wright, et al. *The Puerto Rican Journey: New York's Newest Migrants*. New York: Russell and Russell, 1950.

Miller, Floyd. *The Search for Black Nationality: Black Colonization and Emigration, 1987–1863*. Urbana-Champaign: University of Illinois Press, 1975.

Miller, James. *Democracy Is in the Streets: From Port Huron to the Siege of Chicago*. New York: Simon and Schuster, 1987.

Mintz, Sidney. *Caribbean Transformations*. New York: Columbia University Press, 1989.

Mir, Roberto E. Capote. "La evolución de los servicios de salud y la estructura socioeconómica en Cuba. 2a Parte: Periódo posrevolucionario." Instituto de Desarollo de la Salud: La Habana, 1979.

Mirabal, Nancy Raquel. "Melba Alvarado, El Club Cubano Inter-Americano, and the Creation of Afro-Cubanidad." In *The Afro-Latin@ Reader: History and Culture in the United States*, edited by Miriam Jiménez Román and Juan Flores, 120–26. Durham, N.C.: Duke University Press, 2010.

Mollenkopf, John Hull. *The Contested City*. Princeton, N.J.: Princeton University Press, 1983.

———. *Power, Culture, and Place: Essays on New York City*. New York: Russell Sage Foundation, 1988.

Mollenkopf, John Hull, and Manuel Castells, eds. *Dual City: Restructuring New York*. New York: Russell Sage Foundation, 1992.

Monge, José Trías. *Puerto Rico: The Trials of the Oldest Colony in the World*. New Haven, Conn.: Yale University Press, 1997.

Moody, Anne. *Coming of Age in Mississippi*. New York: Dial, 1968.

Moody, Kim. *An Injury to All: The Decline of American Unionism*. London: Verso, 1988.

Morales, Iris. "¡Palante, Siempre Palante! The Young Lords." In *The Puerto Rican Movement: Voices from the Diaspora*, edited by Andrés Torres and Jose E. Velázquez, 210–27. Philadelphia: Temple University Press, 1998.

———. "Puerto Rican Racism." *Palante* 2, no. 7 (July 3, 1970): 6–7.

———. *Through the Eyes of Rebel Women: The Young Lords, 1969–1976*. New York: Red Sugarcane Press, 2016.

Morales Carrion, Arturo. *Puerto Rico: A Political and Cultural History*. New York: W. W. Norton, 1982.

Morgan, Iwan, and Phillip Davies, eds. *From Sit-In to SNCC: The Student Civil Rights Movement in the 1960s*. Gainesville: University Press of Florida, 2012.

Morris, Aldon D. *The Origins of the Civil Rights Movement: Black Communities Organizing for Change*. New York: Free Press, 1970.

Morris, Aldon D., and Carol McClurg Mueller. *Frontiers in Social Movement Theory*. New Haven: Yale University Press, 1992.

Morris, Charles. *The Cost of Good Intentions: New York City and the Liberal Experiment, 1960–1970*. New York: McGraw-Hill, 1980.

Morrison, J. Cayce. *The Puerto Rican Study, 1953–1957: A Report on the Education and Adjustment of Puerto Rican Pupils in the Public Schools of the City of New York*. New York: Board of Education, 1958.

Moynihan, Daniel P. *Maximum Feasible Misunderstanding: Community Action in the War on Poverty*. New York: Free Press, 1970.

Mullan, Fitzhugh. *White Coat, Clenched Fist: The Political Education of an American Physician*. New York: Macmillan, 1976.

Murch, Donna. *Living for the City: Migration, Education, and the Rise of the Black Panther Party in Oakland, California*. Chapel Hill: University of North Carolina Press, 2011.

Muse, Benjamin. *Ten Years of Prelude: The Story of Integration since the Supreme Court's 1954 Decision*. New York: Viking, 1964.

Muzio, Rose. *Radical Imagination, Radical Humanity: Puerto Rican Political Activism in New York*. Albany: State University of New York Press, 2018.

Myrdal, Gunnar. *An American Dilemma: The Negro Problem and Modern Democracy*. New York: Harper and Brothers, 1944.

Nadasen, Premilla. "Expanding the Boundaries of the Women's Movement: Black Feminism and the Struggle for Welfare Rights." *Feminist Studies* 28, no. 2 (2002): 271–301.

Naison, Mark. *Communists in Harlem during the Depression*. Urbana-Champaign: University of Illinois Press, 1983.

Navarro, Armando. *La Raza Unida Party: A Chicano Challenge to the Two-Party Dictatorship*. Philadelphia: Temple University Press, 2000.

Neale, Jonathan. *The American War: Vietnam, 1960–1975*. London: Bookmarks, 2001.

———. *A People's History of the Vietnam War.* New York: New Press, 2003.

Negrón-Muntaner, Frances. "The Look of Sovereignty: Style and Politics in the Young Lords." *CENTRO: Journal of the Center for Puerto Rican Studies* 27, no. 1 (April 2015): 4–33.

Nelson, Alondra. *Body and Soul: The Black Panther Party and the Fight against Medical Discrimination.* Minneapolis: University of Minnesota Press, 2013.

Nelson, Jennifer. *Women of Color and the Reproductive Rights Movement.* New York: New York University Press, 2003.

Nelson, William E. "Government Power as a Tool for Redistributing Wealth in Twentieth-Century New York." In *Law as Culture and Culture as Law: Essays in Honor of John Phillip Reid*, edited by Hendrik Hartog and William E. Nelson, 322–442. Madison, Wis.: Madison House, 2000.

Newton, Huey P. "Manifesto Issued by the Black Panthers." In *Come Out Fighting: A Century of Essential Writing on Gay and Lesbian Liberation*, edited by Chris Bull, 89–91. New York: Nation Books, 2001.

———. "The Women's and Gay Liberation Movements." In *Huey P. Newton Reader*, edited by David Hilliard and Donald Weise, 157–59. New York: Seven Stories, 2002.

New York City Commission on Human Rights. *The Ethnic Survey: A Report on the Number of and Distribution of Negroes, Puerto Ricans, and Others Employed by the City of New York.* New York: New York City Commission on Human Rights, 1964.

New York State Special Commission on Attica. *Attica: The Official Report of the State Special Commission on Attica.* Santa Barbara, Calif.: Praeger, 1972.

Ngai, Mae. *Impossible Subjects: Illegal Aliens and the Making of Modern America.* Princeton, N.J.: Princeton University Press, 2004.

Noble, David F. *Forces of Production: A Social History of Industrial Automation.* New York: Transaction Publishers, 2011.

Nolla-Acosta, Juan Jose. *Puerto Rican Election Statistics, 1899–2008.* Ponce, Puerto Rico: Juan Jose Nolla-Acosta, 2010.

Oboler, Suzanne. "'Establishing an Identity' in the Sixties: the Mexican-American/Chicano and Puerto Rican Movements." Chapter 3 of *Ethnic Labels, Latino Lives: Identity and the Politics of (Re)Presentation in the United States.* Minneapolis: University of Minnesota Press, 1995.

———. *Ethnic Labels, Latino Lives: Identity and the Politics of (Re)Presentation in the United States.*

Minneapolis: University of Minnesota Press, 1995.

Office of the Mayor. *Puerto Ricans Confront the Complex Urban Society: A Design for Change.* Community conference proceedings. New York: Office of the Mayor, 1968.

Ogbar, Jeffrey. "*Puerto Rico en mi Corazón*: The Young Lords, Black Power and Puerto Rican Nationalism in the U.S., 1966–1972." *CENTRO: Journal of the Center for Puerto Rican Studies* 18, no. 1 (2006): 148–69.

Omi, Michael, and Howard Winant. *Racial Formation in the United States.* New York: Routledge, 1994.

Opp, Karl-Dieter. *Theories of Political Protest and Social Movements.* New York: Routledge, 2009.

O'Reilly, Kenneth. *"Racial Matters": The FBI's Secret File on Black America, 1960–1972.* New York: Free Press, 1989.

Orleck, Annelise. *Storming Caesar's Palace.* Boston: Beacon, 2005.

Pach, Chester J. "And That's the Way It Was." In *The Sixties: From Memory to History*, edited by David Farber, 107–11. Chapel Hill: University of North Carolina Press, 1994.

Padilla, Elena. "Puerto Rican Immigrants in New York and Chicago: A Study in Comparative Assimilation." Master's thesis, University of Chicago, 1947.

Padilla, Felix. *Puerto Rican Chicago.* Notre Dame, Ind.: University of Notre Dame Press, 1987.

Painter, Nell Irvin. *The History of White People.* New York: W. W. Norton, 2011.

Palmer, Lon Weldon. "Theological and Moral Theoretical Antecedents of Twentieth-Century American Liberal Evangelical Protestant Personal Ethics." Ph.D. diss., Columbia University, 1992.

Patterson, James T. *Grand Expectations: The United States, 1945–1974.* New York: Oxford University Press, 1996.

Payne, Charles M. *I've Got the Light of Freedom: The Organizing Tradition and the Mississippi Freedom Struggle.* Berkeley: University of California Press, 1995.

Pearson, Hugh. *The Shadow of the Panther: Huey Newton and the Price of Black Power in America.* Reading, Mass.: Addison-Wesley, 1994.

Peck, Abe. *Uncovering the Sixties: The Life and Times of the Underground Press.* New York: Citadel, 1991.

Peck, Abraham. "Young Lords: Serve and Protect. *Rat Subterranean News*, August 28, 1969.

Pensado, Jaime M., and Enrique C. Ochoa, eds. *Mexico beyond 1968: Revolutionaries, Radicals, and Repression during the Global Sixties and*

Subversive Seventies. Tucson: University of Arizona Press, 2018.

Perez, David. "The Chains That Have Been Taken off Slaves' Bodies Are Put Back on Their Minds." In Palante: Young Lords Party, by Young Lords Party and Michael Abramson, 65–68. New York: McGraw-Hill, 1971.

Perez, David, and Arthur Tobier. Long Road from Lares: An Oral History. New York: Community Documentation Workshop, 1979.

Perez, Nelida. "A Community at Risk: Puerto Ricans and Health, East Harlem, 1929–1940." CENTRO: Journal of the Center for Puerto Rican Studies 2, no. 4 (Fall 1988): 16–27.

Perez, Ramon Bosque, and Jose Javier Colón Morera. Puerto Rico under Colonial Rule: Political Persecution and the Quest for Human Rights. Albany: State University of New York Press, 2006.

Perry, Bruce. Malcolm X: The Life of a Man Who Changed Black America. New York: Station Hill, 1991.

Petras, James, and Morris Morley. Latin America in the Time of Cholera. New York: Routledge, 1992.

Phillips-Fein, Kim. Invisible Hands: The Business Crusade against the New Deal. New York: W. W. Norton & Company, 2010.

Pier, Martin, James R. Mahalik, and Malcolm H. Woodland, "The Effects of Racism, African Self Consciousness, and Psychological Functioning on Black Masculinity: A Historical and Social Adaptation Framework." Journal of African American Men 6, no. 2 (Fall 2001): 19–31.

Piven, Francis Fox, and Richard Cloward. Poor People's Movements: Why They Succeed, How They Fail. New York: Vintage, 1978.

Podair, Jerald E. The Strike That Changed New York: Blacks, Whites and the Ocean Hill–Brownsville Crisis. New Haven, Conn.: Yale University Press, 2003.

———. "White Values, Black Values: The Ocean Hill–Brownsville Controversy and New York City Culture, 1965–1975." Radical History Review 59 (1994): 36–59.

Pope, Jackie. "Women in the Welfare Rights Struggle: The Brooklyn Welfare Action Council." In Women and Social Protest, edited by Guida West and Rhoda Lois Blumberg, 57–74. New York: Oxford University Press, 1990.

Poston, Richard W. The Gang and the Establishment. New York: Harper & Row, 1971.

Powers, Mary G., and John J. Maciso Jr. Los puertorriquenos en Nueva York: Un analisis de su participacion laboral y experiencia migratoria. San Juan: Universidad de Puerto Rico, 1982.

Puerto Rican Forum. A Study of Poverty Conditions in the New York Puerto Rican Community. New York: Puerto Rican Forum, 1970.

Pulido, Laura. Black, Brown, Yellow, and Left: Radical Activism in Los Angeles. Berkeley: University of California Press, 2006.

Purnell, Bryan. Fighting Jim Crow in the Country of Kings. Lexington: University Press of Kentucky, 2015.

Quiñonez, Ernesto. Bodega Dreams. New York: Vintage Contemporaries, 2000.

Rabe, Stephen G. The Killing Zone: The United States Wages Cold War in Latin America. New York: Oxford University Press, 2011.

Ralph, James. Northern Protest, Martin Luther King, Jr., Chicago and the Civil Rights Movement. Cambridge, Mass.: Harvard University Press, 1993.

Ramirez, Yasmin. "Nuyorican Vanguards, Political Actions, Poetic Visions: A History of Puerto Rican Artists in New York, 1964–1984." Ph.D. diss., City University of New York, 2005.

Ramírez de Arellano, Annette, and Conrad Scheipp. Colonialism, Catholicism, and Contraception: A History of Birth Control in Puerto Rico. Chapel Hill: University of North Carolina Press, 1983.

Ramsey, Joseph G. "Revolutionary Relatability: Assata: An Autobiography as a Site of Radical Teaching and Learning." Socialism and Democracy 28, no. 3 (November 2014): 118–39.

Reed, Louis. S. "Private Health Insurance: Coverage and Financial Experience, 1940–1966." Social Security Bulletin 30, no. 11 (1967): 3–22.

Reitzes, Donald, and Dietrich Reitzes. "Alinsky Reconsidered: A Reluctant Community Theorist." Social Science Quarterly 63, no. 2 (June 1982): 266–79.

Ribes Trovar, Federico. Albizu Campos Puerto Rican Revolutionary. New York: Plus Ultra Educational Publishers, 1971.

Rice-Maxim, Micheline. "Frantz Fanon and Black American Ideologists in the 1960s." Contemporary French Civilization 5, no. 3 (1981): 369–79.

Rickford, Russell. We Are an African People: Independent Education, Black Power, and the Radical Imagination. New York: Oxford University Press, 2016.

Risse, Guenter. Mending Bodies, Saving Souls: A History of Hospitals. New York: Oxford University Press, 1999.

Rivera, Geraldo. Exposing Myself. New York: Bantam, 1992.

Robinson, Dean E. Black Nationalism in American Politics and Thought. New York: Cambridge University Press, 2001.

Robinson, William I. *Latin America and Global Capitalism: A Critical Globalization Perspective.* Baltimore: Johns Hopkins University Press, 2008.

Rodriguez, Clara E. *Puerto Ricans: Born in the U.S.A.* Boston: Unwin Hyman, 1989.

Rodríguez, Clara E., and Virginia Sanchez Korrol. "Economic Survival in New York City." In *Historical Perspectives on Puerto Rican Survival in the United States,* edited by Clara E. Rodríguez, Virginia Sanchez Korrol, and José Oscar Alers, 37–54. Princeton, N.J.: Markus Wiener, 1996.

Rodríguez, Clara E., Virginia Sanchez Korrol, and José Oscar Alers, eds. *The Puerto Rican Struggle: Essays on Survival in the United States.* Maplewood, N.J.: Waterfront, 1984.

Rodríguez Beruff, J. *Politica militar y dominacion.* Rio Piedras, Puerto Rico: Ediciones Huracán, 1988.

Rodriguez-Fraticelli, Carlos. "Pedro Albizu Campos: Strategies of Struggle and Strategic Struggles." *CENTRO Bulletin* 2 (Summer 1989): 25–33.

Rodriguez-Fraticelli, Carlos, and Amilcar Tirado Aviles. "Notes towards a History of Puerto Rican Community Organizations in New York City." *CENTRO Journal* 2, no. 5 (Summer 1989): 35–47.

Rodriguez-Morazzani, Roberto P. "Political Cultures of the Puerto Rican Left, in the United States." In *The Puerto Rican Movement: Voices from the Diaspora,* edited by Andrés Torres and Jose E. Velázquez, 28–31. Philadelphia: Temple University Press, 1998.

———. "Puerto Rican Political Generations in New York: Pioneers, Young Turks and Radicals." *CENTRO Bulletin* 4, no. 1 (1992): 96–116.

Roediger, David R. *The Wages of Whiteness: Race and the Making of the American Working Class.* New York: Verso, 1991.

Rogers, Kim Lacy. "Oral History and the History of the Civil Rights Movement." *Journal of American History* 75, no. 2 (September 1988): 567–76.

Rogers, Naomi. "Caution: The AMA May Be Dangerous to Your Health; The Student Health Organizations and American Medicine 1965–1970." *Radical History Review* 80 (2001): 5–34.

Róman, Miriam Jiménez, and Juan Flores, eds. *The Afro-Latina Reader: History and Culture in the United States.* Durham, N.C.: Duke University Press, 2010.

Rosen, Ruth. *The World Split Wide Open: How the Modern Women's Movement Changed America.* New York: Viking, 2000.

Rosenberg, Susan. *An American Radical: A Political Prisoner in My Own Country.* New York: Citadel Press Book, 2011.

Rosner, David. *Children, Race, and Power: Kenneth and Mamie Clark's Northside Center.* Charlottesville: University Press of Virginia, 1996.

Rosner, David, and Gerald Markowitz. "Hospitals, Insurance, and the American Labor Movement: The Case of New York in the Postwar Decades." *Journal of Policy History* 9, no. 1 (1997): 74–95.

Rotella, Carlo. *October Cities: The Redevelopment of Urban Literature.* Berkeley: University of California Press, 1998.

Rudolph, Jennifer Domino. "Masculinities." In *Routledge Companion to Latino/a Literature,* edited by Suzanne Bost and Frances R. Aparicio, 67–74. New York: Routledge, 2015.

Rustin, Bayard. *Down the Line: The Collected Works of Bayard Rustin.* Chicago: Quadrangle Books, 1971.

———. "From Protest to Politics: The Future of the Civil Rights Movement." *Commentary* 39, no. 2 (February 1965).

Sale, Kirkpatrick. *SDS.* New York: Vintage Books, 1973.

Sales, William, Jr. *From Civil Rights to Black Liberation: Malcolm X and the Organization of Afro-American Unity.* Boston: South End, 1994.

Sargeant, Clara Bernice. "Project Demonstrating Excellence: An Examination of the First Eight Years of the SEEK Program at Bernard M. Baruch College, 1969–1977." Ph.D. diss., Union Graduate School, 1978.

Sayres, Sohnya, Anders Stephanson, Stanley Aronowitz, and Fredric Jameson. *The 60s without Apology.* Minneapolis: University of Minnesota Press, 1984.

Schneider, Eric C. *Vampires, Dragons, and Egyptian Kings: Youth Gangs in Postwar New York.* Princeton, N.J.: Princeton University Press, 1999.

"School Begins." *Puck,* January 25, 1899, centerfold.

Sealander, Judith, and Smith, Dorothy. "The Rise and Fall of Feminist Organizations in the 1970s." *Feminist Studies* 12, no. 2 (1986): 320–41.

Seale, Bobby. *Seize the Time: The Story of the Black Panther Party and Huey Newton.* New York: Random House, 1968.

Self, Robert O. *American Babylon: Race and the Struggle for Postwar Oakland.* Princeton, N.J.: Princeton University Press, 2003.

Seligman, Amanda. *Block by Block: Neighborhoods and Public Policy on Chicago's West Side.* Chicago: University of Chicago, 2005.

Sellers, Cleveland. *The River of No Return: The*

Autobiography of a Black Militant and the Death of SNCC. New York: Morrow, 1973.

Senior, Clarence. Puerto Rican Emigration. Rio Piedras: Social Science Research Center of the University of Puerto Rico, 1947.

Shakur, Assata. Assata: An Autobiography. Chicago: Lawrence Hill Books, 2001.

Shawki, Ahmed. "Black Liberation and Socialism in the United States." International Socialism: A Quarterly Journal of Socialist Theory 47 (Summer 1990): 3–110.

Simroth, Peter. Perversion of Justice: The Prosecution and Acquittal of the Panther 21. New York: Viking, 1974.

Sitkoff, Harvard. The Struggle for Black Equality, 1954–1980. New York: Hill and Wang, 1981.

Sklair, Leslie. Assembling for Development: The Maquiladora Industry in Mexico and the United States. San Diego: Center for US-Mexican Studies, University of California, San Diego, 1993.

Smith, Peter. Talons of the Eagle: Dynamics of U.S.–Latin American Relations. New York: Oxford University Press, 2000.

Solomon, Mark I. The Cry Was Unity: Communists and African Americans, 1917–36. Jackson: University Press of Mississippi, 1998.

Spencer, Robyn C. The Revolution Has Come: Black Power, Gender, and the Black Panther Party in Oakland. Durham, N.C.: Duke University Press, 2016.

Springer, Kimberly. Living for the Revolution: Black Feminist Organizing, 1968–1980. Durham, N.C.: Duke University Press, 2005.

Starr, Meg. "'Hit Them Harder': Leadership, Solidarity, and the Puerto Rican Independence Movement." In The Hidden Sixties: Histories of Radicalism, edited by Dan Berger, 135–54. New Brunswick, N.J.: Rutgers University Press, 2010.

State of New York Commission of Investigation. Recommendations of the New York State Commission of Investigation Concerning New York City's Municipal Hospitals and the Affiliation Program. New York: Community Council of Greater New York, 1968.

Staudenmaier, Michael. "'Mostly of Spanish Extraction': Second-Class Citizenship and Racial Formation in Puerto Rican Chicago, 1940–1965." Journal of American History 104, no. 3 (December 2017): 681–706.

Steigerwald, David. The Sixties and the End of Modern America. New York: St. Martin's, 1995.

Stern, Mark. "Calculating Visions: Civil Rights Legislation in the Kennedy and Johnson Years." Journal of Policy History 5, no. 2 (1993): 231–47.

Stevens, Rosemary. American Medicine and the Public Interest. New Haven, Conn., and London: Yale University Press, 1971.

———. "History and Health Policy in the United States: The Making of a Health Care Industry, 1948–2008." Social History of Medicine 21, no. 3 (December 1, 2008): 461–83.

———. In Sickness and in Wealth: American Hospitals in the Twentieth Century. Baltimore: Johns Hopkins University Press, 1999.

Sugrue, Thomas J. The Origins of the Urban Crisis: Race and Inequality in Postwar Detroit. Princeton, N.J.: Princeton University Press, 1996.

———. Sweet Land of Liberty: The Forgotten Struggle for Civil Rights in the North. New York: Random House, 2008.

Suri, Jeremi. Power and Protest: Global Revolution and the Rise of Détente. Cambridge, Mass.: Harvard University Press, 2003.

Suttles, Gerald D. The Social Order of the Slum. Chicago: University of Chicago Press, 1970.

Tauber and Tauber. "The Negro as an Immigrant Group: Recent Trends in Racial and Ethnic Segregation in Chicago." American Journal of Sociology 69, no. 4 (1964): 374–83.

Taylor, Clarence. Fight the Power: African Americans and the Long History of Police Brutality in New York City. New York: New York University Press, 2019.

———. Knocking at Our Own Door: Milton A. Galamison and the Struggle to Integrate New York City Schools. New York: Columbia University Press, 1997.

———. Reds at the Blackboard: Communism, Civil Rights, and the New York Teachers Union. New York: Columbia University Press, 2013.

Taylor, Keeanga-Yamahtta, ed. How We Get Free: Black Feminism and the Combahee River Collective. New York: Haymarket Press, 2017.

Teaford, Jon C. The Twentieth-Century American City. Baltimore: Johns Hopkins University Press, 1993.

Terry, Wallace. Bloods: Black Veterans of the Vietnam War, An Oral History. New York: Presidio Press, 1984.

Theoharis, Jeanne, and Komozi Woodard, eds. Freedom North: Black Freedom Struggles outside the South, 1940–1980. New York: Palgrave Macmillan, 2003.

Thomas, Lorrin. Puerto Rican Citizen: History and Political Identity in Twentieth-Century New York City. Chicago: University of Chicago Press, 2010.

Thompson, Heather Ann. Blood in the Water: The Attica Prison Uprising of 1971 and Its Legacy. New York: Pantheon, 2016.

Thrasher, Frederic M. The Gang: A Study of 1,313 Gangs in Chicago. Peotone, Ill.: New Chicago School Press, 2000.

Tibbs, Donald F. *From Black Power to Prison Power: The Making of Jones v. North Carolina Prisoners' Labor Union*. New York: Palgrave Macmillan, 2012.

Tinson, Christopher. *Radical Intellect: Liberator Magazine and Black Activism in the 1960s*. Chapel Hill: University of North Carolina Press, 2017.

Torres, Andrés. *Between Melting Pot and Mosaic: African Americans and Puerto Ricans in the New York Political Economy*. Philadelphia: Temple University Press, 1995.

Torres, Andrés, and Jose E. Velázquez, eds. *The Puerto Rican Movement: Voices from the Diaspora*. Philadelphia: Temple University Press, 1998.

Torres, Arlene. "La gran familia puertorriqueña 'Ej Prieta De Beldá' (The Great Puerto Rican Family Is Really Really Black)." In *Blackness in Latin America and the Caribbean*, vol. 2, edited by Arlene Torres and Norman E. Whitten, 285–306. Bloomington: Indiana University Press, 1998.

Trevizo, Dolores. *Rural Protest and the Making of Democracy in Mexico, 1968–2000*. University Park: Pennsylvania State University Press, 2012.

Trotsky, Leon. *My Life: An Attempt at an Autobiography*. New York: Dover Publications, 2007.

Trotter, Joe William, and Jared N. Day. *Race and Renaissance: African-Americans in Pittsburgh since World War II*. Pittsburgh, Pa.: University of Pittsburgh Press, 2010.

Tucker, Robert J., ed. *The Marx-Engels Reader*. 2nd ed. New York: Norton, 1978.

Tyson, Timothy B. *The Blood of Emmett Till*. New York: Simon and Schuster, 2017.

———. *Radio Free Dixie: Robert F. Williams and the Roots of Black Power*. Chapel Hill: University of North Carolina Press, 2001.

Unger, Irwin, and Debi Unger. *The Movement: A History of the American New Left, 1959–1972*. New York: Dodd, Mead, 1974.

U.S. Bureau of the Census. *U.S. Census of Population: 1960; Subject Reports, Puerto Ricans in the United States*. Final Report PC(2)-1D. Washington, D.C.: U.S. Government Printing Office, 1963.

U.S. Department of Labor. *Changing Patterns of Employment, Income and Living Standards in New York City*. Bureau of Labor Statistics. Regional Report 10. New York: U.S. Department of Labor, 1968.

———. *Labor Force Experience of the Puerto Rican Worker*. Bureau of Labor Statistics. Regional Report 9. New York: U.S. Department of Labor, 1968.

Valk, Anne M. *Radical Sisters: Second Wave Feminism and Black Liberation in Washington, D.C.* Urbana: University of Illinois Press, 2008.

Van Deburg, William. *Modern Black Nationalism: From Marcus Garvey to Louis Farrakhan*. New York: New York University Press, 1996.

———. *New Day in Babylon: The Black Power Movement and American Culture, 1965–1975*. Chicago: University of Chicago Press, 1992.

Vanden Heuvel, William J. *Crisis in the Prisons: New York City Responds*. Annual Report of the New York City Board of Corrections to the Mayor, 1971.

———. *A Report to the Mayor of New York on the Death of a Citizen, Julio Roldán*. New York: Board of Corrections, 1970.

Vaughan, Roger. "Real Great Society." *Life*, September 9, 1967, 76–91.

Velázquez, José E. "Another West Side Story: An Interview with Members of El Comité-MINP." In *The Puerto Rican Movement: Voices from the Diaspora*, edited by Andrés Torres and Jose E. Velázquez, 88–106. Philadelphia: Temple University Press, 1998.

———. "Coming Full Circle: The Puerto Rican Socialist Party, U.S. Branch." In *The Puerto Rican Movement: Voices from the Diaspora*, edited by Andrés Torres and Jose E. Velázquez, 48–68. Philadelphia: Temple University Press, 1998.

Veltmeyer, Henry, James Petras, and Steve Vieux. *Neoliberalism and Class Conflict in Latin America: A Comparative Perspective on the Political Economy of Structural Adjustment*. New York: MacMillan, 1997.

Venator-Santiago, Charles. "Mapping the Contours of the History of the Extension of U.S. Citizenship to Puerto Rico, 1898–Present." *CENTRO Journal* 29, no. 1 (Spring 2017), 38–55.

———. *Puerto Rico and the Origins of U.S. Global Empire: The Disembodied Shade*. New York: Routledge, 2015.

Vigil, Ernesto B. *The Crusade for Justice: Chicano Militancy and the Government War on Dissent*. Madison: University of Wisconsin Press, 1999.

Wachsberger, Ken, ed. *Voices from the Underground*. vol. 1, *Insider Histories of the Vietnam Era*. Tempe, Ariz.: Mica, 1993.

Wagenheim, Kal. *A Survey of Puerto Ricans on the U.S. Mainland in the 1970s*. New York: Praeger, 1975.

Wagenheim, Kal, and U.S. Commission on Civil Rights. "Puerto Ricans in the Continental United States: An Uncertain Future." College Park: University of Maryland, 1976.

Wakefield, Dan. *Island in the City: The World of Spanish Harlem*. New York: Houghton Mifflin, 1959.

Wallace, Terry. *Bloods: Black Veterans of the Vietnam War—an Oral History.* New York: Ballantine, 1985.

Wanzer-Serrano, Darrel. *The New York Young Lords and the Struggle for Liberation.* Philadelphia: Temple University Press, 2015.

Warren, Christian. *Brush with Death: A Social History of Lead Poisoning.* Baltimore: Johns Hopkins University Press, 2000.

Webb, Gary. *Dark Alliance: The CIA, the Contras, and the Crack Cocaine Explosion.* New York: Seven Stories Press, 1998.

Weigand, Kate. *Red Feminism.* Baltimore: Johns Hopkins Press, 2002.

Weiss, Robert P. "Attica: The 'Bitter Lessons' Forgotten." *Social Justice* 18, no. 3 (1991): 1–12.

West, Guida, and Rhoda Lois Blumberg, eds. *Women and Social Protest.* New York: Oxford University Press, 1990.

West-Dúran, Alan, ed. *Cuba: People, Culture, and History.* New York: Charles Scribner and Sons, 2011.

Westheider, James E. *Fighting on Two Fronts: African Americans and the Vietnam War.* New York: New York University Press, 1997.

Whalen, Carmen, and Victor Vásquez-Hernández. *The Puerto Rican Diaspora: Historical Perspectives.* Philadelphia: Temple University Press, 2005.

Whalen, Carmen Teresa. "Bridging Homeland and Barrio Politics: The Young Lords in Philadelphia." In *The Puerto Rican Movement: Voices from the Diaspora,* edited by Andrés Torres and Jose E. Velázquez, 107–23. Philadelphia: Temple University Press, 1998.

White, Gray. *Too Heavy a Load.* New York: W. W. Norton & Company, 1999.

Whitten, Norman E., Jr., and Arlene Torres, eds. *Blackness in Latin America and the Caribbean: Social Dynamics and Cultural Transformations.* Vol. 1. Bloomington: Indiana University Press, 1998.

Wiener, Jon. "The New Left as History." *Radical History Review* 42 (1988): 173–87.

Wilder, Craig S. *A Covenant with Color, Race and Social Power in Brooklyn.* New York: Columbia University Press, 2000.

Williams, Jakobi. *From the Bullet to the Ballot: The Illinois Chapter of the Black Panther Party and Racial Coalition Politics in Chicago.* Chapel Hill: University of North Carolina Press, 2013.

Williams, Raymond. *Marxism and Literature.* New York: Oxford University Press, 2009.

Wilson, Gregory. "Deindustrialization, Poverty, and Federal Area Redevelopment in the United States, 1945–1965." In *Beyond the Ruins: The Meaning of Deindustrialization,* edited by Jefferson Cowie and Joseph Heathcott, 181–200. Ithaca, N.Y.: Cornell University Press, 2003.

Wilson, William. *When Work Disappears: The World of the New Urban Poor.* New York: Vintage Books, 1997.

Wilson, Robert L. *The First Spanish United Methodist Church and the Young Lords.* New York: Department of Research and Survey National Division of the Board of Missions, 1970.

Wilson, William Julius. *The Declining Significance of Race: Blacks and Changing American Institutions.* Chicago: University of Chicago Press, 1980.

———. *The Truly Disadvantaged: The Inner City, the Underclass, and Public Policy.* Chicago: University of Chicago, 1987.

Witt, Andrew. *The Black Panthers in the Midwest: The Community Programs and Services of the Black Panther Party in Milwaukee, 1966–1977.* New York: Routledge, 2007.

Woodard, Komozi. *Nation within a Nation: Amiri Baraka and Black Power Politics.* Chapel Hill: University of North Carolina Press, 1999.

Woodward, C. Vann. *The Strange Career of Jim Crow.* New York: Oxford University Press, 1978.

Young Lords Party. *The Ideology of the Young Lords Party.* New York: Young Lords Party, 1970.

———. *Resolutions and Speeches: 1st Congress of the Puerto Rican Revolutionary Workers Organization.* New York: Young Lords Party, 1972.

———. "Young Lords Party 13 Point Program and Platform." In *Palante: Young Lords Party,* by Young Lords Party and Michael Abramson, 150. New York: McGraw-Hill, 1971.

Young Lords Party and Michael Abramson. *Palante: Young Lords Party.* New York: McGraw-Hill, 1971.

Zavala, Iris, and Rafael Rodriguez. *The Intellectual Roots of Independence: An Anthology of Puerto Rican Political Essays.* New York: Monthly Review Press, 1980.

Zipp, Samuel. *Manhattan Projects: The Rise and Fall of Urban Renewal in Cold War New York.* New York: Oxford University Press, 2012.

Zumoff, Jacob A. *The Communist International and U.S. Communism 1919–1929.* New York: Haymarket Books, 2015.

Audiovisual Sources

Baldwin, James. "James Baldwin Debates William F. Buckley." Filmed 1965 at Cambridge University. October 27, 2012. https://www.youtube.com/watch?v=0FeoS41xe7w.

The Case against Lincoln Center. New York: Third World Newsreel, 1968. Video, 12 min.

El pueblo se levanta. New York: Third World Newsreel, 1971. Video, 50 min.

Garbage. New York: Newsreel, 1968. Video, 10 min.

González, Juan, West Side Story 1971. Achter Het Niews, Document ID 24914, Beeld en Geluid, Internaal Instituut voor Sociale Geschiedenis, Amsterdam [International Institute of Social History, Amsterdam].

"Leader of New York Young Lords: Felipe Luciano, Yoruba, Rafael Viera, and David Perez." Archive No. BB3583. Broadcast WBAI, December 26, 1969. Los Angeles: Pacifica Radio Archives. Audiocassette.

Luna, Elizabeth Perez. "The Young Lords." Prod. Archive No. SZ0215. Broadcast KPFK, August 5, 1977. Los Angeles: Pacifica Radio Archives. Audiocassette.

Morales, Iris, dir. *¡Palante, Siempre Palante!* New York: Latino Education Network Service, 1996. Documentary film, 48 min.

Paterson, David. "Remembering the Harlem Riot of 1964." *The Brian Lehrer Show*. July 16, 2014.

"Revolution for Breakfast." Archive No. BB2540. Broadcast KPFA, August 14, 1970. Los Angeles: Pacific Radio Archives. Audiocassette.

Rothschild, Edmund. "Lincoln Hospital: The Decline of Health Care." By Bruce Solloway. WBAI, Pacifica Radio, April 22, 1971.

"Self Determination for the Puerto Rican Colony in New York City." Archive No. BB3835.03. Series *Palante* no. 3. Broadcast WBAI, April 6, 1970. Los Angeles: Pacifica Radio Archives. Audiocassette.

Silvers, Cleo. "Lincoln Hospital: The Decline of Healthcare." By Bruce Solloway. WBAI Broadcast, Pacifica Radio, April 22, 1971. www.socialmedicine.org/audio/lincolnhospital.mp3.

Starzenski, Gene, dir. *Freedom House: Street Saviors*. Gena Stars Productions, 2009.

"Women of the Colonies." Archive No. BB3835.02. Series *Palante*, nos. 2 and 3. Broadcast WBAI, 1970. Los Angeles: Pacifica Radio Archives. Audiocassette.

"The Young Lords: Ines Benitez and Felipe Luciano." Archive No. BB3835.01. Series *Palante* no. 1. Broadcast WBAI, March 27, 1970. Los Angeles: Pacifica Radio Archives. Audiocassette.

"The Young Lords Organization: Raphael Viera and Felipe Luciano." Archive No. BB2357. Interview by Denny Smithson. February 7, 1970. Broadcast KPFA. Los Angeles: Pacifica Radio Archives. Audiocassette.

Index

Page numbers appearing in italics refer to illustrations.

abortion, 267, 268, 293–94
Abu-Jamal, Mumia, 60–61, 128
affiliation system in healthcare, 138–39, 141, 144, 276, 294–95, 297, 422n20
African Blood Brotherhood (ABB), 213
Aguadilla Young Lords branch, 11, 350–51
Alan, Howard, 47
Alba, Panama, 219
Albert Einstein College of Medicine, 276, 280, 297
Alberti, G., 164
Albizu Campos, Don Pedro, 59, 84, 128, 146, 214, 349
Alexander, Deacon, 206
Algarin, Miguel, 191
Alinsky, Saul, 112
alternative newspapers, 223. See also specific newspapers
Althusser, Louis, 249
Amazing Adventures (Lee), 383
"American dilemma, the," 56
American Health Empire, The (Ehrenreich), 290
American Jewish Congress, 298
American Journal of Public Health, 153, 382–83
American Servicemen's Union (ASU), 236, 418n2
Andy Boy Farms, 16, 394n11
antiblack racism, 20, 25, 203, 213, 242, 249, 381. See color prejudice
Antonetty, Evelina Lopez, 58–59, 63, 202–3, 206
Aponte, Carlos, 184, 274, 308, 354, 375, 376
appearance of Young Lords, 28–29, 130–31, 200, 363
Armed Forces of National Liberation, 369
Armed Revolutionary Independence Movement, 369
armed struggle, 94, 128–29, 133, 313, 323–25
Armitage Avenue Methodist Church occupation, 47–48, 86
arms, taking up, 323–25
arrest interference, 104–5
arts and the Church Offensive, 180–81, 183, 190–91, 413–14n119, 415n158
Art Steel Company strike, 226, 342–43
Asch, Richard, 190
Asian activism, 218
Attica Liberation Faction, 359
Attica Prison uprising, 358–61, 429n80, 429n83

Auburn State Prison rebellion, 359
Audy Home, 27
August, Bella, 143–45, 149, 173
automobiles, 25–26

Baden, Michael, 320
Badilla, Victor, 164
Badillo, Herman, 78, 191, 327, 360
Baldwin, James, 23, 206
Baller, Arthur A., 164
Batista, Fulgencio, 34, 88
Benitez, Iris, 2, 238
beret, Cuban Revolution origins of, 130
Berkeley Tribe, 362
Biaggi, Mario, 236
Bio-Rad Laboratories, 148, 151–52
Black, Active, and Determined, 42
black American membership in Young Lords, 242–43
Black Panther Bill, 44
Black Panther Party (BPP), 7, 43, 44, 84, 94, 131, 373; armed patrol units of, 125–26; Cha Cha and, 8, 16, 36–37; Church Offensive and, 165, 184; deaths of Clark and Hampton and, 163; feminism and, 269; guerrilla war and, 130, 206, 416n57; health justice and, 140, 278, 281–82; lumpen thesis of, 219–20, 222, 386; Panther 21 and, 3, 99, 314, 326–27, 425n42; prison rebellions and, 327, 328, 360; repression of, 325, 361; revolutionary nationalism and, 6, 210, 212; sanctuary abroad of, 344; social programs of, 10, 100, 123, 157, 341; split within, 242–43, 340, 353–54; Weather Underground and, 312, 313; YL connection to, 4, 5, 42–44, 48, 115, 128, 202, 218–19, 381. See also specific members of
black power movement, 7–8, 9, 83, 246, 247, 393n16
Black Stone Rangers, 38, 46
Black Workers Congress, 363, 368, 429n80
"Black Workers Take the Lead" slogan, 371
blockbusting, 20
Board of Education, New York, 62–67, 68, 69, 70, 395n28, 401nn84–85
Board of Mediation for Community Disputes, 191
Bolsheviks, 94, 201, 212, 213
bomba y plena, 180

boogaloo, 244

Book of Discipline of the United Methodist Church, The, 187–88

BPP (Black Panther Party). *See* Black Panther Party (BPP)

Braasch, Clarence, 40, 41

bracero program, 394n13

branch offices of Young Lords: closings of, 354, 368; criticism of, 338–39; in Puerto Rico, 310, 335–37, 343, 345, 346, 349–51; U.S. openings of, 227–28, 305. *See also specific branch offices*

breakfast programs, free: BPP and, 10, 44, 123; Church Offensive and, 163–64, 167, 171, 175, 177, 178, 191; LIT and, 195; YL establishment of, 10, 45, 117, 123, *124*, 157

Broderick, Vincent, 74

Bronx, the, 274–75, 421–22n7

Bronx Science High School, 86

Bronx Young Lord branch, 224, 227, 234, 274, *380*

Brooklyn House of Detention, 327

Brown, H. Rap, 96, 184, 202

Brown v. Board of Education, 62–63, 64, 65, 66

Buckley, James, 293, 297, 305

Buonoagura, Pauline, 65

Burden, Carter, 147

building the Young Lords Party, 93–95, 200–202; in the face of repression, 117; newspaper as major organ for, 223–32, 342–43

busing program, 63–64, 371

cadre of Young Lords, 121, 128, 195–96; Maoism and, 339; YL organization shift and, 339, 340, 341–42, 364, 375–76

cadre organizations, 44, 133–34, 226

Cambrelen, Huey, 88

Canales, Blanca, 215

Canarsie Chaplains, 95–96

capitalism: as cause of oppression, 51, 112, 176; challenge to, 5, 341, 382; lumpen thesis and, 220, 222; Operation Bootstrap and, 54; revolutionary nationalism and, 210–11; women's rights and, 257, 266

Carl Sandburg Village, 17

Carmichael, Stokely, 7, 96, 130, 206

Carrazana, Humberto: church take-over and occupation and, 173, 175, 179, 185, 187; early YL encounters with, 159–61; Loyalty Sunday brawl and aftermath and, 164, 166, 167–68, 412n51, 412n59; post church occupation and, 191

car theft, 25–26

cartoons in *Palante*, 224, *283*

Casitas Criollas del Bronx, Las, 191

Castro, Fidel, 34, 88, 201

CCRB (civilian complaint review boards), 74–75, 218, 312, 331, 333, 403n125

Central Committee of PRRWO, 371

Central Committee of Young Lords, 87; closed

retreat of, 338–40; demise of YL and, 362, 365; Garbage Offensive and, 99; Luciano scandal and, 305–8, 309–10; mass organizations and, 356–57; model of organization and, 115; organization shift and, 340–42; Party Congress and, 368; Puerto Rico and, 310, 367, 375; racial make-up of, 242; second occupation of FSUMC and, 325; structure of, 127; women and, 255, 259, 263, 265–66, 340. *See also specific members of*

Central Intelligence Agency (CIA), 199, 221, 322, 424n105, 425n21

centralization of Young Lords, 338–39, 364, 376

Chapman, Robert, 166, 179–80

Che-Lumumba Club, 206

Chicago: gang culture in, 19–21, 395n40; Puerto Ricans in, 17–19, 33; racism in, 27–28, 32; social services in, 29–30

Chicago conference of Young Lords, 128

Chicano Youth Liberation Conference, 82–84

children: as interpreters, 59–60, 400n48; as protesters, 172

China, radical delegation to, 363–64, 365

Chivera, Alberto, 48

Christianity, 161

Church Offensive, 155–91; arrests and clash with the police on December 7, 1969, and, 163–66; arrests on January 7, 1970, 188–90; arts and, 180–83; background and overview of, 155–57; blood in the church, 165–66; church take-over of, 172–76; effects of, 190–91, 193; in the context of Fred Hampton's assassination, 163, 172; culture of poverty debates during, 168–70; end of occupation of, 186–90, *189*, 414n136; first visits to FSUMC of, 155–63; liberation school at, 178–80; Loyalty Sunday brawl aftermath, 166–72, 412n51; Loyalty Sunday brawl of, 163–66; Martin Luther and symbolism of, 173; occupation of, 176–81, 183, 185–86; outside support of, 183–85; parishioners' reactions to, 162–63, 165, 168–70; Second Church Offensive, 322–26, 328–29, 332, 339–40; women in, 254; youth parishioners and, 162, 167–68; 172–73, 186–87.

church protests, 166. *See also* Church Offensive

Cinquemani, Anthony, 76

Cintron, Marlene, 238, 250, 252

Citizens Committee Against Civilian Review Boards, 74–75

Citizens Committee to End Lead Poisoning, 147

citizenship of Puerto Ricans, 16, 394n8

City, The, 64–65

City University of New York (CUNY), 51, 240, 310, 398n8

civil disobedience, 102, 110, 123. *See also specific instances of*

civilian complaint review boards (CCRB), 74–75, 218, 312, 331, 333, 403n125

Claridad, 349
Clark, Kenneth and Mamie, 66
Clark, Mark, 163, 231
class politics, 219–23, 228–29, 230–31
Cleaver, Eldridge, 128, 220, 308, 340, 353, 416n57
Cleaver, Kathleen, 184
clinical pathological conference, 295
clothing drives, 86, 123, *136*
coalition politics, 299–302, 393n4
COINTELPRO, 125; BPP and, 128, 129, 314, 333, 340; Church Offensive and, 165, 170, 172, 176; PRRWO and, 377; Puerto Rico independence movement and, 350; YL demise and, 373–74, 377; YL surveillance and exploitation by, 308, 350, 367, 370
Cole, Fischer, Rogow, 74–75
collective living, 196, *197*, 197–99
College Discovery, 51, 398n8
Collier, Bob, 82, 280
Colón, Gilbert, 404n10; PRRWO and, 370, 371; race and culture and, 65, 243–45; on YL, 94; YL Puerto Rico expansion and, 341, 342, 343, 364, 367–68
Colón, Gloria, *118*
Colón, Jesús, 57, 241, 248
colonialism: decolonization and, 10, 93–94, 132, 312, 363; Fanon's writings on, 174, 344; identity and, 247–48; Puerto Rican migrants and, 4, 53, 56, 132; Puerto Rico and, 349; racism and, 5, 19, 51, 57, 206–9; revolutionary nationalism and, 210, 211–12, 214, 225
colonized mentality, 68, 204, 208–9, 248–49, 344
colorism. *See* color prejudice
color prejudice, among Puerto Ricans, 22, 25, 162, 248–49; becoming aware of, 241, 242, 247–49; Felipe Luciano and family challenges to, 88, 95; by Puerto Ricans against black Americans, 24, 25, 31; within the Young Lords, 245, 248
Columbia University, 2, 80–81, 88
Comité MINP, El, 105, 216, 348, 369–70
Commission on Integration, 62, 68
commitment, 195, 196, 199, 200, 226, 355
Committee on Juvenile Delinquency, 82
Committee to Defend the Community, 356
communal living, 196, *197*, 197–99
Communist International, 213
Communist Party (CP), U.S., 40, 204, 205–6, 213–14, 400n35, 427nn28–29
Community Action Programs (CAPs), 34, 80, 82
community control: of healthcare, 141, 145, 267, 279–81, 286–88, 292, 295, 297, 304; of public schools, 37, 123
community participation, 93, 107, 117, 124, 141, 356
complaint review boards, civilian (CCRB), 74–75, 218, 312, 331, 333, 403n125
complaint tables, hospital, 284–85, 291, 296, 298
Concerned Citizens of Lincoln Park (CCLP), 38–39

conclusions, 372–77
Congress on Racial Equality, 71, 73, 219, 406n67
conservatives in Puerto Rico, 350, 428n47
Constantine, Anthony, 144–46
continuity clinics, 295
Cornely, Paul B., 151, 410n73
Corretjer, Juan Antonio, 206, 214
corteja, la, 266
Council of Hometown Clubs, 58, 71
court-martial hearings, 236, 419n15
criticism and self-criticism, Maoist exercise of, 226–27, 307, 308, 338
Crusade for Justice, 82
Cruz, Andres, 87
Cruz, Arcelis, 33
Cruz, Benjamin, 165, 314
Cruz, Gregory, 73, 402n122
Cuascut, Aida, *129*
Cuba, 34–35, 88, 143–44, 159, 394n7, 404n193
Cuban Revolution, 88, 143, 154, 404n193
cultural production, 183
culture of poverty, 67, 169–70, 176, 274
culture of Young Lords, 196–99
CUNY (City University of New York), 51, 240, 310, 398n8
Cuza, Luis, 45, 46

Daley, Richard J., 148
dance parties, 25, 29, 38, 84
Davidoff, Sid, 175–76, 292, 293
Davila, Anibal, 321
Dávila, Orlando, 14, 24, 26, 27, 28, 38
Dayton Boys, 23
deaths in prison, 321–22, 331–32
deindustrialization, 21, 55–56, 80, 207, 218, 274
demise of Young Lords: branch closures and, 354; conclusions on, 373–77; mass organizations and, 355–57; overview of, 361–63; working class and, 354–55, 357–58, 365–66. *See also* Puerto Rico, Young Lords expansion into
demonstrations of 2006, 379, 429n1
Department of Health, 112, 148–49, 151–52, 153
Department of Sanitation, 100–101, 103, 110, 111–12, 407n73
desegregation of schools. *See* integration of schools
Devine, Patricia, 38–39, 40
Devlin, John F., 320
dialectical materialism, 344, 370
Diario La Prensa, El, 4, 78, 171, 239, 240–41, 320
Diaz, Jose "Pai," 88, 113
Dilot, Miriam, 264
diseases: in East Harlem, 136–37, 140; lead poisoning (*See* lead poisoning); sickle cell anemia, 44, 153, 278; tuberculosis, 44, 137, 149, *150*, 271–73
diseases of poverty (term), 144

displacement: emotional fallout of, 60; impact on schooling, 18; Operation Bootstrap and, 53, 54; urban renewal and, 17–18, 21, 38–40, 351, 395n28
"Divided Nation Thesis," 343–45
Division Street riots, 33–34
Dodge Revolutionary Union Movement (DRUM), 142–43, 281, 423n42
dominant ideology, 180, 183, 200, 414n122
door-to-door health services, 142, 148–51, 150, 153–54, 271, 274, 291, 296
double consciousness, 31, 239
Down These Mean Streets (Thomas), 241
Draper, Hal, 405–6n39
dress style of Young Lords, 29, 130–31, 200, 363
drug addiction, 140, 220–22, 275, 302–3
drug detoxification center, 302–3
drug trafficking, 221, 303, 424n105
DRUM (Dodge Revolutionary Union Movement), 142–43, 281, 423n42
Duany, Jorge, 31
Duarte, Marta, 264
Du Bois, W. E. B., 31
Du Brul, Paul, 147
Dunbar-Ortiz, Roxanne, 125

Eagle Electric, 369
Easter Rising of 1916, 207
East Harlem, 5, 96–98, 103; health and healthcare in, 136–37, 140, 408n3; Puerto Ricans in (See Puerto Ricans in East Harlem); riots in, 75–79
East Harlem Health Council (EHHC), 139–40, 141–42, 409n20
East Harlem Prep, 69, 81
East Wind, 218
economy: Operation Bootstrap and, 54–55; U.S., 20–21, 196–97, 222–23; politics of the Young Lords and, 217–20.
Eddy, Norman, 175
education: racism in, 65–68, 401nn84–85, 401n87; school boycott and, 68, 402nn94–95; school decentralization and protest and, 68–70; school integration and, 62–65, 68, 400–401n61, 401n68; YL's political (See political education)
EHHC (East Harlem Health Council), 139–40, 141–42, 409n20
Ehrenreich, Barbara, 290
Eighteenth District Police station meeting, 40–41
Einhorn, Arnold, 287, 293, 297–98, 301
El Caño Young Lords branch, 11, 351–52
El Loco, Mingo, 125–26, 135
Emergency Repair Program, 153
Emmaus House, 123, 157
employment of Young Lord members, 197
Engel, Friedrich, 256, 414n122
environmental awareness, 154

environmental racism, 108, 137, 157
Erwin, Hubert, 315, 316
ethnicity, 83, 46–47; race and, 24–25
eugenics movement, 67, 267

Faction Leaves Young Lords Party, 366–68
Fanon, Frantz, 66, 94, 175, 208–9, 248, 344, 417n74
FBI: campaign against New Left and, 227, 373; Fort Dix Thirty-Eight and, 236; lumpens and, 222; police collaboration with, 316–17, 403n125; PRRWO and, 370; surveillance of Young Lords by, 113, 117; Wright and, 372. See also COINTELPRO
feeding Young Lord members, 197–99
Fein, Charlotte, 287
Fein, Oliver, 320–21
feminist movement, 238–39, 250, 255–56, 261, 261–63, 266, 269. See also women's equality
Fernández, Lilia, 24
festivals of the oppressed, 2, 190
field ministry of Young Lords, 127, 227–28
Fields, Barbara, 381
fighting, gang, 26
film screenings, 179, 196, 274
Fire Department, New York City, 104, 406n48
First Source, 161, 169
First Spanish United Methodist Church (FSUMC): background and overview of, 1, 155–58, 411n15, 411–12n28; end of occupation of, 186–90, 189, 414n136; Humberto Carrazana (head pastor) and, 159; Loyalty Sunday brawl aftermath and, 166–72, 412n51; Loyalty Sunday brawl at, 163–66; Martin Luther and symbolism of protest at, 173; occupation of, 176–81, 183, 185–86; parishioners' reactions to the Young Lords, 162–63, 165, 168–70; post occupation of, 191; second occupation of, 322–26, 328–29, 332, 339–40, 383; take-over of, 172–76; YL first visits to, 159–63; youth parishioners and, 162, 167–68; 172–73, 186–88. See also Church Offensive; Second Church Offensive
flag of Puerto Rico, 78, 104, 214, 382
Flores, Hernan "Huracan," 371, 372
Flores, Juan, 243
Fontanez, Gloria, 142, 202, 310, 337, 340; HRUM and, 142–43, 283; Luciano demotion and, 308, 309, 340; Party Congress and, 368; PRRWO and, 371; Roldán and, 330; Wright and, 365, 369, 372; YL's Puerto Rico expansion and, 337, 341, 345, 348–49, 364, 367
Ford Foundation, 82
Forman, James, 166
Fort Dix stockade rebellion and Young Lord protest, 233–38, 418n2
For the People's Health, 281
fragging, 234

Franklin, Gregory, 147–48
Free Puerto Rico Now march, 312
free speech, 69, 311
Freire, Paulo, 174–75
Frente Unido, 348
Frente Universitario Pro-Independecia, 310–11
FSUMC (First Spanish United Methodist Church). *See* First Spanish United Methodist Church (FSUMC)
Fuerzas Armadas de Liberación Nacional, 216
Fullilove, Mindy Thompson, 60
fundraising, 38, 119, 345–46

Gaddis, Henry "Poison," 42
Gag Law, 78, 204–5
Gamboa, Hilda, 34
gangs, 15; colors of, 29; first generation Puerto Rican and, 21; formation of, 19–21, 24–25, 395n35, 395n40; as form of self-defense, 21; La Hacha Vieja, 21; masculinity and, 25; as outlet of consumer culture, 25; petty crime and, 25–26; postwar migrants and, 21; race pride and, 25; radicalization of, 14–15; white Americans and, 19–21
garbage-dumping demonstrations, 111, 285–86, 406n67. *See also* Garbage Offensive
Garbage Offensive, 91–114, *105*; background and overview of, 91–93; creative disruption of city life and, 110; demands, 107; different from other garbage protests, 111; effects of, 106–9, 112–14, 382; elections and, 109–12; garbage dumping phase of, 101–6; "in service to" phase of, 96–101, *97*, 405n22; origins of name of, 91; political impact of, 109–12; theory and praxis of, 93–95, 405n75; women in, 252
Garcia, David, 166
Garcia, Ralph, 83, 87
Garelik, Sanford D., 305, 312, 424n1
Garry, Charles, 184
gay caucus, 263–65
Gay Liberation Front, 264
gender inequality. *See* women's equality
gender oppression, 250, 254, 256, 257, 258. *See also* women's equality
genocide, 70, 267, 268, 295, 331
Gerena Valentin, Gilberto, 58, 68, 70, 71, 206, 402n114
Giap, Vo Nguyen, 94, 207
Gilligan, Thomas, 72, 73
González, Corky, 82, 83
González, Juan, 49, *50*, 65, *87*, 242, 300, 337; Church Offensive and, 164, 172, 174, 178–79, 186; contributions to documenting the lessons of independence movement, 214, 216; Garbage Offensive and, 112; healthcare and, 140, 141, 142, 149; NLC and, 369; Puerto Rico independence and, 310; on SDS, 217; suspension, demotion and resignation of, 307, 369, 371;

taking up arms and, 324–25; Thirteen-Point Program and, 131; War on Poverty programs and, 80–81; on YL, 93, 127, 354; YL demise and, 355–56, 362; YL organization shift and, 335, 341, 343–44; YL politics and, 200, 202, 203, 204, 205, 214; YL's Puerto Rico expansion and, 345, 364, 365
González, Minerva, 345
González, Mirta, 165, 233
González-Suarez, Oscar, 187
"Goodbye to All That" (Morgan), 261
Goodman, Carol, 315
Gottehrer, Barry, 111, 152, 327, 381
Gray, Jesse, 73, 82
grievance tables, hospital, 284–85, 291, 296, 298
Grito de Lares, El, 214, 311, 418n129
Guardian conference, 368–69
Guerra, Rory, 23, 42–45
guerrillas (term), 312
guerrilla warfare, 94, 102, 106, 130, 206–7, 416n57
Guevara, Ernesto Che, 34, 47, 100, 176, 219, 238, 250, 271
Guzmán, Pablo "Yoruba," *43*, 49, 86, *87*, *120*, 127, 242; on arming, 313; China trip of, 363–64, 365; Church Offensives and, 161–62, 167, 169, 174, 176, 188, 330; Garbage Offensive and, 99, 106, 108; on international struggle, 3; LGBTQ equality and, 264–65; Lincoln Offensive and, 292, 297; Luciano scandal and, 305–7; media and, 148, 300; neighborhood watch and, 125, 126; *Palante* and, 224; resignation of, 371; Roldán death and, 321; welfare rights and, 123; on YL, 94–95, 100, 231, 366; YL expansion to Puerto Rico and, 341, 358, 363–64; YL politics and, 131, 201–2, 203, 208, 220

Hacha Vieja, La, 21
Haddock, Emma, 76
Hagedorn, John M., 19
Halpern, Milton, 320
Hampton, Fred, 42–43, *43*, 44–45; Chicago march and, 128–29; death of, 163, 231; Ramos death and, 46; YL and, 42
Handschu, Barbara, 315–16, 425n42
Handschu files, 12, 407n9, 425n42
Harlem on My Mind, 180–81
Harlem Parents Committee, 63, 68
Harlemville, 291
Harrington, Michael, 169–70, 412n69
Harris, David, 149
HARYOU-ACT, 96
Haywood, Harry, 213–14
headquarters office of Young Lords, 9, 115, 117–21, *118*, *198*, 228
health advisory boards, 141
Health and Hospital Corporation (HHC), 283–84, 285, 292
healthcare: affiliation system in, 138–39, 141,

144, 276, 294–95, 297, 422n20; in Aguadilla, 351; background and overview of, 135–40, 409n8; community control of, 141, 145, 267, 279–81, 286–88, 292, 295, 297, 304; conclusions on, 153–54; health program platform and demands, 141–43; in Cuba, 143–44; door-to-door services of, 142, 148–51, 150, 153–54, 271, 274, 291, 296; Metropolitan Hospital and, 137, 139–40, 141, 144–46; in South Bronx, 272, 274–76; unions and, 278–80; Young Lords activism beginnings in, 139–46. *See also* diseases; healthcare workers; lead poisoning; Ten-Point Health Program and Platform; tuberculosis; *specific hospitals*

healthcare workers: HRUM and, 143, 278–79; at Lincoln Hospital, 276, 277–81, 283, 284; sit-ins and, 144–45, 149; TLC and, 284, 286; unions of, 223, 278–80

health clinic at FSUMC, 178

health insurance, 137, 138

Health Policy Advisory Center of the Institute for Policy Studies, 140–41, 321

Health Revolutionary Unity Movement (HRUM), 143, 149, 280–82, 423n42, 423n70; coalition politics and, 300; HHC and, 284; Lincoln Offensive and, 288, 290; patient bill of rights and, 298–99; restraining order against, 296; TLC and, 283; as a YL subsidiary, 302

Hernández, Vicente, 108–9

heroin, 220–22, 275, 293, 303, 424n105

Hertzberg, Hendrik, 235

HHC (Health and Hospital Corporation), 283–84, 285, 292

Hill, Joseph, 164

Hirsch, Arnold, 20, 27

home ownership, 15, 19, 64, 217

home visit health services, 142, 148–51, 150, 153–54, 271, 274, 291, 296

Hoover, J. Edgar, 316–17, 373

hospitals as employers, 139, 142

housing codes, 146, 152, 153

Housing Development Administration, 153

housing displacement. *See* displacement

hypermasculinity, 262

identity: of mainland Puerto Ricans, 247–48, 419n50; Nuyorican, 190–91, 240–41, 244; racism and, 24–25, 31–32, 242

Ideology and Ideological State Apparatuses (Althusser), 249

Ideology of the Black Panther Party, The, 344

Ideology of the Young Lords Party, The, 248–49, 344

ILF (Inmates Liberation Front), 328, 358–59, 360

imperialism, 88, 132, 206–9, 212, 367

Impressions, The, 177

incarceration, 210, 329

independence movement of Puerto Rico.
  See Puerto Rico independence movement

Indians of All Tribes Coalition, 218

individuality, 210–11, 384–85

industrializing (term), 358

informants, COINTELPRO, 350

Inmates Liberation Front (ILF), 328, 358–59, 360

integration of schools, 62–65, 68, 70, 400–401n61, 401n68

International Women's Day, 258

International Workers' Order, 57, 400n35

intern strike at Lincoln Hospital, 296–98

Ivany, Sonia, 165, 238, 252

ivory tower approach of PRRWO, 370

I Wor Kuen, 218, 322, 369

Jackson, George, 360

Jacobi Hospital, 287, 296, 297

Jacobs, David "Pelu," 313–14

Jaja, 245

Ja-Ja, Che, 234

Jewish Defense League, 298

"Jíbaro, My Pretty Little Nigger" (Luciano), 88–89

jíbaros, 32, 211, 214

Jiménez, Antonio, 16–17, 21

Jiménez, Eugenia, 17, 18, 22–23

Jiménez, José "Cha Cha": as an organizer, 41–42, 43; background and overview of, 13–14, 14, 15–16; becoming an activist, 35–40; becoming a Young Lord, 22–30; becoming Puerto Rican, 30–32; BPP newspaper article of, 50–51, 81; New York/Chicago YL split and, 229–30, 231; RGS and radicalization of, 51; SAC and, 84, 87; theory and praxis of, 94

Johnson, Bruce, 40, 48, 231

Jones, Thomas, 273

Jung, Huey, 224

Justicia Boricua, 348

juvenile delinquency, 21, 82

Kamen, Jeff, 191

Kehl, T. William, 188

Kent State University, 314

Kew Gardens, 327

King, Martin Luther, Jr., 32, 35, 110, 160, 208, 424n10

Kirk, David, 157, 167

Klonsky, Mike, 43

Koch, Edward, 147–48, 426n80

Korn, Hyman, 186

KPFA radio, 178

Kramansky, Wenner H., 147, 152

Kroplinicki, Charles, 165

Kunstler, William, 327, 360

La Clark, 17, 18

Lacot, Antero, 282, 285, 291, 292, 293, 294, 296, 303

la jara (term), 70–71

Lamb, James, 46

language: children as interpreters of, 59–60, 400n48; in the school system, 67–68
Last Poets, 96, 181
Latin American Boys Club, 34
Latin American Defense Organization (LADO), 34, 45, 85
Latinos: as term, 132, 382; Thirteen-Point Program and, 132; U.S. growth of, 311, 425n21; Young Lords inclusion of, 83, 219, 249
Lavon, Raymond, 321–22
law and order, 69, 73, 316, 333
"Lay Lady Lay" (Dylan), 155, 157, 410n2
lead poisoning, 146–54; background and overview of, 146–48; hospital workers and, 276, 277–78; Lincoln Hospital and, 275; YL offensive against, 148–53, 383
lead-screening kits, 148–49
Lebron, Lolita, 119, 215, 260, 405n15
Lee, Bobby, 42
Lee, Robert E., 186
Lee, Stan, 383
legacy of Young Lords, 380–84, 386–87
Legal Aid Society, 329
legal defense center, 326, 328–29, 332
Lemus, Robert "Bobby," 315–18, 319
Lenin, V. I., 190, 201, 207, 212, 382, 404–5n13, 416n31; self-determination's origins and, 207, 212
lessons for organizers, 384–86
Levin, Stephen, 300–301, 303
Lewis, Oscar, 67, 169–70
Ley de la Mordaza, 78, 204–5
LGBTQ equality, 263–65
Liberate Puerto Rico Now, 311
Liberation News Service, 119, 346, 348, 358, 366, 407n5
liberation schools, 68, 159, 178–80
liberation theology, 160, 411n20
Lincoln Collective, 286–88, 290–91, 295, 298, 299, 301, 302, 423n60
Lincoln Hospital, 275–76; drug detoxification center at, 302–3; garbage protest at, 285–86; intern strike at, 296–98; LHMHS, 276–78; Lincoln Collective and, 286–88, 290–91, 295, 298, 299, 301, 302, 423n60; mental health clinic take-over at, 279–82, 422–23n33, 423n35; nurses' residences occupation at, 332; Palante cartoon on, 224; reform at, 276–78; Section K of, 284, 291; sit-in at, 282; TLC and, 283–86; unionization at, 278–79. See also Lincoln Offensive
Lincoln Hospital Mental Health Service (LHMHS), 276–78
Lincoln Offensive: aftermath of, 293–98, 383; background and overview of, 271, 282–88; coalition politics and, 299–302; conclusions on, 303–4; hospital occupation of, 288–92, 289
Lincoln Park, 17–18, 20, 23–24, 27, 38–40, 395n24

Lincoln Park Conservation Association (LPCA), 18, 38, 39–40
Lindsay, John V.: antipoverty programs of, 74, 80; CCRB and, 74; Church Offensive and, 175; East Harlem riots and, 76–77, 79; garbage collection and, 109, 112; lead poisoning and, 191, 407n73; lead poisoning and, 152; prisons and, 317, 326, 327, 330, 383; TLC and, 292, 293
literature read by Young Lords, 94
Little Red Book (Mao Tse-tung), 94, 404–5n13
local movement's connection to national, 385
logo of Young Lords Party, 336; on button, 99, 108
Logos, 293
Lopez, Obed, 34, 42
Lopez, Omar, 33, 34, 37, 41–42, 45
Lordettes, 38
Lords in training (LIT), 128, 193, 195
los peluses (term), 162
Lower East Side branch of Young Lords, 227–28, 305, 354, 356–57, 404n9
Loyalty Sunday brawl, 163–66; aftermath of, 166–72, 412n51
LPCA (Lincoln Park Conservation Association), 18, 38, 39–40
Luchadora, La, 268
Luciano, Felipe, 95–96, 116, 127, 242, 300; arts and, 181; Church Offensives and, 164, 165, 168, 170–72, 325; demotion and exit of, 305–10; Garbage Offensive and, 99, 102, 106–7, 110; Lincoln Offensive and, 288; Morales and, 253; on Oliver, 265–66; race hybridity and, 243; YL New York formation and, 49, 86, 87, 88–89; YL politics and, 202, 207, 208, 209, 210–12, 214; YL theory and praxis and, 93, 94, 96
lumpenproletariat, 219–22, 228, 230–31, 342–43, 366, 374, 386
lumpen thesis, 219–20, 222
Lumpen Unidos Rompecadenas, 356
Lurie, Ellen, 64–65

machismo, 238, 250, 255, 258, 262, 263, 309, 381
Mafia, 222
Malcolm X, 32–33, 36, 71, 200, 208, 407n9
male chauvinism, 151, 238, 257, 263, 309, 339–40
male privilege, 257
Mancussi, Vincent R., 360
Manhattan House of Detention for Men, 317–22, 326, 327, 329, 331, 383
Maoism, 201, 226, 312, 339, 376, 429n117
Mao Tse-tung, 94, 100, 339, 376, 415n18, 429n117
marches: Chicago march honoring Hampton, 128–29; March on Washington, 71, 402n114; Puerto Rico independence, 305, 312, 424n2; Rainbow Coalition's Chicago march, 128–29
March on Washington, 71, 402n114
Marcuse, Herbert, 222
Mari Bras, Juan, 349

Marin, Luis Muñoz, 54, 211
Maristany, Hiram, 76–77, 88, 177
marriage, institution of, 266
Martinez, Jose, 87–88
Martinez, Myrna, 252, 256
Martinez, Victor, 328–29
Marxism, 193–94, 201, 205, 209, 219, 343, 366, 370; training of Young Lords by black and Puerto Rican Marxists, 205–6.
masculinity, 25, 26, 250, 262. *See also* machismo
mass organizations, 355, 356–57, 359, 362, 366, 428n69
"maximum feasible participation" dictum, 76, 80, 107, 141, 277, 304
Mayfield, Curtis, 177–78
mayoral elections of 1969, 109
McCall, Jack, 314
McCarthyism, 75, 82, 215
McCormick Theological Seminary occupation, 47, 86, 166
McGrath, George, 326
McLaughlin, Mary, 152
meals for Young Lord members, 197–99
media, the, 168, 176, 269, 381
Medical Committee for Human Rights, 143, 297, 423n60
medical discrimination, 136, 138–39
medical empires, 290
medical practitioners, 137, 409n8
medical training, 138, 139, 287, 295
Melendez, Mickey, 53, 84–85, *184*, 390; Church Offensive and, 173; founder of the New York Young Lords, 49, 84; La Sociedad Albizu Campos and, 84–88, 252; Luciano scandal and, 308; SAC and, 84–86; War on Poverty programs and, 81; YLO headquarters and, 119; YLO New York formation and, 49, 81, 84–86, 87–88
membership of Young Lords, 117, 185, 193, 195–99; decline of, 352, 354, 362, 368; demographics of, 382; growth of, 185, 193, 305, 322, 339; mass organizations and, 357; overview of, 11; political education and, 202–6; race and, 242–43, 249; requirements of, 117, 374; vetting and integrating and, 196–99; women and, 185, 254
men's caucus, 263
mental healthcare, 276–82
Merton, Thomas, 36
Messinger, Eli C., 297
mestizaje, 65, 240, 420n59
methadone, 303
Methodist Church, 158–59, 167, 179, 186, 187–88, 325. *See also* First Spanish United Methodist Church (FSUMC)
Metropolitan Hospital, 137; activism and, 141, 144–46; Church Offensive and, 178; lead poisoning and, 147, 148; Medicaid cuts and, 139–40

Metropolitan Hospital Workers' Movement, 144
Metropolitan Museum, 180–81
Meyers, Daniel, 190
middle class: guilt of, 301–2; Puerto Rico independence movement and, 215–16; view of YL of, 300–301; women's movement and, 256–57, 258, 262
"Mighty, Mighty, Spade and Whitey" (Mayfield), 177–78
migration, gang formation as a result of, 15; antiblack racism and, 24–25; generational differences amplified by, 23; impact on children, 59- 61; impact on consciousness of second generation, 16; radicalizing effect of, 16; reasons for, 16
Migration Division, 15, 16, 33, 57
migration to U.S., 3–4, 16, 31, 53, 241, 379, 393n4, 399n12
military stockade protests, 233–36, 418–19n12
Ministerio de Salud Pública, 143
ministries of Young Lords, 127–28, 227–28
Minter, Bernie, 278–79
Mitchell, Charlene, 206
Moberg, David, 112
Mobilization for Youth (MFY), 82
Model Cities Program, 351
Moeller, Griswold, 107
Monestero, Phil, 26
Monserrat, Joseph, 57
Morales, Iris, 49, 243, 252–54, 259; Chicano Youth Liberation Conference and, 83; Church Offensive and, 178–79; healthcare and, 144, 151; Luciano scandal and, 308; on paternalism, 217; political education and, *194*, 203, 204; on racism, 246, 247–48; resignation of, 371; SAC and, 84; as a social mediator, 59, 60, 61, 400n48; women's equality and, 252–55, 257, 259–60, 263, 265; on YL, 227
Morales, Ramon, 224, 364
morality, 155–56
Moreno, Carmen "Flaca," 264
Moreno, Rita, 185
Morgan, Robin, 261
Morgan, Thomas B., 152
mortality, 137, 275
Movimiento de Liberación Nacional, 216
Movimiento Libertador, 215
Movimiento Pro Independencia (MPI), 6, 130, 215–16, 337, 348–49, 369, 408n44
Moynihan, Daniel Patrick, 170
Mullan, Fitzhugh, 287–88, 301
Murphy, James, 315
Museo del Barrio, El, 191, 415n158
music: Church Offensive and, 177–78, 180, 181, 191; festivals of the oppressed and, 2; race and class and, 243–44
Myrdal, Gunnar, 56

Naison, Mark, 81
National Community Mental Health Center Act, 276–77
National Council of Churches, 161
National Institute for Mental Health, 279
nationalism: black, 83, 308, 393n16; on the mainland, 343; postwar structural changes as basis for, 217–18; in Thirteen-Point Program, 132. *See also* revolutionary nationalism
Nationalist Party of Puerto Rico, 214–15; demise of, 204, 215, 216; YL and, 6, 214, 341, 346–48, 349–50
National Lawyers Guild, 2, 165, 316
National Liaison Committee (NLC), 369, 370–71
National Liberation Front, 91, 176, 418n3
National Puerto Rican Civil Rights Association, 71, 73
national staff of Young Lords, 363, 365, 429n87
Nation of Islam, 36, 195, 360
"nation within a nation," 207, 213–14, 345, 427n28
Native Americans: activism of, 218; migration of, 3, 16, 393n4; *Palante* and, 245–46; YL solidarity with, 132, 218
Nazario, Victor, 37
Neighborhood Youth Corps, 147
neoliberalism, 54, 399n23
Newark Young Lords office, 227
New Careers program, 277
Newfield, Jack, 149, 151–52
New Left, 6–7, 385, 386; challenge to capitalism of, 222; communal living and, 196; ideology and politics of, 107, 132, 141, 159, 414n122; morality and, 155–56; origins of intellectual arrogance of white students in, 205; racial identity and, 249; white paternalism within, 217; Young Lords as distinct manifestation of and contribution to, 7, 59–61, 99–100, 113, 133–34, 153–54, 249, 268–69, 333. *See also specific groups of*
New Negro movement, 208
New Rican Village, 190–91
New Right, 155–56
New Sixty-Fifth Infantry, 357
Newton, Huey P., 44, 45, 129, 131, 184, 340, 353, 363
New York Daily News, 96–98, 123, 275
New York Police Department (NYPD): arrests of Roldán and Lemus and, 315–16; BPP and, 314, 425n42; Church Offensives and, 164–66, 173, 185–86, 330; repression by, 313, 314, 333; surveillance by, 195, 227
New York Post, 177, 186, 297
New York Times: bearing arms and, 323; on Church Offensive, 186, 190; on East Harlem riots, 76, 78–79; on Garbage Offensive, 104, 106, 108–9, 111; on integration, 64; June 1970 riots and, 314; on lead poisoning, 151; on Lincoln Hospital, 282, 296–97; on Luciano

scandal, 308; on Metropolitan Hospital, 145; on poetry, 181; on prison rebellions, 327, 328; on radical activism, 312–13; on Roldán death, 331; on YL split, 231
New York World-Telegram, 67
Nieves, Josephina, 400n38
NLC (National Liaison Committee), 369, 370–71
Normalists, 34
North Cell House, Cha Cha at, 35–37
North Side Cooperative Ministry, 39
Nuevo Dia, El, 347
Nuñez, Luis, 178
nurses' residences occupation at Lincoln Hospital, 332
Nuyorican identity, 190–91, 240–41, 244
Nuyorican Poets Cafe, 191
NYPD (New York Police Department). *See* New York Police Department (NYPD)

observation and participation, 94–95
office headquarters of Young Lords, 9, 115, 117–21, 118, 198, 228
Office of Economic Opportunity (OEO), 80, 276–77, 279
officers of the day (OD), 121, 258–59
Ohio National Guard, 314
Oliver, Denise, 49, 81–82, 85, 259, 300, 340; abortion and, 267; Church Offensive and, 164, 168, 173, 178; conduct codes and, 226–27; drug crisis and, 221; education and, 63–64, 69–70; healthcare and, 151, 283; LGBTQ equality and, 264–65; Luciano scandal and, 306, 307; *Palante* and, 224; prisoners' rights and, 328–29; race hybridity and, 244; Roldán and, 306; SAC and, 86; women's equality and, 250–52, 254, 258–59, 262, 263, 265–66; YL departure of, 353–54; YL expansion to Puerto Rico and, 341; YL politics and, 200–202, 205
Oliver, George Bodine, 81
"On Revolutionary Nationalism" (Luciano), 210, 214
open admissions, 310, 425n19
Operation Bootstrap, 53–54, 211, 266–67, 379
oral history program, 366
Organization of Latin American Solidarity, 130
Origin of the Family, Private Property and the State, The (Engel), 256
Ortiz, Juan "Fi," 43, 87, 88, 121, 127, 242, 300; Church Offensive and, 173; McCall and, 314; prisoners and, 360–61; Puerto Rico independence and, 310; YL direction shift and, 335, 341; YL exit of, 367; YL Puerto Rico expansion and, 364, 365, 366–68
Osborne, Harold, 286–87, 299–302
Osborne, Wesley, 183–84, 187
Oswald, Russell G., 359, 360
Other America, The (Harrington), 169–70, 412n69

Pabon, Diego, 86
Pacifica Radio, 93, 99, 191, 194
paddy wagon, 396n93
Padilla, Felix, 18–19
Palante (newspaper), 50, 59, 133, 223–27, 225, 251, 418n137; on Chicago group split, 230; demise of YL and, 354, 362; *Faction Leaves Young Lords Party* issue of, 366–68; "Gorilla on Your Back," 220; "Letter from Puerto Rico," 337; on Malcolm X, 208; "On Revolutionary Nationalism," 210; "Pig of the Week," 282; Ponce Massacre commemoration and, 347–48; prisoners and, 360; public health and, 271, 282, 283, 283, 290; racism and, 245–46; sales in Puerto Rico of, 352; "South Bronx Time Bomb," 274–75; women's equality and, 260–61, 269
Palante (radio show), 194, 256–58
palante (term), 223
Palante: The Young Lords Party, 203–4
Panama Canal, 54
Panther 21, 3, 99, 314, 326–27, 425n42
Pantoja, Antonio, 57
Paragons, the, 25
paramilitary image and structure of Young Lords, 130–31, 193, 196, 273, 347, 348, 363, 408n47
Parents and Taxpayers, 64
Paris, Jose, 360–61
Parrilla, Antulio, 332
participation, community, 93, 107, 117, 124, 141, 356
participatory democracy, 107, 141, 161
Passalacqua, Juan M. García, 348
paternalism, 33, 217, 262, 276, 285, 302
Paterson, Basil, 191
patient bill of rights, 298–99, 383
patriarchy, 25, 123, 250, 256, 258, 262
Patrolmen's Benevolent Association (PBA), 74–75
Paulino, Mario, 86, 404n189
Peace and Freedom Party, 308
Peck, Harris B., 279
Pediatric Collective, 140, 296
Pediatric Parents' Association, 298
Peña, Roy "Debenya," 88
People's Church by the Young Lords: activities of, 176–81, 183, 185–86; background and overview of, 1–3, 4; end of occupation of, 186–91, 189, 414n136; gay coalition at, 264; outside support of, 183–85; second occupation and, 124, 322–26, 328–29, 332. *See also* Church Offensive
Perez, Benny, 14, 43
Perez, David, 49, 85, 87, 127, 242, 300; abuse of, 372; Garbage Offensive and, 98, 106; on language, 67–68; organization shift and, 340–41; on repression, 314; resignation of, 371; SAC and, 84, 86; Second Church Offensive and, 325; Wright and, 372; YL branch offices and, 227; YL expansion to Puerto Rico and, 341, 363–64; YL politics and, 202, 209

Perez, Fermin, 14
Perez, Jose, 321
Perez, Richie: on Fort Dix brawl, 236–37; healthcare and, 272, 274; on LIT process, 128, 195; *Palante* and, 224; PRRWO and, 371; YL as a home for, 185; YL politics and, 200, 209, 342–43
personal is political, the, 10, 203, 269, 414n122
Photography Workshop, 76, 88, 93
physical fitness, 196
Pietri, Carmen, 162, 168–69, 172–73, 187
Pietri, Frank, 187
Pietri, Joe, 168, 173, 187
Pietri, Pedro, 162, 181–83, 187
Pietri, Petra Aponte de, 162, 165
pig (term), 131
plumbism. *See* lead poisoning
Pochoda, Dan, 316
poetry, 2, 88–89, 96, 181–83
police brutality, 33, 70–74, 76, 383, 402n116, 402n120, 402n122, 403n125; civilian complaint review board as response to, 74–75; Chicago Young Lord protest against, 40–41, 46–47; connected to Spanish mainland idiom, *la jara*, 70–71; origins of the term "pig" and, 131; protest by Puerto Ricans against, 71, 75–79, 104–5, 125–27
police precinct storming, 104–5
police watch operation: of the Black Panthers, 44; of the Young Lords, 117, 125–27
political education: drug addiction and, 221, 303; film screenings and, 274; liberation school and, 178–80, 413n107; LIT and, 195; Marxism course and, 366; overview of, 193–94, 194; *Palante* and, 225; racism and, 246–47; retreat and, 228; YL politics and, 201, 202–6
political shift of Young Lords Party: background and overview of, 338–42; supporting documents of, 343–45
politics of Young Lords: background and overview of, 193–94; class and lumpen orientation of, 219–23; *Palante* and, 223–27; postwar conditions as basis for, 217–19; retreat and, 228–29; revolutionary nationalism and, 6, 210–17; revolutionary nationalism roots and, 206–10; style and form of, 199–202
Ponce, Puerto Rico, 211, 349–50
Ponce Massacre commemoration demonstration, 341, 346–48
Poor People's Coalition (PPC), 47, 86
Popular Democratic Party, 54
Position Paper on Women, 151, 266–67
poverty, 67, 169–70, 176, 267, 274, 422n22. *See also* War on Poverty programs
Powell, James, 71–72, 73
PPC (Poor People's Coalition), 47, 86
Presidio stockade sit-down strike, 236, 418n12
prison conditions, 317–19, 322–29

prison deaths, 321–22, 331–32
prisoners' rights, 328–29, 332, 383
prison rebellions, 326–29, 332, 333, 358–61, 383, 429n80, 429n83
Procaccino, Mario, 109
Prospect Hospital, 271–73
PRRWO (Puerto Rican Revolutionary Workers' Organization), 368–72, 377
PRSU (Puerto Rican Student Union), 310–11, 348, 357
psychotropic substances, 279, 280
Puerto Rican Day Parade, 130, *184*
Puerto Rican Leadership Forum, 57–58
Puerto Rican Left, 6, 57, 204–5
Puerto Rican Nationalist Party, 214–15
"Puerto Rican Obituary" (Pietro), 181–83
"Puerto Rican problem, the," 52, 56–59
Puerto Rican Progressive Movement, 37
Puerto Rican Revolutionary Workers' Organization (PRRWO), 368–72, 377
Puerto Rican Ruling Elite, 228–29
Puerto Ricans in Chicago, 17–19, 33; race and ethnicity and, 24–25
Puerto Ricans in East Harlem, 22, 216, 381; employment of, 55–56, 80, 107, 399–400n29, 400n31; housing conditions, 98; Luciano on, 171; politics of, 204–5; poverty of, 56; race and ethnicity and, 239, 241; socioeconomic conditions, 56, 103
Puerto Ricans Involved in Student Action, 254
Puerto Rican Socialist Party, 216, 369
Puerto Rican Student Conference, 310–12
Puerto Rican Student Union (PRSU), 310–11, 348, 357
Puerto Rican Study, The (New York Board of Education), 65, 401n85
Puerto Rico, 3, 16, 394nn7–8, 420n59; colonization of, 53–54, 56; conservatives in, 350, 428n47; flag of, 78, 104, 214, 382; independence movement of (*See* Puerto Rico independence movement); industrialization of, 54, 399n22; Jiménez expulsion to, 30–31; migration from, 3–4, 16, 31, 53, 399n12; YL organizing in (*See* Puerto Rico, Young Lords expansion into)
Puerto Rico, Young Lords expansion into: background and overview of, 335–37, 338, 341; building of, 345–53, 365; challenges to, 352–53, 358; conclusions on, 374–75, 385–86; opposition to, 363–65, 366–68; YL documents supporting, 343–45
Puerto Rico independence movement: background and overview of, 4, 5–6, 58, 335–37, 382, 427n2; education and, 193, 247; New York march and, 305, 424n2; Puerto Rican Student Conference at Columbia and, 310–11; revolutionary nationalism and, 211–12, 214–16; suppression of, 53, 54, 78, 204–5, 346–47, 350;

YL in New York and, 183, 193, 232, 310, 311, 312; YL in Puerto Rico and, 335–37, 344–50, 375. *See also specific organizations of*

Queens House of Detention, 326–27
Quintana, Harry, 82

race: Chicanos and, 82–83; ideology, 67, 74–75, 240, 247–49, 312, 381, 419n49, 429n2; mainland experience of black Puerto Ricans and, 24, 65, 83, 88, 95–96, 162, 233–36, 241–42, 248–49; migrant Puerto Rican and Latinx parents and, 24–25; Puerto Ricans and, 22, 83, 162, 239–41; Spanish colonial rule and, 240; Young Lords and, 239–50
race, hybrid experience of, 239–45; conflict of, 245–49
race mixing, 65, 240, 420n59
racial formation, in Puerto Rico, 247, 396n60, 396n98, 419n49
racialization, of Puerto Ricans in the U.S. mainland, 18–19, 22, 241, 394n10; Puerto Rican nationalism as challenge to, 78, 209
racism: against Puerto Ricans, 15, 21–25, 56–57, 67, 71; colonialism and, 206, 208–9; in education, 65–68, 401nn84–85, 401n87; gang formation and, 19–21, 395n33, 395n40; in healthcare, 139; in hierarchy with sexism, 262, 309; identity and, 24–25, 31–32, 242; internalized by the oppressed, 31–32, 67–68, 203–4, 248–49; nationalism and, 211, 213, 217; northern character of, 32; parent/child relationship and, 22–23; race mixing and, 240; revolution and, 213, 371; social status and, 108, 170; in Vietnam War, 233–34; YL politics of, 132, 245–50, 269
radical (term), 11, 50
radicalization: Cha Cha and seeds of, 15, 48; contradictions of morality in the church and, 18, 22, 23; experience of migration as seed of, 59–61; experience of social class and, 80; of gangs, 14–15; imprisonment and, 35; latent race pride and, 33; medical discrimination and seeds of, 139; schools and, 62, 63–64, 66–67, 70; structural displacement as seeds of, 18, 26–28; through popular culture, 29; travel as seed of, 30–32
Rainbow Coalition, 42, *43*, 128–29
Ramirez, Ramon, 64
Ramón Emeterio Betances Health Truck, 273
Ramos, Juan, 365, 366–68
Ramos, Manuel, 46–47
Ramos faction, 366–68
Ramparts, 116
Randall's Island concert, 306, 424n4
RAT, 261
Reader's Digest, 279
Real Great Society (RGS), 49, 69, 81, 142, 398n1
recruits, Young Lord, 195–99, 203

Red Scare, 52, 204–5, 398n10
rehabilitation, drug, 191, 221–22
Report to the Mayor of New York on the Death of a Citizen, Julio Roldán, 331
repression of Left groups, heightened, 125, 312–15, 325, 333, 373, 383
reproductive rights, 267
Resistencia Puertorriqueña, 216
retreats of the Young Lords, 228–29, 337–40, 341
Revolutionary Action Movement, 206
revolutionary awakening, global, 372–73
revolutionary machismo, 238, 258, 263, 309
revolutionary nationalism, 206–17; critique of cultural nationalism, 209–10; critique of the indigenous managers of colonialism in Puerto Rico, 211; background and overview of, 5–6, 11, 84; embodying ideas of, 206–10; MPI criticism of, 349; *Palante* and, 225; postwar conditions as basis for, 217–19; RU and, 371; women's equality and, 256–57, 261; of the YL, 5, 6, 210–17
revolutionary potential, 219, 374–75, 429n116
Revolutionary Union (RU), 363, 365, 369, 370–71
Reyes, Chiqui, 250
RGS (Real Great Society), 49, 69, 81, 142, 398n1
right to bear arms, 125, 130
riots: in Chicago, 33–34; distinct character of postwar riots, 72; in East Harlem, 75–79; in Harlem, 71–73; of June 1970, 313–14; and law-and-order backlash, 73; against police brutality, 72–73, 402n116, 402n120
Rising Up Angry, 42
Rivera, David, 14, 26
Rivera, Geraldo, 239, 330, 427n99
Rivera, Oscar Garcia, 330, 400n36
Rivera, Oscar Garcia, Jr., 330
Rivera, Pete, 45
Rivera, Rafael, 46
Rivera, Ralph, 39
Rivera, Sylvia, 264
Rivero, Sal del, 14, 23, 25, 30
Riverside Church, 166
Robles, Olguie, 255
Rockefeller, Nelson, 112, 141, 191, 360, 361, 407n73
Rodriguez, Carmen, 266, 267, 293–95
Rodriguez, Ezra, 159
Rodriguez, Gloria, 185, 289, 341–42
Rodriguez, Pete, 244
Rodriguez, Reinaldo, 76
Rodriguez, Victor, 71
Rodriguez-Torres, Carlos, 233–35, 236
Rojas, Wilfredo, 59–60
Roldán, Julio: arrest of, 315–19; death of, 306, 319–23, 323, 333, 347, 351, 374; inquiry into death of, 329–30; as YL cook, 197–99
root shock, 60
Rosado brothers, 345
Rossman, Michael, 220–21

Rovira, Carlito, 66–67, 87, 121; arrest of, 121, 122–23; Chicano Youth Liberation Conference and, 83–84; Church Offensive and, 165, 185; on Fort Dix brawl, 237; healthcare and, 140, 145; on Jaja, 245; LGBTQ equality and, 264; PRRWO and, 371, 372; race hybridity and, 244; on YL, 131; YLO headquarters and, 117, 119
RU (Revolutionary Union), 363, 365, 369, 370–71
Rules of Discipline, 196, 308, 356, 415n10
Ryan, Thomas, 76

SAC (Sociedad Albizu Campos), 84–88, 252
SACC (Spanish Action Committee of Chicago), 34
Santiago, Ildefenso, 104, 110
Santiago, William, 288
Schomburg, Arturo, 241
schools and housing displacement, 18, 395n28
SDS (Students for a Democratic Society), 49, 81, 87, 217, 335, 365, 416n49
Seale, Bobby, 44, 353
Second Amendment, 125, 133; exercised by the Black Panthers, 44; exercised by the Young Lords, 323–25; a right reserved for European Americans, 324
Second Church Offensive, 322–26, 328–29, 332, 339–40, 383
Section K of Lincoln Hospital, 284, 291
SEEK program, 96
Segarra, Arnie, 79, 111, 175–76, 187
segregation: in housing, 32, 217; of schools, 58, 62–63, 218 (*See also* integration of schools); urban, 10, 18, 19, 20, 395n27
self-defense: armed, 7, 100, 129–30, 133, 200, 313, 314, 323–25; gangs and, 15, 21
self-determination: black power and, 7, 129; revolutionary nationalism and, 210, 211, 212, 217; as term, 207–8; Third World and, 10, 324, 346; YL and, 5, 126, 132, 292
Senidez, Julio, 328
Service Employees International Union Local 1199, 278–80
service model of activism, 92, 99–100, 376
Seven Storey Mountain, The (Merton), 36
sexual fascism, 255
sexuality, 255–56, 263, 266
sexual revolution, 155, 410n2
Shakur, Assata, 61
sickle cell anemia, 44, 153, 278
Silvers, Cleo, 142–43, 277, 279, 283, 293, 295, 302, 303
sit-ins: at Department of Health, 10, 149; at FSUMC, 184–85; at Lincoln Hospital, 282; at Metropolitan Hospital, 144–46
skin color, 22, 24, 248
Smigiel, Stanley, 64
Smith, J. J., 294, 295–96, 297
Smith, Mike, 277, 279, 293–94

SNCC (Student Nonviolent Coordinating
   Committee), 7, 83, 140, 166, 217
socialism, 5, 102, 382, 386, 405–6n39, 415n18
Socialist Workers Party, 40
social mediators, migrants' children as, 59–61,
   400n48
Social Security Act of 1965, 137
Sociedad Albizu Campos (SAC), 84–88, 252
Solero, Maximo, 71
solidarity: of black Americans and Puerto
   Ricans, 84, 88, 244, 249, 417n107; Cha Cha
   and, 35–36, 51, 86; with mothers, 123–24; with
   prisoners, 328, 359; with racially oppressed
   international groups, 206, 212, 218–19; in
   Thirteen-Point Program, 131, 132; with whites,
   107
Solniker, Hyman, 316
sources, book, 11–12
South Bronx Drug Coalition, 302–3
South Bronx Young Lord branch, 224, 227, 234,
   274, 380
Spain, David, 320
Spanish Action Committee of Chicago (SACC),
   34
Special Commission on Attica, 359–60
spheres of influence, 212, 399n22
split of Chicago and New York Young Lords
   organizations, 229–31
spoken word poetry, 2, 88–89, 96, 181
Stapp, Andy, 236
Starke, Walter, 327
Statue of Liberty superimposed poster, 92
Stead, David, 287
Stein, Marty, 287
Stein, Will, 81
sterilization of women, 255, 260, 266–67, 268
St. Michael's Catholic School, 28
Stone, Richard, 144, 146, 178
Stonewall Inn protests, 264
Store Front, 277, 422n23
Straus, Gene, 149, 178
Streit, Saul S., 190
strikes, labor: in healthcare, 279–81, 296;
   Operation Bootstrap and, 53; revolution and,
   342–43; of sanitation workers, 101, 407n73; of
   teachers, 253, 427n29; wildcat, 222, 357–58, 370,
   423n42, 428n70; working-class consciousness
   and, 222–23
structural unemployment, 55–56, 80, 399–400n29
St. Theresa Junior High School, 22, 26
Student Nonviolent Coordinating Committee
   (SNCC), 7, 83, 140, 166, 217
student organizing of Young Lords, 310–11
Students for a Democratic Society (SDS), 49, 81,
   87, 217, 335, 365, 416n49
subemployment, 55
suicide in prison, 319–22, 332
SUNY Old Westbury, 85, 250–52

surveillance, government, 40, 113, 312, 325, 350,
   405n15. See also Handschu files
sweaters, Young Lord, 28–29

Tabor, Michael, 221
Tactical Patrol Force (TPF), 76, 77, 403n139
Taller Boricua, 119, 224
Taylor, Ronald, 164
Ten-Point Health Program and Platform, 135,
   141–42, 143, 144, 145, 149
Ten-Point Program of Black Panther Party, 42,
   44, 45, 131
terror, white, 20, 23
terrorists, 312
Tet Offensive, 91, 176, 199, 373
theft of cars, 25–26
Think Lincoln Committee (TLC), 283–84,
   298, 303–4; coalition politics and, 299, 302;
   demands of, 286, 292; efforts of, 284–86;
   Lincoln Hospital occupation and, 288, 290,
   292; Rodriguez death and, 294, 295, 296
Third World Gay Revolution, 264–65
Third World Liberation Front, 218
Third World socialism, 10, 39
Third World Students' League, 357
Third World unity, 38, 42, 72
Third World Unity Conference, 42
Third World Women's Alliance, 257
Thirteen-Point Program and Platform, 5, 115,
   131–33, 219; Palante and, 194; women's equality
   and, 250, 262, 263, 309
Thomas, Piri, 241
Three Kings' Day, 188
Tlatelolco massacre, 34
TLC (Think Lincoln Committee). See Think
   Lincoln Committee (TLC)
Tombs, the, 317–22, 326, 327, 329, 331, 383
Trias, Helen Rodriguez, 298
Trinidad, Carlos, 24
tuberculosis, 44, 137, 149, 150, 271–73
Tuberculosis Association of New York, 273
Tuskegee Institute, 86, 404n189
twelve-point program on women, 268–69
Twenty-Sixth of July Movement, 34

unemployment, structural, 55–56, 80, 399–400n29
unions, labor, 101, 204, 222–23, 278–80, 370.
   See also strikes, labor
Union Theological Seminary, 184–85, 188
United Brethren Church, 158
University of Puerto Rico protests, 310
University of the Streets, 82, 178
Urban Action Task Force, 81, 153, 314
urban guerrilla war, 3, 91, 102, 106, 206–7, 312,
   416n57
urban renewal, 13, 17–18, 21, 38–40, 351–52
Urban Training Center, 37, 42
U.S. Congress shooting, 215

Valdes, Ramon, 41
Valle, Marta, 79, 400n38
vanden Heuvel, William J., 330
Vasquez, Nancy, 187
Vasquez-Ignatin, Hilda, 45
Velazquez, Felix, 66
Velez, Ramon, 282
Vicente, Joe, 14, 24
Viera, Rafael, 149, 249
Vietnam War, 91, 199, 233–35, 330, 373, 418n3
Village Voice, 149, 151
Villanueva, Jesus, 322
voluntarism, 341
Volunteers in Service to America, 42

wages, 56, 107, 196, 210, 291, 359
Wagner, Robert, 58, 72, 73, 276, 333
Waithe, Eldridge, 330
Walker, Lucius, 166
War on Poverty programs, 34, 76, 80–82, 304
WBAI radio, 194, 221, 245, 346
WBLS radio, 244
WBON radio, 36
Weather Underground, 128, 312, 313
welfare, 34, 40, 45, 121–23, 407n15, 408n16
welfare rights movement, 45, 121–23, 397n110;
    as anchor for breakfast program of the Black
    Panthers and the Young Lords, 123–24;
    the Young Lords and, 121–23
Westside Block Association, 253
West Side Story, 29
wetback (term), 16, 394n10
We Took the Streets (Melendez), 119
"What Road to Building a New Communist
    Party?" conference, 368–69
white flight, 20–21, 100, 137, 207, 217, 387
white reaction, 64, 74–75, 101, 213; origins of,
    19–21, 27, 396n80
white separation from activists of color, 217–18
Wicke, Lloyd, 187, 188
Wicker, Tom, 360
"wildcat" strikes, 223, 357, 370, 423n42
Wilkerson, Doxey, 66
Wofford, Harris, 85
women in Young Lords: Church Offensive and,
    185; Luciano scandal and, 307; participation
    of, 238–39, 250–56, 251, 268, 340; public health
    crisis and, 151; women's equality and (*See*
    women's equality)
"Women of the Colonies," 256–58, 417n117
women's caucus, 255–56, 259, 262, 263, 265, 307–9
women's equality: background and overview of,
    250–55, 381–82, 420n88; Fontanez and, 371;
    Luciano scandal and, 307–9; *Palante* radio
    show panel on, 256–58; YL changing positions
    on, 133, 260–63, 265–67; YL women's caucus
    and, 255–56, 259, 262, 263, 265, 307–9; YL
    women's union and, 267–69, 357

Women's Union (mass organization), 357
Workers' Federation, 357
working class: divided nation and, 342–45,
    427nn28–29; Leninism and, 201; lumpen
    thesis and, 222, 228–29; RU and, 371; YL
    embracement of, 354–55, 357–58, 363, 365–66,
    385
Wright, Donald Herbert, 365, 369, 370–71, 372

X-ray truck hijacking, 273

Yamasaki, Masao, 29–30
Yglesias, Jose, 193
YLO (newspaper), 45, 47, 135, 223, 229, 230,
    418n137
YMCA's Chicago Area Project, 29–30
Young Lords (gang): background and overview
    of, 1–5, 14–15; colors and style, 29; formation
    of, 24–25; gang activity of, 25–30; political
    transformation of, 41–44, 45–48; transition to
    activism of, 35, 37–40
Young Lords Organization (YLO) Chicago, 50;
    adoption of Black Panther structure by, 86–87;
    Chicano Youth Conference in Colorado
    and, 82–84; formation of, 49, 51–52; Fred
    Hampton and, 42–45, 43, 46; killing of Manuel
    Ramos and, 46–47; McCormick Theological
    Seminary and, 47; New York group split with,
    229–31; SAC and, 84, 86–88
Young Lords Organization (YLO) New York:
    Chicago-inspired style of, 28–29, 130–31,
    200, 363; branches of (*See* branch offices of
    Young Lords); Chicago group split with,
    229–31; building up of, 93–95; Chicano Youth
    Conference in Colorado and, 82–84; culture
    of, 196–99; demise of (*See* demise of Young
    Lords); formation of, 84–89, 87, 404n191;
    founding members, 49; headquarters of (*See*
    headquarters office of Young Lords); heirs of
    Malcolm X, 208; legacy of, 380–84, 386–87;
    membership of (*See* membership of Young
    Lords); Mickey Melendez and, 49, 53, 84–86;
    paramilitary image of, 130–31, 193, 196, 273,
    347, 348, 363, 408n47; politics of (*See* politics
    of Young Lords); structure and organization
    of, 113, 115–17, 127–28 (*See also specific elements
    of*); student base and working-class character
    of founding members, 51; theory, policy, and
    praxis of, 93–95, 130, 405n75; women in (*See*
    women in Young Lords)
Young Lords Party, 230, 340, 341–42, 376–77.
    See also demise of Young Lords
Young Lords Party Congress, 368
Young Patriots, 4, 42, 128, 239, 393n8
Young Socialist Alliance, 40
Young Warriors, 383

Zemann, Daniel, 327